LAY PEOPLE IN THE CHURCH

LAY PEOPLE

in

THE CHURCH

A Study for a Theology of the Laity

By
YVES M. J. CONGAR, O.P.

Translated by
DONALD ATTWATER

NEWMAN PRESS
WESTMINSTER MARYLAND

Originally published in French by Les
Editions du Cerf under the title *Jalons
pour une theologie du laicat.* First published
in English 1957

Nihil Obstat: Joannes M. T. Barton, s.t.d., l.s.s.
                                        Censor Deputatus

Imprimatur: ✠ Georgius L. Craven
                                        Epus Sebastopolis
                                        Vic. Cap. Westmon.

Westmonasterii, die 19a Nov. 1956

Library of Congress Catalog Card Number: 56-10002

Printed in Great Britain by The Ditchling Press, Hassocks, Sussex

IN the course of his Introduction to this book Father Congar expresses his regret that time did not allow him to rewrite and compress certain parts of it. Accordingly, and in spite of what the author says at the end of the previous paragraph, the liberty has been taken of omitting some of the more detailed documentation, especially from the beginning of Part Two onwards. The text itself is complete, except for four brief omissions, which are noted and explained where they occur.

Owing to an unfortunate combination of circumstances, the translator of this book did not have the opportunity to read and revise the proofs of his work in either galley or page form.

FOREWORD

THE idea of a theology of the laity was not included in my course at the seminary, far away and long ago. That is not to say it was a poor course, however poorly I profited from it. It is only to remark that the development of theological studies during the past quarter-century has brought out many facets of a science which was never intended to be static. In the consecrated phrase, dear to generations of clerical preface-writers, this book of Father Congar 'fills a long-felt need'.

That is not entirely accurate. This book, translated for English-speaking Catholics, answers rather a need which has only of late years impinged upon our awareness. We are not much given to speculation, theological or otherwise. It might be said that, in America at least, we have been acting on the implications of a theology of the laity without bothering overmuch about its exact content. We have understood for a long time that the man in the pew is not merely a passive object but an active subject. We have even conceded that he has a few rights beyond Christian burial and a few duties beyond contributing his dollar-a-Sunday.

Father Congar wrote his book for a milieu (precious word!) far different from our own. His occasional torrential outbursts of oratory on the theme of the layman's place in the Church, purple patches in the aridity of his theological learning, might even strike the American reader as more nervous than useful. It is a criticism which is frequently voiced of modern French Catholic writers. We do not have their sense of the immediate necessity for action, of the tremendous urgency of the moment, lest everything be lost and the darkness envelop us. Where we are content to take the comfortable view of gradual development, Father Congar wants Action Now.

He disclaims any intention of presenting this as a definitive work on the subject. It may well be that the book lacks a certain closeness of organization, or that the threads of his discourse have not been drawn together tight enough, but these technical faults are virtues to far as we are concerned. They let us see the man behind the book, she eager, intense apostle of the Church more deeply integrated, more consciously aware of the vital unity of the mystical body. His personal engagement with this theme is given eloquent expression on every page. For all its massive learning this is no grim textbook reeking of decayed calfskin, but the plea of a priestly heart.

The theory of the place of the layman in the Church is Father Congar's business in this admirably discursive book. The practical application of the place of the layman has been the business of the Church in America for all the generations of her corporate existence. This is not the place to launch forth into a discussion of the problems which have confronted her in seeking a satisfactory solution, or to enlarge upon the tensions which were created by the trustee system and the reaction which followed its general suppression. The fact that the Church has been building ceaselessly from the days of Bishop John Carroll has inevitably involved the close association of the clergy and laity. The further factor of the enormous development of the Catholic educational system, as a joint undertaking of priests and people, has notably welded the 'duo genera Christianorum' into a working unity. And it would be false to conclude that this unity has been confined to material concerns. It has flowed over into a genuine spiritual co-operation which is marvellously exemplified in the life of thousands of parishes from one end of the nation to the other.

The American priesthood, moreover, has always remained close to the predominant social element from which it has sprung. There has never been a tradition of aristocracy, on the one hand, to combat, nor of crabbed poverty on the other to ameliorate. The relations of priests and people have been unstrained. If 'The Bells of St Mary's', to cite an example which may be commonly understood if not universally appreciated, presented too optimistic an interpretation of this reality, it erred, shall we say, on the side of the angels. The pastor and his assistant in the average American parish not only speak a different language but breathe a different air from the Country Curate of Bernanos. If they lack something in depth psychology one is tempted to say that they make up for it in breadth.

The last twenty-five years of American Catholic life have been distinguished by a rapid growth of lay organizations. The closed fraternalism of those earlier societies set up rather specifically to counter the influence of the Masonic and allied groups has yielded to the concept of lay bodies dedicated to the inclusive objectives of Catholic Action, in the particular sense of co-operation with the hierarchy in the work of the Church. The National Council of Catholic Women now emerges as one of the largest coherent groups in the country, while the similar Council of Catholic Men, after a delayed start, is making commendable progress. Granted that there is still a great deal of confusion as to the exact area of the interest and activities of these organizations, it remains true that there is manifest a congenial spirit of exploring the possibilities as between the members of the American hierarchy and the lay leaders.

These aspects of the American scene are mentioned not by way of suggesting that we have reached a solution of the problems rehearsed by Father Congar. Much less do they imply that we can make shift without a concern for an exact theology of the laity. While it may be true generally that American Catholics, clerical and lay, are more immediately interested in results than in theory, it is equally true that an increasing number of priests and people are seriously in search of a reasoned theology of lay participation. They know something of the salutary warnings issued by His Holiness, Pope Pius XII, in his encyclical *Mediator Dei*, and they have learned caution from the blunders of those who would press the liturgical revival beyond the norms of prudence. In a word, they have a pretty clear notion of what the priesthood of the laity is not, and can never be, but they still seek to know further what, in its theological limitations, it is.

It is this field which the distinguished French Dominican sets out to explore. How the theologian must be at the same time a profound historian is fully illustrated in this study, for the place of the layman in the Church is clarified even more by what in fact he has done than by what the theologians have said he might or might not do. What is past being prologue, it may be surmised that the result of this and kindred studies will be to give a needed assurance to our whole approach to the subject. The layman of the fourth century and the layman of the thirteenth are not essentially different from the layman of today. We got our pews, they tell us, from the Protestants, but the people who occupy them now in our churches are as fully members of the mystical body as those who joined the Apostles in the first agape in Jerusalem.

It is traditional, again, in the closing paragraph of a foreword, to wish a book well. Certainly, the Newman Press, in introducing Father Congar's study to the American public, has undertaken a major service in intelligent Catholic Action. This is not only to wish it well, but to wish it many readers.

✠ROBERT J. DWYER
Bishop of Reno

CONTENTS

More positive characterisation of the lay condition: Lay people do God's work in doing the world's work . . . p. 15. – They are people who have to consider things *in themselves*, and who recognise second causes . . . p. 17. – Historically and ideologically, this characteristic is the basis of the contemporary world as lay world . . . p. 18. – The distinction between 'laicism' and 'laicity'. . . p. 20.

Chapter II

POSITION OF A THEOLOGY OF LAITY

Two Aspects in the Church . . . p. 22.

The Church is the collectivity of the faithful and, on this title, is made by her members. This aspect is expressed in the word *Ecclesia* and in her traditional definition as *Societas fidelium* . . . p. 22.

The Church is also the aggregate of the means instituted by the Lord in order to make of men a community of faithful. Thus the Church as institution precedes the Church as society of faithful, and makes it . . . p. 23.

Tradition has energetically maintained both aspects together . . . p. 26.

Indications of this in early Christianity and patristic ecclesiology . . . p. 27.

There is in tradition a very corporative idea of the Church as society of faithful and of the active role of the whole community. But the *fidelis* exists only in and through the ecclesial sacramentary institution . . . p. 29. – In tradition, the mystical Body is not a purely spiritual fellowship but embraces the visible organism, the order of means to salvation . . . p. 31.

Exaggeration and alteration of the aspect of the Church as made by her members . . . p. 32.

This tendency in the antihierarchical 'spiritual' sects and in the communal movement . . . p. 32. – Individualist-representative theories; conciliarism; Gallicanism; the Protestant Reformation . . . p. 34.

The treatise De Ecclesia in reaction: whence a certain one-sidedness . . . p. 36.

The treatise on the Church was constituted a separate treatise in reaction against errors all of which in various ways involved the Church's hierarchical structure . . . p. 36. – It was elaborated especially as a 'hierarchology' . . . p. 39. – And this at the time when the human community was being 'laicised' . . . p. 41.

The onesidedness of these Catholic treatises is not on the same plane as that of the later tendencies to emphasise the 'society' aspect of the faithful . . . p. 41. – But the ecclesiological and, especially, pastoral importance of this onesidedness is considerable . . . p. 44. – The laity in the Church are treated rather *en masse*; in the Church's relations with the world, they tend to be passive and timid . . . p. 46.

REDISCOVERIES. TOWARDS A MORE INTEGRAL SYNTHESIS . . . p. 48.

Various causes for the renewed appreciation of that aspect of the Church wherein she is made by her members. Illustrations, including the word 'ecclesial' . . . p. 48. – The meaning of the contemporary pastoral movement is that it has been rediscovered that the Church is also made from below, through the co-operation of the religious subject . . . p. 51.

Chapter III

POSITION OF THE LAITY

KINGDOM, CHURCH AND WORLD . . . p. 53.

God's purpose and the way of its realisation: Jesus Christ in the fullness of his messianic power as king, priest and prophet . . . p. 53.

Christ's kingly power, not only over the faithful but over the world, dominating alike the cosmic order and the spiritual order . . . p. 57.

The Kingdom corresponds to the total exercise of this power, the order in which, by virtue of the *Pneuma*, all things will find their perfection and be reconciled . . . p. 59.

God's design involves two successive stages; the cause of salvation is first given in Christ, and the whole fruits of salvation will be given at his second coming . . . p. 61. – So, after the coming of salvation and before the coming of glory, there is a 'space-between' in which what has been done for all by One may be done also through men: the meaning of history . . . p. 62.

Two great consequences of this: (1) To the two stages of God's design and Christ's work there correspond two states in the exercise of Christ's priestly kingship: as triumphing through the Cross and as ruling in power. Two different exertions of his priesthood also: in sacrificial form, according to the order of Aaron, in kingly form, according to the order of Melchizedek . . . p. 66; (2) During the earthly 'space-between', there is a duality of Church and World, because of the limitation that Christ has put on the exercise of his power and the twofold participation he has accorded, to a spiritual and to a temporal authority . . . p. 73.

Each of these two orders has a relation to the one final term, the Kingdom. What is the world's relation? . . . p. 77. – Dualist and eschatological thesis of discontinuity; incarnational thesis . . . p. 78.

There is connexion and a certain continuity between the cosmic work and the Kingdom: this world will be the subject of the final restoration, just as it was Christ's body born of Mary that rose from the tomb . . . p. 81. – And the energies of the Kingdom are already at work here . . . p. 84. – So there is a relation of the world to the Kingdom of God which will bring to things that integrity and reconciliation for which they strive . . . p. 87. – Church and world, each on its own plane and in its own way, are preparing the Kingdom:

The Church participates directly in the sacred powers through which Christ brings about God's purpose for the world. Her influence may be seen at work increasingly according to three spheres of operation: her priestly power, the priesthood and magisterium, and, with them, jurisdictional authority . . . p. 88.

In as much as the *World*, or *History*, seek to attain a state of integrity and reconciliation, they strive towards the Kingdom . . . p. 92. – Three great shortcomings militate against this effort: ambivalence and ambiguity; ignorance that the wisdom of God is the wisdom of the Cross, and ignorance that success can come only from on high . . . p. 92. – This gift from above will however, have some continuity with the effort: not simply the continuity of a sketch with a finished picture, but that of a preparation for the gift, without which preparation the world would not have all its dimensions as receiving subject in respect of the gift . . . p. 95. – Criticism of hierocratic Christianity . . . p. 98.

Hierarchy and faithful people . . . p. 102.

In the space-between we see God's work already done in Christ and still to be done in and through us: everything comes from the fullness of the *acta et passa Christi in carne* and moves towards the parousial fulfilment. The situation of the Christian can then be considered in relation to the Pasch and to the Parousia . . . p. 102.

The hierarchy's role in the Church as means of grace. – To the two

PART TWO

Chapter I

THE LAITY AND THE CHURCH'S PRIESTLY FUNCTION

(A) *THE PRIESTLY FUNCTION IN THE CHRISTIAN ECONOMY* . . . p. 112.

duality will cease when the end is reached and the means is swallowed up therein, the *sacramentum* in its *res* . . . p. 157. – A threefold priestly quality in the Church . . . p. 159.

Hierarchical regime: Some things are given to some only . . . p. 160. – The hierarchical fact is bound to outwardness, the regime of the 'space-between' . . . p. 161; its function and meaning are to unite and make one with the historic Christ, from whom the Church lives . . . p. 162. – Complex structure of Christian priesthood . . . p. 163.

The content and object of Christian priesthood are not simply the sacramental offering of the eucharistic sacrifice, but also men's spiritual sacrifice . . . p. 164. – Only thus does the apostolic priesthood attain the 'truth', that is, the fullness of its function relative to the Pasch of the Lord . . . p. 165. – The ancient discipline of ordination and its theology, still effective, support this New Testament datum . . . p. 167. – Exposition and appreciation of Canon Masure's position . . . p. 169.

The difference between priest and lay person from the point of view of priesthood. Only the hierarchical priest, more particularly the bishop, can constitute the whole ecclesial *sacramentum* . . . p. 171.

The various terms used in talking about the priesthood of lay Christians and that of priests . . . p. 175.

(B) *THE LAITY'S PART IN THE CHURCH'S PRIESTLY FUNCTION* . . . p. 181.

DIFFERENT aspects of Christian priesthood according to St Thomas: summary table . . . p. 181. – The ten chief elements:

(1) The whole moral life as dedicated life. Holiness . . . p. 184.

(2) Mortification and offering up of the body. Death; martyrdom . . . p. 186.

(3) Activity and responsibility of each according to his state. But all are responsible for the whole world: intercession . . . p. 189.

(4) Priesthood of parents. Marriage as a dedicated state, and the family as a cell of the Church . . . p. 192.

(5) The spiritual priesthood of holiness and its close relation to spiritual kingship. The religious life as an exercise of spiritual priesthood . . . p. 195.

(6) Confession of the faith (and martyrdom); the sacrament and consecration of confirmation . . . p. 196.

(7) The Church's public worship (liturgy), in which are distinguished a worship from above (that of Jesus Christ sacramentally

Chapter II

THE LAITY AND THE CHURCH'S
KINGLY FUNCTION

Chapter III

THE LAITY AND THE CHURCH'S PROPHETICAL FUNCTION

kind of law in all God's work . . . p. 267. – Accordingly, there is co-operation of the whole Church in her dogmatic life, in the conservation and development of the deposit whose guardianship appertains to the hierarchy. The role of the faithful in this matter; the *sensus fidelium* . . . p. 271.

Infallibility of the body of the faithful and infallibility of the body of their pastors. Criticism of a too narrow interpretation . . . p. 276. – In the Church all are animated by the Holy Spirit according to their place and part: the hierarchy to teach, the laity to believe. The laity not thereby reduced to passivity; faith is living and active, and by exerting it they contribute to the doctrinal wealth of the Church. But their part is in the order of living, and is made up of all that comes from a true interior faith . . . p. 277.

(B) *TEACHING ACTIVITIES OF THE LAITY* . . . p. 281.

Three forms and two modes of teaching . . . p. 281.

Teaching of divine revelation with authority. Doctrinal authority in its public form belongs to the episcopal body. In some degree it is shared by priests and preachers, and more remotely by lay people (catechists, godparents) . . . p. 281. – There are charisms of knowledge and revelation which contribute to doctrinal development and enlightenment; but they do not constitute a public authority for giving their structure of belief to the people of God as such . . . p. 283.

Hortatory and apostolic teaching. Three historical stages, culminating in a distinction between preaching proper and exhortation, to which is added apologetic . . . p. 285.

Restrictive discipline of today. But apostolic teaching activity (exhortation and apologetics) remains to a considerable degree open to the laity, (*a*) in private, (*b*) publicly, ratified by a mission, *e.g.*, Catholic Action . . . p. 288.

Scientific teaching. Here the position of the laity is the same as that of the clergy. Every one of the faithful is free to express his thought in a private capacity. Some, including lay people, are given a mission of theological teaching . . . p. 294.

Theological work done by lay people. It has varied according to the vicissitudes of their religious culture. They can contribute much, and they have a mission of mediation between the Church and the actual world. There is, however, in theology, danger of their lacking the nicety and balance of clergy . . . p. 294.

Chapter IV

THE LAITY AND THE CHURCH'S COMMUNAL LIFE

B

Chapter V

THE LAITY AND THE CHURCH'S APOSTOLIC FUNCTION

The Pope spoke essentially of *action*, and organised and extended activity that had been going on among lay Catholics for a century . . . p. 346. – It is a participation (taking one's part) in the *content* of the apostolate, not in the hierarchy's apostolic mandate and its powers. Meaning of the words 'hierarchical apostolate' . . . p. 347. – This is why Pius XII could substitute the word 'participation' for 'co-operation', without altering the meaning of his predecessor's definition . . . p. 348. – The Catholic Action mandate embodies the apostleship of the faithful with that of their instituted pastors; it does not create an entirely new apostleship in relation to that which they could already exercise at will . . . p. 349.

On the basis of the sacramental and extra-sacramental gifts which make the Christian, there is a lay apostleship anterior to Catholic Action, and in some respects wider than it . . . p. 349. – In Catholic Action, on the basis of its mandate, this anterior apostleship is raised to the level of a fully ecclesial instituted activity; it becomes a matter of public law . . . p. 350. – The 'mandate'. . . p. 352. – The mission of Catholic Action is to exert Christian influence in a given *milieu* . . . p. 355. – The laity's proper mission complements that of the clergy . . . p. 356. In what sense the laity can be spoken of as forming, with the clergy, the total 'subject' of the Church's apostolic mission . . . p. 358.

THE DUTY OF CATHOLIC ACTION . . . p. 359.

Various aspects . . . p. 361.

Different possibilities. The properly missionary plane: communication of the faith to other men. Its primacy . . . p. 362.

Action on social structures: this is necessary in the name of apostolic realism and is justified by many papal declarations and by the very nature of the Church's mission. Pius XII quoted . . . p. 364. – This Christian influence leaves the intrinsically secular nature of structures untouched. Relation of Catholic Action, a spiritual effort of the Church, with substantially temporal action on structures. Distinction between the end of him who does the work and the intrinsic end of the work itself. Catholic Action is the intrinsically spiritual part that gives its meaning to the Christian's temporal engagement, while respecting the proper nature and intrinsic laws of the temporal. This is not to sacralise it but to observe its authenticity and integrity . . . p. 369.

There is then a sphere proper to the laity, wherein they have a Christian mission which the clergy are unable to fulfil. Their mission is complementary to that of the priesthood . . . p. 373.

Chapter VI

IN THE WORLD AND NOT OF THE WORLD

SANCTIFICATION IN THE WORLD . . . p. 399.

Chapter VII

CONCLUSION

principles needs to be expressed in outward signs; value of liturgical expressions . . . p. 435.

Introduction

TODAY'S PROBLEM OF A THEOLOGY OF LAITY[1]

IN an essay called 'The Layman in the Pre-Reformation Parish', published forty years ago in a Catholic Truth Society pamphlet, Cardinal Aidan Gasquet relates the anecdote of an inquirer who asked a priest what was the position of the layman in the Catholic Church. 'The layman has two positions', answered the priest. 'He kneels before the altar; that is one. And he sits below the pulpit; that is the other.' The cardinal adds that there is a third that the priest had forgotten: The layman also puts his hand in his purse.

In a sense that is still so, and always will be so: there will never be a time when lay men and women are not on their knees before the altar and sitting before the pulpit, and for a long time yet they will have to put hand into purse. Nevertheless, now and for the future they do these things in a different way; or at least, doing these things, they feel differently about their position as a body in the Church.

According to Arnold Toynbee, a proletarian is not made by being in a subordinate condition, but by living in a society of which he does not feel himself to be organically an active member, with his own rights. Lay people will always be a subordinate order in the Church; but they are on the way to the recovery of a fuller consciousness of being organically active members thereof, by right and in fact.

We can see signs of this everywhere. It is sufficient to recall the world congress for lay apostleship held at Rome in 1951, in which the present writer had the happiness of taking part as an 'expert', along with the representatives of seventy-two countries and thirty-eight international organisations. It is hardly possible to imagine a

[1] The word 'laity' without the article is used herein to designate the state, condition and implications of being a lay person, 'layhood'. Compare 'priesthood' and 'the priesthood'—TR.

more telling expression of the fact that something has happened during the past few decades, namely, a veritable rediscovery of the crucial truth that lay people are fully 'of the Church'.

To mark the stages of this rediscovery would mean writing the inner history of the Church for the last hundred years. First of all there were the great nineteenth-century leaders, with the first ideas of what was to become Catholic Action. Nearer our own time there was the double movement, liturgical and apostolic or missionary, which is still expanding in all directions. With a return to liturgical sources people here and there began more and more to realise that the laity is indeed that *plebs sancta*, that consecrated people, of which the canon of the Mass speaks, and that this people has an active part in public worship, the central act of the Church's life. It is in the liturgical movement that we first find a renewed consciousness of the mystery of the Church and of the ecclesial[2] character of laity. There followed a renewing of the theology and spirituality of marriage thanks to which marriage was seen, above and beyond the juridical dispositions that regulate it, as the formation of a cell of the Church.

In the field of apostolic expansion of the Church, the faithful were at the same time rediscovering both the great dignity and the demands of the Christian obligation. They heard the pope and their bishops invite them to 'take part in the hierarchical apostolate', that is, in that sacred activity—and not in something else—which defines the Church's proper task and mission; they regained consciousness that they also have a responsibility to tell the world about the Saviour, to themselves co-operate in the work of Christ and his Church. To be complete, yet other things would have to be referred to: the renewed interest in mysticism, the demand for religious books, the importance given to holiness lived in the world, the return to the Bible; and, as regards the clergy, the momentous beginning of a change in the matter of clericalism and clerical attitudes. Such are the main components of a history which we are living in, and so of a history which we are making . . .

But beside this history which is internal to the Church there is a whole historical and human context which would have to be brought out too, for movements in the Church, and even in theology, are not unconnected with the general movement of ideas and of the world. Such expressions as 'The laity has come of age', or 'arrival of the masses' are not very acceptable: they belong to realms of ideas different from those with which we are concerned here, they have not

[2][*Ecclesial*. There is no such word in English: 'ecclesiastical' does not quite express it, nor does 'churchly' altogether meet the case. Cf. page 50.—TR.]

much meaning in the Church, so we will not use them. But there are analogies from one field to the other, and even a certain solidarity. And anyhow the development of Christian action by the faithful, and the theological research that goes therewith, is now a general fact in the Christian world, even among those who are not Catholics.

Arising from all this, and in a wide context of ecclesiological renewal, the need for a theology of laity becomes more and more evident. Having sometimes spoken or written a little on the subject, the writer of these pages is repeatedly asked on all hands to speak and write more about it. Not that good books are lacking. The past thirty or forty years have seen the appearance of excellent works, on liturgical life, on marriage in Christ, on Catholic Action, on the Church and the mystical Body, on lay people's Christian responsibilities. But for all that many people are still hungry. There is still a void clamouring to be filled.

There are many who put the blame for this deficiency on canon law. A German Protestant specialist says it is almost exclusively a code for clerics;[3] Mgr Simon complains that only one canon, no. 282, speaks of the rights of the laity,[4] and this runs: 'Lay people have the right to receive spiritual goods, and above all the helps necessary for salvation, from the clergy, according to the rules of ecclesiastical discipline' (cf. canon 948). Actually, supposing this canon were the only one concerned with the laity, it contains more possibilities than might be thought, for it has been shrewdly pointed out that almost everything the law lays down as a duty of the clergy could be transposed into terms of rights of the laity: a right to careful preaching, to spiritual guides who are men of prayer, to well-ordered services—these are certainly not worthless things. Still, it must be agreed that in this view lay people appear only as passive, the objects of the clergy's ministry. There ought to be something else.

And in fact the Code of Canon Law itself provides plenty of more

[3]U. Stutz, 'Der Geist des Codex iuris canonici . . .' in *Kirchenrechtl. Abhandlg.*, 92–93 (Stuttgart, 1918), p. 83 and cf. p. 40. Cf. K. Neundorfer, *Zwischen Kirche und Welt* (Frankfurt a. M., 1927), p. 45; G. Brom, 'De Leek in de Kerkgeschiedenis' in *Annalen van het Thijmgenootschap*, 37 (1949), p. 27. In 'Der Laie in der Kirche' in *Theol. Quartalsch.*, 130 (1950), pp. 184–196, R. Muller notes that in Wetzer and Welte's *Kirchenlexikon* (1891) it says under the word 'Laien'—'Siehe Clerus'. There is no entry under 'Laïc' in the *Dict. de theol. cath.*

[4]P. Simon, *Das Menschliche in der Kirche Christi* (Freiburg i. B., 1936; French tr., 1951), p. 111.

positive elements.[5] Over forty canons (682-725) are expressly devoted to lay people, though only from the point of view of those religious societies—third orders, confraternities, etc.—which they can form or join. Thirty years after the Code was promulgated the constitution 'Provida mater' of 1947 gave many precise directions about secular religious institutes. But since the Code the popes in laying down regulations for Catholic Action have several times been careful clearly to distinguish it from purely 'pious groups' such as third orders and confraternities—Catholic Action is a participation in the Church's apostleship.[6] The Code treats of religious societies but it came out a few years too soon to give its place to Catholic Action, which is an organism of the Church as planned and ordered as, and doubtless more important as well as more adaptable than, religious societies; and the laity's part in it is crucial. This *lacuna* in the Code will of course be made good sooner or later.[7]

The laity's place in the Church's law is not so slight as some people allege, but it is little enough. But indeed the Code is not the place to look for an adequate answer to questions about the laity. In its origins, history and very nature canon law is principally a systematising of sacramental *cultus*, and it is normal that it should be chiefly a code for clerics and sacred matters. The unfortunate thing is that since the thirteenth century, and especially since the sixteenth, the

[5]While we await an article 'Laic' in the *Dict. de Droit can.*, there is an account of the relative dispositions of the Code in E. Roser, *op. cit.*; H. Keller and O. von Nell-Breuning, *Das Recht der Laien in der Kirche* (Heidelberg, 1950); and O. Kohler, 'Der Laie im katholischen Kirchenrecht' in *Stimmen der Zeit*, April 1950. Apart from the right to receive the Church's means of grace (canons 682, 948) and freely to participate in all her acts, within the limits of discipline (a right which can be lost through certain ecclesiastical censures and punishments), lay people are entitled to co-operate in the religious instruction of children (canon 1333 §1), to take charge of its temporalities on behalf of a church (canon 1521), and to be entrusted with certain duties in the Church's administration and judicial organisation (canons 373, 1592, 1657 and cf. below, ch. V). There also still exist some remnants of the right of presentation and nomination. The passage of the constitution 'Sede vacante', according to which a man need not be a priest in order to be elected pope, is generally interpreted to mean that a layman could be chosen. The present work will develop other aspects of lay people's rights, especially where worship is concerned.

[6]Pius XI's letter to Cardinal Bertram, 1928 (in the 'Documentation catholique' collection, *L'Action catholique*, Paris, 1933, p. 48); Cardinal Pacelli's letter of March 30, 1930 (*ibid.*, p. 227); Pius XI's letter to the Argentinian bishops, 1931 (*ibid.*, pp. 388, 394). Notice, however, that Pius XII's letter to the father general of the Society of Jesus (April 15, 1950) declares emphatically that the Marian congregations with apostolical aims that are directed by the Society are a part of Catholic Action, whatever anybody says (*Acta Ap. Sed.*, 1950, pp. 437ff.; *Doc cath.*, 1950, cc. 577-580).

[7]The matter is already being worked on and there are short references to it in manuals, *e.g.*, in Vermeersch-Creusen, *Epitome juris can.* (7th ed., 1949), vol. i, n. 842.

canonical point of view has increasingly taken over the mind of the clergy and become the essential determinant in their attitude to pastoral matters; in both the pastoral and liturgical fields it is very often deemed sufficient simply to add a complement of devotion, of the 'spirit of faith', of zeal, to a structure of canonical positions, and this cannot entirely make up for the loss of a real theology of laity. Or the laity is confined solely to the purely secular tasks of temporal activity. The old medieval comparison of the two parts of the body Christian, sacerdotal and lay, corresponding respectively to the spiritual and the temporal, perhaps accounts for this state of mind. St Robert Bellarmine considered the laity only under the temporal aspect and its submission to the spiritual (Cf. below, ch. ii, n. 22). Many people do not realise sufficiently that a big space is left empty between, on the one hand, a rigid canonical attitude in sacred things, wherein all the emphasis is on the receptive position of the faithful and their subordination to the clergy, and, on the other hand, the field of social and international secular activity. Nowadays lay people are becoming conscious that it is their business too to fill that empty space, through a properly spiritual activity, an active role *in the Church*. They are everywhere asking for a proper theology of laity to instruct them in their uncontentious approach to this task.

To provide that is not a light undertaking. So far-reaching a request is not met simply by putting out a number of special theses on particular points. The requirement is very closely bound up with so many problems which today no longer confront only a few thoughtful people in the Schools but press upon the great body of lay people consciously engaged in the Christian warfare, and with them those clergy whose studies have given them insufficient equipment: such matters as the relations of the Church with the world, an up-to-date pastoral theology,[8] formation of the clergy and the meaning of their priesthood, the nature of the laity's obligation, the Christian meaning of history and of earthly realities. Such are the difficult questions—and there are others—involved in a theology of laity. But its central problem goes beyond the sum of these big questions: the real difficulty is that such a theology supposes the existence of a whole ecclesiological synthesis wherein the mystery of the Church has been given all its dimensions, including fully the ecclesial reality of laity. It is not just a matter of adding a paragraph or a chapter to an ecclesiological exposition which from beginning to end ignores

[8]'The pastoral theology of the past is indeed not enough', said Pius XI in 1933 to the ecclesiastical assistants of Italian women's Catholic Action; quoted by C. Noppel in *Aedificatio corporis Christi* . . . (Freiburg i. B., 1949), preface.

the principles on which a 'laicology' really depends. Without those principles, we should have, confronting a laicised world, only a clerical Church, which would not be the people of God in the fullness of its truth. At bottom there can be only one sound and sufficient theology of laity, and that is a 'total ecclesiology'.

However, we are not offering a complete treatise on the Church here. Ecclesiology keeps on cropping up, and when the reader meets certain seemingly rather irrelevant and laboured explanations, he must remember that they are necessary in order to tie up particular applications with general principles. Much repetition would have been avoided had we been able to refer him to a complete treatise on the Church. At many points the subject is new, and we had to give our arguments and our documentary support, and the more carefully since positions strongly emphasised by some have been consistently minimised by others; for example, in the question of the priesthood of the faithful. This question, like several others, looks simple at a first glance; but the more it is studied the more delicate it is seen to be, and it involves several matters that cannot be set out clearly without serious research. We have not hesitated to include the essentials of our documentation, though by doing so we risk over-weighting the volume: the chief object of this is to make it useful to those who, not having our time for research and our aids to work, have a claim to this service from a theologian who is somewhat removed from the toil and danger of the front line.

This has helped to make the book very long, and we would gladly have avoided more of the prolixities and repetitions. Some of them were necessary; others, however, are due to the preparation of the book having been spread over two years, with frequent and long interruptions by the call of all kinds of other duties. We would like to have had time to rewrite certain chapters, feeling that, with all dossiers put aside, they could have been made simpler, clearer and more effective. We hope one day to be able to recast the whole thing in a style more attractive to the general reader and without the technical references. Meanwhile, sincere apologies are offered for so heavy and undigested a work . . .

In spite of the size of this book and the labour put into it, it is offered as no more than a first essay, simply 'signposts', and it makes no claim to completeness or to the presentation of what is definitive. Under the first head, we are only too well aware of the omissions which prevent us from calling it a theology of laity pure and simple. There is nothing here about women, as such, nothing about religious life in the world, nothing about the laity in the foreign missions, almost nothing about marriage and Christian life in the home. Some of these important matters will be taken up, at any rate in the form of documentation, in a volume of *Etudes conjointes*, for which is also kept a number of technical excursuses and learned notes.[9] We have said that a complete theology of laity will be a total ecclesiology: it will also be an anthropology, and even a theology of the creation in its relation to Christology.

As for definitive statements, it is clear enough that amid so many difficult questions theological opinions can differ. The present work is offered for the consideration and discussion of all informed people, at the same time as it is submitted to the judgment of the bishops, guardians of the tradition on which we have endeavoured abundantly to nourish it. There may perhaps be some people who will scent danger in the very attempt to work out a theology of laity;[10] for their benefit I quote the reply of the bishop of Dijon, Mgr Dadolle, to a similar objection in 1907:

It is very possible that in the past we bishops did not understand your role sufficiently and completely enough. We used to appeal to your purse for our material needs, to your devotedness, to your knowledge for the management of our property, to your devotion for the carrying of a candle in a eucharistic procession. If that was nearly all, it was not, or at any rate it is not, enough. . . . Over centuries, apostleship was looked upon as a 'reserved occupation', and at least in practice the distinction between teachers and taught, priests and lay folk, increased to excess. . . . Here, there and everywhere there is discussion of the delicate question of co-ordinating the two apostleships, ours, hierarchical, and yours, lay.

[9]Subject to modifications that may be made while the work is in progress, this volume of *Etudes conjointes* will comprise the following: (*a*) *Studies*. The theme of the temple. – The Christian idea of property and employment. – Religious life in the world. – 'Being lay' and 'being secularist'. – Woman among the faithful people. – Witness. (*b*) *Excursuses and documentary notes*. 'Laicus' in the middle ages. – The definition of the Church as 'Societas fidelium'. – The principle of consent: 'Quod omnes tangit ab omnibus tractari et approbari debet'. – What is 'one of the faithful' in Christian tradition? – 'Plebs' and 'Populus'. – The lay and the married states as 'orders' in the Mystical Body. – Communion under both kinds.

[10]A certain Father A. Parego included two articles of mine in *Etudes* (January and February 1948) among the demoralising agitations which have led to that '*monstrum*' (Well, well!) the 'new theology', a thing essentially and exclusively French (It would be!), now happily torpedoed by the encyclical letter '*Humani generis*' (We agree!). See 'La nuova teologia . . .' in *Divus Thomas*, 53 (Piacenza, 1950), pp. 436–465.

People talk of the dangers, of the possibility of meddling—oh! Gentlemen, I am well aware of all the dangers that there are. The only way to avoid them is to do nothing, to allow nothing to be done. But that is to resign ourselves to the worst evil of all, standing aloof: the part chosen by those useless souls to whom Dante in his Hell would vouchsafe no gleam of pity, but 'Look, and pass by.'[11]

The dangers referred to are not imaginary. There is no difficulty about finding evidence of exaggeration: as when, for example, lay people think and say that matters of marriage or social morality are *their* affair, and nothing to do with their clergy; or when they exclude their priest from this meeting or that Bible-study circle; or when, rather disregarding the common and ordered character of ecclesial life, they themselves choose a priest to suit the group they have formed. As we go along we shall come across other examples of excess or deviation. But the existence of minor dangers of this kind does not mean that we ought to refrain from putting forward a doctrine of laity, or that it should be set out only in a softened and emasculated form. It simply emphasises the duty of producing a serious work, solid, balanced, grounded in tradition, one that includes in the solidity and balance of one same truth both the inspiring fearlessness of Christian life and the indefeasible limits or conditions outside of which, with all the enthusiasm in the world, the course we take is useless (Galatians ii, 2). We have said elsewhere, in writing of ecumenism and of the problem of reforms in the Church, problems of life and fullness, that her *life* must grow in the setting and framework of her *structure*. Where a doctrinal study is concerned, one must not venture on a doctrine of life until a sound theology of the structure has been established. And here again, in this problem of the laity, we have tried to do just that, to reconnect life with structure, a work of assimilation to principles, so that that *fullness* that we seek, which is the great attraction for our time, may be nothing else than the fullness *of the apostolic Church*.

We are convinced that if this reconnexion be made, if the Church, secure on her foundations, boldly throws herself open to lay activity, she will experience such a springtime as we cannot imagine. The general body of faithful people has been a great reservoir of decisive

[11]Address on the laity's role in the Church in France after the separation of church and state. Text in *L'avenir des travailleurs*, 14 April, 1907; quoted in *Demain*, 3 May, 1907, p. 445.

energies in every age. 'In all times', wrote John Henry Newman, 'the laity have been the measure of the Catholic spirit; they saved the Irish Church three centuries ago, and they betrayed the Church in England.'[12] Today perhaps more than ever lay people are called on to give in full measure those energies by which they are in very truth 'of the Church' and, as Pope Pius XII has said, 'make the Church'. In that huge area that we refer to as 'behind the iron curtain'—over a quarter of the land surface and nearly a third of the population of the world—it is possible that the faith will be for a long time upheld by the faithful laity alone. On another hand, today perhaps more than ever the Holy Spirit moves the world towards an ideal of fullness: there are glorious and unsullied forces only waiting to be used. There are many things that can take on a new and wider life. There is movement in the Lord's vineyard as of a breath of promise. May we not be on the eve of a new spring, a vigil of Pentecost?[13]

The demands of a laity awakening to consciousness of its place and responsibilities in the Church already give us clergy some inkling of what the welcoming, the cultivation and the ripening of such crops will call for from us. It is much easier to keep an eye, if not on an empty cradle, on a sleeping child, than it is to answer the questions of a growing boy who is beginning to feel his feet. The laity are asking a lot from us; they are making us bring all that placid and formalised area of Christianity of which we are the ministers under the demanding influence of what, contained in it, is forever young: of that faith, 'received from the Church, which we treasure; which through the Spirit of God is like something very valuable, in a condition of perpetual youth, kept in a precious vessel, which never ceases to rejuvenate the vessel itself'.[14] A putting into operation of the fullness of God's people through lay activity will call for an extraordinary effort on the part of all the structural elements. Speaking generally, the contemporary world makes demands on the priest that are truly superhuman. But what man who is called to the priesthood, to be a working muscle or joint in the body of Christ, is not

[12]*Lectures on the Present Position of Catholics in England* (London, 1908), p. 398. – We venture to add the words of J. Guehenno in *Caliban parle* (Paris, 1928, p. 144): 'Without the Calibans there can be no Catholic renaissance. We alone are numerous enough to fill the churches, and Mass is badly sung so long as our voices are missing.'

[13]Among other writers who think that the Church will greatly profit if the laity are given trust and opportunity are R. Müller, *art. cit.*, pp. 194ff., and J. Thomé, *Der mündige Christ* (Frankfurt a. M., 1949), pp. 108ff.

[14]St Irenaeus, *Adv. Haer.* iii, 24, 1 (PG., vii, 966).

ready, with the grace of the same Christ, for every effort, for every over-strain if need be, required for loyal co-operation in the growth of the whole organism? (Cf. Ephesians iv, 16).

*   *   *

The plan of this study is ruled by its purpose. After a preliminary chapter giving an elementary idea of what a lay person is, the subject is treated in two parts. The first gives the general position of things and ensures the regularity of structure without which there is risk of going astray. We first consider the place of a theology of laity, and then the place of the laity itself in God's purpose. In the second part we study the laity in action in the Church's life. This we do first in the framework of those three functions among which it is more and more agreed to assign the Church's acts as those of Christ: the priestly, the kingly and the prophetic functions. There was a temptation to keep to this convenient trilogy. But having tried various distributions, it became clear that it is not possible rigorously to bring all lay activity under these heads without doing violence to them. Catholic Action, in particular, involves all three. So we resisted the temptation to make clear-cut distinctions which would appear exact only because of a failure to be completely submissive to the nature of things; instead, we have given a special chapter respectively to lay people in the life of the Church as community and to lay people in regard to the Church's apostolic mission. These rather vague terms were chosen on purpose to label examinations which we hope are not themselves vague. The chapters are all kept under one numeration to mark the continuity of their development, and a chapter has been added on a subject of much interest at present, 'spirituality' and the sactification of lay people amid the distractions of 'the world'. A final section endeavours to summarise the results of investigations which will have been sometimes rather hard going, even if not far too technical.

fr Yves M. J. Congar

Le Saulchoir
December 22, 1951

PART ONE

Chapter I

WHAT IS A LAYMAN?

THE word κλῆρος, from which the English words 'cleric' and 'clerk' are ultimately derived, is of frequent occurrence in the Bible, especially in the Old Testament. Its primary meaning is 'lot', and then 'portion' or 'heritage'. In I Peter v, 3 the word in the plural designates the community allotted to each of the presbyters. The word λαϊκός, whence our 'lay', is not found anywhere in the Bible,[1] but the use of λαός, of which λαϊκός is the adjective, is frequent. A meaning given to this word is 'people', especially in the Bible: in the Old Testament λαός is often opposed to τὰ ἔθνη, and expressly designates the people *of God*, distinct from the gentiles (the *goim*).[2] Our word 'lay', then, is connected with a word that for Jews, and then for Christians, properly meant the sacred people in opposition to the peoples who were not consecrated, a nuance of meaning that was familiar, at any rate to those who speak Greek, for the first four centuries and more.[3]

[1]Except in one or two places in the versions of Aquila, Theodotion and Symmachus. Cf. Hatch and Redpath's Concordance.

[2]E.g., in the Old Testament, Exodus xix 4–7; Deut. vii 6–12; in the New Testament, with application to the Christian community, which is the new and veritable Israel, Luke ii, 32; Rom. ix, 23; 2 Cor. vi, 14. Cf. the article ἔθνος in Kittel's *Worterbuch*, ii, pp. 362–370, and λαός, iv, pp. 29–57, especially 32–37 and 53–57.

[3]In Justin, *Dial.*, 123, λαός = the people of the New Covenant; in 1 *Apol.*, 67, the λαός answers to 'the president'. G. Dix, in *The Shape of the Liturgy* (London, 1945), p. 480, and *The Apostolic Ministry* (London, 1946), p. 285, states, without offering proofs, that λαϊκός still signifies a member of God's people in the East about the year 300; by about 450 it has almost come to mean 'profane' as opposed to sacred. This would be associated with those ideas which, in public worship, ended in the separation of the celebrant from the congregation (rood-screen, eikonostasis). Among other terms used in the East to signify lay people were ἰδιῶται (Chrysostom), corresponding to the *laicus* = *idiota* = illiterate of the middle ages; and βιωτικοί (*Nomokanon*), corresponding to the Latin *saeculares*. Cf. N. Milasch, *Das Kirchenrecht der morgenlandischen Kirche* (Mostar, 1905), p. 216, n. 8; P. G. Caron, *I poteri giuridici del laicato vella Chiesa primitiva* (Milan, 1948), p. 40.

I

We see then that there is no distinction between 'lay people' and
'clerics' in the vocabulary of the New Testament. Nineteenth-century
Protestant historians—Hase, Hatch, Achelis, Harnack—have dog-
matised a lot about this as a fact that supports their theory of an
undifferentiated primitive community living under a charismatic
regime. But another fact does not favour their interpretation of history, namely that the first use of the word 'layman' as opposed to
'priest' is found in a Roman document, the letter to the community
at Corinth, written by Clement.[4] An examination of the views of the
historians just named would involve a full consideration of the constitution and nature of the apostolic Church, its ministries, its relations with the Synagogue, a field where history and theology must
come together and talk if sound conclusions are to be reached; a
field too wherein questions of method are involved, themselves subject to doctrinal choices. A particular point in mind here, which the
writer has touched on elsewhere,[5] is this: in what degree does the
analysis of terms used authorise the making of a judgment about a
reality? Concretely, in what degree does the absence of our words
'cleric' and 'lay', and of the word 'priest' (*hiereus*; cf. ch. iv below),
from her vocabulary allow us to affirm that the Church in apostolic
times was an undifferentiated community with a charismatic regime,
a stranger to what we express, and what Clement, contemporary
with the Apostles, expresses, by the words 'cleric', 'layman' and
'priest'?

We cannot go into such questions here. For our purpose it is
sufficient to grasp the difference between clerics and lay people when
it occurs in the vocabulary. We have seen Clement of Rome's text;
and it is the first of many. Evidence abounds at the beginning and
middle of the third century and, expressed in various terms, the distinction is quite clear: in the East, for example, in Clement of

[4]Clement, xl, 5: 'Special ministries have been assigned to the high-priest; a
special place has been allotted to the priests; and the levites have their own duties.
Lay people are bound by rules laid down for the laity'. In a note on this passage
Hemmer refers to Jer. xxxiv, 19, one of the O.T. texts (there are others in the N.T.)
where λαός designates the people in distinction from their leaders, priests, levites
and scribes. It should be noticed that in referring to a member of the community
distinct from priests and levites Clement gave the faithful a name that directly
expresses their membership in the consecrated people. The Latin translation of
Clement's letter, dating from the first half of the second century, renders λαϊκός by
plebeius, one of the *plebs*, that is, of the Christian community. *Plebs* is constantly used
in this sense by Tertullian and St Cyprian, and by later writers.

[5]*Vraie et fausse reforme dans l'Eglise* (Paris, 1950), pp. 499ff.

Alexandria and Origen, in the West in Tertullian and St Cyprian.[6]
With Cyprian, moreover, we have for the first time the broad lines
of an ecclesiology properly so called, that is, of a theory not concerned solely with Christ and the relation of the faithful with him by
salvation and grace, but with the ecclesial institution in the order of
means of the calling to salvation.

We have got our landmarks. From vocabulary we can go on to an
interpretation. This, directly it begins to be formulated a little systematically, confronts us, not with two terms only, but with three.
We find between clerics and lay people a third category, that of
monks. From the time of Clement of Rome, doubtless from that of
the Apostles, there were ascetics, 'continent ones' and virgins in the
Christian community. Monachism properly so called began about
the middle of the third century, while Origen and Cyprian were
still alive, for we find that when St Antony wanted to go into the
wilderness, around 250-257, he met a man who had already led the
solitary life for several years.

So from the middle of the third century three states could be distinguished in the Church, which were obviously there in fact before
they were subjected to formula and code, but which did not have to
wait long for formulation and, in the most exact sense, canonical
existence. From then on the Church not only lives—she has done
that since she received the breath of the Spirit at Pentecost; she not
only has her essential structure—the Lord gave her that at different
times during his earthly life: but she has her permanent pattern. If

[6]Clement of Alexandria (d. 211-216): St Paul 'allows the marriage of a man
with one woman, whether he be priest, deacon or layman . . .' (*Strom.*, iii, 12;
PG., viii, 1189). Origen (d. 254-255), on Jer. xii, 13: 'Others have commented on
this passage before me, and as I agree with their interpretation I pass it on to you. . . .
Being set up as your presidents because we are clerics, we think we are somebody,
so that certain other people want to have that attribute too. Know then that every
cleric is not necessarily saved: more than one priest will be lost and more than one
layman will be acclaimed blessed. For that reason, because there are some clerics
who live in such a way as not to profit by their office and not to be an honour to
it, those who have expounded this text declare that he wrote as he did: "their
kleros was no advantage to them" ' (*In Jerem.*, hom. xi, 3; PG., xiii, 369). Tertullian
(d. 217-222), before he became a Montanist: among the heretics, 'alius hodie
episcopus, cras alius; hodie diaconus, qui cras lector; hodie presbyter, qui cras
laicus; nam et laicis sacerdotalia munera injungunt' (*Praescr.*, xli, 8). After becoming a Montanist in 205 he writes: 'Differentiam interordinem et plebem constituit
Ecclesiae auctoritas' (*De exhort. castitatis*, 7). 'Si non omnes monogamiae tenentur,
unde monogami in clerum? An ordo aliquis seorsum debebit institui monogam-
orum, de quo adlectio fiat in clerum? Sed cum extollimur et inflamur adversus
clerum, tunc unum omnes sumus, tunc omnes sacerdotes . . .', etc. (*De monogamia*,
12; PL., ii, 948—clearly a poor text). St Cyprian (d. 258): 'clero et plebi' (*Ep.*,
45, 2; Hartel, 602); 'qui se a cleri ejus et plebis societate secernit' (*De unitate*, c. 17;
Hartel, 226), etc.

the distinction between clergy and laity is essential in the Church's structure and life, her permanent pattern includes a distinction between three states or conditions, lay, clerical, monastic.[7]

The lay condition is not so much a matter of definition as of something immediately given as a basis, the condition of Christians who are working out their salvation in the everyday life of the world. The clerical condition is defined by the service of the altar and the religious service of the Christian people. Clericature itself then is an office, a function, not a state of life. It is brought about by entry into the ministry, the 'diaconia', the service of sacred things; and the entry is made by being 'ordained' to this service, that is, in all strictness, by ordinations properly so called. The monastic condition is not defined by service of sacred things, not even by service of the altar: the first monks in the East had hardly any 'liturgical' life (the 'liturgy' is by definition a public service, and therefore the business of clerics), and in some medieval Western monasteries the part of the monastic church used by the laity was put in charge of clerics who were not monks.[8] The monk as such is not a cleric, though of course he can become one by ordination. His condition is not defined by an office or function but as a state or way of life: in order that he shall not live for the world and in the world's way but rather so much as possible for God and in God's way, this consists in living apart from the world, leading so far as may be a heavenly or angelic life, the life of the Kingdom that is not of this world.

In principle, then, clerics and monks were sharply differentiated: 'cleric' indicates a function, 'monk' a state or way of life. A man is a cleric by ordination to the sacred ministry, a monk by personal renouncement of the world. The two things are not unrelated, however, and in the West the relationships have been understood in such a way that the two conditions reinforce one another. The reasons for this can be brought under three heads.

[7] I shall explain in a measure later on about the distinction between the Church's structure, life and permanent pattern: the last comes between the first two, a little like temperament between essential human nature and our daily activities. The place here given to monasticism ecclesiologically can be supported by reference to Pope Pius XII's 'Provida mater', in A.A.S., 1947, p. 116.

[8] Cf. U. Berlière, 'La "familia" dans les monastères bénédictins du moyen-age' in Memoires de la Cl. des Lettres, Acad. de Belgique, 29 (1931). Priests have always been few among the monks of the East, and these not much given to pastoral work: Viller and Rahner, op. cit., pp. 282–283, referring to C. Baur, 'Der weltfluchtige und welttatige Gedanke in der Entwicklung des Mönchtums' in Bonner Zeitschrift, 7 (1930), pp. 113–123. St Jerome, a monk, did not wish to be a priest, and after he had been ordained he had his brother Paulinian priested to take care of the services of the monastery (F. Cavallera, S. Jerome, i, pp. 56, 210–213). Cf. too E. Dekkers's study, 'Les anciens moines cultivaientils la liturgie?' in Vom Christl. Mysterium: Gesam. Arbeiten z. Gedachtnis von O. Casel (Dusseldorf, 1951), pp. 97–114.

(1) Monastic life being, in its widest connotation, a life of holiness and total personal consecration to God, it was fitting that clerics dedicated to the service of the altar and the sacred ministry should have the spirit and virtues of monks. This fittingness was very soon seen and formulated in the West. On the one hand, communities of clerics living monastically, in the wide sense, were formed around their bishop, as in the case of St Eusebius of Vercelli, of St Ambrose, of St Martin and especially of St Augustine (his *De vita et moribus clericorum* and certain texts, under the title of *Regula*, came to exercise a very strong influence that subsists to our day). On the other hand, a whole body of ideas—we could say a whole 'spirituality'—was developed in connexion with the idea of clerical life, starting from the etymology of the word. Here it was not St Augustine who was decisive: his explanation of the word *clerus*, given in passing, as deriving from the idea of the choice and election of Matthias by drawing lots, did not catch on. But the following text of St Jerome became immensely popular: 'The cleric who serves the Church of Christ should in the first place construe and ponder his name and, when he has explained it, try to be what the title means. The Greek word *kleros* signifies 'portion', a part drawn by lot; and he bears the name of cleric either because he is the Lord's portion, or because he has the Lord for his portion. The man who professes the one or the other should show by his behaviour that he possesses the Lord or that he is possessed by the Lord. But he who possesses the Lord, and says with the Prophet 'the Lord is the portion of my inheritance' (Ps. xv, 5, lxxii, 26), can have nothing outside the Lord . . .'[9] The idea of being the Lord's portion and of having a portion in him has been as it were the soul of the clerical state through an age-long tradition that is impressive in its unchangingness. Psalm xv is the 'tonsure psalm', and for centuries consecration to the service of the altar and the faithful of Christ has been expressed in the words, 'Dominus pars haereditatis meae et calicis mei. Tu es qui restitues haereditatem meam mihi.'

Indeed, the very fact of the tonsure, with the spiritual significance attached to it, was calculated to soften any too sharp distinction between cleric and monk. From the fourth century the tonsure, whatever form it took, was the token of monks *and* of clerics. It was materially the same for both even if it did not have exactly the same

---

[9] *Ep.* 52 (PL., xxii, 531). Jerome argues similarly from the word 'monk': 'Interpretare vocabulum monachi, hoc est nomen tuum: quid facis in turba, qui solus es?' (*Ep.* 14; PL., xxii, 350). Jerome's text was not unknown in the East; in the West it has been repeated time and time again.

meaning for both—it is sometimes said that the monastic tonsure is not *signum clericale, sed poenitentiale*. From the point of view of collation to the tonsure, *clericum facere* and *monachum facere* were the same thing.[10] So it is not surprising that their 'crowns', sign of their institution and their condition, were confused.

(2) In the West still more than in the East monks, who have been very generally cenobites, have been given a thoroughly liturgical rule of life. Doubtless Cluny went further than the Rule of St Benedict and the regulations given to monks by the synod of Aachen in 817, but it cannot be said that she was not developing an authentic element of Benedictinism. One is inclined to say that in the West there were scarcely any monks who were not, if not clerics, at least in line with the clericature. We have seen that the cleric is specified by service of the altar, the ministry of sacred things; and certainly, strictly and canonically speaking, monks became clerics only by subsequent ordination, whether properly sacramental ordination to the diaconate and priesthood or lesser consecration for some office in public worship. But as soon as the religious life, monastic life in the wide sense, has a marked liturgical orientation, the monk becomes a man in the service of the altar. The canons regular and clerks regular not only developed extensively in the West, they influenced monastic institutions as well, contributing to their taking on a complexion of cleric-monks, dedicated to the liturgical office and sometimes even to the ministry. And we often see monks assimilated to clerics when they actually and habitually exercise liturgical functions.

(3) This assimilation has often been made on account of circumstances or to meet the requirements of controversy. Thus importance has been given to one category of texts, which originally had in view the other category; faced by the canons regular of the twelfth century the monks claimed the title of cleric, with the help of certain distinctions;[11] or, taking this last claim as a starting-point, it was acknowledged that at bottom monks were clerics who added a form of life under a rule to the clericature. In any case *clericus* and *monachus*

---

[10]Cf. for example the Siena *Pontificale* cited by Du Cange, ii, p. 393, col. 1 (edn of 1842).

[11]Cf. that very curious *Dialogus inter Cluniacensem* . . . (v, 1620–1626, 1644–1647). The religious of Prémontré claimed that they were clerics *ex debito*, while monks, even if priests, were so only *ex indulgentia*. The Cistercian lays claim to the clericature on the strength of his rule, and not *ex indulgentia*, and at the Cluniac's request gives a perfect definition of clericature: 'Officium altaris, quod non facit sanctam vitam, sed requirit sanctam vitam.' To end up, the Cistercian distinguishes three meanings of 'cleric': wide, 'omnis coronatus per sacerdotis benedictionem'; strict, 'episcopi et eorum co-operatores quibus est commissa cura animarum in populo Dei'; and between them, 'officium altaris', which monks exercise within their monastery.

are sometimes taken purely and simply one for the other.

The details of all this are of no concern for our purpose here. What matters to us is that the triple division into lay people, clerics and monks became, by a process of assimilation of clerics to monks and of monks to clerics, a double division into men of religion and men of the world. 'Duo sunt genera christianorum', says Gratian in a canon of which he makes St Jerome the father; and in the first category he puts both those who are dedicated to divine worship, clerics, and those who simply seek the improvement of their own lives, monks.[12]   *   *   *

Although, in distinction from the lay state understood as a secular condition, that of clerics and that of monks tend sometimes to be fused into a single condition of men of religion, the duality of clericature and monasticism nevertheless remains in the nature of things and in canonical definition. The monastic condition has reference to a manner of life having evangelical perfection in view; the clerical condition has reference to function, a ministry or service. From the canonical point of view, and speaking exactly, neither 'lay' nor 'cleric' is inconsistent with 'monk', for one can be a monk (form of life) and at the same time a cleric (ordained for liturgical service) or a lay person. Canonically, the layman can be defined only by distinction from the cleric: Fathers Vermeersch and Creusen can define him in no other way than they do (note 24, below) because they are concerned only for a canonical definition. But this point of view cannot supply a complete positive notion of the lay condition; and we, with a comprehensive grasp of it, need to find a more detailed and accurate conception of that condition.

The fact is that the Church's tradition offers us three notions which, without being all on the same level or being opposed to one another in strict logic, are distinct. During the course of history the lay condition has sometimes been defined from the point of view of way of life, in opposition to the condition of monks and of churchmen, monks and clerics being grouped together indiscriminately; and sometimes it has been defined from the point of view of function or, more exactly, of competence [A][13] in opposition to the condition of

[12]'Duo sunt genera christianorum. Est autem genus unum, quod mancipatum divino officio, et deditum contemplationi et orationi, ab omni strepitu temporalium, cessare convenit, ut sunt clerici, et Deo devoti, videlicet conversi. Κλῆρος enim graece, latine sors. Inde hujusmodi homines vocantur clerici, id est sorte electi. Omnes enim Deus in suos elegit. Hi namque sunt reges, id est se et alios regentes virtitibus, et ita in Deo regnum habent. Et hoc designat corona in capite . . .' (VII, xii, 1; Friedberg, i, p. 678. The quotation is continued below).

[13]Capital letters enclosed in square brackets, [A], [B], etc., refer to the glossary at the end, Appendix I.

clerks. These are two different approaches, leading to two notions of the laity that are complementary: what may be called the monastic notion, defined by way of life, and the canonical notion, defined by function and competence.

The Monastic Notion. – Here the distinction is made in terms of state of life, of the manner or means of sanctification. Clerics and monks are men given over to the holy, so far as may be they live in the divine world. The laity lives among earthly things. At the same time not only holy people but true contemplatives may be found among them: this has always been recognised, even by upholders of the solitary life. God has often made known to some hermit or other distinguished for his austere life, that this married woman, that confirmed thief who helps his neighbour in distress, equal him in holiness in God's sight. Inversely, there are always clerics and monks to be found who are full of worldly preoccupations, and sometimes corrupted by vice. But these are personal situations; they do not affect the difference between states of life that Christian tradition, up to the Protestant criticism of the sixteenth century, has looked on as in themselves representing different conditions of holiness. It still remains true that the cleric (and the monk) is *by his very state* dedicated to divine things, and the layman, by *his* state, to human things —*et divisus est* (1 Corinthians vii, 33). This is not the place to show that these great convictions of the Christian consciousness, if properly understood, are neither a transposition of philosophical attitudes nor a self-interested invention of churchmen, but a conclusion from a literal observance of the deepest imperatives of the Gospel. This will be referred to later.

In defining the layman by state of life obviously we must range alongside the clerics certain people who are not clerics strictly speaking, in the sense that they have no hierarchical grade—unordained monks, lay-brothers (*conversi*) and lay religious, nuns.

This way of regarding the lay condition seems to have been specially in favour during the twelfth century. There had been a great religious renewal in the previous century: even before the Gregorian reform, and still more in consequence of it, a wide-ranging movement impelled souls towards an evangelical, 'apostolic', life of poverty, charity and apostleship. There were 'Apostolic' lay movements; especially were there many movements of renewal of clerical life, modelled on the early Church, through the observance of poverty and chastity within a framework of common life under a rule. Then there was the action of the papacy, aimed at enforcing the celibacy of clerics. Thus clerical life was renewed in a monastic sense; and it certainly seems that this fact encouraged a twofold division of Christians into lay people on one side, monks and clerics on the other.[14]

We have already met Gratian's text 'Duo sunt genera christianorum'. Here is the continuation of the quotation given above (note 12): 'There is another sort of Christians, who are called lay folk. Λαός means "people". These are allowed to possess temporal goods, but only what they need for use. For nothing is more wretched than to set God at naught for the sake of money. They are allowed to marry, to till the earth, to pronounce judgment on men's disputes and plead in court, to lay their offerings on the altar, to pay their tithes: and so they can be saved, if they do good and avoid evil.' From our angle of interest here two things are particularly noticeable in this passage: the lay position is presented as a concession, and its general tendency is to deny that the laity, concerned in temporal affairs, have any active part in the sphere of sacred things.

(1) The lay condition is presented as a concession to human weakness. 'His licet . . ., his concessum est', says Gratian. Other texts of about the same time reflect the same idea. There is, for instance, Urban II's bull of 1092 confirming the foundation of the canons of Raitenbach, a document which, Canon Petit tells us, was afterwards often reproduced or invoked, as when Honorius II confirmed the Order of Prémontré: 'From her beginning the Church has offered two kinds of life to her children: one to help the insufficiency of the weak, another to perfect the goodness of the strong . . .'. Or again the words of Gerhoh of Reichersberg (d. 1169), with their echo of the boundless desire to be remade in the spirit and letter of the primitive Church which was moving western Christendom from the middle of the eleventh to the middle of the thirteenth centuries: in the primitive Church, he says, those who were perfectly converted pooled their property for the benefit of the poor. And he goes on: 'So, excepting those who, being married, used this world as if they did not use it, bought as not owning, rejoiced as not making merry, people whose place was among the imperfect . . ., excepting them, I say, who are numbered among the women who followed the Lord from afar, the people who entirely cleaved to Christ with his disciples, and deserved that name by excellence, were those only who put themselves under the yoke of continence and at one stroke left all they had for the Lord's sake'. Gerhoh's style is clumsy, even in

[14]It is worth noticing that in St Peter Damian's *Vita Romualdi* (PL., cxliv, 986; quoted by Dereine in *Rev. hist. eccles.*, 1946, p. 368) 'communiter vivere' is opposed to 'saeculariter habitare.'

Latin, but his meaning is clear: from the Christian point of view life
in the world is a compromise. A Christian who is completely consistent with the gospel principles that he professes ought normally to
leave the world that he may lead the 'apostolic life', a life according
to the gospel ideal and in accord with the laws of the kingdom of
God.

Only at the expense of ignoring the whole of history can it be
denied that this idea is in conformity with Christian tradition and,
in the last resort, with the nature of things. Christian life led integrally and without compromise in accordance with its proper requirements is what is traditionally called the angelic or apostolic life, that
is, the monastic life (in the wide sense). But one cannot but feel a
certain unsatisfactoriness about an estimate of Christian life so
exclusively dominated by the ideas of renunciation and the wickedness of the world; we shall come back to this in Chapter IX. One
may well ask whether all the aspects of New Testament teaching
have been given their weight; from the point of view of a theology
of laity its pages have been turned rather too quickly.

(2) The idea that the laity, concerned in temporal affairs, have no
part in the sphere of sacred things. *Duo genera christianorum*. Certainly
it was well understood that clergy and laity are both part of the one
Church. Master Vacarius replied to his former fellow-pupil Speroni
(who gave to the twelfth-century so many of the theses of the sixteenth-century Reformers with surprising closeness) that laity and
clergy are united in the faith and that the distinction between them
in no way compromises the unity of the Church. But for the mind of
the middle ages this unity in the faith had a depth and realism that
we can no longer easily appreciate. Towards the end of the century
Stephen of Tournai joined affirmations of unity and duality in the
same passage: 'In one city and under one king there are two peoples
whose difference corresponds to two sorts of life; and to them correspond two sovereignties, a double order of jurisdiction. The city
is the Church; her king is Christ; the two peoples are the two orders
of clergy and laity; the two sorts of life are the spiritual and the
fleshly; the two sovereignties are the priesthood and the kingship;
the two jurisdictions the divine and the human.'[15] Hugh of Saint-
Victor expressed this idea by an image which came to be widely

[15]Prologue to the *Summa super Decreta*, in Mirbt, *Quellen zur Geschichte des Papsttums*,
n. 318.

used, that of the two sides of a human body.[16] Hugh and his followers understood the unity of the Church, or more exactly of the *respublica christiana* (*corpus christianum*, *christianitas* was used more rarely), in this way: Church and society form one single body, in which two powers are operative and two lives are led, somewhat as a man's body has a right side and a left side. All right; but one may be allowed to point out some objections against this way of looking at things. What are they?

Essentially, what has already been said, that it does not show the laity's place in the building together of the Church, in the specifically Christian achievement worked out in human history (and not above it, in some vague Platonic universe). That call and those problems felt so acutely today, which are referred to in our introduction and to which this book seeks to give some elements of a reply where theology is concerned, these hardly have a place in that calm distribution of roles between the spiritual and the temporal—or what Stephen of Tournai calls 'the fleshly'.

Already in the eleventh century (in the *Exultet*-rolls in the British Museum and among the Barberini MSS. of the Vatican Library), and more frequently in the fifteenth and sixteenth, the Church is represented according to Hugh of Saint-Victor's scheme, under the form of two peoples. One, behind the pope, is made up of bishops, priests and monks; the other, behind the emperor, of princes, knights, peasants, men and women. It is true that the middle ages looked on the emperor (or king) as a church person, at any rate when the Church was considered also as *respublica christiana*.[17] In accordance with the mind of Hugh and of Boniface VIII the diagram of the two sides was meant to affirm unity. But in the critical and antihierarchical currents of the fourteenth and fifteenth centuries, which prepared the way for state laicism and the ecclesiology of the Reformers, it lent itself to quite another interpretation. Instead of two sides, a figure of unity, the fourteenth-century critics spoke of two bodies, each with its own head, of one side the emperor or king,

[16]Hugh of Saint-Victor, *De sacramentis*, ii, 2, 2 (PL., clxxvi, 417). This image crops up already in Walafrid Strabo, *De exordiis et incrementis rerum ecclesiast.*, c. 32 (*Mon. Germ. Cap. reg. Franc.*, ii, p. 515; cited by Sohm, *Kirchenrecht*, ii, p. 247). After Hugh it is found, *e.g.*, in Vincent of Beauvais (*Speculum doctr.*, viii, 31), James of Viterbo (*De regimine christ.*, ii, 10; ed. Arquillière, p. 280), and Boniface VIII, who depends closely on Hugh ('*Unam sanctam*'; Denzinger, n. 469).

[17]On this see J. Hashagen, *Staat und Kirche vor der Reformation* (Essen, 1931), pp. 481ff., 505ff.

of the other the pope, and later on a head for each country.[18] Two
bodies, two heads. . . . The mind loves unity, and will perforce
restore it. Starting with this untoward dualism, there was plenty to
draw the Church towards one extreme or the other. In one direction,
we shall see in the next chapter how some arrived at conceiving the
Church theologically as a church of clergy, consisting in the hierarchy alone; we shall produce texts which clearly insinuate this idea.
In the other direction one-sidedness became more catastrophic still
—we shall see why. Princes will lay claim to the headship of the
Christian body, and so of the Church; they will find theologians
ready to recognise their claim, even to offer it to them, as Nicholas
of Dinkelsbuhl did to King Sigismund at the council of Constance
in 1414. Or a theology of the Church will develop, in line with certain elements of medieval ecclesiology, which conceives her purely
as the congregation of the faithful; that is the path the Reformers
will take. 'Christ has not got two bodies, nor two kinds of body, one
temporal and the other spiritual', wrote Luther.[19] So while some
tended to see the Church actualised in a priesthood without people,
others came to see it as a people without a priesthood. For the sixteenth-century Reformers the Church tended to be simply lay society
as submitted to the law of God.[20] The reaction against a too over-
powering development of the aspect of hierarchical mediation and

[18]*Songe du Vergier*, c. 307 (Goldast, *Monarchia*, i, p. 200); William of Occam,
Octo quaestiones (Goldast, ii, pp. 314, 319): cited by H. de Lubac, *Corpus mysticum*
(Paris, 1944), p. 133. In the *Songe du Vergier* the Soldier's thesis is that there are
'duo capita diversorum corporum, scilicet clericorum et laicorum' (c. 307), but
the Cleric answers, 'Quamvis sint duo genera hominum clerici et laici, tamen unum
corpus sunt' (c. 308). Mme J. Fichet, 'Histoire du laïcat dans l'Eglise' in *Le rôle des
laics dans l'Eglise*. *Carrefour* 1951 (Montreal, 1952), p. 20, writes: 'Gregory VII distinguished the spiritual and the temporal in order to bring them closer together.
But instead of that, passion inflamed the situation, spiritual and temporal were
opposed, and one was separated from the other.' She quotes the text of Cardinal
Humbert (*Adv. simoniacos*, iii, 9): 'Laici sua tantum, id est saecularia, clerici autem
sua tantum, id est ecclesiastica negotia, disponant et provideant. . . . Sicut clerici
saecularia negotia, sic et laici ecclesiastica praesumere prohibeantur' (*Mon. Germ.
Hist.*, *Libelli de lite*, i, p. 208). Here can be seen the danger there was of shutting
the laity up in secular pursuits and failing to see that it is their part also, in a
certain way, to fashion the Church.

[19]In his Appeal to the German Nobility (Weimar edn, vi, 408).

[20]That was more and more clearly Zwingli's idea, and eventually Luther's: cf.
A. Farner, *Die Lehre von Kirche und Staat bei Zwingli* (Tübingen, 1930), pp. 7ff.;
E. Foerster, 'Fragen zu Luthers Kirchenbegriff aus der Gedankenwelt seines
Altes' in *Festgabe J. Kaftan* (Tubingen, 1920), pp. 87–102. There were points of
contact in this sense with medieval thought and the fourteenth-century German
preachers; cf. W. Schwer, *Stände und Ständeordnung im Weltbild des Mittelalters*
(Paderborn, 1934), pp. 38, 78–79. The Reformers were led in this direction by the
inner logic of their doctrinal choices (*ibid.*, p. 36). But the importance of sociological
and economic factors can hardly be overestimated.

the clergy's part took the form of elimination of this order of things. We may well think that the remedy was worse than the disease. But for Protestants the glory of the Reformers is that they brought into lay life, into everyday life, the holiness which had formerly been kept in the cloister; that they denounced the distinction between an ordinary goodness and morality, just sufficient for salvation, and a higher morality available only to churchmen; that they restored dignity and Christian value to the various activities of secular life, and particularly to man's trades and professions. There is no need to give references; they would be endless, for these ideas were found everywhere.

Neither shall we undertake an apology for the Catholic middle ages or an account of holiness attained in secular life: this will be the concern of several chapters later on and of a special treatment of the medieval idea of 'estates' or 'orders' and of the Christian conception of occupational calling.

The Canonical Notion. – This rubric does not imply that the conception just dealt with is not canonical, but it is dominated by moral considerations. The view to be set out now is more juridical.[21]

We start with some words of St Bonaventure, who is giving an account of the sacramental characters [B] conferred by baptism, confirmation and holy order.[22] 'Character', he says, 'is a sign distinguishing the faithful in the spiritual people of the New Covenant: he discriminates between different states in respect of faith, and includes in the same state those who are marked with the same character. There are three states in respect of faith, according as that faith is simple, forceful or fruitful. Baptism distinguished the faithful from the non-faithful; among the faithful, confirmation denotes the strong; by holy order 'homo ut sanctus ad ministerium templi a laicis separatur'. – So the cleric is distinguished from the layman as having the charge, not only of living by faith and upholding it, but of imparting it. That the emphasis is put more on the prophetical than on the properly liturgical aspect of the clerical function follows from the point of view from which Bonaventure was writing, a point of view normal in a mendicant teacher. The fact remains, and it is the point here, that the layman's condition is defined by function and not by way of life.

Elsewhere St Bonaventure says: 'For him who is engaged in the

[21]The onesided emphasis given it in such a work as A. Hagen's *Prinzipien des katholischen Kirchenrechts* (Würzburg, 1949) shows to what a degree the canonical point of view finds the distinction in a sacred power. The author goes so far as to say that religious cannot constitute a special 'estate' in the Church (p. 102).

[22]*Sent.*, lib. iv, d. 6, p. 1, art. unicus, q. 4 (Quaracchi edn, iv, p. 143).

Church's service or who becomes a cleric, renunciation of temporal
things belongs to perfection and not to necessity. We see it done in
the early Church . . . and we still see it done today in religious perfection, but neither divine nor human law imposes it on a cleric. All
the same, it is right and proper that clerics should not bother so
much about temporal things as do lay people, who have got to think
about their children. . . . Moreover, temporal preoccupations are
bad for spiritual ones. That is why the texts appealed to speak as if
the clergy ought to give up all earthly things. They don't mean that
with respect to ownership but only with respect to attachment.[23]
This last comment shows a shift of emphasis. The point of view is no
longer that of clericature as a form of life in which clergy approximate to monks, but that of active duties, of an office, of a competence: we have moved from a monastic world to one which is
sociologically and culturally much nearer our own.

For it is this writer's conviction that the deep change that took
place between the end of the eleventh century and the beginning of
the thirteenth had consequences that persist down to our own time.
The synthetical and symbolical intellectuality of the patristic age
and monastic culture became analytical and dialectical. Predominantly moral considerations gave way to those that are predominantly juridical. The idea of *forum externum* was disentangled
from that of *forum internum*, with all that that involves for a theology
of excommunication and for an ecclesiology. In considering the
Church, jurisdictional and sociological elements were developed and,
vis-a-vis the more mystical and sacramental views of the preceding
age, were on the way to becoming pretty well preponderant. So it
can be said that, if 'in the eleventh century the accent was put on the
monk, not on the priest', in the thirteenth it threatened to be put on
the prelate and on ecclesiastical power. All this is of no great importance for our present purpose, however. All we need do is to
grasp a notion of the lay condition different from (and complementary to) the previous one: one no longer looking at way of life but at
function or competence.

From the canonical point of view it is this second notion that is
formal and exact. Where conditions of life are concerned, the layman
is he who lives 'in the world', as opposed to the monk. But canonically a layman can be a monk, for he is defined as 'one who has no
part in the power of jurisdiction and, especially, of holy order',[24] as
opposed to the cleric. The principal canons of the Code that speak

[23]*Sent.*, lib. iv, d. 24, p. 1, a. 2, q. 3 (Quaracchi edn, iv, p. 612.)
[24] Vermeersch and Creusen, *Epitome juris can.*, (1927), i, n. 199 (1933 edn, n. 231).

of lay people in a general way show them as having to receive, as having the right to receive, spiritual goods from the clergy, especially the helps necessary for salvation.[25] This will be shown to be normal when we come to define the laity's position theologically. It could also be demonstrated from the very nature of canon law, which in the first place is a law of the sacraments. This last is an historical truth which, it seems to us, may be taken as established by Sohn and his school (without, however, adopting their systematic construction), and a theological analysis of the content of canon law leads to a similar conclusion. It would be easy enough to find a basis for it in ecclesiology, but this is not the place to do it.

Obviously if we stop there our idea of laity will be rather negative; going from one definition to another has not helped us much in that respect. According to the monastic view, lay people only exist by favour of a concession; according to the canonical view, they are negative creatures. . . . It is always the same old stumbling-block, which this book is trying to do something to remove.

However, there is no need to suppose that the distinction between laymen and clerics (canonical view), coincides with a distinction between people who have only a secular field of action and people who have a sacred or holy field of action. Lay people too exercise sacred activities. Not for a moment may we entertain any idea of them that is inconsistent with their membership in the people of God to which the very etymology of their name bears witness. Once again, the purpose of this book is precisely to study the sacred state of Christian laity, first in its constitution (*statut*) as a whole and then in the detail of its substance.

*   *   *

When we attempt, if not to define, at any rate to outline the characteristics of the lay condition, we see that our two notions of it eventually reach down to one same point, which we will try to indicate by two successive approximations.

First approximation. — As members of the people of God, lay persons are, like clerics and monks, by their state and directly, ordered to heavenly things. All of them have been made fit 'for our portion of the inheritance of the saints in light' (Colossians i, 12). But they are not all ordered in exactly the same way. It would be biblically, dogmatically and in fact inaccurate to say: Clerics and monks are, by their state and directly, ordered to heavenly things; lay people are, by their state and directly (though not exclusively), ordered to earthly things. But it is true to say that: (1) Lay people do not live

[25]Cf. in particular canons 682, 948.

exclusively for heavenly things; that is, so far as present circumstances allow, the condition of monks; (2) Lay people are Christians to the fullest extent as touching life in Christ, but they have no competence, or only a limited competence, touching the properly ecclesial means to life in Christ; these means belong to the competence of clerics.

Lay people are called to the same end as clergy or monks—to the enjoyment of our inheritance as sons of God; but they have to pursue and attain this end without cutting down their involvement in the activities of the world, in the realities of the primal creation, in the disappointments, the achievements, the stuff of history. The laity is called to do God's work in the world; not merely in the sense that its members should move heaven and earth to introduce into lay life what monks and nuns do in the cloister; or not again in the sense that, having to do the works and adopt the form of holiness of the religious life, they *in addition* do the work of the world, which religious don't have to do. There is a certain type of hagiography, not unknown in the *legendae* of the Divine Office, that perhaps turns the mind in this direction; and moreover there is too much truth and depth in it for it to be lightly dismissed. But there are indications that God wills something quite different. Lay people are Christians in the world, there to do God's work *in so far as it must be done in and through the work of the world.* We believe that this is necessary, in accordance with God's purpose, and that his work can be actualised as he wills it should be only through a full, real participation in the world's travail. This is what we shall seek to establish in our third chapter. For the fullness of her work in accordance with the purpose of the living God, the Church has to have laity, faithful who do the work of the world and reach their last end in dedication to that work. This is essential to the Church. She has to have some members who are directly and exclusively dedicated to the work of God's kingdom, and for that purpose are dispensed from the world's work: such are monks and priests. So, too, in Israel the levites were given no allotment when the land was shared out. But the total mission of the Church, corresponding to God's design, requires that the Lord's reign be prepared in and through that creation in the perfecting of which man must co-operate. Therefore do God's design and the Church's mission call for the existence of lay faithful; they need a laity which, in its wholeness, is called to glorify God without lessening its engagement in the work of the world. The laity's relation to the one last end is perhaps less immediate, certainly less exclusive, than that of clergy and monks; but it partakes of theirs in a secondary sense, with reference to the decisive fact that the *whole* of God's people is advancing towards its Promised Land.

Second approximation. The layman then is one for whom, through the very work which God has entrusted to him, the substance of things in themselves is real and interesting. The cleric, still more the monk, is a man for whom things are not really interesting *in themselves*, but for something other than themselves, namely, their relation to God, whereby he may be better known and which can help towards his service. This parallel could be prolonged with the aid of those passages wherein St Thomas Aquinas contrasts the points of view of the philosopher and the *fidelis*.[26] The philosopher, that is, the man of learning, is interested in a thing's own nature, the *fidelis* in its transcendent reference; the philosopher seeks the explanation of things, the *fidelis* their meaning. The subject could be carried further by looking in history for types and movements representative respectively of the attitude of the *fidelis* and that of the learned man, in other words, of the cleric and of the layman. Our attention would probably be caught particularly by two great movements: firstly, what has been called the 'Albertino-Thomist revolution';[27] then, by the upsurge of modern 'laicism' (in the sense that will be explained in a moment), the reconquest by reason of fields in which she had been unduly held in tutelage by the authority of clerics.

The clerical condition as we have described it is full of danger. First of all, so uninterested an attitude towards earthly things as such commands respect only when it is genuine and uncontaminated, especially in a world so concerned with sincerity as ours. Everybody respects Father de Foucauld. But there is great danger that an attitude adopted in the name of one's state, one's calling, should be too theoretical; that one should lay claim to its honour and benefits without having its spirit or taking up its burdens. And the scandal becomes glaring if a man claims to be disinterested towards the process of history and of the world, when he is really seeking power, wealth (in any of its forms, which are many), advantageous influence in secular things.

That, however, is not the biggest danger. That lies in a loss of respect for the true inwardness of things. The man concerned with the transcendent relationship of things with their principle and end, the *fidelis* and more especially the cleric through his profession, runs the risk of forgetting that things exist in themselves, with their own

[26]Cf. Prologus in *II Sent.*; *Contra Gentiles*, ii, 4.
[27]Father M. D. Chenu, following a *scheme* of Father Mandonnet. Cf. Father Congar's article 'Theologie' in *Dict. du theol. cath.*, cc. 386ff.

D

proper nature and needs. The temptation is to make these things simply occasions or starting-points for an affirmation of the sovereignty of the Principle, or as mere means towards the carrying-out of some religious programme. When earthly disinterestedness is total, when it is truly a matter of pure religious relation, such attitudes, though perhaps still irritating, have something about them that is not only religious but unexceptionable. In the concrete, however, the religious relationship is actualised in a Church, through the ministry of churchmen. Church and churchmen have an historical, sociological existence, and for religious ends they make use of means borrowed from historical and sociological life. The danger, then, is of withholding full respect for earthly human things on the ground that they are being given a transcendent reference, whereas concretely they are simply being used among the sociological and historical means of the Church—as when they are referred and made subservient to 'accepted ideas' more than to the faith, to the conventions of 'the Christian world' more than to the requirements of Christianity, to the 'politics' of Catholicism more than to its mystery. From the minute the (historical) Church is thought of in this way we go from one thing to the other on the temporal plane without hesitation or discrimination. Perhaps, even certainly, this is a sign of the Church's transcendence; but there is also unquestionably a danger that the temporal engagement should not be treated seriously, and that the nature and truth of the earthly things that compose it are not fully respected. This is particularly serious when it is a question, not of practical action, whose truth is less objectively determined, but of objective truth: in that case any sharp practice 'in the good cause' is a betrayal that no apologetic or allegedly apostolic advantage can excuse.

Historically, the Christian regime of the West after the dissolution of the Roman empire, and especially from Charlemagne till the coming of the modern world—which began during the last third of the twelfth century, had its age of power, spiritually, at the Renaissance, politically, after the French Revolution and is not yet over—this Christian regime, 'Christendom', was marked by the organisation of the whole of temporal life under the supreme regulation of the Church and in her setting; and this meant that all relative realities were brought under tutelage. It is no part of our present purpose to set forth the benefits that accrued to human society from this state of affairs, nor to examine the theoretical question of relations between the temporal and the spiritual. We will simply note two points. (1) In this regulation of earthly matters—the sciences as well as civil affairs

—by religious authority, interpreter of the absolute, there was an element of confiscation or, to use a Marxist word, alienation. This alienation was never complete, these earthly matters always had a relative autonomy; but, having been taken into the service of the faith, they were never considered and developed for their own sakes. (2) Guardianship is good for children; but it was unduly prolonged in fields wherein men had, as we now say, come of age. The most typical example—which the clergy can never think about too much —is clearly that of Galileo, threatened with torture when he was seventy years old and made to retract in a scientific matter, and when he was right: this in the name of Revelation—but actually in the name of certain 'accepted ideas' which were taken for revealed truth and sound philosophy.

It is against the confiscation of the internal truth of second causes by the First Cause that modern laicism rebelled; fundamentally it was a movement to recapture rights in second causes, that is, in earthly things. The various priesthoods of second causes rose against the alienation of their domain into the hands of the priesthood of the First Cause. A superabundance of proofs could be adduced that this is the true, profound meaning of the lay movement—and of the modern world too. But are any proofs needed when the evidence is so clear? It would be embarrassing to have to choose among all the statements of leaders in the priesthoods of second causes—statesmen, philosophers, scholars, medical men, philanthropists. The following passage from Lavisse has often been quoted: 'To be secular (*laique*) . . . is not to make the best of ignorance about anything. It is to believe that life is worth the trouble of being lived, to love life, to refuse to look on the world as a 'vale of tears', to deny that tears are necessary and beneficial, that suffering may be providential; it is not to make the best of any unhappiness. It is not to leave feeding the hungry, giving drink to the thirsty, righting injustice, consoling the sorrowful, to a judge seated outside of this life: it is to join battle with evil in the name of justice.'[28] Forget the mockery and the irreverence: it is accidental and peripheral to the meaning and essential intention of the words. The real affirmation is this: To be

[28]*Annales de la jeunesse laique* (1902), quoted by L. Caperan in *Foi laique et foi chrétienne* . . . (Paris, 1937), p. 10. I will add only this, from Proudhon: 'I acknowledge the absolute in metaphysics; consequently I acknowledge God, but also in metaphysics, provided he does not leave the absolute.. . . Did the man who invented the lightning-conductor, religious man as he was, use to fall on his knees in a storm and implore God that he should not be struck? . . . I believe that recourse to the absolute, to invisible powers, is the right way to destroy the fruits of knowledge in us' (*Justice*, 7e etude, ch. ii, in L. Maury, *La pensée vivante de Proudhon*, Paris, 1942, i, p. 155).

secular is to use all the resources within us in that pursuit of justice and truth for which we hunger, the very stuff of human history.

Have we then been asking 'What is a layman?' only to end up with a definition of 'lay' in the sense of laicism? Of course the answer is No. But in a sense the answer could be Yes. Because there is laicism (*laicisme*) and there is laicity (*laicité*), a distinction made classical by a declaration of the cardinals and archbishops of France; it is something like 'scientism' and science, the 'modern world' in the sense of Pius XI's Syllabus of Errors and the modern world to which we belong; or somewhat as there is clericalism and there is the Church. There has been, and there still is, a laicism whose foundation-stone is a doctrinal, metaphysical affirmation that there is no God in the sense of the positive Judaeo-Christian revelation; or at all events, no 'supernatural' according to the Church's meaning. But there is also a lay affirmation which does not exclude the supernatural: it simply requires the relative not to be absorbed by the absolute to the point of evaporation; it says that reference to the First Cause should not do away with the reality of second causes and the internal truth of all that fashions the world and the history of men. This 'laicality' (if so barbarous a word may be allowed) does not refuse to believe in God; it simply asks for belief in things as well. It wants to respect their nature, their laws, their needs; it thinks that, given the unique Absolute, the one thing necessary, men as a whole ought to make their way to God without taking short cuts or minimising their passage through history and the things of the world.

Believers are often reproached for not interesting themselves in things, for being content with purifying their intentions in view of God's law, and for not believing in good or evil *in things*: people today, since they belong to the world and to their age, have become hypersensitive to this reproach.[29] Many Christians—in France, at any rate, Christians as a whole—are conscious of this peremptory problem, and it has often found expression in the self-criticisms that have been so common since the war. They see it as one of the bigger questions they have to answer, and perhaps the most important element in their insistent need to know the function of Christian lay people—or of lay Christians.

[29]Its classical expression is criticism of charity; a more technical expression is criticism of a 'morality of intention' and the theory of efficaciousness. A literary expression is the scene in *Prélude à Verdun* where Jules Romains confronts the consciences of two men, Brimont, a Christian, and Clanricard, a *laic*, with a stupid order to attack, which will mean the death of many men but will gain the regiment a mention in dispatches: ' "No, Brimont, you don't understand. I'm not worried about quieting my conscience, but about"—and he laboured each syllable—"*preventing a crime*".'

A few pages back St Thomas Aquinas was invoked. This Christian genius was providentially set at the junction of the ancient world, sacral and monastic (but also feudal), with the modern world, scientific and positive, to help educate the second in respect for what was of everlasting worth in the first. He himself began as an oblate of the great family of Monte Cassino; but his own intellectual beginnings were philosophical and naturalist and, the 'Arts-men' [C] of Paris looked on him so much as one of themselves that when he died they wanted his body, as well as the treatises he had promised them. At one and the same time Aquinas appreciated the ordered unity of things—the most fundamental and universal idea of the middle ages —and the particularity of their nature, each one having its specific note and its content of truth. He is a model and a peerless guide for a world given over to technique and particular explanations without any unifying references, and suffering accordingly. He may be said to have been authentically lay, even though a cleric.

Can the same be said of St Thomas's spiritual children? That fine man Theophile Foisset remarks several times that there was something of the layman about Lacordaire (whose friend and biographer Foisset was). For example, when his lectures at the College Stanislas were interrupted Lacordaire wrote to the archbishop of Paris, Mgr de Quelen: 'I ask the Church, in the person of my bishop, to trust me and to honour my priesthood. . . . I claim what is the priest's sole good and sole honour, freedom to preach Jesus Christ. . . .' On which Foisset comments: 'There was something manly, something of the layman, in these words.' That reflexion is significant. It looks as if people think one is 'lay' when one asks respect for what is human and natural, but that the priestly office is bound entirely to absorb the human man: that office not only in its spiritual and divine aspect but also in the aspect which involves submissiveness to a system whose pattern is one of authority and submission. That that is an altogether happy view may be questioned, but this is not the place to discuss it. The point, however, brings us round once more to this idea: a lay person is one for whom things exist, for whom their truth is not as it were swallowed up and destroyed by a higher reference. For to him or her, Christianly speaking, what is to be referred to the Absolute is the very reality of the elements of this world whose outward form passes away.

Chapter II

POSITION OF A THEOLOGY OF LAITY

Two Aspects in the Church

THE reality represented by the word 'Church' in Christian usage has two aspects, which must be carefully distinguished. The point is so important, and has such consequences in ecclesiology, that in order to explain it properly one must accept the risk of making an exposition that is rather austere.

In her ultimate reality the Church is men's fellowship with God and with one another in Christ. She is also the totality of the means to this fellowship. From this fellowship aspect, her ultimate reality, the Church is the aggregate of those who are 'in Christ Jesus'. This aggregate is quite a different thing from a simple juxtaposition of individuals in a group: it is a people, the people of God. Better still, it is the body of Christ, and people of God precisely because body of Christ, as we shall see in our treatise on the Church. Here we are interested, not so much in the nature of the bond of fellowship in Christ, as in this simple fact: the Church in her ultimate reality is a fellowship of persons. And she is made up of these persons as a nation is made up of its citizens or a body of its members.

This aspect of the Church is the one formally expressed by the very word *Ἐκκλησία, Ecclesia*, which means 'convocation', 'assembly'. At least that is what it means etymologically. In the Septuagint the word has a religious value and designates the community of chosen people gathered together to give worship to God or to listen to his word. In the Greek world it designated any assembly or gathering, especially that of citizens meeting to deliberate. In the Acts of the Apostles and in St Paul the word both remains dependent on the ideas of the people of God and, in that Hellenic atmosphere, is adapted to the usual Greek sense. *Ecclesia* has sometimes the secular sense of assembly, often that of the actual local congregation of the faithful, but it also means—and doubtless did from the first[1]—the messianic community or people, raised up by God, a meaning derived from certain characteristic usages of the Septuagint. There *Ecclesia* goes beyond the simple meaning of an actual local congregation.[2] Nevertheless the semantic value of the word is that of an assembly called together. That the assembly exists on the basis of an act of God does not prevent it being made up, as such, of its members. We shall see that this semantic value of the word *Ecclesia* has carried weight in ecclesiological teaching, as it was normal and even more as it had been normal.

The semantic value was faithfully held in honour by the Fathers, by the earlier Scholasticism (mystical and monastic) and by the later (analytic, rational, of the schools), which continues on the whole today. Not only was it usual to add a translation to the bare transcription *Ecclesia*, but the Church was commonly defined as the society or community of the faithful. *Congregatio fidelium, Societas fidelium,* or *Collectio, Coetus, Adunatio, Collegium, Unitas, Corpus, Communio, Universitas, Populus fidelium* (or *christianorum, catholicorum*), with other variants: these formulas are clearly equivalents, and they express the definition that is commonest and, we may say, traditional in the Church. The idea they represent is more complex than the clearness of the words would lead us to suspect. These different terms are pregnant with a whole 'corporative' ideology, of which the middle ages were very conscious and which can be found, in a wide sense and more diffusely, in all Christian writings. And the notion of *fidelis* is much fuller than is supposed if one has not penetrated to the meaning behind this simple formula in ancient ecclesiology: it carries a Christian realism and an ecclesial realism that are equally profound. About all that we shall learn a little more as we go along. The traditional definition, then, carrying on the very meaning of the word *Ecclesia*, above all expresses that aspect of the Church in which she is made up of her members and represents the aggregate of them.   *   *   *

According to another aspect, the Church is the totality of the means provided by the Lord to bring men to his fellowship. This is

[1]Cf. L. Cerfaux, *La theologie de l'Eglise suivant S. Paul* (Unam Sanctam, 10; Paris, 1942). The interpretation only as the concrete local congregation also has its supporters: see, *e.g.* J. G. Campbell in the *Journal of Theological Studies*, 1948, pp. 130–142.

[2]This is evident, *e.g.*, in Acts viii, 1, 3; ix, 31; 1 Cor. xv, 9.

at the heart of the ecclesial reality, and from the point of view of the
Church's sociological structure radically distinguishes her from every
society that is purely earthly or human. A human society has not got
to make its members, it receives them from families; it simply brings
to families the access of good which results from a pooling of energies;
even from the point of view of public authority it produces and
organises itself. Whereas the Church does not receive her members
from families; structurally she is not made up of parishes (local
communities), which themselves are made up of individual faithful.
The Church exists antecedently to the faithful, to constitute them,
and precisely as their mother.

We have shown elsewhere,[3] and it seems obvious, that Protestants
regard only the transcendent action of God, of the Holy Spirit, as
truly forming the faithful. According to them, only the Holy Spirit
and the faithful constitute the Church, in such a way that their
position can be schematised thus: God transcendent in Heaven ——→
faithful ——→ Church, assembly of the faithful. But, whilst the faithful
so constituted by God's transcendent act form visible churches when
they join together, they also constitute, in a way beyond our knowledge, an invisible Church: and this invisible Church depends on
God's act alone (for Zwingli and Calvin, predestination). Hence
those categories present in certain publications of the Ecumenical
Council of Churches which give them an unconscious but real
Protestant tinge: the Church and the churches. The Church, an
invisible reality living in dependence on an act of God; the churches,
visible realities of human making.

It must then be made clear what we mean when we say that the
Church is there before the faithful and the community which they
form. The Church precedes them by that in her which is on the part
of God, or by that in her which pre-exists in Jesus Christ. The two
ways in which the Church exists in God without yet existing in herself are these: (1) in divine predestination, whence the Church exists
in a free and eternal idea and decree, whose actualisation must be
unfolded in created time: (2) in Christ, who in becoming man virtually takes on the whole of human nature and contains the whole
Church; who as the Anointed of God and in his threefold capacity of
king, priest and prophet had in himself all the properties or energies
by which the Church was to exist and live; who throughout his life
on this earth kept the church in his thoughts and in his heart,
enabling her to exist and to live in him, a little in the same way as
the common good of a people lives in the mind of its king or of an

[3] *Vraie et fausse reforme*, part iii.

army in the mind of its commander. Little by little Jesus actualised his purpose, and the Church accordingly began to exist, no longer only in God or in Christ, but in herself. It is very important to understand how Jesus actualised his purpose, that is, founded the Church. It was principally by giving God's people a new dispensation and thus forming a new Israel, the messianic community. We will not follow all the actions of his earthly life, his death, his risen life and finally the sending of his Spirit, by which Jesus gradually gave this new dispensation, founded in his blood,[4] which opens the way to the new Temple and to God's presence. It is enough to indicate the three essential heads of its institution: (1) by the revelation of the mystery of the Trinity and of the Kingdom, Jesus established the messianic people in respect of its faith; (2) by his baptism, by his celebration of the Supper, by his other priestly acts, at last and supremely by his death followed by the outpouring of water and blood, he instituted the sacraments by which his people enter into the fellowship of communal life; (3) by the calling of his disciples, the promises made to Peter before (Matthew xvi) and after the Passion (John xxi), the different actions establishing the Twelve in their apostolical powers, finally by the solemn and definitive sending of them forth, he gave the messianic community the structure of the apostolical ministry and of its hierarchical powers. Those, very briefly, are the elements that Christ instituted to form the messianic community, the *Societas fidelium*, that is to say, the Church under the first of the aspects we have identified: the deposit of faith, the deposit of the sacraments, the deposit of ministries or of apostolical powers. Those are the means of grace, the elements of the order of salvation, in virtue of which—without prejudice to the action of the Holy Spirit, but rather in co-operation with it[5]—God raises up the *faithful individuals* who constitute the Church as *Societas fidelium*.

And so the Church is built up from God and from Christ from end to end: 'von Gott her, von Christus her', as Karl Barth says. But Protestants, and particularly those of the Barthian school, stop short of seeing the following point, which nevertheless has for ecclesiology the value of an *articulus stantis vel cadentis Ecclesiae*: the elements in the threefold deposit of faith, sacraments and powers of the apostolical ministry, which are begetters of the faithful and their community, exist *in the Church*. They are entrusted to the Church, they give rise to the Church's activities. There is that in the Church, entering into

[4] Matt. xxvi, 28; Mark xiv, 24; Luke xxii, 20; 1 Cor. xi, 25.
[5] Cf. in general 1 John v, 7–8; Acts v, 32; John xv, 26–27. For acts of priesthood, John xx, 22–23; Acts viii, 14–17; xiii, 1–4. For those of magisterium, Acts xv, 28. For those of government, Acts xiv, 22, compared with xx, 28.

her definition, which constitutes the *Ecclesia* as the fellowship of men in Christ; it is not simply the fact of a transcendent act of God, of an operation of Christ invisible in Heaven or of his Spirit: it is the fact of realities or energies which originate in God but which have entered into the world and man's history with the incarnation of the Word. God's design is not to do his work by purely heavenly means used *in the setting* of mankind; it is to do it by a *humanisation of his action*, communicating to an institution of human form the exercise, with him, of activities by which men can enter into communion with him on a basis of faith. That is what the Church is. In her ultimate reality she is, and will be unto everlasting, the fellowship of saved men and women; but she is also the institution that brings such a fellowship about. Not, of course, in the first instance: the Church does not save us, Christ saves us. But in virtue of what she has received from him she hands on and applies, everywhere and throughout the ages, that which Christ has done for us.

As the community of the faithful the Church is the *reality* of salvation (*Heilsgemeinschaft*) [D]; she is also the aggregate of the means of the calling to salvation—one may say, using the word in its wide sense, the *sacrament* of that reality (*Heilsanstalt*) [E]. In fact, according to their classical use in Western theology, the categories 'sacrament' and 'reality' are useful for showing the relationship between the two aspects of the Church that we have distinguished. A sacrament precedes its fruit; it is ministered to procure it. But it can happen that it does not produce it, remaining complete in its ritual form but without living substance; just as inversely it is possible for the reality of salvation to be given by God without the mediation of the sacrament. It would require a treatise on the Church to develop the whole of this theology, which is the very heart of ecclesiology, and to show its applications and consequences, which we have done elsewhere.[6] It suffices here to have set out the two aspects, of the Church as made by her members and of the Church as making and preceding her members. The sequel will make clear that this distinction is one of the supports for a theology of laity.

TRADITION HAS ENERGETICALLY MAINTAINED BOTH ASPECTS TOGETHER

A VERY striking thing about the thought concerning the Church of the first Christian generations and the Fathers is the way the two

[6]The distinction (without separation) between these two aspects is at the bottom of what we have said about sin and holiness in the Church in *Vraie et fausse reforme*. . . . Or again in the matter of the benefit that the Church herself and as such would draw from a general reunion of dissidents; cf. *Divided Christendom* (London, 1939), ch. viii.

aspects we have indicated are considered as depending on the same ecclesial organism. The same single Church is declared to be both visible and invisible, to be a hierarchically constituted society and a mystery of heavenly life. The texts are so many and so unanimous[7] that the burden of proof of any dissociation rests on those who assert it.[8] The point of view of the inspired New Testament writings is so much the same that one wonders how Protestant authors have been able to miss the evidence for so long; nowadays they are recognising it more and more: for the Holy Scriptures it is the visible, organised body of Christians that is the Body of Christ.[9] There is nothing in the texts to suggest a dissociation between a community of faithful that is a pure creation of the Spirit and the system, still rudimentary but very solid, of dogmas, sacraments, powers and ministries exercised under apostolical authority. The way in which public penance was carried out and excommunication understood clearly shows the close compenetration of the idea 'community of faithful' with the idea 'ecclesial institution'. Every ancient ecclesiological theme gives evidence of the same thing. It is extremely remarkable—we shall draw conclusions from it elsewhere—how easily these old texts pass from the bishop, hierarchical reality, to the Church or community: the Church is in the bishop, says St Cyprian as, fundamentally, St Ignatius had already said.[10] The Church is the *pleroma* of the bishop, say the Fathers, and St Gregory Nazianzen adds that the bishop is the *pleroma* [F] of the Church.[11]

The following is an impressive example from early times of the fact that the Church is not only the community of the faithful but the pre-existing institution: When after the era of persecution the Church was juridically recognised by public authority and was in some way registered in law, the only category available to define her juridical position was that of *Collegium, Corpus, Universitas personarum.* But the Church was and knew she was something other than an

[7]See, for example, Darwell Stone, *The Christian Church* (London, 1915), and the testimony of F. Kattenbusch in his remarkable article 'Der Quellort der Kirchenidee' in *Festgabe f. A. Harnack* (Tubingen, 1921), pp. 143–172.

[8]Most of the texts that Protestant historians and theologians quote in the sense of a certain idea of 'Church invisible' are perfectly understandable and have their correspondence in this or that category of the classical theology. One thinks, for example, of the texts quoted by E. Seeberg in *Studien zur Geschichte des Begriffes der Kirche* . . . (Erlangen, 1885).

[9]This has been forcibly put by L. Cerfaux, *op. cit.*, n. 1 above.

[10]The Church is made by the bishop and his clergy: Cyprian, *Ep.*, 33, 1 (Hartel, p. 566); Ignatius, *Trall.*, 3, 1, cf. below n. 26.

[11]Pseudo-Dionysius, *De eccles. hier.*, 3, 14 (PG., iii, 444–445); Chrysostom, *De prophet. obscur.*, 2, 10 (PG., lvi, 192); Nazianzen, *Orat.*, 2, 4 and 99 (PG., xxxvi, 412 and 502). Texts cited by P. Tromp in *Gregorianum*, 1937, p. 25. Cf. below, n. 48.

association of people, a religious *collegium* as paganism understood it, she was something other than a community of man's belief and worship. She was and is an institution formed from on high, hierarchically built. This has enabled Otto van Gierke to maintain that Christianity's great contribution to law has been the notion of institution, that is, beyond a simple association or corporation, the idea of an ideal reality above and antecedent to its individual members. While thinking of herself as a *collegium*, a *corpus*, a *universitas*, and going a long way in that direction, the Church has always been profoundly conscious that the society of faithful exists only through its institution, and that the two aspects of her reality are organically united, in the way we have said.

There is a very important point that has often been noticed, but seems never to have been the object of a particular study, namely, that Christian tradition, the tradition of the Fathers, takes the corporative direction, whereas pagan philosophical and juridical influences, especially that of imperial Roman law, have tended to favour an absolutist point of view which is not that of properly ecclesiastical tradition. The Roman juridical idea, which has sometimes prevailed, is of a sovereign power exercising dominion over a given territory, imposing a uniform system and itself ruling the life of the whole body. In the corporative idea, which has been well-rooted for a long time, the principle of unity is not so much rule by a territorial authority as the relation of many diverse parts with a spiritual principle of order: idea or purpose. The *congregatio*, *collectio*, *collegium* is precisely a collective unity thus realised. Where the Church is concerned the spiritual principle of unity is faith, the total giving up and adhering of the human person to God. *Societas fidelium*: the Church was traditionally considered as a body organised and built together at each level of its being, whose total unity was assured by this adhesion to God which faith effects in a deeply realistic way.[12] In the concrete regime of ecclesial life all this was expressed—here and there from the tenth century but very definitely from the twelfth, in the ordering of communal life—by a whole graduated and hierarchically-organised system of councils, by which each community itself regulated its daily life in accordance with custom and traditional principles. This can be followed from the parish right up to the

[12]Father Darquennes remarks on this realism in the thought of St Thomas. It is in virtue of this realism of the adhesion of faith that theological tradition unanimously affirms the Church's unity throughout the Old and New Covenants, which often takes the form of the affirmation *Ab Abel justo*. See Father Congar's article under this title in *Abhandl. über Theol. u. Kirche: Fetsch. f. K. Adam* (Düsseldorf, 1951), pp. 79–108.

general council which, in the golden age of the corporative principle, was thought of in the West as a sort of supreme council of the 'Christian Republic', the hierarchical society of the faithful.[13]

In continuity with the oldest characteristics of Roman law, Christianity organised its own communities on the principle of collegiality; later on, when the theologians embarked on a theory of political society, they saw the people itself as the body politic, the public service of this body politic appertaining to the highest levels of society, what we call an Estate. This conception of things has from time to time been battered and breached by developments of later Roman law, those of Justinian's code, those of imperial absolutism. This was particularly the case at the end of the fifteenth and beginning of the sixteenth centuries, when the ideological current of modern absolutism and 'stateism' began. This Roman law envisaged society, not as a people organising itself, but as a given domain over which a sovereign central authority exercised power. In the best period of medieval times that would have been called tyranny. The people were a docile mass for whom the king's will was law. While not forgetting that the Church has her own constitution and that, as we shall have occasion to emphasise, her hierarchy is of divine institution, it may well be thought that these ideas, which flourished throughout a whole age, were not without influence on canonists and theologians at this very time when the lines of our treatises *de Ecclesia* were being fixed. In them the hierarchical principle (which we are not questioning for a moment) is emphasised, but not the principle of collective life which is no less at the heart of the ancient tradition.

On the other hand, from the age of the Fathers till the Counter-Reformation the idea of the Church as the community of the faithful, made by its members, was very much alive. That this idea went far is seen when we consider the long use made of this principle of Roman law: 'Whatever affects everybody ought to be corporately approved by everybody'. Who invokes this principle? The upholders of conciliar theories? No indeed. It was, at the beginning and the end of the thirteenth century, two of the most authoritarian of popes, two of the most conscious of their prerogatives, Innocent III and Boniface VIII.[14] Like many others, they were only resorting to a principle which is part of the old Catholic tradition, that of consent

[13]A. Hauck writes on this well and illuminatingly in 'Die Rezeption und Umbildung der allgemeinen Synode im Mittelalter', *Histor. Vierteljahrschrift*, 10 (1907), pp. 465–482.

[14]On this principle, which does not touch the Church's constitution but her concrete life and especially the law of process, see Excursus C of the future *Etudes conjointes*.

of the whole community: we shall find applications of it in the threefold domain of the Church's priestly, kingly and prophetical life, and
shall then examine its exact significance. For the moment let us
simply register the picture it suggests of a Church building herself up
in a measure from below, a Church in which the community aspect
of the faithful is strongly developed.

It would, however, be a mistake to suppose that this 'society of
faithful' aspect was at all detrimental to the insitutional aspect
among the Fathers and in the middle ages: it is clear that for a very
long time unity and balance were held between these ecclesiological
poles. This begins to be understood when a close study is made of the
notion of *fidelis*, in the traditional definition, *Societas fidelium*. From
the start the word has quite an aura of sociological significance, shot
through with religion. It evokes faithfulness as the principle of social
agreement, of the unity and strength of society; but especially is it
inseparable from an ecclesial and sacramental foundation. It takes
rather an effort for us to understand this nowadays. We live in a
world that is desacralised, individualistic, analytical and academic,
a world in which ideas are investigated for their own sake and easily
separated from their signs or their sensible embodiments. For us, one
of the faithful is a 'believer', one who holds intellectually certain
transcendent maxims, who has 'religious convictions'. But in the
Christian tradition with which thought was impregnated at least till
the thirteenth century a *fidelis* was someone sacramentally incorporated in the ecclesial reality. Not only was the faith he professed
essentially the trinitarian faith of the Symbol, it was the reality in
him of baptism and his being part of the Church which, after having
brought him to birth, formed him, nourished his life, governed all
his actions, consecrated and united every moment of his existence to
Christ. The sixteenth-century Reformers kept the material identity
of the formula and an external continuity with the tradition, but
how much they really altered its meaning when they put the *fidelis*
into immediate association with an act of God: the word (Luther),
predestination and salvation (Zwingli, Calvin). For classical theology
was said to be constituted, made, instituted, consecrated, founded by
faith *and the sacraments* of faith.[15] And faith was set in order by the
preaching *of the Church*, through a ministry that was sprung from

[15]Keeping to texts of St Thomas: 'per fidem et fidei sacramenta constituta,
fabricata est Ecclesia Christi' (*Sum. theol.*, III, q. lxiv, a. 2, ad 3); 'sacramenta
quibus est Ecclesia instituta' (I, q. xcii, a. 3), 'quibus consecratur Ecclesia' (*Com.
in Joan.*, c. 20, lect. 5, n. 4); 'Ecclesia fundatur in fide et sacramenta' (*Com. in IV
Sent.*, d. 17, q. 3, a. 1, sol. 5; d. 27, q. 3, a. 3, ad 2), and cf. *Com. in Hebr.*, c. 3, lect.
3, etc.

Christ and was generative of his Body.

Catholic tradition does not identify the mystical Body with the aggregate of men whom Christ spiritually and invisibly quickens by his grace. Here again it has been shown, at any rate as regards Luther, that the Reformers altered this tradition that is so solidly grounded in early Christianity and the way St Paul speaks of the Body of Christ. Traditionally the mystical Body is not solely the order of inward holiness, the spiritual community of the saved; it is at the same time the visible organism, the order of means to salvation. A word will be said further on about the tendency, turning up throughout the middle ages and often using St Augustine's name, to reduce Christianity simply to a spiritual fellowship, thus betraying a profound lack of understanding of the ecclesial means of grace. Nor is this the place to examine the delicate theological problems raised by a rigorous identification of the body of Christ with the visible Church; on this point the encyclical letter '*Mystici corporis*'. of 29 June 1949, propounds teaching very profitable for theological reflexion. What matters here is to notice that, following tradition, the Church is the body of Christ *under the two aspects* that we have distinguished: as community of the faithful *and* as institution or order of the means to salvation, at the same time. These aspects are necessary for the realisation of the double relation Christ has with the Church, by which he makes her his body: as her founder, ruling and building her up by his power; as her life, quickening her by his Spirit —a double relation that the gospels express separately (the Synoptists [G] on one hand, St John on the other), but St Paul unites under the one idea of 'head'.

We shall have occasion to set forth several aspects of the far-reaching law that truth can be held only in the communion of the whole. From a purely objective point of view heresy can be defined as the negation of a truth proposed or defined by the Church as divinely revealed. But if it be considered in the subject, as an error produced and lived by a mind, we then have to characterise it as a schism in the understanding, a breaking of communion with all the values or aspects whose truth is held only when they are held in their connexion and equilibrium with all the others. That is why the one-sided development of one aspect nearly always provokes a onesidedness in an opposite sense: when a balance is upset it results in compensations that are sometimes unexpected. This is what happened in many fields from the end of the thirteenth century. The two aspects of the Church, which we have seen Catholic tradition holding in a living synthesis, began to develop apart from one another. In some

respects these separate developments went on side by side, each
enlivening the other by reaction; but on the whole the position was
this: during the fourteenth and fifteenth centuries, then at the
Reformation and in certain Catholic currents of thought, there was
an exclusive and seriously aberrant development of the aspect
whereby the Church is made by her members. In opposition to this,
the theology *de Ecclesia* was elaborated rather onesidedly as a theology
only of her institution and hierarchical power of mediation.

EXAGGERATION AND ALTERATION OF THE ASPECT OF THE CHURCH AS MADE BY HER MEMBERS

FROM the twelfth century on there were two currents preparing the
ground for this process, an antihierarchical spiritual movement and
the communal movement.

There was an underworld of the middle ages that is still known
only imperfectly. What exactly were the first stirrings of the dualist
heresies? From the twelfth century movements appear which, however various, make up a stream of relative unity, at any rate from the
ecclesiological point of view, characterised by an antihierarchical
attitude. There were the different groups of 'Apostolics', whose
common denominator, says their most recent historian, L. Spatling,
was the confounding of authority or function with personal goodness
of life, a position that reduces the whole of Christianity to the order
of salvation and of what is personal to individuals; which, consequently, disregards the order of means of the calling to salvation,
that of the ecclesial institution. Nineteenth-century Protestants were
right when they looked on some of the twelfth-century reformers as
Vorreformatoren. There is continuity from the ecclesiological point of
view, logically and also in fact, through channels that are known to
history. The 'apostolic' sects represent a first reduction of the
Church to an assembly of faithful. 'Quod nomen ecclesiae, non
structuram parietum sed congregationem fidelium signaret': thus
spoke the Petrobrusians, in words whose equivalent can be found
among the most orthodox theologians but which lend themselves to
a onesided interpretation at the expense of the ecclesial institution.

The communal movement belongs to general history; it involved
a whole society, and its factors were as much economic as political
and cultural. But theologians cannot live altogether outside the
rhythm of their times. As Augustine Thierry said, the movement of
the Communes represented something else than a measure of administrative reorganisation: it was people's desire to organise and

administer themselves. The influence of the ideas that nourished the communal movement made themselves felt in the Church during the thirteenth century, particularly in the constitutions of the Friars Preachers, which were afterwards imitated by other orders; in conjunction with that of the political ideas of scholastic theology on the nature and origin of power, this influence was not lacking in the English constitution and even, more remotely, the American.[16] Modern democracies are not always aware of their true pedigree; this goes back along several lines to what could be called, were the word not rather anachronistic, the democratic stream of the middle ages, which was very real and powerful before it was smothered by absolutist notions nourished on imperial Roman law. The stream itself helped towards a greater appreciation of the aspect of *Societas fidelium* in the Church, a community made by its members.

As regards ecclesiological theories, connexions with the communal movement, if they exist, are loose. It is a matter of participation in common contexts much more than of direct connexion. These contexts were, on the one hand, the communal or 'democratic' tendency; on the other, Aristotelean political ideas following the translation of the *Politics* about 1260. But the application of 'democratic' ideas to the Church was principally aroused by a particular conjunction of events: these were, at the beginning of the fourteenth century, the conflicts between Pope Boniface VIII and King Philip the Fair,[17] then between King Lewis II and Pope John XXII; and,

[16]For the English constitution, cf. Ernest Barker, *The Dominican Order and Convocation* . . . (Oxford, 1913). This thesis of an influence from the Dominican constitutions through the intermediary of the ecclesiastical Convocations has been criticised by E. M. Sait in *Political Institutions: a Preface* (New York, 1938); rightly, we think, Mr Sait looks rather to a common origin in the urban representative institutions of Spain and southern France in the twelfth and perhaps even in the eleventh century. However, see also H. P. Tunmore, 'The Dominican Order and Parliament' in the *Cath. Hist. Rev.*, 26 (1941), pp. 479-489. Influence from the classic theses of Catholic theology, from Aquinas and Bellarmine, has been claimed for the American constitution: C. Smith and V. Ryan, *Catholic Traditions in American Democracy* (1945), p. 6; E. A. Ryan, 'Bellarmine and American Political Theory' in *Miscellanea hist. De Meyer* (Louvain, 1946), ii, pp. 985-992; and cf. P. Blanshard, *American Freedom and Catholic Power* (Boston, 1950), pp. 236, 333, n. 42. Mr Blanshard criticises this thesis, but too cursorily; he ignores indirect influence through several channels, Anglican (Hooker) and Nonconformist, which have transmitted received ideas of Scholasticism.

[17]In opposing the curialist theologians (*e.g.* Giles of Rome, quoted below, n. 40) who gave the same value to the pope as to the whole Church, Philip the Fair declared with much reason that, 'Ecclesia non solum est ex clericis, sed etiam ex laicis' (declaration '*Antequam essent clerici*'. Cf. W. Ullmann, *Medieval Papalism* . . . (London, 1949), p. 214, with sources noted). It was a mournful epoch when a pope himself could declare in a solemn bull that from early times, and then more than ever, laymen were hostile towards the clergy (Boniface VIII in '*Clericis laicos*'; cf. Mirbt, *Quellen*, n. 369).

B

a century later, the schism in the West and the searching crisis it entailed for the Catholic conscience. The history of all this is extremely complex; it is landmarked by the names of theologians, each with his own opinions, which were not infrequently set out in writing that was copious. We mention only those of them who are directly relevant to our purpose.

The theological opponents of John XXII, Marsiglio of Padua, John of Janduno and William of Ockham, developed a purely individualist and representative theory of the Church. They kept only the aspect of *Societas fidelium*, ignoring the aspect of mystery and institution, almost entirely. And even the *societas* aspect is interpreted according to pure nominalist individualism, without reference to the organic corporative sense that it had in the thirteenth century: the Church is only the sum of faithful individuals, a sum that adds nothing qualitatively to the individual by himself. Council and pope are only representatives of the faithful, who can, as faithful, judge them. So, at any rate in theory, Marsiglio of Padua and William of Ockham put the laity on a level with the clergy. The institutional aspect had no part at all in their conception of the Church; the collective aspect itself was corroded by a radical nominalism, and it was understood that the Church could subsist in the faith of one soul alone, even were it a newly baptised baby.

The conciliar theories of the end of the fourteenth and of the fifteenth century were, immediately, much less favourable towards lay people: they were notions advanced by clerics, churchmen and professors, forming a theory of clerical power more or less seriously detrimental to the pope. The question, raised as much by the conjunction of the Great Schism with unsatisfied needs for reform as by an uncertain canonical tradition, was to know who was the supreme authority, at any rate at a time of crisis: pope or council, and more radically still, pope or Church? The principle of authority was not itself brought into question. Nevertheless, the hierarchical structure of the institution was an object of concern. A tree is judged by its fruit; and without any doubt the fruit was a shock, one could even say a kind of disintegration of the Christian conscience, with regard to capital points concerning the Church's hierarchical structure. On the other hand, the aspect as *Societas fidelium* was stressed onesidedly and sometimes wedded to representative individualism, as is manifest in Conrad of Gelnhausen, Dietrich of Nieheim, John Wessel, even a Nicholas of Cusa in his 'earlier manner'.

Gallicanism has gone through several phases. There are variations, even very considerable differences, between the Gallicanism of the council of Paris in 1406, of Bossuet and of Fleury, of Bordas-Demoulin in the last century. Here again we will not go into detail; but let us remember that in the great debate that dominated ecclesiological theory from the eleventh to the nineteenth century in the West, which can be characterised as a tension between two poles, 'Pontifical Monarchy' and 'Church', Gallicanism gave the importance to Church; and accordingly, clerical as was the Gallicanism of priests, episcopal the Gallicanism of bishops, it had a fundamental sympathy with the idea of Church as *Collegium fidelium*. It was not by chance but in the logic of things that John Launoi should draw up that long memorandum in which he shows, in a very interesting way, that the traditional definition of the Church is *Societas fidelium*. Analogous observations could be made about the Jansenism of the eighteenth century, then often Gallican, and about the Synod of Pistoia, which even after its condemnation was far from being heretical through and through. The ecclesiological positions taken up in many of its theses are obviously inspired by anxiety to give value to the 'Church pole' and by a conception of *Societas fidelium*.

But of course it is at the Reformation that the view of the Church as assembly of the faithful is developed most one-sidedly. This is explained in part by a reaction against an invasion of religious life by a multiplying of external forms. In the order of theological thought, uncertainty about the hierarchical structure of the Church and insistence on her aspect as *Societas fidelium* paved the way for the Reformation, nearly all of whose theses had been anticipated by this or that theologian during the two preceding centuries; but in the order of concrete religious life there had been an increase in the external apparatus of Catholicism: unimportant outward forms of devotion, a sociological rather than religious authority attaching to prelates, begging religious and clerics, and so forth. From the beginning the Reformers were in reaction against a stifling of faith by pious practices, against a prevalence of ecclesiastical machinery over inward Christianity, in favour of a direct religious contact, interior and personal: that is partly the reason why their success was so rapid and so big. Ecclesiologically, this reaction took the form of reducing the notion of the Church to that of a holy assembly of the faithful, a proceeding that the very word *Ecclesia* supported and in which the Reformers hoped to realise their programme of a return to the Bible only. At all events they were realising the programme of the rising urban class, the burghers and artisans, who readily adopted the reform in the sixteenth century. From the later middle ages they had been taking the place of clerics in various duties

formerly discharged by the Church, notably in works of charity;
here, as in the urban councils, everything was organised according
to rules of an associational, non-institutional type, a law from below,
thus providing a framework for the reformed communities.

For Luther, for Zwingli particularly, or for Cranmer the Church
was hardly more than civil society gone over to the Gospel and acknowledging the rule of Jesus Christ: a people, not an institution.
Here once more we will not go into the factors and influences at
work in this new conception of the Church. It is no longer a matter
of examining an aspect or even an exaggeration: it is a case of very
far-reaching change. The reality of the Church as institution for
salvation is fundamentally disregarded; the ecclesial institution, true
mother of the faithful, consists in the order of the means of grace, but
attention is given only to the final reality of salvation wrought in
each faithful soul by an act *of God* alone. Thus the part of bishops and
clergy dissolves into air, reduced to the two terms between which it
is traditionally a mediation, the Holy Spirit on one side, the faithful
on the other. The universal priesthood of believers came to exclude
all ministerial or hierarchical priesthood and, at any rate in principle, a purely synodal and presbyterian ecclesiastical system was set
up. In this way, under a materially identical formula, *Ecclesia, id est
(sancta) congregatio fidelium, sanctorum communio*, the traditional ecclesiology was in fact rejected. The laity was given substantial promotion, but of a kind that Catholic tradition, whether Eastern or
Western, had never known, except in the deviations of a Montanist
Tertullian or of those medieval sects we have referred to, which in
their own fashion heralded and prepared for the Reformation.

THE TREATISE DE ECCLESIA IN REACTION, WHENCE A CERTAIN ONE-SIDEDNESS

IT is noticeable that the more or the less serious ecclesiological errors
that we have summarised, occurring over four centuries from the
fourteenth to the seventeenth, all represent a tendency in the same
direction, that is, towards considering the Church under her aspect
of an association in which the members have an active part. There
was always to some extent a questioning, even a disregarding, of
some point affecting the Church's hierarchical structure. When her
structure, her internal principles by which she lived (even if she had
not yet worked them out perfectly clearly), were thus called in question it was inevitable, it was right and proper, that the Church
should reassert and defend those things that she felt were threatened:

her hierarchical structure, the reality of her institution antecedent to and superior to the faithful and the community that they form.

In any field we take a good look at ourselves when we are criticised; opposition teaches us what we are or what we want to be. That is why each generation in finding its place in life goes through a crisis of nonconformity. And so it was normal that the ecclesiological problems raised by men and events should be occasions for the Church to define herself better. Now, curious as it may seem, up to about the year 1300, when regalist Gallicanism began the series of errors we have noted, there was no treatise expressly dealing with the Church. Christian antiquity, the Fathers, monastic theology, the earlier Scholasticism, the analytical theology of the great thirteenth-century scholastics, all had had a solid body of ecclesiological thought; but, in spite of some formally ecclesiological writings such as St Cyprian's *De unitate* and especially of the considerations on the Church in many treatises of the ninth, eleventh and twelfth centuries, there was no treatise *de Ecclesia* as we understand it today. There are plenty of ecclesiological data among the 3,113 articles of St Thomas's *Summa*, but no *ensemble* of questions *de Ecclesia* as there is *de Trinitate, de Angelis, de Christo, de Sacramentis*, etc. It can be said of the middle ages in general, and of St Thomas in particular, that the mystery of the Church was the heart of their thought, yet we see no treatise on the Church in the modern sense until about 1300.

So Mgr Arquilliere was able to give the title 'The Oldest Treatise on the Church' to his edition of James of Viterbo's *De regimine christiano*, from whose first appearance in 1301 or 1302 similar treatises were multiplied. A few months later came Giles of Rome's *De ecclesiastica potestate* (edited not long ago by R. Scholz) and *De potestate regia et papali* by John of Paris (edited by Dom J. Leclercq). These three works were occasioned by the conflict between Philip the Fair and Boniface VIII, but though written *ad hoc* they were not hack-work or purely polemical: their authors were real theologians dealing with principles, and so produced a sort of 'treatise on the Church'. But observe their titles. It is a question only of power and government: they are treatises on the Church's authority and rightfulness. When regalist Gallicanism calls forth a first express and separate treatise on the Church its content is special and particular, as it were a theology of ecclesiastical authority. It was similar with the treatises that were provoked a few years later by the pretensions of parish-priests; an example by a respectable theologian is the *De potestate papae* of Hervé Nédellec.

It was again a theology of pontifical power that was to be worked out against William of Ockham, Marsiglio of Padua and John of Janduno, and then against the upholders of conciliar supremacy. The talented men at that time were mostly on the conciliarist side; but the best fifteenth-century Catholic apologists, men like Thomas Netter of Saffron Walden against Wyclif, John of Ragusa against John of Rokyzana, John of Turrecremata faced by the Great Schism and the conciliarists, did not fail to present a general picture of the Church, and they cannot be fairly accused of onesidedness. Rather was it later, in the writings of the Counter-Reformation and those directed against the Gallicanism of the seventeenth and eighteenth centuries, that the problems raised in the fourteenth and fifteenth were treated with a marked insistence on hierarchical powers, most especially papal power. This emphasis was all the more marked because of the process that had been going on since the thirteenth century whereby a juridical point of view and juridical categories of thought had become predominant in clerical circles; such a man as Dante was well aware of this, and it was on the increase at the very time when the separate treatise on the Church was taking its final form.

Protestantism rejected the whole of the Church's mediation: magisterium, priesthood, sacraments, the authority of tradition and the role of the teaching Church in the rule of faith, prelatical authority, the episcopal dignity, the pope's primacy. Of the institution, not one stone was left standing. Instead, there was offered the notion of the Church as holy assembly of the faithful, wherein, moreover, the ecclesial reality was split into two parts whose organic unity was ignored: on one side, a communion of saints (the true faithful, the predestined), which was the real Church but was invisible; on the other, an organisation that was visible but wholly human, and that was not truly the Church. Catholics replied in treatises apologetical and polemical, or as was said from 1560, controversial: treatises in which the points at issue were debated, and which were not necessarily offered as complete treatises on the Church. This controversial literature was to have such a success that, at least in ecclesiological questions, it unhappily came to determine the content of Catholic theology as taught in the schools. Ecclesiologically, this theology was polemical, anti-Gallican and anti-Protestant throughout, even when it was presented eirenically and with quiet scholarship. This could be easily proved by following the exceptional fortunes of that part of St Robert Bellarmine's *Disputationes de controversiis* . . . that is concerned with the pope, the Church and the members of the Church Militant. That is not to be undertaken here; it will be enough briefly to describe this ecclesiology that was hence-forth to hold the field, its matter, its autonomy as a special treatise, its themes and its documentation.

The chief matter of these treatises is provided by the points questioned or denied by the errors against which the works were written. Essentially it is a question of the authority of the Church as rule of faith,[18] of hierarchical powers and very particularly of the papal primacy,[19] and of the visibility of the Church and her members. To these master questions others were added later and form part of our modern treatises: vindication of the Church as a 'perfect society' in face of the civil power, and, in face of liberal Protestantism and its modernist extensions, proof that Christ founded a church as a visible hierarchical society, juridically instituted. In opposition to the Protestant theory of the invisible Church, Catholic apologists pressed the doctrine of her visibility to its furthest consequences, and developed the aspect of the Church's objectively constituted external and juridical machinery, the aspect of *societas externarum rerum ac rituum*, to quote the Augsburg Confession. Thus whilst Protestants were reducing the Church to an inward Christianity, to salvation, and by so doing were dissolving ecclesiology, Catholic apologists were looking at her above all as the machinery of the means of grace, as the hierarchical mediation of the means to salvation.

The treatise on the Church is a particular treatise composed in answer to Gallicanism, to conciliarism, to the purely spiritual ecclesiology of Wyclif and Hus, to Protestant negations, later on to those of secular 'stateism', Modernism and so on. It follows that it is composed in reaction against errors all of which call the hierarchical structure of the Church in question. The *de Ecclesia* was principally, sometimes almost exclusively, a defence and affirmation of the reality of the Church as machinery of hierarchical mediation, of the powers and primacy of the Roman see, in a word, a 'hierarchology'. On the other hand, the two terms between which that mediation comes, the Holy Spirit on one side, the faithful people or the religious subject on the other, were as it were kept out of ecclesiological consideration: there were plenty of apologetical works—and for a long time there

---

[18]Here is a typical formulation of the question (perfectly sound taken in itself): '. . . an potius, erecto aliquo organismo ecclesiastico, cui munus fideliter custodiendi sacrum revelationis depositum tradiderit, quae est conceptio catholica' (T. Zapelena, *De Ecclesia Christi* (Rome, 1940), Pars apologetica, p.v.).

[19]The more so as the apologists often engage Gallicans or conciliarists at the same time as Protestants. Cajetan did this, and often those eighteenth-century writers from whom many modern treatises directly derive.

was no other teaching (*enseignement*) on the Church other than apologetical—in which the aspects of living depth, wherein the Church is
seen as a body alive and energising throughout, were passed over in
silence, if not sometimes suspected of being 'not really Catholic'.[20]

The deficiencies of ecclesiological consideration were unhappily
rather strengthened by the later history of the treatise *de Ecclesia*.
Dean F. X. Arnold has made a study of the idea of the Church as it
appears in catechisms and works of pastoral theology during the
second half of the eighteenth century and the first of the nineteenth.[21]
He finds that these writers, starting from a philosophical and juridical point of view, have the same defect as some of the Counter-
Reformation controversialists—they do not say a word about the
Church's mystical aspect, they are concerned only with her organisation as a society and the exercising of her hierarchical powers. They
do not point out that it is the whole Church quickened by the Holy
Spirit, the whole faithful people, that co-operates in the work of
sanctification and praise of God; they talk only about the priest and
the hierarchy, and the believing, praying people appears to be

[20]We are still without a general study of this evolution of ecclesiology. For some
references relevant to our subject, see G. Thils (one of the best judges of this
literature), 'De taak van de lek in onze opvatting van de Kerk' in *Het Christelijk
Oosten en Hereniging*, 1949, pp. 229–233; and cf. M. J. Congar's study 'Ecclesia ab
Abel' in *op. cit.* n. 18 above. The following points may be noted: Such great apologists as Bellarmine and Cardinal du Perron say nothing of the relation of the
eucharist to the Church: yet this was central in the consciousness that medieval
theology had of the mystery of the Church. Cf. H. de Lubac, *Corpus mysticum* (Paris,
1944), pp. 291–292. – In later times any request favourable to lay initiative or to
a mystical view of the Church was taxed with Jansenism. This was the case with
any reforming tendency in Mohler's time, around 1820; cf. E. Vermeil, *J. A.
Mohler et l'école catholique de Tubingue* (Paris, 1913), p. 315. At the Vatican Council
several bishops wanted to avoid the idea of the mystical Body, as savouring to them
of Jansenism (Mansi, li, 761). – In such a manual as L. Brugère's *De Ecclesia Christi*
(1878), which I mention because it is one of the best and still very useful for
reference, the Church's close relationship with Christ is mentioned only as a
'remark' when dealing with the mark of holiness: it takes up 27 lines (pp. 282–283)
in a book of 470 pages. – I do not, however, want the facts that I mention, which
I believe to be unquestionable, to give the impression that after the Reformation
the doctrine of the mystical Body and the profound supernatural reality of the
Church were forgotten among us. There are texts of the Counter-Reformation
itself that are strong evidence to the contrary, for example, the Catechism of St
Peter Canisius, and that called 'of the Council of Trent'; cf. also J. Willen, 'Zur
Idee des Corpus Christi mysticum in der Theologie des 16 Jahrhunderts' in
Catholica, 4 (1935), pp. 75–86; F. X. Arnold, *Grundstzaliches . . ., e.g.*, pp. 80, 115ff.

[21]F. X. Arnold, 'Das gott-menschliche Prinzip der Seelsorge in pastoralges-
chichtlicher Entfaltung' in *Theologische Quartalschrift*, 1943, pp. 99–133, and 1944,
pp. 57–80; *Grundsatzliches und Geschichtliches zur Theologie der Seelsorge* (Freiburg i,
B., 1949). Cf. also M. Ramsauer, 'Die Kirche in den Katechismen' in *Zeitsch. f.
kath. Theol.*, 73 (1951), pp. 129–169, 313–346.

passive in a church that it does not affect and is not expected to affect.

This narrowing down of the treatise on the Church solely to her hierarchical powers was the more regrettable in that it happened at a time when in many parts of ancient Christendom human society was being secularised. During the middle ages the ecclesiastical institution included and formed human society; but from the beginning of the fourteenth century society began slowly to assert its independence. First to cut loose were rulers and their politics, then various activities of urban life and welfare, then thought and the sciences, then morality and spirituality itself, finally, and much more radically, the common consciousness of the people in their daily life of sorrows, joys, hope. . . . We referred in the previous chapter to the old image of a body of which clergy and laity respectively form the two sides, left and right. Now there was a kind of divorce between those two sides, between a community of men who were hardly the faithful any longer and an institution of clerics whose problems, activities, interests, language were no longer those of the living human community. So whilst ecclesiological thought was settling down to the consideration of hierarchical machinery in concrete actuality on the plane of the pastoral or apostolic situation, the Church was losing part of her human substance. In this place and in that she was being as it were reduced to her 'formal cause', that is, of course, to her essential, somewhat as cadres, regulations and matériel are the essential of an army. Her public worship, to confine ourselves to that example, always remained the institution's own worship, conformed with its rubrics, but in many places at least it ceased to be the worship *of men, of living consciousness, of the human community.* Whilst Protestantism was making the Church a people without a priesthood and Catholic apologists were replying by establishing the rightfulness of priesthood and institution, the Church in more than one place was finding herself reduced to the state of a priestly system without a Christian people.

Thus it was that of the Church's two aspects which Catholic tradition requires to be held together—that in which the Church is an institution that precedes and makes its members, and that in which she is the community made by its members—the theological treatises practically ignored that one according to which a role of the laity could be *a priori* conceivable.

* * *

It must be carefully noticed that this onesidedness is not heretical, or even really erroneous, while onesidedness in the sense of assembly of the faithful is erroneous and even, as worked out in Protestantism, heretical. And this principally for two reasons.

(1) In order to show the neglect of and need for a theology of laity more clearly, we have treated our matter very schematically, and strongly emphasised the lines of our schema. We believe that that schema as a whole is correct—otherwise it would not have been put forward. But there must be no exaggeration. Even when and where tendency to identify the Church with the hierarchy has been most obvious,[22] the affirmation of the aspect of institution has *never* been to the *exclusion* of the aspect of community made by its members. *This aspect has never been denied*, either directly or indirectly. Thus on one hand the Church in her law has always recognised the existence of communities set up from below, as related groups; on the other,

[22]There is a certain number of twelfth to sixteenth century texts wherein the word Church is used to mean hierarchy. According to Hauck (*op. cit.*, n. 19, p.471) *tota Ecclesia* often indicates the episcopate for Pope Alexander III, and there are traces of the same sense in Innocent III (*Reg.*, i, 27; vii, 42, etc.). In both England and France in the thirteenth and fourteenth centuries clerics were the 'gens de sainte Eglise'; and even in thinking of the Church as society of the faithful it is the 'gens d'Eglise' who are thought of essentially: 'Ecclesia dicitur dupliciter. Vel congregatio fidelium constans ad minus ex episcopo, presbytero, diacono et sub-diacono; vel domus materialis . . .' (Moneta of Cremona, *Summa adv. Catharos et Valdenses*, l. v, c. 8, §3; ed. Richini, 1743, p. 456). Later, William Amidani writes: 'Accipitur Ecclesia pro potiori parte Ecclesiae, scilicet pro clericis seu pro universitate clericorum. Non quia laici non sint ecclesiastici, immo sunt, sed quia non sunt ita nobiles in Ecclesia sicut clerici' (Quoted by Hauck, *Kirchengesch. Deutschlands*, v, p. 505, n. 5). And Joan of Arc's judges ask her whether she is ready to submit to the Church, that is to the pope, the cardinals, the bishops and other prelates. That is why we find in such a document as the Act in Restraint of Appeals of February 1533 that *the clergy* is taken for the whole English church (cf. F. M. Powicke, *The Reformation in England* (Oxford, 1941), pp. 44–46). That is why today still nine out of ten Anglicans say of a young man who has taken orders that 'He has gone into the Church' (cf. H. Burn-Murdoch, *Church, Continuity and Unity* (Cambridge, 1945, p. 1). Among theologians of the papal *plenitudo potestatis* the assimilation of the hierarchy to the Church found its special application of course in the pope: 'Summus pontifex qui tenet apicem Ecclesiae et qui potest dici Ecclesia', writes Giles of Rome in *De eccl. potest.*, l. iii, c. 12 (ed. Scholz, p. 209). – Such applications have often been made within the perspective of ideas of representation; cf. Gierke, *Theories polit.*, tr. De Pange, p. 208 (*Genossenschaftsrecht*, vol. iii, 1881, p. 596: see particularly n. 214, Huguccio's words, 'papa ipsa ecclesia'): the hierarchy, and eventually for the curialists the Roman church and the pope, were then considered as summing up and so containing the whole Church. Cardinal Peter Ameli of Embrun wrote in the fourteenth century: 'Papa et domini cardinales ita sunt in Romana Ecclesia quod etiam ipsi sunt eadem Romana Ecclesia. . . .' (*Contra petentes concilium generale*, in Bliemetzrieder, *Literarische Polemik* . . . p. 110). Among the canonists, this way of talking, joined with the conception of the Church as a corporation, was given frequent expression in questions of ecclesiastical property: *e.g.*, in the *Summa Parisiensis* (c. 1170) on patrimony—'ecclesia enim nihil aliud dicitur, nisi clerici' (quoted by Giercke, *op. cit.*, iii, p. 254, n. 31, and see pp. 255ff.). In the fifteenth century a question often discussed was the attribute—one could say the ecclesiological attribute—*of the Roman Church*, which in a last analysis meant the Curia. The position of theologians favourable to papal power (the conciliarists of course took a different view) can be summed up in the words of Silvester Prieras:

the laity has always been expressly included in the ecclesial reality, and expressly referred to. Bellarmine does this when he divides his *Controversia de Ecclesia militante* into three books concerned respectively with the militant order of clerics, the militant order of lay people, and the order, made up of clerics and lay persons, whose spiritual warfare is carried on in a special state of life under a rule, monks, nuns and other religious.[23] Besides, going beyond the writings of the 'Ecclesia universalis virtualiter est Ecclesia Romana, Ecclesia Romana repraesentative est collegium cardinalium, virtualiter autem pontifex maximus' (*Dialogus*, quoted by Luther's editors, Weimar edn, i, p. 656, n. 1). To this Luther replied: 'Ego ecclesiam virtualiter non scio nisi in Christo, repraesentative non nisi in concilio' (*Ad dial. S. Prieratis . . . responsio ;ibid.*, p. 656ff.). Protestants could not but accuse Catholics of calling the hierarchy the Church: for instance Turretini later, quoted by A. Krauss, *Das protestantische Dogma von d. unsichtbaren Kirche* (Gotha, 1876), p. 70. Paul Sarpi, whose ecclesiological principles were Protestant and in whom a theology of the Church as assembly of the faithful is found in a pure state, wrote: 'Il famoso e augusto nom edi chiesa, che era commune a tutti li fedeli anticamente cosi clerici come laici, adesso pare chiesa ristretto per lo piu a significar li clerici solamente' (*Opere*, ed. Gambarin, i, p. 195). Cf. V. M. Buffon, *Chiesa di Cristo e Chiesa Romana nelle Opere . . . di fra P. Sarpi* (Louvain, 1941), p. 41, n. 3, where he quotes a letter of 29 September 1609: 'Nunc Ecclesiam accipio pro fidelium convocatione, non vero pro clericis solis, quod si pro his accipiatur non est regnum Christi sed pars reipublicae terrenae'. – Obviously no Catholic theologian has ever *identified* the Church with the clergy or the hierarchy. The admirable Catechism of the Council of Trent makes it quite clear that by the word Church must be understood 'nec praesides tantum sed eos etiam qui parere debent' (pt i, c. 9, n. 13). We all know that perfectly well. Nevertheless we often use the word Church in a sense that really refers to the government of the Church, so that Mgr Chevrot observes that: 'They do what the Church tells them. They speak of "the Church" as if they were speaking of the government, as if they were not part of it' ('Pour une prédication évangélique' in *Congrès des Œuvres* (Bordeaux, 1947), p. 74. Here are some commonplace examples: 'This question [the fate of children dying unbaptised], of which the Church is the sole judge. . . . The Church, who alone is competent in this field . . .' (E. Boudes, in *Nouv. Rev. théol.*, June 1949, p. 589); 'the Church as theologian' (V. Berto, in *La pensée cath.*, n. 3, 1947, p. 27); 'the role of historian which the Church takes up in the beatification and canonisation of holy people . . .' (E. Catta, *ibid.*, n. 7, 1948, p. 76). This sense of the word *Ecclesia* can be found often enough in official documents: see, *e.g.*, the constitution '*Provida mater*', in *A.A.S.*, 1947, p. 116. – The sense is quite justified. One of the two places in the gospels where the word Church is found (Matt. xviii) is in its favour if, with Chrysostom, we accept the equivalence of *Dic ecclesiae* with *Dic praesulibus* (*Com. in Matt.*, hom. 60, 2; PG., lviii, 586). Most importantly, this sense can be 'placed' among those senses that the word Church includes, as this writer has done elsewhere: cf. *Vie intellectuelle*, November 1947, and *Vraie et fausse reforme*, pt i, ch. 1. But one must be careful not to identify Church with hierarchy *and no more*, or the fact of being Catholic with the fact of obeying. This is the mistake we had occasion to take exception to in A. Doerner's *Sentire cum Ecclesia* (Munchen-Gladbach, 1941). St Ignatius Loyola's 'Sentire vere in Ecclesia' is much to be preferred. There is considerable *ecclesiological* difference between the two expressions.

[23]But we must be exact. For Bellarmine, all disputed points about the laity 'ad disputationem de magistratu politico revocari possunt' (in the said *Controversia*, l. iii, c. 1; *Opera*, ii, p. 313). He in fact speaks only of the civil power and its obligations towards the true religion; he does not say a word about the laity's part in directly forwarding the work of God's kingdom or of its place in the Church as a spiritual organism.

theologians in every direction, there has been the Church's life as it was lived. It might not be mentioned at all or too little might be said about it; but it was there. The lay people sanctifying themselves in the Church, taking their part in parish life, meeting in societies and confraternities; the renewal that followed the Catholic Reformation and the Council of Trent produced that *invasion mystique* of which Bremond wrote, and began a new chapter in the history of Christian action, the women's apostolate[24] (though at first there was question only of the religious life for them, and St Angela Merici herself formed her daughters into a congregation). If there has been one-sidedness in a clerical direction it has been in theoretical ecclesiology much more than in the lived reality of Catholicism.

(2) Onesidedness in a Gallican or Protestant sense touches the *structure* of the Church, it affects her in her very being, it involves an *essential* negation. We have just seen that onesidedness in favour of the institution has never been anything but a matter of emphasis, touching the *life* of the Church; if it threatens anything, it is not her being but her *fullness*. Did not the Fathers call the faithful people the *pleroma* of the bishop (above, n. 15)? It has been shown elsewhere[25] how, when matters of her life were called in question, the Church was above all concerned to safeguard her principles, how she was more ready to insist on stability than on development, on permanence than on adaptation, though she really holds on to both. If development or adaptation be in a measure disregarded, life and fullness suffer; but the essential of the Church is safeguarded. If, however, some element of her structure be compromised, her very existence is endangered. That is why, supposing (*dato, non concesso*) the two forms of onesidedness to be equally unbalanced, they have not at all the same importance or, therefore, the same seriousness.

*   *   *

Nevertheless the ecclesiological and, especially, pastoral importance of a certain overweighting of the institution is considerable. It

[24]Cf. M. Chalendard, *La promotion de la femme à l'apostolat*, 1540-1650 (Colmar, 1950), and see the pertinent study in the *Etudes conjointes*. – In his address to the international lay congress at Rome in 1951 Pope Pius XII said: 'Some people like to tell us often that during the past four centuries the Church has been exclusively "clerical", in reaction from the crisis in the sixteenth century which professed to have simply abolished the hierarchy; and thereupon they suggest it is time she made room for others as well. The judgement is so far from the truth that it is precisely since the holy Council of Trent that the laity has taken its place and advanced in apostolic activity. This can easily be proved. It is enough to remember two obvious historical facts out of many: the Marian congregations of men exercising an active lay apostleship in every field of public life, and the ever-increasing entrance of women into the modern apostolate'.

[25]*Vraie et fausse reforme*, pp. 540ff. and pp. 243ff.

is one of the principles of our ecclesiology that the hierarchy is an element of the Church's being and structure, as we shall have occasion to emphasise more than once. St Cyprian's 'Ecclesia est in episcopo' has its profound truth. But if theology *de Ecclesia* be practically reduced to a 'hierarchology' or, more generally, be made a theology only of the Church's structure, without reference to her life, there is a risk of the laity being regarded as simply an accident, an appendage of the Church, at most necessary to her *bene esse*. It must be admitted that in this respect the essentially hierarchical structure of the Catholic Church presents a serious question, the same raised by the following passage from Bismarck, which in a way sums up what we have been saying in this chapter: 'The two churches, Protestant and Catholic, have very different bases. The whole being of the Catholic Church is in her clergy, she exists and fulfils herself through them; she could go on without a community, Mass can be celebrated without a congregation; the community is useful for the affirmation of the Christian function of the Catholic Church, but it is not at all necessary for the existence of that Church. In the Protestant Church on the contrary the community is the entire foundation of the whole Church: worship is unthinkable without it, the whole Protestant Church constitution rests on the community.'[26]

This is not the place to discuss why Protestant communions, starting from strict congregationalist premisses and an associational and community basis, are in practice almost as clericalised as the Catholic Church. It is a fact for which there is plenty of evidence, and Protestants deplore it. No doubt there are sociological laws in virtue of which the most 'charismatic' religious communities, those most made 'from below', quite soon become organisations with authority, traditions, a 'church' sociological structure. That does not concern us here for, whatever the unquestionable contributions of history to the concrete development of the Catholic Church, she has not received her essential structure through history but from the Lord and his apostles: that structure of the Church is her apostolicity. At the same time it belongs to our subject to point out some pastoral consequences that follow from an ecclesiological view that is too onesidedly concerned with the institutional aspect. Nowhere perhaps is it more evident that pastoral things are at bottom an extension or application of ecclesiology. Here we can grasp those

[26]*Politische Reden*, xii, p. 376, quoted by E. Siegmund-Schultze in *Die Einigung der christlichen Kirchen* (Bale, 1942), p. 54. Cf. D. T. Jenkins, *The Nature of Catholicity* (London, 1943) p. 114; and, from the point of view of the nature of the Mass, F. Heiler on Prayer (French trans., p. 502).

consequences whether in the sacral domain, that is, in the inner life
of the Church herself, or in the function she exercises in relation to
the world.

If the Church were to be considered solely from the point of view
of institution, of her formal hierarchical cause, she would in fact
exist, without laity; a faithful people would be required only as
materia circa quam, *materia cui*, object and beneficiary of her hierarchical actions. The faithful would not form, organically united with
their clergy, one single active subject of the work of God's kingdom
—that union of the people with their bishop which, on the testimony
of St Cyprian, constitutes the Church.[27] They would be, rather,
those who are ministered to, the matter upon which clerical action
is exercised, a sort of *homo religiosus* analogous to the much-criticised
homo oeconomicus or to the *homo politicus* under a totalitarian regime.
They would have nothing to do but to receive, and, as Father de
Montcheuil wrote, they would be in the Church solely for their own
good and not for the Church's good as well: they would form a sort
of undifferentiated substance for 'the Church' to work on; they
would be a 'mass' in the sense Pope Pius XII has given the word, in
opposition to a 'people', the *laos* from which the laity etymologically
gets its name. For the pope the 'mass' is amorphous, passive and
uniform; the 'people' is an organic reality and it is active.[28] Inevitably are we reminded of Edouard le Roy's 'The simple faithful have
the same part as the lambs at Candlemas: they are blessed and
shorn!' More sharply still, Marcel Barbu compares the position of
lay people in the Church with that of proletarians in society, and he
connects the fact of the existence of a social proletariat in the world
with that of the existence of a religious proletariat in the Church. . . .
Let us get back to a more exact expression of things. Analysing the
situation in France on the eve of the 1939-1945 war, M. Daniel-Rops
observed that while the German was conscious of a duty unceasingly
to create Germany, while the Italian tried to model himself on Rome

[27]'Illi sunt Ecclesia plebs sacerdoti adunata et pastori suo grex adhaerens. Unde
scire debes episcopum in Ecclesia esse et Ecclesiam in episcopo et si qui cum
episcopo non sit in Ecclesia non esse, et frustra sibi blandiri eos qui pacem cum
sacerdotibus Dei non habentes obrepunt et latenter apud quosdam communicare
se credunt, quando Ecclesia quae catholica una est scissa non sit neque divisa, sed
sit utique connexa et cohaerentium sibi invicem sacerdotum glutino copulata' (*Ep.*,
66, 8; Hartel, p. 733). Cyprian in exile considers the theology of a church whose
bishop is for the time being absent. Cf. above, notes 10, 11.

[28]Christmas address, 1944, in *A.A.S.*, 1945, pp. 13-14. Pope Pius himself has
applied his notion of 'people' to the Church in his address of 20 February, 1946
(*A.A.S.*, 1946, p. 145; *Doc. cath.*, 17 March, 1946, c. 173). Cf. his very remarkable
words about public opinion (*Osservatore Romano*, 18 February, 1950; *Doc. cath.*,
21 March, 1950, cc. 322, 327); and cf. the end of Chapter V herein.

to give life to Italy, the French looked on France as something given once for all, from which they could always receive without having to build her up; they came to think that France could do without them: 'France begets us, we do not beget her'. Had we not reached an analogous state of things in the Church before that reawakening of which our Introduction speaks? Had not the faithful got into the habit of receiving without actively co-operating, leaving to the clergy the charge of *building up* the Church?—like citizens who leave the meaking of their country to civil servants and officials, and the defence of it to the military.

The consequences were likewise serious as regards the Church's relations with the world. Clerics are not able to meet all the requirements of a Christian programme in this field. Their position is that of workmen for the kingdom of God, and this inclines them not to be interested in a kingdom of God in preparation in the world according to *the means and ways of the world*; as we have seen, they are inclined to ignore the order proper to second causes, temporal and historical, which has its own demands—unless, whenever it be possible, to bring about a direct regulation of temporal things by religious interests, which is one of the most essential aspects of clericalism. At bottom, forgetfulness of the true role of lay people leads both to clericalism in the Church and to laicism in the world. Pastorally, clericalism results in this, that lay people, kept in subjection and passivity in the Church, are not formed for their own Christian responsibilities, which it is their business to discharge in the world and in the course of history. There is some truth in parts of Protestant criticism, but they use it to attack the traditional constitution of religion and in the defence of a 'private judgment' that we have good reason to reject. But let us keep to self-criticism voiced by Catholics themselves. On the matter in hand there is a good example in Michael de la Bedoyere's book, *Christianity in the Market-Place*. The author, who was editor first of the *Dublin Review* and now of the *Catholic Herald* (London), is concerned for the effectiveness of Christianity in the temporal world. He rightly thinks that there is no solution of the world's problems to be deduced immediately from Christian dogma: the conscience of lay Christians must mediate between that dogma and an effective action, which to be effective must be directed towards the precise conditions of time and place. Because they are Christians, these people have in themselves the possibility, indeed the necessity, of a widespread outpouring of faith; and because they are lay, engaged in the world's work, they take the order proper to second causes and the forces of history seriously. An evangelical quickening in this world's affairs could be brought about by the personal conscience of Christian lay people.

Unhappily the laity, too accustomed to receiving Christian truth 'ready-made' from their clergy, were for long without initiative in the fields which nevertheless belonged to them, fields wherein it was especially out of place that the clergy should decide for them, relying on an authority whose competence does not in fact extend here. From the point of view of conscience the laity, used practically to reducing all virtues to obedience (and all sins to those of the flesh), often lived by proxy; in things where their clergy did not authoritatively decide their duty, they most often did nothing. Only the most robust kept lay initiative alive; the future was to justify them, but in their lifetime they had many troubles: thanks to them, the Church has never been without lay initiative.

REDISCOVERIES. TOWARDS A MORE INTEGRAL SYNTHESIS

THERE is a call for a theology of laity today because the state of affairs resulting from the onesidedness we have just discussed has changed profoundly, especially during the past twenty-five years. The remote causes of this change go back to the great effort of Catholic restoration that marked the nineteenth century after the collapse of conditions bequeathed by medieval Christianity. This restoration, like any other living work, consisted of new creations rather than the repair of an old building, and was effected finally only by the Thomist revival under Pope Leo XIII, the strengthening of the Church's dogmatic tradition by the defeat of Modernism, and the liturgical movement encouraged by St Pius X. The immediate causes are closer to us, and belong to the history through which we have lived and which many of us have had a hand in making. It is a matter essentially of the renewal of Christian initiative that took place between the wars, of which Catholic Action was then the promising fruit. The laity was invited to energise apostolically in the Church, proportionately to work out and carry through the programme of the Church's relations with the world. There is no need to detail the pronouncements of Pope Pius XI: they are easily found, everybody remembers them, and we quote from them in Part Two Ch. V. Round about 1930 there appeared a very marked revival of the idea of the Church; it was parallel with the rise of Catholic Action and was partly due to it, and partly bound up with more general factors, among which special importance must be given to the liturgical movements. In the ranks of Catholic Action there was a veritable 'craze' for the doctrine of the mystical Body, for active participation of the faithful in the eucharistic liturgy, and so on. People began really to find out again that the Church *must develop*, and develop *through her members*.

The highest authorities expressed themselves in such terms as these: 'Lay people are not outside the Church. They cannot be looked on as a kind of addition to the Church, as if she comprised only the hierarchy' (Cardinal Hlond, Archbishop of Gneizno).[29] And Pope Pius XII declared: 'The faithful, and more especially the laity, are in the front line of the Church's life; it is through them that she is the vital principle of human society. In consequence they, they above all, ought to have an ever more clear consciousness, not only of belonging to the Church, but of being the Church, that is, the community of the faithful on earth under the guidance of its common head, the pope, and of the bishops in communion with him. They are the Church; and therefore from the earliest days of her history the faithful, with the approval of their bishops, have joined together in particular societies interested in the very various manifestations of life.'[30]

These and similar texts set forth the truth that the Church exists from below *as well*, and that in this respect she is made by men. We in France have lived this truth and are still living it with intensity, in consequence of the effort that the apostolic situation in our country has called for. The Introduction to *Vraie et fausse reforme dans l'Eglise* has shown that a first realistic quickening of conscience about the apostolic situation took place during those fine years of Catholic

[29] Pastoral letter on the Parish, in *Questions liturg. et paroiss.*, October 1933, p. 216.

[30] Address to the college of cardinals, 20 February, 1946 (*A.A.S.*, 1946, p. 149; *Doc. cath.*, 1946, c. 176). Cf. this passage of Pius XII's address to the Belgian Christian workers' movement in 1949: 'What you do ought to be a shattering answer to the slanders of adversaries who accuse the Church of jealously keeping the laity in bondage, without allowing them any personal activity or assigning them any work proper to their condition. That is not her attitude and it never has been. We are not here referring to the inward growth of faith and supernatural life, in purity of living, love of God and divine likeness, that is wrought by grace in the depth of souls. It is sufficiently obvious that in that matter every one, whoever he may be and whatever his condition, priest or lay, the lowliest or the most highly placed, has the same rights and privileges without distinction. But glance over the history, already more than a century of it, of modern Belgium: is not the fact that you have been able to attain such good results, to improve, consolidate and perfect Catholic circumstances, for the greater good of your beloved country, is not this due to a great extent to the active part taken by Catholic lay people? And the same could be said of many other countries. Is it not as ridiculous as it is offensive to accuse the clergy of keeping the laity in a humiliating state of inaction? In family, educational or social matters, in science or art, literature or the press, radio or cinema, in political campaigns for the election of legislators or the determination of their constitutional powers and duties—a huge and fertile field of action is open to Catholic lay people in every direction' (*A.A.S.*, 1949, p. 550).

F

Action 1925-1940, thanks to the method of investigation; and that it was followed by a second quickening, one more definite and more acute, during the war and immediately after. Helped by a deep fellow-feeling for the human community (which had been rather lacking among the clergy) and by a kind of sociological realism and a proper respect—a lay people's respect—for temporal circumstances, we at last realised that there was a deep rift, which threatened to get worse, between an ecclesiastical machinery existing in itself, complete, in charge of the clergy, between that and the human community. A priesthood without people; a wonderful liturgy, but which had often ceased to be worship *by some person*, the prayer of a real community of people; a catechism equally excellent—as all the treasures of the Catholic institution are excellent—but behind which it was difficult to find *some person's* living conviction. As an institution, made and given from on high since the time of Christ and his apostles, the Church was still there: as a people, she had got to be renewed, and for that she had to be rediscovered. That, if we see it aright, is the meaning of what is new in the present pastoral movement.[31]

This latest movement is at root only a rediscovery of tradition, and nothing expresses it better than the word 'ecclesial', whose use in France goes back to the war years or soon after, when things were indeed happening in French Catholicism.[32] Before the war the only adjective we used from the word *Ecclesia* (*Eglise*) was 'ecclesiastical'; but while the substantive had kept its full meaning the adjective was reduced simply to the clerical aspect of the Church. It is significant how little need was felt for an adjective that would express belonging to the people of God or to the body of Christ, without recourse to some other turn of speech. It would be interesting to study the different expressions then in use, and the present uses of the word 'ecclesial'. In any case there is no doubt whatever that the bringing into use of this word corresponds to an attitude towards the Church in which—beyond the aspect of her apostolic institution, of rites and formulas—the deep and full mystery of the Church, her community

[31]The above refers principally to France, whose conditions we know best. The *Directoire pour la pastorale des sacraments* issued by the bishops of France in 1951 is in many places animated by the idea that the laity also is actively of the Church and has to take its part in her mission. – The problem diagnosed in France is the same in some other places. Father D. Koster has called the present development a *Volkwerdung* of the Church, in *Die Firmung im Glaubenssinn der Kirche* (Münster, 1908), p. 6; and M. G. Brom, *art. cit.*, p. 31.

[32]I have not made a systematic search, but *ecclesial* was used by Jacques Maritain in 1938 (*Nova et Vetera*, p. 264) to signify a 'being of the Church' which is not 'clerical'; and Father de Lubac is certainly one of those who has done most to acclimatise it.

or people's aspect, and the active part the faithful have in her life, are again very consciously present. None of the valuable precisions that theology has brought to the Church's structure and institution are denied; what people do want to do is to get beyond onesidedness, in so far as it may exist. Cannot all today's efforts be described as a search for completion and integration? Contemporary people strive after fullness of life, whether it be through ecumenism or lay activity or enrichment of mind from the Bible and the Fathers or new forms of pastoral care. The important thing is that extensions or additions should be made on the plan and within the framework defined by the Church's structure. Theology and pastoral care progress together, each benefiting from the contact it can have with the other, and both alike require this taking into account of structure *and* of life.

We are too ready to be satisfied, theologically and pastorally, with considering what can be called, in a wide sense, the sacraments of Christianity as existing in themselves, in their state of something already made, given from on high. We have not considered them enough *in the religious subject*, used and lived by men. We have made a theology, we have sometimes even used a pastoral method, of *sacramentum* [H], of the means of grace as they exist in themselves in the condition of institutions, of administrative processes, of formulas and ceremonies; we have not thought of them much as things that can be and effectively are the *res* [I] of a religious subject, and especially of a collective religious subject, of a community. In the contemporary world things reached a stage where there was not only a sort of divorce between the Church institution and the human community, but the system and forms of the institution were in a way a curtain hiding the profound mystery of the Church. That is why this mystery has so often been rediscovered by being lived from below, in small groups that found the Church in her fullness through little Church cells, in whose constitution the religious subject was personally and communally active. It is not surprising that, seeing these new forms of Church life, plenty of good Catholics have exclaimed, 'This is Protestant!'[33]. There is, of course, nothing Protes-

[33]Two or three examples from among a number that have come under our personal notice: The clergy at P. took to preaching more biblically, and instead of rather formal meetings for the whole parish began small local meetings. This was said to be Protestant. – Certain workers were brought to Christ by Abbé D. When they had to go and work in a remote place they took a Bible with them, read it, and talked about it with their mates. This was said to be Protestant. – Visits of parents to their sons at the junior seminary at C. were arranged. Some of the parents remarked, 'Our boys talk to us about the Mission de Paris, Mission de France, etc. What is this new Protestantism?' But Protestantism is a quite different thing from Church *life* considered as people and community; it is a reduction in theory of the very idea of the Church to that of people and community, and therefore a rejection of the institutional element, as may be seen in E. Brunner's well-known work, *Das Missverstandnis der Kirche* (Zurich, 1951).

tant about it. It is simply a taking back into possession and use of that aspect of the Church which Protestantism developed onesidedly, indeed exclusively, and at the same time deformed: the aspect, that is, whereby the Church is a people, the community of the faithful made by its members.

It is for us catholically to integrate a thing that is in fact Catholic; to conceive of a priesthood and a public worship that shall not be without a people, a sustenance for the Christian mind and a testimony of faith, an apostleship, a shepherding and a guiding of the Church's daily life which shall affect the whole body. Those are things which have always existed, and which now exist in good measure in a lived ecclesial life; some of them, such as the apostleship, provide the laity with a part probably larger than it has ever been before. An effort is called for to give them all their place in ecclesiological thought; and for this the facts of ecclesial life, past and present, are most valuable guides. Provided a solidly grounded structure be respected, ecclesiology can only be the gainer.

Chapter III

POSITION OF THE LAITY
KINGDOM, CHURCH AND WORLD:
HIERARCHY AND FAITHFUL PEOPLE

THE ideas named in the heading of this chapter are of such wide range that it should cause no surprise that in order to see them properly we have to trace them a long way back and invoke very general principles. Helps in the outlining of a theology of laity can be found only at that level. It should be no more surprising that to indicate only the essential matters calls for a chapter as long as a small book. And even so there are many points on which it must suffice to use notions whose justification has been, or will be, set out elsewhere.

KINGDOM, CHURCH AND WORLD

God's design as it is revealed throughout the Bible, from the 'Let us make man, in our own image and likeness' of Genesis to the bridal of the last chapters of the Apocalypse, is to bring mankind into fellowship with his divine life. It is this design that is expressed according to different aspects by those great biblical images in which the mystery of the Church has been revealed to us: Bride, Body, City, Temple. Each of these images has its own shades of significance, but in every one it is a matter of fellowship with God, and all together in God. The images of the Body and the Bride express the fellowship whereby we all, being several, are yet one; that of the City expresses the oneness of many under God's rule; that of the Temple, as it is developed in the Old Testament and in the New, is like a synthesis of the others. This last image is so bound up with several of the fundamental themes of this book that we have felt bound to examine it fully among our *Etudes conjointes*. God wills to make the world the temple of his power and his glory; he wills to make mankind his temple built of living stones, his body made of free persons, in a word, the temple of his fellowship. This is whither it all tends: that God wills to dwell and to be praised in mankind as in a single temple, but the indwelling and the praise are spiritual, living: the indwelling is by communication of himself, the praise is in the relation of sonship or the impulse by which a son returns wholly to his Father.

God brings this all to pass by taking on our human flesh. All God's promises (and aims) are made sure in Jesus Christ (2 Corinthians i, 20). Jesus Christ is the reality of the fellowship-Temple, which is none other than his fellowship-Body (John ii, 21). He is the means of its realisation, a means perfect in its suitability and fittingness, the means willed by him who, 'having spoken of old to the fathers through the prophets by many partial revelations and in various ways, in these last days hath spoken to us by one who is Son, whom he hath set up as heir of all things; by whom also he created the ages' (Hebrews i, 1-2). After the Fathers, those interpreters of Holy Scripture, theology has searched this mystery of Jesus Christ sent from the Father, the sole means for the realisation of God's purpose of fellowship. Here are the broad lines of its teaching.

From the moment that God takes on manhood in order to realise his design of grace and fellowship—taking it on not from the outside but by a hypostatic union in the very being—that manhood receives a dignity and power that put it above all creation. 'Primogenitus omnis creaturae' (Colossians i, 15). When God accomplishes his purpose in respect of creation, not from the height of his godhead but by becoming man, he then ceases to exert his power only as God and exerts it also as man; and the manhood thus joined in him for the fulfilling of his purpose becomes the universal and supreme cause of all that depends on this design of grace.[1] Predestined to fulfil God's purpose and promises, Jesus Christ is established in fullness of power and grace, 'ut sit ipse in omnibus primatum tenens' (Colossians i, 18). It is the absolute plenitude and the absolute primacy of Christ. Scholastic theology has here developed some of the most satisfying considerations in all its work for a scientific account of Revelation: fullness of grace, the grace of headship, the conjoined and living instrument. . . . But these are no concern of ours here.

[1]Father E. Mersch formulates this well: 'By the Incarnation the first cause becomes secondary cause. But as secondary cause it still remains the first cause. And it is secondary cause in a way which is congruous with the first cause: that is to say as being, in the order of secondary causes, the universal principle for that which relates to divinisatian': *Théologie du Corps mystique* (Paris, 1944), i, p. 272 (cf. p. 382, and ii, p. 53). – Think of the implications of the simple prayer-ending in the liturgy: 'through our Lord Jesus Christ, thy Son, who lives *and reigns* with thee in the unity of the Holy Spirit. . . .'

Whatever may have been the conditions in which the systematising of the theology of Christ's three offices was carried out, the idea expressed in this theology may be regarded as traditional.[2] In the supernatural dignity and power that were his as God-man and in his mission as the Christ (anointed as Messias), Jesus confirms the attributes of king, priest and prophet.

It would not be difficult to show that these three functions respond to needs arising from the very structure of things, and in the course of the Old Testament grace is mediated through them between God and his people.[3] Because they typified and in a measure anticipated the reality of the one mediator between God and men, the man Jesus Christ (1 Timothy ii, 5), priests, kings and sometimes prophets were consecrated by anointing.[4] And the Scriptures give them the name of 'christs', which is to say 'anointed ones'. In this as in everything else Christ had to be the truth and fulfilment of all that had prepared for him as well as of all that would come after him. It has been shown[5] how sacred history was marked by a sort of progressive concentration from mankind into one people, from one people into a remnant, and from this remnant into one person, Jesus Christ; and how there followed from him an inverse movement, the mission of the ecclesial apostleship being to carry salvation in Jesus Christ to the ends of the earth. Here there is something analogous. All the mediations and consecrations and ministries that the Old Dispensa-

[2]This systematisation was hardly known till after the sixteenth century, and Protestant theology unquestionably had a certain influence on it: cf. J. Fuchs, *Magisterium, Ministerium, Regimen; Vom Ursprung einer ekklesiologischen Trilogie* (Bonn, 1941). Nevertheless in presystematic days the idea that Christ's anointing is made clear in the threefold office of priest, king and prophet is a common property of tradition. Is it found, expressly or nearly so, in the Old Testament idea that anointing is the proper consecration of priests, kings and prophets; implicitly, in the attribution of kingly, priestly and prophetical quality to Christians consecrated by anointing. This last assertion is very common, and appears practically unanimously in all the ancient liturgies. Cf. the texts collected by P. Dabin in *Le sacerdoce royal des fidèles dans la tradition . . . (Museum Lessianum*, theol. sect., 48. Louvain, 1950), a most valuable work which we shall henceforth cite simply as 'Dabin'.

[3]Cf. F. Prat, *Theologie de S. Paul*, 14th edn., ii, pp. 198ff.; Oepke, art. μεσίτης in Kittel, *Wörterbuch*. See Deut. xvii, 14–xviii, 22. When Jeremiah (viii, 1) wishes to show there has been a universal fall into idolatry, he enumerates these three categories.

[4]This is affirmed unanimously by the ancient liturgies and by many authors quoted by Dabin; I have found twenty-three in this collection, and others could be added, e.g., Innocent III and St Bonaventure. For the priests, cf. Exodus xxx, 30; Lev. viii, 2–12; x, 7. For the kings, 1 Sam. ix, 16; x, 1, 6, 10; xvi, 11–12; 1 Kings i, 34–39; xix, 15–16; 2 Kings ix, 1–6; xi, 12. For the prophets only 1 Kings xix, 16 is referred to, but see Luke iv, 18 (Is. lxi, 1), where the Spirit anoints a man and finally Jesus Christ himself as prophet.

[5]Cf. O Cullmann, *La royauté de Jesus-Christ et l'Eglise dans le N.T.* (Paris, 1941), pp. 35ff.; *Christ et le temps* (Neuchâtel, 1947), pp. 81ff., 127.

tion had known in dispersion are brought together in his fullness as the Christ, and from then on will be shared in the Church amongst a variety of conditions and offices.[6]

Beyond the mediations that it knew, no one of which was able to carry its hope to consummation, Israel awaited a king (2 Samuel vii, and the whole theme of the messianic king), a priest (Psalm cx; Vulg. cix) and a prophet (Deuteronomy xviii). Judaism's expectation of this messianic prophet was such that he was appealed to in advance. There is no point in going over the discussions of the expectation of a Messiah, God's Anointed, who would be both king and prophet, and especially king and priest. In Israel's ethnical and cultural surroundings the combination of priesthood and kingship in the same person was looked on as a sort of ideal; of this there are numerous examples. The Bible makes 'priest-king' one of the most important messianic titles: cf. Zacharias vi, 13, Psalm cx and the episode of Melchizedek in Genesis xiv, 17-20. The last two texts in particular were of the first importance in the Christological thought of the Apostles and the early Church, as may be seen from the use made of Psalm cx in the apostolic catechesis,[7] and of the priesthood of Melchizedek by the Epistle to the Hebrews—a notion that is at the heart of our subject and will be returned to later.

One of the meanings of that mysterious expression 'according to the order of Melchizedek' is that Jesus Christ derives his royal priesthood, not through physical descent from Aaron like the priests of Judaism, but from on high, as Son. He is not made priest by a human qualification, but by an act of God; he is not consecrated by an outward anointing, but by an act of the Holy Spirit, who makes of the Son of man the Son of God: his royal priesthood is his very Sonship. He has not only received anointing, he *is* The Anointed.

Our subject does not require that we should study the three messianic functions for their own sake and in detail. We shall return to the priesthood in our next chapter; but to clarify this chapter, which is the key to all the rest, we must briefly consider Christ's kingship or royal power.

The New Testament has things to say about it that are positive, precise and strikingly forthright. Faith in these assertions has been sealed with the blood of numberless martyrs. That faith was expressed and is still expressed in the fundamental confession, 'Christ

[6] St Thomas may be invoked here: *Sum. theol.*, III, q. 22, a. 1, ad 3, and II-II, q. 183, a. 2.

[7] Cf. Acts ii, 22–36; Mark xii, 35–37; C. H. Dodd, *The Apostolic Preaching . . .* (London, 1944), p. 15.

Jesus is Lord'.[8] He sits at the right hand of God: the *Credo* has made the words so familiar that they sound almost trite, and it takes an effort of mind (but how well worth while!) to realise their tremendous and sovereign content. These simple words involve the whole sweep of Christ's work, the issue of which they express. In studying the theme of the Temple we shall see how God's great design attains its end in the association of mankind with his glorious reign, in that kingly sacerdotal state where the glory in which God dwells is the temple wherein we praise him and have our own abode. But this fulfilment can come to pass for us only because it has first come to pass in Christ, for the whole of Christianity consists in this—that his mystery becomes our mystery, his passing our passing, his sitting at the right hand, ours too; or, if you like, in this—that what has been done for us by one above *(ὑπὲρ ἡμῶν)* is imparted to all. But at the stage of it where we are, not yet joined with our head and king in Heaven, it is not yet a question of our reign with him but of *his* own kingship; we shall be joined with him only if we have been willingly subject to him.

But Christ's sovereign power goes beyond those who by faith submit to him. There where he says that Christ is head of the Church (Ephesians i, 22; Colossians i, 17), St Paul declares he is the head of all creation (Ephesians i, 10; Colossians ii, 10). We have seen that it cannot be otherwise: when God takes manhood to himself he exercises in that manhood the power of kingly government that belongs to his godhead. The world's sovereign is no longer God only, but Jesus Christ, who is God made man: 'Regnat Deus, Dei caro', we sing at the Ascension. It is by that ascension that our mediator Jesus Christ, who was born and has suffered, enters into the enjoyment of the kingly power which is his as Son of God and conqueror of sin and death. Then it is that he declares that 'All power in heaven and on earth hath been given me (Matthew xxviii, 18); words which St Paul takes and expounds when he writes: '. . . that same strength he ["the God of our Lord Jesus Christ, the Father of glory"] hath wrought in Christ, raising him from the dead, and "seating him at his right hand" in the heavenly places, above every principality and power and virtue and domination, above every name that is named not only in this world but also in that which is to come. And "he hath subjected all things beneath his feet", and hath given him for supreme head to the Church . . .' (Ephesians i, 20-22). Paul writes

[8]Phil. ii, 9–11. L. Cerfaux, 'Le titre "Kyrios" et la dignité royale de Jésus' in *Revue des sciences phil. théol.* 11 (1922), pp. 40–71; 12 (1923), 125–153, has shown that *kyrios* signifies king, sovereign. See also O. Cullmann, *Les premières confessions de foi chrétiennes* (Paris, 1943).

in the same chapter that God's 'good pleasure' is to unite or subsume 'both the things in the heavens and the things upon the earth' in Jesus Christ as under one sole head.[9]

The decisive conclusion of these texts is Jesus Christ's total universal sovereignty. He is the head of the Church, but the head of all creation as well. He is the supreme head of the body of the saved who will be glorified, he is the principle of salvation, of fellowship with God; but he has also a cosmic sovereignty, which extends to the whole of creation, seen and unseen;[10] the 'powers' are subject to him (Ephesians i, 20-22; 1 Peter iii, 22); he is king of all the ages, now and hereafter (1 Timothy i, 17), he is Pantokrator (Apocalypse i, 8; iv, 8; xix, 6). If, then, we think of the great divisions of all that is created—things visible and invisible, things heavenly and things earthly, the order of creation and the order of the purpose of grace,[11] or, if you will, 'the natural' and 'the supernatural'—Christ's kingly power is seen to be precisely dominion over them all. This is of capital importance for our subject.

This kingly power, which is also priestly (cf. below), is perfectly adjusted to the aim of God's purpose for the world, perfectly fitted to carry it to its high end. The name 'finisher' given to Christ by the Epistle to the Hebrews (xii, 2; cf. ii, 10; x, 14), which Westcott made

[9]With Festugière, Cullmann and others I translate ἀνακεφαλαιώςαςθαι by *récapiter*, to put under a new head. The latest monograph (Protestant) on Eph. i, 10 is by E. Walter, *Christus und der Kosmos* . . . (Stuttgart, 1948). On the Resurrection and the Ascension establishing Jesus as Son-of-God-invested-with-power, cf. Rom. i, 4; Eph. i, 20-23. That that is the meaning of these texts, see P. Michalon, L'Eglise, corps mystique du Christ glorieux' in *Nouv. rev. théol.*, 1952, pp. 673-687.

[10]Everything is through him and for him: 1 Cor. viii, 6; Col. i, 16; Heb. i, 2; John i, 10; Apoc. xi, 15, 17. He is *A* and *Ω*: Apoc. i, 8; xxi, 6, xxii, 13. This cosmic character of the Messiah's kingship is declared in the O.T.: Ps. lxxii, 8-12 (Vulg. lxxi); Dan. vii, 13-14, etc.

[11]This is the great division of Holy Scripture, beginning with its first book. Genesis falls into two parts, from chapter i to xi and from xii to l. The first part shows God in his sovereign creative power, associating therewith the great realities of nature: the cosmos, man and his mind, work, punishment, the family, diversity of peoples and languages; it is dominated by the ideas of creation and of the sovereignty of the divine overruling, and by the covenant with Noah, which bears on the regularity of creation's order and laws (Gen. ix, 9ff.). With chapter xii there begins another order of things which is properly sacred history, and the 'unveiling' (Revelation) goes on till the last verse of the last book, which is called precisely The Unveiling (Apocalypse). This part is concerned with God's purpose or design of grace, no longer with the order of nature and its laws but with that of the vocation communicated by the word of God, which is received in faith. The beginning of this history or design is, 'The Lord said to Abram, Go forth out of thy country . . . and come into the land which I shall shew thee . . . and in thee shall all the kindred of the earth be blessed' (Gen. xii, 1-3); and the end is the bridal of the Lamb, who associates the Church with his reign, and 'the Lord God almighty is the sanctuary thereof, and the Lamb' (Apoc. xxi, 22). It is over this twofold order of things (in theological terms, nature and grace) that our texts declare Christ's unique sway.

the title of a little work of 'popularisation', is one of those that best expresses his attribute as *Christus*, anointed as prophet, king and priest according to the order of Melchizedek. Truly is he Alpha and Omega [J], the fulfilment of all God's promises. He is *the* means devised and put to work by God to bring about his unconstrained purpose of creation and fellowship.

The Kingdom is the reality that corresponds to Christ's kingly power, as its final and sufficient effect. In terms really equivalent, but having reference to his priestly power, we may say that this final and sufficient effect is the Temple of fellowship of which we have spoken above. That in both cases (we repeat, they are really identical) the work, taken beyond Christ, is on account of the Father,[12] makes no difference to what we have to say here. In restoring everything to the Father from whom he is sprung, Christ is only bringing all over which he has been set as priest and king into the movement by which he himself lives his life as Son, heir, partner of the Father in blessedness and glory. His kingdom is thus brought to the exact goal to which his kingly power is directed; this is the work of that kingly and priestly power. What does that imply?

Study and interpretation of the texts lead us to these conclusions. The expression Kingdom of God denotes a reality which has several aspects. There is an eschatological [K] aspect and a dynamic or progressive aspect; and in the last an inward and an outward aspect. Before all that and in all that, the expression *malcouth* that is found behind βασιλεία is susceptible of two translations: in an active sense, 'God's royal government'; in a passive sense, 'the kingdom'. Since Dalman's *Worte Jesu*, critics agree that the first sense was that of Jewish thought and of the New Testament. But we must not oversimplify. The active sense predominates and we must speak first of *reign*; but there is during the dynamic and preparatory phase, and especially will there be at the eschatological (that is, the last) stage, an *effect* of this act of God, an order of things—a *kingdom*. We are here speaking of this kingdom, the state of things created by the perfect exercise of Christ's royal power, and we will try to specify its most general characteristics.

The kingdom will be an order of things in which man and creation will be condemned to the will of God. All things will be gathered

[12]On one hand, Christ must deliver up his kingdom to God, his Father (1 Cor. xv, 24, 28); on the other, if the true temple is the body of Christ (John ii, 21), yet the Epistle to the Hebrews (ix, 11-12, 24) and the Apocalypse (xxi, 22, vii, 15) show us a final state where there is no other temple but God himself. Jesus Christ, the eternal priest, is a path to the throne of God (Heb. x, 20, vii, 19; and cf. Schrenk in Kittel, iii, p. 276).

under Christ as their one head: a single, hierarchical, total order,
consequent on the perfect dominance of the higher principle over
lower elements, and finally on perfect dominance of the *Pneuma* [L],
the gift that belongs to the messianic era. Not for nothing was it said
that Jesus was made Lord and Christ at his resurrection-ascension
(Acts ii, 36). The Resurrection, consummated in the Ascension, is
the very first achievement in the triumph of the *Pneuma* over nature
itself, the reconciliation in Christ of the cosmic order with the order
of God's free grace. With it there indeed begins the renewing of the
Kingdom, which in the fullness of time will be the perfect fruition of
the Easter victory: the ascendancy, the triumph, of justice over
injustice, truth over falsehood, good over evil, life over all that can
do works of death and be called death, grace over nature, of the
Pneuma over the flesh and over all things.

An important fact at once emerges, namely, that it is through this
influence of a higher principle, and in the hierarchy that actualises
the dominance of this principle, that the lower elements find their
perfection, the perfection proper to their own nature. This has an
important place in the theological synthesis of St Thomas, particularly in the way he conceives the 'natural desire' to behold God
and the relationship of nature to the gift of grace. Things do not
exist just in a state of juxtaposition, but in an order. It follows that
their perfection, to which they are called by nature, involves not
only the being or the doing that they can attain by the exercise of
the energies whose active principle they have, but also the being or
the doing that comes to them from their conjunction with a higher
principle. Their nature is in themselves, but the *integrity* of their
perfection is found only through the influence of this principle.
Following up what has just been said about the Resurrection, consider the theme of immortality in the Fathers. They unanimously
look upon the immortality of man (rather than 'of the soul') as an
effect of grace. So what nature desires and what is, in its strongest
sense, man's integrity is seen also to be an effect of the triumph of the
Spirit which raised Jesus from the dead, which has to restore in the
world and in man, from one end to the other, the integrity of the
vestiges or image of God which are in them. Such will be the fruit
of Christ's cosmic power and of that re-establishing of all things
under him [M] of which St Paul speaks. Such will be the Kingdom,
the sufficient and proper effect of Jesus Christ's universal kingship.

Equally will the Kingdom be a world that is *reconciled*, for the perfect order in God will pour out a perfect order among things, a
harmony that will spread to the tiniest realities. A world brought to

oneness, a reconciled world, without antagonisms and painful conflicts—that is just how the prophets describe the messianic era. The English word Atonement—which some theologians like to write atone-ment—is very expressive, 'bringing together into one'. It is used to signify Christ's expiatory work with its reconciling effect. From that we see how Christ's kingdom is priestly, the fruit not only of his kingly power but also of his sacerdotal work of expiation, redemption, forgiveness and union with God. But this belongs to the theme of the temple and its worship, which I hope to deal with in *Etudes conjointes*.

    *   *   **

Such is the goal of God's work, such will be the final work of Christ when, exerting all the might of his kingly and priestly power, he will have fulfilled in us as well as in himself that for which he received the kingly, priestly and prophetical anointing. But God's design as the Bible has revealed it has two stages; and this point, which determines what may be called the constitution (*statut*) of Christianity, is of capital importance, having decisive consequences not only for our subject but for the whole of ecclesiology. Moreover, this point is becoming at the present time (like so many other important points, thank God) almost a commonplace, a matter of general agreement, among Christian theologians.

The work of grace towards which God's purpose is directed is concerned with one advent, but he ordains that it shall be unfolded in two times. Whilst always recognising this, at least implicitly and latently, Catholic theology more or less lost living perception of several aspects of its own positions after it had more or less lost the eschatological sense (which means something more than an aggregate of theses *de novissimis*) [N]. In this matter the eschatologism of Protestant exegetes and theologians in the past fifty or sixty years, when stripped of whatever is exaggerated and onesided, has produced some extremely interesting views among Protestants,[13] and has not failed to bring a healthy stimulus to more than one Catholic theologian.[14] It has been better understood, on the one hand, that

[13]I am thinking (with some important reservations) of C. H. Dodd's 'realised eschatology' in *The Apostolic Preaching* (London, 1938), ch. v, app., History and the Gospel, and of Edwin Hoskyns in *Cambridge Sermons* (London, 1938); but even more of O. Cullmann, *Christ et le temps* (Neuchâtel, 1947). See J. Danielou in *Etudes*, 1950, pp. 359–368.

[14]For example, G. Feurerer, *Unsere Kirche im Kommen: Begegnung von Jetztzeit und Endzeit* (Freiburg i. B., 1937); R. Grosche, *Pilgernde Kirche* (Freiburg i. B., 1938). But among Catholics some of the rediscovery of the eschatological dimension has been in direct contact with the Bible and the Fathers, e.g., H. de Lubac, *Catholicisme* (Paris, 1938; English trans.). Note the convergence of dates: 1937–1938.

Christianity is inconceivable without reference to the final realities, the eschatological consummation, and on the other hand that these eschatological realities are not only things which chronologically will come at the end, they are also present throughout the time of the Church [O] and give this time its inner meaning. The Apostles' preaching never tires in its insistence that we are living in the last days: but this must not be interpreted apocalyptically as the imminence in time of the end of this world, but in the sense that in a way we are already under that definitive dispensation after which there will be no other, for it is the rule of the Son of God himself. The final realities are in a sense present and active among us here and now. This is because of Christ and the economy [P] of the messianic work. The Jews saw the passage of time in terms of an eschatology that should be the consummation of all things, but they conceived it as happening all at once in a single event that should mark the end of earthly history. God would reign, and everything would come under his sway together with his faithful people.

This is what John the Baptist and the Apostles had in mind, for they shared the mentality of their fellow Jews.[15] But between his coming and the fulfilment of his work in the Kingdom, Jesus puts an intermediate time which was outside Jewish thought. His utterances here indeed present that mixture of obscurity and light which surrounded the foretelling of the Christ in the Old Testament, and that goes with the revelation of the Kingdom and of all the Christian mystery in the New. Nevertheless Jesus suggested clearly enough the idea of a twofold coming and of two stages in his work, separated by a period of unknown duration (Cf. for example Luke xvii, 20-21; xix, 11; Matthew xvi, 19); and especially, when the time came to leave his disciples, did he separate the two 'moments' which John the Baptist had still combined, distinguishing between a baptism of the Spirit which must take place 'in a few days' and palingenesy [Q] whose time it does not belong to man to know. Thus there was determined a period that can be called the 'space-between', since it lies between the two comings of Jesus, between his ascension (Pent-e cost) and his *parousia* [R], which in one sense belongs to the last days, the final reign of the Messias, but which nevertheless is also a time of expectation and preparation, awaiting the fulfilment of the end.

It is all bound up with the fact of Jesus, God incarnate. Fellowship with God, his indwelling, salvation, the Father's inheritance are already present and given to the world in him. The fullness of divine

[15]For John the Baptist, cf. Matt. iii, 11–12; Luke iii, 16–17 (cf. Luke iii, 9; Matt. iii, 10). For the Apostles, Acts i, 3–8 and such episodes as in Matt. xx, 20ff.

good things is no longer far away in the future: it is here, coming into the world just there when the Incarnation took place and the passing of Jesus through his passion and resurrection. There is a sense in which Jesus is himself the Kingdom of God, *autobasileia*, to use Origen's fine expression. He is the Kingdom virtually, in its principle, a principle which in a sense contains all its developments. We must look at this more closely, for it throws light on all that is to follow.

St Thomas, whose interpretation of the times of the Christian economy is far better than that of more recent scholastics, formulates these things in a way that contemporary biblical studies can greatly enrich but can only confirm. He distinguished three successive states or stages of interior religion (*Summa theol*. I-II, q. 103, a. 3). Under the Old Dispensation [S], he says, man had relation, by faith, with the promised heavenly benefits and the means to attain them, as things *to come*; the blessed in the Kingdom have relation to these same benefits and their means as *present*, enjoyed realities; we, who are under the New Law but in that space-between to which reference has been made above, we have relation with these benefits, by faith and hope, as things yet to come; but the means to their attainment has been given and is with us, namely, Jesus Christ. The age of the Synagogue is altogether one of expectation and preparation; the age of the Kingdom will be one of full possession of the promised good things: the characteristic of the intermediate time is that the principle of salvation is now given and active, but all its effects have not yet emerged. That is indeed the state in which we are and to which the Scriptures bear witness: that of a people of God still only moving towards the complete fulfilment of the promises made to them, but who have in Jesus Christ, dead and risen for them, the principle of all those goods whose fullness they still await, happy meanwhile in a beginning of their inheritance (Colossians i, 12-14). The principle of the Kingdom has been given, and already we taste of its firstfruits; the full harvest has yet to ripen and the full enjoyment of it is eschatological. The Lord has planted his vine and we are its branches: the whole must grow until the time of God's gathering.

We can now understand something of God's design, of which we have said that it is concerned with one advent but involves two times or stages. God very often at first gives and confides only to one what later is to be given to many. We can, with W. Vischer, call this sort of constant of the divine wisdom the law of *pars pro toto*, and it is wonderfully exemplified in Jesus Christ. He makes for us, ὑπὲρ ἡμῶν, that passing-over into the Father's bosom by which we are enabled to enter into possession of 'the light which saints inherit' (Colossians i, 12): one death is died 'to bring together into one all God's children, scattered far and wide' (John xi, 52), there is one going-up into Heaven (John iii, 13); to make ours what has thus been accomplished on our behalf, we have but to make with Jesus Christ one single body of death to sin and rebirth to everlasting life. So in the work of Jesus Christ there is an aspect of 'done' and an aspect of 'still to be done': already done by one, once for all; still to be done by many, throughout space and time, until he comes again.

The space-between that separates his Ascension from his Return, which we have called the time of the Church, is necessary in order that what has been done once for all in Christ may be done by everybody, or at any rate by very many. There are two times in God's work because it requires that what is to be achieved and dis-played in its fruit shall be first done in the seed. All is in Jesus Christ as in the principle, and it has no other term than his body, the temple and kingdom of God. He is in very truth Alpha and Omega; the parousial mystery is substantially the same as the paschal mys-tery. But, in the principle, Jesus included us only virtually, without our counting for anything in it; in the term, he will include actually those who have come to him by a free decision of faith, ratified and fulfilled in the sacraments of the faith. The parousial mystery is the mystery of the Pasch [T] of Jesus become ours by the grace of the Holy Spirit and with our free collaboration. In a sense, there is nothing in the term that was not in the principle: we add nothing to Christ, and St Thomas is able to write that Jesus Christ plus the Church is no more than Jesus Christ by himself.[16] But this does not exhaust the truth of the matter and of God's design. In another sense we do 'add' to Jesus Christ and 'complete' him;[17] Christ plus our-selves is more than Christ alone, and his communal body is not simply a doublet of his physical body, mechanically reproduced and kept in being. From principle to term there is development, through action of the principle to which the elements—who are persons—respond by their unconstrained collaboration. Jesus is indeed the Alpha of all, 'Primogenitus omnis creaturae', and he will be the Omega of all: all creatures are *through* him and all are *for* him (Colossians i, 15-16); but between the sovereign act by which all

[16]*Com. in IV Sent.*, d. 49, q. 4, a. 3, ad 4. Cf. *De veritate*, q. 29, a. 5; *Com. in Ephes.*, c. 1 lect. 8; and elsewhere.

[17] Col. i, 24; Eph. i, 23 (no doubt the passive sense is not exclusive, but it seems certainly intended), iv, 13ff., etc.

began and the effective kingship in which all will be fulfilled all things must grow towards him, and free beings freely.

All this throws light on the meaning of time and history that must be noted and treasured. When we speak of the 'time of the Church' we certainly understand thereby a certain regime, conditions of Christian life and work, but we also understand a duration of time, days, years, centuries. What is the meaning of this time? Is it something accidental and indifferent for Christianity and its final working out in the Parousia and the Kingdom, or has it a positive value and a part to play?

If God or Christ did everything alone, if there were no positive intervention by man in the final result, then one does not see what value this time would have; it would seem to be only a meaningless delay ('delay of grace', say the Protestants) unless some value be attributed to man's 'doing'.[18] The Christian meaning of time as the time of the Church (and also, as we shall see, as the time and history of the world) is to be found in man's co-operation or 'doing' as bearing positively on the final result, the Kingdom of God (or equivalently, the Temple). The Christian mystery is the fulfilment of the Second Adam in the substance of the First, the conjunction of the two; it is the entry of time into eternity, on the basis of eternity coming down into time; or a return of the creature to God—and as regards men, a return of free persons—on the basis of that down-coming and of the gift of *agape* [U]. Since the vigour of the return is entirely derived from the movement of descent (the grace of the Holy Spirit, Jesus tells us, is a spring of water that carries us to everlasting life: John iv, 14), since all that is developed in the Church is derived from the Lord's revelation (John xvi, 13-15) and the sacraments are simply the celebration of his Pasch (1 Corinthians xi, 26), in short, since all our 'doing' comes from God's 'giving', our explanation does full justice to the oneness of salvation which Cullmann so strongly emphasises in his pages on ἐφάπαξ, the *Einmaligkeit* [V]. But it must be emphasised no less strongly that our situation in the midst of the 'time of the Church', between the Pasch that has gone by and the Parousia that is to come, is not one of inert things, for the simple reason that it is not a question of 'things'. The Church is, in this

[18]When, for example, Pastor P. Balmer writes ('Le fondement de l'Eglise' in *L'Eglise parmi nous*, Neuchâtel, 1947, p. 18): 'God's work is finished and there is no need for us to complete it or to conduct it to victory. God is conqueror, God has done all. There remains now the time of his forbearance, during which we accept, recognise and bear witness to that divine work', it is clear that we *have* something to do, viz., to accept, to recognise, to bear witness; at the very least we can fail to do these things and so wreck the work in us. But something still more positive is called for; cf. e.g., the parable of the talents, Luke xix, 11-27.

G

space-between, the body of Christ, in which Christ lives in the world and 'completes' himself from the world's substance. In order to grow to the stature of Christ and the parousial temple to which we belong, on the strength of the unique gift of the Father who so loved the *world* (John iii, 16), we have to draw upon the Incarnation and Pasch in all the fullness of their meaning, and to bring to this (Yes, this must be said) the fruits of our free activities as beings made in God's image.

Such are, Christianly speaking, the reason and meaning of time or of history.

The work of Christ, the Anointed of God, is then disposed over two periods: a time during which the principle is active but does not exert the fullness of its power, and a time when this fullness will be manifested in all its extent and the Kingdom will be really established. Two important consequences follow, of which the second is connected through the first to their common foundation: (1) Two states of Christ's priestly kingship correspond to the two stages in God's design or the work of Jesus; (2) In the earthly stage which is equivalent to what we have called the space-between, there is the duality of church and world, two realities each of which has its own relationship to the one final Kingdom.

(1) THE TWO STATES OF CHRIST'S PRIESTLY KINGSHIP

This expression must be rightly understood. Christ's priestly kingship is always perfect as regards itself: but as regards its exercise it has two very different states, that of overcoming by the Cross and that of ruling in power. This follows at once from the fact that Christ's work is in two stages: the first when the cause of universal salvation is present but does not produce all its effects; the second when Christ's kingly, priestly and prohetical power comes to its rightful and complete fruition in reconciliation, integrity, praise of God and glory for men. Using a comparison which, without his knowing it, occurs in the Fathers and the scholastics, Cullmann presents this traditional point well in a figure that appeals to men who knew the hopes and conflicts of the second world war. Christ is the victor, Easter for him is like the decisive victory in war that brings mortal hurt to the enemy; but that enemy has not yet lost all his strength, he can still do serious damage, and there must still be much fighting and suffering before he will give in. The day of his unconditional surrender and of the victor's triumph, V-day, is when Christ comes again in power and majesty.

Such are the biblical declarations—of Jesus himself in the gospels,[19] of St Paul,[20] of the Epistle to the Hebrews,[21] of the Apocalypse —as Father Allo expounds them in his fine commentary (1921). There are other concordant passages to be found in the Bible, and it seems to me that the type figures of David and Solomon can be interpreted in this sense. We will, then, consider Christ from this point of view, first as priestly king, then as priest.

We have noticed a number of texts which declare that one day, a day known only to God, Christ will show forth all the fullness of his kingly power. Then will he subdue *all things* to himself, that thereby homage may be given to God. In subduing, he will be reigning in power and majesty, as painters and carvers tried to show us in antiquity and the middle ages; in giving his kingdom's homage to God, he will be fulfilling the priestly office of worship. But his priesthood is a royal priesthood, and it is seen as such in his entry into the very sanctuary of God, there to share in the glory and governance of God. We shall go in with him and shall be associated with him—in his reign sitting at God's right hand. Hence St John's insistence, in the Apocalypse, on calling us 'kings and priests' (i, 6; iii, 21; v. 10; xx, 6). We shall be (we are ready by faith and hope) enthroned above the heavens with Christ, says St Paul (Ephesians ii, 6), and adds that 'we shall judge angels' (1 Corinthians vi, 3), that is, the Powers. . . . Christ's glorious reign will begin with justice: he will render to each according to his works and will mightily put down those who have refused to submit to the order of his love during the time of mercy.

The power that Christ shows forth then will be his thenceforward. It is true that he has already overcome death, overcome and passed judgment on the powers that set themselves up against God's order (Satan means 'contradictor', 'adversary'). But though victor he still has enemies, and the Scriptures show him setting out to conquer them again, this time finally and completely (Cf. Hebrews x, 11-14; Apocalypse vi, 2). Psalm cx, which apostolic Christianity used to express its faith in Christ's sovereign kingship, shows him victorious at the Ascension, but provisionally and incompletely, sitting at God's right hand until his enemies shall be thrust beneath his feet (cf. Acts

[19]On one hand, Luke x, 18, xi, 20; all the texts that proclaim the beginning of the messianic reign; John xii, 31, xvi, 11. On the other, Matt. viii, 29; John xviii, 36, and the texts where Jesus speaks to his disciples about the conflict with Satan who is not yet disarmed.

[20]On one hand, Eph. i, 21–22; Col. ii, 10–15; 2 Tim. i, 10. On the other, 1 Cor. ii, 6, xv, 25–26.

[21]On one hand, ii, 8, viii, 1. On the other, x, 13, and cf. the use of Psalm cx in Acts ii, 34–36.

ii, 35, etc.). His kingship is triumphant and established in Heaven, but for the present it knows certain limits. He has universal dominion (Apocalypse i, 8; iv, 8; xix, 6), but there are also 'the world-rulers of this darkness' (Ephesians vi, 12); he is 'king of the ages' (1 Timothy i, 17), but there are other princes, a Prince of this world.[22] These are active, organised, have followers, forming a sort of 'anti-kingdom', a world of Antichrist—Tychonius, St Augustine, St Gregory and the middle ages used to speak of a *corpus Diaboli*. Only on the day of judgment at the Second Coming, the day of justice, might and majesty, shall Satan and the satanic powers—already beaten but not disarmed—lose all their ability to do harm. Here and now they have that ability, and Christian life, the life of the Church as well as individuals, is a warfare amid temptations.

In the same way Christ, who henceforward has sovereign power over the cosmos by which he will one day make of it a reconciled world wherein each thing will find its integrity, does not exert that power in its fullness, or at least does so only in short passing antici-pations, by way of a sign, or by a kind of inward healing and trans-formation, which is now one of the fruits of grace but remains incom-plete, and rarely leads to a shattering triumph. But the healing and transforming power now shown forth by Christ's grace must not be under-estimated. All action of the Holy Spirit, who is the gift proper to the new and never-ending covenant, to eschatological time, is as it were an anticipation of the Kingdom. What was wrought so powerfully in Jesus during his earthly life is continued in the Church. Cures, miracles, manifestation of heavenly things, some experience of the wonders of the world to come (Hebrews vi, 5), transfiguration of lives—all such things, throughout the centuries as in the time of Jesus and the Apostles, are signs that the Kingdom will come in power, and a foretaste, a far-off anticipation, of that which will be. That is one of the reasons why miracles, cures, even raisings from the dead, occupy such a place in the gospels. We shall come back to this again later.

It must, however, be noticed here, firstly, that this transformation of the world takes place in a priestly rather than a kingly way and on an essentially religious basis, on that of the Cross (This too is referred to further on). There is the healing and transforming power exercised through the Church's priestly mediation, particularly in the sacraments;[23] and there is the wonderworking power of the

[22]'Who are being brought to nought', St Paul adds (1 Cor. ii, 6, 8). Cf. John xii, 31, xiv, 30, vi, 11.

[23]Which in some respects continue the gospel miracles.

saints and of spiritual gifts, which are the seed of holiness. Secondly, this transformation, though it already has some cosmic value, leaves the earthly order untouched in what may be called its Noachic [W] and anteparousial state. The cosmos is in a measure affected through man and in relation to him, but this does not change its economy as the coming of Christ in power will do. Death in particular is overcome and has lost its sting (1 Corinthians xv, 55), but it still holds sway and will be destroyed only at the last (1 Corinthians xv, 26).

Certain episodes in the gospels better than anything else explain Christ's kingly power in its anteparousial stage and put us on the way to understanding its regime. Jesus both declares his power and chooses to keep its exercise and manifestation within certain limits. We know that he declared his power by word and by deed, and his avowal before Pilate tells us so again. But on the other hand he refuses to be proclaimed king (John vi, 15), forbids evil spirits to hail him as the Christ (Luke iv, 41), prevents Peter from defending him by force, saying that if he willed his Father would send more than twelve legions of angels (Matthew xxvi, 53), tells Pilate that if his kingdom were of this world his soldiery would be fighting for him (John xviii, 36). . . . Again, he declares that there is no glory (future) without cross (present). His temptation in the wilderness bore precisely on this point: the Devil wanted to call forth manifestations of power that should exclude the Cross; and it is this spirit again that Christ opposes in Peter (Matthew xvi, 23), in James and John (Matthew xx, 22), and on the road to Emmaus (Luke xxiv, 26). . . . Christ's kingship exists here below in its fullness, but its manifestations are restricted and as it were disguised by his mission as saviour through the Cross, and also (as Dostoevsky points out in his interpretation of the temptations and the incident on Calvary, Matthew xxvii, 40) by his will not to violate man's freedom, to maintain the integrity of which he makes his own divine power not too conspicuous.[24]

It may be said that on this earth Christ is more priest than king, more saviour than ruler: it is a consequence of that work of restoration of which St Paul says: 'As through one offence condemnation came to all men, so also through a single justifying act there cometh to all men life-giving justification' (Romans v, 18). Adam sacrificed the order of submissiveness to kingship, Christ sacrifices kingship to

[24]God's respect for our freedom, his positive will that our response to his call shall be free, is a mystery on which we cannot meditate too much. In a novel of the future, *Der achte Tag* (Innsbruck, 1950), H. Godhe writes, speaking of God: 'Weil er die Freiheit liebt, er der grosste Fanatiker der Freiheit . . . weil er die Freiheit mehr liebt als seine Konigswurde, als sein Herrschaftsamt . . .' (p. 242).

the order of submissiveness. All this corresponds to the regime of the time of seed-sowing and mercy, before the time of retribution and power; the time, too, of our unconstrained co-operation, when our freedom must not be coerced by what is evident. During this regime the final realities are present as mystery and *in virtute*, that is to say, in their principles, at work without showing forth their power clearly and in its fullness. God has made everything subject to Christ, but we do not see all things subject to him yet (Hebrews ii, 8); 'now we are children of God, and it hath not yet been manifested what we shall be' (i John iii, 2); 'your life is hidden with Christ in God: when Christ, our life, shall appear, then also shall ye appear with him in glory' (Colossians iii, 3-4). These texts are clear and hang together; and a whole theology of the sacraments and working of the Church can be evoked from them, recalling the way in which the Fathers and scholastics interpreted this biblical material. We will simply remark how, after what our Lord himself said about baptism and the eucharist, they testify that these two sacraments already contain *in virtute* our resurrection to glory.[25] We always come back to the same point: a regime wherein the cause is present and active, but in which the triumphant manifestation of all its effects is still awaited in toil and conflict.

Turning from Christ's kingly power, which is priestly because of its finality of reconciliation and praise, to his priesthood properly speaking, we find that here too there are two conditions corresponding to the two stages of God's design. Here we follow B. F. Westcott's exegesis of the Epistle to the Hebrews.[26] From this epistle Jesus seems to become priest according to the order of Melchizedek at his ascension.[27] Now the Scriptures present Melchizedek as a priest but say nothing about his offering sacrifice,[28] while the Epistle to the Hebrews attributes a priestly character and the value of a sacrifice to the death of Jesus (vii, 27; cf. ii, 17-18). Does not Christ's priesthood

[25] Cf. John vi, 54; Gal. iii, 29. – Two witnesses only: St Irenaeus, *Adv. haer.*, iv, 18, 5 (PG., vii, 1029), and St Thomas, *Sum. theol.*, III, q. 79, a. 2. The eucharist is *pignus resurrectionis et gloriae.*

[26] *The Epistle to the Hebrews* (London, 1902), pp. 201ff., 229–230. I am aware that this exegesis does not convince everybody. On careful thought it seems to be well founded and in accord with a view of things equally well founded.

[27] Cf. Heb. vi, 20; comp. v, 9ff.; vii, 28, and Westcott, pp. 166, 199.

[28] Westcott, pp. 202ff. L. Soubigou in *Lumières sur le sacerdoce de Jésus-Christ . . .* (Paris, 1948), p. 12, remarks that the term used in Gen. xiv 18 for Melchizedek's presentation of bread and wine *never* has a sacrificial value in the verbal form in which it is used. He tries, however, to establish the idea of a sacrifice by Melchizedek, of which indeed the Fathers and the canon of the Roman Mass speak.

then present two aspects? Or, like his kingship, exist successively under two conditions, one on earth, the other in Heaven?

The wealth of meaning in the expression 'priest according to the order of Melchizedek' cannot be exhausted by one explanation alone; but to see in it reference to the *heavenly order of priesthood* certainly touches the essential point, because of two things that are radically connected. On the one hand, Melchizedek's priesthood, unlike the levitical priesthood, does not come through a temporal succession by bodily generation but is from above ('without father, without mother . . .'), and it does not allow of succession; on the other hand, it is a kingly priesthood. The common root of these two things is that Christ's priesthood comes to him as Son, as the one who is 'heir of all things' (Heb. i, 2-4), whose generation is from everlasting and of Heaven, who has by right a place in the Father's house, even at his right hand. It should be noticed, Westcott observes, that in the Epistle to the Hebrews the sitting at the right hand is, with one exception (i, 13), linked with Christ's royal-sacerdotal character and with the accomplishment of his priestly office.[29] This leads us to think that Christ's priesthood according to the order of Melchizedek is his priesthood in its kingly phase, ushered in by his going up into Heaven and sitting at the right hand of God, whereas before his ascension he had fulfilled the office of high priest according to the type of Aaron, less royal than sacrificial.

As high priest fulfilling the type of Aaron, Christ has offered up himself (Hebrews vii, 27; viii, 3; ix, 14, 26; x, 10-12) and has truly and effectively 'gone in to God's presence'.[30] The whole of his earthly life was like a sacrifice (Hebrews ii, 17-18; x, 5), which had to culminate in the Cross. When he cried 'It is finished', Christ testified to the accomplishment of everything, he had gone in to God's presence through his own blood. By so doing he fulfilled the Aaronic sacrificial priesthood, whose service was summed up in the observances of the Day of Atonement, and the Epistle to the Hebrews applies the whole liturgy of that day to Christ. On that day the high priest *alone* represented the whole people of Israel—Jesus in his passion bore in himself alone the whole people of the children of God (cf. John xi, 51-52). The high priest offered a twofold sacrifice, one for his own sins—

[29]Cf. i, 3; viii, 1; x, 12; xii, 2. Hebrews is perhaps the only book in the Bible which itself fixes the essential matter of its content (viii, 1–2).

[30]Heb. iv, 14; vi, 20; vii, 12, 16; ix, 12, 23ff. 'Go in to God's presence' and 'stand before God' are Old Testament 'cultual' expressions (and what fine ones!), and not strictly sacerdotal. For 'draw near', see ἐγγύς, ἐγγίζω in Kittel. 'To stand' in Hebrew is *kun*, the root of *kohen*, priest.

Jesus had none—the other for those of the people. Then, and it was the only time in the year, he went in to the Holy of Holies, the place of God's presence, and reconciled the people with God by sprinkling the blood of the sacrifice. Such was the character of Christ's priesthood before he sat at God's right hand: sacrificial, and likewise as thing sacrificed. Christian tradition has often deduced (or rather 'induced') Christ's priesthood from his victimhood (especially St Augustine and St Chrysostom; cf. Hebrews ix, 12, 25).

As high priest and king Jesus is enthroned at the right hand of God where he reigns henceforward, priest of the final sanctuary that is not made by human hands (cf. Hebrews viii, 1-2, already quoted). He gathers the fruits of his victory (Hebrews i, 13; x, 12); but though his reign is undisturbed, he does not cease to be a priest. Not that we have to imagine some heavenly sacrifice in the sense of a sacrificial act properly so called.[31] Christ is no longer priest after the manner of the Aaronic high priest but of the kingly kind, according to the order of Melchizedek, who did not offer sacrifice: he *blessed* Abraham; his priestly action consisted in blessing, that is, the *communication of the fruits of an offered sacrifice* (Westcott, pp. 202-203). So Christ, gone up into Heaven, gives largesse to men, *dedit dona hominibus*, 'that he might fill all things'.[32] For the future his priestly activity consists in making intercession on our behalf as he represents us before God (Hebrews vii, 25, 27; ix, 24; comp. xiii, 15), offering our prayer and our praise made one with his (xiii, 15), by his blood ensuring our admittance before the Father (iv, 16; x, 19-22), conferring spiritual gifts, that is, the Spirit, the fruits of his sacrifice: from the breath that he breathed on Mary and John, then representing the Church, was to come the Spirit of Pentecost;[33] the blood and water that flowed from his stricken side while his body was yet warm are the sacraments that bring to us that reconciliation which is the harvest of his death.[34]

[31]Cf. Westcott, p. 232. – There is an altar in Heaven: cf. Is. vi, 6; Apoc. viii, 3; and the Christian liturgies (cf. H. W. Codrington, 'The Heavenly Altar in the Byzantine Liturgy' in *Eastern Churches Quarterly*, 1938, pp. 125–130). But according to Hebrews (v, 5ff.; ix, 12, 14; xiii, 20) the sacrifice as action has taken place on earth once for all, though its fruits remain and Christ is, εἰς τὸν αἰῶνα, the supreme *pontifex* of their application to men. In his *Key to the Doctrine of the Eucharist* Abbot Vonier remarks that according to Apoc. viii, 3–5 worship in Heaven is not sacrificial but of prayer and praise: the altar there is of incense, not of burnt-offerings.

[32]Eph. iv, 8–10; notice the use made of this text in the Ascension liturgy.

[33]The spirit that Jesus Christ breathed forth (John xix, 30) after having bowed his head (towards Mary and John) is the realisation of John vii, 37–39 and should be brought into relation with 1 John v, 8; cf. E. C. Hoskyns, *The Fourth Gospel* (London, 1947), p. 532.

[34]Tradition unanimously interprets John xix, 34 in this sense. In 1 John v, 6–8 the water and the blood are, with the Spirit, the three earthly witnesses to Jesus.

Thus, in his priesthood now clothed in power, Christ in Heaven is the minister of all the gifts that he gained for us in his Day of Atonement.

(2) A DUALITY OF CHURCH AND WORLD IN THE EARTHLY STAGE OF CHRIST'S KINGLY POWER

In the final order, then, answering to the fullest exercise of Christ's kingly power, the whole of creation will be subject to the *Pneuma*, and in that subjection nature itself will find its perfection and integrity. It is characteristic of the time of 'space-between' that Jesus Christ, while having power over them, leaves natural laws to work in their own way and allows forces that oppose him ability still to do harm, the 'Prince of this world' still to exercise his sway. So throughout the time that passes between the Ascension and the Parousia, Christ's kingship allows certain bounds to be set to itself, which correspond respectively to the two meanings given in the Bible to the word 'world', namely, the cosmos as the order of nature and the world as the realm of Satan, the Contradictor.

This last aspect we must put aside, as it is not strictly germane to our subject: the world in this sense is not identical with the world of the natural order and, in the concrete, it exists also in the Church.[35] Our concern is this: we no longer belong to a paradisial order wherein all nature was a temple of God and a friendly thing to man; we are not yet in the Kingdom of God wherein this order will be restored under Christ's kingly and priestly rule. That is why there is on the one side a universe over which Christ is king but does not reign, and on the other a Church over which Christ is king and over which he does reign, for it is made up of those who by faith choose to submit to him.[36] James of Viterbo, author of 'the first treatise on the Church', remarked on this when he wrote: 'All creation is Christ's kingdom in

[35]There is some ambiguity about the use of the word 'world' in the N.T. Sasse (in Kittel, iii, pp. 383ff.) distinguishes three meanings: creation as a whole; man's earth, the stage of history; fallen creation, stage of the history of salvation. – In any case the world of Satan's rule must not be confused with the world God so loves that he gave his Son for it, any more than we may confuse the carnal man (*carnalis*, σαρκικός) with the man made of flesh (*carneus*, σάρκινος). Comp. C. Journet: 'The world of time could be represented as divided into three regions by two planes: one horizontal, separating the temporal from the spiritual, to distinguish them; the other vertical, separating the spiritual area of grace and love from the spiritual area of sin and hate, to oppose them' (*Nova et Vetera*, 16, 1941, p. 310).

[36]I have applied these considerations in an essay on the theology of the church building. It is because the world is no longer (or not yet) God's temple that *special* temples are needed: 'La maison du Peuple de Dieu' in *L'art sacré*, 1947, pp. 205ff.

a different sense from that in which the Church is. All creation can be called his kingdom with reference to the might of his godhead; the Church is his kingdom in accordance with the quality of faith, whose object Christ is and by which he reigns among his faithful' (*De regimine christiano*, pars i, c. 1).

Nothing is more significant in this connexion than the entry into Jerusalem. The people hail Jesus as the messianic king and greet him with leafy branches—products of nature—and woven stuffs— products of human skill; and the Latin liturgy for Palm Sunday takes up with sober lyricism the theme of the Lord's cosmic sovereignty. But the gospels show us how ephemeral was that day's triumph: those same people who were cheering Jesus would clamour for his death four or five days later. The real kingship of Jesus over the earth was not in the morning's triumph; St Mark's gospel opens up a vista that is full of meaning when it shows him in the evening of that trying day, withdrawing to Bethany (xi, 11. But see Matthew xxi, 17). There he was indeed king, reigning in the hearts of his friends, Lazarus, Martha and Mary; amidst a world that did not recognise him he found there—as he was soon to find in the Upper Room— his little Church, the community of the faithful.

Jesus did not stop at intimating to, and then clearly telling, his apostles that the establishment of the Kingdom was not to be at that coming; he did not stop at putting between his ascension and his return an era that should be the time of the Church, of the apostolic ministry of the word and the sacraments:[37] he went further and made a sharp distinction between the Church, the spiritual kingdom of faith, and the natural world of men and of history. Everybody knows the texts: 'Render therefore to Caesar the things that are Caesar's ...' (Matthew xxii, 21); 'My kingdom is not of this world' (John xviii, 36); 'O man, who hath appointed me judge or divider over you?' (Luke xii, 14). And over and above those words there is the attitude of Jesus and of his apostles. In getting at true religious significance, which in inward and spiritual, they recognise the character in *things* and therefore their value simply as things. To eat or not to eat is an indifferent matter, says St Paul, and it only concerns Christianity when the inward principle of faithfulness and love is involved. This

[37]The decisive text is at the Ascension (Acts i, 6–8): 'They therefore that were assembled asked him, saying, "Lord, wilt thou at this time restore the kingdom to Israel?" He said to them: "It is not for you to know times or seasons which the Father hath appointed by his own authority; but ye shall receive power from the coming of the Holy Spiirt upon you, and ye shall be my witnesses in Jerusalem, and in all Judaea and Samaria, and unto the end of the earth" '. Cf. the Synoptists: Matt. xxviii, 18–19, Mark xvi, 15–16, Luke xxiv, 46ff.

was to put *things* in the order that is not sacred, where they are governed by their own proper laws. So the attitude of Christ and his apostles was at the same time a vindication of Christ's universal lordship and one of absolute respect for the two domains (cf. the characteristic episode in Matthew xvii, 24ff.). It has often been pointed out that this was Christianity's great innovation and a decisive contribution to a world which either looked on religion as an appurtenance of public life and authority (the pagan world) or else organised all aspects of life solely from the point of view and according to the laws of the worship of God, leaving nothing to 'the secular' (Judaism).

It must not be overlooked that Christ's kingship is by right universal, and many of the writings that followed the encyclical letter on Christ the King (*Quas primas*, 11 December 1925) recalled that his authority extends over temporal things. But we know he has willed not to exercise this authority, leaving the civil power sovereignty in its own sphere so long as the anteparousial space-between shall endure (cf. Acts iii, 21). And whatever dreams there may have been of a unitary order, from Constantine down to the modern age, whatever appeals have been made on its behalf to the royal and priestly figure of Melchizedek, sometimes in favour of kings, sometimes of the pope,[38] it remains true that Jesus separated the apostolic from the temporal dominion, withheld the Church from all political subjection, and equally refrained from giving that Church any authority whatever in properly temporal affairs. Though we cannot avoid touching on it here and there, this is not the place to discuss this matter or the problem of the relations between the two spheres and their activities; that must be done fully elsewhere. On the other hand, it is pertinent to observe that the two authorities, exercised respectively in the Church and in the temporal order, both derive from Christ's supreme kingship.

Treatises *de Ecclesia* show how authority *in the Church* derives from that of Christ, who instituted a ruling authority, a priestly ministry and a prophetical office as participations in his own messianic functions. Equally do these treatises relate temporal authority to God's authority: 'omnis potestas a Deo' (cf. Romans xiii, 1; comp. John xix, 11; Prov. viii, 15). It is less usual to give a Christological basis to civil power and to consider it as deriving from Christ's universal

---

[38]For these arguments from Melchizedek in the East, see J. Kampers, 'Rex et sacerdos' in *Hist. Jahrbuch*, 45 (1925), pp. 495–515; in the medieval West, J. Hashagen, *Staat und Kirche vor der Reformation* (Essen, 1931), pp. 504–505; J. Leclercq, *Jean de Paris et l'ecclesiologie du xiiie siecle* (Paris, 1942), pp. 99ff.

kingship. There is, however, a tradition in this sense which, as befits traditions, rests on the interpretation of New Testament evidence.[39] We saw at the beginning of this chapter that God's power and government over the world after the Incarnation were relayed, so to speak, by Christ in his sacred manhood. Moreover, the very positive statements, of which some have been quoted, about Christ's sovereignty over all the 'powers', and yet other texts, encourage us to

[39]It would have been better had Catholic tradition developed more scrupulously along the line laid out by Pope Gelasius I, not only in his letter 'Famuli vestrae pietatis' of 494 to the Emperor Anastasius (Jaffé, 632) but also in his treatise *Ne forte quod solent* or *Tomus de anathematis vinculo* of 495–496, c. 11 (Jaffé, 701), wherein the two persons he distinguishes so well are both referred to Christ. This Gelasian tradition is found among the bishops at the synod of Paris in 829, in Jonas of Orleans and, a little later, in Hincmar of Rheims (cf. R. W. and A. J. Carlyle, *A Hist. of Med. Pol. Theory in the West*, vol. i, pp. 254–255); in the same century the popes and the emperor were represented in the apse of the church of St Susanna at Rome, each seated on an eminence, receiving their respective emblems, the keys and the banner, *from Christ*. But the development of a Christological basis for the power of kings was hampered by the struggle for supremacy between clergy and civil power, and then, in the epoch of the canonists and the scholastics, by the idea of natural law. The struggle between princes and pontiffs was not between a profane power and a sacred power, but between two sacred powers, and it was expressed in theological categories. Appeal was made to the idea that kings were vicars *of God*, or of Christ as God (The Anonymous of York and several texts cited by J. Rivière in app. vi of his *Probl. de l'Eglise et de l'Etat au temps de Philippe le Bel*, Louvain, 1926), while bishops were vicars only of Christ, representatives of his earthly priesthood. The clergy sometimes argued from Christ's universal kingship, but claimed that it had been handed over to his vicar St Peter entirely, and after him to the pope . . . Not long after the mosaic in St Susanna, an image in the Lateran showed, not Christ, but St Peter giving the *pallium* to the pope on the right and the *labarum* to the emperor on the left. Later on, the effect of the notion of natural law can be seen in such a one as Francis of Vitoria; and a certain lack of historical sense and of the meaning of the different times in the divine economy prevented the scholastics from properly appreciating the anteparousial condition of Christ's kingship. However, see, for St Thomas, above, nn. 28, 33, and, in James of Viterbo himself, *De regim. Christ.*, pars ii, c. 1 (ed. Scholz, p. 156). – The position touched on by St Thomas is all the more noteworthy: 'Ipse [Christus] est rex regum, per quem omnes regnant' (*Comm. in Matt.*, c. 17, and cf. J. Leclercq, *op. cit.*, p. 100); and this seems to be found also among his immediate disciples, Ptolemy of Lucca (continuation of St Thomas's *De regim. princ.*, iii, 13) and John of Paris (Leclercq, *op. cit.*, p. 103). But the last-named had difficulty in relating the temporal order to Christ: he sees kingly and priestly (in the human order) too much as natural and supernatural (*De pot. regia et papali*, c. 2); and he denies power over the temporal to Christ as man (c. 8), doubtless because in his time too many theologians and all the curialists, while they recognised that temporal power comes from Christ, attributed it directly to the pope as Christ's vicar: see the treatises for John XXII against Lewis of Bavaria in Scholz, *Unbekannte kirchenpolit. Streitschriften . . .*, vol ii (*e.g.*, that of Opicinus de Canistris). This 'tie-up' was so strong that it even embarrassed Occam (*Allegationes de pot. imp.*; Scholz, *op. cit.*, pp. 417ff.). – A monograph is needed on this question of the Christological basis of power. The great decretalist Huguccio (d. 1210) looked on it favourably: cf. the quotation from his unpublished *Summa* in S. Mochi Onory, *Fonti canonistiche dell' idea moderna dello Stato* (Milan, 1951), pp. 148–149. At the time of the Council of Trent, Cardinal Pole taught very remarkable doctrine on this point, which also deserves a study: cf. his *De concilio*, quoted in Dabin, p. 347.

interpret Christologically the motives given by St Paul (Romans xiii, 1ff.) and St Peter (1 Peter ii, 13ff.) to inspire Christians with respect for the temporal authorities. We hold then that Christ's kingship, until his return in glory, takes two different directions, which do not encroach on one another: as spiritual authority in the Church (and spiritual does not mean nebulous or disembodied), as temporal authority in whatever concerns the order of this world.

It may be said in passing that this way of looking at things, so far from undermining the independence and stability of the temporal order, actually establishes them. It is not uncommon to find Christians, more enthusiastic than realist and often belonging to some sect (such as the Watch Tower, *alias* Jehovah's Witnesses, *alias* Bible Students), who carry over just as they are into the sphere of temporal things certain attitudes or requirements that properly belong to the Christian order, to the Beatitudes and to behaviour in the Mystical Body. This too was the mistake of Tolstoyism, which is being revived by some upholders of non-violence or of absolute conscientious objection to war. It is not sufficiently understood that during the anteparousial era Christ's kingship is shared and ought to be honoured, not only in a church which is his body, but also in a world which has its own proper needs. In the Mystical Body (*as such*) there is no longer man or woman, Greek or barbarian, bond or free; but in the temporal order these categories exist and should be respected for what they are. Just so do methods of force have their place therein, and a hundred other techniques with their own special requirements.

That this duality of orders gives rise to many problems and entails much hardship is all part of the state of suffering and manifold tensions that belong to the time before the establishment of the Kingdom. In that alone, the mirror of Jesus Christ's priestly kingship, will justice and mercy kiss, holiness be clothed in power and power in holiness: we repeat, the Kingdom is the reconciliation into one order of all that we know as disunited and often opposed and at variance. There Pascal's three orders will be made one under the sway of him who, himself king, prophet and priest, is the supreme ruler of captains and scholars and saints. Those three orders often follow different roads in this world: nevertheless they are all dependent on Jesus Christ, and each in its own way is helping to prepare his kingdom.

*   *   *

And that is what we must now examine: the Church's function

and the function of the world in regard to the Kingdom, and their relative unity that follows from this common reference.

Many are preoccupied by this question today, and it is approached sometimes as the theology of history, sometimes as the theology of earthly things. The problem is to know whether what we do in the secular sphere of this world is. altogether irrelevant and without importance for what will be the Kingdom of God. Do our interior spiritual dispositions alone signify for that Kingdom? Is the world only the occasion or the background (how often tragic!) of our charitable deeds and spiritual purification? Or does the world in its texture of temporal earthly work add something to them? Education, increase of knowledge, advance in techniques and methods of production, use of the world's resources, development of our physical bodies—has all that a relationship, some continuity, with the final reality of God's Kingdom? And if so, what?

It has been and it still is maintained that there is total discontinuity between them: that is the argument of the dualism and eschatologism of a Luther or a Barth. It would certainly be misleading to overlook what is positive in these theologians regarding a happy carrying-out of temporal duties (Luther: notion of 'orders' and of *Beruf*; *Das Gebet der Hausfrau*) or the taking seriously of the earthly situation in which God has put us to be his witnesses (Barth). But their fundamental point is that there is a division, more, an opposition, between a strongly eschatological Christianity and 'this world' which is completely under the judgment and sentence of God. All that may be asked of the world is to be allowed to preach the gospel in order by faith to prepare people who will be saved. We are aboard a vessel whose destiny is to go to the bottom; men will be saved by journeying in another ship built wholly by God.

What may be called the dualist-eschatological view has also existed and goes on existing in the Catholic Church. This does not imply any solidarity with the teaching of Luther or Barth, but simply taking seriously of certain texts in the New Testament. A forceful formulation of them can be found, for example, in some articles of Father L. Bouyer.[40] In opposition to a certain apostolic optimism according to which the world is not so much hostile to the gospel as secretly attached to it, Father Bouyer emphasises what may be called the Christian paradox: pessimism about *this* world and

---

[40]'Christianisme et eschatologie' in *Vie intellectuelle*, October 1948, pp. 6–38; 'Où en est la théologie du Corps mystique?' in *Rev. des sciences relig.*, 22 (1948), pp. 313–333.

optimism based simply on the eschatological victory of him whom the world crucified but God raised from the dead. 'Since the Incarnation', he writes, 'the continuance of the world has meaning only for so long as is necessary for the gospel to enable everyone to have the opportunity for a fresh decision. When that point is reached, everything will be ready for a second intervention of God. Do not misunderstand me. I do not mean that God will only have to gather what we have got all ready, like a ripe fruit dropping into the hand. Eternity is not by any means a fruit of which the present time is the flower. . . .' This stresses not only the transcendence of the Kingdom in relation to the process of history and all earthly progress (it will be seen that we are in complete agreement about this), but also that it is foreign to such a process of preparation and development.

Without its being theoretically upheld in some such terms as these, it is substantially a dualist-eschatological view that is put into practice by monks. We have seen that monasticism is part of the life and permanent pattern of the Church. It answers to the indefeasible needs of a Christian conscience that has been gripped by the absolute demands of 'the one thing necessary'. – 'For what shall it profit a man if he gain the whole world, and lose his soul?' asks our Lord; 'The world as we see it is passing', says St Paul. So we will shut our eyes and think only of eternity. . . . Wherever and whenever monastic life is led in its integrity there is therefore a contempt for the world which leaves no room for a positive value in the temporal order with respect to the Kingdom of God.[41] The only thing to do is to die to this world in order to share in the life of the Spirit that is in Christ, dead and risen again. . . .

The thing to be noticed is that the monks and holy people who regard the world as nothing in comparison with the Kingdom of God have never said that the creation is evil and life 'in the world' a sin. In this they differ from many sectaries. Nevertheless it was inevitable that there should be a certain depreciation of life in the

[41]The most typical and perfect examples are certainly the fathers of Eastern monachism, such as St Antony (see his Life by St Athanasius in PG., xxvi, pp. 837ff.), and St Paul of Thebes (his Life by St Jerome is regrettably lacking in sobriety). Fusebius describes the life of these monks thus: They 'are as if dead to mortal life; only their bodies live on this earth, their souls and thoughts are in Heaven. As if they were themselves heavenly beings, they despise the way of life of most people . . .' (Demonstr. evang., i, 8). Cf. the office of Confessors: 'in hac terra solo corpore constitutus. . . .' The life and words of many holy people are to the same effect: St Boniface calls the body a prison from which death delivers us (cf. Theol. Quartlasch., 1940, p. 135); Bd Jordan of Saxony, though so 'human', said when he lost an eye, 'There goes one of my enemies'.

world.[42] In obedience to the gospel, Christian life has always been looked on as requiring conduct in conformity with the City that is to come; at the same time most of those leading it have always been doing so 'in the world', amid the activities and distractions of the city that now is.[43] The monastic answer has its place in the Church, and it 'shall never be taken away from her'; but it is still a particular solution, which leaves the problem of principle in the relation between the world and the Kingdom still to be solved.

In recent times an affirmative and optimist solution has been offered, especially by men thinking towards a better contact between the Church and the contemporary world. There is talk of incarnational theology, and the names of Father Teilhard de Chardin, Father de Saint-Seine, Mgr de Solages, Father M. I. Montuclard, Canon Thils are mentioned.[44] From diverse points of view, and with *nuances* that must not be ignored, these writers see a certain continuity between the work of this world, the cosmic process, and the eschatological Kingdom. Within a great evolutionist design, Father Teilhard de Chardin sees the human effort as one of the ascending stages—whose achievement and excellence of course only a transcendent intervention can ensure—which leads on through a succession of preparatory degrees to man's divinisation, to the Mystical Body and to the Kingdom of God. Canon Thils, taking his stand on the biblical idea of the unity of the universe and its subjection to redemption by Christ, and adopting the Thomist idea that things are not simply means but have their own value as beings, sees in the

---

[42]M. Viller and K. Rahner, *Aszese und Mystik in der Vaterzeit* (Freiburg i. B., 1939, p. 278ff.), remark that early monastic writings often point out that lay people engaged in the most secular occupations can equal and even surpass the ascetics in holiness: cf., for example, the stories of Paphnutius, in Rufinus, *Hist. monach.*, 16 (PL., xxi, p. 439), and of Macarius. They also quote Chrysostom (pp. 283–284). He, however, perhaps carried away by rhetorical maximising, sometimes depreciated lay life and used words that were not exactly laudatory when comparing it with monastic life: *e.g.*, *In Matt.*, hom. 68 and 69 (PG., lviii, pp. 645, 652ff.). See especially below, Part Two, Ch. VI.

[43]*The Letter to Diognetus*, v and vi, has significance here. Christians do not live according to the world but they live in the world, mingling indiscriminately with other men in the world's activities. Cf. Tertullian, *Apol.*, 42, and Newman, *Historical Sketches*, ii, pp. 94ff.

[44]The scientific, religious and poetical synthesis of Father Teilhard de Chardin is available only in a roneoed form, but its broad lines have been set out by Mgr M. de Solages, 'La pensée chrétienne face à l'évolution' in *Bull. de litterat. eccles.*, 1947, pp. ciii-cxvi. – See also E. Rideau, *Consécration: le Christianisme et l'activité humaine* (Paris, 1945); Fr de Saint-Seine, *Découverte de la vie* (Paris, 1946); M. I. Montuclard, 'La médiation de l'Eglise et la médiation de l'histoire' in *Déliverance de l'homme* (Paris, 1947), pp. 9–33.

Christian regime a progressive spiritualisation of earthly realities, a transforming influence of grace that extends to the social and cultural plane and is an anticipation of the final work of the Spirit. For Father Montuclard, Christ's saving mediation comes through 'history' as well as through the Church, which has spiritually to quicken the historical process and show it its meaning as a fulfilling of God's purpose and a possible intermediary of salvation, of the redemptive salvation.

It seems to us that in a sense these interpretations put too much continuity between the secular work and the Christian reality that will be fulfilled in the Kingdom. Canon Thils appears to find too great a continuity between the relative and human spiritualisation which goes on in earthly history and the 'pneumatical' order of the Kingdom; he does not sufficiently appreciate the ambivalence of this business of the liberation of man and the control of things, nor how, through this process, a redeemed universe and a sinful universe are being simultaneously produced, as Father D. Dubarle has properly stressed. Father Montuclard gives the impression of over-much attributing to history and the Church, as intermediaries of Christ's unique mediation, the same end of religious salvation; the particular viewpoint of his very interesting work leads him insufficiently to emphasise that, if they serve the same end, they do so by ways that are specifically different and not equivalent. The Kingdom will indeed be, in one sense, the attainment by the world of its end, but not by its own efforts, and not without a purifying of history, which in so many ways is corrupt and false. God's final order, thanks to which, we believe, the world itself will be saved, does not come from history but from on high, beginning with a specific principle of holiness which is active in the world but has to be bestowed on it. As for Father Teilhard de Chardin's interpretation and others like it, we would underline the truths that Father Bouyer has recalled so forcefully (but too onesidedly), namely, that God alone will make the Kingdom, from above; that there will be no regeneration without first undergoing death ('victory was given by the Father raising his Son only after having let him suffer and die'); that the whole existence of the world and the evangelical leaven working in it is branded with the sign of contradiction and disturbed by a war of the Contradictor against God's governance.

*   *   *

Nevertheless it seems to me that there is a certain continuity between the human work of this world on the one side and the Kingdom of God on the other, which the dualist-eschatological position

H

this time misses. This continuity arises from the fact of what I will call God's unitary plan. It appears to me grounded in this, that between the world and the Kingdom there is unity through final object, at least partial unity of subject or material cause, unity of agent, namely, the Word of God and his Holy Spirit. There is unity through man, with whose fate the world is associated, whether in catastrophe or in hope and in transfiguration. Thus the world forms with man, though 'in the lump' and not strictly, a single object of divine intervention, a single beneficiary of redemption and transfiguration.[45] That is why the whole of creation is waiting and 'doth groan and travail together to this hour' (Romans viii, 18-22); that is why man, with whom creation is linked in fall, in redemption and in movement towards a common end, has to 'make all things grow towards him who is the head'.[46] Over against this association of all creation with man-made-in-God's-image is the universal and expressly cosmic power of Christ: for his mission is to the world; when he takes up the work of salvation he takes up the work of restoring its meaning to creation, and of bringing it effectively to the term whose germ and vocation he has, as Word and Wisdom of God, already given to it. There is indeed unity of last end, relative unity of subject, unity of agent; and there may be added unity of (quasi-) form, that is to say, unity in the quality of the created thing that is renewed in the integrity of its nature and made God's temple by the Spirit of the Lord. And so we get the cosmic praise of Apocalypse v, 13, which furthermore is none other than the realisation of the expectation of the Old Testament, which so often associates all nature with the deliverance of the redeemed.[47]

At the heart of all this is Jesus Christ and the fact that his risen and glorified body is the same as that in which he took flesh and suffered. Certainly his body is transformed, it was reborn at the resurrection 'a spiritual body'; but it bears the scars of the passion (Cf. John xx, 27; Apocalypse v, 6) and recognises its own. The same will happen with us. Rightly do we expect the redemption of our bodies (Romans viii, 23), for the Spirit of him who raised Christ from the dead will restore life *to our perishable bodies too* (Romans viii, 11); the Lord Jesus

[45]As formulated, this seems to me solidly established by biblical and liturgical texts, such as those cited by A. Frank-Duquesne in *Cosmos et Gloire* ... (Paris, 1947). See too H. Biedermann, *Die Erlosung der Schopfung beim Apostel Paulus* ... (Wurzburg, 1940); E. Scharl, *Recapitulatio mundi* ... (Freiburg i. B., 1941).

[46]So at least H. Schlier translates Eph. iv, 15 (art. κεφαλή in Kittel). Cf. 1 Cor. viii, 6; Rom. xi, 36; and the doxology that ends the canon of the Roman Mass.

[47]Cf. Ps. xcvi, 11-13; xcviii, 7-9; Is. xxxv, 1ff.; xli, 18ff.; xliv, 23; xlix, 13; lv, 12-13.

Christ will change this wretched body of ours into a likeness of his own glorified body, by virtue of the power whereby all things are subject to him (Philippians iii, 21; cf. 1 Corinthians xv, 42).

But surely these things, which are true for Jesus, which will be true for us, must be extended to the whole of creation. St Paul says that 'flesh and blood cannot inherit the kingdom of God, neither doth corruption inherit incorruption' (1 Corinthians xv, 50); there must be death and then a transformation. And it is our pitiful bodies that are going to be thus changed. So it may well be asked whether, when Holy Writ speaks of a new heaven and a new earth, 'all things new',[48] it does not mean the cosmos of the first creation as submitted to the Spirit, who is the agent proper to the second creation, and transformed by him into the image of Christ's glorified body. Not, assuredly, without purifications and changes, as witnessed by the Bible: a final intervention of God, which the Scriptures compare to a cleansing fire, will separate the good from the bad; many things in the existing cosmic order will be brought to an end.[49] What matters to us here is that beneath these blissful changes there remains a substantial identity of subject, that that which is to be changed is the same earthly cosmos with which we are associated as much in the order of the new creation as in that of the old, wherein we have to complete it. The Scriptures speak of a *restoration* of all things (Acts iii, 21) and associate the new heaven and the new earth with the new name (and, in the Apocalypse, the new hymn: v, 9). But the new name signifies a new nature, of such a kind that safeguards the substantial identity of beings.[50]

[48]Apoc. xxi, 1–5; 2 Peter iii, 13; cf. Is. lxv, 17; lxvi, 22. Perhaps Behm's note may be applied here (art. καινός, in Kittel, iii, p. 450): 'The word used in these texts is not νεός, which signifies the newness of that which was not there before and is new because of its appearance in time, but καινός, which signifies the newness of that which is new in its mode of being or in reference to what is usual and to a previous state'.

[49]Cf. 2 Peter iii, 10 and parallels, as cited, *e.g.*, in A. Charue's excellent commentary, coll. *La Sainte Bible*, vol. xii (Paris, 1938); Apoc. xx, 1, etc. (The sea often appears as a hostile and forbidding element in the Bible); Apoc. xx, 11 (cf. Ps. cxiv, 7, 3): and cf. J. Theissing, 'Gottesreich und Vollendung' in *Amt und Sendung* (Freiburg i. B., 1950), p. 186.

[50]Cf. Is. lxv, 15, 17; in Apoc., the new name of ii, 17, iii, 12 corresponds to the new things of xxi, 1, 5: cf. Father Allo's commentary. In 1 Cor. vii, 31 it is the *figura* of this world that passes. – The scholastic theologians are clearly for continuity of subject between our world and that of the new heaven and new earth: cf. *e.g.*, St Thomas, *Sent.*, d. 48, q. 2 (and *Summa*, suppl., q. 91); *Contra Gent.*, iv, 97; Suarez, *De incarn.*, disp. 23, sect. 1, n. 9–10 (Paris, 1860, p. 649); E. Mersch, *Le corps mystique* . . . 2nd edn, vol. ii, pp. 243ff. St Albert the Great observes on the subject of the great cosmic eschatological changes that nothing can be known about them: 'in veritate hic potius est divinatio quam quaestio habens scientiam aliquam: quia neminem puto scire qualiter hoc erit nisi qui viderit quando fiet . . .' (*IV Sent.*, d. 47, a. 7; Borgnet, 30, 649).

There is more yet. The Kingdom is already in some fashion present and active in our world. St Paul speaks of the new creation as having begun at Christ's resurrection and as having begun in us.[51] It is true that, instead of the new external order that the Jews looked for from the Messias, we have received a new life, a new life as regards man inwardly (2 Corinthians iv, 16; Ephesians iii, 16). It is true too that Paul is looking to the eschatological perfection of our bodily transformation by the Spirit, and next to nothing can already be given of that. At any rate, expectation of this complete redemption produces groaning in us, and in all creation as well, as it awaits with us the transforming work.[52] But Paul allows, he even considers normal, a transformation in the bodies of those who have had contact and communion with the body of the risen Christ in the eucharist.[53] It is a little surprising not to find in his letters any echo of the cosmic activity of the Spirit conferred on the faithful such as the Acts of the Apostles tells us about, miracles and healings, representing in our fleeting state so many fragmentary anticipations of a universal rebirth (Matthew xix, 28). It is clear that, from the time the faithful received the gift of the Spirit, Christians have experienced a certain transformation of earthly things; but to appreciate the full extent of this experience it would be necessary to go beyond the limits, narrow in time, of the Bible. It has been remarked how St John already was able to explain many aspects of Christ's work and utterances in the light of a pentecostal experience deeply lived (see H. B. Swete's fine book, *The Holy Spirit in the New Testament*). It is not matter for surprise—rather is it to be expected—that the Church, with the time and the experiences which are hers, should have found occasions and circumstances when her spiritual resources prove to have a certain power of transforming the things of this world. It is a fact which no narrow 'biblicism' can exclude that postapostolic generations (especially St Irenaeus) experienced and bore witness (as St Paul did not) to a healing and hallowing of the whole man, down to his very flesh; that Christians of old felt they were living in a world where God's hand often intervened and miracles were everywhere; that before the persecutions were over a Christian

[51]2 Cor. v, 16ff., Gal. vi, 15; Eph. ii, 10, 14–15, iv, 24. Of course everyone agrees in so far as it is a question of man and of grace or charity. Cf. also Titus iii, 5.

[52]Rom. viii, 19–23. Actually St Paul's thought works the other way: he begins with creation's groaning, and goes on 'not only so, but ourselves too', although we have the first-fruits of the Spirit, so that he seems to limit those first-fruits to the faithful. But he makes the common expectation quite clear, and the solidarity of destiny between us and creation.

[53]So Cullmann interprets 1 Cor. x, 16ff., and xi, 29–30. The interpretation is consistent with tradition theology: cf. above, n. 25.

intellectual activity had begun to develop to which subsequent ages have only added, and so much so that, to say nothing of strictly religious thought, one could speak of 'a Christian state of philosophy' (J. Maritain) and of 'Christian philosophy' (E. Gilson); that after the Peace of Constantine there developed a whole Christian culture, with institutions that were Christian or notably changed by Christianity; and that since then down to our own day Christians have become more and more conscious of the healing power of grace, which St Paul refers to as the foretaste of the Spirit. Has all this no meaning?

Over the centuries the Church has had an ever-growing historical experience of the transforming power with which the forces of the Kingdom exert over this world. She experienced the Christian leaven at work, no longer in the highly civilised world of Hellenism and the Roman empire, but among barbarian peoples; in the West in the twelfth and thirteenth centuries she took account of the consistency of the natural order and elaborated a theology of the relations of nature and grace (Thomas Aquinas, Albert the Great); then again, in a world grown restive and more expressly secular, she has formulated a doctrine of these relations more officially through the voice of the last five popes, and it contains things bearing directly on our subject.[54] The following is its general import.

God has bestowed various different forces as participations in his goodness and these are the energies proper to things themselves: their aggregate constitutes the cosmos. But he has done more. There is a highest participation in God's goodness, not as the proper constitutive force of any creature, but one which unites with God the created spirit who is made in his image: by it God establishes man in a relationship with himself of a similar kind to the relationship between father and son in a family, one of indwelling, of life together, of knowledge and love, in short, of communion and fellowship. This is grace. It creates in man a new relation with the whole world in regard to its principle and end; things are not changed physically, but man is endowed with new energies corresponding to

[54] St Albert the Great's theology provides specially notable views on all this: cf. H. Doms, *Die Gnadenlehre des sel Albertus Magnus* (Breslau, 1929) and Father Congar's article, 'Albert le Grand, theologien de la grace sanctifiante' in *Vie spirituelle*, January 1933, pp. 109–140. See too J. Maritain, *Religion et culture* (Paris, 1930) and *Humanisme integral* (Paris, 1936). – There is no study devoted to recent papal teaching on the healing of nature by grace, and consequently the Church's relationship with the world, more particularly with human civilisation. The point has been studied historically in numerous separate monographs, and as a whole by E. Chenon, *Le rôle social de l'Eglise* (Paris, 1911). Some of the more important passages from Leo XIII and Pius X, XI and XII will be found in Part Two, Ch. V, herein and in Appendix.

his supreme destiny, and the use he makes of things is no longer quite the same as before. Thus all the world, which forms a whole, is changed there where it is bound up with man. The gifts of grace, the object of the Church's ministry, do not yet have full cosmic effect, but they already bear on things through man's ties with things and the use he makes of them, a mark of consecration and, in the measure that they are humanised, a reflexion of God's reign. This is not much—and it is a great deal. It is enough to show us the connexion of the earthly cosmos with the regeneration of the Kingdom. As the Church sings on the feast of Christ the King:

> Te nationum praesides
> Honore tollant publico.
> Colant magistri, judices,
> Leges et artes exprimant.

We believe we are justified in concluding that (1) Ontologically, this is the world that, transformed and renewed, will pass into the Kingdom; so the figure in which we expressed the dualist position is wrong: final salvation will be achieved by a wonderful refloating of our earthly vessel rather than by a transfer of the survivors to another ship wholly built by God; (2) The regenerating power that will finally operate is already at work in our world, transiently, precariously, fragmentarily, and generally unperceived.

Shall we then recognise that there will be a progressive transformation of the world in the sense of a liberation and spiritualisation anticipating or beginning the work of the Spirit? Shall we invoke in support certain parables in the gospels that indubitably present the Kingdom as actual and dynamic? We would not dare to do so; and when later on we write about 'ripening' it is not exactly in this sense. It seems to us that the parables in question (the leaven in the dough, the grain of mustard-seed) are parables of the Kingdom as beginning *in the Church*, or equivalently, parables of faith, which certainly imply a development *in* the world but do not allude to a development *of* the world or to a properly cosmic aspect of Christ's spiritual work. In a general way, what elements of transformation or anticipation of the final renewal that there really are in this world seem to us to be too closely connected with the spiritual life of individual persons to be very socialised, or to be computed somehow objectively, independently of the strictly spiritual activities of the Church (the *sancta*) and of the holiness of holy people (the *sancti*): a point on which Jacques Maritain dwells very happily in his notion of an 'integral humanism'. Is not the scholastic theologians' idea applicable here? Corruption is transmitted from nature to persons; the restoration within the Christian economy goes out from persons to nature, from the spiritual man to his surroundings and institutions (Cf. St Thomas, *Sum. theol.*, III, q. 8, a. 5, ad 1; q. 69, a. 3, ad 3).

*   *   *

We are now in a position to interpret positively and on our own account the relationship to the Kingdom, on the one hand of the world and history, on the other, of the Church.

We have said that the Kingdom will be an order wherein each thing will be in possession of its integrity and all will be at peace with one another because they are at peace with God, and this through perfect submissiveness to God, the power of Jesus Christ and the full influence of the Spirit. This clearly is to consider the Kingdom less from the properly spiritual or religious point of view—when we shall have to speak above all of God's glory, his dwelling in the righteous as in his fellowship-temple, his perfect presentation to their under-standing, their blissful transformation, the love which makes all the heavenly Jerusalem one—less from this point of view than from that of the world and of creatures. Our subject requires this, but it does not involve us in anything that might be untrue or even out of accord with the right balance of truth. We will add somewhat only to the second of the characteristics referred to above: integrity and reconciliation. It touches what is perhaps deepest in man's present state and in his state that is to be. In this world we suffer—and in some way all creatures suffer with us—through our being external to one another and not forming a fellowship which makes of all one whole, each thing being nevertheless respected for its own sake (Solovyev's 'uniplurality'). Made in God's image, which is perfectly one in many and many in one, we long to overcome the exteriorities and sometimes intense oppositions from which we suffer. I am not thinking only of the numberless disagreements of daily life, but of those deeper oppositions, grounded in otherness (*extériorité*), onto-logical, which are a kind of disintegration for us beings who thirst for unity: otherness of man and of nature, of one man and of another, of man and of woman, of power in relation to life, of public duties and of authority in relation to persons and their life, the supreme otherness of man and of God. . . . Over against all this there are the Mystical Body, on a purely spiritual plane, and the Kingdom, integrally, rising above all oppositions and exterior otherness and actualising that unity towards which we aspire. The law of the Mystical Body is: 'That they may be one, as we are one—I in them, and thou in me—that they may be perfected in unity' (John xvii, 22-23); and the law of the Kingdom is: 'God all in all' (1 Corinthians

xv, 28): which is as much as to say that, through the Spirit of God,
the law by and in which all things will live will be a law of fellowship,
insight, communication, harmony. There is a swarm of texts expressing, more or less symbolically (and how else can you suggest what
can be only spoken of prophetically?), this supreme effect of the
Spirit's unchallenged hold on creation.[55] A creation overflowing in
its multifariousness, yet wherein each one has found, in subjection
to God, his own integrity, a creation wherein all are reconciled and
have fellowship one with another: such seems to us to be what the
Kingdom finally is.

In God's unitary design the Church and the world are both
ordered to this Kingdom in the end, but by different ways and on
different accounts. Church and world have the same end, but only
the same *ultimate* end. That they should have the same end is due to
God's unitary plan and to the fact that the whole cosmos is united
with man in a shared destiny. That they should have only the same
ultimate end prevents a confusion that would be bad for the Church,
as raising a risk of dissolving her own proper mission in that of history, and bad for the world, as raising a risk of misunderstanding and
hindering its own proper development (cf. criticism of the hierocratic type of Christianity, below). Church and world (or 'history',
to borrow from Father Montuclard's suggestive vocabulary) have
the same ultimate end, but they do not have the same immediate,
and therefore specifying, end. They serve the same end by different
means and on different planes, each keeping its own nature and its
own constitution (*statut*). The constitution proper to each must now
be examined more closely.

The Church. – The Church's constitution (*statut*) is in this, that she
already has within herself, and as the very things that make her
Church, the self-same and decisive causes of that renewal of which
the Kingdom will be the consummation: the kingly, priestly and
prophetical power of Christ, and the Holy Spirit. Therefore the
Church co-operates *directly* in the constitution of the Kingdom,
through the exercise of energies that are her own and constitute her
reality as Church. The three chief forms of this co-operation would
seem to be prayer, participation in the messianic offices, and the
active presence of the Holy Spirit with his gifts.

[55]'They shall teach no more every man his neighbour . . .' (Jer. xxxi, 34; cf. Heb.
viii, 11); the prophetic descriptions of messianic peace (Is. xi, 6–9 and numerous
parallels); the agraphon reported by 11 Clem., xii 2: 'When someone asked the
Lord himself when his kingdom would come, he replied: "When two [things] shall
make only one, when the outside shall be like the inside, when in the commerce
of man with woman there shall no longer be man or woman" ' (As it is already in
the Mystical Body: Gal. iii, 28). These are a few only.

In his profound theology of prayer St Thomas declares that when we pray we feeble Christians, knowing ourselves to be merely creatures, take our place in the order that God has willed and thus identify ourselves with his cause: for in fulfilling one of the conditions willed, foreseen and upheld by him we co-operate with him in the governance of the world, by grace as well as by nature.[56] This is a noble and immensely interesting theme, but it cannot be dwelt on now; it will suffice to recall it when considering the various zones in which ecclesial mediation takes place.

We have already something of the active presence of the Holy Spirit and his gifts, which are the earnest of our inheritance and a beginning of the renewal of all things, though in a fragmentary, undeveloped and uncertain way. Elsewhere, too, we have said a word on the substantial indwelling of the Holy Spirit in the Church as the gift proper to the New Covenant which is to have no successor. Thus there is already present and active in the Church, as the dowry befitting the Bride of Christ, that Principle which will calm the world's groaning and dry our tears; which brooded over creation at its beginning (Genesis i, 2) and always has been and is the quickening of the second creation, the Church; which makes and one day will make all things new.

The Church's participation in the offices, in the causality of grace, that Christ received by his anointing makes the ecclesial institution a divine organ for the realisation of God's purpose; the three sacred 'capacities' (hierarchy) of priesthood, government and prophetical office are thereby established in the Church. It is not yet time to define the nature and exact conditions of these 'capacities': they will be considered in the later part of this chapter and in the three that follow. Through these 'capacities' the Church participates directly and properly in the sacred powers by which Christ is God's supreme human organ for the realisation of the divine purpose, which is to make the whole world his temple and mankind his fellowship-temple. And the Church's participation is within the same limits within which Christ exercised his powers, and still exercises them in this *aeon* [X] of anteparousial time: not, that is, in the fullness which in God's time will produce the last effects and whole fruit of the Kingdom, but 'in mystery' and in a way that produces only the germ of the Kingdom, the spiritual and almost solely inward earnest of the 'inheritance of the saints in light'. This is why the argument that in the middle ages sometimes led from the idea of Christ's universal

---

[56]See *Contra Gent.* iii, 95, 96; *Sum. theol.*, II-II, q. 83, a. 1, 2.

kingship to that of an equally universal kingship of the Church, and so to a papal authority over temporal things, is absolutely false—and God knows what mischief it has done.[57]

There seem to be three zones or degrees in the Church's exercise of her sacred powers of priesthood, magisterium and jurisdiction, which can be distinguished in accordance with a diminishing influence, the Church acting in a given sphere firstly with the fullness of her three powers, then with two only, finally with one. Where there is complete obedience of faith, that is, entry into the Church and submission to the apostolic 'capacities' by faith, professed in full and ratified by baptism, the sacrament of faith, there the Church operates through, in addition to prayer, her three 'capacities' of magisterium, priesthood (sacraments, sacramentals) and spiritual government. She thus brings all her energies into play with a view to the bringing about of the Kingdom, at any rate spiritually and in germ.

Where there is partial obedience of faith, by an orientation in the Church's direction (the *voto* of the theologians) or by some acceptance of her influence, there the Church is acting (always of course in addition to prayer) on people and things that are not expressly subject to her: the people because they have not been baptised, have adhered to dissident communions or abandoned Christianity; the things because Christ's temporal kingship over the world has not been given to the Church and *things* as such are not subject to her.[58] In this case, then, her jurisdiction is not involved and she cannot employ those priestly and magisterial activities that presuppose jurisdictional authority. But she does her utmost through her priesthood, which is continually offering up, sanctifying, interceding for, blessing, sustaining and nourishing a thousand works of mercy, and through her magisterium, which enlightens, proffers, warns, testifies. . . . When we look at the Church in action we see that she is unwearying in her efforts to extend the sphere of her influence, and in the concrete, pastorally, she is as much concerned with this as with the full exercise of her influence: and not from any lust for power (though this sin may sometimes intrude among individuals),

[57]This line of reasoning can be met in Gregory VII, Innocent IV, and the curialist theologians Giles of Rome and Augustine Trionfo. There is a sort of echo of it in L. Veuillot (d. 1883), *L'illusion liberale* §ix.

[58]Except, of course, those things that are strictly necessary to her existence in the world. Ecclesiastical property and, canonically, the ecclesiastical *forum* are grounded on Christ's kingly power and the positive divine law according to which he instituted the Church.

but through the logic of her high mission, of what she is and what she has. The Church is the direct preparation for the Kingdom, having within herself the strength of the Holy Spirit, and she cannot but strive to transform the world to the utmost. Of necessity she seeks as much as possible to reduce the evil in the world, to rebuild it in good order, to make operative the healing, uplifting, transforming force of which we have spoken above, the gifts of grace. By so using the lesser forms of her priesthood and prophetical office, the Church exerts a kind of kingship, not of an authority and power which are not hers, but of influence and service, and this answers to her true position in regard to the world. For it can be said that she is responsible for it, without really having authority over it.

That anticipates what must be said about the sphere wherein the Church is unknown and nothing is looked for from her. She has charge of that, too, an essentially apostolic charge. Here she uses her priestly grace in a wide sense, by prayer and intercession which includes everything—'Mercy for Katharine, mercy for the Church, mercy for the world' was the threefold supplication of St Katharine of Siena; but here the Church's specific work is apostolic witness and preaching, in accordance with the apostolic or missionary form of her magisterium (see below, Part Two, Ch III, second section). Thus does she obey the word of her Lord: 'Go ye, therefore, make disciples of all the nations . . .', 'Preach the gospel to the whole creation'. This second text suggests that there is a certain cosmic value in such activity, as do the analogous facts of St Francis preaching to the fish and the birds. However, it is for human creatures that apostolic preaching seeks to open the way to faith, aided by the *paraklesis* [Y] of the Holy Spirit.

Because of all these activities the Church indeed deserves the name of seed or germ-cell of the Kingdom that theologians who write in German particularly like to give her (*Keimzelle*). The idea is formally biblical,[59] and it well expresses the Church's role, positive and active, in regard to the Kingdom; moreover, any study of the conception of the Kingdom of God in the New Testament leads to the recognition that it includes a dynamic earthly phase which corresponds to the Church and the time of the Church.

It would be very interesting to study this last as being, not simply the period of earthly time during which the Church exists, but as properly *the Church's time*, the measure of her own earthly duration

[59]Cf. James i, 18: 'Of his own free will hath he begotten us through the word of truth, that we might be, as it were, the firstfruits of his own creatures'; Rom. viii, 19–23, etc.

and inner life. As such, it is rather a 'metahistory' than a history properly speaking, determined by the original meeting of the supra-temporal with human time, by the active presence of the Christian mysteries, which are beyond time, in the recurring time of nature. But this belongs rather to a theology of the liturgy, or again to a serious study of Christian development or of the 'dialectic of giving and doing' as we understand it and have referred to it above.

The World or History. – History and the world strive to attain wholeness and that state of reconciliation in which all the opposi-tions from which we suffer shall have been overcome; and that is to say that they seek the Kingdom, not so much on its spiritual and religious, as on its cosmic side. The meaning of history (which is the world's movement) and the meaning of culture (which is history's attainments) is the quest for this triumph of good over evil, truth over falsehood, justice over injustice, life over death, which we have called collectively the state of integrity. When we say 'of life over death' it is not just a manner of speaking. Man's amibition must not stop short of that, and in fact his efforts have already, at more than one point, pushed back the frontiers of divers forerunners of death. Fundamentally the meaning of history and the content of culture correspond to this struggle for perfect knowledge, perfect justice, perfect health, perfect control of good over evil, of life over sickness and over all that belongs to death and does its work; this striving for the dominance of mind over matter, for victory over heaviness, coarseness, opacity, time. . . . The recurrence and beginning again that characterises our earthly time itself represents a reaching-out towards a fullness that eludes us and that only eternity can bring.

Simultaneously and in the same movement history tries to over-come the oppositions and 'othernesses' that man feels to be so many limitations and absurdities bringing suffering upon him—we have mentioned some of them: spirit and nature, the person and social authority, between classes, between nations. . . . Not for nothing has man been made in God's image and allowed a part in world dominion! He longs to make it real, to recover what he has lost; being many, to find himself one, even as God is one. . . .

Clearly, in this twofold quest, for integrity and for complete reconciliation, the world without knowing it tends towards realisa-tion of the Kingdom, at any rate in its terrestrial and quasi-secular aspect. But as regards its realisation as God sees it, the world's endeavour suffers from three major defects.

(1) First of all, there is something ambivalent and ambiguous about it. Ambivalent because, as Father D. Dubarle has well

shown,[60] a sinful universe is engendered simultaneously with a redeemed universe, so that they are at variance before there is, eschatologically, rupture and separation between them: accordingly, there is nearly as much reason for pessimism as for optimism when we look at this world. Ambiguous because even authentic values can be wrongly developed. It is easy for the world to seek its integrity not only through itself but *in* itself, forgetting or denying that integrity can be ordered only to God. The history of modern culture is exceedingly instructive on this point. It is dominated by various forms of immanentism, rationalism, the spirit of Faust; and eventually there is Marxism, the most consistent endeavour that has ever been made to give the world a purely immanent meaning, excluding all transcendence; an endeavour to overcome all contradictions and to attain integrity without any reference whatever to God. Even things that are in themselves good and true, authentic earthly values, are susceptible of becoming idols and a 'home-ground' for the Prince of this world. Think what can happen to country, production, progress, class, race, the body and sport, domestic comfort; and how many names can be given today to Egypt, Canaan or Babylon. . . .

It may be remarked in passing that, if we must seek a form of action that is as unsullied as possible in the light of God's word and the Church's teaching, we must also be on our guard against setting up as judge and arbiter before the time that God decrees. As we have seen, it is not till the end of the time that he has put between his ascension and his coming again that the Son of man will take his winnowing-fan and sweep clean his threshing-floor. 'Nolite ante tempus judicare', says St Paul, 'Pass no judgment, therefore, before the time, until the Lord come, who shall both bring to light what is hidden in darkness and manifest the counsels of hearts; and then shall every man have due praise from God' (1 Corinthians iv, 5). The Portuguese proverb that Father F. Portal loved to quote, and that Claudel inscribed at the beginning of *The Satin Slipper*, 'God writes straight with crooked lines', is a remarkable version of one of the deepest truths of Christian wisdom. We believe that Christ alone holds the secret of the ambivalent world in which the history of salvation is worked out; there was reason perhaps in St John's tears before the sealed book (Apocalypse v, 1ff.), but it is precisely in the fact that only He breaks the seals that the sovereign power of the immolated and conquering Lamb is made manifest. We are not able to know which of the forces in history may not in the end work for

---

[60] *Optimisme devant ce monde* (Paris, 1949). Cf. too, W. A. Visser 't Hooft, *La rovauté de Jésus-Christ* (Geneva, 1948), pp. 131ff., 137.

the Kingdom. God, who is lord of the world of nature as well as of grace, has everywhere sown seed which by his power contributes to his work, and it is beyond question that we shall one day be very surprised to see in what ways it has been done.

(2) The world simply follows its instinct to live, it is not aware that God's wisdom is the wisdom of the Cross. As St Paul says, we want to put on a body of glory over our old clothes, so to say, without first undergoing death (2 Corinthians v, 4). But there is no continuity for the aspirations and strivings of the man who does not have to accept the Cross and undergo a death. St Paul, who stresses the aspect of continuity, speaks rather of the pains of childbirth.[61] This aspect of the Cross does not apply only at the last, when there will be no choice, but each time some new part of nature has to surrender to an advance of Christianity. There can be no higher life except on a foundation of renunciation and death, no renewal in which there is not something old that has to disappear. The rightful order between nature and grace is certainly a harmony, the order which the Creator has willed and the Saviour will re-establish. But this rightful order is obstructed by a factual order, the order of sin and redemption by the Cross. Hence the tension inherent in Christianity and the kind of dialectical character of the pattern it imposes: '. . . use the world as not using it to the full'; 'he that hath lost his life for my sake shall find it'.

This tension cannot be got rid of, and when it seems to have been avoided it is always a temporary, partial and precarious avoidance. Often man does not meet even with a limited success, but a check. In our personal life, one of the meanings of sacrifice is to prevent us from being complacent about our own actions and from taking the means for the end, led away by our interest in those means. In history, deadlocks and reverses remind man that *the* full solution is in God's hands. Pagans, Celsus, for instance, objected to Christians, and Christians sometimes objected to themselves, 'Why was Christ so long in coming? Should he not have come at once after the Fall?' The Fathers replied that, 'It was necessary that man should experience his need for a redeemer'. In the same way we may ask, 'Why is the Parousia so long in coming?' And surely the answer must be: In the first place, because the world must have time to develop in the degree that God wills for it. But also so that the world may learn through efforts that fail and experiments that lead nowhere that it stands in need of Jesus Christ to come again and give all it longs for

---

[61]Rom. viii, 14ff.; cf. Gal. iv, 9; John xvi, 21; and already in Is. lxvi, 7ff., for the New Jerusalem.

—peace, life, fellowship, light! The world has got to learn to say with the Church and the Spirit, 'Come!' (Apocalypse xxii, 17). And so, in explaining why God delays, we again find life and the Cross—together.

(3) We can now see the resemblance that there is between our idea of the Kingdom and the term that Marxism assigns to the historical process. This should be borne in mind when looking for the nature and causes of contemporary unbelief. At the beginning of modern times Christian thought was rather losing sight of the eschatological sense that gives movement and balance to the economy of salvation, *in Christo et in ecclesia*; while at the same time men were beginning to discover history, not simply events and their chronological order, but history as a movement towards something—the eighteenth century said towards enlightenment and reason, towards progress. By so doing men were really providing an eschatology for themselves, an equivalent of the Kingdom; they were giving themselves a hope, the equivalent of a religion. But it was a religion of man and a kingdom of the world and of history.

The Christian position is that final integrity and a reconciled life with oppositions overcome, the end that corresponds to the cosmic aspect of the Kingdom, cannot be attained simply by the power of the natures that make up the world. This term is a result of an order, and an order always comes from above, from a principle to which the elements are referred. There is no complete order of the world if there be not an order of man himself, and this order can be realised only by reference to God, who alone can provide it, as a gift of his grace. Man's nature is such, and the nature of the cosmos, if man be included, is such that it cannot fulfil its *integral* programme without a 'wholly gratuitous' taking of the work by God: the natures of things contain the energies necessary for their own operation as expressed by their bare definition, but they are ordered to something higher than themselves and they reach their fullness only by a means that comes from that 'something higher', namely, what Catholic theology calls the preternatural or else the (strictly) supernatural.[62] It is not for nothing that a whole apologetic can be grounded in the analysis of what Cardinal Dechamps called 'the interior fact', which is a simple expression of man's need of a renewal, of a free gift from God, to enable him *integrally* to realise the possibilities of perfection that are in his nature.

[62]The word 'grace' can cover them both (and even sometimes include the act of creation), or it may designate simply 'supernatural', properly speaking.

The Bible is our principal witness to the story of salvation, and in a general way God's plan seems to unfold thus: By an exercise of pure grace God in Heaven brings the happy outcome which an effort begun here below, itself not without the help of grace, could not reach by itself. This is what happens throughout the whole economy of salvation, and not only in the spiritual life of each individual (St Teresa of Lisieux's little child, whose father, seeing the boy can't get up the stairs, picks him up and in one swoop puts him on the landing). The Bible shows us God responding to man's gropings after him (cf. Acts xvii, 27). It shows him calling a people to himself by his word, but in the end Israel could actualise itself as the people of God only by becoming the Body of Christ, on the basis of God's Son coming in the flesh. Israel could offer to God only a movement of penitence whose last gesture was the baptism given by John; but Jesus brings a baptism by water and the Spirit (John i, 26; iii, 5). So too the worship and sacrifices that went up to God from Israel are fulfilled by the eucharistic gift, the bread that comes down from Heaven. It is the same with the temple; it is the same with the kingdom, which the book of Daniel taught Israel would not in the end be a result of man's efforts, but a gift from on high; it is the same, the same mystery under another name, with Jerusalem, for the earthly city will be completed only by the gift of that from above. Rightly does Father Bouyer say that 'The Bride of the Lamb will appear at the end of time *coming down from Heaven*. It is not we who will offer to God "the city where righteousness shall dwell". It will come, all ready built, from him to us.' But who will venture to say that the gift has here no continuity of substance with the effort? Is not the gift rather the issue, given from on high, towards which the effort tended, the effort already directed by him who would give all, but an issue which the effort would never have been able to attain by itself? If this be so, does it not suggest a certain conciliation, even a *rapprochement*, of the eschatological and evolutionist-incarnationist theses which would be disadvantageous to neither? For our part, it is the conclusion we have reached.

Father L. Malevez makes use of the following comparison: 'A master puts a student to work on an exercise made up of difficult problems. The student does not find the answer, though he tries very hard and comes more or less near it. The master will give him the answer, but only when, through his own efforts to find it, the student has improved his mind and abilities in a way that would have never entered his head had the answer been given him at once. The student will in a way have brought himself up to the level of the answer; he will *receive* it really only because, in the course of his efforts, he has risen to its standard' (*Etudes*, February 1948, p. 214).

This comparison adds something to the idea of pedagogy or of rough sketch by which, Father Danielou tells us, the Fathers of Christian antiquity answered our question. The patristic theme is that of pedagogy, or of sketches, which are not kept as such in the finished work but represent necessary stages which could not be gone through without them. But here the Fathers were thinking less of the relation of the work of this world to the eschatological reality than of the relation of Old Testament things to the truth that had come in Jesus Christ. Father Danielou transposes this relation, of its herald-ing and prefiguration to the true reality, into our problem.[63] Cer-tainly there is an analogy between the relation of Old Testament to gospel and that of Church to Kingdom; but is it more than an analogy? Surely under the new and definitive dispensation the rela-tion of the world as well as of the Church to the Kingdom is some-thing different from and rather more than a prophetical relationship of announcement and prefiguration?

Personally we would simply complete or clarify this way of looking at things by saying that the results of man's efforts and the positive substance of his sketches are taken up and returned to him in the final gift. It is as if a master should get his pupil to make a sketch and should then take it over himself, transfiguring it with matchless skill but not failing to work into his picture what the unskilled hand had tried to draw. God indeed will give all from on high, and all will be new, but he purposes that we should have nothing in which we have not been enabled to co-operate. What then exactly is this human co-operation and what of it will be taken up into the Kingdom?

First of all, of course, the whole order of charity, of which St Paul says that it endures (1 Corinthians xiii, 8). There is no difficulty about that. Then, the earthly work, and that in two ways: co-opera-tion by making ready the material of the Kingdom, and by striving after integrity and unity. We have touched on the second of these and seen that whatever of value under this head shall have been produced by human effort will be taken up and fulfilled at the last; but there are things to be said about the first point.

It is not a matter merely of the numerical multiplication of men. It is not a matter of imagining that our buildings and our machines, or even our cultures and our institutions, will as such be received

---

[63]'Christianisme et histoire' in *Etudes*, September 1947, pp. 166–184, cf. p. 172; 'Perspectives eschatologiques . . .', in *Etudes*, March 1950, pp. 359–368, cf. pp. 360–361.

I

into the Kingdom of God. The only ones of our earthly institutions that we know will endure in Heaven, though in different conditions, are the marriage union and the Church; it does not look as if countries (*patries*) will subsist otherwise than in the charity of those who have loved them in a Christian fashion. And the Church and the marriage union (especially this last) will continue only under profoundly changed conditions (for the second, see Matthew xxii, 23-30; Mark xii, 18-25). We are not here thinking of *things* as such but of their relation to man, of their development of authentically human qualities in him or of humanised, and therefore spiritualised, quality in the world. We are thinking of what has been shown elsewhere (*Divided Christendom*, Ch. III) to correspond with a qualitative notion of the Church's catholicity or, if you will, with its material cause. The whole work of this world is necessary in order that the first creation, and above all the men for whom it was made, may make full use of all that is in them, which has to be put under Christ as under a new head.

Medieval Christendom, which M. Maritain calls sacral and we should call, less poetically but more accurately, hierocratic and jurisdictional, was an undeniably imposing attempt to actualise a sort of kingdom of God on earth. Israel long before had tried to establish God's reign under the form of secular life, and in fact medieval Christendom often appealed to the Old Testament. It came near a maximum domination of the temporal by the spiritual, of nature by grace, approximating as closely as possible to that union of two worlds in a single order that characterises the Kingdom. In the Carolingian age, for example, there was no longer a church *and* a world in the West, there was no 'outside' to the Church: the world existed and built itself up according to the Church and within the Church.[64]

A great deal could be said about this Christendom. The fact that (in principle) the Church absorbed the world and imposed on it regulations proper to herself eventually meant the ignoring of the secularity of what is secular; preoccupation solely with the last end —the normal point of view of clergy—led to the disregarding of

[64]Two important pieces of evidence: (a) While Gelasius's famous text of 494 ran, 'duo sunt quibus principaliter mundus hic regitur', from Carolingian times theologians and churchmen quoted it as 'quibus Ecclesia regitur': thus the synod at Paris in 829, Hincmar of Rheims, Hugh of Saint-Victor, St Bernard, Innocent III, Boniface VIII, etc. (b) In the middle of the twelfth century Otto of Freising wrote in his *Chroni-on*, 'From that time [Constantine], seeing that all people, including emperors, were with few exceptions Catholics, I feel that I have written the history not of two cities but as it were of one, the Church . . .' (quoted by E. Gilson, *Dante et la philosophie*, p. 203).

secondary causes, the proper and immediate causes of things. We can but recall what has been said at the end of our first chapter. Medieval Christendom was, very generally speaking, a sacral regime, and by its hold of the spiritual over the temporal it brought about a union of the two that was in some ways premature and bought too cheaply. Earthly things were hardly considered except for their use in the Church's sacred work, hardly at all in their own reality and causalities, and so they were not taken really seriously and received neither the attention they deserve nor the development they call for. The truth of the first creation was too quickly swallowed up in the second, of grace, and one may well ask whether in these circumstances the second creation itself is able to bring all its own truth into play (the cosmic value of 'recapitation', putting under a new head). Looked at in this way, it seems that a giving back to 'the secular' of whatever in the present economy belongs to the world is a necessary condition if the world is to arrive at the Kingdom in a state of full development and activity. Without that, it will still be immature and childish when it offers itself to the Spirit's embrace.[65]

From the aspect then of allowing the earthly work to develop to the full for the Kingdom, a Christendom of the sacral or hierocratic pattern is seen to be undesirable. But from the aspect of the earthly work's quest for basic integrity and unity *a certain* Christendom, that is, an influence of the spiritual over the secular order, is necessary. Necessary: first of all in itself since, as we have seen, integrity and unity can truly come to the world only from the Spirit of God; then necessary concretely, because a duality of unalloyed separation is profoundly at variance with the demands of Christianity in Christian

[65]Here are two illustrations of these ideas, one from history or the economy of God's plan, the other from priestly experience. (*a*) Israel had a pure religious vocation, independent of all cultural values, in which Israel was very poor. If the Messiah had brought the Kingdom at once it would have been realised without the developments, and the acceptance of the developments, of history. But between Israel and the Kingdom there is the Church, constituted by the sending of the 'apostles' to the 'Nations' (cf. E. Peterson, *Die Kirche*). God's design includes a 'Church' stage that is essentially correlative to a 'Nations' reality and to a development of the 'World'. Jesus is 'inheritor of the Nations' and of 'all things' (cf. Ps. ii, 8; Heb. i, 2). It is the whole idea of 'recapitulation' (cf. above, n. 9), and according to the liturgy one of the deepest meanings of the feast of the Epiphany. (*b*) People intimately concerned have often remarked that youths brought up for the priesthood in an apostolic school or junior seminary of a narrowly clerical type lack the support to their priesthood provided by a certain human development which can be acquired only by a cultivation of secular things *for their own sake*. The most effective priests are often those who, before their clerical training, made secular studies or followed some human activity for its own sake. On respect for things, which can serve God only if they are first authentically themselves, we quote in Part Two, Chs. V and VI Gilson's very sound article, 'L'intelligence au service du Christ-roi'.

hearts. The faithful soul busy in the world cannot but seek for himself a harmony of the two cities to which he belongs, he cannot but want to change the world in some measure. This is forced upon him by love; but it also follows from what experience has taught him about the weight of social pressure and the conditioning of our moral and religious attitudes by our environment. He is conscious of God's authority over everything and of his own duty to do all he can to forward Christ's reign; he has to seek to forward that reign in earthly institutions and over earthly things themselves. The Christian has to energise in the earthly city in accordance with what he is, as a Christian; he cannot do otherwise than make use of the Christian powers that are in him and direct what he does towards the Christian end.

He is prompted to do this by his fidelity towards him to whom he has given his faith, and his fidelity towards created things requires that he should fully respect their truth. We no longer live in a world of the identical-with-Christendom pattern of the middle ages, and the Christian today is called to live a twofold loyalty, to God and the world, a state of tension for whose solution there is no ready-made formula. Only since the end of sacral Christendom, with its monastic and clerical set-up, have we been able to get the full measure of the extent and requirements of the secularity of things and of the fidelity we owe to them. Now the danger is to see only what appertains to the nature of 'profane' things, to know only the techniques, and to forget the wisdom which, while respecting its own truth that is in every reality, has to order and 'hierarchise' everything in dependence on the supreme Principle. Respect for the Principle as principle, respect for the elements as elements, each in proportion to its truth —such is the providential grace of Thomism, as we have pointed out at the end of our first chapter. Respect for the truth of things is called for alike by love of God and love of man. By love of man, because in a laicised world there is no longer unanimity of religious faith, very far from it; and it is through and on the basis of this respect that men can still live closely and work together. By love of God, because the existence of things and their realisation as fully and frankly as possible, each according to its nature, is the first condition of their homage and service to his sovereignty.

*   *   *

We shall end this chapter by trying, in the light of the whole, to get an idea of lay people's role in the Church and in the world as regards the Kingdom of God. But first we will, allowing a little modification, make use of a very significant comparison which not long ago was offered by two Protestant writers independently of one another: the Church, they said, is the *maquis* of the world.[66] This metaphor, like Oscar Cullmann's of the decisive battle and V-day, is so expressive that we must take the risk, inherent in the use of topical figures, of a certain triviality.

The crucial battle has been fought, and Christ is victorious. But the struggle still goes on, the enemy is still in occupation, and he is still strong enough to do damage. In the occupied country everybody perhaps in a confused way may look forward to liberation, but many people have adjusted themselves and are content to live not too badly under prevailing conditions. Others have gone underground. These refuse to recognise the occupier's rule and put all their faith and hope in the Power, still far away, who has achieved a victory that may not have looked much but was in fact decisive. The Liberator already reigns over these men who are working for the freeing of themselves and everybody else, who are already spiritually living in freedom, oppressed and harried as they still are. When full and final liberation comes, it comes from outside, through a landing, a 'parousia' of the Liberator—but it also comes from the *maquis*, which gets to work with fresh energy; it would have been helpless by itself, but it is integrated into the final triumph.

If experiments for a new order have been planned or tried out during the days of oppression, whatever has proved good in them also is integrated into the victorious regime, and their best workers are associated with the Liberator in his reign. Here the figure of the Church as *maquis* of the world does not quite fit. The actual *maquis* withdraws from society altogether and collaborates neither with the occupying power nor even with the precariously balanced institutions of the occupied country. The *Maquis* of the World says rather: 'Resistance *in* the world! Mix with the crowd of people who just don't care, mix with the ordinary decent folk, yes, mix with the "collaborators" themselves, working in the world's conditions and amidst all its business that it may be set free by Jesus Christ'. Not an ideal situation, and one that sometimes leads to activities of a somewhat equivocal kind. Yes, indeed! Christian action in the world calls

[66] J. J. von Allmen, 'L'Eglise ou le maquis du monde' in *In Extremis*, 1945, no. 7—8; R. de Pury, 'L'Eglise, maquis du monde' in *Le Semeur*, 1945, no. 8–9. Compare these expressive words of the Italian former communist A. Rossi, a convert to Catholicism: 'Every true communist henceforth regards himself as a citizen of another country and subject to its laws, whilst he awaits the time when he will be able to confer them on others' (*Le Parti communiste en action*). Is not this the Christian's position to this extent, that his other (and true) country not being an earthly one, it is not in competition with his natural country *on the same plane*, and therefore does not involve him in treason: for his true country is supernatural.

for great single-mindedness and a continual strengthening in faith.

HIERARCHY AND FAITHFUL PEOPLE

What I am about to put forward now will be examined in more
detail in the five chapters that follow. A certain amount of repetition is inevitable; but if we are successfully to define the *place of the
laity* it is necessary to give a general account here of the respective
roles in the Church of the lay order or function and of the hierarchical order or function. 'Lay religious' are reserved for consideration in the volume of *Etudes conjointes*; while lay-brothers,
such as the *conversi* or coadjutors of the great orders, or the members of non-clerical congregations (Brothers of the Christian
Schools, most of the Brothers of St John of God, the Little Brothers
of Jesus), they continue to belong to the lay order and to fulfil lay
functions, for they live 'in the world' and do its work; but they
have no original significance in the Church's structure, inasmuch
as its fundamental distinction is between the lay and the hierarchical order or function.

The intermediate situation characteristic of the Church enables us
to understand the place and part respectively of laity and hierarchy.
The situation itself follows from the fact that God's work is at the
same time already done and still to be done, since all the substance
of it is given us in Jesus Christ and yet it has still to be carried out by
us. Jesus Christ is in himself alone the Temple and the Kingdom,[67]
but we have to become Temple and Kingdom in him or, what comes
to the same thing, he has to become so also in us, though not without
our having personally *done* that which he *gives* us the ability to do.[68]
He is the fullness from which we draw all our spiritual existence, but
we too are his fullness, in whom, by whose contribution and co-
operation, he fulfils himself.[69] In other words, Jesus Christ is the

[67]For the Temple, cf. John ii, 19–21. For the Kingdom, exegetes are agreed that
Origen's word for Christ as Kingdom, αὐτοβασιλεία (*In Matt.* xiv, 7, on Matt.
xviii, 23), exactly interprets the indications of the gospel where the same affirmations are made about the Kingdom and about Jesus. Cf. *e.g.*, Kittel's *Worterbuch*,
art. βασιλεία, vol. i, pp. 590ff.; art. Εὐαγγέλιον, vol. ii, p. 725; art. Ἐκκλησία,
vol. iii, p. 525; A. M. Hunter, *The Message of the N.T.* (Philadelphia, 1944),
pp. 19, 56: eyc.

[68]We have referred more than once to this 'dialectic of giving and doing'. Cf.
Divided Christendom, pp. 69, n. 2, 96–97, 103; *Esquisses du mystère de l'Eglise* (1941),
pp. 26, 29–30 (written in 1937); 'Sacerdoce et laicat dans l'Eglise' in *Vie intellectuelle*, Decr 1946, p. 11; etc.

[69]Principal references: John i, 14; Col. i, 19, ii, 9; and again, Eph. i, 23, iv, 13;
Col. i, 24.

whole Temple and Kingdom, a first time by himself, and he will be so a second time with us, in whom and—we need not hesitate to say —through whom he will have attained his full stature.

The Christian position can therefore be considered in relation to the fullness of the Pasch, wherein he receives everything, and in relation to the fullness of the Parousia, to which he has something to bring. As regards the Pasch, we receive everything from the unique fact of Jesus Christ in his historical incarnation, his *acta et passa pro nobis* [Z], a well-spring of holiness established outside ourselves at a certain moment in history. The Church is the aggregate of the means whereby these waters reach us (before she is the community of men in whom is the truth and grace of Jesus), and there we find the function of the apostolic hierarchy. As regards the Parousia, we, on the basis of what we have received, have to bring to God through Christ the modest riches of creation and of our free co-operation, or, if you will, the produce of the talents God has given us, 'the interest on his outlay'. Here is the lay state contributing actively to the building up of the Temple.

These two aspects are organically connected; we will examine them in turn.

The Hierarchy's Role in the Church as Means of Grace. – One of the keys of a Catholic ecclesiology is to hold that the Church, the same Church, is both communion with God in Christ *and* the means for attaining this fellowship. That in her which is communion already realised will endure for ever in Heaven, and so we can say that she is one same Body of Christ, one same Church of God, in two different states, here of pilgrimage and warfare, there of happiness and glory. That in her which is means to communion belongs to her earthly condition, and will pass away when Christ delivers up the Kingdom to his Father that God may be all in all. These are the formative realities of the ecclesial institution (the *Heilsanstalt* of German theologians), which one can, with tradition, establish in the deposit of faith, in the deposit of the sacraments of the faith, with the corresponding apostolic powers.[70] Patristic ecclesiology, which is followed fundamentally by St Augustine and Western scholasticism, conceives the Church essentially as a fellowship in heavenly things, in Christ, through the sacraments, preaching, acts of the visible ministry and of the authority that derive from the Apostles. In this sense we could adopt Augustine's categories, *communio sanctorum,*

---

[70]To attempt to do more than sketch the theology of these things would be to write a treatise on the Church. There are some precisions in the three following chapters. We like to associate these elements of the ecclesial institution with the pregnant text in Acts, ii 42: cf. *Esquisses*, pp. 35ff.

communio sacramentorum; but the best instrument of formulation is perhaps that of which the medieval theologians found the principle: it has in fact become classic in the West under the terms *res* and *sacramentum*.[71]

The *sacramentum* is the sacramental rite, the outward sign, the visible institution; the *res* is the spiritual fruit that the sacrament hiddenly procures. Thus the Church as Body of Christ is the reality in which he takes form in order to live and to act there; as institution, the Church is the visible form of his action, and as fellowship, of his life.

There correspond to these two co-existent aspects, two participations in the messianic energies that we have associated with the offices of priest, king and prophet. In the Church as communion these functions exist *as form or dignity of life* qualifying all her members as such. In the Church as institution and means of grace, the three functions qualify certain members only, giving them a charge or ministry for the benefit of all the others, and they then exist *as powers*, active means for promoting the life of the body. We are reminded here of Christ's relationship to his body the Church according to the gospels and epistles, a twofold relationship, of power and of quickening: he is head over the body and he is the immanent life of the body. This duality is repeated in the Church, particularly in the application just indicated.

The Church can be compared to a building under construction, say a place of worship. The world is the quarry that supplies the stone. A whole organisation is necessary to bring the rough stone to its final state in the finished building: hammer and chisels, means of transport, scaffolding and ladders, cranes, an architect to give orders and industrious workmen. When the church is finished, every stone in its place according to the architect's design, the scaffolding and everything else that is no longer wanted is taken away, and the workmen have a rest. When the Body of Christ has reached its final state in Heaven there will no longer be any mediating activity of the hierarchical priesthood, no magisterium of the faith, no ruling authority, no 'dogma', no law, no sacrament: for God will be all in all (1 Corinthians xv, 28). For man now saved and reborn, external things will have ceased, there will be an end to the machinery of the earthly Church, her hierarchy, temples, powers, her aspect of law and synagogue, all the things that belonged to a time of waiting and

[71] In St Augustine, Christ is the *res* of all the *sacramenta*; but he does not carry over these categories into the efficaciousness of properly sacramental rites: cf. H. M. Feret, 'Sacramentum, res, dans la langue theologique de S. Augustin' in *Rev. des sciences philos. et theol.*, 29 (1940), pp. 218–243.

change, when the *sacramentum* was not yet completely *res*. Or, if there
be still some outward expression of spiritual realities, it will not be
in order to procure those realities, by a movement from without to
within, making them dependent on an external thing for their
existence: rather will it be by supererogation, in order to instruct
and enlighten, or by way of manifestation and as an element of
glory:[72] that is, by a movement from within to without, and so in
no wise opposed to the perfect inwardness of truth and life. That is
why St John describes the Heavenly Jerusalem (which is perfectly
free: Galatians iv, 26) thus: 'I saw no sanctuary therein, for the
Lord God almighty is the sanctuary thereof, and the Lamb. And the
city hath no need of the sun or of the moon to shine upon it, for the
glory of the Lord enlighteneth it, and the lamp thereof is the Lamb'
(Apocalypse xxi, 22-23; cf. xxii 3-5). There we see the full realisation
of the messianic promises (Isaias lx, 19) and the effects of the New
Covenant as declared by Jeremy: 'I will give my law in their bowels
and I will write it in their heart: and I will be their God, and they
shall be my people. And they shall teach no more every man his
neighbour, and every man his brother, saying: Know the Lord. For
all shall know me from the least of them even to the greatest . . .'
(Jeremias xxxi, 33-34; cf. Hebrews viii, 10-11).

But Jerusalem below is only the beginning and an earnest of
Jerusalem above. In as much as it is in a state of becoming and men
are on their pilgrimage to God, it has an element of outwardness
and, in this sense, of 'law' (though this word would raise certain
difficulties in regard to some passages of the epistle to the Galatians).
Metaphysically, the relevant principle is this: so far as action does
not coincide with its norm, a rule exterior to it is at work: a law or a
pedagogy, so far as good does not fully reside in our freedom; an

---

[72]We think that the hierarchical or sacramental priesthood will continue in
Heaven as a dignity, as a closer likening to Christ, as an 'aureole'. In the honour
given to Christ's members the liturgy distinguishes between simple confessors and
confessor-bishops. – The teaching that there will be no other hierarchy than that
of holiness in Heaven, and that the ecclesial apparatus of powers and external
means will have disappeared, is classical in the Fathers and in theology. Cf., *e.g.*,
H. de Lubac, *Corpus mysticum* . . . (Paris, 1944), pp. 227ff.; and for St Thoma see
IV Sent., d. 24, q. 1, a. 1, aq 1, ad 3; *Sum. theol.*, III, q. 61, a. 4, ad 1; q. 63, a. 1,
ad 1; a. 3, ad 3; a. 5, ad 3. Comp. Giles of Rome, *De eccl. potest.*, ii, c. 13 (ed.
Scholz, p. 121). And these texts of Cajetan: 'As there will be neither sacrifice nor
temple in our heavenly home, as is said in Apoc. xxi, 22, "I saw no temple in it",
so our text [Apoc. i, 6: He "made us a royal race of priests, to serve God, his
Father"] says nothing about any priestly *action* in that future, though the priestly
dignity itself endures for ever' (*Jentaculum tertium: De sacerdotio*). 'The whole finality
of the Church is to engender, nourish and defend faith [he means, living faith];
the rest is destined to be made into bundles and burnt (Matt. xiii, 30).' (*Com. in
I-II*, q. 33, a. 4, n. 2).

instruction, so far as truth does not fill the mind; a nourishing from without, so far as the fountain of Life does not gush forth from the living person himself. Theologically and christianly, we are here only interpreting God's design, the law of his saving economy. Its object is that he shall be all in all, that his creation shall be his temple and men the associates of his life; and to realise it he has adopted a means in our world, or more accurately, *in the depth of human nature*—the Incarnation. So from the start he has joined the oneness of the communion we must have with him to the means of realising it: the mediation of the man Jesus Christ (1 Timothy ii, 5). Thus in communicating his life to us, God acts not according to *his* mode, but according to *ours*. Whatever is given us of the final reality of divine life is through the *sacramentum humanitatis (Christi)*: there will be nothing in Omega that has not come from Alpha, that is, from what Christ has been and has done and has suffered for us in his incarnation.[73]

And so it will be until Christ shall have given back all things to the Father, in a 'Consummatum est' of which that uttered alone on the cross is only the 'sacrament'; only then will God be truly all in all; only then will there be an end to the regime of mediation under which men live so long as the night shall last, *donec auferetur luna*.

The Church as institution has no other meaning than to carry on this mediation (in traditional symbolism she is compared to the moon). Those people who misunderstand the Church as institution are the same people who misunderstand the existence of an element of externality or 'law', and their misjudgment arises from the same basic attitude. It is for the same reason that they completely misunderstand the meaning of the hierarchical fact, which is an aspect of the Church as institution and of the existing regime of mediation. Protestants in particular believe and say that hierarchy and sacraments as presented by the Catholic Church are so many human mediations that obscure the unique mediation by Christ on which St Paul insists. This, as we will show, is profoundly to misunderstand the meaning of the hierarchical fact; but also, we think, it is to mis-

---

[73]In his fine study, 'Mystique: Essai sur l'histoire d'un mot' (*Vie spirituelle*, suppl., May 1949, pp. 3–23), Father Bouyer shows that the Fathers use the word 'mystic' of everything that relates to the fulfilment of God's hidden purpose, and that this purpose, and therefore all 'mystic', is linked with Jesus Christ. There will be nothing in the *eschaton* [AA] that is not from the hapax *(ἐφάπαξ)* of Christ, come in the flesh. This explains the value that Catholics put on the historical Church, which surprises Protestants: she is the bond between the root and the fruit, between Christ (alone) as Alpha and Christ (with us) as Omega. – For all this paragraph I venture to refer the reader to *Divided Christendom*, pp. 64ff. On the referring of all to the historical Incarnation, see St Thomas, *Sum. theol.*, I-II, q. 108, a. 1.

understand the exact role of the Incarnation and of Christ's *human* mediation. In their anxiety not to make salvation depend on anything but an act of God, the Protestant reformers seem to have joined the Church immediately and as it were vertically to Christ in Heaven; they seem to have overlooked to what an extent everything comes from the *acta et passa Christi in carne*, from the Incarnation and the Calvary of history, through a continuity of 'sacraments' in which the mediation of the man Jesus is prolonged: as St Augustine says, until the Kingdom of God, whatever we drink comes from Christ's stricken side. Protestant theology understands by 'Church' the aggregate of those who are the object of God's grace-giving act; it sees in actual earthly churches so many man-made assemblies, whose ministries are a delegation by the community of faithful. This last mistake has not been confined to Protestants. We saw in the previous chapter how theories of representation led to disregard of the hierarchical fact, which in turn led by reaction to a strong emphasis on hierarchical mediation in Catholic theology.

The meaning of the hierarchical fact is bound up with this regime of God's people who are under the new and final dispensation, but upon whom the Parousia has not yet come; the regime during which the Body, receiving the fullness of grace and truth that is given in Christ Jesus, is progressively built together in Heaven, where its Head is. This grace and this truth come to us through the exercise of a priesthood, of an *hierarchical* governance and teaching, and this is so because grace and truth are not fully 'interiorised' in us, and to that extent we have to receive them from outside and above. So far from obscuring the unique mediation of the man Jesus Christ, sacramental and hierarchical mediation realises it; that mediation is sign and cause, manifestation and ensurance that all is bound to come to us from on high; it is the extension, or rather the sacrament, of Christ's mediation. In Chapter XVII of St John's gospel the Apostles are sent out as a sequel to the sending of Christ into the world . . .

Consequently the hierarchical functions in the Church are by no means organs of the body, a creation of the immanent powers of the organism. They are not referred to the aspect or 'moment' wherein the faithful make the Church (community), but to that wherein the Church (institution) makes the faithful. Undoubtedly the Church has both these aspects, and it would be false to say that hierarchical persons never in any way represent the faithful. Bishops in council, priests celebrating the eucharist, have a certain role as representatives of the believing and praying community. But in the properly hierarchical acts of defining the Church's tradition, consecrating the

holy gifts or ministering the sacraments, they are acting as ministers
and delegates, not of the faithful, but of Jesus Christ.[74] Their role
therefore corresponds not to the activity of a living man who expresses
what is in him, but to a body that must receive from outside itself in
order to live. In as much as they are hierarchical persons and not
simply members of the faithful (which of course they are, but under
another aspect) they do not exert the life of Jesus Christ but his
power and action.

A few pages back we ventured on a comparison from building;
here is another and perhaps better analogy, that of a growing blade
of corn. Only the ear will be gathered; in terms of religion, only the
ear will form the great offering of praise for ever in Heaven. But
until it has ripened it cannot live without its stalk, which one day
will be ploughed in or trodden underfoot. The Church on earth is
both the growing ear and the stalk that supports it and is a channel
for its nourishment.

This estimate of things answers to all the circumstances. It has the
great advantage of establishing the hierarchical form of the kingly,
priestly and prophetical functions and their common form, immanent in the whole body, in a single truth taken from the very heart of
Christianity. The Church is hierarchically royal, sacerdotal and
prophetical in order that she may transmit the life that is in Christ to
men; the faithful, incorporated in him, live spiritually by a life that
is kingly, priestly and prophetical. That is how the respective parts
of the clergy and the laity are distributed, or preferably, of the
hierarchy and faithful people, it being understood that hierarchical
persons are firstly and always remain, simply as persons, among the
faithful.[75] The two simultaneous truths, a clear inequality on account
of function and a radical equality as members of the one body, living
the same Christian life, are thus brought together and reconciled.

The Laity's Role in the Building of the Temple and the Kingdom. – Looking at it from the above point of view it would appear that lay people
have only to receive, that they are Christians thanks to hierarchical
mediations, and that their function in the Church is solely to be the

[74]All that must be set forth in more detail in a treatise on the Church. Cf.
'Mission de la paroisse' in *Structures sociales et pastorale paroissiale* (Paris, 1948),
pp. 49ff. – The encyclical letter '*Mediator Dei*' (1947) underlines the fact that the
hierarchical priesthood does not represent or derive from the people; the priest as
such acts 'in persona Christi capitis'.

[75]Notice these words of Aeneas Silvius Piccolomini (afterwards Pope Pius II):
'Debemus duplicam considerare Ecclesiam: alteram quae laicos cum clericis in se
habet, alteram quae solos clericos, et ad secundam pertinet docere, purgare,
illuminare, dirigere, corrigere, pascere et perficere primam' (*De gestis Basil. conc.*,
i; in Brown, *Fasciculus rerum expectandarum . . .*, vol. i, p. 15).

object of ministry. Such conclusions would show scant respect for apostolic teaching: 'For as in our one body we have many members, and all the members have not the same function, even so we many are one body in Christ, and members each of the other. But we have gifts which vary according to the grace that hath been given us . . .' (Romans xii, 4-8); 'Now ye are the body of Christ, and severally his members' (I Corinthians xii, 27; cf. 18-30). This teaching was taken up by Pope Pius XII: 'It must not be supposed that this co-ordinated, or organic, structure of the body of the Church is confined exclusively to the grades of the hierarchy. . . . When the fathers of the Church mention the ministries of this body, its grades, professions, states, orders and offices, they rightly have in mind not only persons in sacred orders, but also . . .' etc.[76] Lay people, each one according to the conditions of his life and his state in the Mystical Body, truly bring something to God's Temple and help to build it up. It is in and through the life of the faithful (and of the clergy as members of the faithful) that Christ's saving powers are made manifest within the dimensions of history and of the world, so as to bring back to God all the richness of his creation, of which Christ is the first-born and the king.

To this theme Part Two of this book will be devoted: in Chapter I, from the point of view of the priestly offering; in II, of spiritual kingship; in III, of the development of Christian understanding; in IV, of each one's contribution to the building up of the Church according to his gifts and charisms [BB]; in V, of apostleship and influence on what is temporal; in VI, of a spirituality governed by the ideas of each person's vocation and responsibility 'in that state of life to which it has pleased God to call him'; and in the concluding section, from the point of view of the idea of the Church as organism and fulfilment.

By God's positive institution the role of the hierarchy is to bring us the fullness of the Pasch, of the Incarnation; the role of the faithful thus quickened by Christ is to spread this quickening in the world, a world given us by God together with a call to co-operate in its completion. The Church is at once ear and stalk, sprung from the noble Seed from whose solitary sowing the whole harvest must come; or again, she is at once a building and all that is needed for its erection. We have used these figures to illustrate the part played by the institution or priestly hierarchy; we will now use them to illustrate the active part of the faithful. The Church is at the same time ear

[76]Encyclical letter 'Mystici corporis Christi'; A.A.S. (1943), pp. 200-201; C.T.S. English trans., p. 15.

and roots, roots which draw nourishment from the earth, the world, that the grain may swell and ripen; or she is both the building and its stones, quarried from history and the world (cf. I Corinthians iii, 10-15). For, once again, she is made from above and from below. From above, as from a source of holiness given by God as a positive principle, not included among the world's possibilities, which thus constitutes a special sacred and saving order. That is why the Church is a different thing from the world or history attaining a perfect maturity through their own development (which moreover is impossible since, as we have seen, their perfection must be given them from above). At the same time the Church is formed also from below, from history and the world, whose contributions, redeemed, restored, cleansed, have to return to God in Christ, their royal firstfruits.

This giving-back is done by man and in the heart of man. Man is naturally the measure of the world, for he is its supreme outcome;[77] he is also its epitome, and in regard to all we are saying here the old idea of microcosm, found so often in the Fathers and in medieval days, could still teach us something useful. Before the fulfilment of Christ's kingship at the Parousia there is no direct dominion of the spiritual over the cosmic order; so long as the duality of Church and world continues there is simply a 'christofinalisation' of the temporal, working in the life and hearts of the faithful. Recall what has been said above about the two concentric zones of Christ's kingship here below, zones that do not overlap: he reigns in the Church, in the hearts of his own; he is king of the cosmos, but leaves that sovereign power as it were in abeyance. Pope Pius XI decreed that the feast of Christ the King should be celebrated on the Sunday next before All Saints, thus emphasising that in this life the Lord's reign is in the souls of his holy ones. For the great circle of the world and the lesser circle of the Church to have the same centre, it is enough that the Church really should be the germinal cell of the Kingdom, in which the bounds of the two circles will coincide completely. This too is the foundation of the Christians' obligation *spiritually* to realise God's universal reign in their hearts, their human hearts. And how is this to be done?

In the first place by giving oneself up to his reign by faith and becoming his spiritual temple by charity, and that means freeing oneself from sin and service of the Devil. Then by doing all we can to

[77]In recent times this idea, which is certainly traditional, has received a new lease of life from philosophers and other learned men; *e.g.*, Bergson (*Les deux sources de la morale et de la religion*), Lecomte du Noüy (*L'homme et sa destinée*), Teilhard de Chardin and others referred to above, n. 44.

'christofinalise' temporal civilisation (cf. Chapter V), and for
that purpose to humanise it to the utmost. Then by offering up the
cosmic world, firstly by an affective offering, a consecration by intention which is eventually translated into symbolic actions, as the
liturgy does with such meaning and impressiveness; but not less by
preparing, anticipating, imitating so far as may be, the control of the
cosmos by spirit: by christianising history's efforts towards integrity
and unity, by seeking so far as possible to bring *things* into the life of
the spirit (instead of alienating man from things), and at the same
time trying to free man from his bondage to nature and the world.
And so we come full circle, back to freedom from sin and enslave-
ment to the Evil One, and to the giving up of self to God in the
spiritual sacrifice spoken of in the next chapter.

It would seem that according to God's design the one supreme
mediation of Jesus Christ is exerted through a twofold mediation by
men, corresponding to the double participation in Christ's messianic
energies, as powers and as form of life. From the time that Heaven
received him until the day when all will be restored anew (Acts iii,
21), Christ's kingly, priestly and prophetical mediation is at work in
two ways: through the apostolic hierarchy, for the formation of a
faithful people; through the whole body, in respect of the world. In
the first case, mediation takes the form of powers and is applied to
the Church; the second case, answering to the life of the ecclesial
body, is essentially spiritual and applies to the world of men. The
hierarchy exercises the mediation of the means of grace between
Christ and the faithful; the latter exercise a mediation of life between
the Body of Christ and the world, and this also is a means of grace
in its order. The world is drawn to Christ in and through the faithful,
its human part to be transformed in him, its cosmic part to find its
end in him.

In this way then are their respective parts allotted so that the
hierarchy and the faithful may form one Church and carry out her
mission to the full. The hierarchy is a means by which Christ's
specific and properly divine life is brought to the stalk of the corn;
through the faithful, the measure of Christ comes to the teeming
substance of mankind and the world. The resuming of everything in
Christ is realise by the two together, so far, that is, as we are called
on to bring it about. The sacrifice of praise both takes the form of the
Pasch and is as all-embracing as that of the final harvest; from their
roots in Christ the man all things grow up to the stature of Christ in
Heaven, who is their Head (Ephesians iv, 15).

PART TWO

Chapter I

THE LAITY AND THE CHURCH'S PRIESTLY FUNCTION

(A) *THE PRIESTLY FUNCTION IN THE CHRISTIAN ECONOMY*

JESUS CHRIST, the Word of God made flesh, is the only true wisdom —yet there was wisdom in the world before him. Jesus Christ is the only true priest—yet there was already a natural priesthood, drawing all its worth from him, referred to him and subsisting in him ('Omnia in ipso constant': Colossians i, 17). Holy Writ itself bears witness to the existence of a natural priesthood.[1] Each man was his own priest,[2] or, more usually, a man was priest of a group, in which he ranked as head: in patriarchal days, the father or patriarch;[3] under a wider social regime, the leader (judge)[4] or the king;[5] or again someone might be designated for a public sacrificial occasion.[6] Natural priesthood can be illustrated endlessly from the history of religions, and we shall return to it when we speak of the priesthood of fathers of families.

God has not allowed the world to lack witness to himself, he has always provided that he shall be honoured, he has always been

[1]Cf. B. F. Westcott, *The Epistle to the Hebrews* (London, 1903), pp. 140ff.

[2]*E.g.*, Abel (Gen. iv, 4), whose sacrifice is referred to in the canon of the Roman Mass.

[3]Noah (Gen. viii, 20ff. Cf. Eccl. xliv, 17), Abraham (Gen. xiii, 4), Isaac (xxvi, 25), Jacob (xxxv, 1), with whom can be connected the cases of Job (Job i, 5), Manue, Samson's father (Judges xiii, 19) and perhaps Melchizedek (Gen. xiv, 8ff.) and Jethro (Exod. ii, 16; xviii, 1, 12).

[4]Gideon (Judges vi, 19ff.).

[5]Saul (1 Sam. xiii, 9ff., xiv, 34–35), David (2 Sam. vi, 13ff., xxiv, 25), Solomon (1 Kings ix, 25), Achaz (2 Kings xvi, 12ff.).

[6]The young men after the covenant of Sinai (Exod. xxiv, 5).

recognised by men in some way or other and been given their wor-ship and sacrifice: but in his love for men he himself has instituted a form of worship and of sacrifice, just as, after giving them under-standing, he has further given his word and his Spirit. In the eleven first chapters of Genesis the elements of the world's development are shown under the hand of God, and he intervened in a new and gratuitous way when he put in its midst and there unfolded his free purpose of grace, whose fulfilment is Jesus Christ and to which the scriptural revelation bears witness. By this gift of grace we live, and we must now endeavour to understand its economy, especially from the point of view of worship, sacrifice and priesthood.

At the beginning of the previous chapter we said that the aim and object of God's design is to make mankind his temple of living stones: a temple wherein he shall not only dwell by being there, but by communicating himself, a spiritual Person, to other persons at once spiritual and physical, whose worship shall alike be spiritual (and physical). We shall see from what follows that it may be said that the Church or Body of Christ is simply the reality of this temple and this worship: God's spiritual temple, Christ's spiritual body, God's temple of fellowship, Christ's body of fellowship. The pattern of grace is realised in Christ, who is the fulfilment of all the promises (2 Corinthians i, 20). He is the heart and achievement of everything: it all leads to him, from Abraham throughout the history of Israel; it all comes from him, through the Apostles throughout the history of the Church, till the day when all shall be accomplished, and Alpha, having fulfilled all the Scriptures, shall have become our Omega. We must then consider this way upward to Christ's priest-hood, his priesthood itself, and the Church's participation in it.

We cannot study the sacrificial system and worship of the Old Dispensation in detail, though it would be very interesting to do so. It was not for nothing that St Thomas commented on it minutely in the *Summa* (I-II, qq. 101-103). Did not God reveal his will concern-ing this worship of himself down to the smallest item? Are not its different aspects valuable for the understanding of what has been done and given to us in Jesus Christ, who abolished the prescriptions of the law only by 'accomplishing' them? But, again at the risk of making it as long as a small book, this chapter has got to consider priesthood at some length, and it is no more its business to present a detailed study of Jewish rites of worship than to do the same for the Christian liturgy. Such studies can easily be found elsewhere. For our purpose it is more useful to look at the general lines and charac-teristics of priesthood and sacrificial worship in Israel.

J

In the first place, there is something priestly about all Israel. This vocation and quality attach to the people as such: God cohoses this people to be set apart, to be associated with him and to be dedicated as his particular people.[7] The grand name 'people of God', *Laos tor Theou*, denotes as one whole the sovereignty of God, to whom all peoples belong and who calls whom he pleases, and the state of holiness in which Israel is put by his choice: as chosen, Israel is indeed 'of God', and therefore she is holy;[8] she is a consecrated people, a religious people, a praising and worshipping people. This priestly quality also implies that Israel has a part to play among the nations: to them she is to be a revealer and a witness of the true God, a leader in praising him, a privileged minister of his worship. That idea was to be particularly developed later on by Philo, and adapted by St Peter to Christians (1 Peter ii, 9), but it cannot be looked on as foreign to the meaning of Old Testament passages about Israel's priestly quality,[9] and it fits in with that *pars pro toto* that is found at so many stages and in the basic vocation of the people of God.

Israel's worship is a sacrificial worship, and the sacrifice generally has an expiatory value. There are also sacrifices of thanksgiving, simple offerings of first-fruits, and their value (found also in the others) is exclusively as an acknowledgement of God's sovereignty and holiness. But many of the other sacrifices which mark the personal, family and national life of the Israelites have reference to a state of sinfulness and are expiatory. The same word is used both for sin and sacrifice.[10] Israel's consciousness of having to live in holiness as a people belonging to God and bound to his service was accompanied by a very strong feeling of endless transgression and back-

[7]The fundamental text, when the covenant is made at Sinai, is Exodus xix, 3, 5–6; 'Thus shalt thou say to the house of Jacob, and tell the children of Israel: . . . If therefore you will hear my voice and keep my covenant, you shall be my peculiar possession above all people, for all the earth is mine. And you shall be to me a kingdom of priests and a consecrated nation'. The Hebrew text should be translated thus; the Greek version made at Alexandria translates as if it were a royal priesthood', which brings in a new idea and reflects an orientation to which we shall return.

[8]'Because thou art a holy people to the Lord thy God. The Lord thy God has chosen thee to be his peculiar people of all peoples that are upon the earth. . . . Keep therefore the laws and ordinances and decrees which I command thee this day to do' (Deut. vii, 6, 11; the rest of the text expresses the absolute freedom of the divine choice; cf. xiv, 2).

[9]Cf. Is. lxi, 6. Several exegetes (*e.g.*, Condamin) include this text among the Jehovah's Servant poems. The idea of Israel as God's witness to men is not common in the O.T., but it is found expressly in the Servant poems: Is. xliii,8-13; lv, 4ff. Sometimes the expression ʿ*ēd* (witness) is not used, but some such equivalent as 'servant' or 'messenger'.

[10]The verb *hatta'*: cf. *e.g.*, Ps. li, 9, 'Cleanse me with hyssop'.

sliding, of a constant need for purification and restoration of communion with her God.

Priesthood in Israel is at the same time both a collective quality and an office in which a few men are mediators for all the rest. Are we 'reconstructing' too logically if (with Westcott) we see this regime unfolding in an orderly way from the priestly dignity of all up to that of the high priest? There is first, bound up with Jehovah's covenant with the people as such, the priestly quality of the sacred totality of Israel, as expressed in the texts of Exodus and Isaias quoted above (notes 7, 9). From there, there is a sort of contraction of the priesthood of all into the person of one man, analogous to the progressive concentration of religious mankind into the Messiah (above, Chapter III, note 5). Here again there is a logic of substitution, leading from all to one and prophetically heralding the Cross on which One alone was to hang for the whole people (John xi, 50-52). Instead of the first-born, the tribe of Levi is appointed and dedicated (Numbers iii, 12); and from among this tribe Aaron and his sons are designated to properly sacrificial duties (Exodus xxix, 5-7). So the priestly quality of the whole people does not prevent there being a functional or hierarchical priesthood which God protects and surrounds with honour.[11] The Old Testament imposed the observance of this honour as much on the people as on the priests, and Jesus respected it even in the persons of those who persecuted and condemned him, whose function he was himself bringing to an end. But nothing speaks more eloquently under this head than chapters xvi-xvii of Numbers, about the rebellion of Korah, Dathan and Abiram, a rebellion against the constituted priesthood, the priesthood of office, in the name of the general priesthood: God's punishment—whose meaning is completed by the miracle of Aaron's rod—shows how jealously he watches over the order he has established among his people.

At the head of the Aaronic priesthood stood the high priest, whose office and its insignia passed from father to son (Numbers xx, 26-28). The high priest summed up the whole people in himself and represented them; everything about him expressed this representativeness, to the extent of a kind of equivalence of religious function between him and them. He carried the names of the tribes on his shoulders and breast (Exodus xxviii, 12, 29); on his forehead were words that expressed the nation's consecration: 'Holiness to the

[11] It is to be noticed that the books that affirm Israel's collective priesthood are the same books that affirm the dignity of the priesthood of office: respectively, Exod. xix, 6 and Is. lxi, 6, and Exod. xxix, 5-7 and Is. lxvi, 21. For the N.T., cf. Conclusion below.

Lord' (Exodus xxviii, 36ff.). And this in a spirit of bearing before
God both the failings of all the people and their will to expiate
them.[12] The same offering was due for the high priest's transgressions
through inadvertence as for the transgressions of all Israel (Leviticus
iv, 3, 13-14). On the Day of Atonement the high priest went alone
into God's presence to fulfil his office as representative of the whole
people in a specially clear and solemn way, to offer up the sacrifice
for sin and renew communion with God the all-holy. This has already
been referred to, and we ought here to reread together chapter xvi
of Leviticus and the Epistle to the Hebrews, particularly viii, 1 to x,
8. We are at the heart of the economy of priesthood as God prophetically established it in Israel before its fulfilment in Jesus Christ. All
these sacrifices and mediations of the Old Testament were in fact
steps towards the one and only sacrifice and the one and only
mediation of Christ.

There was still a stage to be gone through in this preparatory and
anticipatory process: that of the prophets, whose mission, here as
elsewhere, is by a sort of dialectic to forward the development of
God's purpose beyond the forms in which it is realised at a given
moment. We are thinking here of the notion of sacrifice to which, as
we shall see, that of priesthood is strictly correlative. We are confronted by two series of opposed texts. On the one hand, God says
through the mouth of his prophets that he does not desire sacrifices
and turns away from them: 'To what purpose do you offer me the
multitude of your victims? saith the Lord. I am full, I desire not
burnt-offerings of rams and fat of fatlings and blood of calves and
lambs and he-goats. . . . Who required these things at your hands? . . .
Offer sacrifice no more in vain; incense is an abomination to me.
The new moons and the sabbaths and other festivals I will not abide:
your assemblies are wicked. . . . When you stretch forth your hands,
I will turn away my eyes from you; and when you multiply prayers,
I will not hear' (Isaias i, 11-15).

But the same prophets tell us that there will still be sacrifices and
all the business of outward worship in an Israel cleansed and
renewed after the captivity. Moreover, the prophet Malachy (i, 11)
proclaims a new incense and a pure offering in contrast with the
spoiled victims offered to God by the post-exilic priests. Here, God
wishes sacrifice; there, he does not wish it. Is this a contradiction? . . .
No, not a contradiction, but a simultaneous affirmation in respect of

---

[12]'And the Lord said to Aaron: Thou and thy sons and thy father's house with
thee shall bear the iniquity of the sanctuary. And thou and thy sons with thee
shall bear the sins of your priesthood . . .' (Numbers xviii, 1).

the same thing, of a Yes and a No that express the dialectic of progress which is at the heart of the prophetic mission. The Yes and the No are concerned with the same reality; but the No is looking at an aspect of it that must be rejected and left behind, while the Yes is looking at a deeper aspect which must be proved in a new state of things. It is the prophets' business to state plainly what this dialectic conceals. God desires sacrifices, but not such as are offered in a spirit of unrighteousness; he wants mercifulness and not outward observance, inward godliness and not the equivocal carrying out of a rite. He wants, indeed, the offering, not of material things, animals and first-fruits, but of the living man himself:

> Not for thy sacrifices will I reprove thee:
>> Thy holocausts are ever before me.
> I will take no bull from out thy farm,
>> Nor he-goats from out thy folds:
> For mine are all the beasts of the forest,
>> And the cattle upon a thousand mountains:
> I know all the birds of the heavens,
>> And all that moveth in the fields is in my mind.
> If I were hungry, I would not tell thee,
>> For mine is the world and the fullness thereof.
> Am I to eat the flesh of bulls,
>> Or to drink the blood of goats?
> Nay, sacrifice a thank-offering to God,
>> And pay thy vows to the Most High . . .
>>>> (Psalm l, 8-14; Vulg. xlix)

> In sacrifice and grain-offering thou hadst no delight . . .
> For holocaust and sin-offering thou didst not ask:
>> Then said I, 'Lo, I am come.
> In the book-roll it is prescribed to me
>> That I do thy pleasure, my God . . .'
>>>> (Psalm xl, 7-9; Vulg. xxxix).

What God wants offered is nothing but the man himself: not irrational beasts but the spiritual, 'rational', worship and sacrifice of his reasoning creature, who is made that he may as a son render up again to God the Image that he bears. Wherefore does St Paul apply to Christ, and puts into his mouth, the psalm verse that has just been quoted: 'Hence he saith when entering into the world: Sacrifice and offering thou hast not desired, but a body hast thou prepared for me. In holocausts and sin-offerings thou hast taken no pleasure: then

I said: Behold, I am come . . . to do, O God, thy will' (Hebrews x, 5-9).

With the penetrating insight of genius St Augustine saw and set forth the sacrifice of Christ and of Christians in relation to the great biblical landscape just summarised. In two brilliant chapters of the *City of God*[13] he expounds sacrifice not only on the speculative or ideological plane but also in the setting of the great story of salvation, or of the whole great curve of God's design from its beginnings to its goal in the Land of the Blessed. Sacrifice, like grace itself, seems to him completely whole only if it tends towards its full and final fruit. Taking up the prophetical dialectic whereby God both desires and does not desire sacrifice, he arrives at the famous definition which Aquinas and so many others have adopted: 'True sacrifice is every work done with the aim of uniting us with God in a holy fellowship, that is to say, every work that is referred as its end to the good which can make us truly blessed'. Holding to this idea of a total Godward movement that excludes the wretchedness of being separated from him, associating with it the many biblical texts that equate true sacrifice with mercy, Augustine shows that total sacrifice is the realising of the adherence to God of the 'tota redempta civitas, hoc est congregatio societasque sanctorum'; this community of the holy people alone forms the 'universale' sacrificium [quod] offeratur Deo per sacerdotem magnum qui etiam seipsum obtulit in passione pro nobis, ut tanti capitis corpus essemus'. And so we reach this sequence of ideas: It is not a matter of external gifts (of which God does not stand in need) but of spiritual deeds which work together to draw us, us and the others, out of misery and direct us to God that we may enter into a fellowship with him which is our true bliss. And through these spiritual deeds we constitute the one and only universal city of the saints, the body on behalf of which Christ is offered up. So are we able to lay down these equivalents of the 'true' sacrifice, equivalents so sublime ideally and so concretely real—'totum sacrificium ipsi nos sumus;[14] 'hoc est sacrificium christianorum: multi unum corpus in Christo'.[15] At this point Augustine associates with the sacrificial theme, as well as the sacrifice of Christ's communal body and that of his cross, the

[13]Bk x, c. 5, 6 (PL., xli, 281-284); cf. c. 16, and St Irenaeus, *Adv. haer.*, iv, 17, 4 (PG., vii, 1023).

[14]*Civ. Dei*, x, 6; cf. x, 19 and *Sermo xix*, c. 5, n. 3 (PL., xxxviii, 133–134); *Sermo xlviii*, c. 2, n. 2 (PL., xxxviii, 317: 'Quaerebas quid offeres pro te, offer te. Quid enim Dominus quaerit a te, nisi te'); *Sermones ccxxvii, cclxxii* (PL., xxxviii, 1101, 1247).

[15]*Civ. Dei*, x, 6; a formula adopted in the middle ages: cf., *e.g.*, the gloss *in* 1 *Cor. xii*, 3 (PL., cxiv, 510d).

sacrifice of the altar, which is the 'sacrament' of our oneness in him: 'ubi ei Ecclesiae demonstratur quod in ea re quam offert, ipsa offeratur'; and all Augustine's magnificent passages on the eucharist find their place here. We cannot even touch on them, though later on we shall have to take up their essential theme, for it certainly seems that St Augustine's treatment exceedingly well expresses the workings of the designs of grace to which the Bible bears witness. There is to be found therein the movement of inwardness which has been mentioned, the referring to Jesus Christ of all that has gone before him, and the unique reality of his sacrifice—a unique reality, but such that it becomes fully ours, we enter into it and take part in it.

Yes, all sacrifice and priesthood belongs to Jesus Christ, finds its worth in him, and from him passes into participation in the Church. The value of all the Old Testament worship, and especially of its sacrifices, as types is set out in detail by the Fathers. The Bible and the Fathers declare that the *truth*, the *unique* truth, of sacrifice, altar, priesthood and temple is realised in Christ. Before him, there were *sacramenta* of him; since he came, there are participations in him which, 'taking of that which is his' (cf. John xvi, 14), reach the measure of his fullness (Ephesians iv, 13): the perfect stature of the one and only sacrifice, of the one and only temple, of the one and only priest—the body of Christ. 'Sacrifice and offering thou hast not desired, but a body thou hast prepared for me . . .', says the priestly Christ of the Epistle to the Hebrews (x, 5). St Augustine's commentary on this declaration of the finality of the Incarnation perhaps goes beyond a strict exegesis of the text, but it expresses its full theological meaning: the body God has fashioned is at the same time Christ's personal body, his fellowship-body—the body of which we are the members—and, making a living bond between these two, his sacramental body.[16] Christ's body is complete only when considered in these three states dynamically linked with one another;[17] but considered in the fullness of its principle, the Alpha of Christ offered up on the cross to the Omega of the 'whole Christ', *unus Christus amans Patrem*, this body is at the same time the one true

[16]Cf. *Enarr. in Ps. xxxix*, n. 12, 13 (PL., xxxvi, 442: 'in hoc corpore sumus, hujus corporis participes sumus, quod accipimus novimus. . . . Perfectum est nobis corpus, perficiamur in corpore. . .'). Doubtless it would not be difficult to justify this commentary exegetically by a study of the word σῶμα in the N.T.: Christ's *immolated* body (on the cross and in the eucharist) and the body-temple or sanctuary, which is the Church; cf. C.F.D. Moule, 'Sanctuary and Sacrifice in the Church of the N.T.' in *Journal of Theol. Studies*, 1950, pp. 29–41: cf. pp. 31–32.

[17]The aim of Father de Lubac's wise and enlightening book, *Corpus mysticum* (Paris, 1949), is to restore the meaning of this linking-up in prescholastic theology.

temple, the one true sacrifice, the one true priest. Putting aside the
temple aspect for the present, there is nothing more strongly
emphasised in the Bible than the unique reality and definitive work
of Christ's priesthood and of his redemptive sacrifice for sin. The
Epistle to the Hebrews connects this affirmation with the fact that
it is a question of acquiring the benefits of the new and final covenant,
good things that are nothing less than heavenly, eternal, properly
divine. Among such goods, communion in the divine life itself, can
result only from a relationship wherein the Son of God made man
is both priest and victim: a wholly spiritual victim (and, in this
sense, 'made sin for us'[18]), consisting not in the substitution of human
flesh or life for those of an animal, but in giving to God the living
person himself, a Son entirely dedicated to doing his Father's will.[19]
Of this sacrifice which makes his temple—or at least opens the way
into it—Jesus is the sole sufficient priest: priest by virtue of God's
oath and will, but priest also as God-man, whereby he is essentially
a mediator, uniting in himself both parties to the covenant, God and
man.

The Bible and the Apostolic Fathers bear explicit witness to the
oneness (*unicite*) of Christ's priesthood and, more relatively, of his
sacrifice. There is and there can be no argument about this matter.
Yet the texts apply priestly terms to Christians and to the Church as
well. There is of course nothing contradictory about that: there is
only one Christ, there are many Christians. It is precisely God's
purpose that many should have part in Christ and that, being persons, they should freely and really co-operate in such participation.
We must look at these things more closely from the point of view of
the subject of this chapter.

SCRIPTURAL AND PATRISTIC DATA ON THE CHRISTIAN SYSTEM OF PRIESTHOOD

Perhaps the question will seem simple when it is answered, but it
does not look like that at the beginning if we consider all its data
seriously, as we must. And so we have to look first at what we are

[18]2 Cor. v, 21. Cf. above, n. 10. Christ is made 'sin' because he is made the
sacrifice and propitiation for sin. This seems to us the only interpretation which
allows of agreement between 2 Cor. v, 21 and Heb. iv, 15, ix, 28, and it is that of
St Augustine: cf. *Sermo clii*, n. 10–11 (PL., xxxviii, 824–825), *Sermo clv*, n. 8 (PL.,
xxxviii, 845), *Tract. xli in Joan.*, n. 5 (PL., xxxv, 1695), *De Trin.*, bk iv, c. 13, n. 17
(PL., xlii, 899), *Enchir.*, c. 41 (PL., xl, 253), *De pecc. orig.*, c. 32 (PL., xliv, 403).
[19]In Kittel's *Worterbuch*, vol. iii, p. 281, Schrenk rightly remarks that the statements about Christ's offering of *himself* (Heb. vii, 27; ix, 12, 25, 28) must be understood in the light of Heb. x, 5ff., quoting Ps. xl, 7ff., where the Hebrew has 'You
have pierced my ears', the mark of a servant's dependence (cf. Exod. xxi, 5) and
symbol of the obedience clearly stated in verse 9.

told in the Bible and by Tradition. The matter cannot be dealt with in a few lines, even if we keep to the point and consider conclusions rather than make researches, but the task is made much easier by a considerable number of monographs and studies.

The New Testament texts are easily got at, but their import must be kept well in mind. They apply the terms 'priest' and 'priesthood' to Christ (Hebrews: cf. above) and also to Christians as such. The passages concerning these last are as follows:

And drawing nigh unto him, the living stone, rejected by men but with God chosen and honourable, yourselves also as living stones be ye built up into a spiritual house, to be a holy priesthood, to offer spiritual sacrifices well-pleasing to God through Jesus Christ. . . . But ye are a chosen race, a royal priesthood, a holy nation, God's own people, that ye may proclaim the perfections of him who hath called you out of darkness into his wondrous light; yet who were once not his people but now are the people of God, who once had not found mercy but now have found it (1 Peter ii, 4-5, 9-10. Perhaps it is allowable here to invoke Luke i, 75: λατρεύειν αὐτῷ?)

To him who loveth us and hath loosed us from our sins in his blood, and made us to be a kingdom, priests to God and his Father—to him be the glory and the might for ever and ever: Amen! (Apocalypse i, 5-6. Or 'made us a royal race of priests to . . .').

Worthy art thou to take the volume and to open its seals, for thou wast slain, and didst redeem to God through thy blood men from every tribe and tongue and people and nation, and hast made them a kingdom and priests to our God, and they shall reign upon the earth! (Apocalypse v, 9-10; same alternative).

Blessed and holy is he that hath part in the first resurrection! Over these the second death hath no power, but they shall be priests of God and of Christ, and they shall reign with him for a thousand years (Apocalypse xx, 6; see also xxii, 3-5).

We shall see in the sequel that to these texts must be added, as well as several passages from the Epistle to the Hebrews, those verses of St Paul wherein expressions pertinent to worship are stressed, but not the words priest or priesthood:

. . . through him *we have access* in one Spirit to the Father. Therefore ye are no longer strangers and foreigners, but ye are fellow-citizens of the saints and members of the household of God: ye are built upon the foundation of the apostles and prophets: Christ

Jesus himself is the corner-stone. In him the whole building is duly
fitted together and groweth into *a temple holy* in the Lord; in him
ye also are being built together unto a spiritual *dwelling-place of God*
(Ephesians ii, 18-22).

For we are the circumcision, who *worship* by the Spirit of God . . .
(Philippians iii, 3. Another reading is 'serve God in the spirit'.)

I exhort you, therefore, brethren, by the compassion of God, to
present your bodies a *sacrifice*, living, holy, well-pleasing to God,
your *spiritual service* (Romans xii, 1; cf. vi, 13).

Through him, therefore, let us at all times *offer sacrifice of praise*
to God, that is, the fruit of lips that praise his name. And forget
not kindness and fellowship, for in such *sacrifices* God taketh
pleasure (Hebrews xiii, 15-16).

There are several points to notice about these texts.

(1) The joining and combination of the theme of priesthood with
that of temple. To be a holy priesthood, to make spiritual offerings,
is equivalent to building the sanctuary wherein God dwells and is
honoured. This is formally expressed only in 1 Peter, but it is implicit
in Ephesians, through the 'cultural' character of the words 'have
access', and it is to be found in the general sense of Hebrews. There is
nothing surprising in this: with reference to Christ we have already met
this bond between sacrifice and temple, united in the idea of body.

(2) The kingly and the priestly qualities are joined in those
passages of the New Testament that speak expressly of the priesthood
of Christians. In 1 Peter this is clearly in dependence on Exodus xix,
6 as it appears in the Septuagint; in the Apocalypse the kingship of
the faithful has an eschatological flavour (even 'millenarist'—but
there is no need to go into that here).

(3) The priesthood of Christians is evidently 'spiritual'. But the
word must be properly understood, for it could be as misleading
here as in the matter of what is sometimes called spiritual exegesis.
Some people read the passages about the priesthood of the faithful
with a background of the levitical or Judaic priesthood and of the
'spiritual' interpretation given to it at Alexandria (Philo), in a context of the spiritualising process in worship which in the apostolic
age was at work not only in Judaism but in paganism as well:
Christians, then, would be priests 'spiritually', that is, in the moral
sense. We shall come back to this point when we consider the reality
of the priesthood of the faithful and what it means. Meanwhile we
will only say that, using the same word and with a certain material
likeness, this interpretation differs from that which we are adopting

here. The general process of Revelation, as shown forth by the prophets and formulated by a St Augustine, is that of a thing outlined at first which moves on to its full realisation, which is spiritual: that is, inward to man himself, the work of the Holy Spirit in him. When the Christian regime of temple, sacrifice and priesthood is reached it is not the interpretation alone that becomes spiritual, it is the reality. That is why the way the New Testament and the Fathers, even Origen, speak of the spiritual nature of Christian worship is altogether different from the way a Philo speaks of it.[20] The 'spiritual' of Christian worship is not formally an idealisation, a 'moral' transposition, of Judaic worship: it is the *reality* of which Judaic worship was the herald. Therefore do we characterise the corresponding priesthood by the words 'spiritual real'.

That much said, we can tackle the content of the passages of the New Testament, and of the Fathers who bear witness to the Tradition, touching first the priesthood of the faithful and then the priesthood of the hierarchical ministers. For the moment we consider them simply as statements; later we will try to justify them, to expound them intellectually, and in so doing to arrive at their meaning.

(A) *The Priesthood of the Faithful*

A verbal study is not a sufficient guide to the Church's faith: the Christian reality handed on in the Church as the full content of her *traditio* goes beyond what is stated in the texts and is not necessarily limited by their silence. Nevertheless these texts, principally and as a norm those of Holy Writ, are the record of that tradition, and for its understanding a careful study of the content and expression of the texts is of the utmost value.

Here a very important observation must be made.[21] In the New Testament and the writings of the Apostolic and Subapostolic Fathers the words ἱερεύς and ἀρχιερεύς are used to denote the priests of the levitical priesthood (or in quoting the Old Testament) and also pagan priests; in the Christian context these words are applied only to Christ on the one hand and to all the faithful on the other. With one exception,[22] they do not use these names of the

[20]St Ambrose wrote that 'His Judaic mind prevented Philo from grasping spiritual things and he kept to the moral sense' (*De paradiso*, iv, 25: quoted by J. Daniélou, *Sacromentum futuri* . . ., p. 45). For Origen, cf. H. de Lubac, *Esprit et histoire* . . . (Paris, 1950), pp. 150-166, 267-270.

[21]For what follows we turn, and shall return, to 'Un essai théologique sur le sacerdoce catholique: La thèse de l'abbé Long-Hasselmans: Texte et remarques critiques' in *Revue des sciences relig.*, 25 (1951) pp. 187-199, 288-304.

[22]St Clement, *Cor.*, xl, 5. The abbé Long lessens the significance of this text when, arguing from the Jewish context, he stresses the language of accommodation, moralistic aims and the unusualness of such usage even in Clement.

ministers whom we call 'priests', a word that signifies simply 'elders'. In this connexion the Reformers and Protestant controversialists used a handle against certain Catholic apologists—and philologically we cannot say they were wrong—when they proposed to render πρεσβύτερος by 'elder' and ἱερεύς by 'sacrificer'. In the New Testament, and by Christian writers to the end of the second century, ministers are called by the name of the *function* for which they have been 'ordained': bishops (superintendents), presbyters (elders, advisers), deacons (ministers), higumens (heads), presidents. But the names denoting *sacerdotal rank*, ἱερεύς and ἀρχιερεύς, are reserved for Christ on one side, to Christians (the faithful) on the other; and in such a way that it cannot be overlooked that the usage was intentional.

Examination of the use of the word θυσιαστήριον, altar, leads to analogous conclusions. The altar is Christ, or the community of the faithful, or an individual member thereof; down to St Irenaeus the application of the word θυσιαστήριον to the table of liturgical celebration was exceptional (*e.g.*, St Ignatius, *To the Philadelphians*, iv).

Leaving aside for the moment the problem that the priesthood of the ministers is not *expressly and directly* spoken of in the New Testament, we have this fundamental statement that there is a spiritual and real—real because spiritual—sacerdotal quality which, belonging properly to Christ, is communicated to all the members of his body (by baptism; cf. Hebrews x, 22). Here we have a far-reaching characteristic of the structure of the divine economy: what is given to one alone of behalf of all is then extended and communicated to all; what has been done by one alone on behalf of all must still be, in a way, done by all. Christ is Son, and as such, heir: we become *filii in Filio* and *cohaeredes Christi*. Christ alone is temple: the faithful are temples with him. Christ alone is priest: the faithful are priests with him. This is the place for those passages from the Epistle to the Hebrews referred to but not quoted above.

Now to crown what we have said: Such a High Priest we have, who hath taken his seat at the right hand of the throne of Majesty in heaven as priestly servant ['liturgiser'] of the sanctuary, and of the true tabernacle, which the Lord, and not man, hath set up (viii, 1-2).

As Westcott observes, these verses give the foundation for Apocalypse iii, 21: it is because we have a High Priest who fulfils his office with kingly eminence in Heaven that we ourselves are kings and priests.

Since, then, we have a great High Priest who hath passed through the heavens, Jesus the Son of God, let us hold firmly to what we confess. For we have not a high priest who is unable to realise in himself our weaknesses, but rather one who hath been tried in every way like ourselves, short of sin. Let us, therefore, *approach* with confidence to the throne of grace . . . (iv, 14-16).

On the one hand there is here a rejection of an earlier command . . . for indeed the law brought nothing to *perfection* . . . on the other hand it is the introduction of a better hope, through which we *draw nigh* unto God (vii, 18-19).

Since, therefore, brethren, we have full freedom *to enter the sanctuary* in virtue of the blood of Jesus, a new and living way which he hath inaugurated for us through the veil, that is to say, his flesh, and since we have a great High Priest over the house of God, let us *come forward* with a true heart in full assurance of faith, purified through the besprinkling of our heart from an evil conscience, and with body cleansed in pure water (x, 19-22).

We have stressed the expressions that are pertinent to public worship, 'draw nigh', 'approach'. Under the old dispensation only a few drew near to God, or at least to his sanctuary; and only the high priest, once a year, had access to the Holy of Holies. Jesus has not only gone into the true Holy of Holies, the temple not made with hands, but he has opened it to us and allows us to go in with him, freely and confidently. The last text quoted alludes to the washing at the consecration of Aaron and his sons (Leviticus viii, 6) and on the day of Atonement (Leviticus xvi, 4), washing that for us is baptism, which allows us just as we are to enter into the true Holy of Holies with our high priest. It could not be made plainer that we are all priests in the one high priest, Jesus Christ.

And what is the worship that goes with this priesthood? Our texts do not say much about this, but they are quite clear and unambiguous: we need only read over those that we have transcribed. In addition to the biblical ones there are those of the Fathers, the liturgies and the theologians, now easy to get at thanks to the nearly complete collection made by Father Paul Dabin, s.j.[23] For the moment we will inquire of this material only to what order the wor-

[23]See Chapter III, note 2. There is also a good collection of patristic and scholastic testimony in E. Niebecker, *Das allgemeine Priestertum der Glaubigen* (Paderborn, 1936); and see J. Lecuyer, 'Essai sur le sacerdoce des fidèles chez les Pères' in *Le Maison Dieu*, 27 (1951-53), pp. 7-50, which contains some new texts suggestively arranged.

ship, and so the priesthood, of the faithful corresponds; in the second
part of this chapter we will examine what the acts of this worship
and this priesthood represent in the concrete.

We read of a spiritual ('pneumatic') worship, of spiritual sacrifices
acceptable to God (Romans xii, 1; Philippians iii, 3; 1 Peter ii, 5),
of living, holy offerings (Romans); concretely, of a sacrifice of praise,
the tribute of lips (Hebrews xiii, 15), of confession of faith (1 Peter)
and of works of mercy, as the prophets of Israel spoke: charity,
generosity, alms-deeds,[24] and *the* work of spiritual mercy—teaching,
the handing-on of saving truth by word of mouth.[25] St Paul uses
very strong 'cultual' expressions about the ministry of the gospel that
he exercised: not only *diakonia* but 'liturgiser', sacrificing, oblation
(Romans xv, 16, 31). Service has passed from an offering-up of
things in a material temple into the building-up of a spiritual temple
in the faith of the *fideles*, wherein the living man himself freely offers
himself in sacrifice. Nowhere in the New Testament is there any
express reference to the worship and priesthood of the faithful in the
eucharist or even in the sacraments (except for what has been said
above about baptism), or in the Church's public worship.[26]

A conclusion emerging from all this is that the worship and sacrifice of the faithful, and therefore their corresponding priesthood, are
essentially those of a holy life, an apostolic life of religion, prayer,
dedication, charity, compassion. This worship, these sacrifices, the
corresponding priesthood are not thought of at a properly liturgical
or sacramental level—at the most that aspect of things is only implicit in the texts. The offering and priesthood of the faithful are
spiritual. But this epithet must be understood in its biblical sense, and
not as equivalent to metaphorical or simply moral: we have said,

[24]Heb. xiii, 16; cf. Hosea vi, 6, xiv, 3, and Chrysostom on the 'altar of alms' and
'the poor' (*In* 2 *Cor.*, hom. 20: PG., lxi, 540). On spiritual sacrifice, see O. Casel,
'Oblatio rationabilis' in *Theol. Quartalsch.*, 99 (1917–18), pp. 429–439; 'Die λογική
θυσία in *Jahrb. f. Liturgiewiss.*, 4 (1924), pp. 37–47; *Le memorial du Seigneur . . .*
(Paris, 1945), pp. 31, 57.

[25]Cf. 1 Peter ii, 9 and, because of what goes before, Heb. x, 24. Chrysostom calls
exercise of the ministry of the word 'the greatest and noblest of sacrifices' (*Sermo
cum presb. factus fuerit*: PG., xlviii, 694).

[26]We say an *express* reference. It seems difficult not to see an implicit reference in
Heb. xiii, 10 (followed at once by a passage about the spiritual priesthood of the
faithful), and also in Heb. x, 19–22: when we consider the 'cultual' sense of 'draw
near' and what we know of the eucharistic celebration at the dawn of every
'Sunday' at least, in memory of the Lord's resurrection, it would appear that there
is here a reference to the cultual—sacramental—participation of the faithful in the
one sacrifice of Christ who is the high priest of our offerings, now gone into the
heavenly sanctuary for ever. Cf. also 1 Cor. x, 17–22; Heb. vi, 4). – The eucharistic
reference of the priesthood of the faithful is found explicit in Justin, *Dial.*, cxvi,
3-cxvii; for the theology, see below.

and we say it again, that the priesthood of the faithful ought much
rather to be called 'spiritual real'. But it does not belong to the order
of the celebration of the Church's public or sacramental worship:
no ancient text (except perhaps in Tertullian after he had become a
Montanist) supports a transference of the worship and priesthood of
the faithful from the place of Christian life to that of liturgical celebration. When we say that, we do not at all mean to deny any
relationship between the priesthood of the faithful and the Church's
liturgical life, especially with the offering of the eucharist; such a
relationship was to become more explicit, notably in our own time,
without yet being perfectly clear, and we shall have to return to it.
But if we keep to the New Testament and originating texts we have
to recognise that the worship and priesthood of the faithful belong
to the order of Christian life and cannot be *defined* as properly
liturgical things. In so far as the question of the priesthood of the
faithful was afterwards considered in relation to properly sacramental worship, and especially to the eucharistic celebration, people
were led to stress its reference and organic subordination to the
hierarchical and properly liturgical priesthood if the bounds of
Catholic truth were to be observed. This was done by the Catholic
apologists who opposed Luther, by certain promoters of the liturgical movement, and by those who, combating certain marginal
exaggerations, went so far as to define the priesthood of the faithful
by its relationship and subordination to the hierarchical priesthood
—a rather surprising attitude when compared with that of the New
Testament: but it is explained by the necessity of keeping within
orthodox bounds an idea that was straying from its true order of
reality.[27] Others, however,[28] have joined with the present writer in
carefully maintaining the definition of this idea in its own order, that
of the acts of a holy, Christian life.[29]

[27]Against Luther: Cajetan in part, Catharinus (Dabin, p. 344), Cornelius a
Lapide a little (*id.*, p. 402) and Father de Clorivière (*id.*, p. 455). See also A.
Robeyns in *La particip. active des fideles* (Louvain, 1934), p. 51. – Promoters of active
participation: J. Casper, *Berufung Eine Laienpastoral* ... (Paderborn, 1940), pp. 83ff.;
J. E. Rea, *The Common Priesthood* ... (Westminster, Md., 1947), especially pp. 222ff.
– Against exaggerations: Mgr Grober in his report of January 1943 (text in *La
penséé cath.*, 15 (1948), p. 66), who quotes Palmieri in the same sense (*Tract. de Rom.
Pont.*, p. 71): 'Est enim Ecclesia regale et sanctum sacerdotium quia est regnum
quod a sacerdotibus regiture, quodque ad cultum divinum per actus hierarchicos
speciatim exhibendum ordinatur.' It is not easy to see how such words agree with
those of the New Testament.
[28]Particularly B. Capelle, B. Botte, L. Charlier, A. Robeyns, *op. cit.*
[29]In the name of tradition we have always emphasised that the priesthood of the
faithful is not to be *defined* by a relationship with the eucharist. See, *e.g.*, our
theological bulletins in *Revue des sc. philos. et theol.*, 1934, p. 685; 1936, p. 758; 1937,
p. 789; 1949, p. 459.

Tradition is solid and continuous in this sense, from the Apostolic Fathers[30] and Apologists to those of the classical age, from these to the high middle ages,[31] from the earliest scholastics to those of the great epoch. It is not possible to reproduce even the chief items of this evidence here. There is no doubt at all that the priesthood of the faithful corresponds to the spiritual worship that the offering of a good life is; and we are often told that every righteous person is a priest, or that one is a priest by faith and charity, by belonging to Christ's mystical body.[32] In short, we are in the climate of that great Augustinian conception already invoked: that the priesthood and sacrifice of the faithful consist in self being ordered to God. It causes no surprise to find that the offering-up of life itself, the supreme confession of faith made by martyrs, has often been specially instanced as a Christian priestly act; and this not only in the era of the persecutions but in the patristic age, in the liturgies, and by theologians down to our own day. Nor would it be difficult to illustrate this special regard for martyrdom by apostolic texts.[33]

* * *

We should however be mistaken and we should be impoverishing Christian tradition were we to confine ourselves to the rather elementary proposition that the spiritual priesthood of the faithful consists in the offering or the reference of our Christian life to God; and still more so if we limited Christian priesthood to that.

[30]Their idea of spiritual sacrifices agrees perfectly with that of the N.T. But in fact there is not much about it in the Apostolic Fathers and before the middle of the second century.

[31]Cf. F. Holbock *Der eucharistische und der mystiche Leib Christi* . . . (Rome, 1941), pp. 227ff. After an exhaustive inquiry over the period from Berengarius to Innocent III the author concludes that the active participation of the faithful in the eucharist was put into relation, not with the royal priesthood, but with the fact of incorporation in Christ and of making a unity with all the faithful in him. – See in Dabin the texts of Ambrose Autpert (pp. 157ff.), Berangaud (p. 175), St Bruno (p. 211), Raoul Ardent (p. 213), and others.

[32]Whence St Irenaeus's famous declaration: 'Omnes enim justi sacerdotalem habent ordinem . . .' (*Adv. haer.*, iv, 8, 3; PG., vii, 995. He is speaking of David eating the shew-bread). Cf. *Opus imperf. in Matt* (Dabin, p. 549), and the Decree of Gratian (*id.*, p. 550). St Thomas attaches the priesthood of the faithful to that anointing which is the grace of the Holy Spirit (*Com. in 2 Cor.*, i, lect. 5), or to union with Christ by faith and charity (*Sum. theol.*, III, q. 82, a. 1, ad 2). Like Augustine, Prosper of Aquitaine, Bede and Amalarius before him, he sees it as a consequence of belonging to the Mystical Body (*De reg. princ.*, i, 14). – It is unquestionable that this application of the priestly idea to Christian life materially covers the field of a moral priesthood; the Fathers sometimes speak of priesthood in a purely metaphorical and moral sense, *a propos*, for example, virtues or virtuous dispositions: thus Irenaeus, *loc. cit.*, and St Leo (Dabin, pp. 126ff.).

[33]*E.g.*, Phil., ii, 17; iv, 18. The sacrificial aspect of martyrdom is found, in the very words used, in Ignatius, *Rom.*, and in the *Mart. Polyc.*, xiv, 1.

The fact of the matter is that the priesthood of the faithful is a reality so rich in content that no single aspect or statement exhausts it. We see this clearly when we read one of those fairly detailed formulations made for scientific or pedagogical purposes at various moments in the development of the tradition: for instance, the writer we call Honorius of Autun (Dabin, pp. 247ff.) at the dawn of scholasticism, or Salmeron (Dabin, pp. 367ff.) just after the Protestant Reformation, or that very instructive document called the Catechism of the Council of Trent (Dabin, pp. 355ff.). In writings such as these we find the data of the tradition that are held and developed in the Church's life; and it is these that Father Dabin, after exploring the records and evidence of the tradition, seeks to systematise and interpret in all their richness and complexity. There is a moral priesthood, which consists in living and doing with a priestly soul, in a spirit of religion; there is a real but wholly inward and spiritual priesthood, that of prayer and ascetical life; there is a priesthood with a sacramental reference and import, associated not only with righteous life but with baptismal consecration, and whose supreme activity is participation in the eucharistic offering. All these are authentic aspects of the tradition's deposit.

The last of them did not become clear all at once, and perhaps has not even yet found a perfect expression in the Church's consciousness.[34] From the beginning, in the apostolic texts themselves (cf. above, with reference to Hebrews x, 19-22; and cf. Galatians iii, 27), the origin of the priesthood of the faithful is referred to baptism. Liturgically, this is made clear by a rite. It was necessary to express participation in and conformity with the Messias, the Christ, whom God anointed to his threefold office of king, priest and prophet, and it was natural that this should be done liturgically by an anointing. Anyone who was not anointed was hardly looked on as a Christian by the Christianity of ancient and patristic times (which was a liturgical Christianity);[35] and in the Fathers and in many liturgies the kingly and priestly quality of the faithful Christian is connected with an anointing, just as Christ, fulfilling the Old Testament types, was made priest and king by the anointing of the Holy Spirit. The

[34]Several excellent monographs have recently examined this question of the relationship of the priesthood of the faithful with the eucharist: A. F. Krueger, *Synthesis of Sacrifice* . . . (Mundelein, 1950), J. E. Rea, *The Common Priesthood* . . . (Westminster, Md., 1947), etc.

[35]See, for example, Tertullian, *De bapt.*, 7; St Cyril of Jer. (?), *Cat. myst.*, iii, 1-5 (PG., xxxiii, 1088ff.); St Augustine, *Enarr. in Ps. civ*, n. 10 (PL., xxxvii, 1395); *Quaest. evang.*, 2, 40 (PL., xxxv, 1355); *Civ. Dei*, xx, 10 (PL., xli, 676). And cf. P. Galtier in *Revue asc. et myst.*, 4 (1923), pp. 1-12. The idea was often referred to in the middle ages, e.g., by Agobard, *Lib. adv. Fredegisum*, nn. 19, 20 (PL., civ, 171).

evidential texts are very numerous, but they vary somewhat.[36] Some, following Origen, connect the kingly priesthood with confirmation; others speak of baptism without being more explicit; others again refer to the anointing in the baptismal rite; yet others—the most numerous and weighty—associate the priesthood of the faithful with a post-baptismal anointing, but in the later references it is difficult to tell whether this refers to the baptismal rite or to confirmation.

No doubt this diversity accounts for the lack of unanimity among modern theologians as to which liturgical action is associated with the priestly consecration of the faithful. It seems to us difficult to dissociate it from baptism on any showing. The exact ritual moment in baptism is surely of secondary importance from a doctrinal point of view:[37] this is a matter of the liturgical expression of one of the effects of the sacrament. The rites of ordination, for example, detail different aspects of a single thing by giving each its own dramatic expression, but that does not mean that the sacramental act itself has to be distributed and divided among these separate moments.[38] There is no need to look for an exactness in which it would be difficult not to be arbitrary: it is enough for us that the priesthood of the faithful is connected in the first place and principally with the baptismal consecration.

It is worth nothing that St Augustine expressed himself plainly and fully on this point. Unquestionably he evolved a deeply spiritual and personalist meaning in Christianity and handed it on to the Western middle ages. Equally unquestionably he brought the priesthood of the faithful strongly into relationship with their character as

[36]See in Dabin the passages of Tertullian (p. 70), St Ambrose (pp. 77–78), Prudentius (p. 80), Rufinus of Aquileia (p. 81), St Jerome, who calls baptism 'sacerdotium laici' in *Adv. Lucif.*, 4 (p. 83), Fastidius (p. 87), St Augustine (pp. 94, 98–99), St Maximus of Turin (p. 128), John the Deacon (p. 131), St Isidore and St Ildephonsus (pp. 145ff.), Amalarius (p. 178), Ratramnus (p. 187), Innocent III (p. 282), William of Auxerre (p. 291), etc.; and the liturgical texts on pp. 601ff., to say nothing of modern theologians. Father Dabin sketches a systematic classification on pp. 44ff., but surely a liturgico-historical classification would have been better.

[37]Here I am in agreement with E. Niebecker, *Das allg. Priestertum* . . . p. 97. Some contemporary theologians link the priestly quality of the faithful with baptism (so D. Winzen in the treatise on the sacraments of the 'Thomas Ausgabe', vol. xxix, pp. 534ff.); others with confirmation (the tendency of M. Laros, *Pfingstgeist über uns*, Regensburg, 1934). E. Scheller, *Das Priestertum Christi* . . ., pp. 412–415, sees the priesthood of the faithful conferred *in actu primo* at baptism, *in actu secundo* at confirmation.

[38]This consideration has often been applied to the question of the epiklesis in the eucharistic rite: see, *e.g.*, Bossuet, *Explication de quelques difficultés sur les prières de la messe*, § §xlv–xlvi.

members of Christ,[39] and this character with the life of grace, of faith and of charity (Cf. St Thomas, *Sum. Theol.*, III, q. 8, a. 3). So then, since the faithful become priests through their incorporation in Christ, is not their spiritual priesthood to be quite simply identified with sanctifying grace? Looked at this way, 'our priesthood adds nothing effectively to our state as children of God or to the reality of our divine life'.[40] The consequences of this would be important: in particular, we should be able to speak of a spiritual priesthood for the heathen who are justified by good faith, which would seem to accord with 1 Peter. There are some who believe that Augustine himself admitted this conclusion, and it is possible that he did.[41]

It must however be remembered that Augustine expressly associates the priestly quality of the faithful with the sacrament of baptism,[42] more particularly with the anointing.[43] This is important. It shows that Augustine's theological synthesis, centred in the *Christus totus*, is profoundly sacramental, as will be still more apparent when we see what a strong eucharistic sacramental reference he gives to the spiritual sacrifice of the Mystical Body. But it also evinces what may be called the dualism, even ambiguity, of Augustinian ecclesiology, which developed historically along two lines that were not always successfully harmonised; harmonisation indeed was not even always attempted. One line is concerned above all with inward spiritual reality, and as touching our question can be followed up in St

[39]'Sicut omnes christos dicimus propter mysticum chrisma, sic omnes sacerdotes, quoniam membra sunt unius sacerdotis' (*Civ. Dei.* xx, 10; cf. St Thomas, *De reg. princ.*, i, 14.

[40]P. Glorieux, *Dans le Prêtre unique* (Paris, 1938), p. 46. Father Glorieux himself goes further than this quality of child of God by grace, but he does not show that Augustine did so.

[41]See, *e.g.*, Dabin (p. 100): 'Even without anointing and outward rites indicating union with the visible Church, there is an invisible royal priesthood constituted by all souls of good will who have desired Christ, whether before or after his coming...' The text of St Augustine that Father Dabin glosses thus (*Enarr. in Ps. cxviii*, sermo 20, 1: PL., xxxvii, 1557) seems to us to envisage only the justified of the O.T. Still, Augustine's very strong spiritualist and personalist feeling, together with his spiritual conception of history, disinclined him to emphasise the newness of the Christian regime in successive time (cf. our study 'Ecclesia ab Abel' in the *Festschrift K. Adam*). This is also a particular application of the question of Augustine's thought on salvation outside visible membership of the Church. On this, see J. Mausbach, *Die Ethik des h. Augustinus*, vol. ii (1929), pp. 300–329; and cf. G. Spanedda, *Il mistero della Chiesa nel pensiero S. Agostino* (Sassari, 1944); and C. Romeis, *Das Heil der Christen* ... (Paderborn, 1908).

[42]Cf. *Quaest. in Evang.*, ii, q. 48 (PL., xxxv, 1356).

[43]*Enarr. in Ps. xxvi*, ii, n. 2 (PL., xxxvi, 199–200); *Quaest. in Evang.*, ii, q. 40 (PL., xxxv, 1355); cf. Dabin, pp. 98–99, and Krueger, *Synthesis of Sacrifice* ... pp. 118–119, 157.

Gregory, St Prosper of Aquitaine, St Bede and Amalarius;[44] later on
it inspired some far less Catholic thought. The other line is concerned
above all with the earthly mechanism of ecclesial and sacramental
things, and one of its ripe fruits was seen in the theocratic ideologies
of the Middle Ages. We may borrow terms from Augustine himself
and call these 'lines' the ecclesiology of *res* and the ecclesiology of
sacramentum.

The idea of the sacramental characters as participations in the
priesthood of Christ proposed by St Thomas in his *Summa Theologiae*
is a fine fruit—late in time, alas! and almost unique—of St Augustine
as theologian of the sacraments and ecclesiologist of the *sacramentum*.
The idea has become so much a part of theology, particularly in
modern times, that it is looked on as if it were received from tradition
and almost a part of the common teaching.[45] St Thomas recognised
spiritual priesthood in the wholly inward sense of the offering of
spiritual sacrifices, a priesthood which has no explicit relation to the
sacramental or liturgical order; and it is to that, and that alone, that
he refers the well-known biblical texts, Psalm li, 19, Romans xii, 1,
1 Peter ii, 5, Apocalypse v, 1.[46] But he does not stop there: he also
recognises another title to priesthood in the baptised person, namely,
his baptismal character: he does not invoke the biblical texts cited
above, but he declares that this character is a participation in

[44] I do not know whether the fact that some more recent theologians have conceived the kingly priesthood solely as the life of grace must be attributed to a
special influence from St Augustine: thus N. Ysambert, who died in 1642 (Dabin,
p. 411).

[45] The texts are in *Sum. theol.*, III, q. 63, a. 2–6. There are several works on this
point, but none of them completely satisfying as historical disquisition or speculative
commentary. Dominic Soto's strikes us as the best commentary. Among modern
works, see F. Brommer, *Die Lehre vom sakramentalen Charakter* . . . (Paderborn, 1908);
C. V. Héris, *Le mystère du Christ* (Paris, 1928), pp. 259ff.; L. Audet, 'Notre participation au sacerdoce du Christ' in *Laval théologique*, 2 (1946), pp. 110–130; J. E. Rea,
The Common Priesthood, pp. 172–201. – Father J. Lécuyer (*art. cit.*, n. 23) shows how
St Thomas's idea of a participation (unequal, analogical) in Christ's priesthood in
baptism, confirmation and order has a solid basis in patristic tradition, itself interpreting biblical facts or texts. – What we have said above about the value of
St Thomas's idea as quasi-common teaching is based on its very frequent use by
contemporary theologians and on several passages in papal encyclicals (cf. Pius XII
in '*Mediator Dei*'; and see Suhard in *Le prêtre dans la Cité*, p. 14). Many theologians
of our day do not hesitate to refer to it as common teaching: *e.g.*, E. Puzik in the
collection *Amt und Sendung* (Freiburg i. B., 1950), p. 41; H. F. Davis, 'The Priesthood of the Faithful' in the *Downside Review*, 69 (1951), pp. 155–170, cf. p. 164. But
we must not exaggerate, and especially we must not turn this *theological* notion into
a *dogmatic* datum. The dogmatic position on this matter of character lacks clarity:
cf. K. Adam in *Theolog. Quartalsch.*, 1941, pp. 161ff. (criticising M. D. Koster's
maximising in *Ekklesiologie im Werden*); and H. Lennerz, *De sacramentis in genere*
(Rome, 1950), nn. 338, 29.

[46] See *IV Sent.*, d. 13, q. 1, a. 1, qa 1, ad 1; *Sum. theol.*, III, q. 82, a. 1, ad 2; *Com.
in 2 Cor.*, c. 1, lect. 5. Cf. L. Charlier, *op. cit.*, pp. 30ff.

Christ's priesthood. That is his own contribution, and we must try to fathom its meaning.

* * *

The idea of the *Summa Theologiae* is man's return to God from whom he comes. There is therefore a sort of coincidence of matter or content between man's spiritual doing, minutely analysed in the Second part, and the 'sacrifice' described by St Augustine (and by St Thomas),[47] 'every thing done in order to realise our communion with God'. The moral life—more widely the whole spiritual life— is thus able to rank as spiritual worship—but more of that later. But when in his Third part St Thomas has considered Christ, who through all he did and suffered is the way by which we return to God,[48] he faces the properly and specifically Christian aspect and reality of this return. It is not simply a matter of Christ's faithful offering up the spiritual worship of a righteous life to the God of the wise and learned; or even of offering up the spiritual worship of Jesus Christ to the God of Jesus Christ. What has happened is that Jesus 'has ushered in the worship or rite of the Christian religion by offering himself up as an oblation and sacrifice to God'.[49] I think that these careful words are something other and more than a simple statement of the beginning of the Church or of the New Covenant on Calvary; they bear on the content and character of the new, Christian worship, and the important word is *seipsum*, 'offering up *himself*'. Instead of legal worship, the sacrifice of animals and of first-fruits, of external *things*, Christ 'fulfils' the word of the prophets: he inaugurates the *true* worship, in spirit and in truth, wherein there is no sacrifice but that of the man *himself*; 'per passionem suam initiavit ritum christianae religionis offerens *seipsum* oblationem et hostiam Deo'.

But to grasp the whole of St Thomas's thought there is another word to be emphasised, namely, *ritum*. In adjacent places he uses the words *cultus*, *religio*, obviously in the same sense, or fuller expressions, 'cultus secundum religionem vitae christianae' (q. 62, a. 5), 'cultus Dei secundum ritum Christianae vitae' (q. 63, a. 1), 'cultus Dei secundum ritum christianae religionis . . . ritus christianae religionis' (q. 63, a. 3): in this last passage he says that this *ritus* derives entirely from Christ's priesthood. So we must join St Thomas in a second

---

[47]*Sum. theol.*, II-II, q. 85, a. 2; a. 3, ad 1; III, q. 22, a. 2; q. 48, a. 3; *III Sent.*, d. 9, q. 1, a. 1, qa 2, ad 1; *In Boet. de Trin.*, q. 3, a. 2.

[48]'Acts et passa (Christi)' (III, prol.); Christus 'via est nobis tendendi in Deum' (I, q. 2, prol.).

[49]III, q. 62, a. 5, quoting Eph. v, 2; cf. q. 22, a. 2; *Com. in Ps. xliv*, 5; *In Hebr.*, c. 5, lect. 1.

affirmation, viz., that the worship and sacrifice begun by Christ are 'organised'. Christ has not simply put an end to positive religions in favour of a purely personal, human, inwardness; he has ushered in a worship and a sacrifice as a *positive, social, institutional religion*. The new worship 'according to the rite of the Christian religion', or— and it is equivalent—'according to the rite [religion] of Christian life', is not something purely personal, private and altogether interior: it is truly a religion, a worshipping and sacrificial order, with its high priest or head, Christ, the sole *verus sacerdos*;[50] it also has its ministers, its *sacramenta*, and its faithful people are by implication ordered, consecrated, appointed and united to it.

That appears to be the background against which St Thomas sets the sacramental characters of baptism, confirmation and order as participations in Christ's priesthood. For 'the whole rite of the Christian religion springs from Christ's priesthood' (q. 63, a. 3) or from 'the worship of Christ's priesthood' (q. 63, a. 6, ad 1), that is, the worship that appertains to Christ as priest. St Thomas is very realistic in the way he sees Christ as head of mankind and, in respect of those who give him their faith, head of a priestly body. Subtended by precise and forceful notions of fulfilment, first in a given kind, participation, instrumentality, of all that the word *auctor* can mean, St Thomas's thought here follows lines that are unfortunately only outlined. So Christ is the principle of the whole Christian order, or as we should say today, of all Christian existence. If we are thinking of the personal action of the faithful, their virtuous deeds, then Christ is its principle in the sense that it is all a sharing in him under the twofold title of exemplary causality and efficient causality;[51] if we are thinking of properly ecclesial actions, particularly those that are sacramental, pertaining to worship proper, then Christ is principle as their *auctor*, the person rightly and ultimately responsible, on whose efficacious will these things depend. We thus see that Christian worship in as much as it is institutional, organised and social, is

---

[50] Cf. *IV Sent.*, d. 17, q. 3, a. 3, qa 2, ad 1 (if, confession to a priest being impossible, one does all that one can for oneself, 'defectum sacerdotis Summus sacerdos supplet'); *Sum. theol.*, III, q. 22, a. 4 and *Contra gent.*, iv, 76, where we read: 'Omnia ecclesiastica sacramenta ipse Christus perficit; ipse enim est qui baptisat, ipse est qui peccata remittit, ipse est verus sacerdos, qui se obtulit in ara crucis et cujus virtute corpus ejus in altari quotidie consecratur; et tamen, quia corporaliter non cum omnibus fidelibus praesentialiter erat futurus, elegit ministros per quos praedicta fidelibus dispensaret'. It is Christ who 'dispenses' everything; there are in the Church only 'ministers' of his priesthood. – This is already in St Augustine: cf. D. Zahringer, *Das kirchliche Priestertum nach dem hl. Augustinus* (Paderborn, 1932), pp. 115ff.

[51] For this wider aspect the chief references are *De verit.*, q. 29, a. 5; *Sum. theol.*, III, q. 7, a. 9; q. 24, a. 3, 4; *In symbol.*, a. 10 (*Sanct. commun.*).

celebrated by Jesus Christ, *verus sacerdos*, as its supreme author; and
when it is public, 'institutional', ecclesial form of worship, the celebration is 'vice ipsius', 'in virtute Christi', 'in persona Christ'. In the
measure that Christ communicates to men the power to celebrate
his priestly worship with him—and we have seen that the Epistle to
the Hebrews shows that this is in fact the economy of God's grace—
he dedicates and deputes them by making them share in his priesthood. Such is the priestly value for worship that St Thomas sees
realised in the sacramental characters of baptism, confirmation and
order, the truly consecratory sacraments by which the continuance
of Christ's worship is ensured in the Church.

This worship is Christ's worship in and through the Church; it is
then ecclesial, that is, social and communal in its very structure. Its
celebrant is the whole body with the head, Christ—that is why those
of the body who are specially the ministers of worship are called
ministers not solely of Christ but of the Church.[52] This body is
socially organised, and everything goes to show that Christ willed
and constituted it so. Therefore, whilst all the members are active in
the sacramental worship it celebrates as the body of the high priest
Christ, there are some who are specially described as ministers and,
in the proper etymological sense of the word, functionaries or
'liturgists'. As St Thomas says, some members are active in order to
receive, others in order to give; or again, the members are active
either to perfect themselves or to perfect others. There are then two
degrees, one linked with consecration by baptism (and confirmation), the other with consecration by holy orders, in the priestly
quality through which the fellowship-body—and temple—of Christ
celebrates on earth, with its head, the worship of the New Covenant.
So far as the priestly quality or the power of Christian worship is
concerned, holy orders is simply the exalted rank by virtue of which
some members of the body are ministers of the *Unus sacerdos* for the
others.[53]

From St Thomas's careful elaboration of the traditional assertion
that associates the priesthood of the faithful with baptism (and confirmation), we naturally turn to a second aspect of the tradition, of
which we have not met an express formulation in our biblical sources:
viz., the existence of another title to participation in Christ's priest-

[52]Cf. *Contra gent.*, iv, 73: 'Si tamen unus presbyter adsit, intelligitur hoc sacramentum perficere in virtute totius Ecclesiae, cujus minister existit et cujus personam
gerit'. Cf. *IV Sent.*, d. 19, q. 1, a. 2, qa 2, ad 4; d. 24, q. 2, a. 2, ad 2; *Sum. theol.*,
III, q. 64, a. 1, ad 2; a. 8, ad 2.

[53]'Gradus eminens per potestatem spiritualem ordo nominatur' (*IV Sent.*, d. 24,
q. 1, a. 1, qa 2, ad 4).

hood besides that of baptism common to all the faithful, that of ordination or the ministry.

(B) *The Priesthood of the Ministers*

As we have briefly noted already, the writings of the New Testament and of the Apostolic Fathers or Apologists not only do not use but seem deliberately to avoid using the words ἱερεύς and ἀρχιερεύς of the ministers of the Christian Church. There is one exception, St Clement of Rome (*circa* 95):

> We are obliged to carry out in fullest detail what the Master has commanded us to do at stated times. He has ordered the sacrifices to be offered and the services to be held (*προσφορὰς καὶ λειτουργίας*), and this not in a random and irregular fashion, but at definite times and seasons. He has, moreover, himself, by his sovereign will determined where and by whom he wants them to be carried out, in order that all things may be done religiously according to his good pleasure and be agreeable to his will. . . . Special ministries have been assigned to the high-priest; a special place has been allotted to the priests; and the levites have their own duties. Lay people are bound by rules laid down for the laity.[54]

Actually, even in this passage the priestly title is less accorded directly to ministers of the Christian Church as the name of their function, than called up from its Old Testament context to support the general idea of respect for the hierarchical order and discipline of the Church. Under the Old Dispensation the hierarchical order instituted by God was of high priest, priests, levites and members of the people. What is it in the Christian Church? Clement does not tell us; and we know that contemporary writings mention only bishops, presbyters, deacons, higumens and presidents.

But at the end of the second century we find Hippolytus of Rome applying priestly titles to bishops without circumlocution, and most probably to presbyters too, whilst about the same time Polycrates of Ephesus was calling the apostle John a '*ἱερεύς* wearing the breast-

---

[54]*Cor.*, xl, 1–3, 5. I do not count *Didache*, xiii, 3, as an exception: there the use of the title high priest of the prophets has in view the establishment of the obligation of first-fruits and is simply a transcription from the O.T. For what follows, see also the study noted above, note 21.

plate'.[55] Hippolytus uses the word as if referring to something well-known and certain in the state of things that he knew personally in his youth; there is no suggestion of innovation, even in his vocabulary. We may in passing notice an idea of his that seems to have been quite familiar to Christian antiquity, for we have met it in Clement and shall meet it again in, for instance, the *Sacramentarium Serapionis*: namely, that God has always provided that he should be honoured, that worship should be given to him; and that he does this still in the Church, through the order and succession of the ministry. As well as a fine idea about the economy of the purpose of grace, this shows consciousness that the hierarchical order of ministry also concerned the domain of worship, of the λειτουργία.

The *Apostolic Tradition* is the oldest liturgical document that we have and the only one of the age before Constantine, and it gives some very important information along this line. It establishes a difference between the institution of a bishop, a presbyter and a deacon on the one hand and that of a widow, a reader, a subdeacon on the other (cf. c. 11, 12, 14). The last three offices are conferred by a simple *katastasis*, the word by which is designated institution to a public activity simply by nomination. But the bishop (c. 2), the presbyter (c. 8) and the deacon (c. 9) receive a real ordination, a *kheirotonia*. The passage about the widows tells us why: 'When a widow is instituted *(καθίσταται)* she is not ordained *(οὐ χειροτονεῖται)* but is designated by this name. . . . A widow is instituted by words alone, to be numbered among the widows; but she is not ordained because she does not offer the oblation *(προσφορά)* and has no liturgical duty *(λειτουργία)*. Ordination *(χειροτονία)* is for the clergy because of their liturgical office, while the widow is instituted for the prayer that is common to all'.[56]

[55]Eusebius, *Hist. eccl.*, v, 24, 2. In the *Philosophoumena* of Hippolytus, bishops are successors of the Apostles and of their *charis*, sharing their priesthood, μετέχοντες sἀρχιερατείας. On the other hand, we read in *Trad. apost.*, 3 (prayers of consecration of a bishop): God 'who has established leaders and priests [Latin: *principes et sacerdotes*. Greek of the *Const. apost.*: ἀρχοντάς τε καὶ ἱερεῖς] and has not left your sanctuary without servants. . . . May he feed your holy flock and exert your sovereign priesthood [ἀρχιερατεύειν] without reproach'. – In *Trad. apost.*, 9, Hippolytus explains why the bishop alone lays on hands at the ordination of a deacon: because a deacon 'is not ordained to the priesthood but to the service of the bishop'. G. Dix observes in his *Apostolic Ministry* (London, 1946), p. 225, n. 2, that there may be there an express allusion to the priesthood of the presbyters: given the meaning B. Botte attaches to the passage (*Sources chret.*, pp. 28–29), this seems to us certain.

[56]*Trad. apost.*, c. 11. The original meaning of χειροτονεῖν is 'to elect with uplifted hand'. There was sometimes, elsewhere and later on, an imposition of hands on deaconesses, but this does not affect the testimony of Hippolytus. – It will be noticed that, in Hippolytus as in Clement of Rome (xliv, 4), to offer the gifts pertains to episcopacy.

So the ministers engaged in the liturgical service whose highest action is the eucharistic oblation are instituted by a laying-on of hands, which the text reserves to the bishop; while those who carry out duties not properly or directly concerned with the liturgical offering are instituted simply by appointment. Ecclesiastical offices are on a different plane not only because they are (clearly enough) distinct and 'hierarchised', but also in respect of their ontology, if I may put it so. There is an institution to the service of the Church by way of appointment; and there is another, in respect of liturgical or eucharistic service, by way of an episcopal consecration which may properly be called sacramental. Associating what Hippolytus tells us with the application of the words ἀρχιερεύς and ἱερεύς to the episcopal ministry (and apparently to the presbyteral), we can say that the documents of the end of the second century provide the first explicit testimony to the existence of another source of priesthood besides baptism, namely, ordination of higher ministers by an episcopal laying-on of hands.

From the beginning of the third century there is an increasing amount of evidence. The exact meaning or significance of such and such a passage of Tertullian or St Cyprian may be matter of dispute; we may notice how the title *sacerdos* is not given to simple presbyters without mentioning that they are subordinate to bishops; or how still in the fifth and sixth centuries, and perhaps later, there is a tendency to confine the word *sacerdos* to the bishop: these things have little importance for our subject. It suffices for us to grasp, as part of a 'datum' that theology has to interpret and 'construct', the truth that there is in the Christian economy another modality, title, source of priestly quality besides those of baptism. There is a ministerial or hierarchical priesthood.

As faithful and as theologians, that is, recognising the continuity of development and infallibility of the Church as a principle, we can grasp this truth of tradition, not at the point where it begins to emerge in written records, but when it is proposed for our acceptance in its fully developed and 'defined' form, for example, in the texts of the Council of Trent. The essential content is the same, and it can be summed up thus: There are spiritual gifts given for the building-up of the body of Christ (the true temple of God), and these gifts are new and original participations in Christ's priestly power through the power of baptismal consecration or righteous life. Particular aspects can be reduced to these:[57] The hierarchical priesthood is not simply a function instituted by men to meet the requirements of good order and of the theological competence of ministers; it is a matter of a hierarchical rank which entails 'sacred capacities'. These powers are to consecrate the eucharist, to forgive sins and to minister the sacraments; other powers are joined with these, in respect of teaching and ruling. The divinely instituted hierarchy consists of the episcopate, the presbyterate and the diaconate. Sacramental ordination confers a character that can neither be lost nor taken away.

This teaching of the Council of Trent is the developed expression of the Church's teaching. Nevertheless we cannot but refer, however rapidly, to the problem of continuity, about which the least inquiring mind asks questions since history tells us so little. What we have said above makes the problem unavoidable. It can be put from the point of view of historical continuity or from that of Catholic theological principles.

(1) *The Historical Problem.* This arises from the fact that the application of a sacrificial and sacerdotal vocabulary to external Christian worship is relatively late, and at the beginning was obviously shunned.

In the first place it must be noticed that the gospels themselves do not give the name 'priest' either to Christ or to the faithful; the Apostolic Fathers give it to Christ but not expressly to the faithful, and this last application was rare even in the second century.[58] But it is certainly not in the use of the words priest and high priest that evidence for continuity must be looked for. That continuity is clear from the eucharist and its sacrificial import: from Irenaeus back to Justin, from Justin to Ignatius and the *Didache*, from thence to Clement and the apostolic writings, the celebration of the eucharist as a sacrificial worship can be followed.

The reasons why the earlier generations of Christians at first refrained from speaking of ἱερεῖς but later developed a sacrificial and sacerdotal terminology can apparently be explained as follows: Christian consciousness was at the beginning struck by the fact that Christianity, unlike Judaism (and still more unlike any form of

---

[57]Council of Trent, sess. xxiii (Denzinger, 957–968) All the points of this teaching are common to East and West, except perhaps the last, about the indelible character. But even on this point several weighty Eastern Orthodox authorities take the Catholic position, e.g., the Confession of Dositheus and the Orthodox Confession of Peter Mogila.

[58]The ἀρχιερατικὸν τὸ ἀληθινὸν γένος of St Justin (*Dial.*, cxvi, 3) is exceptional.

paganism), is not a religion of this world, but it is nevertheless comparable with these other religions as touching its 'cultual' and sociologico-religious structure. Those first Christian generations were very strongly conscious that the Church is at bottom a *heavenly* thing, existing through a gift from on high and relating to things on high: our altar, they said to themselves, is in Heaven, so is our Priest, our one and only priest, and there he offers up our gifts. For the most part they lived, like the Epistle to the Hebrews, in an atmosphere of comparison between the Christian spiritual economy and Judaism.

In a general way the Apostles and faithful of the earliest generations were very conscious of the newness of Christianity, in contrast both with the pagan world around them and with Judaism.[59] In the face of Judaism they declared that the promises were fulfilled; but like the prophets before them (Joel, Jeremy, xxxi) they had a tendency somewhat to telescope what belongs to the age between Pentecost and Parousia, the time of the earthly Church: the new and heavenly life seems to have driven out everything else (see what Peter said at Pentecost). This feeling that our life, the activities that qualify a man as citizen, belong to Heaven (Philippians iii, 20) applied particularly to worship and priesthood. If it pertained to a ἱερεύς, whether in Judaism or paganism, to immolate a victim in offering and so to be a 'sacrificer', then in Christianity there was only one deserving that name, Christ, who offered up his own life to God, and every living faithful soul who made a drink-offering of his life poured it out to God drop by drop or all at once. The ministers of the eucharist were not acting as 'sacrificers' because, in celebrating that efficacious memorial as the Lord had given his Apostles power and commandment to do, they were simply making Christ's one sacrifice actual and present to the faithful.[60]

The 'cultual' and priestly terminology seems to have arisen from the eucharist as the sacrament of the Lord's sacrifice, and therefore the Church's liturgical sacrifice. It was not long before this consciousness of having a pure and perfect sacrifice in the eucharist came to be expressed by reference to Malachy i, 11; and soon a sacrificial vocabulary was applied to the Church's worship. The

---

[59]K. Prumm, *Christentum als Neuheitserlebnis* (Freiburg i. B., 1939). Christians often avoided adopting words associated with pagan religion, but not always (*e.g.*, *aquae* for baptism); and the whole history of Judaism lay behind *hiereus*

[60]The expression of the eucharistic institution τοῦτο ποιεῖτε εἰς τὴν ἐμὴν ἀνάμνησιν (1 Cor. xi, 24-25; Luke xxii, 19), refers to a Hebrew word, from the radical *zkr*, whose O.T. usages convey the idea of a commemoration that is equivalent to a showing-forth of presence (cf. *e.g.*, Exod. iii, 15; xx, 24; Ps. cxi, 4). Cf. J. Pedersen, *Israel* i–ii, pp. 106ff., 245ff.

word $\theta v\sigma\iota\alpha\sigma\tau\acute{\eta}\rho\iota o\nu$ was treated at first with a reserve similar to that accorded to $\iota\epsilon\rho\epsilon\acute{v}s$, but it came to be used of the eucharistic table, as can be seen in Irenaeus, a generation before Hippolytus, without its reference to the altar in Heaven being lost to sight.

Ideas had to be more carefully developed in this sense when it became necessary to meet the criticism of pagans who treated Christians as atheists and accused them of not offering sacrifice. At first apologists answered from the heart of Christian truth, new and old, that God, the creator of all things, is in need of nothing, and that the truest and noblest sacrifice man can offer him is a righteous life for the good of others. But soon they were adding that Christians have a sacrifice, the eucharist, a sort of first-fruits of creation. From then on the terminological development spread from worship to the ministry, and Hippolytus speaks of the priesthood of bishops and even of presbyters as of something well-known and taken for granted. Nevertheless it is probable—and perhaps there is an echo of it in Origen— that for a time the faithful kept the feeling that it could be truly said either that Christianity had priests or that it did not have them. Fundamentally Christians had a sort of living continuity with the prophets: they could speak in the present tense of things which had been announced for the future; but, themselves witnesses of the new things of God, they, like the prophets, could say both Yes and No about many things of which the heavenly reality was theirs but which had to be called by clumsy names with earthly connotations. They had priests, yes, because they had ministers set apart for the celebration of a sacrificial worship, the sacrament of Christ's sacrifice; at the same time they had no priests except the Lord in Heaven and the faithful as a whole, for their ministers did not immolate anything after the manner of Jewish or pagan $\iota\epsilon\rho\epsilon\hat{\iota}s$.

The real Christian idea was that there is only one high priest, Christ, priest in Heaven for evermore; that all the faithful have a real priestly quality, being incorporated in Christ by the sacramental consecration of baptism and by a living faith; and that for the Church's benefit bishops and presbyters (and deacons) have a ministry of Christ's priestly actions, most particularly of the eucharistic memorial, a ministry to which they are consecrated by a sacrament, whereby they receive a third participation in the priesthood of Christ. There seems no doubt at all that this view of things, which is the view of St Thomas Aquinas[61] and of the Fathers of the classical

---

[61]This follows from what has been said above and from St Thomas's vocabulary: to Christ's *auctoritas* (or *principalitas*) corresponds man's *ministerium* which is applied to different *officia*: cf. *e.g.*, the texts cited above, nn. 79–87.

age,[62] is also that of the ancient tradition, whose historical continuity can be seen at least in the leaning towards objective 'cultual' reality, the same which the Lord instituted in the upper room. We hold these points to be certain: The sacrificial value of the Supper, its celebration by the ministers of the Church, and then, in the second half of the second century, the application of priestly terms to ministers ordained by the bishops for the liturgical service. Between the two, apart from certain external tokens bearing on the priestliness of hierarchical ministers, there are the significant indications of Christian worship as a sacrificial worship. In the apostolic age we see the Apostles themselves and apostolic men such as Titus and Timothy instituting ministers by laying their hands on them; and we find the same gesture used by bishops in the second century. Can it be doubted that all reasonable likelihood is on the side of continuity?

(2) *The Theological Problem*. This arises from the questions raised by and principles involved in the Catholic position, and by the fact that the ministerial priesthood, with all that it means in the Church's structure and her sacramental and hierarchical regime, is not *expressly* attested in Holy Scripture. Here we can only point out the problems; they have been considered elsewhere (*Vraie et fausse reforme*, third part). There are two principles involved.

(*a*) Concerning herself, the Catholic Church presupposes continuity and infallibility; and this not through any trust in herself as a work of man but through trust in herself as the realisation of God's word and God's promises, in as much as the Holy Spirit, the gift proper to the New and final Dispensation, has been given to her, dwells in her and is at work in her. *Credo in Spiritum sanctum, sanctam Ecclesiam.* . . . The scholastics tell us that these two terms are bound together in such a way that the second derives all its truth from the first. We have a solid assurance that the Church has not erred and will not err because the Lord has so promised, and that his Spirit is with his Body in all the workings of that body (See *ibid.*, pp. 475ff.; cf. 101ff.).

(*b*) With the question of the real objective continuity of the Church there goes that of our knowledge of such continuity. There we come up against the monumental problem of the Scriptures and their relationship with Tradition for the knowledge of truth, as well

---

[62]See, *e.g.*, for St Augustine, D. Zahringer, *op. cit*. There are many magnificent passages in St Leo, displaying a perfect balance, expressed in unforgettable language, between the eternal sovereign priesthood of Christ, the dignity of the hierarchical ministry and the dignity of the priesthood of all.

as the problem of the criteria of homogeneous dogmatic development. Can the truth of Christianity be established through a critical
study of the Bible and of historical sources? What is the test of
Christian truth? Is it properly only Tradition? Here again the reader
must be referred to the book mentioned above, pp. 482ff., 498ff., and
503ff., and to Newman's classical work.

That finishes our basic statement; it is very elementary, I am
afraid, but complete so far as it goes. We now have to 'construct' it,
that is, to interpret it into a coherent synthesis, endeavouring to get
at the meaning of things, the connexions and harmony between different parts—the proper business of theology.

THEOLOGICAL INTERPRETATION

Definition of Priesthood. – There have been two approaches, and
perhaps more, to the notion of priesthood in Catholic tradition. Those
lay people who have read Cardinal Suhard's pastoral letter on the
Priest[63] have become aware of this, and some of them were a little
disconcerted. But it is a sign, not of contradiction, but of richness,
for there is continuity and transition between the aspects, and the
same minds, especially the greatest, hold both points of view together.

Some would define priesthood by mediatorship: the priest essentially is he who stands in between man and God to reconcile man
with God. In the New Testament mediatorship is very properly
brought into relation with the covenant, the establishment of an
economy of salvation, as in the Epistle to the Hebrews (viii, 6; ix, 15;
xii, 24). The economy of the salvation of which Christ is the mediator
rests on his sacrifice (1 Timothy ii, 5ff.). The idea of mediator
($\mu\epsilon\sigma\iota\tau\eta\varsigma$) plays hardly any part in theology before the Council of
Nicaea, whereas St Augustine put it at the centre of his synthesis of
the saving economy: to him we owe the fine expression *sacrificium
mediatoris*. He thus prepared that great synthesis of Catholic theology
which was brought together and digested in so masterly a fashion in
the encyclical letter of 1947, '*Mediator*'. When St Thomas speaks of
Christ's priesthood he finds its proper function in being mediator
between God and the people, giving out divine gifts to them and
sending up prayer and satisfaction to God (*Sum. theol.*, III, q. 22,
a. 1; q. 82, a. 3). Are then those interpreters of Aquinas right who
build their whole notion of priesthood on mediation? We shall see
that St Thomas himself was less committed to this idea. We are told

[63]*Le prêtre dans la Cité* (Paris, 1949), pp. 10–11.

that had only one individual been created he would not have been
priest because he would not have been mediator (Father de Finance).
Is that certain? The canon of the Roman Mass refers to Abel's
sacrifice—was he not his own priest? In any case mediatorship is not
enough to define priesthood, for there are mediators of teaching and
of guidance and of ruling. So we must turn for help to the idea of
reconciliation brought about by some sacrificial offering.

Biblically speaking, the idea of priesthood is bound up with sacrifice, whether it be suggested, without being formally expressed, that
the priestly quality in Christ arises from his being victim (1 Peter i,
19; ii, 24; iii, 18; John xvii, 19), or whether his priesthood be
expressly defined by his sacrificial function (Hebrews v, 1; viii, 3;
cf. ii, 17; ix, 11-14; x, 11). The chain of testimony in this sense
makes up an impressive tradition. Some texts simply set out the
identity of victim with priest; but there are magnificent passages
wherein St Augustine, often after speaking of the Mediator, associates Christ's priesthood, and priesthood in general, with sacrifice:
'Ideo sacerdos quia sacrificium' (*Confess*. x, c. 43, n. 69); 'Si nullum
sacrificium, nullus sacerdos' (*Enarr. in Ps. cxxx*, n. 4). St Thomas
writes cautiously in the *Summa*, 'in sacrificio offerendo potissime
sacerdotis consistit officium' (III, q. 22, a. 4, sed c; cf. ad 2), and
comments frankly on Hebrews, 'dicit *sacerdos*, quia se obtulit Deo
Patri' (*In Hebraeos*, c. 5, lect. 1); and many theologians, sometimes
expressly following him, define priesthood by the office or competency of offering sacrifice. And this is what the Council of Trent
teaches when, going back to the connexions so clearly indicated in
the Epistle to the Hebrews, it declares that 'Sacerdotium et sacrificium ita Dei ordinatione conjuncta sunt, ut utrumque in omni lege
exstiterit' (Denzinger, 957).

It is quite certain that there is a bond between mediator, sacrifice
and priest in the priesthood *of Christ*. St Augustine puts the matter
exactly when he says that Christ is mediator in the sacrifice for which,
in which—we may add, through which—he is priest. When we regard the mystery of salvation and consider the mediator in his
mediation and the priest exercising his priesthood, we see that they
are made one in the sacrifice.

There are those who advance a third approach to the notion of
priesthood, starting neither from mediation nor from sacrifice but
from consecration. This is the line followed by the French school.
The priest is the man of God set apart and consecrated to carry on
the mission of the Incarnate Word: a mission of adoration, as
Condren particularly insists (the priest as God's religious), as St

Vincent de Paul insists still more; the priest ought in every way to be completely divested of self, dedicated and given up to the carrying on of Christ's prayer and charity. When this idea is deeply impressed on the clergy during their time of formation it renews the ideas of the priest as man of sacrifice and of the priest as mediator and carries them over into the spiritual life. Priests of today's missionary generation are fond of pointing out that the mediator is the point where God and men meet; and for that one must cease to live for self, self must be emptied away, there must be a complete surrender to the two extremes that have got to be brought together: a priest must be possessed by them, eaten up by them, be himself no longer for self's sake but totally God's man and men's man. It is to them, following Christ who was wholly and entirely given up to them, it is to them that we must give ourselves, at this moment in space and time whereat we have been put that we may actualise Christ's priesthood: for through our priestly consecration we are a moment in that work whose Principle was laid down two thousand years ago.

Everybody must admire this impressive ideal and hope that it may spread for the nurturing of priestly life; its potentiality for good in the formation of a missionary clergy such as the Holy Spirit is raising up in the Church today must be apparent to all. But its limitations cannot be overlooked: it is not so much a definition of priesthood as a spirituality for the clergy. We may say that, theologically as well as historically, it represents the thought of seminary-directors whose responsibility it is to train priests in the spirit of their charge. To say that is not to depreciate a very lofty doctrine: it is simply to identify its 'position'.

In our opinion, faithfulness to Holy Scripture and sound theology requires that priesthood be defined as the quality which enables a man to come before God to gain his grace, and therefore fellowship with him, by offering up a sacrifice acceptable to him.[64] Such a definition allows a place to values which, while not a strictly essential part of it, may have their place as an adjunct—consecration, for instance—or as a condition qualifying a priesthood that has a social or public bearing—instituted, mediatory. Obviously those texts that speak of the levitical priesthood or the priesthood of Jesus Christ refer to a public priesthood, therefore one that is instituted (by God) and mediatory. Moreover, they are concerned with the priesthood of a revealed religion, depending on a positive order of sin and grace:

---

[64] If one finds this definition well-grounded and right, the fact that it happens to agree pretty exactly with Calvin's (Catechism, §38) does not seem a good reason for giving it up.

to establish fellowship therefore means here to reconcile sinners, and implies that their sins are covered up or that satisfaction is made for them.[65] The English word Atonement, 'at-one-ment', admirably expresses these different aspects of an action that established communion, reunites and reconciles, and is at the same time expiatory or propitiatory.[66]

The Idea of Sacrifice. – Priesthood then is the sacrificial office and, after what we have already written, we can start a consideration of sacrifice from St Augustine's definition: Every work done with the aim of uniting us with God in a holy fellowship. Some repetition is unavoidable, but we will try to advance our understanding of Christian priesthood and of the part in it of the members of God's λαός.

Every sacrifice implies a person, matter and, at least in its properly 'cultual' sense, a consecratory rite. In current speech the word 'sacrifice' is sometimes used much too narrowly, sometimes very broadly. Narrowly, when children are taught the way of 'little sacrifices', which reduces the word to meaning 'anything that is not easy'; broadly, but significantly, when we speak, for example, of a girl who has not married so that she could look after her old father or mother, as 'sacrificed to her parents', or of a soldier who 'sacrifices his life' for his country. There are two things to notice in these last examples. First, that the idea of 'sacrificing oneself' implies putting oneself in a right relation towards another, determined by what he is to me and by what I am to him. Second, it is a matter of disposing oneself aright in respect of things more important than myself, things which in the examples given are even responsible for my being. Obviously this is not always the case, for we speak of a mother sacrificing herself for her child, and even of a politician sacrificing himself to maintain his party's majority. But in every case something is preferred before self, and this preference is the price we pay for the spiritual good of a right relation towards another.[67]

This preference of another over self is not essentially or necessarily

---

[65]Cf. Heb. v, 1–3; vii, 27, and all the typology of the Day of Atonement; unlike the levitical priesthood, that of Christ really opens the way to God and obtains communion with him (τελείωσις); vii, 11, 19; ix, 9. Cf. also 1 John ii, 2.

[66]The following writings by Anglicans are particularly valuable: R. C. Moberly, *Atonement and Personality* (London, 1911); F. Weston, *The Fulness of Christ* (London, 1916; especially pp. 12ff.); V. Taylor, *The Atonement in N.T. Teaching* (London, 1940); W. J. Phythian-Adams, *The Way of At-one-ment* (London, 1944).

[67]As an illustration I quote L. Blum (*A l'échelle humaine*, p. 120): 'Man must know the value of life, but he must also know how to subordinate it to ideal ends, collective ends—justice, human freedom, national independence, peace. Such subordination in practice is called sacrifice'.

painful. A man can sacrifice himself light-heartedly; or he can do it unconsciously and without experiencing any suffering. Normally our total turning to God, answering to the highest realisation of self, should be accompanied by feelings of happiness and fulfilment. But sin makes us refer everything to self alone, our own sensitive being becomes the only pole of attraction and criterion of values, and it is then inevitable that the ordering of ourselves to something other and higher, and therefore sacrifice, should have an element of painful deprivation: in practice, sacrifice is generally something that hurts. But good can be drawn out of evil. We can offer up to God these lesser goods to which we are overmuch attached and turn them into matter of atonement, in the sense that the movement of love and generosity that makes us take up a burdensome duty compensates for our former disorders and sinfulness. Expiation and satisfaction are at the heart of sacrifice, understood in its widest and most positive sense.

When it is a question of our right relation with God—our creator, from whom comes *all* that we are and have—then it is oneself, the totality of one's being, doing and having, that must be the 'sacrifice'. That is evidently the work of a lifetime, one which literally can be fully carried out only if it includes our death in the offering of our life; but this work is made concrete in particular actions and things, in the offering of which we are able to express and so to make actual our relationship to God as to our absolute source. Thus do our sacrifices have their soul and their matter.

Their soul is the free and loving acceptance of our absolute dependence on God, that we are his and must be turned towards him: in short, it is man's spiritual movement towards God. Whether, with St Thomas, we speak of turning to God, of religion, of inward sacrifice, or, with St Augustine, of man himself as consecrated and dedicated to God, invisible sacrifice, these are but different names for the soul of all sacrifice. For the great doctors the essential thing in sacrifice lies there: outward action will follow, but it is not by that that sacrifice is primarily *defined*.[68] As for the matter, that includes

---

[68]Cf. St Thomas, II-II, q. 85, a. 2. Cf. a. 4 and q. 81, a. 7; q. 93, a. 2, obj. 2; q. 94, a. 1, ad 1; III, q. 82, a. 4; *Contra gent.*, III, 120 ('exterius sacrificium repraesentativum est interioris veri sacrificii, secundum quod mens humana seipsam offert Deo'). – I am then unable to agree on this point with G. de Broglie, 'La messe, oblation collective . . .' in *Gregorianum*, 30 (1949), pp. 536ff., who defines sacrifice by the external action (making something pass under the dominion of another), though there must be internal dispositions (p. 538, n. 1) Father de Broglie's criticism of the French school (p. 539, n. 4) arises from the same idea that sacrifice (and virtue: p. 538, n. 3) *consists* in the outward act. One must be more Augustinian than that! See B. Durst in *Benedikt. Monatsch.*, 25 (1949), pp. 348ff.; and G. L. Bauer in *Divus Thomas*, 1950, pp. 5-31.

everything which is capable of being offered up: 'every work done
with the aim of uniting oneself with God in a holy fellowship', says
St Augustine, every good, every virtuous work, says St Thomas; but
also material things as well, as we see from the Bible and in all
religions.

It may be objected that this is an over-spiritualised conception of
sacrifice, but it is not so, for there is a third element, at any rate
when we consider properly 'cultual' sacrifice, namely, the consecratory rite. St Thomas clearly states the principle that every sacrifice is an oblation but every oblation is not a sacrifice (*Com. in Ps. xix*,
7; II-II, q. 85, a. 3, ad 3). It is proper to speak of sacrifice when,
with regard to the things offered, *aliquid fit*.[69] St Thomas's thought
seems to be this: That for sacrifice properly speaking there must not
only be a purpose of referring or ordering to God, not only something offered, *res oblata*, but an action by which the thing offered is
the subject of an expressly authorised change, in a word, is 'sacralised'; this is normally brought about by a rite that sets the offering
in order. The thing offered is consecrated, it is assigned to God by a
public expression of determination henceforth not to make use of it.
So, for instance, celibacy publicly vowed takes on a sacrificial
character to a greater degree than does a simple inward offering up
of chastity. The offering of food to God in recognition of having
received it from him becomes a sacrifice in the strong sense if,
instead of consuming it, one 'sacralises' it, by a libation, for example.
It is clear that in the liturgical sacrifices of public worship this
'sacralising' of the thing offered by a sacrificial action is a necessary
element.

The Forms of Christian Priesthood. – Priesthood being essentially
relative to sacrifice, the kinds of priesthood are distinguished according to the kinds of sacrifice. All the various Christian sacrifices or
priesthoods are *true* and *spiritual*, and these two qualifications go
together: if they be taken in their biblical sense, as they ought to be
and as they are here, they overlap one another. That is 'spiritual'
which comes not by flesh and blood but is put in motion by a working of the Holy Spirit, the gift proper to the New and final Dis-

---

[69]II-II, q. 85, a. 1; a. 3, ad 3. Doubtless there is some influence here from
Isidore's definition, 'sacrificium dictum quasi sacrum factum' (*Etym.*, vi, n. 38, in
PL., lxxxii, 255).

pensation.[70] The word 'spiritual' is opposed to carnal, 'psychical', purely natural; it is not opposed to visible or sensible: the eucharist is an essentially sensible and social celebration, and it is also eminently 'spiritual'. The word does not mean symbolical, figurative, 'not really', though when applied to Old Testament types or the Church's sacraments it can have the *nuance* of reference to something else that the words mystery, mystical, sacrament have in the language of the Fathers. The meaning will have to be brought out later on, but it was necessary first to point out that all Christian forms of sacrifice and priesthood are concerned with worship 'in spirit and in truth' and are accordingly 'spiritual': by the same token they are also 'acceptable to God'.

What these forms are is well enough known—the trouble is to set them forth adequately. There are first of all, shining down on all the rest, the sacrifice and the priesthood of Jesus Christ, absolute, unique and universal. And they are so, not because they could be exclusive of any others, unique in solitariness, but because they are the fullness of true sacrifice and of true priesthood, of those which God accepts; not, again, because they could be a sum total, but because they are the principle, *the* reality in which all the others share and have their being. Whatever can attain to God—really *to God*—can do so only in and through the priesthood and sacrifice of Jesus Christ: *de lis quae sunt ad Deum, omnia in ipso constant*, if we may join and accommodate two sentences of St Paul (Hebrews v, 1 and Colossians i, 17). This has all been interpreted with unequalled care in St Thomas's theology of the fullness of grace, Christ's grace of headship, his *auctoritas* and his *principalitas*.

The chief characteristics, six of them, of Christ's sacrifice (and therefore of his priesthood in action) can be detailed thus: It embraces the sacrifice of all men and even of God; it was outward and inward; it was the sacrifice of his whole life and that of the single act of his 'pasch'.

To set out even an elementary theology of its embracingness it is

[70]An article on πνεῦμα, πνευματικός not having yet (Novr 1950) appeared in Kittel's *Wörterbuch*, see W. Bauer's *Griechisch-deutsches Wörterbuch z.d. Schriften d. N.T.* (Berlin, 1937) or a similar work (C.L.W. Grimm, F. Zorrell); and a good summary in E. Niebecker, *Das allg. Priestertum*, pp. 9off. See also O. Casel, 'Oblatio rationabilis' in *Theol. Quartalsch.*, 99 (1917–18), pp. 429ff.; the same, 'Die λογική θυσία der antiken Mystik . . .' in *Jahrbuch f. Liturgiewiss.*, 4 (1924), pp. 37–47; C. Mohrmann, 'Rationabilis λογικός in *Revue internat. des droits de l'antiquite*, 5 (1950), pp. 225–234, on the word *rationabilis* in St Ambrose; C. F. D. Moule in the *Journal of Theol. Studies*, 1950, pp. 29–41, an article which brings out the connexion between λογική or *spiritual* and *acceptable* (to God). On πνευματικός, *spiritualis*, as an attribute of the Church, the body of Christ, cf. S. Tromp. *Corpus Christi quod est Ecclesia*, vol. i (Rome, 1946), pp. 98ff.

needful to advert to the question of mankind's inclusion in Christ, distinguishing the moment of his incarnation and the moment of his redeeming acts, with which we are associated: we are here concerned with the last. St Paul does not say that we are 'born with', 'incarnate with' Christ; he says that we are dead with, crucified with, buried with, raised again with, gone up into Heaven with, set at God's right hand with him: that which was done for us and includes us is precisely the passing of Jesus to his Father, his pasch. Christ's sacrifice is ours; one is dead for all, then all are dead, exactly in order that all shall share the deep reality of sacrifice, which is the making of one's centre in someone else, to live for another (Cf. 2 Corinthians v, 14-15, 21). In his pasch, which is his sacrifice, Christ returns to God so that we may return in him; our sacrifice, our return, are possible only in his, which already contain them and give worth to them in advance: None goes up into Heaven but he who has come down from Heaven, the Son of man, who must 'be lifted up' so that those who believe may have eternal life in him (John iii, 13-15; Vogels' text).

It may seem surprising that we should say that Christ's sacrifice embraces even God's, but Holy Writ itself moves us to do so, in the same passage from 2 Corinthians referred to above: 'But all things [referring to the fact of being a new creature] are of God, who hath reconciled us to himself through Christ and hath given us the ministry of reconciliation [at-one-ment]; God, as it were, was reconciling the world to himself in Christ, by not reckoning against men their transgressions, and by the word of reconciliation wherewith he had entrusted us' (v, 18-19). There is action from God in the Cross: reconciliation, the fruit of sacrifice, comes from God who, as it were, leaning down towards us, is himself at work in the victim of Calvary. Jesus is Lamb *of God* not simply because he is in all things conformed to God, but because he is given, sent, sacrificed by God: 'Agnus Dei, filius Patris', we sing in the *Gloria in excelsis*; 'Sic Deus dilexit mundum . . .' says St John (iii, 16). And again: 'Herein doth lie the love, not in our having loved God, but in his having loved us, and having sent his Son as a propitiation for our sins' (1 John iv, 10).

Exteriorly Christ's sacrifice lay, for instance, in all the prayer deeds that were seen of men; but above all of course it was in his passion and death in the presence of a great multitude and of the representatives of public authority: the Saviour gave ample evidence that he was giving his life freely for a determined end, as a ransom and as a covenant, that he was making his passion and death a sacrifice. Of the intensity of his spiritual resolution the psalmist spoke in prophecy: 'Sacrifice and offering thou hast not desired, but a body thou hast prepared for me. In holocausts and sin-offerings thou hast taken no pleasure: then I said: Behold I come . . . to do, O God, thy will' (Hebrews x, 5-7—Psalm xl, 7-9). The inner soul of the sacrifice of Jesus is his 'Yea, Father, because so it hath been well pleasing in thine eyes' (Matthew xi, 26), his spirit of sonship. We have seen that according to the Epistle to the Hebrews Christ is priest in as much as he is Son, and that he realises his priesthood by his maintenance of an attitude of sonship, of watchfulness and obedience towards the Father, whatever befalls. Here we might consider Christ's filial soul, filial personality, filial obedience—in a word, his complete, total reference to his Father, precisely in which 'being filial' consists: πρὸς τὸν Θεόν, πρὸς τὸν πατέρα.[71] We might also consider the connexion between Jesus' life of sonship and the economy of salvation of which we are the beneficiaries and, in a sense, the agents. For in the end it is a matter of making the incarnate Son and us one single filial being, one single being returned to, praising, acknowledging the Father, one single heir at last, joined together in glory at the Father's right hand: 'Erit unus Christus amans Patrem' we may say, adapting St Augustine, and with St Paul, 'O altitudo . . .', 'O the depth of the riches of God!' And we must add that the soul of Christ's sacrifice is also his love for men, which is inseparable from his filial obedience as the first and second commandments are inseparable and, in the sacrifice of the cross, Jesus' priestly act towards his Father and his priestly act towards men. We must not forget this indissoluble union of love of God and love of men, of fellowship with God and fellowship among men, which characterises Christ's sacrifice in its root and in its fruit.

That sacrifice was the sacrifice of his whole life and that of the single act of his 'pasch'. The first of these points is obvious from the fact that the soul of Christ's sacrifice is his disposition as son, co-extensive with his existence, which is why Berulle and the French school after him considered the religion or priesthood of Christ through all the mysteries, from his conception and earliest life in Mary's womb. The second point is also obvious, from the sacrificial and properly soteriological [CC] purpose that apostolic teaching and all theology recognises in Christ's passion, or rather his 'passover', that moment that the Lord himself calls 'my hour'. It is the sacrifice

[71]It is very remarkable that priesthood is defined as competence concerning τὰ πρὸς τὸν θεόν. that which must be referred to God (Heb. ii, 17; v, 1), and that for St John the Word is he who is πρὸς τὸν πατέρα (John i, 1; 1 John i, 2). Cultual actions, approach (Eph. ii, 18), prayer (Acts viii, 24; xii, 5; Rom. x, 1; xv, 30; 2 Cor. xiii, 7), are done πρὸς τὸν θεόν.

accomplished once for all on the cross that is chiefly Christ's sacrifice, which includes ours, whose fruit endures for ever and through which we are able to come into God's presence; but the whole of his life is meritorious, exemplary, efficacious for our return to God. The liturgy both celebrates the different mysteries of the Saviour's life and declares that Easter is 'the feast of feasts' (which means much more than a degree of solemnity), and it centres the whole of worship in the eucharistic commemoration of the Passion. That is the meaning of the theology that St Thomas set forth in so precise and balanced a fashion.[72]

It was necessary to examine these different aspects of Christ's sacrifice separately in order to understand them; they must now be brought back into one. Comprising the sacrifice of all mankind; interior and outward at the same time; accomplished on the Cross but recapitulating the whole of the Saviour's earthly life—it was as this one thing that on Maundy Thursday evening the sacrifice was anticipated and instituted as a sacrament, to be men's worship and food always and everywhere. This is where all the threads of the Christian economy of priesthood are gathered into one, and we must try to see how. As with the problems considered in the previous chapter, as for all ecclesiology, so here—everything depends on an exact appreciation of our situation between the pasch of Christ and his parousia.

Christ has gone up into Heaven: his sacrifice and his priesthood have become outside of time and space. The Epistle to the Hebrews is full of this: by shedding his blood once for all Jesus has given an inexhaustible spring of grace; gone into the Holy of Holies, his priesthood is eternal, appointed 'in the power of an unending life'. This is the image that dominated Christian art up to about the twelfth century: Christ lifted above time, become by his sacrifice the Lord of all grace, Celebrant supreme and universal in God's presence. Sometimes there was shown simply a great cross filling the sky above the Church;[73] sometimes Christ was represented together as ruler of

[72]He attained this balance by giving its fullest value (as also in the question of Christ's universal merit) to the positive will of the Father. For his thought on the part played by the passion and the other mysteries of Christ, see C. Journet in Nova et Vetera, 16 (1941), pp. 319–329.

[73]E.g., the mosaic of St Pudentiana at Rome (5-cent.), the tomb of Galla Placidia (mid. 5-cent.) and the baptistry 'of the Arians' (end 5-cent.) at Ravenna, the mosaic apse at Casaranello (c. 490) and in St Apollinaris at Ravenna (c. 549). I am inclined to think that the cross-shaped division of some ceilings in the catacombs is not simply ornamental but intended to represent the mystery of salvation. – The Cross has often been represented in the form of a living cross or tree of life. The Cross with its fruits is Alpha become Omega.

all things (*Pantokrator*) and lover of men;[74] sometimes we see the reign of the Lamb, signifying the Saviour both as victim and priest.[75] Christ is shown in image always as sole author of grace, as sole priest celebrant in Heaven, through whom all prayer, worship and praise must pass if it is to be acceptable to God. Not that we must imagine a heavenly sacrifice of the same kind as the expiatory sacrifice on Calvary: that happened once for all at a given moment in history, 'under Pontius Pilate'. But there is indeed an altar in Heaven,[76] whereat Christ celebrates, and there our gifts must be offered by him: lifted up from the earth (first on the cross, then by his ascension, in the single movement of his 'passing over' to his Father), he draws all men to himself (John xii, 32; cf. iii, 13-15). Our good is in Heaven, our head is in Heaven, and we press towards union with them.[77] There is however no sacrifice in Heaven in the sense in which the cross was Christ's sacrifice, offered once for all; but the result of that sacrifice remains, with Christ, throughout eternity, and with men it is applied in time. So, properly speaking, there is no heavenly *sacrifice*. The celebrant, the victim and the fruit of the sacrifice are for ever in Heaven, but the sacrifice itself as a work, as 'omne opus quod agitur ut sancta societate inhaereamus Deo', took place only on earth. As Abbot Vonier rightly says in his *Key to the Doctrine of the Eucharist*, the heavenly altar referred to in the Apocalypse (viii, 3-5) is not an altar of burnt-offerings but an altar of incense, an altar of fulfilment, not of propitiation: worship in Heaven is not properly sacrificial, it is prayer and praise. But on the part of Christ, seated at the Father's right hand, there is continuance of his quality of victim immolated on the cross (Apocalypse iv, 7; Hebrews ix, 14, verb in the aorist), application of the fruits of his sacrifice, and sacerdotal action by which he is the high-priest of all our gifts and offerings—for, as Theodoret writes, 'he is the head of those who offer, calling the Church his body'. The fulfilment of the elect in the

[74]*E.g.*, the mosaic in the cupola of the Palatine chapel at Palermo (12-cent.). Cf. C. Panfoeder, *Christus unser Liturge* (Mainz, 1924); J. Jungmann, *Die Stellung Christi im liturg. Gebet* . . . (Munster, 1925), p. 215, n. 24; J. Kollwitz in *Theol. u. Glaube*, 1947-48, pp. 106ff.

[75]*E.g.*, St Vitalis at Ravenna (*c.* 530) and the *diakonikon* of Torcello cathedral (639).

[76]The Bible (Is. vi, 6; Apoc. viii, 3), the Fathers and the liturgies speak of the heavenly altar. Cf. the canon of the Roman Mass and the Eastern liturgies (H. W. Codrington, 'The Heavenly Altar . . .' in *Eastern Churches Quarterly*, 1938, pp. 125–130).

[77]'. . . Ut per haec sacramenta quae sumpsimus, illuc tendat nostrae devotionis affectus quo tecum est nostra substantia Jesus Christus Dominus noster' (Postcommunion for the eve of the Ascension). The same idea is often developed by the Fathers in terms of the Pauline theme of head-body.

fellowship of God will be the work of Christ's priesthood simply as the eternal (spiritual) fruit of his sacrifice, not as a sacrificial act.

Christ is the Alpha and the Omega of the whole relation of man with God, which has to be a relation of fellowship (God's fellowship-temple).[78] But he is its Alpha only through all his *acta et passa in carne*, *for* us *(ὑπὲρ ἡμῶν)*, whilst he is its Omega *with* us, not only in the body of flesh that was born of Mary and was crucified, but in his fellowship-body which we compose with him and in him—and he in us. He is its Alpha as principle and root, and his powers of hallowing, ruling and revealing consequently endure a state of abasement (Chapter III above); he will be Omega as effect and fruit, in a state of fullness, of opening out, of unfolding ('apocalypse') all the powers of the Shoot.[79] So the mystery of Alpha and the mystery of Omega or, if it be preferred, the paschal mystery and the parousial mystery,[80] are the same mystery, but under two differing conditions: the first a state of root and principle, wherein Christ is all and does all, alone, for us; the second a state of fruition and result, wherein Christ is still all and still does all, but not alone—he with us and we with him. Or one could speak of two states of fullness: the first wherein Christ is our fullness and we can only receive from him; the second wherein we also are his fullness, because he wills to 'complete himself' in us and to take his full stature from and through us.[81]

The space between these two moments of the one fundamental mystery is the time of the Church, filled with the action of the Holy Spirit and of the ecclesial institution, sacraments and apostolic body. It is for these two agents of Christ's work to draw on him, Christ Alpha, on his *acta et passa (et dicta) in carne*, that his body may grow to his Omega; at the same time this growth takes place also through man's contribution and 'doing', which as we have seen is the true Christian meaning of time. For the present we are not concerned

[78]Apoc. i, 8; xxi, 6; xxii, 13. In Eph. ii, 20–22 the theme of this paragraph is expressed with considerable force; there we see that the temple we help to build is as it were the expansion of its foundation stone, Christ.

[79]'Shoot' is a messianic name for Christ: Is. iv, 2; xi, 1; liii, 2; Jer. xxiii, 5; xxxiii, 15; and especially Zach. iii, 8; vi, 12. – Comp. 'Principium, Primogenitus mortuorum' in Col. i, 18.

[80]This is the terminology of F. X. Durrwell, *La resurrection de Jesus* . . . (Le Puy, 1950). This book must be recommended to whoever wants a good understanding of the fundamental identity of the two mysteries. Our text will show that this is how the Fathers understood it; there is an example from St Gregory in the Easter office: 'Nostrae dicamus, an suae solemnitatis? Sed ut fateamur verius: ut suae dicamus et nostrae' (PL., lxxvi, 1170).

[81]For the first aspect, Col. ii, 9; Eph. iii, 19; iv, 10: for the second, Eph. i, 23 (passive); iv, 12–13.

with this 'doing' but with the bond wherewith Jesus joins the Alpha of his *acta et passa in carne* and the Omega of the *tota redempta civitas*, his final fellowship-body. Inwardly, this bond is his Spirit; outwardly it is the sacraments and the apostolic body that ministers them. Among the sacraments, one forms this bond in a very special way, since it not only contains the power of Christ's *acta et passa* but also the active reality of his body as our Alpha and its intended reality as his Omega and ours: we refer, of course, to the eucharist or sacramental body, which shares the name of Body of Christ with his fleshly body (A) and his fellowship-body *(Ω)*.[82] This sacramental mystery which the Apostles were told to celebrate 'until he comes [again]' (I Corinthians xi, 26) is the bond between the fleshly body of the incarnate Word and his fellowship-body, between the temple that he alone is and the temple that we are to be together. This is just the old traditional meaning of things so well restored by Father de Lubac, who, after quoting uplifting words of St Augustine on the sacrament of the body, himself writes: 'The end coincides with the beginning, the Church rejoins Christ in perfection'.[83] Only he who has come down from Heaven goes up to Heaven, the Son of man, who dwells in Heaven: yes, but this Son of man, who is all our good, becomes sacramentally present on earth as our food in order to join, throughout earthly time and subject to it, his incarnate body to his body of fellowship and glory.

Let us go back to the point where all the threads of the Christian

[82]It may be supposed that the term has followed the dynamic order of things and that the name 'body' has passed from the historic Christ [DD] to the sacrament and from thence to the Church.

[83]*Corpus mysticum*, p. 203. The Augustinian texts, rather beyond those who do not share the patristic idea of *sacramentum*, speak of the eucharistic body and the fellowship-body as of one same thing. Apart from the benefits of erudition, the great gain to be had from a study of this difficult book is a better understanding of what the Fathers (and the middle ages till at least the twelfth century) understood by *sacramentum* and *mysticum*, words that are extremely close in meaning. – See also pp. 287ff., and, *passim*, texts like the following, which contain all that we have been explaining: '. . . Hoc agit universa Ecclesia, quae in peregrinatione mortalitatis inventa est, expectans in finem saeculi quod Domini nostri Jesu Christi corpore praemonstratum est, qui est Primogenitus mortuorum' (Rudolf of Bourges, d. 866; PL., cxix, 716). Augustine's commentary on 'corpus autem perfecisti mihi' now receives its full meaning. – To the restored meaning of *sacramentum* and *mysticum* may be added the traditional significance of 'mystical': see L. Bouyer's 'Mystique: essai sur l'histoire d'un mot' in *Vie spirituelle*, suppl., May 1949, pp. 3–23. The Fathers use 'mystical' of whatever relates to the fulfilment of God's design, that is, of the mystery of Christ. But for them this fulfilment is only in reference to the Christ of God's economy, Christ incarnate and crucified. Those things are 'mystical: which, like the sacraments, go on between the Alpha and the Omega. Cf. what C. Journet, interpreting St Thomas, says on the plane of speculative construction: all the workings of grace of Christ in Heaven have a reference to his passion on earth (Cf. *Nova et Vetera*, 1941, pp. 318–329).

economy of priesthood are gathered together: on the evening before, the sacrifice of the cross, which integrated all the aspects of Christ's sacrifice and priesthood, was anticipated and appointed as a sacrament wherein men were to worship and receive strength always and everywhere, from the Lord's pasch to his parousia. *The Apostles* were commanded—and this command, giving what it ordered, was a creation or institution of power—to do by way of commemoration the *same thing* that Jesus Christ had done and to show forth his death sacramentally. Catholic tradition is unanimous that Christ instituted a properly sacramental priesthood at the same time as the sacrament of his sacrifice, and also that the priests of this priesthood are such only in order to represent Christ sacramentally: with reference to the Celebrant they are what the mystery of the sacred gifts is with reference to the Sacrifice—simply the sacramental channel, a commemoration and re-presentation.[84] That is why in all these numberless sacramental celebrations there is always the same host and the same offering, as the Council of Trent declared; and why Chrysostom can say that the words of institution, which truly make the gifts the body and blood of Christ, have been pronounced only once, by Christ, and operate through the minister who, in the sacramental sense of the word, represents him. Jesus Christ's *sacramental* sacrifice and priesthood, like the stalk between the root and the fruit, are the link between his sacrifice and priesthood in his suffering flesh (the seed and root of all—'unless the grain first dies . . .') and that priesthood and sacrifice in glory which will be the achieved fruit of all (wherefore there will no longer be any expiatory sacrifice).

The sacraments belong to the 'space-between' in which the

[84]'We do not make another sacrifice, like the high-priest in the past; it is always the same one that we make, or rather, commemorate' (Chrysostom, *Hom.* 17 *in Hebr.*, n. 3; PG., lxiii, 131). This passage, which met with Luther's approval (Scholia on Hebrews, i, 1ff.), would have to be given in full were we making a theology of the eucharist, for it is one of the most pithy in Catholic tradition and has often been quoted, sometimes under the name of St Ambrose. See O Casel's commentary on it in *Jahrb. f. Liturgiewiss.*, 6 (1926), pp. 151–152. – 'If priesthood according to the Law has come to an end, a priest according to the order of Melchizedek having accepted sacrifice and made other sacrifices useless, why do the priests of the New Testament carry out a mystical liturgy? It is clear to those who have some theological competence that we do not offer another sacrifice, but simply carry out a memorial of this unique and saving sacrifice' (Theodoret, *In Hebr.*, viii, 5; PG., lxxxii, 736). St Maximus the Confessor affirms that only Christ is fully priest and that presbyters are such only representatively and by participation (*Eccl. Hist.*, 5; *Epist. Dionys.*, 8; PG., iv, 164, 545). Cf. H. Urs von Balthasar, *Liturgie cosmique: Maxime le Confesseur* (Paris, 1947), p. 247. In the West, see St Augustine (Krueger, *Synthesis of Sacrifice* . . ., pp. 103–115); St Thomas, *Sum. theol.*, III, q. xxii, a. 3, ad 2; etc. Other references for the priest as sacramental reality are given by J. Lécuyer his 'Essai sur le sacerdoce des fidèles chez les Pères', in *La Maison-Dieu*, 27 (1951), pp. 34, n. 82, and 49.

Church's mission is carried out. On the one hand, theirs it is very specially to link up the operations of grace with their historical source, the life and death of the Word made flesh. On the other, they partake of both terms, the beginning and the end. (1) They share Christ's condition of being both a visible human thing and a spiritual object of faith; they follow on from his incarnation; they represent and apply his redeeming mysteries in the life of man under conditions of earthly time. Therefore these sacraments, and the liturgy with them, conform to a law of both sameness and beginning anew, for they organically unite a spiritual reality which corresponds to Christ's *hapax* [V] with a sensible celebration that recurs in space and time. Like Peguy's 'temporally eternal', they are what has been done *once for all* actualised and made present in the order of ever-recurring things. (2) Springing from the single root of Christ, the sacraments enable us to partake of his fruits here and now. As sacraments they effect the reality that they signify, they represent a process that involves its own end, that does more than foretell it—it anticipates it. Hence the idea of 'realised eschatology', recovered by contemporary Protestant exegetes in a context and with a meaning which are not in all respects beyond discussion; 'recovered', then, to the degree that it corresponds with the affirmations of liturgical and theological tradition about the relationship of the sacraments to grace and to glory.[85]

Because God's economy is what we have seen it to be (Chapter III), comprising two 'times', and because the space between those times, which both separates and joins the root and its fruits, carries with it an economy of sacraments, the Church participates in Christ —who is our way as well as our Alpha and Omega—in two ways. Firstly, Christ is the *reality* of the Church's *life* in the measure that she is his fellowship-body, that is to say, in the measure that Christians form with him one single being in a life of sonship, πρὸς τὸν πατέρα. It will be so in eternity, and it is so now, but not fully and not unless something else goes with it. Secondly, Christ is no less the *means* and the *way* whereby the Church may realise this communion in the life of sonship. Principle of everything, Christ is shared in as end and as means.

This twofold participation corresponds to the twofold relationship, of authority and quickening, which, as we learn from the New

[85]Nothing shows better how the sacraments belong to the 'space-between' than the classical doctrine of their threefold symbolico-real relation, to Christ's passion as the cause of holiness, to eschatology as to his fulfilment, to present grace (Cf. *Sum. theol.*, III, q. 60, a. 3; q. 73, a. 4; etc.).

Testament, subsists between the Lord and his Church. No doubt this double relationship could be grounded on the two espousals that tradition has seen respectively in Christ's incarnation, when he was wedded with human nature, and his baptism, when he was dedicated to the ministry; but we do not dwell on this since, in default of space to expound it fittingly, it might appear far-fetched.[86] The gospels show Jesus as having *authority over* his Church: it is rather the line of the Synoptists and particularly Matthew, the ecclesiological gospel, with the Petrine passage in chapter xvi and its conclusion, xxviii, 18; but they also show him as the *life* of his Church, dwelling in her by his Spirit—and that is rather St John's line, all irradiated by the fact of Pentecost. Jesus is the Lord, the authority on whom the ministers depend (1 Corinthians xii, 5), and he is the vine, who dwells in his own and they in him. It is clear that this dual relationship does not affect the unity of the ecclesial reality, as can be seen from the simple fact that St Paul unites the two aspects in the idea of the Church as the *body* of Christ and Christ as *head* of the Church. The one Christ is both transcendent to his body the Church by his power and immanent by his life; the one body is both fellowship in the reconciled life of sonship and means, ministry or sacrament of that life.

This means a duality of aspects in the Church, the proper understanding of which is the key to Catholic ecclesiology. There are two subordinate common Goods in the Church, fellowship of grace and sharing in the means to salvation, and likewise two unities, two laws, two authorities. So we can understand the existence of a double participation in Christ as priest (and also as prophet and king): one in respect of his quickening relationship with his body, the relationship of fellowship pure and simple; the other in respect of his authority over the body and of the means to fellowship.

This duality will cease when the duality of means and end ceases: that is, when the end shall have been reached, when, his work as 'way' to the Father finished, Christ shall yield up the Kingdom to him and God shall be all in all (1 Corinthians xv, 28). The law of the economy of *fulfilled* grace is one of perfect inwardness: there will no longer be any *external* law, for this pertains to a state of things wherein good is exterior to the will; nor will there be any sacraments, for these pertain to a state of things wherein the source of grace is exterior to the soul—when a pool is fed from a spring in its midst there is no need to direct water to it from outside. The priesthood of

---

[86]But we shall return to it when we show that through his incarnation Jesus weds the Church to make *una caro* with her, and through his baptism weds her as the means of man's regeneration by the sacraments and ministry.

holiness and the priesthood of authority will coincide exactly—or rather, the second will be submerged in the first, for it will no longer have to mediate grace, as it does in our present state of 'exodus' as we journey from our Egypt to our Promised Land. We need not dwell on this point; it has already been touched on and references to traditional theology given (in the second part of Chapter III). In this life we live under a regime of outwardness and duality, that of a priesthood of inner holiness and a priesthood of celebration of a sacramental worship.

Here we may remember something that will be useful when we come to consider the priesthood of the ministers and of the faithful respectively: all priesthood is relative to a sacrifice, if not to a mediation. Now, when all things are fulfilled there will no longer be sacrifice: there will be its consequences, but not the doing of it; fellowship with God, but not the *opus* done *ut sancta soctetate inhaereamus Deo*. There is an altar in Heaven, and worship of praise, but not properly sacrifice. We are, then, driven to the conclusion that the priesthood of holiness, which is real and even higher than the other, is less strictly and less properly priestly than the sacramental priesthood, which is referred to Christ as means to fellowship and to a sacrifice strictly and properly so called.

But it must not be supposed that participation in Christ in the order of living and participation in the order of sacramental means are to be simply identified respectively with the priesthood of the faithful and the priesthood of the ministers. That would be to simplify at the expense of precision. St Thomas's position is more subtle and can be set out as follows (We will come back to the explanation and justification of this teaching later, when it will enable us to clarify the meaning and place of the hierarchical priesthood.)

There is a priesthood of the life of grace, of life lived in Christ, lived by the Holy Spirit: this is the priesthood of the righteous as such, the priesthood of communion with God. It offers up sacrifices that are called spiritual, not solely in the biblical sense recalled above, but as consisting of acts arising from the personal spiritual life. To this St Thomas applies the scriptural texts about the *sacerdotium regale*. There is also a sacramental priesthood which is a sharing in the priestly office of Christ; it is acquired through the sacraments that confer a character, baptism, confirmation, order. Here, living communion with God through grace and divine predestination do not formally come into the picture: it is a matter of consecration to sacramental worship, to the liturgy of the Church—the

present Church, here on this earth. In this worship, some are qualified
to celebrate and to give, others to take part by assistance and to
receive; the first are thus qualified by the character of holy order, the
second by the character of baptism and confirmation. St Thomas
writes of this sacramental priesthood with its two organic parts, the
baptismal priesthood of the faithful and the ministerial priesthood,
in *Summa theologiae*, III, q. 63, a. 3, and related texts.[87] It seems then
inevitable that in Thomism we must speak, as Abbot Bernard Durst
does,[88] of a threefold priestly title in Christianity: the wholly spiritual
priesthood of a righteous life; the baptismal priesthood (which is
sacramental relative to the order of sacramental means of worship
and communion); and the hierarchical priesthood of the ministers.
We will examine the last first.

We have seen that in God's economy of grace what is communicated to many (or to all) is at first given to one only. At its beginning
the New Dispensation consists in Jesus Christ alone, who contains the
whole Christian order within himself: all salvation, the whole Kingdom, all worship, all the world's peace—*Ipse est pax nostra*.[89] But
certain of the things that Jesus is or includes are extended to all,
other things to some. The gifts of salvation and fellowship are communicated to *all*: *all* are to be sons and heirs, to enter into the Holy
of Holies, and so to be priests, to go up into Heaven, to sit at God's
right hand and to reign: in short, whatever concerns the personal
life, which is at the same time the life of a member of a body. To
some men only is it given to be sent (John xvii, 17-19; xx, 19ff.); to
be bishops as Jesus is (1 Peter ii, 25); to be shepherds (John x; xxi,
15ff.; 1 Peter v, 2ff.); to be foundations of a church which is God's
house (1 Corinthians iii, 11; Ephesians ii, 20; cf. the article θεμέλιος
in Kittel, *Worterbuch*, vol. iii, pp. 63-64); to be a door (John x;
Apocalypse xxi, 12-14); to preach and baptise (Matthew xxviii,
19-20; Mark xvi, 15-16); to strengthen or confirm (Luke xxii, 32);
to forgive sins (John xx, 23), as God does (Mark ii, 7; Luke v, 21;

[87]III, q. 63, a. 3, c. and ad 3; cf. a. 1, obj. 1 and ad 1, where he takes his stand
against an ecclesiology dominated by the idea of predestination (Wyclif, Hus,
Zwingli), which ends up in an invisible church, and against an ecclesiology that
looks on the Church as the order of salvation or of Christian life instead of as the
order of means to salvation (Luther; cf. *Vraie et fausse reforme*, pt iii). That it is a
question of worship *praesentis Ecclesiae* is very notably stressed in both texts (Cf.
a. 5, obj. 3, and above, Chapter III, n. 68). See also III, q. 65, a. 3, ad 2, 4.

[88]*Dreifaches Priestertum* (Neresheim, 1947). Using a slightly different vocabulary,
other thomists reach a similar conclusion; *e.g.*, H. Bouësse, *Théologie et sacerdoce*
(Chambéry, 1938), pp. 106-110.

[89]This passage of Eph. ii, 14-15, is one of those that best express what is being
said here: the wall of separation between Jews and Gentiles is first thrown down in
Jesus, then in all the world.

vii, 49) and as he has given authority to the Son of man to do
(Matthew ix, 6; Mark ii, 10; Luke v, 24); to 'do this in memory of
me' (Luke xxii, 19; 1 Corinthians xi, 24-26).

This list could be made longer and the whole thing looked at more
closely, but it is enough for our purpose to gather the general sense:
those energies in Jesus Christ which represent a personal good
(without prejudice to the person's 'communal' aspect and his
orientation towards 'others': John xiii, 34-35, etc.), a good concerned
with salvation and fellowship, are communicated to everybody: but
the mission and competency to do certain acts for or upon others, the
charge of the institutional means to salvation, in a word, the ministry, is communicated only to some and this, moreover, sets them
apart from the rest. Whether one speaks in purely biblical terms of
saliah and διακονία and the rest, or in theological terms of ministry,
mission, powers and hierarchy, or in canonical terms of mission of
right (distinct from and complementary to the mission of grace), it is
all at bottom the same thing—a twofold participation in Christ's
saving energies, as a good of grace and as a means of grace. In
Augustinian terminology one would speak on one hand of the *res*,
on the other of the *sacramentum*, at least in the wide sense of those
words.

The significance of the hierarchical fact is now clear.[90] It is twofold, in accordance with the two terms to which the fact is referred,
placed as it is in the 'space-between'. In relation to the final fulfilment, hierarchical representation and mediation is bound to outwardness, to our state as beings still plodding on far from home: it
will come to an end when God is all in all. In relation to the Principle, to the incarnate Christ, the deep meaning of this representation and mediation is to make real to us, in and throughout the
'space-between', the way through which that which will be harvested
at the last comes from the Principle, namely, the *acta et passa Christi
in carne*. Our immediate problem is to know whether we are joined
to the Cause of salvation by the wholly spiritual, personal, 'vertical'
link of an act of Christ glorious in Heaven; or whether by a sensible,
ecclesial, historical, 'horizontal' link joining us to the Christ of the
incarnation, of the baptism in Jordan, of the sending out of the
Apostles, of the supper, the passion and the pasch.[91] Theologically

[90]Apart from this *significance* at the heart of the Christian economy, there are of
course ecclesio-sociological *reasons* for the hierarchical fact: they can be found in
any treatise *de Ecclesia*.

[91]This is also the essential ecclesiological issue between Protestants and Catholics:
cf. the author's *Vraie et fausse réforme*, pt iii; *Marie, l'Eglise et le Christ* . . . in *Vie
intellectuelle*, Octr, Novr 1951, or volume form, 1952; and especially *Chalkedon:
Geschichte und Gegenwart*, vol. iii (Frankfurt a. M.).

M

the meaning of the hierarchical fact, and historically of the apostolic succession which is the consequence and expression of it, is to show forth and make real to us that everything comes from the incarnate Christ, and him crucified. We say 'historically', because the idea of apostolic succession made itself felt at the moment when a sacrificial and priestly terminology was developing in the Church, the idea being formulated precisely against Gnosticism, a heresy that sought a *mystique* outside the Economy [P], a fellowship or Omega apart from the one only Alpha, Jesus, the incarnate Word. Against these heretics St Irenaeus brought his theory of the succession as an important element in the dependence and continuity of all teaching and all sanctification on the unique historical fact of the Incarnation. Theologically, the apostolic institutional mediation manifests and realises that grace and truth come to man from outside and on high, from Jesus who was born, who lived and who died.

We will not repeat what has been written in the second part of the previous chapter, and amplified in the preceding pages; but there is a very important conclusion to be drawn from what has been said here and there. The ministerial or hierarchical priesthood does not come from below, from the community, but from above, from Christ as the Church's Lord who has authority *over* her. Christ is our priest and in a sense our representative, but he is not our delegate. The ministerial priesthood's significance lies just here—visibly, sacramentally, to bring *Christ's* action to bear on us. In certain circumstances it acts as delegate of the community, and to that we shall return at the end of this long chapter; and on any showing the hierarchical priests are priests *in* and *for* a community. In that sense the minister is priest *of* a community, but his priesthood does not derive from it. In celebrating the sacraments the priest acts as president of the community of the faithful; but the power he uses comes not from it but from Christ, whose representative he is. (Cf. the encyclical letter '*Mediator Dei*' of Pope Pius XII). The Church is like any other body politic in the detailed organisation of her canonical forms and the provision of organs for her daily life. But in relation to her essential structure her hierarchy pertains to her sacramental being; it represents a mystery given to her from above and ontologically anterior to the existence of a community: the Apostles were appointed to preach the gospel and minister the sacraments before there was any community of faithful. The Protestant idea of a clergy delegated by the community can only be upheld on exegetical hypotheses that the texts do not support.

We shall indicate the faithful's part in liturgical services later on, and after what has been said it will be easy to see the principles involved. The participation of the faithful in and, in a strong sense, their consent to what the ministerial priesthood does cannot be considered as validating those ministerial actions, for the power and authority to do them does not come from the people but from Christ, the head of the Church. It is very important to be clear on this point, especially if one is to emphasise—as it is desirable that we should— the union of the hierarchical priesthood and the priesthood of the faithful in a priesthood *of the Church*. There is a by no means imaginary danger[92] of seeing no more than an obscure and, basically, single priesthood, of the Church, a priesthood to be organically exercised only by a community on the one hand and by ministers, organs of that community, on the other. A point can be reached—and Abbé Long-Hasselmans reaches it—where it is difficult to see how the ministry represents a special title to participation in Christ's priesthood,[93] or why the Anglican position, for instance,[94] should not be in accord with the traditional Catholic position.

The Abbé Long puts the problem of Christian priesthood thus: How organically to connect the three statements of Holy Writ that

> One alone is priest, $\iota\epsilon\rho\epsilon\dot{\upsilon}s$;
> All are priest (singular), $\iota\epsilon\rho\epsilon\dot{\upsilon}s$;
> Some are 'priests', $\pi\rho\epsilon\sigma\beta\dot{\upsilon}\tau\epsilon\rho\omega$.

He sees the 'ordination' of presbyters simply as the provision of a qualified organ made in an entirely priestly body for the right exercise of priesthood in that body. We agree with this in one way, but there is a certain ambiguity in it: its view of the Church, under the name of priestly body or body of Christ the Priest, is confused: it does not distinguish the aspect or moment of the body as fellowship and its aspect or moment as sacrament. In consequence it fails to see clearly enough how two participations in Christ's priesthood correspond to these two aspects, or how the Church as sacrament logically precedes the Church as fellowship: this was the order even in its origins, for she was a church of priests before she was a church

[92]The danger seems not to have been always avoided, not only in such 'reformist' gatherings as the Synod of Pistoia or, in a very much more Catholic sense, by the Möhler of 1825 (Cf. *e.g.*, *Die Einheit in der Kirche* . . . §64), but in our own day. See, *e.g.*, the essay of G. Long-Hasselmans cited above, n. 21, or that of E. Walter, 'Weihe- und Laienpriestertum . . .' in *Volksliturgie und Seelsorge* (Colmar, 1942), pp. 31–47. In his *Diener der neuen Bundes* . . . (1940), Walter began with the priesthood *of the Church*.

[93]Cf. these words of St Prosper of Aquitaine, himself a layman: 'Totus populus christianus sacerdotalis est. Verum plenius hoc ipsi rectores plebis accipiunt qui specialius summi pontificis et mediatoris personam gerunt' (*Ps. expos.*, cxxxi; PL., li, 381).

[94]As expressed in *Doctrine in the Church of England* . . . (London, 1938), pp. 156–159.

of faithful. In addition, the Abbé Long's view takes insufficient account of how the ministerial priesthood is, on the one hand, cause and begetter for the body, a properly hierarchical mediation between Alpha and Omega, and on the other hand is simply the advancement and expression of the body's immanent generalised priesthood, organ of a life that is entirely priestly. We will summarise what we have written elsewhere about what is called for when a Catholic position is confronted by one that suggests Protestantism, by examining the following formulation.

One alone is priest, Christ, who is Alpha, Omega and the Way.

Between Alpha and Omega, his priesthood is shared in sacramentally, with a view to the sacramental celebration of his sacrifice, (a) by all at baptism (confirmation), in order to join in that celebration; (b) by some, hierarchically, at ordination, in order to carry out that celebration.

All are priests through their spiritual life in Christ, and in Heaven they will exercise only this priesthood, which is the priesthood of the last and final reality.

This formulation is more complex than the simplified one of the Abbé Long. The texts of the third century, emanating from a Church wherein the theology of the means of grace was already developing, are more precise than those of the apostolical writings, when interest was chiefly directed towards the new reality of a heavenly calling and grace given to all.[95] Furthermore, texts do not tell us everything: we receive the content of Christianity more from actuality than from writings, tradition is a handing on of realities more than of statements. It is natural that a complex and detailed formulation should be required to express all the richness of the priestly reality of Christianity. We therefore do not so much mind appearing to complicate things by putting forward a more complete picture, in accordance with the above formulation, in which we try to do justice to all the basic aspects of Christian priesthood: for in spite of our considerable developments, not all has yet been said.

With our Augustinian background, which seems so happily adapted for the co-ordinating of biblical data, definition of priesthood cannot stop at the offering of the eucharistic sacrifice. If we turn to the gospels again we find we have to include something else in the proper work of the Christian priesthood, a matter of charity

[95]Cf. W. Manson, 'Grace in the N.T.' in *The Doctrine of Grace*, ed. W. T. Whitley (London, 1932), p. 60: the N.T. is concerned with grace and God's action, not with the means to grace and the ecclesial means to spiritual life.

and mercy. We find Jesus making his own the words of the prophet Hosea, 'I desired mercy and not sacrifice'. Like the prophets themselves, he did not do this to exclude all outward worship, but in opposition to a spirit of pharisaical observance. But we get an impression that there was more in it than this and that Jesus was *substituting* the exercise of mercy for the old worship and its sacrifices. The passing away of the Temple and of the Judaic system of worship that he announced was not to come about simply through the coming of a new sacrifice, a new worship and a new temple, those of his own body, but also through the giving of a new law, the law of *agape*. Such episodes as that of the ears of corn plucked on a Sabbath day (especially as given by Matthew) are significant, and their theology goes a long way. And this impression is strengthened at the very moment of the institution of the apostolic priesthood at the Last Supper.

The institution of the Eucharist is related by the Synoptists and by St Paul, but not by St John. Not that John ignores the eucharist, for he records (vi, 48-58) the Lord's words at Capharnaum about the bread of life, and is the only one to do so. But he often seeks to give the inner meaning of what the other evangelists simply record, and at the point in the Last Supper where they narrate the eucharistic institution he does not simply leave a blank: he tells us something else, which again the Synoptists leave out—the washing of the Apostles' feet. Is not John here giving us the meaning of the eucharist, and also throwing light on the institution of the apostolic priesthood? The 'As I have done to you, so you do also' of the washing corresponds to the 'Do this for a commemoration of me' of the institution. Is it not true that the sublime liturgy of the Upper Room follows that sort of law of so many liturgical actions whereby the full significance of what is done by a simple act is conveyed under several forms? Is not the content of Christian priesthood conveyed by two complementary actions, a sacramental celebration of the covenant in Christ's blood and that of the ministry or loving service? A sacrificial office of Christ's body of flesh and a sacrificial office of his fellowship-body?

The question arises again when we find St Paul, who had not been sent to baptise but to preach the gospel (1 Corinthians i, 17), using priestly and sacrificial terms when speaking both of his ministry and of the collection for the faithful of Jerusalem: '. . . that I should be a priest of Jesus Christ unto the gentiles—that I should sacrifice in the service of God's gospel, and that my [sacrificial] offering of the gentiles should be acceptable, being sanctified in the Holy Spirit'

(Romans xv, 16); 'Even if I am to be poured out over the sacrifice
and offering of your faith . . .' (Philippians ii, 17); and for the
'liturgical' signification of the collection, cf. Romans xv, 27, and
2 Corinthians viii, 4 and ix, 12.[96]

Doubtless it would not be difficult to find the Fathers using
analogous terminology with reference to ministerial acts other than
those of a properly sacramental character.[97] After all, the eucharistic
liturgy envisages the celebration of the sacrifice and the preaching of
the gospel together—the twofold object of the hierarchical ministry
to which a man is dedicated by the priesthood (*fides et fidei sacramenta . . .*).

We are not writing a theology of the ministry, but it is relevant to
notice how the inclusion in the notion of priesthood of the ministry
of spiritual mercy, inasmuch as it is a sacrificial office of men joined
to the sacrificial office of Christ, corresponds to the two sources and
objects of Christian sacrifice: Christ and the faithful, the Son of man
and man.

[96]Strathmann (in Kittel, iv, 232ff.) considers that the word λειτουργέω has
hardly any meaning beyond 'public service' in these texts, except Phil. ii, 17,
because of the association with θυσία. In *La théol. de l'Eglise suivant S. Paul* (Paris,
1942), pp. 107ff., L. Cerfaux gives reasons for a more religious, 'cultual', character.
The word λειτουργία, which in the N.T. signifies 'service of God', takes on its
full eucharistic sense in the Apostolic Fathers: cf. A. Romeo in *Miscell. liturg. in hon.
L. C. Mohlberg*, vol. ii (Rome, 1949), pp. 467–519. The ἱερουργοῦντα of Rom. xv, 16,
which is an *hapax* [V], put in association with προσφορά . . . εὐπρόσδεκτος supports
the strong meaning of priestly service more certainly. Cf. Chrysostom, quoted in
the following note.

[97]Systematic research is desirable but I have not made it. A few references are:
Clement of Alexandria and Origen 'spiritualise' the bread of life of John vi, interpreting it simply as the bread of the word (Cf. *Pedag.*, i, 6, 46–47; Origen, *Com. in
Joan.*, vi, 43; x, 17; xx, 41–43); often enough they interpret the eucharist in the
same sense: the Lord's body is his teaching (Clement, *ibid.*; Origen, *In Num.*, 17, 9;
and cf. *Dict. theol. cath.*, xi, c. 1559). But before Clement, Ignatius of Antioch had
written to the Tralleans (viii, 1): '. . . in faith, which is the flesh of the Lord, and
in charity, which is the blood of Jesus Christ'. So there is a line of thought which
approximates faith, hope and charity to the eucharist. – Chrysostom has been
quoted (n. 25) as calling the ministry of the word the 'greatest, noblest and most
excellent of sacrifices', and he remarks, *a propos* Rom. xv, 16, that 'Paul . . . speaks
no longer only of worship, as at the beginning (λατρεύω: i, 9), but of liturgy and
hierurgy—his sacrifice that he offers is to preach the gospel'. Cf. also St Cyril of
Alexandria, expounding Heb. viii, 1–2 (PG., lxxvi, 1396ff.). St Gregory says that
no sacrifice is more acceptable to God than zeal for souls (PL., lxxvi, 932), and
St Thomas follows him (*Sum. theol.*, II-II, q. 182, a. 2, ad 3). Many texts make
doctrine an act of priesthood. – Another series of texts that deserve attention is those
of the middle ages which give the word a sort of practical primacy over the sacrament, *e.g.*, Humbert of Romans; John Eck (and St Bernardine of Siena) says that
if in one place Mass were celebrated for thirty years without preaching, and if in
another place there were preaching for thirty years without Mass, the people would
be better Christians in the place where the preaching had been: cf. E. Iserloh,
Die Eucharistie in der Darstellung des J. Eck . . . (Münster, 1950), pp. 286ff.

The purpose of God's economy of salvation is to bring men, made in his image, back to himself, putting them under the headship of his incarnate Son in such a way that they make a single body with him, a single being in the life of sonship, communion, glory and inheritance. All that is indeed accomplished, as we know, but virtually and in such a way that men have still to effect it in themselves throughout space and time, freely bringing to the work all that has grown up in them since the first Adam. So the fullness of the Omega of the work of grace has to come both from Christ and from man, as has been shown at the end of Chapter III. It follows that the apostolic priesthood instituted on Maundy Thursday is at the same time a single and a double sacrificial office. One as to its end, it is concerned with two sacrifices that are not adequately distinct, since in their real nature they cannot be conceived apart from one another: that of Christ in a way[98] comprising that of man, and that of man not being what it ought to be unless it is that of the members and body of Christ, of members united and integrated with their head, of a body in which the head is fulfilled ('Adimpleo ea quae desunt': Colossians i, 24). Every Christian as priest is ordered to the celebration of the sacrament of the Lord's pasch, each according to his priestly condition in the body, ordered therefore to procure the truth of that sacrament, the fullness of that pasch. Christian priesthood—I mean the sacramental priesthood which celebrates Christ's worship—Christian priesthood cannot be defined without reference to the sacrifice of the faithful, that is, to all that they do to unite themselves all together to God in one holy fellowship. For us today, the way the ancient texts bring together the realisation of the unity of the faithful in one single body and the eucharistic celebration is rather difficult to understand and explain.[99] Here St Augustine is unsurpassed: for him, as for the Holy Scriptures, the content of the sacrifice is the exertion of that brotherly mercy through which we implement our determination that all unhappiness shall be taken

[98]How is this way to be understood? It would be possible to combine several answers, no one of which alone is fully adequate. One can speak of virtual presence, of efficient, final and exemplary causality. In the order of a transcendent cause, Christ is all that is in his members. St Thomas has recourse to a comparison with the relationship of a universal cause to particular causes in a given order: for example, a teacher who stirs up a notion in his pupils' minds, but in such a way that they will never understand, however hard they work, unless they use and share their knowledge.

[99]The well-known eucharistic texts of the *Didache*: over the cup: 'We give thanks to thee, our Father, for the holy vine of David thy servant'; and over the bread: 'As this broken bread was scattered upon the hills, and was gathered together and made one, so let thy Church be gathered together into thy kingdom from the ends of the earth'.

away by the return to and fellowship with God of everybody and everything; for him the eucharist is the sacrament and sacrifice both of Christ and of his body: when she offers up the sacrifice of Christ, the Church offers up the sacrifice of herself, the two sacrifices becoming one under a single sacramental sign.[100] The ministerial priesthood celebrates Christ's sacrifice liturgically only in making it the Church's sacrifice. This does not necessarily involve the *effective* exercise of a pastoral ministry or even *effective* participation in the celebration by the congregation (validity and allowableness of so-called 'private' Masses): it is enough—and, normally, according to present discipline it is necessary—that the Church should be represented by *one other* than the hierarchical celebrant, namely, his server. The act proper to the ministerial priesthood is at least shown to involve reference to the people's sacrifice, the liturgical service of the ecclesial community.

This is seen more clearly still in the customs of the early Church and of the classical age of the Fathers. Normally there was no ordination without reference to service or ministry: the exceptions remain exceptions. As well as priestly powers, ordination gave those of teacher and pastor: thus the celebrant was president of the ecclesial assembly and in many old documents he is not called anything else. Later, often much later (end of the twelfth century), distinctions were made, bringing with them both the benefits and inconveniences of analysis. Canon law today still retains more than one witness to the old interpretation of the priesthood,[101] and the theology of hierarchical powers shows the principle of other powers among them, constituting the hierarchy and giving it its unity.

In spite of some undeniable modifications of outlook, particularly a predominance of the dignity or personal quality of the hierarchical priest over his function in respect of a given ecclesial community, the developed Scholasticism of the thirteenth century maintained in its theology of priesthood elements that are crucial as we understand them. To each order it attributed some act relative to Christ's 'mystical body', side by side with an act relative to his 'true body' (sacramental), the first in dependence on the second. Some thought

---

[100]Cf. H. de Lubac, *op. cit.*, p. 79; Krueger, *op. cit.* This fundamentally biblical idea is already found in Irenaeus and Cyprian: cf. E. Mersch, *Le corps mystique du Christ*, vol. ii (1936), pp. 25–26; *Morale et corps mystique* (1937), pp. 150ff.; *Théol. du corps mystique*, vol. ii (1944), pp. 315ff. In reference to this doctrine, '*Mediator Dei*' very happily quotes St Robert Bellarmine side by side with St Augustine.

[101]*E.g.*, canon 948: 'Ordo Christi institutione clericos a laicis distinguit ad fidelium regimen et cultus divini ministerium'. But the canonical sense of *ordo* does not necessarily include the sacrament of holy order.

that the idea of the sacramentality of the minor orders could be sufficiently justified by attributing to them activity in respect of the mystical body without any activity in respect of the eucharist. In defining the priesthood of priests as a certain *potestas*, classical theology brought in the power of the keys, which certainly relates to the faithful.

For these reasons, and for other lesser ones, it would seem that an adequate definition of Christian priesthood must go beyond an exclusive reference to the power of consecrating the eucharist, as indeed some writers have firmly maintained.

Let us see how Canon Masure, and several other theologians with him, have recently treated this question of the hierarchical priesthood.[102] These authors start from a practical problem of the spiritual and pastoral order, that of the spiritual life of priests working directly with their bishops in the parochial ministry; and from the technical and theological point of view they invoke the following ideas: priesthood, a permanent quality, goes beyond the offering of the eucharistic sacrifice, which is an action (Masure, p. 27); the ministerial priesthood is a sharing in the priesthood of the Apostles, itself an extension of the priesthood of Christ. Now Christ was a priest before the sacramental anticipation of his sacrifice on Maundy Thursday, priest as mediator of salvation, and throughout his ministry he was initiating the Twelve into his priesthood, his mediating office, which is a religion of love and adoration as regards God and an apostleship and a ministry of salvation as regards man: in the Upper Room he simply instituted a sacramental and efficacious ritual sign of a priesthood into the reality (what the sign signified) of which the Apostles were already initiated. Christ's priesthood was communicated to them by the authority he there gave them to consecrate the eucharist. But as with Christ, so with the Apostles, priesthood was more than this power, since it was only the sign of the underlying realities, which went beyond it:[103] the liturgical celebration of the sacrifice of the Cross is a ritual sign of all that is involved in the priestly function of mediation—love and worship towards God, apostolic love and ministry of salvation towards men. This shared priesthood of Christ

[102]E. Masure, *Prêtres diocésains* (Lille, 1947), a work anticipated in *De l'éminente dignité du sacerdoce diocésain* (Paris, 1938) and a number of articles; P. Glorieux, *Dans le prêtre unique* (Paris, 1938) pp. 95ff. N. Rocholl's *Vom Laien-priestertum* (Paderborn, 1940), though concerned with the priesthood of the faithful, is relevant here, because of its concern to associate Christ's priesthood with his redeeming love.

[103]Masure, pp. 52–53. On p. 56 this eucharistic action is presented as 'the conclusion and efficacious sign of a reality prefigured in the souls of the Apostles long before . . .'

in the Church is that of the Apostles as such, continued in the episcopal office. The priest is the bishop as carrier on of the apostolic
function, who finds food for holiness in the discharge of his office;
and simple priests have to seek both their sanctification and the idea
of their priesthood in their union with him and their co-operation in
his apostleship.

This attitude has been criticised'from the thomist point of view
that priesthood is defined solely by competence to offer the eucharist,
and also on the ground that it is too negative where religious are in
question. Here I need do no more than indicate my agreement with
Canon Masure and the limits of that agreement.

We agree to look for a definition of sacramental priesthood that is
not confined to the power *conficere sacramentum*, and this because of
what we learn from the New Testament and because of actual
priestly duties. The Cross is the crucial earthly act of Christ's
priesthood in which priests share, but as its definitive act that priesthood comprises the reality, contained in that oblation, of man's
entry into the Holy of Holies. A power cannot be defined by the successful obtaining of its object, any more than a law by its effectiveness, or the allowableness of something by its good results; a sacrament is good independently of what follows: a definition of priesthood does not have to include the obtaining of the spiritual good that
it aims at. But it does have to include the powers and abilities, duties
and mission which enable priesthood to aim at that good. Man's
effective *vita in Christo* is no more included in the definition of priesthood than is man's conversion in that of apologetics; but priesthood
can no more be separated from the good promised by sacraments
than apologetics from devising a body of arguments suitable to its
purpose. A sacrament is not a 'thing' existing in and for itself; it
differs from the 'things' of the natural physical world not only in
corresponding to a particular category of being (symbolico-real) but
in involving a reality beyond itself. Were the power of consecrating
the eucharistic gifts no more than a power of transubstantiating
bread and wine it would be a participation in Christ's kingly power
rather than in his priesthood: it is a participation in that priesthood
only if it be the active commemoration of the offering by which
Jesus included us in his obedience and made us an offering to the
Father with himself. Doubtless that is why St Thomas and theological tradition do not separate priestly action over the 'mystical body'
of Christ from priestly action over his 'real body'—the first being the
act of preparing the faithful to be offered with Christ, to share in his
'passing over.' Theologically as well as historically the different

hierarchical competences are seen to derive from the priestly power of celebrating the sacraments, particularly the eucharist; ecclesiastical communion is an extension, a concrete realisation and application, of sacramental communion.[104] One cannot define priesthood by competence and at the same time exclude from that competence those acts through which there may be formed a fellowship of communicants, in which alone the sacrament can, sacramentally speaking, find its 'reality'.

Having defined sacramental priesthood by the offering of Christ's sacrifice, it is one thing to include therein all that it comprises and another to give a description of the duties of the apostolic ministry as a definition of priesthood. We define it by its object, sacrifice, and we give this object its fullest extension. Canon Masure, proceeding descriptively and having in view a particular problem which he perhaps does not put in quite its right setting, seems to us to offer as a definition *of priesthood* what is in fact the activity *of priests*, more precisely, of priests engaged in the cure of souls under the authority of the bishops and as direct associates and co-operators of them in their pastoral charge. He posits a kind of special privileged priesthood consisting of diocesan priests, which is a disregard of tradition. He himself is conscious of passing from the concrete duties and activities of pastors of souls to a definition of priesthood itself, below which the priesthood of religious who have not the pastoral charge falls somewhat. It seems to us that we can keep all that is best in Canon Masure's thought, and that surely is its essential part, without entering into the particular problems that prompted his work.

* * *

And now at last we are in a position to get some idea of the difference between the priest (bishop) and the lay person from the point of view of priesthood. But first we must state a very important truth that must never be lost sight of: a priest, a bishop, a pope is first of all a layman. He has to be baptised, to become a Christian, to offer his life as a spiritual sacrifice, to receive communion, to do penance, to be blessed, to work out his salvation. It is impossible to separate his personal religious life, that of layman, and the religious

[104]Historically there is that much truth in the thesis of Sohm and his school that the rights of magisterium and jurisdiction derive from the sacerdotal competence of the sacraments. Cf. R. Sohm, *Kirchenrecht* (Leipzig. 2 vols, 1892, 1923), and in *Festschrift f. A. Wach* (Leipzig, 1918); W. Maurer, *Bekenntis und Sakrament . . .* (Berlin, 1939). In *Scholastik*, 17 (1942), pp. 342-384, H. Keller shows what is sound in this thesis from the point of view of canon law. Theologically, there is only one hierarchy and it springs from the priestly power: cf. C. Journet, *L'Eglise du Verbe incarné*, vol. i, pp. 34, 601ff. and indexes; J. Fuchs in *Scholastik*, 16 (1941), pp. 496–526).

life of his office, that of priest or of bishop: the two are united in one single destiny, the destiny of one single person. The *personal* religious life, the *personal* holiness of a priest or bishop are those of a priest or bishop, as regards duties, material, sources, graces—somewhat as the sensitive life of a man is not that of an animal, though he is sensitive because animal, but of a man.

Hierarchical priests are alone able to celebrate the sacramental 'beginning anew' (in the sense we have explained) of *Christ's* worship, *in persona Christi*. This is extremely important, for it is the application of Christ's passion and the union with his sacrifice in the sacrament (at least *voto*) that gives value to all the rest;[105] and because, though the temple, the sacrifice, the priesthood of the New Dispensation are spiritual, God nevertheless has explicitly provided a *sacramentum* to forward their realisation: instead of leaving their spiritual 'reality', man's return, to him, to come about 'all anyhow', he appointed a means to its visible realisation to which we are bound to have recourse.[106] There is a visible economy of salvation, comprising not simply the one only mediator, Christ, but the Church as the great sacrament of what he did for us: such words as those of our Lord in Mark xvi, 16, Luke x, 16, John vi, 53, and others, are the real equivalent of that too-famous formula, 'Outside the Church, no salvation'. The root of the matter is that there is a divinely-appointed economy, joining the Omega to Christ as Alpha and as means, and that, if it is to be accepted, man's inward spiritual sacrifice must (at least *voto*) pass through the *sacramentum* of which the hierarchical priesthood has been given the competence and ministry.

If we now turn to the field of 'doing', the apostolate, we at once see that this is not peculiar to the priest: every Christian can exercise apostleship, a lay person as much as anybody else, and that not only *ex spiritu*, by personal vocation, but in a way *ex officio*, as a member of the Church. What more then has a priest in this field, over and above specialisation, professional training, acquired skills, and particularly the 'graces of his state'? Well, in the first place, he has an *officium*, an apostolic charge and mission that is much more definite, formal and pressing, much more closely connected with the work of Christ and the Twelve. But he also has things that his very quality as

---

[105] A truth of common teaching. Cf. *e.g.*, St Cyril of Alexandria: 'We are not fulfilled otherwise than by being acceptable to God the Father in the churches, Christ as priest offering us up' (PG., lxviii, 1016a; cf. L. Bouyer, *Le mystère pascal*, p. 461; Eng. trans.); for St Augustine, God receives 'caro sacrificii nostri corpus effectum sacerdotis nostri' (PL., xlii, 901). And cf. Mersch, above, n. 100.

[106] This idea, underlying St Paul's words on the Unknown God (Acts xvii, 22–31), seems to have been familiar to early Christianity: cf. Clement, *Cor.*, xl; Hippolytus, *Trad. apost.*, 3; *Sacr. Serapionis*, n. 14.

hierarchical priest brings to the order of apostolic competence: properly hierarchical powers, with the pertinent charisms, a certain sharing in the spiritual jurisdiction and teaching authority of bishops. Even in the fields that he has relatively in common with the laity, liturgical prayer, for instance, or the apostolate properly so called, the priest has a higher value of ecclesial capability, *i.e.*, of competence and gifts for the building up of the Church: we shall refer to this again when we speak of the liturgy and of the Church's apostolic function. And finally, in the celebration of the sacraments, and most particularly the eucharist, the priest is able to consummate the whole of man's sacrifice, which his apostleship, with that of the laity, has aroused (cf. Romans xv, 16; Philippians ii, 17) and of which, as priest, he is the appointed sacramental minister: 'constituitur pro hominibus in iis quae sunt "ad Deum" ' (Hebrews v, 1).

History tells us of Christian churches which began without priests —it is almost a commonplace—or which have carried on without priests. It seems clear that in the apostolic age many local churches had their rise from lay apostleship. In the era of the persecutions and afterwards, throughout the Church's missionary history, the seed of the Gospel has often been sown by lay people: by the Christians captured by the Goths about 250, by St Frumentius of Edessa in Ethiopia, by the faithful of Antioch seized by the Sassanids and deported to Persia, by St Nino, the woman apostle of Georgia in the fourth century; the faith was introduced into Korea through books brought from China.[107] Examples of Christianity subsisting without a clergy are relatively numerous. There are the facts found in concentration-camps and the like; there is the case of the Acadians of North America[108] and of the 300 families of Guarani Indians in South America: these last emigrated over the Iguazu after the expulsion of the Jesuits from the Spanish dominions, and eighty-three years later, in 1851, they were found 'carefully continuing the religious observances they had learned in the missions, baptism, marriage, morning and evening prayer, the observance of Sunday'.[109] Many of the Russian Starovery or Old Believers have gone on for centuries without priests or bishops, maintaining a personal and communal life of remarkable purity. And then there were the Japanese Christians: from the time the priesthood ceased to exist in

[107]It seems almost to be a law of Christian apostleship that when the faithful are scattered by persecution they bring the light of the Gospel to places it has not reached before. The first mission outside Jerusalem followed the first persecution and dispersion (Acts viii, 4). For Israel, cf. Tobias xiii, 4.
[108]See T. Maynard, *The Story of American Catholicism* (New York, 1941).
[109]See C. Lugon, *La république . . . des Guaranis* (Paris, 1949), p. 263.

Japan about 1660 lay people maintained their Christian communities, and on 17 March 1865 Father Bernard Petitjean to his amazement came upon their descendants at Nagasaki. Such things are happening again in our own day among Christians behind 'the iron curtain', especially in China, from whence come striking examples redounding to the glory of the laity.

These things are not only moving, they are very interesting theologically, and they put in its true light the question of the difference between a lay apostleship and one that is sacerdotal, or better, episcopal. Lay people can be missionaries: it is very important to recognise this, and to draw the consequences from the fact that the Church is already in a measure existing and at work wherever they carry the faith and bear witness to it: a token and sign of the Church is set up before the world, a seed of God's word, and therefore of faith. This gathering of a community, which has to be completed and confirmed by the priestly word and sacraments, can surely be compared to the first gathering around St John the Baptist and his disciples (Cf. Acts xix, 1-7; viii, 14-17) of a messianic community having faith, baptism of water and of repentance, but still awaiting the gifts of the ministerial hierarchy. Did not the holy women have this part of forerunner in relation to the Apostles on Easter morning? Given the absolute priority of the apostleship of the Twelve and a connexion with that, lay people can keep together or even begin to constitute a community of faithful; they can convert individuals or keep others in the faith, and the congregation of faithful thus formed will be, in a certain degree, Church: they will in a way be realising that aspect of the Church that so appeals to Protestants.[110] But the Church is something much more than a society of people who accept the Gospel: she is the *sacramentum*, willed and appointed by God, of a full reality of fellowship in Christ. And included in this *sacramentum* are the sacraments, above all that of Christ's sacrifice, the priesthood and ability to perpetuate it, participation in the apostolic charism of magisterium. . . . Simple acceptance by individuals of the gospel message is not the aim of apostleship: its aim is to put the believer in touch with God's presence and action as he has realised them through the Incarnation: beyond a baptism of repentance there is a

[110]Protestants see a foreign mission as directed towards the conversion of individuals, who when grouped together will form the Church; whereas Catholics look on a mission as aggregating converts to the Church, which is present from the moment the sacerdotal ministry makes it so by preaching and the sacraments. Cf. Perbal, *Premières leçons de théol. missionnaire* (Paris, 1937), pp. 113ff. – In consequence of their rediscovery of the mystery of the Church, Protestants nowadays often approximate to the Catholic psoition, as may be seen, *e.g.*, in the reports of the Amsterdam Conference (1948).

baptism of water and the Spirit, a eucharist, a laying-on of hands. . . . A lay person cannot complete the work of the mission, for it goes beyond the apostolate strictly so called to the planting of the ecclesial institution, the whole *sacramentum* of the Church.[111]

* * *

In the preceding pages we have sometimes used the term 'hierarchical priesthood', sometimes 'sacramental priesthood', or again 'ministerial priesthood' or 'of the ministers'; and on the other hand, 'priesthood of the faithful' or 'baptismal priesthood'. And other expressions have been freely used as occasion required. In doing this we have followed theological tradition, which makes use of all these expressions, and others as well. We will conclude this long section by examining this point of terminology; not, indeed, with the object of eliminating all the expressions except one, for no one of them has the advantages of all the others, and each appears preferable from some point of view, but in order to size up the respective merits of each and why this one may be preferred to that.

Father Dabin's collection (cf. above, note 23) is a great help on the historical side. But first of all there is this to be said: The Western Fathers[112] and scholastics of course distinguish the two forms of priesthood, those of priests and of faithful; but, even on the relatively rare occasions when they expressly state the difference and refer to the relationship of the second to the first,[113] they do not find it necessary to make the distinction clear by a definite terminology. This necessity hardly made itself felt till the Reformation, or with Wyclif at the earliest. Moreover, the theological treatise *de Sacerdotio* was not developed till late (beginning in the second half of the twelfth century), a little time before the treatise *de Ecclesia*.

St Augustine wrote once, *a propos* Apocalypse xx, 6, 'non utique de solis episcopis et presbyteris dictum est, qui proprie jam vocantur in Ecclesia sacerdotes . . .' (*De civitate Dei*, xx, 10), but he did not develop it further. Correlatively to this *proprie sacerdotes*, we find St

---

[111]For the meaning of 'mission' in this technical sense, see the writer's contribution to *Histoire illustrée de l'Eglise*, vol. ii (Geneva, 1948), pp. 360–361. Cf. also I. Paulon, *Plantatio Ecclesiae* . . . (Rome, 1948), and Pius XII, '*Evangelii praecones*' (1951).

[112]The Eastern writers cited by Dabin distinguish between the priesthood of priests and that of all the faithful, but they have no exact terminology (see *e.g.*, the *Const. apost.*), except Peter Mogila (Dabin, p. 598) who, under the influence of Western scholasticism, speaks of spiritual and sacramental priesthood.

[113]As do St Augustine (Dabin, pp. 108ff., St Prosper of Aquitaine (p. 120), Florus of Lyons (p. 189), Rupert of Deutz (p. 231), Stephen of Baugé and Honorius of Autun (pp. 233–234), Hugh of Saint-Victor (pp. 235–236); and later, James of Viterbo (p. 309), Alvarez Pelayo (p. 313), Thomas Netter (p. 317), Denis the Carthusian (pp. 325ff.).

Thomas calling the priesthood of Christians a 'mystical' priesthood, but the word is very vague and Aquinas himself uses it in several ways without explaining them. Probably in theology the most generally useful and exact terms would be 'priesthood of ministry' and 'priesthood of personal spiritual life'. The curialist theologians of the early fourteenth century distinguished between 'private' priesthood and that which is 'common', *i.e.*, public. However, it was the negations first of Wyclif and then of Protestants that made Catholic theologians set themselves to find a satisfactory formulation of the distinction.

Thomas Netter, whose efforts have several points of interest, on the whole continued the curialist position, the purely private and personal priesthood, offering one's life in sacrifice to God, and priesthood as a public office, ministering holy things to others (Dabin, p. 317). It was along this line that Luther's Franciscan opponent, Caspar Schatzgeyer, in 1522 formulated the distinction (perhaps for the first time) that was popular at the time of the Council of Trent and was to be used in the *Catechismus ad parochos* of 1566: between the inward worship which each one offers up in the temple of his soul, to which corresponds an internal priesthood, and the outward worship celebrated in material temples, to which corresponds a priesthood that is external and 'ecclesiastical' (*i.e.*, of the Church). A number of Catholic apologists used this distinction against Luther, but other theologians preferred other categories. Cajetan said that the Christian community has a priestly dignity which comes to it from the fact that some of its members are chosen to be properly and personally priests; the faithful are personally priests only *similitudinarie*, in a moral sense, through their exertion of the virtue of religion. A considerable number of others spoke of the faithful having a 'metaphorical' as opposed to a 'proper' priesthood (St John Fisher, in Dabin, p. 336); Lessius called it allegorical and spiritual (p. 394), and others, what is much the same thing, priesthood improperly or mystically so called (Cornelius a Lapide, p. 402; cf. pp. 408, 416); yet others called it 'improper' and general or broad, as opposed to 'proper' and particular or special. And this is to say nothing of contemporary theologians, to whom we refer below. But it may be added that some recent writers speak of an inceptive or undeveloped priesthood of the laity: this has the advantage of marking the coherence and relative continuity of the priestly quality in the Church, but perhaps it marks it too much, even taking into consideration the thomist view of the three characters, of baptism, confirmation, order.

As we have said, it is difficult to settle on one single distinction, for each has its good points. For the faithful, 'baptismal priesthood' is good only up to a point, for its very precision leaves out the priesthood of righteous life as such; 'priesthood of the faithful' is less precise, but better from this point of view. 'General and common priesthood', opposed to 'special', is much used in German, sometimes in English, but hardly at all in French;[114] 'universal priesthood' rather suggests a Protestant denial of the hierarchical priesthood. 'Inward' and 'outward' priesthood, or 'personal' and 'public', would not be bad were it not for the danger of confining the thing to one only of its aspects. On the whole, we prefer to speak of 'spiritual priesthood' and of 'ministerial' or 'hierarchical' or 'sacramental priesthood'. We do not call the priesthood of the faithful 'spiritual' in a metaphorical sense, still less with a suggestion that the ministerial priesthood is not spiritual, but in order to suggest the idea of a priesthood in the order of *vita in Christo*, one not involving any 'powers' which distinguish one member of the body from another and put one above another. We call the priesthood of the ministers the 'hierarchical priesthood' precisely to express this aspect that the priesthood of all has not got; or the 'ministerial priesthood' to express its aspect of function[115] and of service (rejecting of course the sense of 'ministerial' as delegation by the faithful, as Febronius and some Anglicans understand the word) ; or the 'sacramental priesthood' to emphasise that it is conferred by the sacrament of order— provided that one remembers that baptismal priesthood is also sacramental in its order.

It is said commonly enough that the priesthood of the ministers is an active power and that of the faithful a passive power. St Thomas himself does so. So far from falsifying his thought, it expresses it more adequately to speak of the priesthood of the faithful as active to share and receive, in order to perfect oneself by receiving, and that of the ministers as active to celebrate and to give, in order to perfect others,[116] at any rate if it be a matter of baptismal priesthood and that of orders. We know that for St Thomas, as basically for St Leo before him, faithful and ministers, baptised and ordained, jointly participate in Christ's priesthood that they may together, these by

[114]It has the support of St Leo: 'generalis dignitas ... specialis ministerii servitus' (PL., liv, 148).
[115]Father Bouëssé says 'functional': *Théologie et sacerdoce* (Chambéry, 1938), pp. 106ff.; Father Mersch says 'ecclesiastical priesthood': *Morale et corps mystique* (Paris, 1937), pp. 153ff.
[116]Cf. *Sum. theol.*, III, q. 63, a. 2; a. 3; a. 6, ad 1; q. 65, a. 2, ad 2. For St Thomas lay people are certainly *recipientes tantum*, bu this *recipere* is not equivalent to passivity.

N

celebrating, those by taking part, make one single celebration of the
Church, or rather of Christ in the Church, and of the Church with
Christ. Along this line of thought, guided and encouraged by the
encyclical letters '*Mystici corporis*' and '*Mediator Dei*', several theologians have recently sought to elaborate the theology of the relations
between the sacramental priesthood of ordained ministers and the
sacramental priesthood of the baptized.[117] In this view of the two
forms of Christian priesthood as organically relative to one another,
the technical scholastic expressions 'active power, passive power' are
as it were left behind (Tradition is far from being unanimous about
them anyhow).

And in any case they concern only the liturgical priesthood. We
have seen that, with Abbot Durst, we have to recognise, not indeed
three priesthoods, but three titles to priesthood, three ways of
realising the attribute whereby we are enabled to stand before God
to acquire his grace and fellowship by the offering of an acceptable
sacrifice (it will be remembered that that is our definition of priesthood): to the sacrifice of ourselves through a life wholly ordered to
God there corresponds a priesthood of holiness which, by reference
to the sense of the biblical Revelation and to the Augustinian synthesis set out above, we call 'spiritual-real'. Christ's sacrifice includes
our own, and ours has to be joined with it in as much as it exists
under a sacramental and liturgical form in the sacraments, particularly the eucharist: and to this sacrifice of Jesus Christ there corresponds a sacramental or liturgical priesthood, that of the sacramental characters. This priesthood is truly liturgical (liturgy = public service), always thoroughly ecclesial and communal, and it is
exercised by a ministerial priesthood which celebrates and a non-
hierarchical priesthood which participates. So we speak of a liturgical or sacramental priesthood of the faithful, which can be called
'common', or 'general', and 'baptismal', and of a liturgical or sacramental priesthood of the ministers, which can be called 'hierarchical'
or 'ministerial'.

Must we after all that takes sides about whether the priesthood of
the faithful is properly or less properly so called, metaphorical or
real? There is a whole literature on the subject, touched on in passing or, in recent years, treated for its own sake. Not proper priesthood, offering up sacrifices, inexactly so called, of prayer and good
works—so said Cornelius a Lapide and others in the past and many
in the present. But how are they not embarrassed by the Holy

[117]Rea, *op. cit.*, pp. 223ff.; Krueger, *op. cit.*, pp. 123ff., 148; Niebecker, *op. cit.*,
pp. 129ff.

Scripture which speaks of no other sacrifices, no other priesthood, but these 'improper' sacrifices and priesthood? Or by the ancient texts which say 'veri sacerdotes'?[118] Or by those of St Augustine that faithfully interpret the Bible on *true* sacrifice?[119] Nearly all modern writers have been fogged by priesthood in its social form and, where the liturgical priesthood itself is concerned, by the hierarchical function. It is curious to watch writers rebuking others for thinking of priesthood of the faithful too much along the line of hierarchical priesthood, and then themselves falling into the same mistake and arriving at an opposite conclusion, less favourable to laity. Here both sides do what the Fathers did not do—consider the priesthood of the faithful in reference to and by comparison with the priesthood of the hierarchical ministers. Holy Writ and the Fathers conceived it with reference to the levitical priesthood, dedicated to external things that were only figurative: and compared with that the 'spiritual' priesthood of Christians was a 'real' priesthood.

The three titles to priesthood that we have distinguished make a person priest in a way that is real and true: but these epithets themselves need definition, for they can be vague and ambiguous. In accordance with the sense of the Bible and of the Augustinian synthesis, real and true can signify that in which the economy of God's gifts reaches its end, is 'realised', attains its truth, within man himself. It is in this sense that we say the priesthood of righteous life is spiritual-real. But real and true can be taken according to the purport of a word that has a well-determined meaning in language (which is really what St Augustine was doing when he wrote 'qui proprie vocantur in Ecclesia sacerdotes'). If then we turn to Littré, we find under 'Priest': '(1) He who presides at the ceremonies of religious worship. ... (3) In the Catholic Church, he who, in virtue of priestly orders, has the power to celebrate Mass and administer the sacraments'.[120] If by the word 'priest' we connote sacrificial function in a worship that is exterior and public, then indeed lay people can be called priests only in a wide sense in the Christian economy of public worship, which is sacramental; and if we include

---

[118]*E.g.*, Minucius Felix (Dabin, p. 69), Tertullian (pp. 70–71).

[119]John-of-St-Thomas Poinsot feels the difficulty and offers an explanation (Dabin, p. 412). What we actually find here is that alteration, that reversal, in the use of the word 'true' that Father de Lubac analyses in a masterly way with reference to the expressions *Corpus verum*, *Corpus mysticum* (in *Corpus mysticum*, ch. ix); and compare the words of Peter Lombard (p. 254) with those of the Fathers quoted (p. 216).

[120][In the *Shorter Oxford English Dictionary*: ' ... (2) A clergyman in the second of the holy orders ... having authority to administer the sacraments and pronounce absolution. ... (4) A sacrificing priest, a minister of the altar ...'—Tr']'

the *power* to consecrate, then only in an improper and metaphorical sense, and indeed not so much metaphorical as improper, even equivocal. According to the teaching of St Thomas, which has become practically common ground among contemporary theologians, the baptised *really* participate in Christ's priesthood, which makes them priests in an improper or inexact sense (for they have not full power to celebrate the worship of Christ sacramentally), but a sense that is not purely metaphorical.

It seems that the following is justified by what has already been said and by what is to come:[121]

Sacramental offering of the sacrifice of Christ, which includes ours:	through an active power to celebrate or consecrate: SACRAMENTAL HIERARCHICAL PRIESTHOOD.
	through an active power to participate: SACRAMENTAL PRIESTHOOD of the faithful, true (not metaphorical) priesthood, but only in the order of living, without hierarchical qualification, which therefore may be called SPIRITUAL or MYSTICAL.
Real offering of the sacrifice of oneself:	SPIRITUAL-REAL PRIESTHOOD, or priesthood of personal righteousness.

[121]The tenor of each man's work leads to his own vocabulary. It is very difficult to establish exact equivalents, and even to have a uniform usage oneself. Still, I feel in real agreement with such writers as R. Grosche ('ein wirkliches Priestertum': *Pilgernde Kirche*, p. 173), B. Durst, P. Dabin and A. F. Kreuger, whose work has been cited; and, subject to small reserves that may be only matters of expression, with B. Capelle, B. Botte and others.

(B) *THE LAITY'S PART IN THE CHURCH'S PRIESTLY FUNCTION*

HOLY SCRIPTURE hardly brings the priestly quality of the faithful into relation with the eucharist but refers it particularly to holy life, good works and apostolic activity. The tradition of the Fathers keeps to the same line but is more explicit about relationship to the eucharist, and modern theologians go further still in this direction. Nevertheless, when we examine the sacrifice and *cultus* to which the priesthood of the faithful is expressly referred, we find that it is chiefly the sacrifice and *cultus* of a good life which are mentioned, often in the very words of the Bible.[122] A good number of texts, too, relate the lay Christian's priesthood to martyrdom. But some of them associate eucharistic *cultus* with that of righteous life, even in those passages which expressly refer to the priesthood of the faithful (the texts which, without directly mentioning this priesthood, envisage a participation by the faithful in the eucharistic offering are much more numerous). Such passages are relatively rare among the Fathers and in the High Middle Ages, more rare still, perhaps, among the great scholastics;[123] but among modern theologians they are more frequent. Sometimes, indeed, they have gone too far, and provoked a reaction among those writers who, as 'guardians of the liturgy', are very properly concerned for the maintenance of the hierarchical sense of the sacramental act.

It is clear that the priesthood of the faithful involves two different applications, one in the order of holiness of life, the offering of oneself, the other in the order of sacramental worship, and very specially of eucharistic worship. When we come to set this out theologically and to give a concrete descriptive explanation, we turn again (as we have done above) to St Thomas Aquinas; we rely on his inspiration for an objective and coherent organisation of the various aspects and acts of the priesthood of the faithful, which admits of a title of sacramental but not hierarchical priesthood, that of baptism.

We first of all distinguish, with St Thomas, an inward *cultus* and an external *cultus*. The first consists in acts of the theologic (*theologale*) virtues, faith, hope and charity, in inward acts of the virtue of religion (devotion and prayer), in the whole moral life in as much as

[122]St Augustine, St Thomas, etc. have already been quoted; Dabin gives others. See also Dom Botte and Father Charlier in *La participation active des fidèles au culte* (Louvain, 1933).

[123]We have seen that St Thomas never associates the biblical passages on the *sacerdotium regale* with the eucharist. It seems that the older scholasticism did not relate the idea of the kingly priesthood with the people's active participation in the eucharistic offering; for this, it was not the baptismal character that was invoked but incorporation in Christ, union with the whole Church in faith and charity.

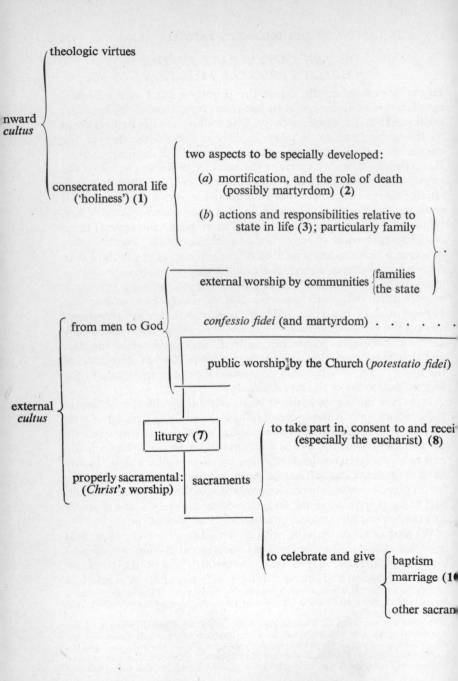

inward
cultus
- theologic virtues
- consecrated moral life
  ('holiness') (**1**)
  - two aspects to be specially developed:
    - (*a*) mortification, and the role of death
      (possibly martyrdom) (**2**)
    - (*b*) actions and responsibilities relative to
      state in life (**3**); particularly family

external
cultus
- from men to God
  - external worship by communities {families, the state}
  - *confessio fidei* (and martyrdom) . . . . . .
  - public worship by the Church (*potestatio fidei*)
- properly sacramental:
  (*Christ's* worship)
  - liturgy (**7**)
  - sacraments
    - to take part in, consent to and recei
      (especially the eucharist) (**8**)
    - to celebrate and give { baptism, marriage (**1**), other sacram

ood of parents **(4)**

ter of confirmation **(6)**

spiritual priesthood of holiness,
very close to spiritual
kingship **(5)**

priesthood
of the lay
faithful **(9)**

sacramental priesthood of the faithful

mal character, 'cultual'
ver of the baptised
son **(8)**

ter of holy orders . . . . hierarchical
priesthood

it is a holy life, offered to God. The second consists in the various *protestationes fidei*, whether they come simply from men or a religious gathering of men, or whether they are properly sacramental. The first of these categories includes outward acts of virtue related to God, in particular of the virtue of religion (prayer, sacrifice, and so on), public confession of the faith, above all by martyrdom, and that public worship which is not properly sacramental. The sacraments themselves are celebrations of the religion and sacrifice of Jesus Christ himself, which they make present and active, applying them to mankind and giving them to men as a means of worship of the Father. We next recall what has already been said about the three-fold title of priesthood according to St Thomas: the spiritual priest-hood of the righteous, participation in Christ's priesthood through the sacramental characters of baptism and confirmation, and the priesthood of holy orders.

These various aspects and acts of the priesthood of the faithful are set out in the appended table. The pages that follow are a com-mentary on them, references to the table being given by number, in bold type.

(**1**) The kingly priesthood spoken of in the Bible is the priesthood of the offering of 'spiritual' sacrifices, which are nothing else than a person's own life, especially in its deeds of praise, confession of faith, kindness to others, sharing what one has, in alms and in spiritual generosity in communicating truth (cf. above pp. 126). All this is referred to in the Fathers, the liturgy, theological tradition and the works of spiritual writers; nor is it matter for surprise that Protestants should be in agreement with us on so clear a point.

In a fashion as striking as it is sober, St Thomas writes of spiritual sacrifice consisting in the offering to God of oneself, no less, and he makes his own Augustine's definition of sacrifice as *omne opus quod agitur ut sancta societate inhaereamus Deo*; to him, then, Christian life has, or at least is able to have, the whole value of worship and even of sacrifice, in as much as it grows under the influence of the virtue of religion and of that faith of which all its acts are a sort of *protestatio*. In his *La vraie vie chrétienne* (Paris, 1934), Father A. Gardeil has shown Christian life making itself a consecrated life, a properly *religious* life, directed by the virtue of religion which, having human actions for its matter but God himself for its end, is a sort of joint between moral life and theologic life. This consecrated or religious life is also a *holy* life, in the technical sense of the word. Faithful interpreter of tradi-tion that he is (even if his etymologies are not quite right), St Thomas sees in holiness a consecrated or religious life which especially actualises the notes of innocence and stability or continuance (*Sum. theol.*, II-II, q. 81, a. 8; *in Hebr.*, c. 7, lect. 4).

This view fits in noticeably well with the biblical idea of a people consecrated to God, a people pure and holy, which is thereby made a sacred temple, God's dwelling-place, a priestly people. Israel had to be pure because she was chosen to be God's people, to do his work and to be the nation from whom the Messias should come. Surely it is more than a coincidence or a verbal accommodation that all mystics who attribute a sort of messianic destiny, or value as a chosen group, to a particular people or nationality or class also attribute to it a character of holiness, and particularly of purity. Under the new dispensation, God's gifts, attaining the spiritual truth of those that the Mosaic dispensation foretold, are more internal: the collective aspect of holiness, of God's in-dwelling, of priestly rank, remains real, but it is combined with an aspect of inwardness and personal assimilation. There is indeed the 'tota redempta civitas' which is offered to God in a 'universale sacrificium per sacerdotem magnum', of which Augustine speaks (*Civ. Dei*, x, c. 6), which is as well the temple, which is pure: but every soul also is the Church, every soul is temple and bride. It is on our attributes as members of Christ and temples of the Holy Spirit that St Paul bases the Christian necessity of purity: 'Know ye not that your bodies are members of Christ? . . . Know ye not that your body is the temple of the Holy Spirit? . . . and ye are not your own . . .' (2 Corinthians vi, 15, 19; cf. iii, 16-17). These motives, indeed, are the last and strongest we can have for undertaking and maintaining purity, not simply in the particular field of sensual and sexual impulses but also in life as a whole. (The contemporary application is often developed with reference to eucharistic communion.) Our spiritual-real priesthood, of which we are priests by the title of holiness, is actualised and exercised in the offering of all that we can do to put ourselves in a right order with God.

Since in all this the Fathers and theology have kept very close to the letter of the biblical revelation, which is coherent with itself, the notion of the priesthood of holy life harmonises and is bound up with the heart of Christianity and its gospel. The uncovering of such agreements is one of the great joys of the religious mind, as it is of theological study. The gospel is the religion of God's *agape* shown forth in Jesus Christ, who died for us and for each one of us. It is by faith that we lay hold on this gift of *agape*, this grace done in Christ Jesus. And in faith we find or receive the two great imperatives that determine the matter of our spiritual offerings: on the one hand, love and mercy towards our neighbour, the humble service of love, for the mystery of Christ is there present in our neighbour; on the other, thanksgiving to God, loving movement towards him, confession of faith by both praise and witness. If we re-read those passages of the New Testament that express the content of our spiritual worship, concisely, indeed, but coherently and exactly; if we relate them to the theme of *agape*, to the Sermon on the Mount, to the words about the new commandment and those addressed to the Pharisees: then we shall get an idea of what is meant by this holy life offered in spiritual sacrifices. Moreover, these are things that must not be forgotten when we have to talk about a 'lay spirituality'.

(2) When St Paul speaks on this matter, one cannot but be struck by the importance he gives to the offering or sacrifice of the body.

Let not sin, then, reign in your mortal body, so that ye obey the lusts thereof, neither offer ye your members as tools of wickedness to sin; but offer yourselves to God . . . and your members to God as tools of justness (Romans vi, 12-13; cf. 19).

I exhort you . . . to present your bodies a sacrifice, living, holy, well-pleasing to God, your spiritual service (*Ibid*. xii, 1).

Know ye not that ye are the temple of God, and that the Spirit of God dwelleth in you? If any man destroyeth the temple of God, him shall God destroy; for the temple of God is holy, which temple yourselves are (1 Corinthians iii, 16-17; see also vi, 15, 19 quoted above, and v, 20).

For a Jew, the body was in the first place, not so much the sensible companion and opposite of the soul, as that in which man lives and is able to act: the ensemble of conditions and possibilities in accordance with which he leads his life. So St Paul was saying in effect: 'Offer to God all that you are and do'. But there is something else more precise. First, an insistence on one aspect of sacrifice, the struggle with that in the 'body' which takes form in the 'flesh'. In baptism, says Chrysostom, 'you are made king, priest and prophet. . . . Priest when you have offered yourself to God, when you have immolated your body and have been yourself immolated: "If we have died with him, we shall also live with him".' Other Pauline texts can be joined with this from 2 Timothy ii, 11: *e.g.*, Romans viii, 13; 1 Corinthians ix, 27; xv, 31; 2 Corinthians iv, 16; Galatians v, 24; Colossians iii, 5, and all the texts on the flesh. This struggle with a carnal self, of which the body is the particular abettor, provides plenty of occasions for the priesthood of living victims that St Paul talks about. This association was expressly made by many Fathers and early theologians. In more recent times, the offering of oneself, with its difficulties, mortifications and 'sacrifices', has been developed with reference to our membership of Christ's body, with the idea of a co-operation in his satisfactory work: 'I . . . make up in my flesh what is lacking to the sufferings of Christ, on behalf of his body, which is the Church' (Colossians i, 24). In his encyclical letter *'Miserentissimus Redemptor'*, in a pregnant passage that would be better expounded than summarised, Pope Pius XI joins together the ideas of our satisfactions, sacrifices and battles with the flesh, of the eucharistic sacrifice, and of our kingly priesthood, under the ensign of the mystical Body, of the communion of saints, of our union and co-operation with Jesus Christ, our High Priest.

But there is more. After all offering of self, all *quotidie morior*, all *licet is qui foris est noster homo corrumpatur*, comes death. When St Paul writes of being 'poured out over the sacrifice (Philippians ii, 17), he is doubtless thinking of the spiritual sacrifice of the living victim wherein in one moment all the other sacrifices are subsumed. The supreme example is martyrdom, and the Fathers and theological writers specially indicated martyrdom among Christian priestly deeds. But if everything that we do to unite ourselves in holy fellow-ship with God has sacrificial value, and if the decisive characteristic of spiritual sacrifice is that it is made voluntarily (cf. Hebrews x, 7), then all giving up of life to God, all acceptance of death, is the ful-filling of our sacrifice, for each one of us. We are not able to want death or to be glad to die; but we are able intensely to desire one day to offer God this definitive and total worship, this 'pasch'. Only man can thus offer it, for he alone is a spiritual person freely disposing of a mortal life; the angels cannot do it. And when he took on our flesh, Jesus gave himself the ability freely to offer death (cf. Hebrews ii, 14-18).

Not without reason then does St Paul insist so much on this point of the offering of our body as a living sacrifice; and here and there he applies it to chastity. It is sometimes asked why such exceptional importance is attached to chastity in ascetical and pastoral teaching. Exaggerated language is indeed not unknown, to a degree where all sin seems to be reduced to impurity (as all virtue seems sometimes to be reduced to obedience); there are teachers who give the impres-sion of being almost obsessed by it, and of having ideas of the human body and the things of love that are more manichean than Christian.

This does not alter the fact that, in accord with Christian tradition
and with experience that anybody can gain in his own person or by
observation or as shepherd of souls, man's attitude to his own body
and the bodies of others, and finally to sexual matters, is of the utmost
importance for his relationship with God; it may even be decisive.

It is there that one begins to be enslaved or free. The aspects of
morality opened out at puberty are almost entirely new; one is faced
with matter for a really personal choice, outside the things of social
behaviour and conformity hitherto known. It presents, too, the
ambiguity of a possibility of simultaneous generosity and selfishness.
Here the sub-titles of Maxence van der Mersch's novel, *Corps et Ames*,
are suggestive: i, *Lié à ton corps;* ii, *Qu'un amour t'emporte*. The body
brings us very strongly into touch with self and with 'the other', and
our attitude with regard to it is decisive in conditioning our choices.
Shall there be giving, a harmony of persons loving one another as
persons, that is, neither treating the other as a means? Or shall there
be a love that is selfish, and to that extent without friendship? Not
that bodies should be excluded from true love and friendship; they
are the very intermediaries through which love and friendship are
brought to birth, nourished and, in one aspect, fulfilled. But, in
respect of others, there is that right order we spoke of in defining
sacrifice only when, bound to our respective bodies and to one
another's, we dominate an instinctive selfishness: then, made royally
free by purity, we can love truly, giving and taking between one
another as persons. Read in this context, St Paul's words are found
to be overflowing with truth and meaning.

Nevertheless, to stop there would be to humanise and restrict that
truth and meaning, since St Paul was chiefly concerned with a worship to be given to God, as when he uses sacrificial and priestly terms
of his activity as an apostle. Despite the clarity of text and context,
the definitely apostolic bearing and sense of what he says about
sacrifice, suffering and death are often overlooked (1 Corinthians ix,
27, xv, 31; Philippians ii, 17; Colossians i, 24): the spiritual priesthood of the offering of himself and his body is bound up with the
mystery of apostleship. But there is something else, perhaps more
radical still. In the Church's tradition, wider and deeper than written
texts, in St Paul himself, we find a very great esteem for virginity, an
esteem that goes beyond morality and has something ontological
about it. The offering of one's body as a living victim seems to find a
preferred and perfected realisation in virginity, maidenhood not
simply physical and material, but maintained for God's sake. To
consecrate is to set apart, to withhold from all secular usage. Conse-

cration of one's body, of one's personality wedded to a body, is supremely real in the giving of one's virginity to God, as temple of the Holy Spirit for his worship, as apostle for his service. In his prophetic description of the new temple, Ezechiel says of the eastern gate: 'This gate shall be shut. It shall not be opened and no man shall pass through it: because the Lord, the God of Israel, hath entered in by it. And it shall be shut' (xliv, 2; the liturgy of the Immaculate Conception applies these words to our Lady).

This far from exhausts traditional teaching about virginity, which includes in particular an eschatological reference to the order of the new, 'pneumatic', creation, whose origin is not of this world but in Heaven. It would certainly not be over-ingenious nor a straying from our subject to relate this to St Paul's 'spiritual' sacrifices. But this is not the place for a treatise on virginity, and enough has been said on the point.

(3) Mgr R. Grosche is one of the few modern theologians who, dealing seriously with the theme of spiritual-real priesthood exercised in the sacrifice of self, is careful to follow it up in the various states or situations of life, martyrdom, virginity, marriage, ill-health (*Pilgernde Kirche*, 1938, pp. 198ff.).[124] The application of what we have said above to a state of sickness, the enunciation of Christian considerations in face of bad health, is so easy that nothing need be said on that head.[125] Here, perhaps even more than elsewhere, the point is not so much to have good ideas as to live them; it is easy to talk, and deeds speak louder than words. 'The blood of martyrs is worth more than the ink of the learned.'

The four states that Mgr Grosche considers are doubtless the most characteristic. But it is needful to see the full extent of the application of spiritual-real priesthood to each person's conditions, life, gifts, responsibilities, for these are all involved in a last analysis; each man offers what he is and what he has in everyday life, and not only on exceptional occasions. At the heart of this big programme there are two aspects of special concrete significance, of which the first is the offering and, in this sense, the sacrifice of our gifts—Hercules and

[124]Many writers are unable to get outside the liturgical aspect, defining the priestly quality of the faithful solely by reference to the eucharist and treating the priesthood of holiness as metaphorical, making it a subject, not of theology, but of 'spirituality'.

[125]The Bible and the Fathers hardly mention it. Here the liturgy may bear witness to a certain evolution: the earlier 'secret' prayers tended to ask God to give us to him through communion; the later ones ask that we be associated with Christ's sacrifice. This seems to mark a recent development of spirituality, perhaps through consideration of the 'states' of Jesus, ideas of compassion and of union with Christ's sufferings and love, the extension of works of corporal mercy, etc.

Christopher offer God their strength, Thomas his understanding, Dante his poetic power, the acrobat his skill. The gifts that we have received have a kingly aspect, because they give us a share of power over the world's wealth; they have a charismatic or prophetical aspect, because they can be put to the service of God, the more so the more we are able thus to use them directly. This is specially true of the gifts of sensibility or intelligence, theology and other sacred sciences or learning auxiliary thereto, and artistic abilities. All these things and many others can bring matter to our spiritual worship, a worship which has its first-fruits and its burnt-offerings.

The second notable aspect is the priestly offering of that in the solidarity—and therefore responsibility—of which one is engaged. During the past half-century there has been a great development of this notion, which is connected with the emergence of a more lively consciousness of collective responsibility. Hardly was he converted when Psichari was praying for the army. . . . In Catholic Action this feeling of responsibility of each for all has given rise to the profound idea of representing before God all those with whom one is solidary, as it were to carry them in one's prayers and lift them up in offering to God. Many of us have experienced those vigils and Masses wherein young workers and students offer up their brethren as well as themselves, emulating Israel's role of *pars pro toto*, or the leaven that leavens all the dough (1 Corinthians v, 6). Just so do parents offer and entrust their children to God.

Israel had a mediatory role in connexion with her collective priesthood. She bore witness to God before the nations and was bearer of salvation to them. Since universal salvation has been confided to the Church, a mission ceaselessly supported by the grace of the Holy Spirit, the new people of God has not only to represent him before the world, to 'proclaim the perfections of him who hath called you out of darkness into his wondrous light (1 Peter ii, 9), to 'be a priest of Christ Jesus unto the gentiles' (Romans xv, 16): she has also to come before God in their name as the first-fruits of the reconciled world.[126] Here, again following St Augustine, one could develop the idea of *the whole Church* as means of grace, that it is *the Church* as such, 'ipsa societas congregatorum fidelium', which puri-

[126]The faithful as first-fruits: 1 Cor. xvi, 15; Apoc. xiv, 4. – The idea of praying for all men is found in the Scriptures (1 Tim. ii, 1–4), and still more, apostolic prayer for those to whom one is sent (Rom. i, 10; Eph. i, 16, iii, 14; Phil. i, 4; 1 Thess. i, 2; 2 Tim. i, 3; Philemon 4, etc.); but so far as I know the idea of a sacred representing of men before God is not found.

fies, remits sin, sanctifies, enables us to live in truth.[127] And with regard to mediation, the representing of God before the world and of the world before God, it is the whole Church that is charged with it. It is an exercise of spiritual priesthood on the part both of the whole body and of its individual members, and is of great concrete importance. May the faithful not neglect this intercessory duty, in which we are associated with our High Priest, Jesus Christ, and with all the saints. Katharine of Siena divided her Dialogue with God between three supplications: Mercy for Katharine, mercy for the Church, mercy for the world.

So we come back to a theological point we have already met in Chapter III: the three great offices that the Church shares with Christ have a wider application in their state of qualification or form of life than in their state of hierarchical 'powers'. The Christian's spiritual kingship—inner reality, not hierarchical qualification—extends to all created things; the power of government is exercised only over the baptised. Spiritual prophecy is directed towards the whole world as its field; the hierarchical magisterium has authority over the faithful. The hierarchical priesthood celebrates the sacraments for the faithful; the Mass is applied only within the Church, while the sacrifice of the Cross belongs to the entire universe—which no doubt is why the eucharistic liturgies, which pray so much for the Church and all her members, pray so little for the conversion of the heathen. But Christian priestly intercession is referred directly to the universality of Christ's mediation and redemptive work, going beyond properly sacramental celebration and embracing the whole world. It goes even beyond the world of men and offers to God all things that are his—space, time and inanimate nature itself.[128] We could quote Paul Claudel's *L'offrande du temps*, wherein a whole theology of the liturgy as a cosmic work and hallowing of time is expressed with an inspiration which is no mere lyricism; or again, certain passages of St Maximus the Confessor. The following, from Bossuet's sermon on the Annunciation (1662), is a faithful echo of the psalms, and its message, sublime as it is, is nevertheless quite simply lived by many religious men and women.

An insensible creature cannot see, but it shows itself; it cannot love, but it moves us; it cannot hear God, but it speaks to us of him. And so, imperfectly but after its own fashion, it gives glory

[127]It cannot be doubted that this is Augustine's thought: see especially *Quaest. in Evang.* l. 2, q. 40 (PL., 35, 1355); *in ev. Joann.*, tr. 124, n. 7 (35, 1976); *Sermo ccxcv*, n. 2 (38, 1349), and the texts that speak of Peter as type of the Church.

[128]Cf. 1 Cor. iii, 22–23, viii, 6; Eph. iv, 15; and the invitatory in the Office for the Dead: 'Deus cui *omnia* vivunt. . . .'

to the heavenly Father. But for its worship to be fulfilled, man must
be its mediator. Man has to lend it voice, understanding, a heart
burning with love for all visible nature, so that in him and through
him it may love the unseen beauty of its Creator. That is why man
is set in the midst of the world, a talented epitome of the world . . .
a big world within the little world, for, though his body keeps him
in the world, man has a heart and spirit greater than the world.
So that, contemplating the whole universe and gathering it up
within himself, he offers it, hallows it, consecrates it to the living
God. Man is the contemplator and mysterious epitome of visible
nature only in order that, through a holy love, he may be its priest
and worshipper before unseeable spiritual nature.

(4) The Church's esteem for virginity does not mean that she
depreciates marriage. The offering up of integrity of body and soul
as a sort of burnt-offering is a most worthy act of our spiritual priesthood; but among the finest and best things of Christian life there is a
priesthood of the fathers and mothers of families.

We showed at the beginning of this chapter that there is a natural
priesthood in virtue of which the head of a community is also its
priest. Hence, in the Bible, the case of Job (i, 5), such expressions as
'Be unto me a father and a priest' (Judges xvii, 10; xviii, 19), and the
family character of the Passover celebration (Exodus xii, 3, etc.).
Now in marriage it is the natural reality itself which is made sacred
or sacramentalised, adopted by a sacred act of the Lord himself: so
much so that, when two heathen are baptised, their natural union is
confirmed 'in Christ' and it becomes *ipso facto* the sacrament of
marriage. That is why the teaching that has now prevailed in Western
theology is that the partners, being the makers of the contract, 'give
themselves the sacrament', the priest being but a witness on behalf
of the Christian community; in certain circumstances his place as
witness can be taken by lay people.[129] Marriage is the sole example
in the Christian economy of a natural institution, in itself and as
such, being taken into the order of grace and made sacred. This
entails important consequences.

[129]The thesis that marriage is a sacrament given by the Church, and by the
priest as minister of the Church, was upheld by Melchoir Cano (d. 1560); Pope
Benedict XIV (d. 1758) still considered it very probable, as did some good theologians in the nineteenth century. This idea was reflected—and is still reflected—
in the marriage rite of the *Rituale Romanum*, wherein the priest says, 'Ego conjugo
vos. . . .' On the other hand, in the new rite approved for Germany in 1950, the
priest says: 'By the authority of the Church I ratify and bless this marriage you
have contracted, in the name of the Father and of the Son and of the Holy Spirit.
Amen. I call on all of you here present to be witnesses of this holy union'.

First of all from the point of view of communicating the faith, the Church's mission of making disciples and baptising all men. As regards the participation of lay people in this charge, parents are in an exceptional position, in that their natural authority and their apostolic responsibility coincide, their natural office and their Christian office merge into one. Their responsibility as Christians occurs at the very root of the life and growth of mankind. When they bring a child to birth, they can bring a disciple to birth too. It is through Christian parents that the substance of the human world, in the very act of its increase, turns into the Body of Christ and into Church. Families are actually and literally cells of the Church.

This is so not only in the sense of cells germinating to increase, but also in the sense of living cells in which the life and mystery of the whole Body exists in an elementary way. A family is a church in little.[130] How could it be otherwise when we find St Paul associating human fatherhood with the fatherhood of God (Ephesians iii, 15), and comparing the relationship of husband and wife with that of Christ and the soul or the Church (1 Corinthians xi, 3ff.; Ephesians v, 22ff.)? The Fathers and other theologians often speak of the priesthood of the father of a family, and of his authority as a true ministry, a sort of 'bishopric'.[131] Not that the priesthood of married Christians may be taken as a kind of priesthood analogous to that of sacramental orders; but it has its own particular position, three things meeting and mingling in it, namely: the natural priesthood of which mention has been made, identified with the father's authority (and how many fathers abdicate their authority and priesthood, leaving it to the mother . . .); the priesthood of holiness, which here has a specially wide application, in view of its exercise according to each one's conditions and responsibilities; and the baptismal priesthood, a true consecration that confers a religious power (*puissance cultuelle*). It is on the foundation of baptism that the contract of the marriage partners becomes a sacrament.

The priesthood of Christian husband and wife is therefore more than a simple application of the spiritual priesthood of holiness to a particular situation, as is found, for instance, in the case of a schoolteacher with reference to his charge. There is something 'instituted'

[130]Cf. Chrysostom, *In Genes.*, sermo 7, 1 (PG., 54, 608) and 2, 4 (53, 31). See *La vie intellectuelle*, 10 July 1939, pp. 9–29); and the Orthodox writer P. Evdokimov, *Le mariage, sacrement d'amour* (Paris, 1945), ch. ix.

[131]Notably St Augustine, quoted by Pope Pius XII in his encyclical '*Summi pontificatus*': 'in domo sua ecclesiasticum et quodammodo episcopale implebit officium ministrans Christo . . .' (*Tract li in Joan. Ev.* c. xii, n. 13; PL., 35, 1768). And the English Bede the Venerable, in *Homiliae*, l. i, h. 6 (PL., 94, 57).

about it, and that not only on the basis of an *officium*, a public responsibility, but of a sacramental consecration, that of baptism being echoed in that of marriage. Marriage is a charism [BB], says St Paul; it is a function in the mystical Body and an *ordo*, says tradition:[132] these statements are fundamentally concordant; but they have reference to the Church considered as organism, a body organically diversified and articulated, and that cannot here be gone into. Priesthood is here our business, and there are two points that must be particularly emphasised.

First, family worship, or as it is sometimes called, using the word in a wide sense, the liturgy of the home. There is prayer in common —grace before and after meals, evening prayers (Compline in some households), and so on; and the parents' personal intercession for their children, now in joy, now in tears, always in faith, hope and love. There is teaching the children themselves to pray and to offer up their own selves and lives. There is Bible-reading, and here perhaps I may be allowed a quotation from an unexpected author, writing what is almost the life of a saint. In his *Vie de mon père*, Restif de la Bretonne tells how his father would every evening read a chapter or two from the Bible to his family and servants; and he would begin by saying, 'Keep quiet and listen: the Holy Spirit is going to speak to us'. Then there are the numerous opportunities for *protestationes fidei*, family testimonies of faith, one of whose uses is to link up family life with the life of the parish and of the Church at large: the occasion may be personal—a baptism, a first communion, a funeral—or general, as at Easter or Christmas.[133] Family worship is necessary in its order, as the completion of what is ordinarily received from the parish, the ecclesial centre of daily life. The pastoral problem involved is that which faces all secondary communities: to be at the same time both closed and open.

Secondly, the state of being husband and wife, inspired by true love and a consent that is free and heart-felt, is very properly a state of 'sacrifice'; it is therefore a priestly state, in the sense of sacrifice and priesthood that we have considered. There are indeed in marriage very many occasions for sacrifice, in the sense of renunciation, and this not only through life's trials and troubles, but as it were in

[132]See the references given by S. Tromp in his annotated edition of the encyclical 'Corporis mystici' (Rome, 1946), p. 76, and in *Corpus Christi quod est Ecclesia* (2nd ed. Rome, 1946), p. 144. In 'Casti connubii', Pope Pius XI compares marriage with the charism given in priestly ordination.

[133]In the absence of all clergy, it is the duty of fathers of families (failing them, the mothers) to conduct some form of worship and to carry on religious instruction, as was done in France during the Terror. And cf. above, pp. 173.

the very structure of marriage. Husband and wife sacrifice much in relation to one another; parents sacrifice themselves for their children, and there again they exercise a sort of episcopacy, as St Augustine puts it, since a bishop weds his church by wholly devoting himself to her in love.[134] But the structural state of marriage is a sacrificial state in a still deeper sense, the sense already explained with the help of Augustine's definition of sacrifice as that which one does in order to put oneself in a right relation towards someone else or someone above oneself, 'Every work done with the aim of uniting oneself with God in a holy fellowship'. It is not for nothing that St Paul calls marriage a mystery whose whole greatness comes from its likeness to Christ's union with his Church. It is nothing less than a matter of Christ's love for and agreement with the Church, and the Church's love for and agreement with Christ. A love and agreement which bind both sides to a death and resurrection; which are realised only in a new birth, the one and the other in one, after a death to the life led only for self: '. . . as Christ also loved the Church and delivered himself up for her. . . . For this shall man leave father and mother, and shall cleave to his wife, and the two shall come to be one flesh.'

(5) From what has been said in this chapter, and especially in the four preceding sections, we can understand how the priesthood of holiness is *kingly* and that there is a close relationship between this priesthood and spiritual kingship. Many of those who would reduce spiritual-real priesthood to something purely metaphorical argue from this relationship thus: just as the faithful are kings but without having any power, just as, compared with real kings, their kingly quality is wholly metaphorical, so in the case of priesthood. . . . No line of reasoning could be more out of accord with the text and meaning of Holy Scripture, which speaks of the kingship and priesthood of the faithful in relation to the true reality given us in Jesus Christ, and not in relation to the sociological thing that human terms refer to.

We have defined priesthood by sacrifice, and sacrifice by ordering to God. But the Christian's spiritual kingship also is defined by ordering, or at any rate derives from it: it is the state of him who (spiritually) dominates all that is below him because, being himself subject to what is above him, he shares its dominance and freedom. Chrysostom can accordingly write: 'At baptism, you were made

[134]Marriage, says St Thomas, is conformed to Christ's passion 'quantum ad caritatem, per quam pro Ecclesia sibi in sponsam conjungenda passus est' (*Sum.*, *Suppl.*, q. xlii, a. 1, ad 3).

king, priest and prophet. King, when you trampled on all evil deeds
and slew sin. Priest, when you offered yourself up to God, when you
immolated your body and were yourself immolated. . . .' (*In 2 Cor.*,
hom. 3, 7).

It is not possible to refer to spiritual kingship without using the
word 'freedom': the two things are so close that they can almost be
regarded as identical. 'The world' is within us, as well as around us
in the form of constraints and restrictions warring against the Spirit;
and Christian freedom is seen in relation to this 'world' as freedom to
be completely for God, to be dedicated and subject to him. It is then
simply a reflex or consequence of the kingly priesthood, of our
ordering to God, with its twofold aspect of self-sacrifice (priesthood)
and of dominance over all below us (kingship).

To that is every Christian called, and in the measure that he is
Christian he makes it real. But the religious life (in the technical
sense) is the state in which the condition of spiritual priesthood,
spiritual kingship and spiritual freedom is systematically provided
for and, normally, best realised; some of the Fathers and other
writers put monastic life or, more widely, the religious life, into
express relation with kingly priesthood, or again, with martyrdom.[135]
May we notice in passing that it is a pity this doctrine is so rarely
brought to the notice of the faithful, or even of religious. In itself, the
religious life is an ideal actualisation of that spiritual-real priesthood
through which every faithful soul is personally and inwardly qualified himself to offer to God the spiritual service that we owe him
(Romans xii, 1) and by which he is well pleased (Hebrews xiii, 16).
But in the religious life, as in the Church at large, appreciation of the
worth and dignity of the hierarchical priesthood has lessened that of
the spiritual-real priesthood of holiness. If their vocation were more
often put before them as a pure realisation of the kingly priesthood
of baptism and grace, nuns and other religious who are not ordained
priests would be encouraged and strengthened in that vocation.

(6) A holy life, martyrdom most especially, the priesthood of
fathers and of mothers, the religious life as a showing-forth of our
royal priesthood, all have their outward acts, and we must now enter
the field of external worship.

In the New Testament and in classical theology, St Thomas in
particular, faith is the principle of all worship, inward or outward.
The second is always characterised as a *professio* or *protestatio fidei*,
and this involves a profound theology of worship, closely connected

---

[135]It is from this point of view that the monastic life is sometimes called a second
baptism, likening it to baptism of blood (not to sacramental baptism!).

with ecclesiology. Traditionally, martyrdom is the outstanding act of spiritual priesthood, as a perfect sacrifice in perfect conformity with Jesus Christ. It is also an act of spiritual kingship and, as the supreme testimony, of Christian prophecy (the New Testament sometimes refers to our Lord's own death as 'bearing witness'; cf. 1 Timothy vi, 13; ii, 6). Martyrdom, indeed, is the noblest act of Christian life, and the true disciple, wanting like St Ignatius of Antioch to become fully such, can but long for the grace of this complete following of his Lord. Short of martyrdom, there is a *sacrificium confessionis*: it may be a sacrifice of praise, such as Augustine offered in his *Confessions*, or an act of worship that bears witness, *protestatio fidei*, according with the two meanings of the word 'confession'. In the second sense, St Thomas speaks of it as an act of worship which is specially associated with that power of worship, a participation in Christ's priesthood, which is the character of the sacrament of confirmation. The Christian who is confirmed, he says, exercises in the Church the *officium* or *ministerium* of publicly professing or confessing the faith; and according to his use of them, the words *officium* and *ministerium* imply an act of Christ in the Christian.[136]

It is not surprising that some theologians and pontifical statements have associated Catholic Action with the sacrament of confirmation, thus giving it a basis in the priestly consecration of the faithful.[137] We have indeed seen that, biblically speaking, the kingly priesthood is directed to the consecrated people's bearing witness to God before the world (1 Peter i, 9, and note 9 above). But Catholic Action has

---

[136]The following two texts represent St Thomas's mature thought: 'Omnia sacramenta sunt quaedam fidei protestationes. Sicut igitur baptizatus accipit potestatem spiritualem ad protestandam fidem per susceptionem aliorum sacramentorum, ita confirmatus accipit potestatem publice fidem Christi verbis profitendi, quasi ex officio' (*Sum. theol.*, III, q. lxxii, a. 5, ad 2). 'Per ordinem et confirmationem deputantur fideles Christi ad aliqua specialia officia. . . . Ordo et confirmatio habent quamdam excellentiam ratione ministerii' (q. lxv, ad 2, 4). See also *IV Sent.*, d. xlix, q. 5, a. 3, qa 2; *Quodl.* ix, a. 14; *Com. in Rom.*, c. 10, lect. 2; *Sum. theol.*, II-II, q. iii; q. clxxvii, a. 1; III, q. lxxii, a. 5, 9.

[137]Pope Pius XI several times presented Catholic Action as an activity of the kingly priesthood of the faithful: *e.g.*, in the encyclicals '*Ubi arcano*' (A.A.S., 1922, p. 695) and '*Ad catholici sacerdotii*' (A.A.S., 1936, pp. 46-47) and cf. the letter '*Cum ex epistula*' (A.A.S., 1928, p. 296). It is also expressly associated with (baptism and) confirmation, understood according to St Thomas: *e.g.*, in the letter '*Ex officiosis libris*' (A.A.S., 1934, p. 629). Apart from the texts of St Thomas just cited, there is the little-known one in II-II, q. clxxxii, a. 2, ad 3: 'Sacrificium spiritualiter Deo offertur cum aliquid ei exhibetur. . . . Offerre autem debit aliquis Deo, primo quidem animam suam . . ., secundo animas aliorum, secundum illud Apoc. (xxii, 17), "Qui audit, dicat, Veni . . .".' The invoking of this last text in the sense of the overcoming of another through the testimony of one who by faith has understood Christ's word, and its association with the theme of spiritual sacrifice, are deserving of notice.

other bases besides that priesthood—lively personal faith, the hierarchical mandate. Moreover, as *action*—and Pius XI insisted strongly
on this—it belongs more to the prophetical office than to the faithful's priesthood. We accordingly reserve this matter to a special
chapter, and now turn our attention to the Church's public worship,
the liturgy properly so called.

(7) In the table given above we indicate two parts in this matter:
man's worship of God, and Christ's own worship, which the Church
celebrates under a sacramental form. Before considering the main
points in the sacramental part that involve the laity, it seems desirable to give a broad summary of the Church's public worship.

As it tends towards its eschatological Omega, the life of the
Church is nourished from two sources, the first and the Second
Adam. What at the end will be God's community-temple is mankind
created in God's image, the increased and multiplied substance of
Adam; but as a body of sonship in Christ it is a body that is spiritually renewed, with a new head, and derives from the incarnate Son.
We may speak of a source of increase, on the side of matter, and of a
source of animation and quality, of which Christ is the sole principle,
chiefly in the mystery of his going to his Father. At one and the same
time it all comes from the *acta et passa Christi in carne* and all from
Adam, in as much as, being in the flesh a race of human beings, it
becomes in the spirit the body of Jesus Christ.

Hence the two aspects of the mystery of the Church. In a sentence,
there is the institution for reconciliation and there is the community
or society of those reconciled. The institution has to communicate
Christ, their Alpha, to men; in the community, the *collectio fidelium*,
the peoples of the earth are raised to God in Christ, whose inheritance they are (Psalm ii, 8; Hebrews i, 2; cf. Apocalypse v, 9; xxi, 26,
and the 'chosen people' of 1 Peter ii, 9). These two aspects are found
also in Christian worship: there is a worship which comes to the
Church from above, and a worship from below; together they make
up the Church's worship and sacrifice to her God.

From above, the Church receives Christ's worship and sacrifice,
which she celebrates sacramentally, that is, under the form of a
spiritual reality of eternal worth made present and applied under
earthly veils. Of this worship and sacrifice, Jesus Christ is alone and
personally the true priest. The Church, however, carries them out
in persona Christi, forming one single celebrant with him: this is due,
on the one hand, to the sacramental reality of the apostolic institution, in accordance with the truth that one sent, a *saliah*, is by right
the same person as he who sends him; and on the other, to the

identity of the power that is at work: *virtus Christi, virtus Spiritus sancti*.

In this celebration, understood 'formally', the priest exercises only a *ministerium*, in the sense of that word in St Augustine and the scholastics, *vis-a-vis* Christ as *auctor* of the sacraments. More exactly, the priest acts as minister *of Jesus Christ*. It is true that even in sacramental actions the priest is minister of the Church and president of the worshipping congregation, but properly speaking he is not acting in virtue of those titles and the powers they confer (see pp. 201ff.). When the Church commemorates Christ's passion she does not simply call him to mind and praise God in so doing: she (sacramentally) makes him present in his immolation and actualises the power of his sacrifice. It is *he* who is the real celebrant; the priest is so only *in persona ejus*.

In the worship that comes from *below*, the priest acts as representing the community, presiding at the assembly for worship. The worship comes from man and goes up to God. The worship we are considering is not that of a particular Christian or of a group of faithful, however large, meeting together under their own leader, for that is still, theologically and canonically speaking, a *private* thing: our concern is public worship, instituted, acknowledged, vouched for by the Church, who is a moral person.[138] The Church as a whole, the universal society of the faithful, one and holy, constitutes as such a real subject of rights and proceedings; she is like a person, a moral person indeed. From this point of view she is not so much the body of Christ as his bride; as body, she forms with him *una caro, una persona mystica*, but when she is considered as herself a person, it is bride that she should be called (Cf. St Thomas, IV *Sent.*, d. xlix, q. 4, a. 3, ad 4). The worship of the Church as such, considered not simply as Christ's worship sacramentally celebrated but as her own worship, is worship as bride, and in this respect a theology of liturgy must learn from an ecclesiology of the Church as bride. Furthermore, just as the Church's moral personality is partially realised in lesser moral persons of one sort or another, so her quality of bride can be attributed in a partial and lesser degree to particular communities, such as dioceses, parishes, religious houses.

Some readers may perhaps be a little shocked, or at least disturbed, by the juridical flavour of the categories and terms used above. This unpleasant impression will be dispelled if they will try to see the realities behind this terminology; they will find that we are

---

[138] The Church is a moral person 'ex ipsa ordinatione divina', and she includes lesser moral persons, of ecclesiastical ordinance (*Codex juris can.*, c. 100).

talking about very concrete and very mystical aspects of the mystery of the Church. The need for precision makes certain demands; perhaps we have not met them in the best way, but it is one way of doing it. . . .

All the faithful are celebrants in the worship of the ecclesial community, but the hierarchical priest is the normal minister, not in the sense of minister of Christ, but *of the Church*. About the conditions of this, St Thomas's teaching is clear. He first distinguishes sharply, and in the Mass itself, between the properly sacramental work done *in persona Christi* and prayer, the sacrifice of praise, done *in persona Ecclesiae* (*Sum. theol.*, III, q. lxxxii, a. 6). He also distinguishes purely personal or private prayer, in which at bottom the priest is simply a *fidelis*, and whose worth depends on his own fervour, and communal prayer wherein the priest takes part as the Church's minister to offer up the people's prayers and join his own thereto (*Com. in* 1 *Cor.*, c. 11, lect. 2; *Sum. theol.*, II-II, q. lxxxiii, a. 12; and elsewhere). In the degree that he does this as the Church's minister, the priest here acts 'in persona Ecclesiae, cujus est minister . . ., in cujus unitate consistit'; the Church as it were takes over his intercession and so gives it a value relatively independent of the priest's personal worthiness and fervour.[139] This does not hold good for a priest separated from the Church's communion by heresy, schism or excommunication, though such a one can always celebrate validly *in persona Christi* (III, q. lxxxii, a. 7, ad 3; cf. a. 5).

But after all, prayer is not an act peculiar to priests; every Christian can and should pray, and for others as well as himself. Now, if certain acts of the Church's non-sacramental public worship seem indeed to depend, if not on a priest, at least on a lesser cleric, still prayers, even communal public prayers, do not appear to call for a properly hierarchical sacred qualification. Sacraments are within the competence of priests, sacramentals within that of lesser hierarchical ministers, such as exorcists; but the ordinary faithful can carry out certain duties of the Church's public worship. In the absence of a priest, they can be witnesses to a sacramental marriage, they can preside at prayer, thousands of nuns without any hierarchical qualifications celebrate the Divine Office. . . . At youth camps and conferences, at meetings of lay groups, in mission countries, in internment camps and at times of persecution, lay people often preside at

---

[139]*Sum. theol.*, III, q. lxxxii, a. 6. The idea of the value in itself of prayer made *in persona Ecclesiae* can be interpreted in too mechanical, juridical and ritualistic a way. Father E. Mersch's pages on the subject (*Morale et Corps mystique*, 1937, pp. 125–126) seem not altogether to escape this danger.

communal prayer, and liturgical prayer at that, Vespers or Compline or the Mass prayers without a consecration.

So an hierarchical priest doing the same thing is, without ceasing to be what he is, simply filling the office of delegate and president of a community. It could not be otherwise. But he is something else as well, and as that something else he is not the delegate of the community. A priest is the official witness at a wedding, he presides at a service of prayer, as having received canonical commission and cure of souls from his bishop, or as having been deputed by his rector. He is an instituted and hierarchical minister even for these 'lay' duties; theologically and canonically he is delegate of the Church as moral person by divine ordinance, not of the Church as community of the faithful. That does not prevent him from being a man among men, a man of God and a man of prayer in the midst of a community of which he is part and to which he can be like a spiritual pacemaker.[140]

It is to be expected that an appreciation of this aspect of the pastoral whole should be very specially called for at the present time, when there is a renewed consciousness of the fact that the Church, *as well as* being built up from above, is also built up from below by men's work and co-operation. We shall return to that yet again, for it touches the heart of our subject. We shall see, too, that nothing is more useless than to set up an opposition—or even a bare separation—between that which comes from above in the Church as body of Christ and that which comes from below. We can see their unity in the two parts of the Church's worship, and this will become yet more clear in the following paragraphs.

There is a give-and-take, a sort of mutual complementing, between these two parts of the Church's worship, so that together they form one single liturgy. Looked at in their celebration or exercise, the sacraments have two aspects: they are a movement of man to God, with their corresponding value as worship, and a gift of God to

[140]Writing theologically and canonically, we have said 'president of prayer'; spiritually and pastorally, we must add 'head of prayer', for there is a difference between president and head. He who is a president of prayer, and no more, may be cut off from this community; it is possible to ensure order and dignity in the services without adding anything to people's spiritual life. A head is one who communicates something to life, someone who does something *with* men and enables them to do something *with* him. In this essential matter of prayer, the priest has to be his people's man, their spiritual trainer, doing something with them, and they with him. As a concrete application, the abbé Michonneau urges that the priest should not be always and only at the altar, but that he should come down among the people sometimes, encouraging them to pray and sing, an active and visible leaven working in the *sacrificium laudis*. – This is a particular point, but it vitally affects the whole pastoral office and priestly attitude.

man, with their corresponding value for sanctification (*Sum. theol.*, III, q. lx, a. 5). The sacrament of penance, for instance, is constituted by sacramental absolution following on a movement of repentance: God's gift comes down on a man who offers him the worship of penitence in accordance with the Church's forms. The same sort of thing can be said of the other sacraments: in marriage, anointing of the sick, confirmation, holy orders, the consecration and the gift (or promise) of grace answers to an offering of self made by man to God in union with Jesus Christ and through his mediation. So, too, in the baptism of adults, and most clearly of all in the celebration of the eucharist. In *The Christian Sacrifice*, Canon Masure shows well how, at Mass, it is the poor gifts of us sinful creatures that are transubstantiated into signs of Christ's perfect gift; and how our return to God through the offering of ourselves, which we are unable to make wholly effective, is taken up by Christ and by him borne to its end in his own return. Our worship is perfected in this celebration of the sacrament—*usus sacramenti*, says St Thomas—wherein, the Holy Spirit appropriating to us the gift of God, all our desire for the grace of the sacrament is divinely answered. *Opus operantis* and *ex opere operato* are made one single spiritual reality of grace. Surely it is a sort of law of the divine economy that man, moved and encouraged by God, has to strive towards an end that he can only reach with the support of a gift of grace. What has been said here is illustrated by what we have said before about 'the dialectic of giving and doing' and about the meaning of history in relation to the Kingdom of God, by the progress of God's people under the old dispensation, and by the Catholic theology of grace.

Man's movement, God's gift, man's use of that gift, are linked up organically. 'Offerimus de tuis donis ac datis', we say at Mass; meaning thereby the oblations taken from among the good things we receive from the Creator (cf. David's prayer in 1 Paralipomenon xxix, 14, 16), but most certainly also Jesus Christ offering himself to God, which the oblations then denote and contain sacramentally. We take God's gifts, but also his perfect Gift, the only-begotten Son, the true Bread come down from Heaven, and offer it to God, making of it our spiritual worship. As well as in the supreme example of the eucharist, we do this too, fundamentally, in our worship of praise (taken almost entirely from Holy Writ, 'de tuis verbis'), and in every act of prayer, for it is God who makes us pray, and in the deepest prayer he prays in us (Romans viii, 26-27). Finally, historically and theologically the whole of the Church's worship—prayers, choir-office, sacramentals, dedications and blessings—flows from the sacraments, the eucharist above all, around which it is organised. This should be true, and it very often is true, also of lay worship, whether of families or individuals.

(8) The faithful, in virtue of their baptismal priesthood, participate in properly sacramental worship, not of course by celebrating as hierarchical ministers, but by consenting thereto, receiving, and uniting themselves therewith. It is a matter principally of the eucharist, and what there is to be said about this can easily be extended, *positis ponendis*, to other sacraments. We will, therefore, simply add a few pages to the many excellent studies that already exist on this question of the participation of the faithful in the eucharistic offering.

It has been noted above that the New Testament hardly brings the priesthood of the faithful into relation with the eucharist; it presupposes the hierarchical priesthood, but hardly says more about that either. We can, then, discuss the matter scripturally only through 'the analogy of faith', that is, by bringing together various data of the Bible and drawing further conclusions therefrom—a perfectly valid way of going to work, which has given good results for other doctrinal points. On the other hand, positive and definitive indications can be obtained from patristic and theological tradition, from liturgy and practice, and (last, but not least) from the actual magisterium.

In early Christianity and the Fathers, (1) the whole Christian community, lay people included, is said to celebrate or offer the Lord's sacrifice.[141] (2) The faithful are not the ministers of the eucharistic celebration.[142] The oldest surviving description of the eucharist, that of St Justin, distinguished between the part played by the hierarchically qualified celebrant and that of the faithful (*Apol.*, i, 65). Later evidence to the same effect is abundant and clear. (3) The people's part is to offer the matter of the holy gifts and to unite themselves spiritually with the sacrifice, which includes the offering of Christ's members and finds its full significance in thus

[141]See St Justin, *Dial.*, 117; St Cyprian, *De orat. dom.* (PL., vol. 4, c. 538), and *De opere et eleem.*, 15 (*ib.* c. 612). And also St Irenaeus, *Adv. haer.*, iv, 17, 5 (PG., 7, 1023); Chrysostom, *In 1 Cor.*, hom. 24 (PG., 61, 200); St Augustine, *Civ. Dei*, x, 6, 20; *Ep.*, 111, n. 8 (PL., 33, 426); and *Contra Faustum*, xx, 18 (PL., 42, 382); St Fulgentius, *De fide ad Petrum*, xix, 60 (PL., 65, 699); St Leo, *Ep. ix, ad Dioscorum*, c. 2 (PL., 54, 626).

[142]A contrary text of Tertullian in his Montanist days (*Exhort. cast.*, 7) has occasionally been rashly set up against the unanimous testimony of tradition. – Evidence for the celebration of the eucharist by confessors under persecution, without ordination by laying-on of hands, all derives from one source, the *Apostolic Tradition* of Hippolytus. The exact meaning of this text is in dispute.

being the sacrifice both of the Church and of her Head.

Especially during the high middle ages, before the development of analytical theology and 'scientific' form had diminished interest in the symbolic expression of spiritual things, there is no end to the texts that set forth the eucharist as the sacrifice of the mystical Body, that it is offered by the whole Church, and that it includes the sacrifice of the faithful as well as of Christ. The most important passages alone would fill a score of pages. In them, however, the people's part in the offering is not attributed to their priestly quality or to a character conferred at baptism or confirmation, but to the fact that as members of the Church they belong to Christ's Body, whose sacrifice is therefore theirs also. Their eucharistic role, frequently and positively affirmed, is therefore found at a spiritual level, that of *life* in holiness. This was expressed in a formula that was carried over into thirteenth-century scholasticism: what priests do *ministerio*, by office and competence [A], the faithful do *voto*, by desire, prayer and fervent union (This has liturgical expression; see below). The writers of this era do not merely say that the faithful unite themselves spiritually with a liturgical action which is carried out alone by a hierarchical priest in virtue of his own personal sacerdotal power (which is the view commonly expressed today); they add that, by their faith and prayer, the faithful contribute to the effective and efficacious celebration of this liturgical act: for, truly enough, this act is not the work of the priest but of the whole Church, in whose unity alone her ministers' powers are authentic.

It seems undeniable that these views had little place in scholasticism after the second third of the thirteenth century. The prevailing idea is well represented by a widely read treatise of Gabriel Biel (*Canonis missae expositio*, lect. 22, 29); according to this, only the hierarchical celebrant truly offers, in the name of the whole Church; the faithful offer only spiritually and mediately (through the celebrant). The controversy with Protestantism accentuated this view. Later spiritual movements, especially in the seventeenth century and during the past fifty years, again took up the theme of the faithful's active participation in the eucharistic offering, and resolutely associated it with life and spiritual fervour; with this difference, that in the contemporary liturgical movement this fervour has again been given its traditional liturgical expressions. But this has not been accompanied by a full restoration (we cannot move backwards in time) of the ecclesiastical and sacramental theology which originally gave life to these expressions.

The evidence provided by the liturgy, especially the text of the

Mass, is particularly positive and rewarding (We confine ourselves here to the Mass of the Roman rite). It has often been used by patristic and theological tradition,[143] and there is no need to enlarge on the excellent use of it made by contemporary liturgists and theologians. Numerous 'secrets', especially medieval and later ones in the *sanctorale*, express the idea of offering oneself with and through Christ. Certainly for the liturgy the offering of the eucharistic sacrifice pertains to the whole Church; only ordained priests are able to carry out the sacramental celebration, but the whole *plebs sancta* unites and co-operates in that celebration (In the Egyptian liturgy the people respond with an acclamation to a passage in the canon that expresses this). Rites sometimes used to give force to this offering may not be beyond question liturgically; presentation of the liturgical gifts belongs to the deacon's office.[144] But the *pastoral* truth of such gestures is so striking, they are so full of meaning, that they cannot be sacrificed to liturgical juridicism, and some bishops have authorised them, at any rate tacitly.

In the doctrinal field, the voice of the bishops could not be more positive or clear. Already two hundred years ago Pope Benedict XIV spoke of the co-oblation of the faithful in the Mass,[145] and since then there have been the magnificent statements of Pope Pius XI and Pope Pius XII.[146] We have then to keep our theological exposition in line with the teaching of the magisterium, of the liturgy and of tradition. Here we need concern ourselves only with those parts of this teaching that are directly concerned with our problem, namely, the participation of the faithful in the holy offering and the exercise of their priestly titles that it involves. For this purpose it is necessary briefly to recall a few theological points about the Mass. Accustomed as the faithful are to unite themselves with the sacrifice as well as they can and in all simplicity, they are apt to be disconcerted by theological analysis; experience shows it to be a difficult task, and too often it is confined to the field of 'spirituality', at the expense of

[143]The liturgists of the high middle ages were especially interested in the 'Orate, fratres', the commemoration of the living, the 'Hanc igitur' and a so n certain actions, such as the offering of bread and wine and of stipends.

[144]But there are solid writers who favour the offering of altar-breads by the people, and even an offertory procession; cf. Fr Clifford Howell in the *Clergy Review*, vol. xxxii (1949), pp. 228–238.

[145]*De Missae sacrificio*, ii, c. 13, n. 12. For the context (communion of the faithful at Mass, normally from hosts consecrated at that Mass), cf. *Quest. liturg. et paroiss.*, 1950, pp. 168–169.

[146]Pius XI: encyclical letter '*Miserentissimus Redemptor*' (A.A.S., 1928, pp. 170ff.). Pius XII: allocution '*In questa vibrante*' (A.A.S., p. 498); encyclical '*Mystici corporis*' (A.A.S., 1943, pp. 232–233); encyclical '*Mediator Dei*' (A.A.S., 1947, pp. 552–560).

properly theological aspects. I ask my readers' forgiveness for the dryness of these pages, but I am trying to be both exact and clear.

(1) Christ was offered up in sacrifice once for all; and in that offering he included the offering of us all. Here in particular is it true that the mystery of Christ cannot be understood unless we see its reference to man and our inclusion in it. Its significance throughout is that of *principle*, of source for a whole people. The Son alone goes up to the Father (John iii, 13), but he does so that he may draw all men with him (*Ibid.*, 15, xii, 32; cf. i, 14, 16). The Fathers understood this profoundly, and St Thomas emphasises it strongly: Christ, he says, is the *auctor* of the whole Christian cultus and worship (Cf. above, pp. 134ff.).

(2) The sacrifice of the Mass is essentially and principally the memorial, the sacramental celebration, of the sacrifice of the Cross; it reproduces Christ's sacrifice sacramentally and applies it, throughout time and space until he shall come again. It has, then, the same content and the same celebrant as the sacrifice of the Cross: its content is Christ's sacrifice for us, the sacrifice of our Head, including that of us all ('*Mystici corporis*', C.T.S., para. 81); its celebrant is Christ, in as much as he has willed that it should be 'done' through the mouth and hands of his Apostles. Thus the Lord continues to be the one true celebrant, joining with himself sacramental celebrants.

The Mass being a sacramental 'recommencement' of *Christ's* one sacrifice, it is carried out only by hierarchical ministers, sacramental ministers *of Christ*. They alone sacramentally effect the consecration of the holy gifts (the Holy Spirit being its true but unseen artificer) and the sacramental immolation on our altars. As the carrying out of the external sacramental act of the eucharistic sacrifice, a sacrifice wherein the victim is immolated, the Mass is rightly the act of that sacramental priesthood which is transmitted by the laying-on of apostolic hands. Pope Pius XII wrote in '*Mediator Dei*': 'The bloodless immolation by which, after the words of consecration have been said, Christ is made present on the altar in the state of victim, is done by the priest alone, and by him as acting in the name of Christ, not as representing the faithful'.

(3) Nevertheless, the Mass is not only Christ's sacrifice as offered by Christ himself. It is also the Church's sacrifice, and that in two ways: (*a*) in as much as *Christ's* sacrifice is offered *by* the Church; (*b*) in as much as the Church offers *her own sacrifice* in and through Christ's. We will consider these two points for themselves, and we shall then see the laity's part in them later.

(a) Wherever there is a sacramental celebration of Christ's sacrifice there is an act of the Church; the Council of Trent tells us that Christ gave himself as a new pasch to be immolated *ab Ecclesia per sacerdotes*, by the Church acting by means of her priests, under visible signs, in memory of his going to the Father (Sess. xxii, c. 1). There is the same victim, the same offerer, but he is not alone in offering since he offers himself *sacerdotum ministerio*, through the ministry of priests (*Ibid.*, c. 2). That, too, is why the Mass is a sacrifice in its own right in relation to the Cross. It is not, it could not be, purely and simply a 'repetition', because it is celebrated in and by the Church: it is a true and proper sacrifice (*Ibid.*, can. 1), in as much as it is Christ's sacrifice. In our opinion it is this offering *by the Church* of *Christ's* sacrifice that '*Mediator*' has in view when it says, immediately after the passage just quoted: 'But precisely because the priest places the divine Victim on the altar[147] he presents it as an oblation to God the Father for the glory of the Blessed Trinity and the good of the whole Church. Now, understood in this restricted sense, the oblation is shared by the faithful in their own way, and in a twofold sense: because they offer the sacrifice through the priest, and because, in a certain sense, they offer with him. This participation of the people makes their offering pertain to liturgical worship itself'.

(b) The liturgical action ends by being the Church's own sacrifice offered in and through Christ's, but in the order in which it takes place it is the earthly celebration of his sacrifice in being the Church's sacrifice first. The daily 'beginning anew' and actualisation of Christ's sacrifice in a sacramental celebration is by means of an insertion into a rite wherein the Church first offers bread and wine, as first-fruits of creation and symbols of her spiritual sacrifice, and at the same time as the symbols or sacramental *species* of Christ's sacrifice, through which 'the lamb standing as it were slain' (Apocalypse v, 6), immolated and raised to life again, will by the change of the elements be made present on the Church's altar. Jesus no longer offers his sacrifice on earth except by means, not only of the priesthood, but of the Church's offering: by adding the Memorial of his death, in the celebration of which the priest acts as sacramental minister *of Christ*, to the Church's rite of worship in which the priest acts as minister *of the Church*. Thus the eucharist is at once both the sacrament of Christ's sacrifice, which includes that of his whole Body, and the sacrament of the Church's sacrifice.

---

[147] *Altari superponit*: i.e., because the priest localises the Victim on the altar by the consecration of the *oblata*.

(4) Let us now see what part the faithful have in these two aspects of the eucharist as offered by the Church.

(a) It is the priest who, having placed the divine Victim on the altar, offers it to God the Father, but the faithful offer it also and, says Pope Pius XII, in two ways. First, they offer in and through the priest. He alone celebrates at the altar, but he acts in the person of Christ considered as Head and as offering in the name of all his members; this is why it is true to say that the whole Church makes the offering of the victim through Christ ('*Mediator*'). Second, only ordained priests have the power to make the Memorial of the Lord; but they have it precisely so that the Memorial may be celebrated in the Church, for the carrying on therein of the work of the Redemption by showing forth the reference of Christ's sacrifice to ours and by actively associating ours with his, the one supreme sacrifice. This double reference means that the consecration (that is, the sacramental 'recommencement' of Christ's immolation), though brought about by the priest alone, truly concerns the whole Church and involves something on the part of the people themselves.

What exactly? Surely, the prayers and aspirations, whether tacit or expressed outwardly, by which the faithful unite themselves in heart to what is going on at the altar. And these prayers and aspirations have a properly ecclesiological and liturgical value; but we don't hear much about that because we are so taken up with the 'spiritual' aspect. Older writings give a reply that repeats and corroborates the teaching of the magisterium, and which can be very valuable for the exercise of the people's liturgical priesthood.

These writers tell us in the first place that the sacramental consecration takes place in the bosom of the Church and is conditioned by her faith and unity. This is clearly expressed canonically in the minimum condition for the validity of sacramental acts, the will to 'do what the Church does'. The power of consecration belongs solely to the hierarchical priesthood; but it is not a magical power to change one thing into another: it is simply a divinely-ordained application of the might of God, who is faithful to his covenant and to his own ordinance. This application and faithfulness, then, exist only in and for the Church. The sacrament implies a relation between the faithfulness of God and the faithfulness of his people, to which the Church is wholly pledged by her faith and prayer. It is true that in time and space she goes far beyond the modest group assembled for the eucharist; but this little gathering represents her, it holds her mystery. And accordingly patristic and theological tradition sees the eucharistic consecration and all other liturgical

celebration as being wrought by the grace of God or the Holy Spirit
in response to the prayer of the Christian people; the tradition declares that
the people do *voto*, by faith, devotion and desire, what in the sacrament the priest effects *mysterio*.[148]

This faith and prayer of the people are not something purely
inward and personal; they have liturgical expression throughout the
sacred action, all during which the people ought to accompany the
priest by their movements, posture and prayers. Particular examples
of this in the Roman Mass are the response to the priest's call for the
congregation's prayers (Cf. '*Mediator*', para. 91), the dialogue which
leads to the preface ('Let us give thanks to the Lord our God'—'It
is meet and right'), and particularly the different Amens by which
the faithful express their unity and agreement in the celebration of
the mystery. Amen signifies 'Yes; it is true; so be it', and it is found
in both the Old and New Testament as the exclamation by which a
gathering assents to something said by one among them. In the early
Church it was much used by the people in liturgical worship: they
said it after the words of consecration (as is still done in all Eastern
liturgies), again, with great emphasis, at the end of the canon, and at
communion after receiving each kind.[149] The consent thus expressed
is very important; as St Augustine says, the faithful thereby sub-
scribe and agree to what is done. Father Tromp points out in his
annotated edition of '*Mystici corporis*' (p. 117), that the older ecclesiology here looked at the Church as the united fellowship of all the
faithful and saw the very validity of the sacraments to be conditioned
by this unity or fellowship; the active consent of the people, expressing itself in prayers, aspirations and acclamations, was an indispensable element in the celebration. Since then, in consequence of
certain errors, it has been found necessary to make clear that rati-
fication by the faithful is not necessary to the strict validity of the

[148]Of the many texts that can be cited, the testimony of the Eastern liturgies is
specially fine and expressive.

[149]For the preface dialogue, see especially Chrysostom, *In ii Cor.*, hom. 18, 3
(PG., 61, 527) quoted later herein; Cyril of Jerusalem (?), *Cat. myst.*, 23, n. 4–5
(PG., 33, 1111); and A. Kolping's articles in *Divus Thomas* (Fr.), vols xxvii and
xxviii (1949–50). – For Amen in the Bible, cf. Kittel's *Wörterbuch*, i, 339–342. – For
Amen after the consecration, see St Augustine's sermon edited by G. Morin in
Miscell. Agost., vol. i, p. 31. – For Amen after the canon: St Justin, *Apol.*, i, 65 and
67; St Jerome, *In Gal.* (PL., 26, 355); Eusebius, *Hist. eccl.*, vii, 9, 4; etc. – For
Amen after communion: St Augustine, *Sermo Guelf.*, 7, 2 (*Miscell. Agost.*, i, 462);
Sermo cclxxii (PL., 38, 1247); Tertullian, *De spectaculis*, c. 25. And see generally
F. Cabrol, art. 'Amen' in D.A.C.L., vol. i; and J. Jungmann, *Missarum sollemnia*,
vol. i, p. 31; vol. ii, pp. 2, 129, 218, 248, 331ff. (German edn). – It may be questioned whether it be in accordance with the norm for the priest to add Amen to the
words of administration at communion, as is now generally done. In several
Eastern liturgies the receiver says it.

sacrament, to the structure as we say in our categories.[150] But those popes and theologians who have most strongly upheld the conditions of the structure against these errors have expressly retained the idea of assent: St Robert Bellarmine, for instance, and '*Mediator*', which quotes him (paras 90, 109).

As we shall again show later on, it is here question of a law, not perhaps of the Church's structure, but of her life, according to which there is in her perpetual hierarchical communication and communal agreement.

(*b*) Not only do the faithful offer the sacrifice of the divine Victim through and with the priest; they also offer the Church's sacrifice, and this again in two chief ways, by offering the *oblata* and by offering themselves.

Offering of the oblata. The oldest writings that deal with the eucharist strongly insist on it as an act of thanksgiving to God who created the world and gave it to us; they emphasise the aspect according to which the bread and wine, destined to become Christ's body and blood, are the first-fruits of creation.[151] Liturgical prayers, too, 'secrets' especially, often ask God that our sacrifice (of which the gifts are the sign) may become his, passing into the sacrament or mystery. When this has been fulfilled by the consecration of the holy things, the liturgy considered as sacrifice of the faithful is accepted and henceforward it is concerned only with the sacrament. Then indeed is realised, with our earnest supplication, the programme of the whole eucharistic institution, corresponding to that of the Redemption: under one single sign, one single sacramental celebration, there takes place one single sacrifice of Christ and his body, of the Head and his members. That which on Calvary was enacted fully and openly in respect of the Head, hiddenly in respect of the members, is now enacted day by day, from one Christian assembly to another throughout space and time, by the members joining their own sacrifice to that of their Head. We may remember what has been said earlier on about the unfolding of Alpha in Omega, and the basic identity of the two. The members develop and bring to pass, and in that sense they add; the sacramental 'recommencement' is not a simple repetition. But what they develop is taken entirely from

---

[150]Pius VI, constitution '*Auctorem fidei*', n. 28 (Denzinger, 1528). Cf. Trent (Denz., 944, 955) and '*Mediator*', paras 89–99, 109.

[151]This at least was one of the thanksgiving themes: cf. St Justin, Clement of Alexandria, St Irenaeus, Tertullian, Anaphora of Sarapion, the Apostolic Constitutions, Leonine Sacramentary, etc. As time went by, thanksgiving for the Redemption became dominant.

what they receive; the growth of the body comes entirely from its Head.

There is a reminder in '*Mediator*' (para. 94) that still sometimes, and in earlier times more often, the faithful offer the bread and wine to the sacred ministers, and they give alms to the priest with the request that he will offer the divine Victim for their intentions. This offering of bread and wine, and often of candles and other things, had an important place in ancient tradition, which saw in them both the first-fruits of creation and the sign of the Church's offering. The liturgical text, hardly changed today, repeatedly says 'We offer thee', 'we' meaning all the people; nor can it be said that this *offerimus* refers solely to the offering of the *oblata*: it also refers to the sacrifice of the divine Victim whose sacramental oblation is made in and through our gifts. As we have seen, the liturgical action is continuous from the sacrifice of the faithful to that of Christ, from the offering of the gifts to the mystical immolation of the Lord.[152]

We are already beginning to see that in the Mass all forms of priesthood work together organically under the one true priest, Jesus Christ. The offering by which the faithful signify the spiritual sacrifice of themselves, which is also the sign of Christ's sacrifice offered here below (each according to its power: the baptismal priesthood of the faithful, the ministerial priesthood of the priest), this fundamentally has the value of first-fruits of creation: for it involves the natural priesthood, which for Christians is entirely subsumed and sublimated in the baptismal consecration by which they are ordered to the religion of Jesus Christ. But it is important to note that the liturgy is truly cosmic, that in the eucharistic sacrifice the offering of the world and of time is integrally and efficaciously taken up by the only One, ultimately, who is able to do it. In it we give thanks to God for all the good things of creation, *semper bona creas*, 'through him and with him and in him . . . all honour and glory'.

This is a point of capital importance for a theology of the liturgy or of the cosmic function of Christ and the Church, and also precisely for a theology of laity. It is what might have been expected that a much decreased consideration of the laity's part in the Church's

---

[152]*Offerre* signifies 'to carry the *oblata* to the altar' (Cf. Jungmann, *op. cit.*, ii, 2). That it includes also the sacrifice of the divine Victim, cf. note 141 above (especially the reference to St Leo); Jungmann, *op. cit.*, i, 218–219; ii, 69, n. 85, 264ff.; and many texts of the liturgy, including the canon of the Mass, where a small but significant modification was made at the beginning of the ninth century: 'qui tibi offerunt' was altered to 'pro quibus tibi offerimus, vel qui tibi offerunt' (Cf. Jungmann, ii, 204). – For the importance of the offering of 'haec dona, haec munera, haec sancta sacrificia', see M. de la Taille, *Mysterium fidei* and *Esquisse du mystère de la foi*.

liturgy should have coincided with a certain neglect of the aspect in which the liturgy is *sacrificium laudis*, an offering going up from below; with, too, an almost exclusive view of the Mass as *Christ's* sacrifice and a certain forgetfulness of its essential meaning as thanksgiving. It was only logical that, the sacrament being seen almost wholly as a movement from above downwards, the gift of heavenly grace, there should have developed a thanksgiving after Mass *pro beneficio accepto*, when the Mass itself is essentially that. In this respect as in so many others, the encyclical letter '*Mediator*', while confirming the more recent acquisitions of devotion, marks a tendency towards a fuller appreciation of sacred tradition. The theology of laity will benefit accordingly. If the laity are those Christians who serve God in and through the work of the world, without being 'of' the world (Chapter I), if this world prepares something of the material of the Kingdom of God and ought even now to be consecrated and offered (Chapter III), if the 'spirituality' of lay people ought to bear particularly on God's will to give us the world as our vocation and our job (Pt. Two Ch. VI)—if these things be so, then it is clear that the Christian priesthood of the faithful, which they have in Christ by baptism, has specially and expressly to take over the natural priesthood of every creature's homage, as a creature, towards its Creator. To do that is not to restore some natural religion or other; on the contrary, for at Mass the path of this homage is wholly through the Cross and is offered in him who, once 'lifted up', draws all things to himself: as is sung at the end of Lauds on Maundy Thursday in the Dominican rite, 'Qui expansis in cruce manibus, traxisti omnia ad te saecula' (Cf. John xii, 32).

Offering of ourselves. The faithful offer themselves in a spiritual (moral) immolation of which they are themselves the priests, which touches the Mass both as content and as fruit. Yes, even as content, for the eucharist is the offering of the members with and in their Head; but most especially as fruit. '*Mediator*' stresses this aspect (paras 103-108), showing how the Mass has its full effect and its full reality (in the Augustinian sense, *res*) only in the hearts of the faithful and when they lead a life offered to God in Christ. The eucharist must be given its whole truth in ourselves and in our daily lives. There is no question here of the ritual validity of the sacrifice (which depends on the power received through the laying-on of apostolic hands), but of its spiritual reality, of the 'soul' of the sacrifice and the spirit in which we should take part in it. To put the whole of life into the Mass, to put the Mass into the whole of life: that, clothed in the varying forms of each age, has always been the very practical truth preached to the faithful by the Church where participation in the eucharist is concerned.

Thus our spiritual-real priesthood, through which we offer ourselves as spiritual victims, is joined with our baptismal priesthood, through which we offer the sacrifice of Christ liturgically. There is a sort of osmosis, presence of each in the other, since as members of the liturgical gathering we offer ourselves with Christ, achieving the act of our inward spiritual priesthood in that of our baptismal priesthood; and then we give the Mass all its reality in our life, thus achieving the act of our baptismal priesthood in that of our inward spiritual priesthood, which is co-extensive with our existence.

(5) Communion crowns all. This is not a treatise on Christian life, so we cannot here give to communion a space in proportion to its incomparable importance. If the faithful participate in the eucharistic oblation as has been said—offering Christ's sacrifice, offering the Church's sacrifice with him, assenting wholeheartedly to the sacred work, offering creation's first-fruits, and offering themselves—it is obvious that their final act of participation will be to unite themselves with the Victim in whom all the other offerings are hallowed and accepted, uniting themselves in such a way as to form but one body with him. He who truly offers sacrifice should also partake of it. That we should be really one with the Lord and, in him, with one another is both the term and the seal of all the sacrifices that the Mass incorporates. Once again St Augustine speaks memorably: after defining sacrifice as 'every work done in order to unite oneself with God in a holy fellowship', he remarks how the Body of Christ is made real in offering and sacrifice, our incorporation with him and our sacrifice being exactly co-extensive.

With the fullest respect for the Church's hierarchy, which has the authority and responsibility in the ordering of the liturgy, may it be added that the participation of the faithful would be more complete in its expression if they could communicate in Christ under both the kinds in which, and by the separation of which, his sacrifice is sacramentally represented and renewed? No difficulty is made about this in the Byzantine and other Eastern liturgies, but since the fourteenth century it has not been done in those of the Western Church. Such differences at times and in places need cause no surprise: '*Mediator*' (paras 53ff.) sets forth how there are in the liturgy divine elements that are absolutely unalterable and human elements that are susceptible of change; among the latter, communion in one or both kinds is expressly mentioned (para. 57). However, this point is of such consequence that we have had to defer it to our *Etudes conjointes*.

(6) To conclude this short sketch it has to be shown that the different title of priesthood are united under Christ's supreme priesthood in the eucharistic celebration. This celebration, beginning as all creation's sacrifice of praise, takes over the duty of natural priesthood, but a natural priesthood that for the laity is entirely subsumed in their inward spiritual priesthood. The exercise of this last, more commonly spread over the whole of life, is in turn here found in the proper work of baptismal priesthood—participation in the worship that Christ instituted in the Church as the highest expression of homage to the Father. But baptismal priesthood can take part in this eucharistic work, and fully carry it out, only in union with ministerial or hierarchical priesthood and in virtue of the sacramental operations of which this last alone has the competence.

Or we could start from the top and show how the hierarchical priest, able to 'make' the Memorial of the Lord, takes the prayers and spiritual offerings of the whole Church into his celebration, particularly those of the little gathering for which he celebrates, and integrates them into the sacrifice of the Head, at the same time giving effect to the homage of creation and its reference to God. Thus the priesthood from below and the priesthood from above unite and complement one another, just as the sacrifice from above and the sacrifice from below unite and fulfil one another, to make one single worshipping organism, with Christ as its one high priest.

This idea of one worshipping organism, taken with that of the assent of the faithful, leads naturally to a general consideration of the right order, the 'position', of the priesthood of the faithful in the Church.

(9) In answering this question, can we make use of the distinction between structure and life? Certainly if Church be identified with Christian life (as was done by Luther), the priestly quality of the faithful and even the exertion of their spiritual priesthood are essential to the Church. Father Dabin has rightly remarked that in the priesthood of the faithful it is a question of *christianitas*, of the quality or form of being Christ: or as Guardini would say, of 'christliche Existenz'. If we are speaking strictly ecclesiologically, certainly we must distinguish. The *priestly qualification* of the faithful as we have tried to explain it is indeed essential to the Church; but their exercise of *the acts of this priesthood* does not properly belong to her structure. Such exercise shows forth the nature of the Church, it helps to fulfil her mission, and to that extent it is necessary; but it does not constitute the Church in so far as she is the institution, holy and quasi-personal, that the New Adam takes as his bride in order that,

through him and for him, she may be the mother of the living unto everlasting life. The priestly *acts* of the unordained faithful pertain to the sphere of liturgical deeds that express the Church, but they do not constitute her.

It may be useful here to summarise the position of Luther and other continental Protestant reformers on the matter of the common priesthood. There is only one priesthood in the New Dispensation, that of Christ. All the faithful share equally in its dignity (*Stand*); the notion of a special priesthood proper to 'priests' is, they say, an invention of the pope. For the orderly conduct of meetings for preaching and worship, it is necessary that certain suitable persons should exercise a function (*Amt*) of direction. They qualify themselves for this by personal study, but they are nominated to office by the secular ruler. Calvin is much more ecclesiastical than Luther on this last point and protected the independence of church discipline more effectively; but fundamentally they, and Zwingli, took exactly the same line.

It could be criticised from the point of view of the early Church, of the undivided Church, of the Church of all places and all times ('quod ubique, quod semper, quod ab omnibus traditum est'); it could be criticised from the point of view of ecclesiology and the theology of the sacraments. For our purpose here, it involves a calamitous passing from the sphere of life to the sphere of structure, that is, the doctrine of the priesthood of the faithful is interpreted as meaning that each and every Christian is in himself qualified to carry out all the functions of the ministry. As Ricker has said, if the priesthood of the faithful were for Protestantism simply 'ein religioses, nicht ein Verfassungsprinzip', we should then be in the sphere of Christianity as life, and an understanding might be possible. But it is not so. In various places Luther attributes all priestly *powers*— to preach, celebrate the Supper, absolve, etc.—to each one of the faithful. It is true that he adds that these powers may not (*non licere*) be used without the approval of the congregation, sanctioned by the leader—but this is precisely because those powers belong to them all. The transfer of ecclesiastical competences to the faithful is so radical because, for Luther, the Church as institution or *ensemble* of the means of grace is swallowed up in the Church as community of the (true) faithful; there is no 'Church' apart from (true) Christianity: she is identified with her mission, and her structure with her life.

Near the end of Chapter II we quoted a remarkable passage from Bismarck (page 45). We are now more able to judge what he said, and to appreciate the importance of the issues raised. Among his

statements were that 'Mass can be celebrated without a congregation'. In a sense, of course, this is true. But only in a sense: for the
whole Church is never totally absent from a solitary celebration, and
also because there is even so something wanting to it, or at least
something wanting if celebration of the liturgy be regularly confined
to hierarchical priests alone. We have only to think of the meaning
of the words 'liturgy' (public service), 'hierarchical or ministerial
priesthood', and 'church' itself. The structure of the Church is from
above, but she lives also from below. She exists in the first place
through her clergy, that is, through the part of herself which, as the
depository of the apostolic ministry, visibly carries on Christ's work
in the building of a community of faithful; but this work is done,
the mission fulfilled, the life of the organism is properly active, only
when the community celebrates with its priests. Bismarck was wrong:
the Church does not begin and end with her clergy.

Again it is the Fathers who put the matter unforgettably. St
Cyprian: 'plebs adunata sacerdoti et pastori suo grex adhaerens';
St John Chrysostom calling the laity the bishop's 'priestly *pleroma*'
[F]. It is indeed that: not a question of existence, but of fulfilment,
plenitude. When it be a matter of worship, or of any other aspect of
her mystery, the Church exists hierarchically in her structure; only
in and through the faithful does she fulfil herself and attain the verity
of her mission and her life.

Later on it will be shown that hierarchy and laity together form
a single subject of apostolic work, the faithful being united and, in
the strongest sense, associated with the hierarchy in one apostolic
body. That is why St Leo the Great, St Peter Damian, Cardinal Pole
and others did not hesitate (and with such men it was no mere
rhetoric) to attribute a priestly role to those who actively exercise a
Christian influence—in times past, kings and princes; nowadays, the
faithful people.[153] How much the more, then, can one speak of a
single subject of worship, praise and liturgical celebration formed of
priests, faithful—'nos servi tui, sed et plebs tua sancta'—and the
Head of them all, Jesus Christ. 'Christ and the Church form one
body', wrote Paschasius Radbertus, 'Without the Church, Christ is
not priest for ever; without Christ, the Church is not offered to the
Father'. And four hundred years earlier, St John Chrysostom (he
again!) said to his people:

Sometimes there is no difference between priest and people, as
in the receiving of the holy mysteries, to which we are all admitted

[153]Cf. Dabin, *Le sacerdoce royal* . . ., pp. 126ff., 205–206, 349. And see F. Dvornik,
Emperors, Popes and General Councils (Harvard, 1951).

on the same footing. It is no longer as it was under the Old Covenant, when certain things were reserved to be eaten by the priest and the people were not allowed to partake of the priestly things. It is very different now: the same Body and the same Cup are offered to all without distinction. It is the same with the prayers, wherein the people have an important part. Priest and people together say the prayers for the energumens and for the penitents, so that there is the one single prayer, overflowing with mercy. In the same way, when those who are not yet permitted to take part in the sacred meal have left the assembly, we begin another prayer, prostrating together and together rising to our feet. When we give and receive the token of peace, each one kisses his neighbour. At the very heart of these holy mysteries the priest wishes well to the people, and the people wish well to him: that is the meaning of 'And with your spirit'. The eucharistic prayer, too, is a common prayer, for the priest does not give thanks [does not 'eucharistify'] alone but the people with him; he does not begin it until the faithful have signified their assent by 'It is meet and right' (*In ii Cor.*, homily 18, n. 3).

(**10**) It remains to examine what part lay people have, or may have, as ministers of the sacraments, in ordinary or in extraordinary circumstances.

The Code of Canon Law and the Roman Ritual recognises that any lay person, man or woman, can administer baptism; it is not even required that this emergency minister should himself be baptised, provided he intends 'to do what the Church does'. There are many references to lay baptism in cases of necessity in early times. Later on, some people proffered in explanation of this practice that 'a man can give what he has himself received'. That principle could be carried a very long way, and in fact it was frequently used by medieval canonists, who invoked it in respect of holy orders. Whoever has received an order, they said, radically has the power himself to confer that order: 'Ex demandatione papae quilibet conferre potest quod habet: unde ordinatus ordinem et confirmatus confirmationem. . . .' If this refers to the sacrament of confirmation—and it looks as if it does—it is clear that an application in this sense of a principle that is highly disputable, in its cast-iron form, has no support in tradition or even in history (though this does not at once settle the impossibility of the thing).

Another tradition, that was commonly received for five centuries (about 800 to 1300 in the East; about 1000 to 1500 in the West), allowed a practice which, if it be still in existence at all, must be

exceedingly rare—confession to lay people. Among theologians,
St Thomas took an exceptionally favourable attitude to this practice,
and he expressly bracketed it with the administration of baptism: it
appeared to him that in both cases necessity for salvation justified
maximum facilities. St Thomas did more than anybody to give full
weight to sacramental action and the (instrumental) role of priestly
power; but he went far beyond most of his contemporaries when he
recognised some sort of sacramental value in confession made to any
of one's neighbours in a case of necessity.[154] For him, the acts of the
penitent (sorrow for sin and self-accusation) enter into the very
constitution and essence of the sacrament. The absence of a priest
deprives the penitent of absolution and the imposition of a properly
sacramental penance; but on the side of the subject, the confession
is all that it could be in the line of a sacramental confession, the
minister being supplied in the person of a lay man or woman, and,
for St Thomas, the confession deserves, *on this title*, to be qualified as
quodammodo sacramentalis.

Among the many authors cited by Father A. Teetaert, in his
exhaustive inquiry (*La confession aux laiques dans l'Eglise latine depuis
le viii^e jusqu'au xiv^e siecle*, Bruges, 1926), none associates the role of a
lay person thus receiving the confession of a fellow Christian with
any priestly character, whether of baptism or of holiness; holiness is
invoked here and there, but without any reference to its priestly
value. Several writers of the early and middle thirteenth century
attribute the non-sacerdotal or non-hierarchical remission of sins
either to the personal holiness of him who is the instrument of it, or
to a sort of undivided force of ecclesial faith and charity, of which
the instrument provided in emergency by God becomes the channel.
Here we touch an ecclesiological aspect of the question; very probably we ought to see in this last explanation a continuation of ideas
current among the Fathers, and still found in the eleventh and
twelfth centuries. According to these ideas, the power of hallowing,
consecrating and absolving resided in the Body of Christ as such, and
it was exercised in this or that man in virtue of his fellowship in that
ecclesial Body, through faith and charity.

But the practice of confession to lay people (sometimes called
fraternal confession) involves the ecclesial mystery, or at any rate the
Christian mystery, yet more closely: it is directly connected with the
mystery of our neighbour, which, lived in the spiritual experience of
the Church, is set out in all its depth in the Bible and in patristic

---

[154] *IV Sent.*, d. xvii, q. 3, a. 3, qa 2, ad 1. St Thomas's position might be assimilated to the received theology of today by the idea of desire (*votum*) for the sacrament (Cf. Trent; Denzinger, n. 847).

commentaries thereon. This is something other and greater than the moral duty of treating other people as brothers: it is a true 'mystery', a sacrament of our neighbour in the sense of a revelation, a presence, a communication of God, of Christ, in and through that neighbour. Beyond the realisation of the mystery of ecclesial unity in faith and charity, there is this mystery of God's presence in our neighbour, through whom we must go if we would know the Lord. When the pseudo-Augustinian *De vera et falsa poenitentia* encouraged among theologians the idea that confession to another has some sort of value in itself, there followed what could be called a happy confusion: it found an echo in the medieval religious mind because in its own way it expressed an essential aspect of the Christian economy, namely, the mediation of creation, and especially of man, our neighbour, in the fellowship with God to which we are called, or in the restoration of that fellowship.

And so, although it has not got full sacramental value (St Thomas), or even if it has no properly sacramental value at all, confession to any fellow Christian in the absence of a priest was and is a desirable practice, blessed by God. The historical examples of it, found mostly in the records of chivalry and of war, are very beautiful, human and Christian alike in their singleminded simplicity.[155] It can hardly be doubted that two world-wars, with their prisoner-of-war, concentration and displaced persons' camps, have seen a revival of a practice which the present writer would not hesitate himself to observe in the appropriate circumstances.

We must now return to more immediately practical matters. The Catholic Church recognises, *positis ponendis*, the existence and validity of the sacraments of baptism and marriage even in those Christian communions that have no priesthood. There the active powers of lay people in the sacramental field come to an end; in particular, they have no power to consecrate the eucharist. In the days of chivalry, there were occasions when lay people, having no priest at hand, were given or gave themselves three blades of grass or a leaf, which they ate 'in place of the Lord's body'[156] That was a perceptible expression of desire for the sacrament, and also of a feeling for the

[155]There is an example in Joinville's memoirs, several times translated into English. Later on, after the practice had been sharply criticised by some theologians, Bayard is found confessing to his steward, 'par faute de prestre'. The soldier Ignatius of Loyola, wounded at Pamplona in May 1521, in the absence of a priest confessed himself to one of his comrades in arms.

[156][At one Easter of World-War I, a small group of Anglican soldiers in France, having no chaplain, met together, prayed, and gave one another bread and wine. —*Translator's note.*]

mediation of things in our reaching-out towards God; it has a deep truth. The sacraments are, indeed, a practical example of the truth that, to reach God, we have to use the mediation of actions, of words, of our fellow men (therefore one cannot baptise oneself), of all creation. It is very understandable that the men of the middle ages should want to objectify their inward penitence or desire for communion in a gesture that should acknowledge the Church represented in the person of a neighbour, or the creation represented in some scrap of living vegetation. But save in a few aberrant instances, recognised as such at the time, no lay person ever claimed to consecrate the holy things; the question was never even raised in canonical, liturgical or theological tradition.

At the same time lay men have, or can have, a ministerial part in respect of the eucharist, independently of the personal liturgical participation of which we have spoken. It is true that the Church's tradition and discipline attribute this to them only as substitutes in the absence of ordained clerics; it is clearly laid down that the laity's place is in the nave, the sanctuary being reserved to clergy. However, the present discipline freely admits lay men to the direct service of the altar, to discharge the duties of an acolyte, even of a lector; those of cantor seem never to have been the object of a special ordination, at any rate in the West. In our own day, the question has been raised whether it would not be a good thing to allow certain liturgical or pastoral ministries to be exercised by lay men, through their collation to a corresponding lesser 'order'.[157]

The Church has had to limit and regulate the handling of the eucharistic species by the laity. In the days before Nicaea, the faithful took the consecrated bread home and gave it to themselves in communion during the week; they also, especially during persecution, carried it to prisoners and to the sick. From time to time there were abuses to be remedied (such as the giving of communion by 'deaconesses'), and the Church was particularly watchful that admitted exceptions should not work to the prejudice of the ordinary law. But exceptions were always allowed, being formally provided for in law, and the pertinent discipline today is homogeneous with that of the first centuries. It is not only in the middle ages that lay people are found carrying the eucharist, to war, for instance; it happens today, in concentration-camps and under persecution. St Clare was not the

---

[157][In the French edition the learned author appends to this chapter an *excursus* entitled 'Des "ordres mineurs" aux laics?' The question cannot be said to be a live issue in English-speaking countries, and in any case a lesser cleric is not a lay man, so the *excursus* is here omitted. – In Eastern rites the lector's duty of singing the epistle at Mass is commonly discharged by a lay man. – *Translator's note.*]

only woman who carried the Blessed Sacrament (solemnly, in her case); at Barcelona, during the revolution of 1909, Sister Mary Mercedes saved it from profanation by taking it away. Often enough the faithful in mission lands or in time of persecution have had the charge of the reserved Sacrament and been authorised to take it from place to place and give it in communion. Such things are multiplied in exceptional circumstances: in a case of necessity, any lay person can give communion as *viaticum* to himself or to another.[158]

Such are the facts, such is the law. We may perhaps speak of the laity having an active part as ministers in the *giving* of certain sacraments; but obviously it would be an exaggeration to the verge of error to speak of a properly sacerdotal role. Non-Christians can become Christ's ministers for baptism provided they associate themselves with the ecclesial organism by having the intention 'to do what the Church does'; a marriage contract made between heathens becomes the sacrament of marriage on their being baptised: these facts show that in the two sacraments that the laity can give there is involved no inherent priestly power. As to confession received by a lay person, even if we follow St Thomas and assign it a place in line with the sacrament, it is not, and has never been taken to be, *the* sacrament of penance; the absolution that a lay person can pronounce no more involves an inherent priestly power than does the administration of baptism to which reference has just been made: the external action simply serves to express, to concretise, to localise the reference to the Church and the appeal to God's almightiness. It is not in such things as these that we find the substance of the priesthood of the faithful, to whose reality, we hope, the whole of this chapter bears witness.

---

[158][Reference may here be made to the parts of Hungary in the sixteenth-eighteenth centuries where for some 150 years, because of lack of clergy due to Turkish oppression, the ecclesiastical authorities appointed lay men as 'semi-pastors' (*licentiati*), with remarkable responsibilities and powers. See H. J. Eggemann in *Social Justice Review* (Saint Louis, Mo.), 1948, pp. 299–303, 337–340. —*Translator's note*.]

Chapter II

THE LAITY AND THE CHURCH'S
KINGLY FUNCTION

THE Church participates in the energies of her divine Head in two ways: as *form of life* in the order of the New Covenant, and as *power* or competence for the leading of God's people to perfect fellowship in Christ. We will, then, examine the part of the faithful in the Church's kingly function under these two aspects in turn.

(A) KINGSHIP AS FORM OF LIFE

Like 'priestly', the epithet 'kingly' belongs to the life of the Christian in the spiritual order, but not in exactly the same way. In itself, priesthood implies nothing external, no superiority of one man over another: *in its proper sense*, priesthood is verified even with respect to a man's own sacrifices. Kingship, however, in itself implies something external and superior; only *metaphorically* is it verified in a man with respect to himself. The meaning of the word 'spiritual' is rather vague, not free from ambiguity, and in applying it to the inward personal priesthood of the righteous we have tried to make it more precise by adding the qualification 'real', in the sense explained on page 127. In applying 'spiritual' to the inward personal kingship which the righteous man exercises *over his powers and deeds*, we give it the moral and metaphorical sense in which Philo and his followers use it (the sense in which Philo also used it of priesthood). But in respect of the kingship that the Christian exercises *over the world*, that, again, we call 'spiritual-real': spiritual because its principle is within, in the soul dedicated to God and indwelt by his Holy Spirit; real, because it has the character of outwardness and superiority that real kingship implies, and because in the conditions of earthly life, it is an exercise of the kingship promised to the elect, of which the Apocalypse, in particular, speaks.

Kingship over Self. The theme is age-long. It is perfectly natural to present the ideal of the sage or the moralist in terms of man's mastery over his body, his passions, his soul, and so in terms of governance or kingship. Were the Fathers literally dependent on the pagan moralists, Stoics especially, or the allegorical transpositions so dear to Philo? It really matters but little. Their common line seems clearly to be that the Christian is king because he triumphs over sin, controls the enticements of the flesh, and rules body and soul.

St Augustine, and others after him, develop a theme in which our rather moralising outline above is as it were expanded from within, from a point of view that is both simple and impressive. He says little about man's spiritual kingship, but writes rather in terms of order, beauty, perfect blessedness. He shows order or disorder working itself out at the different levels of existence, indivisibly, like a chain. The body lives by the soul, and the soul lives by God. When man is submissive to God in his soul, his body is subject to his soul, and he enjoys a kingly freedom with regard to that which is below him. Before sin, the inner man, submissive to God, dominated the outer man, his passions were under control, everything was in harmony: Adam was king of all creation. Afterwards, man had the use of things only through the sweat of his brow, and he will recover his lordship over them only at the final renewal. But when man refers himself and all things to God in a loving and obedient worship, he spiritually restores right order and regains mastery over what is below him. This is as much as to say that the path of spiritual kingship is that of inward priesthood, and that our kingship exists only through the actualisation of this spiritual-real priesthood.

St Augustine's theme[1] is a working-out (sometimes in rather philosophical terms) of two important ideas from the heart of Holy Scripture: that the king is the source of all prosperity for his people, the source of all security and of that fullness of good that the Bible sums up in the word peace (*salom*); and that by submitting to God's rule man himself rules[2]—a very active idea in the expectation of the era of Judaism.

This enables us to give its full scope to the idea of spiritual kingship. It is possible, of course, to limit it to a wholly moral, anthropocentric, 'secular' aspect. This aspect is real, and must not be ignored.

[1]There are many echoes of it in theological literature, including a very personal passage by Cardinal Pole, quoted by Dabin, pp. 348–349.

[2]Cf. what Bernanos says in the *Diary of a Country Priest* about the two petitions of the Lord's Prayer: 'Thy kingdom come; thy will be done. . . .' The second necessarily follows on the first, because God's Kingdom is ours too.

It answers to a legitimate desire not to renounce rule in our own kingdom—so many men are content to submit to external circumstances, the promptings of body and senses, and to be the accomplices or the victims or merely the lookers-on of all these things. . . . It is a good and fine thing to be king of one's own realm through self-mastery (*askesis*). But not even in its moral programme is Christianity a stoicism. Not only is *apatheia* [GG] not its ideal, but it sees order in man only in the close and real dependence of a human order on God: and not any sort of order, not even philosophic, for God is not the god of the philosophers, but the order of Jesus Christ, of a free and positive purpose of grace. The faithful follower of Christ shares in the kingship and holiness of his Head only by submission to and union with God's will, by adjusting himself to the divine purpose for us, for our brethren and for the world. So it is that the Christian's spiritual kingship is properly supernatural and Christian.

In the patristic and monastic spiritual tradition, the idea that there is something kingly about Christian life has a certain context of images referring to the 'king's highway'. The use of this secular expression derives from Philo, developing the theme of Numbers xx, 17 or xxi, 22, where the Israelites in a foreign land promise not to stray from the direct road, the king's highway. Such is the Christian's way to God: the narrow path that is Christ; more generally, and without Numbers being always referred to, the way of the virtues; very specially, monastic life, the way of the Cross; or again, as St Teresa of Avila says, the way of prayer and meditation. But we need not trouble about the variations on a particular theme whose relationship to the idea of spiritual kingship is often rather external.

Kingship over the World: Spiritual Freedom. – The Christian's relation and attitude to the world of external things are bound to be paradoxical—not through love of paradox, but because paradox resides in the Christian position itself. Luther was not playing at paradox when, in his *Liberty of a Christian Man*, he elaborated the contrasting propositions that a Christian is a free lord of all things, subject to nobody, and that a Christian is a bondslave in everything, subject to everybody. We shall show later where Luther was wrong; but it must be recognised that his thought about the Christian condition was far from superficial. Holy Scripture says: 'The time is short: henceforth let those that have wives be as having them not, and those that weep as weeping not, and those that rejoice as rejoicing not, and those that buy as possessing not, and those that use the world as not using it to the full' (1 Corinthians vii, 29-31; cf. 2

Corinthians iv, 7ff.). The Christian is a citizen of two countries. He lives in the one here, but his setting and activities belong to the one there; hence his transcendence and immanence to the world, his life lived in accordance with the absolute value of eschatology but in conditions relative to history. He is bound to avoid becoming a slave to the world; but he has a duty to make use of the world, for the accomplishment of God's will therein, to serve it.... Accordingly, transcendence and engagement *together* make up the Christian's condition, and in virtue of the same truths; they are two aspects of his kingly position, and give rise to the two attitudes that conscience prompts him to adopt—engagement and refusal.

(1) *Engagement*, in order to bring about, so far as we can, the reign of God and the subjection of all things to his Spirit. That is the work of God for the realisation of which the Lord has made us co-operators with himself. When we accept this kingly purpose, when we co-operate in this work of ruling in the conditions willed by God according to the different levels of his design, then we are kings. There seem to be three levels, with corresponding aspects of Christian kingship in relation to the world: the work of creation, the work of redemption, and the meeting of the two—that is, of power and holiness—in the Kingdom.

(a) The first royal power over the world given to man is dominion: 'Increase and multiply, and fill the earth and subdue it, and rule over the fishes of the sea and the fowls of the air and all living creatures that move upon the earth' (Genesis i, 28; cf. ii, 20). This subordination of things to man has indeed been damaged by man's insubordination, things have become a source of trouble to him (Genesis iii, 16-19); but there is still a natural order in things—'everything God hath created is good' (1 Timothy iv, 4)—which man's punishment has not gone so far as to destroy (Genesis viii, 21-22). And so man is still—though now in affliction—God's co-operator for the fulfilling of the divine purpose for the cosmos. Man is a toilful and anxious king, who has to subdue his realm inch by inch, with unceasing labour. He justifies his princely title by subjecting the world's resources to himself, becoming its motive power (and therefore its servant too); through that motive power, the progressive control by mind (*esprit*)—an ineffectual arrangement but providentially willed—becomes the one sovereign control by the Spirit (*Esprit*). Thus the Christian is king in the first place through his engagement by divine ordinance in the work of the world.

(b) In Chapter III it has been shown how power and holiness do not meet in this world. Union with God does not necessarily follow upon the development of natural things; their coming together under the one absolute sovereignty of Christ has to await the eschatological Kingdom. On this earth Christ's kingship is exercised, not through power, but in gentleness and through service: David is the type, not Solomon. Here we feel ourselves to be at the very heart of the Christian condition. We find two truths that are clearly solidary and which characterise Christianity when contrasted with human philosophy: namely, the fact that God's wisdom is a wisdom of the Cross, and the fact of our Master's warning: 'Ye know that they that pass as rulers of the gentiles lord it over them, and their great ones domineer over them. But with you it is not so. Nay, whosoever would become great among you shall be your servant; and whosoever would be first among you shall be the slave of all. For the Son of man also came not to be served but to serve, and to give his life a ransom for many' (Mark x, 42-45; cf. John xiii, 12ff., etc.).

This of course refers to relations with men, not directly with things. Over them, as we have said, man has a dominance as co-operator with the Creator; but they dominate him too, often hurt him, sometimes crush him: he still looks forward to the liberation of his body. As regards other men, a Christian sometimes has a position of power and authority over them. The hierarchy in the Church is of divine institution, and authority in the temporal order is real and good too; moreover, we have seen that it has, as well as its basis in the order of creation, a positive basis that is properly Christological. But the Christian is called to exercise a *spiritual* kingship: he can be spiritually king without having any authoritative charge, however lowly, even oppressed, he may be; or, being in a place of authority, a wielder of power, he can be spiritually what he is in his external position, by using his power as a service. Even sitting 'at the right hand of the throne of Majesty in Heaven', He who, once 'lifted up from the earth', draws all men to himself, reigns by serving, as 'priestly servant of the true tabernacle' (Cf. Hebrews viii, 1-2; John xii, 32). For the Christian, a place of power is an opportunity for serving others. The episcopate is the supreme authority in the Church only through a total consecration to the service of the mystical Body; and within the episcopate, the sovereign trust of the Bishop of Rome is that of Servant of the servants of God.

Obviously there is a great temptation to forget this spiritual kingship, wholly grounded in the wisdom of the Cross, and to yield to the wisdom of this world by seeking to dominate by force. Churchmen have sometimes succumbed to this temptation, particularly towards the end of the Middle Ages, when the pastoral so often gave way

before the prelatical and, among the prelates, the priest before the
official or baron. But God always raises up men who act upon others
through love and service, if need be by sacrificing their own life, and
they were never more effective than at the very time when so many
churchmen were seeking worldly power. St Katharine of Siena
(d. 1380), St Joan of Arc (d. 1431), St Bernardine of Siena (d. 1444),
St Nicholas von Flüe (d. 1487): four saints of whom three were lay
people and two women. They show us spiritual kingship made real
in genius and holiness; we see them dominating and leading by
taking on themselves the burden of people's sins and troubles,
humbly loving and serving them at all costs. 'Beati mites, quoniam
ipsi possidebunt terram.'

This way is not unknown even among men who are not disciples
of Jesus. 'He who bears his country's reproach shall be called the
country's master; he who carries the disasters of his land shall be
called king of the world': Thus spoke Lao Tzu. When two boys of
his school went astray, Gandhi imposed a severe fast on—himself.
As Peguy puts it so well, 'We do not exalt grace by decrying nature'.
Rather must we see in such noble examples a homage given to
Christ without knowing him, testimony to the universal value and
real effectiveness of the path that he teaches.

(c) His teaching, and even more his promises, do not stop there.
They announce the Kingdom, the restoration of all things, the coming of a time that shall see the re-establishment of the order that
subdues death to life, materiality to spirit, darkness to light, and all
things according to their kind to the control of the Spirit of God.
That order, we have seen, is Christ's kingly power in its full exercise.
Holy Scripture, which shows dominion of the world passing 'to our
Lord and to his Christ' (Apocalypse xi, 15), promises the Kingdom
to us too (Matthew xxv, 34, etc.), and puts into the mouth of the
elect praise to God who has made them kings and priests for ever
(Apocalypse i, 6; v, 10). This kingship has to be looked at eschatologically; like Christ's, it is reached through the Cross.[3] St Paul
recalls the self-satisfied Corinthians to reality and reminds them that
there are promises of the Cross as well as of glory: 'Already are ye
satiated, already are ye become rich, without us ye have come to
reign!' (1 Corinthians iv, 8).

But there are anticipations of eschatological things, not only in
the ordinary form of Christian life (which is itself eschatological),
but in the less common form of charisms and miracles. The absoluteness of our dependence on the Lord for everything in a sense sub-

[3] For Christ: Luke xxiv, 26, etc. For us: Rom. viii, 17; 2 Tim. ii, 12.

jects everything to us: 'All things are yours . . . whether the world or
life or death, whether the present or the future—all are yours, and
ye are Christ's, and Christ is God's' (1 Corinthians iii, 22-23). But
sometimes God intervenes to show forth this subjection in some
extraordinary and tangible way: it may be the spiritual man's
dominion over space (movement through space, levitation), over
time (prophecy), over ignorance (knowledge of secrets, gift of
tongues, of counsel), over matter (multiplication of food), over sickness and even death (healings, raisings); or more simply still, over
the elements (tempests stilled), over animals (St Francis of Assisi),
over the most stubborn thing of all, man himself (sudden conversions). Surely the most finished example of spiritual kingship thus
anticipating eschatology is Francis of Assisi—who was also the stig-
matic of Mount Alvernia.

(2) The justification of *refusal* is never in itself: one refuses in
order to keep oneself pure, to safeguard the integrity of an engagement. For the Christian, refusal is simply a requirement of his twofold loyalty, towards God, and towards the world to which he owes
a duty of love and of service through love. For Jesus, the cross was
the consequence of his faithfulness to his mission of love, obstructed
by the refusal of the Jews. What is commonly called sacrifice is only
the painful aspect of an engagement to which one wants to be faithful; or the result of restrictions voluntarily imposed on oneself lest
the work becomes an end in itself and one becomes its slave. In the
spiritual world, sacrifice is the sign of freedom, a kingly act, for it is
an act of dominion. There can be no doubt at all that the major
importance attached to fasting and almsdeeds by the Gospel and
Christian tradition owes something to that fact.[4] Engagement in the
work of the world makes, in its own order, demands of the same
kind: refusal, sacrifices, crosses, disengagements.

How much more then our Godward engagement. Its transcendence makes yet greater demands; while its integrity requires engagement in the world in preparation for the Kingdom, it also imposes
a refusal, even a contempt, of the world, in so far as this is the realm
of the Prince of the world and itself implies refusal of God. The first
form of this contempt is resistance to temptation and sin—an obligation co-extensive with Christian life itself. It is needless to say more
about that. There is joined with it a certain spirit of renunciation
and poverty—'kingly' poverty—which, in view of man's heavenly
destiny, is the condition for a legitimate use of things: having this

[4]On prayer, fasting and almsdeeds as fundamental acts of the Christian life, see
V. Solovyev, *God, Man and the Church* (London, 1938), chs. i–iii.

refining and correcting basis, legitimate use can include frank enjoyment of all things that are good and lovely—'using them as using them not . . .'.

Then there is independence of conscience, freedom to serve God, and in the last resort to serve him only. In divers ways throughout the ages the people of God and each faithful soul have had to repeat the word of Moses to Pharaoh, 'Allow us to worship our God'. Whether it be God's people or the Church as a whole,[5] hierarchical heads or leaders of movements, an individual Christian at odds with his neighbours, with Caesar, with the world—there is always the same victory of faith, even when outwardly defeat appears complete: 'This is the victory which hath conquered the world, our faith (1 John v, 4). Between Herod feasting in his palace amid flunkeys and flatterers, and John the Baptist lying headless in his dungeon, it is John who is victor and king. Martyrdom is the supreme achievement of spiritual kingship resisting worldly power, just as it is the supreme achievement of the spiritual-real priesthood of holiness. In the *Passion of SS. Perpetua and Felicity*,[6] we read that, when it was proposed to dress the victims in the amphitheatre as priests of Saturn and priestesses of Ceres, Perpetua protested to the officers in these words: 'For this cause came we willingly unto this, that our liberty might not be obscured. For this cause we have devoted our lives, that we might do no such thing as this; this we agreed with you.' Even without going so far as martyrdom, it is plain that every affirmation of prophetic or apostolic freedom has value as testimony; it is a spiritual expression of the sovereignty of the absolute over the relative. With St Gregory the Great, we can associate fraternal correction with this exercise of our spiritual kingship. We intervene in the life of our fellows, or even of our superiors, with no other authority or mandate than that of a transcendent truth of which we become as it were the mouthpiece. Much more could be said about this right of remonstrance, that has always been known in Christian tradition. Under this transcendent aspect, spiritual kingship appears, once again, as an anticipation of that eschatological state wherein, says St Paul, we shall judge angels (1 Corinthians vi, 3).

[5] No doubt it is chiefly with reference to the moral and spiritual plane that the old sacramentaries ask for the faithful to 'libera mente servire'; but the Church in her public prayer also asks 'ut destructis adversitatibus et erroribus universis, secura tibi serviat libertate.'

[6] A document not only contemporary but written in part by two of the martyrs concerned. The reference is to xviii, 3, on pp. 17 and 38 in W. H. Shewring's edition (London, 1931).

A third form of refusal is to say No to the world by withdrawing from it. Christians have a sacred right—and the Church has fought and suffered for it—thus to 'contract out' of the sort of common law that involves us in the world's work. Certainly one must be specially called; but such a vocation is a normal thing, and it must be respected as a total engagement in the work of God's Kingdom, *opus Dei*. Most commonly (but without prejudice to other possible calls) this spiritual kingship is found in the monastic life, for which one leaves the world, and in virginity, by which one withholds oneself from the fundamental work of the world, which is to ensure its continuance. The Christian who follows these vocations in a sense anticipates the coming of the Kingdom, with which our Lord expressly puts them into relation.[7]

This refusal of the world is entirely different from that of a man who kills himself. Psychologists, speaking from their own point of view, distinguish between suicide and self-sacrifice; they recognise a form of self-destruction that is not sacrifice because its overruling motive is that of sheer 'escape', with resentment and indifference towards the world of men. It is of course possible for a given case of rejection of marriage or retirement from the world to be actuated by attachment to one's selfish ease. We shall all be judged by God in the scales of love. . . . But the romantic idea of a man turning monk through disappointment or despair is a sorry fiction; it does not correspond to even one in a hundred of the facts.

That tradition, then, was not mistaken that very early applied the royal psalms to monastic life and saw an emblem of spiritual kingship in the clerical or monastic tonsure. Hagiography often shows holy monks and hermits exerting a kind of dominion over the elements and wild beasts and brutal men; whilst historically it is often among the monks that the Church has found a strong support for her freedom in face of wordly power, and this perhaps even more in the East than in the West.

(B) KINGSHIP AS POWER

Here we are concerned with lay people's part in Christ's kingship in its aspect of power properly so called, of governing authority; and this not in temporal society (where authority clearly belongs to lay people) but in properly spiritual society, the Church.

---

[7]Fr D. Thalhammer particularly stresses the eschatological value of the religious life in *Jenseitige Menschen, eine Sinndeutung des Ordensstadnes* (Freiburg i. B., 1937); this is found at its fullest in the properly monastic life.

To hear some statements the question would have to be regarded as settled in advance, in an absolutely negative sense. 'The mass of Christian people is essentially governed, and radically incapable of exercising any spiritual authority, either directly or by delegation ...': thus Dom Gueranger. 'What is the province of the laity? To hunt, to shoot, to entertain. These matters they understand, but to meddle with ecclesiastical matters they have no right at all': thus Mgr Talbot, writing to Cardinal Manning. Both these statements belong to the nineteenth century. Analogous ones can be found in the thirteenth and fourteenth centuries, in the high Middle Ages, in patristic antiquity, and again in contemporary times. But they all have a historical context, which has been briefly outlined in Chapter II of Part One.

On the other hand, there are some in our own day who argue from the part and rights that civil rulers used to have in the direction of ecclesiastical affairs, seeking thus to establish a sort of tradition in favour of the laity: has not the former role of kings and princes today passed to the people as a whole?

One may reject this last argument, but the historical bases invoked cannot be denied. If we look, not only at the general principle of the hierarchical, non-democratic, nature of the Church, but also at the facts, it will be seen that a position favourable to a certain lay activity finds support. It seems to us that a somewhat extensive historical inquiry is required for the understanding of certain elements of the Church's tradition in this matter; these data have then to be interpreted in the light of general ecclesiological principles; and the results can then be applied concretely to some questions with a contemporary background. This order will be followed in the second part of this chapter. The subject is very important and very delicate, and it cannot be touched otherwise than in the only light proper to it: that of the Church's tradition, which in a matter of this kind is expressed by actual facts at least as much as in doctrinal texts. Inquiry into the Church's concrete tradition concentrates attention on five points, as follows.[8]

(1) *Election and Provision to Church Offices*. – We are not concerned with the history and conduct of elections to ecclesiastical charges in general, nor with why this way of designating bishops has disap-

[8]So far as this writer knows, there is no satisfactory general work on the subject. Without prejudice to original documents and writings on particular points, we mention (without committing ourselves to them): P. G. Caron, *I poteri giuridici del laicato nella Chiesa primitiva* (Milan, 1948); ed. W. J. Sparrow Simpson, *The Place of the Laity in the Church* (London, 1910); R. B. Rackham in *Reform in the Church of England* (ed. C. Gore; London, 1915). Cf. note 21, below.

peared almost entirely. Our business is with the part lay people took
in it all, what power this supposes in them, and how it fits into the
Catholic tradition.

The rules for election to the episcopate in the early Church are
well known in their broad lines from the correspondence of St
Cyprian (d. 258), and from the Canons of Hippolytus and the Apostolic Constitutions, documents not so securely dated but here reflecting early third-century tradition. The elements guaranteeing valid
episcopal institution are enumerated by Cyprian thus: judgment of
God, good recommendation by the clergy, suffrage of the people,
consent of other bishops. In what exactly did this suffrage of the
people consist, and what was its bearing? Another text, concerning
ordination proper, is more precise about the object of the people's
assent: 'episcopus deligatur plebe praesente, quae singulorum vitam
plenissime novit et uniuscujusque actum de ejus conversatione per-
spexit' (Cyprian, *Ep. lxvii*, 5). It was a matter of ensuring the
promotion of the *most suitable* person; so the faithful, who were well
acquainted with each one's merits, had to add their opinion to that
of the clergy. The Apostolic Constitutions suggest the same reason,
and it can be found to this day in the text of the ordination rites;[9]
surely, indeed, it is of apostolic inspiration? (Cf. Acts vi, 3-7; 1
Timothy, iii, 7). There is a second aspect of the people's intervention,
as consent. Letter xiv, in which St Cyprian writes that nothing must
be done 'without the advice of the clergy and the consent of the
laity', refers to a context that is examined in our next paragraph; it
directs attention to a general significance of the laity's role. No doubt,
indeed, we must see election, not so much as a majority choice of a
candidate (which is what we mean by an election today), but as an
assent to a person; sometimes that person was already designated by
a sign of some sort, 'Dei et Christi ejus judicio', as happened for
instance at Rome in 236, when a dove hovered over Fabian (Eusebius, *Hist. Eccl.*, vi, 29). At a later time, in the West, an hereditary
succession was sometimes followed by an election, though in this
case it was a consent to a choice brought about in a certain way
rather than the designation of a particular person.

This aspect of things has very deep roots in tradition. For Pope
St Clement I (d. *c.* 100), tried men put in charge by the apostles, or,

[9]Today, the question put solemnly to the people at ordinations usually remains
unanswered—it has become 'a ceremony'. But at an ordination at Colombes in
France in 1950, three lay people came forward to testify that the deacon was worthy
to be made a priest for the Christian people. The observance is still full of meaning;
it needs only to be brought to life. But in the Church everything must be done
'decently and in order'.

after them, by other men of high repute, are instituted 'with the approval of the whole Church'. In Hippolytus (d. *c.* 235) similar expressions occur even thrice in a few lines when the ordination of a bishop is in question. We have seen what Cyprian says, and it was verified for such a bishop as St Augustine. This aspect of assent is the preferred principle of pontifical and canonical tradition. The councils of Orleans in 549 and of Paris in 557 quote this from Pope St Celstine I (d. 432): 'That a bishop must not be imposed on people against their will' (*Ep. iv*, 5). There is more than one example of this principle being applied. It is true that from the fourth century, especially in the East, there was a tendency to restrict the intervention of the local church in favour of the provincial synod; nevertheless the principle remained as it was formulated by Pope St Leo I, 'Qui praefuturus est omnibus ab omnibus eligatur' (*Ep. x*, 4). We have already found this principle of assent at work in the sacramental and liturgical order, and we shall meet it again: it touches the heart of the laity's role in the Church.

We are not going to detail the history of the part lay people have taken in episcopal elections, still less of the prerogatives they have exercised (often through usurpation) in the provision of various ecclesiastical charges (See below, No. 3).[10] Abuses came to such a pass, ecclesiastical affairs were so corrupted by politics, that the

---

[10]So far as episcopal election is concerned, reference may be made to the articles on 'Election des évêques', 'Election des papes' and 'Pape' in *Dict. de theol. cath.*; on 'Election des évêques' in *Dict. apologetique*; and Fliche and Martin, *Histoire de l'Eglise*, vol. vii, pp. 190ff. (this volume is not inappropriately called *L'Eglise au pouvoir des laïques*). – This matter well illustrates a conclusion we reach more than once in this work, viz., that when the Church has ordered her own life freely and in accordance with her own genius, she has put into effect a discipline wherein the whole community is active. After the era of the Apostles and of the men immediately appointed by them, the elements of the nomination of bishops by election were what we have seen. In the fifth century the lay part in the East was already being limited to the *potentes*; but in the West all the laity and lower clergy still testified in favour of a candidate (*testimonium*) and asked that he be consecrated (*petitio*); the metropolitan and his suffragans decided (*judicium*). Unhappily this discipline of the Church became disordered by the exaggerated pretensions of secular authorities, firstly among the rulers of newly converted peoples. In the Frankish dominions, nomination to bishoprics became a monopoly of powerful laymen. Pope St Gregory VII's reform restored the old discipline for a time; but eventually it became necessary to protect the independence of the ecclesiastical order against the princes by making the nomination to bishoprics a purely clerical affair. Election by cathedral chapters eliminated the other clergy, as well as the laity. Moreover the Holy See increasingly asserted rights of intervention, confirmation and even direct nomination; by the beginning of the thirteenth century it was reserving to itself nomination to all benefices, a process completed by the Avignon popes, with deplorable results in the fiscal field. The old tradition, then, wherein the Church spontaneously regulated her life in such a way as actively to involve the whole community, each according to his condition, was brought to an end by powerful laymen abusing their position.

Church so far as possible has got rid of all lay connexion with episcopal elections. What little remains is mostly in the Near East
where, more than in the West, the Church is felt to be a community,
a people, often even a nationality; here there is still a certain participation of lay people in the designation of bishops. Among the
Melkites until 1920, in the other Syrian churches still, the leading
lay men have an advisory voice. Among the Armenians, Pope Leo
XIII recognised the people's right to recommend a candidate. It was
a propos these Armenians that Pope Pius IX expressed the great concern of the Church and the Holy See lest this lay intervention should
become a question of structure, of *constitutional* right.

It is in fact abundantly clear that the lay people's part has never
been looked on as giving the Church her structure as Church, as
constituting the hierarchy by instituting the bishop in the powers of
his office. It can be seen from the first election, that of the Seven in
whom tradition sees the first deacons (Acts vi, 1-3): 'Choose your
men', say the Apostles, 'and we will appoint them'. Not a single
ancient text shows anything but a designation of the best fitted person in which all the people collaborate, and a collation to sacred
powers which is the business of the episcopate alone. There is not,
there never has been, any *power* of ecclesiastical rule among the laity,
nothing that determines or conditions the hierarchical and sacramental structure of the Church. It is infinitely regrettable that false
claims in this sense, made at the dawn of the modern era, should
have comprised a different and important principle, one found in
the oldest, purest and most constant tradition: the principle, namely,
of consent, as a principle, not of structure but of life, as a concrete
law of all the great acts of ecclesial life, beginning with that of designation to the highest offices. As we so often see in this book, the
Church's solid tradition has always been to join with the hierarchical
principle (structure) that of communal agreement (life).

(2) *The Laity and Councils*. – This question is important, but it does
not deserve the reputation it has of being a delicate one, for with the
aid of its ample documentation it is relatively easy to arrive at
coherent facts and sound conclusions, which can be summed up in a
few simple points. This, however, does not mean that the question
of councils themselves is so simple as the simplicity (in both senses of
the word; and add *simplisme*) of many of the accounts in our manuals
lead us to expect. The truth is that, under the same name of council
or synod, there have existed in the course of history several seriously
diverse things: the provincial councils of the third century, the great
oecumenical councils, the national synods of the high Middle Ages,

the Roman synods, the councils of medieval Christendom, diocesan synods—all these differ from one another.

The first synod was that of Jerusalem, about the year 51. The account given of it in the Acts of the Apostles calls for close examination and a careful distinguishing between the different stages of the assembly. It then appears that decision rested solely with 'the brethren who are apostles and priests', while 'the whole multitude held their peace': cf. Acts xv, 6, 12, 24, 28; xvi, 4. But before the decision was taken there was general contact for welcoming and information (xv, 4); and after the decision, arrangements were made for publicising and executing it, and the whole people is expressly mentioned in connexion with these arrangements (xv, 22). Seen thus, the synod at Jerusalem shows a pattern of the discipline which was to prevail in the Church, whose principal stages we will summarise.

Councils were held against Montanism during the years 160-175, and others about the paschal question towards the end of the same century; but there is not enough known about them to say what part the laity took. However, there is plenty of information about the African provincial councils of the middle of the third century. Here, we again meet St Cyprian's demand for wide consultation. He writes to his priests and deacons that his wish is 'to study together [with them] what the government of the Church requires and, after examining everything together, to come to a careful decision . . . for I have made it a rule from the beginning of my episcopate to decide nothing without your advice and the people's agreement, according to my personal opinion' (*nihil sine consilio vestro et sine consensu plebis mea privatim sententia gerere; Ep. xiv*, 1, 2, 4). It is clear that, at least so far as information and advice were concerned, the aim was to bring in the whole community. As for the councils themselves, some texts refer simply to the presence of laity, without suggesting that they were consulted; thus the acts of the council of 256, about heretical baptism: 'Cum in unum Carthagini convenissent . . . episcopi plurimi . . . cum presbyteris et diaconibus, praesente etiam plebis maxima parte . . .'. It certainly seems that, if the people were there, they were not always consulted. On the dogmatic question of heretical baptism, only the bishops were concerned; the laity did not vote, and their opinion does not seem to have been asked. On the other hand, there were some subjects on which their views were valued, notably in the matter of the *lapsi* [EE]. When it was a question of receiving them back, St Cyprian expressly provides for the *sententia* of the faithful (*Ep. xvii*, 3, 2 and elsewhere); they knew the cases intimately, and there could be no reconciliation of *lapsi* without the concurrence of the whole community.

The discipline of the great fourth-century councils was much the same as in those of Africa. At Elvira in Spain in 305, priests were present and signed the acts after the bishops (at Carthage, only bishops signed); deacons also were present (but they did not sit down), and lay people too, but neither deacons nor laity signed. At Arles in 314, deacons and lower clerics sat and signed, it seems in the place of absent bishops; there is no evidence for the presence of laity. At Nicaea in 325, it is certain that St Athanasius took part in several discussions, being still a deacon. It appears certain, too, that the Arian party was supported by lay philosophers, and presumably they were given a hearing. Most importantly, the emperor took a personal part in this council for the first time. But no lay man intervened in the decisions: the council properly so called, as a dogmatic and canonical authority, was composed only of bishops and bishops' representatives, and they alone voted.

After the barbarian invasions, the Church entered into a sort of symbiosis with temporal societies under the protection of their rulers, to form Christendom. Lay men of rank attended church councils in Gaul and Spain in the sixth century, in England in the eighth and ninth; the names of two distinguished lay men are among the signatures to a council at Rome in 495; priests were invited to bring with them 'aliquos de filiis ecclesiae saecularibus' to the Council of Tarragona in 516; at Orange in 529 eight signatures are followed by the words 'vir illustris consensi et subscripsi'. A like custom was observed in the Spanish councils of the seventh century, beginning with Toledo in 589. The centuries after the barbarian invasion were the 'golden age' of what are called mixed councils, that is, those with a lay representation. But it would be a monstrous error—masses of facts and texts are against it—to suppose that this was the inauguration of a new discipline, and that henceforward lay people were constituent members of councils, *ex aequo* with the bishops. The meaning of the presence of laity is sometimes carefully indicated. Convoking the clergy of the province to the Council of Epaone in 517, the bishop of Lyons says: 'Laicos permittimus interesse; ut quae a solis pontificibus ordinanda sunt, et populus possit agnoscere'. The fourth Council of Toledo, in 633, explained the presence of laity by the fact that it gave them an opportunity to disclose abuses. Thus, very interestingly, we are given two reasons, publicity and information. A study of the Frankish and German councils, which from the fifth century functioned as regular organs of church government, shows that the laity assisted standing up and did not take part in the discussions; they made complaints, supplied information, and gave evidence; and when the canons were read they together responded Amen at the end. And this without prejudice to those councils at which no lay person attended at all. Similar conclusions may be drawn from papal synods held in Rome and France and Germany, which Pope St Gregory VII in particular used as an instrument of reform; he required a numerous attendance of lay people thereat, in order to ensure wide approval and co-operation for his reforms.

This, no doubt, is also why the participation of laity, especially of rulers, was regarded as an essential feature of great councils from the Lateran in 1215 to Trent inclusive, when they became essentially councils for reform and, more generally, councils of Christendom, assemblies to ensure unanimity—and so effectiveness—for decisions concerning crusades, the peace of the Christian commonwealth, or some work for the wellbeing of the Church. The widest possible representation of the different 'estates' and corporations, of the chief sovereign or feudal powers, seemed at that time to be essential to a council and its oecumenicity. From the beginning of the thirteenth century till the end of the sixteenth, the presence of kings and princes was looked on as normal at councils 'ubi agitur de fide, reformatione et pace'; the Council of Siena in 1423, which some popes called oecumenical, wished that lay people should be heard in the discussions touching *casus fidei* (Inquisition cases?) and *si tractatur de matrimonio quia tales causae eos tangunt*.[11] Under the regime of Christendom, the Church and temporal society were like two sides of the same body, and it is clear that ancient traditional points of view amalgamated with practices that derived directly from the kind of symbiosis thus brought about between the spiritual and the social. The Vatican Council of 1869-1870 returned to the earlier idea of the dogmatic oecumenical councils, and no lay man was invited thereto, in any capacity whatever.

Our conclusions are these. (1) The Church's concrete regime is traditionally one of councils, not of solitary personal decisions. St Ignatius of Antioch shows us the bishop surrounded by his presbytery. Laity do not form part of councils habitually and by right, but, as St Cyprian and others show, they can do so when they are able to

---

[11]Richardus Anglicus (Richard de Lacy?) and certain other medieval canonists believed that there was decretal support for the principle that 'ubi de causa fidei agitur tam laici quam clerici debent interesse'. Richard's reference to Pope Lucius III's decree *Ad abolendam* confirms us in the idea that judicial and inquisitorial cases of heresy were in question. Cf. W. Ullmann, *Medieval Papalism* (London, 1949), pp. 21, 214.

supply useful information or when the matters to be discussed concern them: e.g., restoration to the Church's communion, mixed questions, marriage, abuses to be reformed. Chrysostom regarded lay people as a bishop's advisers (*In ii Cor.*, hom 18, n. 3). (2) Lay people at a council are not constituent members and are not judges of faith. The old tradition is that they neither vote nor sign the acts. But, as well as information and advice, they have roles of consent and publicity.

Consent. – They have to pronounce Amen to the decisions of the Church and her hierarchical government, as they do to her liturgical action, which also is hierarchical but has its complement in their assent. In neither case is this Amen 'totalitarian' (as it has been put, expressively but not quite exactly); it does not bring about the validity of the hierarchical action: but in both cases it is living, coming from the heart. When decisions are in question, this quality of livingness requires that legitimate requests should have been able to be put forward and explained, that discussion should have been possible. We explain elsewhere the meaning and limits of the juridical principle *Quod omnes tangit ab omnibus tractari et approbari debet.*

Publicity. – Laity are present at councils in order that what should be everybody's concern should in fact become so; they are there in order that the community may be able to express its views in whatever affects them, may know what is being dealt with, may act in accordance with the council's decisions and give them full effect. The *custodia disciplinae* that St John Chrysostom attributes to the laity must doubtless be associated with this role. In his eyes the laity have made the Church's discipline their own to the degree that they are anxious to enforce it: to help the ministers organise assemblies for worship by getting the people there punctually, seeing them to their places, observing the discipline of standing and sitting, etc., to stop secular business during service time, to enforce the rules of public good behaviour in general, and so forth.

The characteristics set out above can be seen distinctly as early as the Jerusalem synod and the African councils' dealings with the *lapsi*. They may be considered as belonging to the Church's regime or concrete form, in the sense we shall give to those words later on.

(3) *Kings in the Church.* – This subject is too big for a whole monograph, much more for a few paragraphs. Even leaving aside the huge question of the Byzantine emperors, and confining oneself to the West during the decisive period from Charlemagne to the Reformation, it is surely an empty gamble to try to convey any useful information in two or three pages. Still, what must be done must be done, so

we will make an attempt; and, without neglecting other sources of information, we will follow J. Hashagen's *Staat und Kirche vor der Reformation: Eine Intersuchung der vorreformatorischen Bedeutung des Laieneinflusses in der Kirche* (Essen, 1931): a work which sketches the subject in six hundred pages. Hashagen sets out to show that the *Kirchenregiment* established by the Lutheran reform, in which the prince governs the concrete life of the Church in his own territory, had been in preparation over seven hundred years, during which a similar arrangement had to a large extent been operative in practice. He provides us with a veritable museum of royal prerogatives and pretensions where the Church is concerned.

Though we cannot discuss the question of the Byzantine emperors, we must, because of their influence on Western ideas, refer to the sacred character with which the emperor appeared to be invested and a certain imperial tradition of royal *jus in sacra* that was solidly established at Constantinople. Charlemagne, the Norman princes, the Germanic emperors, all took an effective hand *in sacris*. In that state of symbiosis between Church and temporal society that characterised Christendom, such a prince as Charlemagne indeed ruled the people of God; he convoked councils, promulgated canons and liturgical ordinances, made his capitularies proper church documents. He really ruled the Church in her ordinary life. It must be noticed, however, that common opinion, and the princes themselves, generally recognised a limit that must not be overstepped, that of divine law and of dogma, the proper sphere of the priesthood. There is abundant evidence of this, and it can be found among the Germanic emperors, the Hohenstaufen, Frederick II himself, and in Lewis of Bavaria. At councils, including those of the conciliar period (whose claims were more in favour of clerics and the learned than of the laity), no voice was given to lay men. But it was during the fourteenth and fifteenth centuries that royal pretensions reached their height. The occasion and setting of this was the chronic confusion of Christendom resulting from the great schism in the West and the continued failure to bring about reforms. The many projects for reform gave temporal rulers opportunity to interfere in properly ecclesiastical affairs, such as public worship, preaching, recruitment and discipline of religious orders. While a sort of right was being thus created, a theory was evolved that, in case of necessity due to ecclesisatical authorities failing in their duty, the prince could act in the Church's domain, and *vice versa*: both were members of the same body, and so could supply each other's deficiencies, by *epieikeia* [FF].

The sacred character of kings and of their royal power was evidently based on their ceremonial sacring. For the clergy, this sacring had been a means of rallying kings to the Church and to acceptance of her sacred power. But kings invoked it as a basis of rights, as well as of duties. Those vestments that were put on them, those anointings and their accompanying prayers, those sacred and priestly titles —these seemed to make veritable ecclesiastical ministers of emperors and kings. In the eleventh century the mysterious Anonymous of York (of Rouen?) completely assimilated the sovereign to the sacerdotal order: 'Quare non est appellandus laicus, quia christus Domini est. . . . Quare et peccata remittere et panem et vinum in sacrificium potest offerre, quod utique facit in die quo coronatur'; such expressions were not all that isolated and unusual.[12]

The Church had reacted. She had declared the emperor to be a son of the Church, not a prelate at her head; she had denied the sacerdotal character of kings. But princes went on legislating and interfering with all their might, and were veritable popes in their own lands. The sixteenth-century reformers had only to collect these testimonies, this kind of jurisprudence, to produce the various theories of *Landeskirchen* and of the *jus reformandi*. *Landeskirchen* are churches, of provinces or countries, whose external life, legislation and even doctrinal expression are regulated and sanctioned by the political authority in a given sovereign territory. Fundamentally, the *jus reformandi* was a public law ratifying existing fact, simply the expression of this regime and of the notorious principle *Cujus regio, illius et religio*. The expression *jus reformandi*, just as it is, is not found before 1540; like the word 'confession' in the sense of a religious body or church, it belongs to the vocabulary of imperial or Germanic public law necissitated by the situation of the imperial territories in Germany. The *jus reformandi exercitium religionis* is the temporal ruler's right to regulate the form of religion and doctrine to be observed in his territory: it underlays but was not mentioned in the Peace of Ausgburg in 1555, and was one of the bases of the Peace of Westphalia in 1648, which is quite certainly one of the reasons why the Holy See protested against the latter.

In all this there was at the same time both a certain material

[12]J. Haller in *Papsttum und Kirchenreform*, vol. i (Berlin, 1903), shows that the example of England determined the ideas of the Parisian teachers at the beginning of the fifteenth century. John Juvenal des Ursins, archbishop of Rheims, wrote to King Charles VII: 'You are not simply a lay person but an ecclesiastical prelate, the leader in your kingdom and, after the pope, right hand of the Church'. [The English jurist Lyndwood (d. 1446) remarks that 'According to some people, an anointed king is not simply a layman, but a "mixed person" '.—*Translator's note.*]

continuity and a deep break with Catholic tradition. It is very difficult for us today to grasp the extent to which the Church under Christian princes acquired form as the people of God concretely identified with political society. It was not for nothing that, particularly in the Carolingian epoch, names and examples from the Old Testament were so often invoked: Charlemagne was Josiah, every 'Christian' king was David and Solomon. Protestant reformers, principally Zwinglians and Lutherans, by eliminating the Church as institution and as aggregate of the mediations of grace, practically reduced the idea of the Church to that of a faithful people under the true law of faith; the Church was to be once more God's people in a given land; there would be new Josiahs, new Hezekiahs.

These Old Testament patterns have certainly bulked largely in Christian consciousness. When Christian kings became a fact, when the fiction of a wholly Christian people was accepted, when under guise of the Empire history seemed to be unrolling in a single movement of the City of God or of the Church,[13] from that moment kings were looked upon as in a way exerting, by means of their own proper power, government over the Church, *regimen Ecclesiae*. It was then inevitable that they should be recognised as having the right, nay, the duty, of taking reforming action in the Church. In the one Christian body, kings and princes were one of the two principal members, and they had to act in it in accordance with their own proper power for the single good of that body.[14] Accordingly the idea of the Christian prince, vicar of God for the *regimen* of his people, had from the first included among the emperor's attributes that of suppressing heresy and 'reforming' the body according to the norms of healthfulness. The verb 'to reform' is already used by Aponius at the beginning of the fifth century. Even those theologians, canonists and churchmen who were the strongest upholders of the independence and priority of the spiritual encouraged the reforming activities of temporal rulers. Even so resolute an opponent of Luther as the Franciscan Thomas Mürner freely acknowledged the right of lay men at that time to concern themselves with Church reform if the clergy failed to do so. And well after Luther's time prelates and good religious turned to the prince to see reforms through, especially those of religious houses.

[13]Cf. the quotation from Otto of Freising, Part One Chapter III, note 64.

[14]The two powers were not confused, they were two powers of the same body directed to the same unique good. Among numberless texts this first sentence of the *De institutione regia* of Jonas of Orleans should be noticed: 'Sciendum . . . quia universalis Ecclesia corpus est Christi . . . et in ea due principaliter exstant eximie persone, sacerdotalis videlicet et regalis. . . .'

R

We see, then, that the role of secular rulers in the Church developed within a framework of ideas that were themselves relative to the fact of 'Christendom'; that is, not of a confusion of powers but of their coming together within a single body, the Christian commonwealth or order, in which the two powers were like the two arms of the same body. These ideas were reinforced, but also weighed down, by the fact that under the feudal regime *power* and *ownership* appeared to be, and were, linked with one another, till we reach the ambivalence of such words as *honor* and *dominium*. This led to increasing royal intervention in ecclesiastical things which, dependent on princes for their temporal stability, seemed insufficiently independent of them in their spiritual reality.

Many abuses followed. Many of the things mentioned above were as much abuses as normal proceedings, especially at times when spiritual institutions were displaying deplorable weakness (fourteenth to fifteenth centuries). And then, especially at times when spiritual institutions were vigorous, there was a great deal of quarrelling. It was not easy to bring about a temporal-spiritual relationship analogous to that of body and soul at a time when the temporal and the spiritual were regarded as the two sides of a body.

The princes' part in the life of the Church was worth whatever the princes were worth. From the statutory point of view, however, it may be said to have remained radically wholesome so long as, concurrently with the idea of the Church as people of God, on which truth it lived, there was a living idea of the Church as institution or order of the means of grace. The boundary of sacred things, the order of properly hierarchical competence, was then maintained. But with the democratic and conciliar movements, and then, decisively, with the Protestant Reformation, the Church came to be by many considered, preponderantly or exclusively, simply as the aggregate of believers, a community of men and women professing true doctrine; and then the power of the king or civil magistrate became exclusive, autonomous and, from the ecclesiastical point of view, anarchical. The statutorily healthy or unhealthy character of the princes' role in ecclesiastical matters has to be considered with reference to what has been said in Chapter II of Part One of this study.

When it comes to applying our data to the laity today we must not lose sight of how things have evolved in modern times. In temporal society, the medieval spiritual unity has been blown to bits. Since the Protestant Reformation, accompanied or followed by the emergence of a non-believing world of men, modern societies as a whole have definitely lost the spiritual unanimity, real or more or less fictitious, which allowed the symbiosis of temporal and spiritual into a single body. It still exists here and there (Spain, Mohammedan countries); but the general current of history is elsewhere. In positive fashion, the meaning of this current can be interpreted as a conquest of its independence by 'the profane', which has progressively denounced the sort of alienation that we have spoken of at the end of Chapter I in Part One.

If we make a positive estimate of the meaning of the historical movement on the side of the spiritual community, the Church, we can speak of a much greater independence and integrity. She has lost nothing in herself: she is simply thrown back on her *own* resources, which are spiritual. She renounces the help of *power*, at least in a large sense, for it is neither desirable nor in fact possible (apart from persecution) that she should be completely unaided in this way, if only in recognition of human sympathy and kindness; she renounces, we repeat, the help of power, and therefore she rejects the use of power or force in herself by lay people. They are brought back to the plane whence the Church herself again brings her action to bear on society: effective action, but with no force to back it, action through devotedness, through the most careful and fullest possible discharge of her responsibilities; action by 'taking charge of', rather than by issuing orders. In a sentence, an exercise of spiritual kingship much more than of government or kingship as power.

(4) *The Life of the Community*. – Here the laity are very effectively active, in the first place (often indirectly) in the legislative and governmental spheres of civil life. When they make and enforce laws, especially in certain fields, they surrender or defend, weaken or strengthen, the Church's defences from without. The parliamentary and legal work, the social and apologetic activity of Catholics engaged in God's warfare at the Church's immediate approaches, are examples of the community's part in the ordering of its own life at this first and elementary level.

We have seen that the laity were able to act directly on the Church's internal order through the part they used to take in councils, without, however, having any decisive voice. And it must be added that, especially from the fourth to the ninth centuries, the influence of the Byzantine emperors was particularly strong. These councils had become a sort of senate of the Empire for religious affairs, and the emperors confirmed their decisions as imperial laws. Things have changed; lay people are no longer invited to councils, and the direction of the *Caeremoniale Episcoporum* that seats should be provided for them thereat is only a dead reminder of the past. We shall see whether there are not living and efficacious things today that answer to these old forms. In any case the laity co-operates actively in the regulation of its life in two ways: custom, and initiative from below.

In origin, objects and nature the canon law that regulates the Church's life is above all a sacramental law: we have already seen that this is the principal reason why it is also primarily a law for clergy. But the Church is not only an institution wherein the faithful simply receive the objective means of grace; she is also a community actively formed by its members on the basis of their baptismal engagement; and this community takes part in the creation of law, for law is often simply a formulation of tradition and custom. Custom, as we shall explain it, is a law from below, which those who use it, namely the laity, *also* make. Gratian's *Decretum* defined it as 'a certain law established by what is done'.

For a long time custom was hardly distinguished from tradition; its value was not looked for anywhere but in the great authority which, through the thick mist of many centuries, was attributed to all traditions whatever. Theorising about it began only towards the middle of the thirteenth century, and it bore the mark of that healthy age, in which there was a remarkable balance between the content of the subject and the needs of the object, between initiative or personal action and datum or authority. (We have seen this in the notion of Church itself and in such a particular case as confession to a lay person.) Was this an influence from Roman law, here favourable to the general community, or was it rather an influence from the sociological ideas of Aristotle?

At that time more than one theoriser, including in a measure St Thomas Aquinas, saw in custom a product of that sovereignty which in the first place resides in the body politic itself, and a fruit of a sort of legislative power immanent in the people.[15] This is the more noteworthy because in those days communities were to a large extent governed by custom. However, what was true in the natural order was much less so in the properly Christian or ecclesial order. In the natural order, authority is, in its positive form, an organ that the body politic (having the capacity) gives itself for organising itself. In the positive order of salvation, authority is given with the Body, in such a way that, at least logically, it is anterior thereto; essentially, the order of law is a positive order bound up with the

[15]For St Thomas, see *Sum. theol.*, I-II, q. xcvii, a. 3, ad 3.

hierarchical fact and having the same meaning as that fact, according with our explanation in Pt. One Ch. III and Two Ch. I. To have applied materially to the Church what is favourable to the community in old Roman law or in Aristotle would have been to dissolve the Catholic order. This has always been finally safeguarded by the proviso of the higher authority of the custom of the Roman Church, or better, of apostolic authority. The profound genius, the very nature, of canon law has an element that is, not more voluntarist, but more positive. Beyond any influence of Roman law or Aristotle's sociology, canonists have set themselves to define the limits and conditions for validity of custom, law-from-below, in the order of ecclesiastical life, which is that of canon law; and after a long and varied history, the provisions of the Code of Canon Law of 1917 were reached (Canons 5, 25-30). All the obligatory or legal worth of custom comes from above, from the approval given by lawful superiors according to the various ways provided for in law. *Properly speaking, there is no law-from-below in the Church.*

But, even from this narrowly legal point of view, it remains true that custom introduces into law-from-above a mode of origination and determination which shows the reality of a source from below in the life of the Church. The people cannot confer a juridical value in law on rules that they impose on themselves. But in many cases this is not the problem. It is rather a matter of finding a way of action in common which can be a form of life and concrete activity for a community: no more than that. Authority has always to intervene, but it is not then the authority of the legislator properly so called that is involved; rather is it the fatherly authority which the Church's law recognises in her 'family' groups—parish, convent, school, private association, etc. Thus communities are continually giving themselves their own regulations, or working them out together: without prejudice to that body of custom with which the Code is concerned and which, contrary to the law or alongside of it, has legal validity only in the conditions laid down.

In *Vraie et fausse réforme dans l'Eglise* (pp. 274-292, 318-325) we analysed how peripheral initiatives, or 'from below', have a large place in the Church and harmonise with her order. There we distinguished from a bad *via facti*, revolutionary and anarchical, a good *via facti*, in which the periphery *proposes* its desires, its hopes, its endeavours to the centre or to authority, submitting everything to the judgment of those who have the office and charism of judging. Throughout this present book we have tried to show the necessity of a twofold consent in the Church: the radically necessary consent of life to incorporate itself in the structure, lacking which we run in vain and life is not the life *of the Church*; and the consent of the structure to welcome life's needs and developments, lacking which the bases remain firm but there is no movement at all, and the Church, while faithful to her fundamental constitution, fails to fulfil her mission. Within what we have explained as the way alike of order and well-being, there are wide lay initiatives, a whole body of achievements through which the faithful truly *make* the Church and shape her historic embodiment and aspect throughout time and space. Everything goes to show that there is the community's role in the regulation of its own life. But it is not properly *power*, authority, participation in ruling or in the kingly function of the Church as power.

(5) *The Church's Executive Power*. – In sections (2) and (4) above we have considered the laity's part in the Church's legislative function; we have now to examine what they have done and can still do in the executive field, whether administrative or judicial.

During the third and fourth centuries there was, at any rate in Africa, an institution of *seniores laici* which is relevant here. P. G. Caron has shown, in the *Revue internationale des droits de l'antiquité*, vol. vi (1951), pp. 7-22, that these *seniores laici* helped in the management of the ecclesiastical patrimony and in the administration of justice. There were for this purpose *presbyteri* (*seniores*) and *laici seniores*, these last probably chosen by the people. They were something more than churchwardens, having a position intermediate between the hierarchy proper and ordinary important laymen. Caron states that there were two categories among them, *seniores ex plebe*, with rank between the presbyters and the deacons, and *seniores ecclesiae*, who ranked below the deacons. The first formed a veritable administrative board for the bishop, summoning the participants to councils and taking part in them themselves. With the bishop, they formed a court with power of judgement, especially when it was a case for excommunication. Was this state of affairs primitive? In the early Church the very logic of things had led to the regarding as a sacred office and veritable 'liturgy' (St Paul's word) of the collection and distribution of goods, a charge whose object was bound up with the mystery of the Lord's life in his members—the faithful, the poor, the neighbour. The whole thing calls for closer examination. In any case, later history, in the fourth and fifth centuries, unquestionably shows us a party bent on taking the management of the Church's temporal goods away from the laity and entrusting it to clerics, sometimes even to priests. The measure seems to have been justified by need for more disinterestedness in the work; and also by the very close link there has always been between the Church's temporal economy and the spiritual ends of the ministry, involving a whole conception of things, expenditure, superfluity, and so on.

Here we will only mention a system, revived even in modern times, which proved disastrous: that of a private lay person, or the lay community, having the proprietorship of the parish church, with all that such a proprietorship entailed. This system of private churches is often called that of *Eigenkirchen*, as it was particularly associated with Germanic feudalism. It was a plague of the tenth century and the beginning of the eleventh, a time when (as the sub-title of volume vii of Fliche and Martin's *Histoire de l'Eglise* emphasises) the Church was so often 'in the power of lay people', from the papacy down to a local chapel. Among the later recrudescences of this abuse was that in the United States in the eighteenth and early nineteenth century, under the trustee-system. Groups of lay people claimed the right to choose and pay their pastor and to con-trol the use and arrangement of the church building and its proper-ties; eventually a claim was even laid to the designation of bishops.[16] It is easily understood that the Church would not be anxious to repeat an experiment from which it had been so difficult to get free, and that she refrains from recognising the community of the faithful as such as a juridical person. Canonically speaking, a parish is not a totality or society of faithful, it is not a moral person capable of rights; it is a certain territory over which the bishop has set a priest with cure of souls as his assistant; the parish priest depends on his bishop, not on his parishioners.

These remarks are calculated to discourage the frequent statement that it would be a good thing were the whole temporal administra-tion of the Church in the hands of the laity. The present provisions of canon law are quite clear. We are not referring to the beneficial right of the laity (Canons 1409-1488), whose interest is wholly speculative in our time and country, nor to the right of patronage (Canons 1448-1471), which affects only specific individuals. Canon law organises the real life of the Church on earth—*Juri canonico, quo sit Christi Ecclesia felix*, says an old inscription over the door of a lecture-room at the University of Salamanca; it regulates the ad-ministration of the Church's necessary temporalities, and it gives plenty of scope therein to the laity. There are institutions, such as

---

[16]See T. Maynard, *The Story of American Catholicism* (New York, 1941). There have been other cases of pastors being chosen by their flocks, e.g., in Switzerland in the seventeenth and eighteenth centuries.

hospitals and orphanages, founded and run by lay people, but with canonical status and so subject to the ordinary (Canons 1489-1494); there are property-management committees (Canons 1183-1184); there is the administration of church estates *nomine Ecclesiae* (Canon 1521; cf. 1495-1551): in all these, canon law provides for large lay participation. It certainly gives the faithful administrative *powers* in the Church.

In each case the law expressly reserves the hierarchical principle which, today as in the day of St Ignatius of Antioch, is finally embodied in the authority of the bishop. There can be no mistake about it: the Church's constitution is fundamentally hierarchical, not democratic. The Church is first of all, in the strong sense, an institution: a man is incorporated with her by baptism, and thus acquires certain rights. She is not in the first place a society formed by the faithful joining together, and as such the subject of rights laid down for itself. Therefore, in the various juridical forms through which she shapes her life, the Church has always been careful jealously to safeguard the fundamental right of the hierarchical principle. In France, the story of the condemnation of the Civil Constitution of the Clergy in 1791, and that of the rejection of the *Associations cultuelles* in 1906, are tragic illustrations.

Some people are surprised when they hear of the part played by lay men in the Church's law of process, not as parties to, say, a matrimonial case, but as judicial personnel. It looks as if there was in the early Church a participation of the community as such in judgements wherein the discipline of public penance involved external with moral aspects (cf. Matthew xviii, 15-17; 1 Corinthians v, 4); evidence for this can be found so late as the fourth century. It is difficult to say whether the community then really participated in the Church's power of judging; or whether its part was confined to giving evidence, information and advice, in other words, to a 'publicity' such as we have seen with reference to councils; or again, to a moral attitude of acceptance or rejection. Plenty of writers seem to limit the exercise of the power of judging to bishops, but these sometimes joined trustworthy lay men with themselves. In ecclesiastical trials today, lay men cannot be judges, defenders of the marriage bond, or officers corresponding to a public prosecutor. But they can be secretaries, notaries (except in proceedings against a cleric) and, above all, advocates, and this is the current practice in the Roman courts, such as the Rota.

We conclude, then, that in administrative and legal matters lay people can have a certain participation in ecclesiastical authority, with fullest respect to the Church's hierarchical constitution; these no doubt are the only examples of a part, and a very small part, in the Church's governing authority, or her kingship as power, falling to them.

One other case could be adduced, though it goes beyond the limits of the lay state: it is generally held that a lay man could be elected pope. At one time this was forbidden (by Stephen III in 769); at other times lay men have in fact been chosen (Benedict VIII in 1012, John XIX in 1024). Nowadays it is generally agreed that the constitution '*Vacante sede*' has incorporated the possibility in canon law. There are several ways of explaining theologically how a lay man, by the fact of his election and before any ordination, would have supreme jurisdiction and authority in the Church; these theoretical problems have their own interest, and this one is not very difficult to solve. But a consideration of it is not essential to a theology of laity. It is much more to the point for us to seek a general interpretation of the data we have collected, and, finally, to put the question of a modern version of what history shows to be the Church's concrete positive tradition as to the laity's role in the direction of her life—which, let us not forget, is the subject of this chapter.

*   *   *

We believe the whole question can be clarified by the distinction between structure and life; on the other hand, disasters happen whenever one gratuitously passes from the plane of life to that of structure. By *structure* we understand the principles which, because they come from Christ, representing with him and in his name the generative causes of the Church, are the things in her, as her *pars formalis*, that constitute men as Christ's Church. These are essentially the deposit of faith, the deposits of the sacraments of faith and the apostolical powers whereby the one and the other are transmitted. Therein resides the Church's essence. By life we understand the activity which men, made Church by the said principles, exercise in order that the Church may fulfil her mission and attain her end, which is, throughout time and space, to make of men and a reconciled world the community-temple of God.

The Church is constructed hierarchically; the life through which she fulfils her mission presupposes the co-operation of the faithful. From the point of view of eucharistic worship, for example, we have seen that to make the presence, participation (communion) and consent ('Amen') of the faithful a condition of valid consecration would be to overturn the Church's structure; while to posit the bare structure of worship, its bare reality juridically constituted and valid,

without participation and consent by the people, is to disregard the
order of life and to fail to forward the Church's mission. In the same
way, to make an act of the body of the faithful the condition for
validity of an hierarchical operation, whether of magisterium
(dogma) or government (decree), is likewise to overturn the structure; and to give no place to the co-operation and assent of the whole
body is to ignore something in the order of life.

It is understandable that, when some element of the structure is
threatened, the Church should seek above all to maintain her integrity and that doctrine should then take little account of life. There is
no doubt at all that this is what explains the rather onesided rigidity
of such a statement as that of Pope St Pius X in his encyclical letter
'*Vehementer*';[17] this was written in 1906 to meet the situation created
by the anti-religious campaign and separation of Church and state
in France. In general, our treatises *de Ecclesia*, born of the need to
combat error (cf. Part One, Ch II), are concerned only with structure;
they do not deal with the operations of life, and above all—what
seems to us of decisive importance—they do not show how structure
requires life and is fulfilled in it, how life has to be integrated in the
structure. Our theology, which is insufficiently inductive and too
often ignores what can be learned from facts, has almost completely
failed to see how the actual Church, whose structure is life-bearing,
follows a law of existence that can be formulated thus: the meeting
and harmonising between an hierarchical communication from
above and a community's consent. The Church is actualised in a
living relationship between two poles, that can be called the hierarchical and the 'communitarian' poles. Once one has seen that, a
crowd of texts and facts are clarified, the history of ecclesiology takes
shape, and one's collection of notes soon becomes a volume. Especially do the texts of early Christianity fall into place: one sees that
they are all at the same time both resolutely hierarchical and
indefeasibly communitarian. Cannot we see this even in the fact
that the letters of the first centuries are written both by a man and a
community, and more often addressed to a community than to a
man? All this cannot be studied here; we will simply quote two
representative texts from St Cyprian: 'Per temporum et success-
ionum vices episcoporum ordinatio et Ecclesiae ratio decurrit ut
Ecclesia super episcopos constituatur et omnis actus Ecclesiae per
eosdem praepositos gubernetur. . . . Quando Ecclesia in episcopo et

[17]'In the pastoral body alone reside the right and authority necessary to advance
and direct all the members towards the end of the society. The multitude has no
other right than to let itself be led and to follow its shepherds as an obedient flock'.

clero et in omnibus stantibus sit constituta' (*Ep. xxxiii*, i, 1-12);
'Quando a principio episcopatus mei statuerim nihil sine consilio
vestro et sine consensu plebis mea privatim sententia gerere' (*Ep.
xiv*, 4).

R. B. Rackham (cf. note 8, above), who has collected many notes
relative to what has just been written, interprets them as if they
denoted the existence of a *duality of authority* in the early Church. He
is severely criticised by G. Bayfield Roberts in *The Place of the
Laity* . . . (same footnote). Actually, Mr Rackham has the answer to
his difficulty in the very passages that he quotes. The texts are what
they are, and it is to be wished that no theologian should write a line
on the Church without having read and reread them. The texts of
themselves fall under the categories of dogmatic truths, which have
only to be given their proper names. What they say in the sense of
the hierarchical principle represents so many statements about the
Church's structure: no Church without an apostolically instituted
bishop; nothing in the Church without the bishop; to the bishop
appertain celebration, preaching, decision; 'Ecclesia est in episcopo'. But the texts—often exactly the same ones—also say: nothing
without the consent of the community, all living by the Spirit of
God; each one can give his opinion; each gives thanks according to
his rank; 'Ecclesia . . . et in omnibus stantibus constituta'. Duality?
Yes; but of what? *Of authority*? Not at all. But the duality of the
hierarchy pole and the community pole: of a hierarchy by which the
Church is constructed, and of a community in which alone she finds
her plenitude and fulfils her life; one single Church made from
above and from below: from above, in order thence to receive the
principles of her structure; from below, in order that those principles
may be accepted and lived by man and thus attain the fullness of
their application.

We can now perhaps understand better the relationship of the
laity to the Church's kingly function, how they are active and really
co-operating, without having any *powers* properly speaking, or very
few. . . . Theirs is not the activity of constituted leaders, but of members whose directive functions are really solidary within a body in
which those members are given life, and use it. . . . Referring back
to the ideas set out in the preceding chapters, we say that the faithful
as such share in Christ's kingship as it is immanent in his Body, not
as transcendent to it, as exercised *in* the Body by way of energy and
dignity rather than *over* it by way of power and authority. It is the
apostolical hierarchy that shares in this second aspect of Christ's

power, by which he fashions his Body and is, as it were from without, its efficient or generative cause.

The faithful can really exercise spiritual kingship, which is from within, by virtue of whatever we have been able to acquire of the life of the Spirit—a firstfruits only, of course, for the fullness of that life belongs to the end of time. But kingship of power and authority in the Church's sphere is an attribute, not of faithful members of the Body as such, but of those instruments of God's work who are chosen to exercise, after Christ and through him, the office of generators of the Body. Considered not solely as the community of Christ's free and conscious members but as order of means to ensure and build up such a community, the Church requires an order of hierarchical mediation in the threefold sphere of priesthood, teaching and government. It is in accordance with *the* norm that the faithful as such should have no part (or a very small part) in the Church's kingship as power. Nevertheless they are active even in respect of *this* kingship. How so?

Not by an improper passing from life to structure, from co-operation of members *in* the body to hierarchical power *over* the body; not (unless in abnormal circumstances) by such unhappy experiments of the past as the trustee-system and so on; but by active consent, a co-operation made manifest as a general characteristic of their life and in certain particular ways.

If they be 'alive', people under authority accept the directions of their governors in a living way and, without talk or formality, a dialogue takes place between the body and its head.[18] It is not here a question of one of those things that are just put up with, regarded as not our affair because we neither effect them nor really agree to them—a tax, for instance, that we pay because we've got to. It is more like the guardianship of a young man who is old enough to know what he is doing but has not yet got his independence. Decisions are still made for him, but they are made with him, with due respect for his character, ideas, wishes and opinions. As they say in the Schools, he is governed *non despotico sed politico principatu*: not by 'giving orders' and arbitrary decisions, but taking him into account, and all the more because he is quite aware that the matters in question are *his* affair. In our case, all the more because the faithful are conscious of being of the Church and even, as Pope Pius XII said, of being the Church. The same pope said to the international congress of the Catholic press at Rome in 1950:

[18]This is well set out by Father A. D. Sertillanges in his excellent book *L'Eglise*, vol. ii, pp. 250–260.

Public opinion is the attribute of every society made up of men who, conscious of their personal and social behaviour, are closely concerned in the community of which they are members. . . . In the eyes of every Christian, to stifle the citizens' voice and force them to be silent is an outrage of man's natural right, a violation of the order of the world as God has established it. . . . We wish, too, to add a word about public opinion within the Church herself (concerning those matters, of course, that are open to free discussion). This can surprise only those who do not know the Church or know her insufficiently. She is a living body, and something would be lacking to her life were there no public opinion in it, a want for which the blame would rest on pastors and faithful. . . .

Public opinion has been called 'queen': a queen without legal prerogatives, but not without power. Even the most autocratic regime cannot entirely ignore it, but has to take it into partnership. In the Church that can be done in no disorderly fashion, through unconsidered and irresponsible expressions of any emotion or enthusiasm that turns up. Like the hierarchy, the faithful speak under the impulse of the Holy Spirit, soul of the whole body, who acts on the one to promote decisions and on the other to promote consent and co-operation, but who works in both for the building up of the body.

Apart from this general activity of service and 'dialogue', lay co-operation in the Church's government may be found in particular activities at different levels of ecclesial life, that of the Church as family and that of the Church as society (*cité*); and in these activities there are the same aspects that we found in the participation of lay people at councils: information or advice, consent, 'publicity' or diffusion.

At the level of the Church as family (parish, good works, everyday apostolic commitments), we put first lay co-operation in obtaining the basic information provided by exact sociological analysis of the apostolic field in which we have to work. This characteristic of modern apostleship, the methodical analysis of what can be called the material cause of the Church's work, after having long been emphasised by far-seeing clergy, was developed in Catholic Action during 1925-1940 by use of the inquiry method, and then more widely and efficiently in the French pastoral research of 1942 and after; reports and text-books have been published on the subject.

Unquestionably this is one modern form of that information and advice which is traditionally required of the laity.

Another thing learnt from tradition is that there is no real community, no common life and dynamism, without a pooling of aims, experience, needs, criticisms, solutions—call it a chapter, synod, 'get-together' or what you will. It is absolutely necessary that the difficulties involved, sometimes very serious ones, be overcome, in order that parochial and clergy deliberations may be given new life in this way. For lack of personal experience, the present writer can only refer to the good results that other priests report. It is certainly in accord with the mind of the Church and with current practice that the laity should not simply take a leading part in but should effectively direct certain undertakings, with due safeguard for the hierarchical principle. We shall come back to this in Chapter V, *à propos* Catholic Action. All this presupposes very healthy relations between clergy and laity and a healthy understanding of the Church by both—and health begets health. *Habenti dabitur. . . .*

That ancient institution the parish began as a living community of men and women, in structure frankly popular and democratic, if that anachronistic word be not misleading; within its framework the faithful were concerned in the running of things and had a voice in many decisions. The basic community, religious as well as civil, had a sort of administrative autonomy in everyday life, thanks to a system of self-managing councils and organisms. In France, the centralisation and uniformity of the Revolution and the Empire were the death of what Montesquieu called *corps intermediaries*; in recent times the need for their restoration under up-to-date forms has been recognised.

We have given our reasons for thinking that it is chimerical to consider handing over the care of the Church's temporalities to the laity. No doubt it could be a great help to the clergy; no doubt, too, it would be advantageous in certain respects in that the laity would be better informed about these things and more concerned in a matter *which is a care of the Church*, and not some shamefaced concession to the spirit of the age. It might be a good thing to restore the functions of deacon and archdeacon in this matter; but that is secondary to the more radical necessity that this task of the Church should be, for its essential part, in the hands of churchmen. As we have seen, in the eyes of canon law itself this does not prevent making considerable use of lay ability and zeal.

There is the same necessity that the laity should be able to make themselves heard at the level of the Church as society (diocese,

Catholic Action, movements, congresses, etc.). There is always the possibility of their doing it from time to time, when, in a sudden access of enthusiasm, they jump the barriers of protocol, and at their risks and perils cross the zone of silence and dignity behind which the priestly hierarchy too often isolates itself in order to protect the prestige of its authority and the stability of tradition. The action of the young university students who, Ozanam at their head, went to ask the archbishop of Paris to inaugurate what were to become the Conferences de Notre-Dame—that was not an unrepeatable or un-repeated happening. If only those concerned had always been Ozanams and Lacordaires! But it is obvious that the well-being of the Church and the nature of things call for something more ordin-ary and more organic. They require that the laity should be able to make themselves heard by the ecclesiastical authorities, by way of information or advice, in everything that concerns them or wherein they may be able to make a useful contribution. We are thinking, for example, about matters of marriage and upbringing of children, and so of schools and education;[19] about questions involving technical experience, and also certain repercussions on social life and public opinion, relevant for instance to the organisation of congresses and demonstrations; even about questions concerning the recruitment and formation of the clergy—obviously a sphere wherein the hier-archy has to judge and alone be finally responsible: but all the faith-ful are concerned in it, their concern indeed is a guarantee of success, and it is not difficult to imagine modern forms corresponding, in respect of the Church's discipline, to the people's former part in elections and ordinations. After all, the investigations by which authority nowadays directs its decisions deserve the final acclama-tions by which the people used to ratify the choice that those with authority had made.

And, inquiry apart, we already have in France lay bodies for information and advice, whether permanent, such as the com-mission which functions with the Secretariate of the Bench of Bishops, or occasional, such as the consultative assembly at the time of the

---

[19]In *Esprit*, 1949, p. 548, J. Vialatoux and A. Latreille rightly point out that recent Roman documents insist on the urgent duty of parents to look after the religious instruction of their children; the encyclical letter '*Acerbo nimis*' of St Pius X (1905) and the decree of the Congregation of the Council of January 12, 1935 are referred to. It seems difficult to ask people to take a more active interest in their children's Christian education without recognising their right to be heard in the matter. In a declaration of the French bishops on education (1951) we read: 'These are the essential demands of educational justice in this country. It is the business chiefly of parental organisations and expert groups to show how they can be met.'

inauguration of Workers' Catholic Action in 1949-1950. When we
come to speak of Catholic Action we shall see how the clergy bear
witness to the amount of information, knowledge of conditions for
apostolic work and even of doctrinal resources, they owe to listening
to their lay fellows; their testimony bears out what such as Scheeben
said from a theological point of view, Newman from a more concrete
and pastoral angle.[20]

So much for information and advice. Where consent and diffusion
are concerned, it seems to call, on the part of the clergy, for a very
sincere effort at the various levels of ecclesial life, an effort which, if
it creates its own difficulties in some circumstances, will nevertheless
be effective. It means 'putting the laity in the picture' and, honestly
and without artifice, making them feel they are there. To do that,
they must not be approached merely as a matter of form, or in some
other way that nobody would use if he wants to be understood and
followed: the approach must be real. They must be told what is
proposed, given so far as possible the reasons for a decision taken,
informed about results, difficulties and new measures required; thus
may their agreement be obtained and their help enlisted in the
spreading of their clergy's aims and decisions. This way of going to
work always gets results, and no other way does. It involves no indis-
cretions or imprudences, no derogation of authority. Relations
between clergy and people are able to have that mutual confidence
and loyalty, those exchanges of views and sharings of ideas, which,
as everything shows, ought to distinguish the Lord's followers today
as they distinguished the Church immediately after the Pasch and
Pentecost.

An historical example of what we mean can be found in St
Augustine's sermons, where he accounts to his people for his line of
conduct and the principles on which he wants to base the co-operation of his clergy with his episcopal office (Nos 355, 356; PL., 39,
1570ff.). He does not hesitate publicly and frankly to lay open a
delicate business, the perfect type of affair which today would be
kept for private discussion behind closed doors: a matter of the over-
adroit arrangement of his personal interests by one of the clergy.
When St Augustine explained to his flock on what terms he expected
his clergy to live with him, he made the whole life of the Church
perfectly clear and ensured the wholehearted assent of the faithful

[20]M. J. Scheeben, *Dogmatik*, §12, n. 159; J. H. Newman in *The Rambler*, May
1851 and July 1859; and cf. W. Ward, *Life of . . . Newman*, vol. ii, pp. 397–398;
L. Bouyer, *Newman* (Paris, 1952), pp. 373ff., 398; and D. Woodruff in the *Dublin
Review*, 1952, pp. 1–25.

to a government for which he did not cease to be wholly responsible.[21]

*   *   *

We have deliberately refrained from mentioning the considerable
extent of a superior's duties in religious congregations of men and
women, which involve a wide participation in the Church's power
of ruling; this is exercised by lay people in congregations without
priests (Brothers of Christian Doctrine, Brothers of St John of God,
etc.), and in all orders and congregations of women. Theologically
and canonically, such religious are lay people, but they are not
altogether so from the point of view of a theology of laity, even (in
our opinion) in the case of 'secular institutes'. Their life is not the
life proper to laity. So it is enough simply to mention this area of
participation in the Church's ruling office, which is large but outside
the scope of our study.

[21]The writer saw Father Lombardi's important *Per un mondo novo* (Rome, 1951)
only when his own work was in the press. Father Lombardi follows ancient tradition and corroborates the considerations expressed here. Among the measures he
proposes for the greater effectiveness of the Catholic religion is that the laity should
inform and advise the clergy at various levels. He suggests that headquarters should
have a representative lay body, a *Senato laico dell' Umanita* (p. 305); in each country
he suggests a *Consulta nazionale* (p. 367), in which representatives of the various
branches of Catholic Action should form a kind of consultative committee for the
bishops of the country; at diocesan level, a *Consulta diocesana* (p. 406) of priests and
lay people, for action in the social and benevolent field, maintenance of public
morality, recruitment for the clergy, and the spreading of religious truth with the
help of modern methods; finally, in the parish (pp. 594–595), collaboration of the
laity 'as a unified body, and not dispersed among various undertakings'.

Chapter III

THE LAITY AND THE CHURCH'S PROPHETICAL FUNCTION

In the threefold division of the Church's powers that corresponds to the same division of Christ's messianic offices, prophecy (*prophetisme*) is equivalent to magisterium or the teaching function. But the word is wider than this, and therefore less precise: it includes activities of knowledge or expression which do not come under the head of magisterium or teaching. In its widest extension the prophetical function of the Church includes all the work of the Holy Spirit in her whereby, in her present state of pilgrimage (*peregrinamur a Domino*), she knows God and his purpose of grace, and makes them known to others. Thus understood, the prophetical function includes mystical knowledge or foretelling of the future and prophetical explanation of events in time, as well as teaching in its ordinary sense. In this chapter the rather vague word 'prophecy' (*prohetisme*) is taken in its fullest extent, though only brief mention will be made of mystical knowledge and the different forms of prophecy (*prophetie*), so that due attention may be given to the part taken by the laity in the Church's teaching function. That is the heart of the matter where these questions are concerned.

These same questions are rarely approached coolly and calmly and they are commonly supposed to be very prickly: they are associated in people's minds with memories of the exaggerated pretensions that appeared in some bastard forms of Gallicanism and at the epoch of Modernism. As so often happens, a few nasty disputes are allowed to impose on people's thought an exclusive and unhealthy concern to avoid the distant appearance of coming to terms with the accursed thing. With a few very remarkable exceptions, one finds an almost obsessive preoccupation with affirming the distinction between the teaching Church and the taught Church, and the complete subjection of the second to the first. Yet things have only to be put in their place to be clear of any suspicion of allowing the laity dangerously to trespass with respect to teaching and dogma. Are we mistaken? In the light of the principles already laid down and used, the thing does not seem difficult.

(A) GENERAL PRINCIPLES

THE DATA

In the sphere of knowledge of faith, as in that of the priesthood, there are two series of complementary assertions: that all receive light and are active, that some have a magisterium. But the second series of texts and facts is here much more explicit, biblically speaking, than appeared for the priesthood.

All receive light and are active. The Old Testament heraldings of a new dispensation in the messianic age are so many promises of knowledge and inwardness addressed to the new people as a whole. They are all repeated or evoked in the New Testament, and put forth as having their fulfilment in the faithful people of Jesus Christ. Here are the chief texts.

Behold the days shall come, saith the Lord, and I will make a new covenant with the house of Israel and with the house of Juda. . . . I will give my law in their bowels and I will write it in their heart: and I will be their God, and they shall be my people. And they shall teach no more every man his neighbour and every man his brother, saying, Know the Lord. For all shall know me from the least of them even to the greatest . . . (Jeremiah xxxi, 31, 33-34). Cf. Hebrews viii, 8-12.

All thy children shall be taught of the Lord . . . (Isaias liv, 13). Cf. John vi, 45.

Thou shalt no more have the sun for thy light by day, neither shall the brightness of the moon enlighten thee: but the Lord shall be unto thee for an everlasting light, and thy God for thy glory (Isaias lx, 19). Cf. Apocalypse xxi, 23.

. . . I shall be sanctified in you before their eyes. . . . I will pour upon you clean water and you shall be cleansed from all your filthiness; and I will cleanse you from all your idols. And I will give you a new heart and put a new spirit within you. . . . I will put my spirit in the midst of you [Cf. 1 John iii, 24; iv, 13] and

I will cause you to walk in my commandments [Cf. *ibid*. i, 5-7; ii, 6, 9-11] and to keep my judgements [Cf. *ibid*. ii, 3-5; iii, 23] and do them [Cf. *ibid*. ii, 29] (Ezechiel xxxvi, 23-27).

. . . I will pour out my spirit upon all flesh; and your sons and your daughters shall prophesy; your old men shall dream dreams, and your young men shall see visions. Moreover upon my servants and handmaids in those days I will pour forth my spirit (Joel ii, 28-29). Cf. Acts ii, 17ff.

The Lord repeated these promises to the apostles with an eye to the whole Church: cf. John xiv, 16-17, 25-26; xvi, 13-14; xvii, 26. And see what apostolic testimony says about their fulfilment. . . . The faithful are established in light and are themselves a light (John iii, 19, etc.). All know the things of faith (1 John ii, 20, 27, etc.); all are taught by God (1 Thessalonians iv, 9, etc.); all drink of one Spirit (1 Corinthians xii, 13); all have received the gifts of understanding and wisdom abundantly (*Ibid*. i, 4-5, etc.). They must be children in faith, but grown men in understanding (Ephesians iv, 14, etc.); and again it is St Paul who wants all to be filled with knowledge (Colossians i, 4-9, etc.)—and this with an insistence that is one of the characteristics (too often little appreciated) of his religion. The strongest speaker is St John: 'Ye indeed have an anointing from the Holy One; ye all do know. . . . In yourselves, the anointing which ye have received from him abideth, and ye have not need that any one teach you; but even as his anointing teacheth you concerning all things, and is true. . . .' (1 John ii, 20, 27). The context of St John's letter suggests that the bearing of these very strong statements is not unlimited, for it indicates the object of their teaching in several ways; it has the character of spiritual experience, a matter of fellowship with God and abiding in him, of sonship and of love and grace present in us. But there are other texts which give the personal knowledge of the *fidelis* a range that is, if one may put it so, more ecclesiastical: the faithful recognise Christ's voice (John x, 4; 1 John iv, 6), they discern Christ and antichrist (1 John ii, 18-27; iv, 1-6), they have the capacity to make a judgement (1 Corinthians ii, 10-16, etc.).

In many passages of the liturgical, patristic and theological tradition these things are repeated and synthesised: the anointing that makes men Christians also makes them prophets; all have the Spirit of God within them, and so are not like a flock of silly sheep, whose understanding is all in the shepherd who looks after them. Rather are they all united to their Shepherd through whose Spirit they are endowed with understanding and discernment.[1]

Some have a magisterium. There seems to be no need to discuss this either with respect to the apostolic Church or later, for it is made clear by the slightest knowledge of the texts. There are many expositions of these testimonies; here we will simply outline the general argument from the economy of God's work, which is a mission economy, one of communication from above. In God's design, many are made partners in the good things which make up his life of blessedness, including, for instance, the good of knowledge of himself. But God does not do this in piecemeal, disorderly, inorganic fashion; he does it by establishing lines of communication between himself and us: from him to us, Jesus Christ, the incarnate Word; from Christ to us, the apostles and all those who, after them, share their mission, carrying it on to the furthest borders of time and space. Thus, beginning from on high, there is through communication, extended to the many by means of some who, as ministers of the divine activity, are the principle of organisation, ordering of life and authority in the spiritual community thus brought about.

That is how the Church's constitution works. Before being the inward Christ of our divine life, Jesus is sent with power, particularly as revealer; between him and any soul whatever living by him, there is the sending of the apostles, who are not only his first followers, the first community (the point at which Protestants stop), but God's ministers, stewards of his house, leaders of his Church. As Jesus was sent, so they are sent, in accordance with that logic of *saliah*, of the one sent forming with his master a single juridical person with mission and authority, of which St John's Gospel in particular is full. Far from obscuring the mission and authority of Jesus, the apostles are seen to continue and use them. Evidence of formal institution is not wanting: Matthew xvi, 19 and xviii, 18; xxviii, 18-20; Mark xvi, 15-16, etc.; and after Pentecost the Church is seen being organised round the apostles' authority: Acts ii, 42; iv, 35; 37; v, 12-15; vi, 1ff.; viii, 14-19; x, 44-48; xi, 15-18; xix, 5-6, etc. Those whom they

---

[1]Hence this in the *Didascalia* (c. 9; 3-cent.): 'If a man calls a lay person crazy or *raca* he is liable [to the judgement] of the assembly, as one who withstands Christ by calling empty a brother in whom dwells Christ, who is not empty but full; or because he calls crazy one in whom dwells the Holy Spirit of God who is fulfilled in all knowledge, as if he were crazy through [the fact of] the Spirit dwelling in him. If then a man falls under so heavy a condemnation for saying such a thing about a lay person, what will it be if he dares speak against the deacon or the bishop. . .?'

have instituted will also teach with authority.[2] To sum up: all the faithful receive light and are active, but this is *through the knowledge received from the apostolic word and set in order by the apostolic authority*. Their light and their activity are in no way equivalent to a revelation, to independent and direct knowledge; they are simply a living personal understanding of the revelation made to and received from the apostles: this appears not only in the context of apostolic vindication of full authority, but also where the inwardness and personal activity of the faithful in knowledge are expressed.[3]

The witness of tradition becomes ever more strong as we go backwards in the Church before Nicaea: from Cyprian to Irenaeus, from Irenaeus to Ignatius, from Ignatius to Clement. It will be enough to give the continuation of the passage from the *Didascalia* quoted in note 1 above: the bishop is 'the intermediary through whom God gives you the Holy Spirit, through whom you learn the Word, know God, and are known by him; by the bishop are you signed, through him you become faithful [children] of light. . . . Reverence bishops, then, who deliver you from sin, who by water bring you to rebirth, who fill you with the Holy Spirit, who nourish you on the Word as milk, who bring you up in doctrine, who strengthen you by teaching. . . .' Who can deny that these lines express the same things as do the texts from the Acts of the Apostles quoted above?

EXPOSITION

(1) It is not difficult to harmonise our two series of statements: they correspond to two different but complementary aspects or moments of one living thing. First, on the side of her generating causes, the Church as society is engendered by that which is minister of Christ and means of grace in her; she exists then as an institution for salvation, associated with God (Christ) to be the mother of the faithful. Second, the apostolic ministers applying the means of grace (faith and its sacraments), the Church exists as community of the faithful, the aggregate of Christ's members living by the fullness of grace and truth which is in him. *Sacramentum*, means of grace; *res*, living fellowship: the two aspects whose simultaneous affirmation and organic combination are the keynote of a Catholic ecclesiology. In its urgency to refer everything to God alone—right in intention, but pushed too far and falsified by wrong categories of thought—

[2]Cf. Acts xx, 28–31; Titus i, 5–9, ii, 15, iii, 10–11, etc. No doctrine is to be listened to (2 Thess. iii, 6; 1 Tim. vi, 3; 2 John 11), none taught (1 Tim. i, 3; 2 Tim. i, 9), except what the apostles have themselves delivered.

[3]Cf. e.g., 2 Cor. xi, 4; Gal. i, 9; Apoc. xxii, 18–19; and then Col. i, 3–10; 1 John i, 1–5; ii, 7, 23–24; iv, 6.

Protestantism puts the faithful into direct relation with Christ by completely telescoping the order of ecclesial means of grace. Hence, as history shows, its congenital inability to produce a real ecclesiology, except when (while rejecting the idea) it comes back to a basis of Catholic principles.

It is clear that, though all the members of the body be living in knowledge of the faith according as they have personally received light and made it their own, that is, the Church as fellowship in Christ, the members are not all equal at the stage, logically anterior, where the Church is engendered by the work of apostolical ministries. If the Church be regarded only as reality and fellowship of grace, then there is no difference between the members beyond their varying degrees of fervour, due to gifts being received and used in unequal measure. But if—as we must—we see the Church also as institution or aggregate of means of grace, then there are differences of ministry among the members, and these differences affect their position in the social body of the Church. So we have the distinction between the teaching Church and the taught Church: this expression is perhaps recent, but the reality for which it stands is indicated, in somewhat similar terms, in very early times and, in equivalent terms, in the New Testament itself. There is then in the Church a combination of inequality of function with equality of life: as St Augustine was fond of saying, the same men are shepherds of the faithful in Christ's name and are also, with and among the faithful, sheep beneath Christ's crook.[4]

From the point of view of revelation and dogma coming to the ecclesial community from without—from the prophets, from Christ and his Apostles—in an objective historical revelation as a deposit to be safeguarded and handed on, we have the competence proper to an hierarchical magisterium; this magisterium resides essentially in the apostolical body continued (apart from the special charisms of the Apostles as founders of the Church) in the episcopal body, with the Apostolic See as its criterion of unity. From the point of

[4]"The inequality produced by the duty of some to command and others to obey does not affect the equality of them all before the one Shepherd whose sheep they are. Ecclesiastical superiors are superiors only as public persons; their superiority is complete with respect to their office, but it is nil as regards their invidual life. They interpret Christ's law with Christ's power, and they alone can do so; but the law they interpret by themselves they have to observe with everybody else. They dispense the means to holiness; but like all the rest they need penance if they sin, the eucharist if they would have life, anointing when they come to die. From this point of view they are in themselves among the faithful: the pope as much as anyone else needs a confessor and a priest to minister to him; as a private person, he is one of the sheep of the flock which he guides as a public person' (E. Mersch, *Théologie du Corps mystique*, vol. ii, p. 218).

view of doctrine received in obedience to faith, lived (and therefore developed) and applied according to man's needs, that is, of Christian truth confessed and shown forth by people who truly live by and for it, to the degree that the Spirit is moving in the individual, from that point of view every faithful soul has grace, initiative and activity. 'Being made a disciple of the Apostles, I become teacher of the peoples', says the writer of the *Letter to Diognetus* (xi, 1). In the whole order of living and showing forth by life, the faithful are active in proportion as they have made saving truth their own.

To the episcopal hierarchy it belongs: (1) to bear the charism of apostolicity in the Church, that is, to ensure that the doctrine of the faith comes to us from Christ and the Apostles; just as, we have seen, the role of the hierarchical priesthood is to signify and to ensure that grace comes to us from the unique historical fact of the Cross: in order that the community of the faithful may truly live 'upon the foundation of the apostles and prophets: Christ Jesus himself [being] the corner-stone' (Ephesians ii, 20). (2) To judge of the confirmity with the deposit of faith of developments, expressions and applications that come to this doctrine through being lived, pondered and shown forth by the faithful; so that all may 'speak the same thing' for the avoidance of divisions and 'become fully united in the one mind and judgement' (1 Corinthians i, 10). It is precisely the business of a public authority to regulate the collective life of a community through acts that are valid as judgements and criteria. In the Church, unlike civil society, collective life is not purely a practical matter but is a life in unity of faith and based on that very unity; so her public authority takes the form of a magisterium, as well as of jurisdiction or government.

The Church is in a state of journeying, her destination not yet reached, and so means do not coincide with end, understanding with truth, our pasch with Christ's pasch. It is, then, needful that there should be an order of means external to the end, of *sacramenta* external to their *res*. A condition precedent of inwardness is a moment of outwardness and mediation, that mediation of grace and truth which is the *raison d'être* of the hierarchical fact. We have seen that this is why Christ's powers are shared under two forms in the Church on earth: the external form of ministry and authority, the inward form of personal life. It is true that the prophets, those 'first Christians', and the Apostles too, were so taken up by the thought of the messianic renewal in its freshness and plenitude that they often spoke of it as if it were even now fulfilled, without dwelling either on the imperfectness of our present state or on the order of means and ecclesial *sacramenta*. Reference to the prophetical texts about the perfect inwardness of the New Dispensation, and to the use made of them by the Apostles, shows that they were, then and there, looking at the perfection of spiritual knowledge, not considering its actual condition; other apostolical texts, however, were explicit enough about this last, as we have seen. Speroni, one of those anti-ecclesiastical spiritualisers whose line runs from the eleventh century to the Reformation, invoked the great passages of Jeremy and Hebrews on the absolute inwardness of knowledge; and his former class-mate, Vacarius, replied just as we have said, that these passages refer to the eschatological consummation of Christ's work.[5] 'For we know in part, and we prophesy in part. . . . For now we see in a mirror, obscurely. . . .' (1 Corinthians xiii, 9, 12).

Failure to distinguish between the Church as institution and means of grace and the Church as life and fellowship is at the bottom of many errors; and it is more than ever necessary to be on one's guard against muddling up these orders, and against improperly carrying over to the plane of the Church's structure or constitution what is sound and right on the plane of living or of the concrete regime of life. Unhappily that has often been done, through one bias or another; and by Martin Luther in particular.

Some of Luther's less developed passages, and others that keep close to the Bible without systematisation, are no doubt susceptible of a good interpretation. He makes much of those biblical passages that attribute to the faithful detection of false teachers and deceivers in the order of salvation: Matthew vii, 15; xxiv, 5; John x, 14, 17, etc. But the general principles, both positive and negative, of his theology give these ideas a calamitous ecclesiological bearing. Every Christian is anointed, he says, and can interpret the word of God, judging any doctor, bishop or pope in the act of teaching. The word of God has got to be propounded, and it is normal that particular men, masters and preachers, should have this duty. If a Christian is alone, he can do it himself; if several are together, they should choose one amongst them to do it. But, it is objected, this belongs to the competence of bishops and other prelates: Paul told Timothy and Titus to appoint priests. Luther replies that, if those prelates who claim to be Paul's successors really take his place and teach the Gospel, if this be all their care, then appointment of ministers of the word can be entrusted to them. Wanting that, even, following New Testament example, when there is no urgency, the community must do it; for it is their business (and he cites Titus i, 7-8 and 1 Timothy

[5] Cf. Fr Ilarino of Milan, *L'eresia di Ugo Speroni* (Rome, 1945), p. 547.

iii, 2-7) to attest that the bishop is without reproach. . . . Thus does
Luther transpose the exercise of the inward anointing, by which the
faithful are enabled to grasp the sense of true doctrine, to the plane
of the structure of the Church's doctrinal life; he uses it to replace
the principle of apostolical function by an apostolicity of content
which every man can judge for himself, and the community above
all. Just as the Church's aspect as institution or order of the means
of grace is set aside, so all hierarchical mediation is eliminated. The
general priesthood, transposed to the plane of a structural ecclesiological principle, becomes private judgement at the level of rule of
faith (whether that expression, 'private judgement', is used or not
is irrelevant).

Similarly with Calvin's notion of the inner witness of the Holy
Spirit. Seen in its true order, that of life, this also corresponds to
something that is authentic, namely what St John calls the anointing
from God (1 John ii, 27). Some Protestant theologians, sticking close
to the text, write of this in a way that would be perfectly acceptable
in a Catholic synthesis. But if one finds in it a structural ecclesiological principle, a part of the rule of faith (as it appears to us Calvin
did), then one falls into the same mistakes or misunderstandings as
Luther, and ends up in private judgement as a principle.

Moderate Gallicanism, such as was upheld by Mgr Maret[6] at the
time of the Vatican Council, also erred by passing from life to structure when it maintained that the consent of the body of the Church
is necessary to a pontifical definition: necessary not simply as a
recorded *fact*—order of life and concrete regime—but as an *act*
conditioning the validity of hierarchical deeds. A very similar position, calling for the same diagnosis and distinction, is taken by some
Anglicans, when they say that a consent expressed by the body of
the Church, finally by the faithful, is necessary to the validity of
synodal decrees, and that a veto by the same annuls them.

A very important position in which it seems that our distinction
could be used with fruitful consequences is surely that of *sobornost'*,
which certain Russian Orthodox of the emigration have made well-
known in the West during the past thirty or so years.[7]

[6][Bishop H. L. C. Maret, dean of the theological faculty of Paris and author of
Du concile générale et de la paix réligieuse (2 vols Paris, 1869).—*Translator's note.*]

[7][In the original work, Father Congar here proceeds to an examination of the
idea of *sobornost'*. He finds in it a very strong foundation of ecclesiological truth, to
which some have added an anthropology, a special religious gnoseology; then
certain polemical considerations have crept in. These developments have led to a
warping of the idea and the giving to it of an ecclesiological interpretation foreign
to the unbroken tradition of the Church and to Orthodox theological tradition.
This highly specialised disquisition is here omitted. Cf. below, page 270.—*Translator's note.*]

(3) The co-operation of the faithful in the Church's teaching function belongs to her life and the actual exercise of apostolic powers, not to her structural powers or acts conditioning the validity of hierarchical actions. What we find in Scripture and the old tradition is the union of an hierarchical structural principle and a principle of corporate exercise. This point is so important and decisive for the very foundations of a theology of laity that it must be dealt with at some little length.

In the first place, this union can be found within what is so happily called 'the Apostolic College'. After all, if the Scriptures sometimes call the faithful 'those who were with the Twelve', the Apostles are sometimes called 'those who were with Peter' (cf. *e.g.*, Mark iv, 10; i, 36). Eastern Orthodox and Protestants generally bring against the Catholic interpretation of the Petrine texts the fact that the powers given to Peter were afterwards extended to the other apostles.[8] As a statement, this is correct; and it is certainly opposed to a 'monarchical' conception of apostolical powers that would make them simply derivations from or participations in powers conferred on Peter *alone*. But it is not opposed to a theology that finds in the texts at the same time both an hierarchical principle *which includes* Peter's apostolic primacy and a principle of corporate exercise of authority, for that is what the texts say. Peter is the first to receive, alone, a power or quality, which is afterwards given to all, including Peter, collectively. While himself part of the building, he is that on which it is built. If all are doors (Apocalypse xi, 13, 21), yet Peter has the keys; if all are foundation, he is the underlying rock; if Christ's prayers are promised to all, he is the object of prayer that his faith may fortify the others. Peter has what the others have, he has it with them and they have it with him; but he has it *as leader*, not only chronologically but hierarchically first.

Nothing, surely, is more significant here than what the New Testament says about the pre-eminent apostolic testimony, to Christ's resurrection, as it is expounded by some recent exegetes. It is mainly a matter of 1 Corinthians xv, 3-8, especially verse 5: 'He appeared to Cephas, and then to the Twelve'. The exegetes referred to take this 'then' in an emphatic sense, which justifies the order, surely hierarchical, in which St Paul enumerates Christ's appearings. That vouchsafed to Peter is, in the strong sense of the word, the principal one, but it allows of a similar one afterwards to all the Twelve, that is, to the apostolic college as such, including Peter.

[8]Matt. xvi, 19: xviii, 18; Matt. xvi, 18: Eph. ii, 20; Luke xxii, 32: John xvii, 9, 20; John xxi, 15-17: Luke xxii, 30.

This interpretation is corroborated by St Luke, who is ecclesiologically so close to St Paul, in his account of events in the evening of
Easter-day: the Apostles' attitude has changed since the morning,
when they thought the myrrh-bearing women's story to be mere
nonsense (Luke xxiv, 11); and when the two disciples get back to
Jerusalem from Emmaus, the same Eleven and their companions
say to them, 'The Lord is risen indeed and hath appeared to Simon'
(*Ibid.*, verse 34).

These texts suggest another consideration that is interesting for
our subject. The Gospels relate a first appearing of our Lord to the
women: it was, so to say, lay people who first came to the tomb,
found it empty and, with Mary Magdalen, saw the risen Jesus. This
privilege is for ever theirs, and we are envious of their blessed fer-
vency. Nevertheless, their testimony is as it were without properly
ecclesial weight, without structural value for that apostolical witness
on which faith is to be based. It belongs rather to the order of personal fervour; their part was to warn Peter—if one may dare to put
it so, they had to get the hierarchy moving. . . . It was rather the
same a little later, by the sea of Tiberias (John xxi, 1ff.), an episode
in which many exegetes see the fulfilment of Mark xvi, 7. John is the
first to recognise Jesus, but he turns to Peter, and it is he who takes
the initiative and is thrice told to feed the Lord's flock. There are
other incidents that follow the same rhythm and have the same
meaning. Surely it is obvious that all members of the Church are
active and are active together and as a whole, but not at the same
level or in the same way. Actions of life are for all; but for some only
is their activity constructional in the Church, contributing to her
solidity and government. Within the apostolical body itself Peter is
the first to be given, alone and in a special way, what is afterwards
given to the others. His testimony does not receive its worth through
and in virtue of the testimony of the Eleven; but neither is it separate
therefrom, and when Peter gives it, it is expressly offered as theirs
also (Cf. *e.g.*, Acts x, 40-41).

The Acts of the Apostles shows us the Church less in her institution by Christ than in the upsurge of her life through the power
of the Holy Spirit; without any diminution of the hierarchical principle, this book displays the communal principle at work. This is
very noticeable when, after studying what the gospels say about
St Peter, one goes on to the Acts: here the hierarchical aspect of
Peter's primacy is less dwelt on and stressed than the communal
aspect of the Church's concrete regime. It is not only those passages
wherein Peter does not seem in any way different from the others;

there is also the emphasis on what may be called the collegiate principle, in accordance with which the disciples act collectively and are
conscious that they together form a single principle of action. This is
true of the Apostles proper not only on such occasions as in Acts viii,
14, and when the Holy Spirit is given to each one at Pentecost, but,
whenever they are all gathered together and of one mind.[9] The
expression 'The Twelve' has itself a collegiate significance. This
collegium is organised within itself: Peter is called to the first place
in the order of apostolical function and its role of 'constructing' the
Church. But this hierarchical principle is combined with a principle
of collegiality, in virtue of which each one acts as a member of the
college, in whose activities all take part—which is what we find in
the life of the early Church, in St Cyprian, for example, in the principle of the episcopate held and exercised *in solidum*.

Properly speaking, the collegiate principle operates within the
hierarchical order, but it is found as communal principle throughout
the Church. The book of the Acts shows the Church assembled,
unanimous, actively assenting to what is done; it calls her members
'the brethren'; it distinguishes these brethren from the hierarchical
parts of the Church, apostles and elders; but this distinction does not
stand in the way of association between the apostles or the bishop,
the elders, and the church or brethren, a regime of which Judaism,
surely, had drawn a first sketch (Cf. *e.g.*, Acts i, 15; ix, 30; xi, 1, 22).

It has often been remarked (and not by Anglicans and Protestants
only) that the early Church comprised a monarchical aspect, in the
authority of the Apostles, of apostolical men or of bishops; an aris-
tocratic aspect in the role of elders and of councils; and a 'popular'
aspect, in the part taken by all the faithful in the assemblies. To put
these different aspects into opposition with one another, and even
separate them, to erect one or another into the principle of the
Church's constitution, as various heresies have done, bringing about
episcopalianism, presbyterianism, congregationalism, this is to misunderstand the living organic reality of the total Church. In life as
it is lived, the hierarchical principle (determinant for structure) combines with the communal principle (which calls for all to be associated together according to their order) for a work which is the work
not of the hierarchs but of the Church. That is why in the writings
of the Apostolic Fathers one passes so often and so easily from very
strong hierarchical statements to communal statements, and *vice
versa*. These writings themselves are at the same time and inseparably

[9]Cf. J. A. Möhler, *Symbolik* . . . §37 (Eng. trans.); *Die Einheit in der Kirche* . . . §63
(French trans.).

the writings of leaders and of communities. They reflect a state of things in which the two principles harmonise.

So much so that we believe the idea of *sobornost'*, when rightly understood, to be profoundly true and Catholic. Members of the Orthodox Church often say that the word is untranslatable. We certainly prefer not to translate it rather than to speak of 'conciliarity' (*sobor* in Russian means council, as well as cathedral). This translation is favoured by polemical usage and by the systematisers of the *sobornost'* idea; but it seems bad to us, because it limits and narrows the idea to an excessively particularised and systematised meaning. And there is something else. *Sobor* comes from the verb *sobirat'* or *sobrat'*, which means to gather, gather together, collect: in fact, exactly what the Western canonical and theological tradition means by the words *colligere, collegium*. *Sobornost'* can be unhesitatingly translated as 'collegiality' or 'collegiate principle'; this includes 'conciliarity', the 'synodal principle', and more than that. The word *sobornost'* expresses or connotes everything that our tradition, social and political as well as theological and canonical, puts into that fine word *collegium*, with its equivalents and relatives: *collectio, congregatio, coetus, universitas, communio, communitas, societas, corpus*, corporation, fellowship, and finally *ecclesia*.

Despite the work of O. von Gierke, R. W. and A. J. Carlyle, and others, we still lack any thoroughly satisfactory study of all that these words can stand for, not so much as juridical institutions as a concrete regime of living together. What is needed is an inclusive monograph on the communal sense and the collegiate principle in the whole tradition of the West from before Nicaea to, say, 1789. It would then be seen that all the different expressions just enumerated carried with them the idea of a relationship of a number of persons to a same principle of life, to a same work; a relationship through which the persons were associated in such a way that each and every one of them had his part in the work, each according to his degree and resources, all being really necessary to one another, joined to one another, thus forming together a veritable transpersonal unity. However, we do not at all mean to suggest any rigorous equivalence between the old corporative idea and *sobornost'*, but simply to justify our proposed translation. The expressions 'collegiality' and 'collegiate' or communal principle need to be given the whole content proper to their ecclesiological application: fellowship, unanimity, Christian life in fellowship and unanimity, in a word, all that we have tried to set out in the first part of this chapter. And, having seen that it was a fact in the life of the apostolic Church, we must try to give a full explanation of it.

This must be looked for no lower than in God himself and in his economy of grace. The two orders of mystery, the necessary and eternal mystery of God and the gratuitous mystery of his economy [P], are founded the one on the other, the second patterned on and revealing the first; and they present the same structure, that of principle of existence given from above (therefore hierarchical) associating itself with another, like to it, together to form one complete whole, a fellowship. We at once recognise the sublime mystery of the Holy Trinity, the blessed unity of the Father—the Principle— the Son and the Holy Spirit, a sort of concelebration, as Dom Gréa says. And that is the law of the whole economy. We are told in Genesis that man was made in God's image. The woman is made in the image of the man, for she is derived from him, dependent on him and, so to say, his 'opposite number', his fellow creature and his partner. Together they are destined to form a living community and finally to be one flesh, while remaining two persons. Later on St Paul will take up these things in his theology of the relations of man and woman, and he will find their relationship analogous to that between God and man; he will go further, and find in it the type of the relationship between the Church and Christ (1 Corinthians xi, 3, 7-8; Ephesians v, 21-33). This involves much deep doctrine, connected with the revelation of that of Christ's ('mystical') body of fellowship. There we see the application to the Church of the law (if one may put it so) of the divine economy whereby a principle of help and fulfilment is joined to a principle of authority or hierarchy; the law whereby the Principle, the Source, has the happiness of communing with as well as communicating to, of giving itself a fellow as partner and helper, with whom a dialogue and co-operation are set up, then a sharing, and finally a communion. All comes from the Principle, but in the economy of grace this does not exhaust everything: the Principle is fulfilled by taking to itself something in some sense feminine, which it determines and fertilises, but only in and by which it reaches fulfilment. This is true not only of man and woman, but of God's grace and man's freedom, of Christ and the Church, and, within the Church, of the apostolical hierarchy and the lesser ministers, of clergy and faithful people. At a time when the active role of the laity is being found again, it is not without significance that the relationship of clergy and laity is often expressed by the word 'couple'.

We hold, then, that there is an analogy between what the Bible

shows to be the law of God's work and what the Bible also shows to
be the Church's concrete regime. Hierarchy and people are like
husband and wife (or the children) in a family. 'The head of the
woman is the man . . . he is the image and glory of God: but woman
is the glory of man' (1 Corinthians xi, 3, 7); but the woman too
sways the man and takes part in his decisions in her own way. What
she thinks is present to and active in the man through the love that
makes them one, through their mutual 'dialogue', through the co-
operation and help the woman gives her husband; his mind and
judgement are full of his wife. St Paul has some hard sayings on this
subject, but he adds: 'Yet, in the Lord, neither is woman a being
independent of man nor man a being independent of woman. For as
woman is from man, so is man through woman; yea, and all things
are from God' (*Ibid.*, verses 11-12). The hierarchical principle is not
by itself the whole of God's design; it involves the complementing
and give-and-take of a community and the fullness that comes from
the association of two. St Paul expresses the mutual relationship
between Christ and the Church by the word *pleroma* [F]; St John
Chrysostom uses the same term for the relationship of the faithful
with their bishop; and it cannot be doubted that St Ignatius of
Antioch or St Cyprian would have accepted the expression. The
Principle is fulfilled in the living organism to which it communicates
itself.

'On those who have a right faith, the Holy Spirit bestows the
perfect grace of knowing how those who are at the head of the
Church must teach and safeguard all things': that was not written
by some slavophil upholder of *sobornost*', but by St Hippolytus (*Trad.
apost.*, c. 1). To some it may sound bold and even dangerous; but it
expresses a real aspect of the Church's tradition and practice. The
master of Hippolytus, St Irenaeus, writes of the Roman Church
itself: 'It is to this Church, because of its more weighty origin, that
every Church—that is, the faithful who are from all parts—must
resort: this Church in which the tradition derived from the Apostles
has been kept by those who come from all parts'.[10]

We will take two important examples; one, from the Arian crisis
in the fourth century, wherein the Church's central magisterium
was not very active (some people found in it an objection against
papal infallibility); the other from the past century, wherein the
supreme magisterium was dogmatically and practically affirmed in

---

[10]*Adv. haer.*, iii, 3, 2 (PG., 7, 849). The correct translation of this passage has been
much discussed. For a recent suggestion, see M. Sagnard in *Sources chret.*, no. 34
(Paris, 1952), pp. 103–107, 414–421.

a way as active as it was striking. The first example was elaborated at length by John Henry Newman in an article that at the time almost excited scandal.[11] This article can in fact be misleading if it is taken as a complete account of the crisis: for it deals with only one aspect of it, using texts which often come from lay historians favourable to the laity, such as Socrates and Sozomen. Nevertheless, although not the only one, this aspect was real, and has been frankly recognised as such by other able Catholic historians.[12] It is unquestionable that throughout the first half of the fourth century the faithful people resisted Arianism and its by-products, a heresy of intellectuals that was often accepted by bishops themselves, whether as theologians or because they followed imperial inclinations. That same Christian people remained faithful to persecuted bishops; in Rome they supported Pope Liberius when he was carried off by the Emperor Constantius, just as they had supported Pope St Cornelius against Novatian, and just as the Alexandrians welcomed back St Athanasius.

Among other characteristics of Catholicism during the nineteenth century were these two: a great development of Marian devotion and doctrine (the dogmas of the Immaculate Conception and the Assumption), and a renewed development of the Roman magisterium, not only in doctrine (the dogma of Papal Infallibility) but also in exercise of this magisterium. Under Gregory XVI and Pius IX this ceased to consist simply of intervention (especially by way of condemnation) at moments of crisis; it took the further form of positive and regular Christian teaching through the medium of encyclical letters, addresses and so on, as it were a day-to-day commentary on and clarification of current questions and ideas. Would these new forms taken by the central and supreme magisterium do away with any positive role of the faithful people? Fear was often expressed that the magisterium of bishops themselves would be made empty and useless. But these things did not happen; the active role

[11]'On consulting the Faithful on matters of Faith', in *The Rambler*, July 1859, pp. 198–230. As well as in the studies of Newman, M. J. Scheeben (*Dogmatik*, n. 168ff.), A. G. Martimort, and others, the question of the co-operation of the faithful in the conversation and especially the development of dogma has been touched on briefly but positively by, *e.g.*, K. Adam, *The Spirit of Catholicism* (London, 1929), pp. 135ff.; J. Leclercq, *La vie du Christ dans son Eglise*, pt i, ch. 8; J. Levie, *Sous les yeux de l'incroyant* (Paris, 1944), pp. 240ff.; P. Broutin, *Mysterium Ecclesiae*, (Paris, 1947), pp. 247ff.

[12]Cf. *e.g.*, L. Lebreton, 'Le désaccord de la foi populaire et de la théologie savante . . .', in *Revue d'hist. eccles.*, vol. xix (1923), pp. 481–506, and vol. xx (1924), pp. 5–37. His title shows that Fr Lebreton puts the break, not between the faithful and the hierarchy (which Newman rather overdid), but between the people's faith and the risky speculations of theologians.

T

and co-operation of the faithful remained, and were seen exercised in matters about which the papal magisterium was specially concerned. As for the acts of the ordinary magisterium, it is known that, to take one example only, preparatory work for Leo XIII's 'Rerum novarum' in 1891 was done by groups of lay people, particularly those of the Fribourg Union; in regard to social problems especially, it is normal that the laity should exercise a function 'preparatory and complementary to that of the hierarchy'.[13]

The properly dogmatic acts whereby our Lady's immaculate conception and taking up into Heaven were defined as dogmas of faith clearly show the part taken by the laity even in the elaboration of dogma. It has often been remarked how the extraordinary development of Marian doctrine has been carried on, sometimes in the teeth of theologians (as in the case of the Immaculate Conception), by the people's faith and devotion, with the encouragement of their bishops. It is to this faith of the Church, the faith of shepherds and flock together, that the constitution 'Munificentissimus Deus' makes appeal to ground the dogmatic quality of the Assumption. Both the above dogmas were solemnly defined only after the pope had consulted the whole Church and received assurance of her belief. No council was called, but there was a veritable 'council by writing', as it has been put, in which the opinion of all the bishops and through them, expressly, of their flocks was asked: on the Immaculate Conception by the encyclical 'Ubi primum' (2 February 1849), on Assumption by the letter 'Deiparae Virginis' (1 May 1946). This last contained a phrase that echoed earlier times, St Cyprian, for instance—'cum clero et populo vestro'. All this constitutes a sort of jurisprudence for the pope's exercise of his infallibility, one moreover anticipated by the Vatican Council; this needs to be taken into consideration by any theology whose aim is correctly to interpret the dogma promulgated by the council (Const. de Ecclesia, c. 4). Papal infallibility, we know, is not the consequence of a *revelation* but of a *help*, by virtue of which the pope is kept from deluding himself and deluding the Church in an act whereby, exerting his authority as supreme teacher and shepherd, he pronounces definitively on a matter of faith or morals. And this help is given him only in order that he may define *the faith of the Church*. The pope has to investigate and ascertain this faith by appropriate means; it exists in the Church more or less obscurely until it is brought into the full light of day by a dogmatic definition.

[13] J. Caryl and V. Portier, *La mission des laics dans l'Eglise* (Lyons, 1949), p. 179. See H. Rollet, 'Les origines de "Rerum novarum" ', in *Vie intellectuelle*, June 1951, pp. 4–21; A. de Gasperi, *I tempi e gli uomini che prepararono la 'Rerum novarum'*.

In this connexion we speak of *sensus* or *consensus fidelium, sensus Ecclesiae, sensus catholicus, sensus fidei*; or, as in '*Munificentissimus Deus*', of *christiani populi fides, communis Ecclesiae fides*. The two sets of terms are not exactly equivalent: they belong to different moments in history and different points of view. But they suppose a common basis, which can be formulated thus: there is a gift of God (of the Holy Spirit) which relates to the twofold reality, objective and subjective, of faith (*fides quae creditur; fides qua creditur*), which is given to the hierarchy and the whole body of faithful together (Cf. below, section 4), and which ensures an indefectible faith to the Church. This gift, we say, relates to the objective reality of faith, that is, the deposit of notions *and of realities* which constitute tradition (*id quod traditur Ecclesiae; id quod tradit Ecclesia*); correlatively, it relates to subjective reality, that is, to the grace of faith in the *fidelis*, or religious subject, the quasi-instinctive ability that faith has to see and adhere to its object (at least within certain limits, as we shall explain presently). This subjective aspect of the grace of faith was specially considered by the great thirteenth-century scholastics. But the aggregate of what we have just briefly analysed, which can be called the infallibility of the Church's faith, is a universal traditional belief. It is found in the Fathers, who often argue from it as from something that it is impossible to challenge. It is found in the authors of the second half of the sixteenth century, who introduced 'the Church universal' or 'the sense of the faithful' among the *loci theologici*, that is, among the criteria of Christian thought. It is found among the general principles of ecclesiology; so much so that, in general terms, Orthodox theologians and those of the Anglo-Catholic wing of Anglicanism are here in agreement with us.

Too much must not be attributed to the *sensus fidelium*, not only in view of the hierarchy's prerogatives (Cf. below, section 4) but in itself. History tells us of widespread failures of faith in the Christian people: in the East of the seventh century in face of Islam, in England and the Scandinavian countries in face of the Protestant Reformation, in unhealthy enthusiasms here and superstitious devotions there, and so on. The treatise on theological criteria [JJ] sets out to determine certain limits, certain rules or conditions within which the infallibility of the *sensus fidelium* is or is not certainly operative, as it tries to do also in respect of the Fathers, for they too were sometimes mistaken. The Church loving and believing, that is, the body of the faithful, is infallible in the living possession of its faith, not in a particular act or judgement. As we shall see, this infallibility is not simply a submissive deference to the hierarchy, a moral act of docility or obedience, but it is of a vital, moral nature, connected with righteous living. An explanation is required in respect of its objects. From that standpoint, it is ordered to the apostolic hierarchy, the guardian of tradition in its reality and its formulations. As Mgr Journet says, the 'right orientation' of the faithful to the faith does not simply involve a kind of internal instinct for submissiveness to the appointed organs of the tradition handed down from Christ and the Apostles. For an Ignatius of Antioch, no less than for St Paul, the oneness of mind of the whole body comes from conformity with its bishop. Doubtless here again the final ecclesiological principles must be looked for in the theology of the missions of Christ and of the Holy Spirit, with their duality and unity. If it be right that the *sensus fidelium* or *sensus catholicus* is a power of adhesion and discernment in the body of the faithful, it is also and conjointly a sense of oneness and fellowship in which an essential element is an obedient attitude towards apostolical authority living in the episcopal body. Such is St Ignatius Loyola's rule, 'Bene sentire in Ecclesia'.[14]

(4) We must now examine more closely the respective place and position of the infallibility of the body of the faithful and that of the body of their pastors. Not for a moment or in the slightest degree do we adopt the proposition censured by the decree '*Lamentabili*' in 1907, *viz.*, 'In the definition of truths the teaching Church and the taught Church collaborate in such a way that the sole task of the teaching Church is to sanction the opinions of the taught'. But neither can we accept as fully and exactly representing tradition and the best authorised teaching the view that the body of the faithful has no other title to infallibility than 'to listen properly to the magisterium'.[15] This is the narrow idea that Tyrrell opposed by upholding the contrary position, which is also false, and even more so. But Catholic theology knows a larger and deeper view which, its intrinsic value apart, has weighty support.[16]

[14] In Appendix II herein will be found an *excursus* on the *sensus fidelium* in the Fathers.
[15] 'The passive infallibility of the faithful consists in listening properly to the magisterium': A. A. Goupil, *La règle de foi* (Paris, 1941), p. 48. This view is very common. See, *e.g.*, Bishop Caixal y Estrade at the Vatican Council (Mansi, 52, 914c); A. Vacant, *Le magistère ordinaire de l'Eglise* (Paris, 1887), p. 109; L. Choupin, *Valeur des décisions . . . du Saint-Siege* (Paris, 1913), pp. 3–4; J. de Guibert, *De Christi Ecclesia* (Rome, 1928), n. 321.
[16] For example: Dom Maurus Cappellari (afterwards Pope Gregory XVI), *Triomphe du Saint-Siège et de l'Eglise*, ch. xxvi, especially n. 2; Bishop V. Gasser, *rapporteur* of the deputation *de fide* at the Vatican Council, answering Mgr Caixal y Estrade (Mansi, 52, 1216b); M. J. Scheeben, *Dogmatik*, §§11–14; J. V. Bainvel, *De magisterio vivo et traditione* (Paris, 1905), n. 94. For the medieval doctors, see *e.g.*, M. Grabmann, *Die Lehre des hl. Thomas von der Kirche als Gotteswerk* (Regensburg, 1903), pp. 169ff.: W. Scherer, *Des sel. Albertus Magnus Lehre von der Kirche* (Freiburg i. B., 1928), ch. v.

The first view is too narrow because, being governed by a momentary debate, it looks at the question only in terms of opposition and choice between hierarchy and faithful; whereas these two poles are relative to one another and integrated with one another in a single organism, within which each receives, from one higher principle, the animation required for its respective place and office. The narrow view fairly reflects the weakness of a certain ecclesiology referred to in our second chapter, in which Möhler saw a result of naturalism: the working of the Holy Spirit is overlooked, leaving in the ecclesiological field only a passive mass and a machinery of mediation; and then all there is to be considered is the running of the mass by the machinery. When, however, all infallibility in the Church is expressly referred to the working of the Holy Spirit which Jesus promised should enable his Church to live in the truth, then the prospect widens out. In that case, each is acted on in view of an infallibility (finally one) according to his place in the body, receiving the infallibility that belongs to him in function of the infallibility of the total organism, rather as each of man's various powers receives its part and pertinent energy from his soul. The episcopal body, heir to the apostolical body, has the help of the Holy Spirit lest it err in discharging its teaching office; it forms a college in whose midst, like Peter amidst the other Apostles, the Bishop of Rome, Peter's heir and successor, has the help of the Holy Spirit in carrying out his part as the final criterion of unity and orthodoxy; the faithful people has the help of the Holy Spirit to be a faithful people, that is, to cleave to God with a living faith in him, but a faith whose objective determinations are, in accordance with the divine economy, brought to the people by the teaching of its hierarchs.

But there is more to be said. The loving and believing Church is infallible only when it listens to the teaching Church and thus partakes of *the teaching Church's* infallibility; again: the loving and believing Church is infallible through the animation received from the Holy Spirit in her quality as loving and believing Church, which implies organic reference and submission to the magisterium. In the first case, the Holy Spirit makes the hierarchy infallible, and the hierarchy, by subjecting the faithful to itself, communicates the benefit of *its* infallibility to them; in the second case, the Holy Spirit makes the Church, as a whole and as such, infallible, and in her each organic part according to what it is—the whole body in order that it may believe and live, the apostolic and magisterial hierarchy in order that it may transmit the apostolical deposit to the body and declare its authentic meaning. We have already pointed out how the hierarchy can be considered from different points of view, as belonging to the generative cause of the Church and so anterior to her, or as formal part (authority) in her. Like so many others, these points can be treated fully only in a comprehensive treatise on the Church.

With reference to the faithful, one often hears of 'passive' infallibility, as one hears of active infallibility with reference to the teaching Church. Franzelin preferred to speak of infallibility *in credendo*, in the order of believing, and of infallibility *in docendo*, in the order of teaching, which is near enough to what Tertullian said seventeen hundred years ago (See Appendix II). 'Passive' is an ambiguous adjective; it too easily suggests the position we have criticised above and the picture drawn by Cappellari of 'a blind man, walking unafraid on his guide's arm, but not knowing where he is going or what he is walking on' (*loc. cit.*, note 16). It would seem to give a new lease of life to that blind man!

To believe is doubtless first of all to listen, but it is also to cleave with heart and mind, to make one's own, to think, to do. Our Lord said: 'Whoso believeth in me, as the Scripture saith, "Out of his belly shall flow rivers of living water". . . He that believeth in me, the works that I do, he also shall do, and greater than these shall he do' (John vii, 38; xiv, 12). And St Paul: 'Now we have not received the spirit of the world, but the Spirit which is from God, that we may realise the graces God hath given us . . . we have the mind of Christ' (1 Corinthians ii, 12, 16). St John tells us that he who believes has everlasting life and the evidence of God is within him (John iii, 15, 36; 1 John v, 10, etc.). These few texts are enough to remind us that the Christian faith is something active in the *fidelis*, and not solely in the realm of morals or mysticism but also in the order of thought, for the faith itself has an intellectual content. The apostolic hierarchy bears witness, it authoritatively imposes formulas that have a content and express the mind's adhesion truly, but that content is put forward 'in the lump'; it is for the faithful, to whom bishops and priests belong as private persons, to take this datum and think about it, construe it, develop it. The magisterial authority keeps an eye on these explications; and if this one or that seems to falsify the meaning or deny the implications of the truths of which that authority is the guardian, then it will interpose, and eventually condemn. But even then such and such a statement is condemned only from the angle at which it endangers the integrity of the deposit: condemnation does not always and necessarily touch the most important aspects of the Christian datum, and it still leaves a good margin for investigation both to right and left.

If faith is a talent that calls for increase, it is also a light that must be shed around. We have seen, and we shall see again (Part Two Ch.V), that priests and lesser ministers, and then the laity, have to be —and are ecclesially instituted to be—transmitters of the apostolic witness, husbandmen of episcopal teaching. How can this be done passively, as by a loud-speaker, without actively adding something to the message being handed on, by word and by deed?[17] Rather do we find, in apostolic souls really dedicated to God, a deep knowledge of the things of God, a sort of spontaneous re-creation of the Gospel which, redeeming Christ's promise to those who believe, is born in them of the Holy Spirit who dwells in them.[18]

Thus do we see the place of the respective parts of the hierarchy and of the faithful in the Church. Those parts have to be looked for in the various aspects of the one faith, in the diverse movements of the Holy Spirit that confront them, and in the different 'moments' of the one Church: '. . . one body and one Spirit . . . one faith, one baptism. . . . But to every one of us is given grace according to the measure of Christ's bestowing. . . . And himself gave some as apostles, some as prophets, some as evangelists, some as shepherds and teachers, for the perfecting of the saints in the work of the ministry, unto the building up of the body of Christ. . . . From him the whole body, welded and compacted together by means of every joint of the system, part working in harmony with part—from him the body deriveth its increase, unto the building up of itself in charity' (Ephesians iv, 4-16).

Inasmuch as the Church is loving and believing, her faith made inward and personally lived, she is a spiritual organism of faith and love and all her members are simply members. Inasmuch as she requires a public authority to uphold and foster the faith and keep it true to the apostolical deposit by teaching, interpreting and watching over it, there is among the members a relationship of authority and 'subjects'. But this relationship is set up precisely *within the Church*; it is not, as some less happy formulations might make one think, between the Church and a laity who are not the Church,[19] but indeed between *the Church* as teaching and *the Church* as taught. At the

---

[17]This point is well dealt with by Scheeben, *Dogmatik*, §12, n. 159 and 13, 168ff., especially 171.

[18]This is very noticeable among the martyrs (for example, the nineteenth-century martyrs in the Far East), who are the finished models of discipleship (Cf. Matt. x, 19).

[19]There is something of this in Cappellari, *loc. cit.*, n. 3., and it is rather suggested by the formula *Sentire cum Ecclesia*—as though the Church were outside the faithful, who adjust themselves to her by accepting her determinations in a purely passive way.

level of the Church's generative causes, it is the office of the apostolic hierarchy infallibly to declare the authentic apostolic deposit; at the level of the constituted Church, as her authority or formal part, its office is to expound and maintain the deposit by way of authoritative judgement. The part of the faithful (among whom the bishops belong as private persons) is to live by the apostolic deposit, to live that deposit; living it, to safeguard it and, safeguarding it, to develop it, to the limits of space and time in which it is given mankind to endure. So we say, with Scheeben (*Dogmatik*, § 13, n. 170; § 15, n. 200), that the hierarchical pastorate alone teaches with authority, but the whole Church transmits the tradition; nor does that tradition consist solely in statements, but, more widely and deeply, in the very reality of Christianity. This is not to say that the faithful people do not teach. They do teach and very actively, but not in virtue of apostolical authority, by imperative decision; they teach in virtue of the faith within, through all the activities of life and mind that it stimulates and develops. 'Credendo docent quodammodo', as Father Bainvel carefully puts it. More exactly still: all the richness of the deposit confided to the Church that can be revealed to a life of active faith objectively ruled and supervised by the apostolic hierarchy—it is through that that the faithful teach.[20]

We have spoken of the Church loving and believing, not because it is an inclusive expression but because of the truth of things; St Thomas's theology justifies us at the level of advanced construction. The faithful maintain tradition by fully living their Christian state, each one according to his calling, that is, conformably to God's will; but they also develop it, instinctively reacting against whatever is harmful to it, and thus they teach mankind, the Church, the hierarchy itself; it is rather like a wife or a child drawing the attention of the head of the household to things wherein authority and decision belong indefeasibly to him. 'Bishops, too, have to learn', said St Cyprian (*Ep. lxxiv*, x, i), which certainly does not lessen their prerogatives.

We have now given a summary of the position in principle of the laity with respect to the Church's prophetical or teaching function. We know that their proper order is that of the living of life; and accordingly we find conditions of exercise for 'prophecy' similar to those found for priesthood and kingship: maybe we have come upon a constitutive law of the Church, an essential characteristic of the

[20][A paragraph is here omitted in which Father Congar refers to what Maurice Blondel wrote on tradition in *La Quinzaine*, vol. lvi (1904), pp. 145–167, 349–373, 433–458.—*Translator's note*.]

divine economy. But we have also come upon an essential characteristic of the Church's concrete regime, collegiality or the combination of the corporative with the hierarchical principle. Again are we
struck by an earthly order that follows the pattern that exists in God
himself, in whom the Father is Principle, but he is not alone. The
witness that God has raised up on the earth, the Church, is also many
and one, a concord, literally a symphony. The fatherly and fertilising
voice of apostolic authority is echoed by the voice of the faithful
people, in such a way that the second voice, while in exact agreement with the first, does not repeat it mechanically: it amplifies it,
carries it further, enriches it and corroborates it. And this concerted
movement stands four-square on Scripture and tradition.

(B) Teaching Activities of the Laity

No doubt different forms of teaching have always been recognised;
but it seems unquestionable that the coming of scientific analytical
theology, at the juncture of the twelfth with the thirteenth century,
strengthened the distinction between a doctoral, university teaching
and a pastoral teaching, episcopal and monastic, that was more
associated with liturgical and contemplative life. Certainly we find
these distinctions more clearly formulated by the thirteenth-century
scholastics, particularly St Thomas, who distinguishes between teaching by pastors, of which the chief activity is preaching, and teaching
by doctors; the first depends on the authority of spiritual government, the second on the scientific qualification of the doctor or
master. To this fundamental distinction St Thomas adds a third
term, teaching by way of private exhortation or personal admoni-
tion, and this, he says, can be exercised by women.

We adopt these common distinctions then, which in any case can
be arrived at by simply looking at the facts. Following an empirical
order, there is first exhortation, a call to repentance with a view to
conversion to the faith, then authoritative teaching given to the
fidelis in either practical or speculative matters, and then purely
objective intellectual teaching, a matter of scientific competence,
which can be addressed to unbelievers as well as to the faithful.
There are various conditions and circumstances within these forms,
and each of the three may be divided into its public and private
exercise.

Teaching of divine revelation with authority. – Authority for the public
teaching of the Christian revelation belongs by right to the apostolical body, whose charisms are inherited by the episcopal body, at

least in part: that is, no longer for the purpose of revelation (*traditio constitutiva*), but in order faithfully to safeguard and unerringly to declare the deposit (*traditio continuativa et explicativa*). *Ex officio* and in virtue of the charisms appertaining to their function, bishops have a public authority in doctrinal matters, and a rightful magisterium. This they exercise by preaching, which tradition regards as the first of their duties, by their supervision of all sacred teaching activity, and as 'judges of faith', a function exerted in the censuring of doctrines and in synods or councils. This authority cannot be delegated, but up to a point it can be participated in. Priests and religious who preach (whether by speech or writing) have a certain share in the doctrinal authority of bishop or pope, as being co-operators with them; but, even when assembled in a synod, they are not 'judges of faith', and their authority is never more than 'borrowed' from and controlled by that of the bishop: it is a reflection or echo, depending entirely on association and conformity with the bishop's public authority.

In an analogous way, lay people can receive a still more tenuous participation in this authority. They are associated, officially *ex missione*, *ex officio*, with the teaching function of the pastoral authority whenever they are given, at least implicitly, some canonical teaching mission under its control. For example, in the institution of lay catechists officially affiliated to some society or confraternity under episcopal authority, or, as in the foreign missions, incorporated canonically in the Church's apostolic organism.[21] Or again, in the office of godparents, nowadays often become a mere memory or theoretical ideal; but it is associated with the hierarchical teaching office (Cf. St Thomas, *IV Sent.*, d. vi, q. 2, a. 2, sol. 2). This teaching duty appertains to the spiritual responsibility assumed at a child's baptism, but it remains latent in the authority, the natural and sacramentalised authority, of the parents, especially of the father, whose

---

[21]For all exercise of a ministry of the word, canon law requires a mission received from the proper authority (Canon 1328). This exercise is by means of catechism classes, sermons and missions. It is expressly laid down (Canon 1333, §1) that the parish-priest may, and even ought to, be helped in his catechetical duties by lay people, particularly by members of the Confraternity of Christian Doctrine: recent popes and decrees of Roman congregations have insisted on these provisions. – On societies of catechists and their position in mission lands, see the encyclopedia *Catholicisme*, vol. ii (Paris, 1950), cc. 656–663. – The canonical mission of teaching is implicitly conferred on teachers of religion in schools by the bishop's approval of their appointment. Some declarations even speak of these teachers sharing in the magisterium (Mgr Tedeschini, nuncio at Madrid, quoted by Dabin, *L'apostolat laïc*, p. 120; Pope Pius XII, quoted in the *Osserv. Rom.*, 7 Septr 1949); no doubt this means participation in the mission of the magisterium, and to that extent in its authority in some way, but not in its power.

responsibility it is to ensure the Christian upbringing of their children.[22] This responsibility too can be seen as a remote participation in the authority of the Church as mother, but without explicit institution or formal control; nor is there anything of *public* authority in it, and there is practically nothing of this in the duties of a godparent or even of a catechist. We have seen that the invitation of lay men to councils did not imply the recognition or bestowal of any power of magisterium; it was an interesting application of the law of association or collegiality, which is profoundly characteristic of the Church and has to be honoured in one way or another. The tradition is that the laity should be joined with the hierarchy for information, advice, and so on. There is no trace here of public doctrinal authority, such as that which gives the Church her rule of faith.

There is no question of any such authority in the purely personal and private sphere of what the faithful may say, even though prompted by God, without mission or public charge. From the very beginning the Church has known inspired souls whose words were able to contribute much to her life, but those words were not the vehicle of any belief that constituted and constructed the people of God as such. The apostolic age and following centuries were particularly rich in visions and prophetical gifts, but every age has had them in one way or another and our own would hardly yield to any other in the matter of visions: it is in modern times that the question of private revelations has been definitely raised.[23] But the distinction has always been made between private revelations and the one and only revelation made to the Apostles that is constitutive of the Church. The early Church distinguished between those appearings of Christ on which apostolical witness was grounded, and the visions vouchsafed to some of the martyrs. However authentically divine, visions and private revelations have never been given place in the rule of faith, those who experienced them have never been put on a level with public teaching authority.

But where living is concerned a great deal has been brought to the Church by such gifts and by those of deep understanding implanted

[22] Cf. Part Two Ch.II, note 19. The parents' mission in respect of their children's religious education is something like marriage itself, a natural thing sacralised by an act of the Church: a sort of delegation of the Church's motherhood added to and coinciding with the natural mission of natural parenthood. H. Keller, in *Scholastik*, vol. 17 (1942), p. 372, calls parents 'Mandatarii Ecclesiae a natura designati et per se inamovibiles'.

[23] On this, see Franzelin, *De div. tradit.*, xxii; M. J. Congar, 'La crédibilité des revelations privées', in *Vie spirituelle*, suppl., Octr 1937, pp. 29–48; and K. Rahner in *Revue ascet. et myst.*, vol. xxv (1949), pp. 506–514.

in the faithful by the Spirit of God, spoken of by the texts quoted at
the beginning of this chapter. They belong with those charisms about
which the New Testament, the writings of the three first centuries,
and continuous experience in the Church sufficiently inform us.
Charisms are referred to in our next chapter. Here it is enough to
remark, following St Paul, that they are gifts of grace or gifts
ordered to the effecting of God's saving purpose, which, on being
manifest, do not come from some regular hierarchical proceeding
such as baptism or the eucharist; but, having to contribute towards
the same end as the Church and the ministry, they belong to the
pattern of unity, and therefore are subjected in use to a certain
regulation by instituted authority (1 Corinthians xii, xiv).

That is exactly how it is with charisms of knowledge and unveiling
of divine mysteries.[24] They do not, or need not, come from any
hierarchical proceeding (though they are often associated with
reception of the sacraments), but from an unpredictable direct visi-
tation of God; and they therefore have, as Scheeben says, a relative
independence with regard to hierarchical apostolic witness. But
their content, like that of any other spiritual pronouncement, is
bound to conform with that apostolic witness, of which the episcopal
body is guardian (in organic conjunction with the body of the faithful, as has been explained above). If anyone be a prophet, let him
prophesy, but 'according to the proportion of our faith' (Romans
xii, 6). What the Apostles preached is a strict norm, and whatever
departs from it is worthless (1 Corinthians xii, 3; Galatians i, 8;
1 John iv, 2-6). Spiritual gifts of knowledge and understanding can
be powerful aids to penetrating its meaning, to developing thought
and nourishing godliness, even to laying bare the true significance of
God's gifts. Nobody will deny that much has been brought to the
Church in respect of knowledge of God by such people as the two
St Teresas (in whom popes have acknowledged a real attribute of
doctor), St Margaret Mary, Barbe Acarie, Pascal, Gaston de Renty,
and more than one contemporary. But their contribution, however
striking and fruitful, draws all its worth from its conformity with the
apostolic rule of teaching, and its subordination to and co-ordination
with hierarchical teaching, even when it exceeds the latter in depth.
Thus, when the faithful are enlightened by the Spirit, they corrobor-
ate hierarchical teaching; in a sense, they add to it, and may even

[24]St Paul speaks of charisms of revelation: Rom. xvi, 26; 1 Cor. xiv, 6, 26; 2 Cor.
xii, 1 (referring to himself). The encyclical '*Mystici Corporis*' shows the place of
charismatic illumination in the Church (sect. 37).

be a guide to its judgement, as Scheeben says.[25] Their contribution is infinitely valuable (we are again reminded of what Chrysostom said about the bishop's *pleroma*); but it does not *by itself* constitute a public authority, having social value as a criterion for the life of God's people in the unity of truth. It comes from God, but it attains its public value only through approval given by the hierarchical magisterium, which recognises in it a development and elaboration of the apostolical deposit confided to that magisterium.[26]

Hortatory and apostolic teaching. – Here we have to consider preaching by lay people, of which the history falls into three stages before we reach modern times. The early days of the founding of the Church were characterised by an abundance, or at least plenty of evidence, of charisms, graces ordered to the building up of the Church. These charisms were certainly often associated with corresponding orders; but sometimes they were given by God to whom he willed, and any one of the faithful might receive the privilege and the responsibility. Differently from liturgical and governmental charisms, those of preaching and evangelisation in particular are seen to be exercised now by ordained and instituted ministers, now by unordained *fideles*. Twice at least the Acts of the Apostles shows the disciples scattered by persecution and seizing the opportunity to preach God's word and increase the Church (viii, 4; xi, 19); this happened often in the early days, and it has been repeated at intervals ever since in the Church's missionary history. Aquila and his wife Priscilla completed the instruction of Apollos (Acts xviii, 26), and became trusted helpers of Paul (Romans xvi, 3); and Apollos himself, who seems never to have received any ministerial consecration, was a vigorous preacher of Christ (Acts xviii, 27-28).

The second stage is that of the Fathers and councils, when the Church was organising her life and fixing her canonical tradition. Not that the process of organisation had not begun in apostolic times —the idea of a primitive regime that was purely charismatic is a figment of the imagination, contradicted not simply by the evidence but by the very nature of an association of human beings. The movement took the form of a stricter subordination of charismatic gifts to hierarchical orders. The Acts of the Apostles already shows a Church in which the gift of tongues no longer has the place it had when St Paul was writing to the community at Corinth; the prophecy that

[25]*Dogmatik*, §12, n. 166–167. Scheeben is one of the very rare theologians who gives their place to charismatic organs of teaching.
[26]There is perhaps an example of this in the famous *Indiculus de gratia* (Denzinger, 129–142), really drawn up, in Rome between 435 and 442, by the lay man, Prosper of Aquitaine: cf. M. Cappuyns in *Revue bénédictine*, vol. xli (1929), pp. 156–170.

St John writes about in the Apocalypse, while he always gives it pre-
eminence, has lost the element of disorder implied by the two letters
to the Corinthians. As for the Pastoral Epistles, they are so 'Catholic'
that plenty of critics have judged them to be of later date.

In the second and third centuries, lay people are found speaking
of Jesus Christ to the heathen, and even still preaching. It is ques-
tionable whether the author of the second-century 'Clementine'
homily was a lay man, but it is certain that Origen was when the
bishops of Caesarea and Jerusalem invited him to expound the
Scriptures to the assembled faithful: Eusebius has preserved a letter
in which the two bishops explain the situation and refer to other
cases of a similar kind. In all these, bishops took the initiative and
kept control. The fact that Eusebius does not quote other examples
suggests that the custom of asking lay men 'who could be useful to
the brethren' to preach in church did not survive the third century.
A passage in the fourth-century *Apostolic Constitutions* (lib. viii, c. 32,
10) shows a certain survival, but it is not clear whether it refers to
preaching strictly so called, or simply to instruction. There is no sort
of preaching by laity at the great councils. St John Chrysostom,
whose pastoral teaching on lay co-operation is notably positive,
finds the field of their teaching activity in apostleship; they have to
instruct others, having first of all instructed themselves. There is
hardly any ancient canonical text on the subject, except the *Statuta
Ecclesiae antiqua* (end of the fifth century), whose regulations are
severely restrictive. Pope St Leo the Great had previously declared
that teaching and preaching belonged to the priestly order—by
which he meant bishops, without excluding simple priests—and not
to monks or lay men, however learned they might be. Anyone may
have learning and understanding of the true faith, but to preach in
church is a priestly activity.

The third stage is connected with the strong spiritual movement
that accompanied and followed the Gregorian reform; this movement came into contact with people's aspirations towards a certain
autonomy and untrammelled initiative, and was particularly expressed in the apostolic currents of the twelfth and thirteenth centuries. These tendencies were no less reforming than apostolic; and
it is easily understood that they included ambiguous elements,
balanced between Catholicity and heresy, or even definitely pledged
to untenable positions: such were the various groups of 'Apostolics'
and the followers of Peter Waldo and others. It was during the
evangelical ferment of the last third of the twelfth century that lay
preaching began again, among the Waldenses and among the

Humiliati of northern Italy. When the archbishop of Lyons forbade the Waldenses to interpret the Scriptures and to preach, Waldo turned to Pope Alexander III, who approved his scheme of evangelical life but directed that Waldo and his fellows were to preach only when asked to do so by a parish priest, 'nisi rogantibus sacerdotibus'. In this way, without being forbidden in principle, lay preaching was subjected to the norm of ecclesial life and brought under a degree of hierarchical control. A similar request to that of Waldo was made in the same year, 1179, by the Humiliati and was refused; in 1184, under Pope Lucius III, this was followed by excommunication. However, negotiations were reopened in 1198-1199, under Pope Innocent III; he had the situation in hand and followed a course that combined firmness with sympathy. This had good results, and in 1201 Innocent reconciled the Humiliati with the Church. He approved the *propositum* of these brotherhoods of lay people living 'in the world'; and, among other things, they were allowed to meet together every Sunday, when one of them could preach with the bishop's permission. But with this restriction, or rather clarification: the discourse must be simply a *verbum exhortationis*, aimed at encouraging right life and religious works, to the exclusion of dogmatic questions *de articulis fidei et sacramentis Ecclesiae*. This was the first enunciation of a distinction which is henceforward found in the terminology of the Curia; it was used in connexion with permissions given to the first Friars Minor, and occurs again in later theologians.[27]

Innocent III was not successful with the Waldenses, who had never been inclined to obedience and who maintained that anybody, even women and illiterates, could preach without permission. But he was completely successful with the Humiliati; in 1216 James of Vitry came across a hundred and fifty of their groups in the diocese of Milan, clergy and lay men who were authorised to preach not only at their own meetings but in church and in public places. There were others for whom the pope made provisions that were equally liberal, and even more so. Among the followers of Durando of Huesca, who became the Poor Catholics, was a good proportion of clergy. When he reconciled these in 1208, Pope Innocent authorised them to preach without having to ask permission individually from

[27]For the Friars Minor, see H. Felder, *Geschichte der wissenschaftlichen Studien im Franziskanerorden* . . . (Freiburg i. B., 1904), pp. 33-57. – St Thomas distinguishes between public and private teaching when he speaks of the witness that can be borne by lay people, particularly women: *Sum. theol.*, II-II, q. clxxvii, q. 2; III, q. lv, a. 1, ad 3; III, q. lxvii, a. 4, ad 1; *Com. in 1 Cor.*, c. 11, lect. 2; c. 14. lect. 7; *In 1 Tim.*, c. 2, lect. 3; *In Tit.*, c. 2, lect. 1; *Quodl.* xii, a. 27 (where he uses the word *exhortatio*).

their bishops; and this not only for the training of members of the
group, in whose *scholae* the word of God could be freely expounded,
but also with an apologetic object, to win Waldenses back to the
Church. In 1212 the society of converts formed under Poor Catholic
influence had a sermon on every Sunday, independently of Mass
apparently, which was directed to the moral ends of the *exhortatio*.
Two years earlier, Innocent III had authorised Bernard Prim's
association of clergy and laity to preach to heretics, with due permission of authority. That permission was also needed for exhortations addressed to the faithful, but this requirement was afterwards
cancelled. The last two cases are specially interesting because of the
apologetical activity added to the addresses and teaching given in
the groups' *scholae*. These particular societies had a good proportion
of clergy members, but laity were expressly included in the authorisa-
tions. And so the Church's jurisprudence was perfected: the laity's
proper part in the ministry of the word is, on the one hand, apostolic
exhortation, and on the other, apologetical exposition.

But later on the excesses of sectaries and of Protestant reformers
brought about a reaction, and the Church imposed narrower
regulations. Canon law forbids lay people, even those who are
religious, to give a sermon in church (Canon 1342 § 2); today this
is the rule for all Catholics, including, it would seem, those of
Eastern rite. But is this forbiddance the whole story? Is there nothing
left of that lay co-operation in exhortation and apologetical speaking
that the Church used expressly to admit? We will again let the facts
and the texts speak for themselves. They can be grouped under the
general headings of (*a*) private apostolic teaching; and (*b*) public
apostolic teaching (presupposing a mission).

(*a*) A Christian's private activity is not without mission, but that
mission is either entirely general, arising from membership of a body
which is as a whole apostolic and prophetic, or particular and personal but wholly inward, 'instinctu Spiritus Sancti', as they used to
say in the Middle Ages.[28] Such a mission may well attain publicity,
but its character and value do not thereby become public, part of an
official function.

Through baptism, each one of the faithful belongs to the people
of God, set apart and consecrated to bear witness before the world
(1 Peter ii, 9). Confirmation is a very special development of the

[28]For example: '. . . sanctae mulieres . . . meruerunt aureolam [praedicationis],
quia etsi missae non erant ab homine sicut a praelato potestatem habente, tamen
instinctu Spiritus Sancti et missae a Spiritu Sancto praedicaverunt . . .' (Eustace
of Arras, *c.* 1265). Cf. *Vraie et fausse reforme*, pp. 534–535, 625. – For the technical
sense of 'mission', cf. Chapter IV, note 111.

baptismal consecration with reference to the Christian's strengthening and activity in the *social* life of the Church and of the world; accordingly, the prophetical function of witness is connected with this sacrament. In virtue of his consecration at baptism and confirmation, and of the gifts of faith and grace that are his, every lay person can and ought to bear that personal witness to which he has been dedicated. 'The laity do not have to wait to be empowered in order to discharge their individual apostolic mission: it is enough that they are the faithful, with the demands made on them by their baptism and confirmation'.[29] Everyone has this common apostolic responsibility and ought to exercise it, in the particular conditions and state of life to which God has called him. According to the time and place of our coming into this world, according to our country, our antecedents, our work, our resources, human and spiritual, according to a hundred other circumstances of our pilgrimage, we have a particular personal responsibility in respect of the Kingdom of God. As the existentialists say, we are *en situation*. Each of us is God's handiwork, 'created in Christ Jesus for good works, which God hath prepared beforehand that therein we may walk' (Ephesians ii, 10). Each of us has been put in a particular place at a particular time, in a personal 'situation' which specifies our Christian responsibility. And in the field of apostolic teaching, this responsibility is discharged by bearing witness in various ways, and by a certain teaching, especially of a kind that can be addressed in an unauthoritative way to those outside.

Witness is at the same time both an activity of lay people (or of clergy considered simply as *fideles*) and an apostolic activity directed to the world outside the Church. Preaching, properly speaking, is directed to the faithful; it presupposes the obedience of faith.[30] Normally, it is a liturgical act, complementary to the celebration of the mysteries. Witness is addressed to those who have not yet entered the ecclesial community and who do not take part in its mysteries. It is the personal communication of a personal conviction, of a shock received, of an experience undergone. Theologically speaking, it is in the strictest correspondence with what we have seen to be the position and role of the laity, and with the position and mission of the Church in relation to the world (Cf. page 282). So once again we find that the voice of the laity is heard more especially

[29]The meeting of French cardinals and archbishops on Catholic Action: *Docum. cath.*, 21 July 1946, col. 742. And see below, Chapter V.

[30]There is no accepted or adequate terminology. The Abbé C. Moeller (in *Irenikon*, 1951, pp. 313–343) calls 'preaching' almost what we here call 'witness' or 'testimony', and he calls 'catechesis' almost what we call 'preaching'.

in the Church's missionary stage, there where she has to establish
herself and where, being as yet without institutional activities, she
exists simply in the living faith of her children and through the
communication of that faith.

Teaching through witness is not given through words alone; often
its more effective form is that of belief translated quite simply into
life, with no attempt at persuasion. St Paul remarks that the behaviour of the faithful had been a pattern teaching others (1
Thessalonians i, 6-8). Day-to-day experience confirms it, as doubtless each one of us can testify: the conduct of how many people has
taught us this or that about Christianity. We reveal God and life in
Christ to one another, and this is part of God's design and the building up of the Church, which we shall discuss in our next chapter.
Here we will simply notice the immense value of the silent witness of
living, whether personal or communal, for apostolic teaching: it is a
wordless call to repentance—that is, to a change of life—to conversion, to faith; it is a most impressive instruction. Of late years
special emphasis has been laid upon the high worth of witness given
by the community as such; we may particularly mention the apostolic and prophetical value of the liturgical celebration of the mysteries according to the rhythm of the yearly cycle of feasts. Any
theology of worship, the sacraments or the liturgy lays stress on the
fundamental aspect of expression and evidence of faith in these
things, as does '*Mediator Dei*'. In the eucharistic celebration, all the
faithful proclaim the death of the Lord;[31] in their observance of the
feasts they testify to the mysteries, showing them forth before those
who are willing to take notice.

But the faithful can teach more explicitly, not only by way of witness but by way of teaching properly so called, directed to those
outside. This public manifestation of their faith by those qualified to
make it takes two main forms, both used very beneficially in our day:
the one is through artistic and cultural symbolical expressions, which
are a sort of mediation between the faith and people; the other is
explanation of and *apologia* for Catholicism. The great eras for faith
have been those in which the Church was able to illumine her teaching by means of authentic creations of poetry, art and culture; other
eras, such as the eighteenth century, though rich in interior life, have
been without this irradiation, for want of talent and initiative. This
mediation through art is for the most part a lay people's business.
We have seen that it is one of the forms of their consecra-

[31]Cf. 1 Cor. xi, 26. Some theologians expressly associate this aspect with the
prophetisme of the faithful, *e.g.*, Salmeron, John Lorain (Dabin, 371, 399).

tion and, when art is directly in the service of sacred things, a certain exertion of spiritual priesthood. Here we emphasise it as a teaching activity whose bearing is truly religious and, in some circumstances, apostolic.

How much more then the other form of mediation between faith and reason, more austere than the first but hardly less necessary, the work of apologetic. Defence and explanation of the faith has been expressly and directly undertaken by many lay people. Pascal in the seventeenth century is not an isolated example; many could be given from the French Revolution down to our own time—Chateaubriand, Joseph de Maistre, Goerres, Donoso Cortès, Auguste Nicolas, Brunetière, G. K. Chesterton are only a few of them, without naming any living persons. It is true that not all the work of these men is above criticism (the limitations of lay religious thought will be referred to later); but it cannot be denied that they produced a real apostolic teaching in the apologetical field. Lay thought and witness elaborate values which are much less well appreciated by the Church's ministers; not being professionals, lay people are given a more ready hearing and can handle things more effectively. Above all, being in closer touch with secular life and more at liberty to experiment in their methods and approaches, their efforts appeal more directly to the needs of their contemporaries; sometimes their work is more satisfactory in meeting that requirement of all living thought, the creation of values; and it is more successful in establishing the spiritual contact between the Church and the world that is so valuable to apostolic work. Pope Leo XIII summed up in eloquent words all that has just been said about the laity's personal part in teaching of an apostolic kind:

Amidst this worldwide flood of opinions it is the Church's mission to defend truth and rescue souls from error; this mission she has to carry out in holiness and ceaselessly, for to her has been entrusted the guardianship of God's honour and man's salvation. But, when circumstances make it necessary, it is not prelates alone who have to watch over the integrity of the faith; as St Thomas says, 'Everyone is bound to show forth his faith publicly, whether for the instruction and encouragement of other faithful or to repel the onslaughts of adversaries'.

The first applications of this duty are to profess Catholic doctrine openly and courageously, and to spread it so far as one is able. It has often been said, and with much truth, that nothing is more prejudicial to Christian wisdom than ignorance of it. Displayed in the light of day, it is by itself strong enough to overcome error. As soon as it is grasped by a straightforward mind free from prejudice, it commands the assent of right reason. Assuredly, faith as a virtue is a precious gift of grace and divine goodness; nevertheless the objects to which faith should be directed can hardly be known otherwise than from preaching: 'How are they to believe in him whom they have not heard? And how are they to hear without a preacher? . . . Faith is by hearing, and hearing is through the word of Christ.' Faith being indispensable to salvation, it follow of necessity that the word of Christ must be preached. By divine ordinance the charge of preaching, that is, of teaching, belongs to doctors, that is, to the bishops whom the Holy Spirit has established to govern the Church of God. It belongs above all to the Roman Pontiff, the vicar of Jesus Christ, appointed with supreme authority in the universal Church, teacher of faith and morals. At the same time one must be careful not to think that private persons are forbidden to co-operate in this apostleship in a certain way, especially in the case of men whom God has endowed with gifts of understanding and the desire to be of service.

Whenever it be needful, such can freely—not, indeed, arrogate to themselves the mission of doctors, but—hand on to others what they have themselves received, an echo, so to speak, of the doctors' teaching. So opportune and fruitful did private co-operation appear to the fathers at the Vatican Council that they did not hesitate to call for it: 'We beseech in the bowels of Jesus Christ, we command in virtue of the authority of the same divine Saviour, that all faithful Christians, especially those who teach or are leaders, should unite their zeal and their endeavours to get rid of these dreadful things and banish them from Holy Church'—that each of them then should remember that he can and ought to spread the Catholic faith by the authority of example, and preach it by unceasing public profession of the obligations it imposes. Thus, among the duties that bind us to God and to the Church, a large place belongs to the zeal with which we ought to work, so far as we are able, for the spread of the Christian faith and the driving away of falsehood.

The faithful will not satisfy these obligations fully and effectively if they engage in this warfare as isolated individuals. Jesus Christ declared plainly that men's rancorous opposition to himself would be perpetuated against his work, so that many souls would be hindered from profiting by the salvation for which we are beholden to his grace. Accordingly he willed, not only to form disciples, but to make of them and their harmonious assemblage one single body, the Church, of which he should be the Head. The life of Jesus Christ flows throughout the organism of this body, strengthening and nourishing each of its members, holding them together in one, and directing the aim of all towards the same end, though they do not all have to fulfil the same functions. It follows that the Church, a perfect society, the highest of all societies, was given a mandate by her Author to fight for the salvation of the human race like an army in order of battle (Encyclical letter *'Sapientiae christianae'*, 1890).

(*b*) The last part of the above quotation seems to be a declaration that the Church recognises and provides for apostolic witness given by lay people in a personal, private capacity. There may be discerned therein at least a possibility that, instead of confining it to the title of personal fervour, such witness can be brought within the setting of the Church in virtue of a certain mission received from her, that is, from the episcopal body which is her authority or public power. This is what happens in Catholic Action. To deal with that here would not be convenient, for it brings in considerations remote from our present subject, the prophetical function. We shall therefore consider Catholic Action in Chapter V, as the apostolate of the laity, their apostolic witness in that they receive the consecration of episcopal public authority, through a mission expressed in the mandate given to the movement. This puts it outside any purely private initiative, even though the movement was already more or less corporate and organised.

At Berlin during the war of 1939-1945, eight hundred of the laity, young men and especially young women, some of whom had done a full course of theological studies, were given a *canonical mission* for apostolic and apologetical work under various forms. In the Italian movement 'Pro Civitate', and in such an institute as the Company of St Paul, lay people give what are properly religious discourses, not in church but in public halls. During a recent week of conferences and sermons on the Faith and the Ten Commandments, held at Essen, the laity gave two hundred and seventy-two conferences in halls, and the clergy preached two hundred sermons in churches. Together with classical Catholic Action, such things are forms of lay

apostolic participation in the prophetical function of the Church, in
virtue of a mission and so of a certain public office.[32]

Scientific teaching. – Every one of the faithful, whether cleric or lay,
who believes he has something to say, may propound teaching of the
scientific or doctoral kind. He is simply subject to the ordinary
criteria, to dogma and the authority of the magisterium where
orthodoxy is concerned, to the rules of scientific work and the judgement of competent men where technique and human value are concerned. As one of the faithful, he is judged by the appointed guardians
of tradition and of the faithful community; from the point of view of
his competence as a teacher, he is judged by the learned in general.
In this respect the lay man is on exactly the same footing as the cleric,
for the cassock, or priesthood itself, does not confer any charism of
theological learning; though it cannot be said that priesthood, with
its accompanying celebration of the mysteries, brings nothing in the
spiritual order to a theologian's work (Cf. below). We have to guard
against the common unconscious tendency to assimilate the scientific work of the theologian or exegete to the dogmatic utterance of
him who can speak with authority (not with ability only), in virtue
of the charisms pertaining to an hierarchical function.[33]

A doctor of proved ability and orthodoxy can receive a teaching
mandate from the Church, that 'canonical mission' spoken of in the
constitution '*Deus scientiarum*' by which the Church in 1931 re-
organised the teaching in her universities and faculties. Such professors can be, and sometimes have been, laymen;[34] but in any case
their teaching is entirely of the scientific order, and its worth is the
worth of the documentation and reasoning that they bring to it. But
it bears a certain public character and, because of the general
approbation given it (under reserve . . .), it enjoys some small
authority, of which, needless to say, the price and the guarantee are
a strict control over its expression on the part of the accrediting
authority.

We must here make a few remarks about lay theological activity.
The first theologians were lay men: Justin, Tertullian, Pantaenus,

---

[32][Compare the work of the Catholic Evidence Guild in England.—*Translator's
note.*]

[33]We have pointed out the difference at the beginning of section (B) above. For
the relationship of doctors to the work and competence of the hierarchical magisterium, see *Vraie et fausse reforme*, pp. 503–536; and a few words on doctoral teaching
in universities, Scheeben, *Dogmatik*, §12, n. 162.

[34]For example, John d'Andrea was professor of canon law at Bologna from 1302
to 1348, and was a great authority; W. G. Ward was professor first of moral
philosophy and then of dogmatic theology at St Edmund's, Ware, from 1851 to
1858.

Clement of Alexandria, Origen (who was ordained priest later). After them we may name Victorinus, Pamphilus, Sextus the African, Lactantius, Firmicus Maternus, Prosper of Aquitaine (one of whose writings was recognised as expressing the doctrine of the Holy See: see above, note 26). In the East, the historian and jurist Socrates, Sozomen and Evagrius were lay men. A number of the Fathers began their theological work while lay men, such as St Cyprian, St Basil, St Gregory Nazianzen, St Jerome, St Paulinus of Nola, St Augustine (*De Genesi*), Diodorus of Tarsus. In the Middle Ages we still come across some lay theologians, for instance Hugh Etherianus, a Tuscan living at Constantinople during the second half of the twelfth century, not to mention the more numerous theologians and writers of homilies who were princes. The truth is that, as H. I. Narrous says, 'the distinction between a religious culture reserved to the clergy alone and a profane culture allowable to the laity is quite a modern idea . . . foreign to the patristic age'. There was only one culture, which used the techniques evolved by the pagans as a basis and directed them to the service of God. Cultured lay people took an active interest in religious matters, and they figured considerably among the correspondents who put theological questions to an Augustine or a Jerome.[35]

It was, in fact, an accident of history that brought about the reservation of high religious culture to the clergy, namely, the over-running of the Roman empire in the West by the barbarians and the saving of a tradition of order and culture by churchmen, bishops and monks. In the East, which escaped this ordeal, theological culture and culture at large were less a clergy monopoly: the state had at its disposal a body of lay officials, an efficient administrative machinery made up of lay men. The laity may or may not have been more closely involved in the celebration of the liturgy, but they were certainly more educated than in the West, where men who often could not read or sign their names were even more ready to busy themselves in the Church's affairs. Claud Fleury associates with this state of things the fact that it was impossible for Eastern clergy to modify certain dispositions of traditional discipline, as was done in the West, because they were faced by a body of well-informed laity; and also, connected with this, the East did not experience the lay criticism of a too dominant ecclesiastical power that arose in the West, says Fleury, from the twelfth century (Arnold of Brescia).[36] The tradition

[35]Cf. H. I. Marrou, *S. Augustin et la fin de la culture antique* (Paris, 1938), pp. 383–385.
[36]*Histoire ecclesiastique* (Paris, 1691–1720), vol. xvi, p. x, and xix, p. xix. Fleury's considerations are worth attention and study in the light of modern knowledge.

of lay theologians has remained alive in the Orthodox East; lay men
hold important chairs in the theological faculty of Athens, the
Russian theological institute at Paris, and elsewhere. But their exact
position as regards the Church's teaching functions has not yet been
cleared up.

The humanist movement, enlarging the world of culture and the
study of the religious sciences among the laity, was favourable to the
reintegration of lay people into the circuit of religious thought and
even to their receiving important posts in the Church's government.
Aeneas Silvius Piccolomini as a lay man wrote treatises on the
Council of Bale. Caspar Contarini wrote *De officio episcopi*, a *Confutatio
articulorum sue quaestionum Lutheri* and *De potestate Pontificio*, and was
still a lay man when Pope Paul III named him cardinal in 1535. In
the following year another lay man was named cardinal—Reginald
Pole. The future Pope Marcellus II (Cervini) was called to the
cardinalate and then to the episcopate while a lay man. And then
the Council of Trent. Frederick Staphylus, a champion of Catholicism against the Protestants, was a lay doctor of theology and of canon
law, and many, including Pope Pius IV, wanted him to assist at the
council as a theologian. He was an advocate of conciliation, and
refused to attend if no Protestants were there. But other laymen took
part: Angelo Massarelli was appointed secretary to the council after
another lay man, Marcantonio Flaminio, had declined the post;
Count Lodovico Nogorola was *rapporteur* for the commissions of
theologians (but not a deliberating member), and he preached on
one occasion.

King Robert II of Naples (d. 1343) left nearly three hundred
sermons, and he was not the only royal theologian: among others
there was Henry VIII of England—did not his answer to Luther
earn the title of Defender of the Faith from Pope Leo X? The succession of lay theologians was continued in the seventeenth and
eighteenth centuries, especially among Jansenists and Gallicans,
which came near to compromising it; but the antigallicanism of such
as Joseph de Maistre and Louis Veuillot retrieved their reputation
in the nineteenth. The restoration of Christian philosophy by Leo
XIII and the renewal of Catholicism and of the religious sciences
have led to an increasing number of lay people who, without claiming to be theologians, deal very ably with religious questions, and so
with theology. Their contribution to the religious sciences is one of
the great blessings of our time.

We must, however, here make a point and perhaps register a
limitation. The laity, giving utterance to the questings and strivings

of the world, can bring a wealth to the Church that it is their mission to dedicate to God. But they never handle theology like priests, they have never quite the same contact with the Church's tradition. It is not simply that the priest, conscious of the pastoral effects and consequences of his words and works, takes nicer account of all the factors and tries to balance them: having the priestly charisms, celebrating the mysteries, he has to a greater degree living contact with the realities of tradition. Theology properly so called is pre-eminently a clerical, priestly, learning. Extensive lay activity in matters of religious thought is very desirable; but, rather than in the domain of theological science, it should be exerted in the immense field that lies between the Church's dogmatic tradition and man's most actual problems, a field wherein the cause of faith and the good of Christian understanding alike require that mediations should be actively undertaken. By mediations we do not at all mean compromises, but endeavours to restate 'the Christian thing', to apply it to secular problems, to present Catholicity as climate or atmosphere, to seek a new cultural creativeness rooted in Christian faith and experience; and all this without neglecting work on theology's auxiliary sciences —philosophy, history, and the rest—for which there can never be too many good workers. In this great field, placed like the laity itself at the juncture of the Church and the world, lay thinkers, artists, scholars, men of inquiring mind, ought to be and to feel more free than the clergy who are dedicated to theology proper. They can work on behalf of sincerely held but unpopular opinions, to which the priest can give himself far less, since he has to be everybody's man; they can more easily be creators, blazing new trails, whereas the clergy, men of tradition, are sometimes tempted to use the method of authority suitable to dogmatics in other fields, where they are out of place.

So the laity's place in Catholic thinking is considerable: engaged in all the life of the world, they can bring a rich harvest of problems and thought to the Church. On the other hand, no attempt should be made to put them in the clergy's place and turn them into doctors of divinity. The faithful 'can and must help towards an ever wider and deeper synthesis through their integration in the thinking and doing whole that we call the Church' (H. Dumery); for that they have certain advantages over the clergy, such as being less influenced by a closed professionalism and more free from *rabies theologica*.[37] But they have their own limitations and dangers. Their theology is

[37]For this reason Erasmus, in face of the Reformation, advised the Holy See to convene a conference which should include lay people.

sometimes too much influenced by their temporal, political and cultural sympathies; it runs the risk of being made to serve theses that do not arise from itself, which throw it out of balance. Something of this sort can be found in de Maistre, Veuillot, Solovyev. . . . The same difference between lay thinker and churchman can be found outside Catholicity, for instance, between Kierkegaard and Grundtvig.

Doubtless it is for these different reasons, and also to bring peripheral initiatives more closely under her direction, as well as, above all, to make the most of their gifts, that the Church has so often integrated great masters into her organism by impelling them towards monastic life and conferring the priesthood on them (sometimes against their wishes): so it was for St Athanasius, St John Chrysostom, St Basil, St Gregory Nazianzen, St Gregory of Nyssa, St Jerome, St Augustine, St Gregory the Great. . . .

*   *   *

As a sort of appendix to this chapter something must be said on a matter which overlaps what has been said about the co-operation of the faithful with the Church's life in truth, and about the different forms or modalities which lay teaching activity can take: namely, Bible-reading. Certain circumstances have made this a ticklish subject, about which some faulty ideas are still current, but it is not troublesome to anybody who is willing to consider it understandingly and objectively.

Should anyone put the general question, Is the reading of the Bible by lay people forbidden or discouraged?—the answer is a firm No! The Church's tradition is to encourage all the faithful who are able to profit by it to read the Bible assiduously. At the time of the early persecutions there are many references to the faithful carrying the sacred books about with them; a fresco at the tomb of St Petronilla at Rome (fourth century) shows her leading a woman named Veneranda into Heaven, and the latter 'has near her some scrolls in a box: they are the holy books which will open Heaven to her'. In the early centuries the faithful read the Scriptures at home when they were not able to hear a sermon. St Jerome urged the religious women whom he guided to study The Book with all their might. It was clearly a question of cultivated groups, the sort of élite which later included the imperial physician, Theodore, to whom Pope St Gregory the Great wrote: 'I have a bone to pick with my very illustrious son Theodore: the Holy Trinity has conferred on him gifts of understanding, of a high position, of mercy and charity, but he is so taken up with worldly business and too many state occasions that he neglects the daily reading of this Redeemer's words. What is sacred Scripture but a sort of letter from Almighty God to his creature? . . . So be sure to ponder your Creator's words every day.' Obviously the illiterate were not given to Bible-reading; but in monasteries and schools it was most actively used from Christian antiquity on throughout the Middle Ages. In those days culture was essentially biblical. Those who have studied the question closely declare very definitely that there was no prohibition of Bible-reading during the medieval times. When anyone took up a restrictive or negative attitude towards it, there were always those who sprang to its defence.[38]

We are not concerned here with translations of Scripture into the common tongue, but this has an obvious importance where the laity are concerned and we must notice some of the conclusions of serious students of the subject. The Bible was translated into vulgar tongues, and so made accessible to lay people who knew no Latin, well before the Reformers of the sixteenth century. The more this point is studied the more evidence is found for the fact, and the greater becomes the number of translations, manuscripts and editions recorded. Still, one gets the impression that for the Middle Ages translation of Holy Writ, as such and in its entirety, was not so urgent and compelling a matter as it becomes when we approach the sixteenth century or for certain individuals; it must be remembered, too, that Latin was the language of culture and plenty of lay people could read it. But there were differences from country to country. It appears that the Bible was translated, at least in part, earlier and more often in Germany than in the lands of Romance language; in that country we have fragments of bilingual texts from the eighth century. In France, or rather Normandy, we have to wait till the twelfth century for translations of the psalter, then of the Apocalypse and of the historical books of the Old Testament. There is, however, no trace of a vernacular Bible among the heretics (Catharists, Albigenses) or itinerant preachers of the twelfth century. Peter Waldo is the first of whom it is known for certain that he translated the Bible; his version was shown to Pope Alexander III in 1179. The thirteenth-century translation by Guyart des Moulins had a wide circulation. Italian and Catalan translations were still later, and sometimes took their rise from French or Provencal versions. The position in England is not clear, though there was certainly something between the Anglo-Saxon versions of the psalms and gospels,

[38]See, e.g., F. Kropatscheck, *Das Schriftprinzip der lutherischen Kirche* . . . (Leipzig, 1904), vol. i, pp. 106, 134–135; C. J. Jellouschek in *Aus der Geisteswelt des Mittelalters* (Munster, 1935), pp. 1181–1199.

made in the eighth and ninth centuries, and Wyclif's translation. The Norman conquest paralysed literary activity in English for a long time. Wyclif's extreme views compromised the cause of vernacular Scripture up to and including the first generation of the Reformation.

Does all this mean that the people's contact with the Bible was feeble during the middle ages? Not at all. Reading and study of its text were done by clergy, who often were the only people who could read and who had access to the manuscript texts (a Bible was nearly as expensive as a horse). Moreover, the culture of the educated was Latin (not only in spiritual but in profane things), and the Latin Bible was at all times widely known. But culture at large, however much 'of the people', was biblical; it was under the guidance of Mother Church, and the works and evidences of the beginnings of national literatures are full of the Bible. Preaching was a tissue of biblical texts and instances; and from the eighth century synodal decrees ordered that the liturgical reading of the scriptural lessons should be followed by an explanation in the mother tongue.

These facts are coherent and their significance is clear. In the Middle Ages the Church never forbade the reading of the Bible; but very few of the laity had the ability to do it. The Church cannot be reproached with not having done all she could to instruct people, but she was not disturbed by the limitations which the facts of the situation imposed on the laity's access to the text of the Bible: for this reason, that she has never given that text the exclusive position, fanatical and almost idolatrous, accorded to it by the teachers of *Scriptura sola*, 'the Bible, and the Bible only', in particular Wyclif and the Protestant reformers. In these matters the point of view of the medieval Church was mainly pastoral, and in relation to actual pastoral conditions. That is why translations of the Bible were relatively late and often incomplete, limited to the psalter, the gospels, the epistles and the Apocalypse, with some historical books of the Old Testament and occasionally the liturgical pericopes: that is why in thirteenth-century France they originated in a sacred history, the *Historia scholastica* of Peter 'le Mangeur'. To teach men saving truth—that was the primary business in hand. Clergy studied doctrine, and for that the Bible was of such decisive importance that one can speak of a certain *Schriftprinzip* (in a different sense from that of the Reformers); but the direct personal reading of the Bible by each one of the faithful was neither the only way nor a necessary way to the learning of that truth. It has always been taught through the Church's tradition and the various forms of her preaching; this does not exclude personal reading of the Bible, but neither does it demand it. For historical reasons, there was much less Bible-reading in the Middle Ages than there is today; but as an Anglican observer has remarked, if some of the faithful now know the Bible much better, people as a whole know it very much less.

Many things have happened between medieval times and ours, among them a series of forbiddances and restrictions. Again the facts are coherent and their significance clear. At first they may appear to contradict what has just been said, for they seem to oppose a No to our Yes. But there is no contradiction; when the Church issued certain prohibitions she did not unsay anything of her basic mind, which is explicitly in favour of Bible-reading by all the faithful who are able to profit by it. The letter of Pope Innocent III to the faithful of the diocese of Metz is very significant from this point of view. It is the first of the series we must look at, and the only one of the Middle Ages that acquired an official general status through being inserted in the canonical *corpus*. Under the influence of Waldensian preachers, many lay men and women in the Metz diocese had brought about the translation into French of the gospels, the epistles of St Paul, the psalms, Job and other books. The pope did not reprove them for this, much less for their wish to understand the Scriptures; rather was he pleased about it. What he did rebuke in the Metz people was their sectarian spirit, their uncatholic goings-on: the secret meetings from which other people were haughtily excluded, the disorderly preachings, opposition to the authority of the clergy and contempt for their flavourless sermons. . . . The mysteries of faith are not anybody's for the asking, no more are those of the Scriptures. . . . The books were impounded and burnt.[39]

It was sectarian abuse of the Bible that here led to censure and restraint, and Du Plessis d'Argentre rightly says the same about the proceedings of the synod held at Toulouse in 1229. This synod forbade lay people to possess any books of the Bible (except a psalter or breviary for the Office or the Hours *de Beata*), and they were again forbidden in the vulgar tongue. There were analogous prohibitions here and there during the thirteenth and fourteenth centuries: a council at Tarragona in 1223 ordered forbidden books to be sent to the bishop to be burnt; a council at Beziers in 1246 extended to the clergy the prohibition of vernacular theological works; in 1369 the Emperor Charles IV, alarmed by the circulation of all sorts of

[39]Innocent's text in PL., ccxiv, 695; and cf. H. Grundmann, *Religiose Bewegungen im Mittelalter* . . . (Berlin, 1935), pp. 70–72, etc.; Congar, *Vraie et fausse reforme*, pp. 275, 285; and L. Hardick in *Wissenschaft und Weisheit*, 1950, p. 135.

writings suspected of error or heresy among lay people and nuns in Germany, ordered these writings to be brought to the inquisitors for destruction. . . . And so we come to the Council of Trent—for it must be noticed that Wyclif, who is claimed as the great champion of the *Schriftprinzip*, was not condemned on that ground. Does this mean that the Council of Constance failed to find it in his teaching, or did not clearly see its heterodoxy?

Bible-reading was discussed twice at Trent, in the fourth session (April 1546), *a propos* the dogmatic question of the objective rules of belief, and in session xxv (December 1563), in a setting of reforms to be introduced, when preparing the decree of 1564 which is the basis of our present legislation about the Index.[40] The decree of the fourth session provides for the publication of texts of the Bible. It lays down that the Latin Vulgate is authoritative for all public teaching. It expressly does not forbid the publication of vernacular translations, provided they are submitted for the approval of the authorities, or the reading of them, provided this is done according to the general principles of orthodoxy. But the discussions preparatory to this decree showed two opposing tendencies. There were those who were worried by the appeals made by heresy from the magisterium of the Church to the authority of the Bible, and in consequence wanted all translation into vulgar tongues to be condemned as an abuse; and there were those who emphasised the excellence of the Bible in itself and appealed to German usage. Foremost among the latter was Cardinal Christopher Madruzzi, bishop of Trent. There was no special question of the laity in this, the clergy were equally concerned. Later on, Cardinal Peter Pacheco, bishop of Jaen in Spain, asked who were able to interpret the Scriptures: certainly the bishops, but also, he said, doctors and masters approved by a university; but lay people could not do it, either in a public or a private capacity. This idea that lay people had not got the education or understanding necessary for an appreciation of the mysteries of faith was rather common at this time. It is found in the Franciscan theologians Alfonso de Castro and Vincent Lunel, in Thomas Campeggio, in a reforming bishop such as Cardinal Claud de Givry, and in Bartholomew Latomus, the one of his adversaries whom Luther seems most to have respected. The idea is clearly connected, particularly in Pacheco and Latomus, with the markedly high

[40]For Trent and vernacular Bibles see, in addition to such classical works as that of S. Ehses (1908), F. Cavallera in *Melanges Podechard* (Lyons, 1945), pp. 37–56; and G. Dunker in *Angelicum*, vol. xxiv (1947), pp. 140–169.

opinion of doctors and professors entertained during the fourteenth-sixteenth centuries; but its excessiveness was a consequence of more weighty things, themselves not without importance for the question of the laity's place in the Church.

From the middle of the thirteenth century (the mendicant friars), indeed, virtually from the coming of scholasticism (Abelard), a university teaching function grew up beside the pastoral teaching function, and in a measure surpassed it in reputation. Now the pastoral function, exercised in close dependence on the bishops, was bound up with ecclesial life and did not isolate the clergy from the laity; but those engaged in the scholastic professorial function were outside the pastoral setting; they formed a world of their own, an influential and attractive world, moreover, which made it the easier for them to get out of touch with new demands of life. Then, from the beginning of the fourteenth century (if not a little earlier), the Church found herself face to face with the formation of nationalities and, from the middle of the fifteenth century, with the invention of printing and all its possibilities.

The question of rendering the Bible into common tongues, made more acute by the discovery of printing, was properly a matter for dogmatic and disciplinary considerations, and also those of ecclesiastical fact and history. But we cannot separate it from the general problem (with which it was contemporary because like causes had produced the two together) presented by the birth of a new society: a society of communes and legal immunities and rights, then of nationalities and national cultures, with an ever-advancing middle class, a society in which there were means to individual and autonomous culture whose critical preoccupations profoundly modified the framework of thought, even in the matter of religion. The Church accepted and 'baptised' the communal or corporative movement, but she was not so quick to understand nationality,[41] and saw a disturbing threat in an autonomous critical culture. On the other hand, it is no matter for surprise that the Reformation found its main support in the urban middle class and the rising artisan class. The two facts of printing and an educated laity, coming together, were almost bound to occasion a crisis for the Church. As an epistemological principle of theology, *Scriptura sola* had been sustained well before the Reformation; but only by clergy in the theological schools, where actual practice allowed, beyond an at least implicit general

[41]These things were very complex and each case has to be carefully examined separately; but it is difficult to forget the condemnation of Magna Carta and of the Sachsenspiegel, the failure to understand the Czech movement, and similar things.

regulation by the Church's tradition, a method of reasoning that went far beyond the literal text. In the new conditions—to which the conclusive factor of humanism must be added—the principle of 'the Bible only' took on a new scope, rigour and critical value, and it appeared dangerously to threaten all regulation by the Church. When the Council of Trent opened, the danger was only too real; when it ended, the response was fully at work and perfecting weapons for the inevitable struggle, in which it was to be to a considerable extent victorious.

One of these weapons was the Index of Forbidden Books. Its regulations were drawn up by a conciliar commission, and published by Pope Pius IV in 1564. Already in 1559 his predecessor, Paul IV, had forbidden the printing and reading of any vernacular translation of the Bible without permission from the office of the Roman Inquisition. The rules (nos 3 and 4) issued by Pius IV slightly modified this truly draconian measure: the local bishop or inquisitor, on the recommendation of parish-priest or confessor, could give written permission for the reading of a vernacular version made by a Catholic translator; infringement of this rule involved refusal of absolution. This severity was justified by definite experience that, such being men's rashness, more harm than good was resulting from indiscriminately authorised reading. In 1590 Pope Sixtus V restored the even stricter provision of Paul IV, and permission had again to be sought from the Holy See itself. Efforts associated with the Jansenist movement to bring about a more liberal practice were censured at the condemnation of Pasquier Quesnel (1713) and of the Synod of Pistoia (1794). Against Quesnel, Pope Clement XI repeated the argument from the obscurity of the Bible, which cuts off its accessibility to the laity.

Nevertheless there was some easing-up in the eighteenth century. In the constitution given to the Index in 1758, Pope Benedict XIV made an addition to rule 4, allowing the use of translations provided they were approved by the Holy See or furnished with notes from the Fathers or other competent Catholic writers. Authorisation was thus given, not to each prospective reader, but once for all to the edition itself. That has been the fundamental regulation in force down to our own day, touched up by a succession of popes and finally by the Code of Canon Law of 1917.

But if one wants to get a correct picture of the position of Bible-reading by the laity since the Protestant outbreak it is necessary to look at actual practice as well as at canonical provisions. Here, as in so many other matters, the Church's attitude is represented as much, or almost as much, by acknowledged facts as by written texts. The facts (like life itself) go further than the texts, making the position that they define wider and more flexible. Nor is this through defiance, inconsistency or double-dealing, but with the consent, at least implicit, of the authority that enacted the laws, and through the exercise of peripheral initiative, the good *via facti* and legitimate adjustments which we have discussed in *Vraie et fausse reforme*. How does this apply to Bible-reading?

First of all, translations of the Scriptures into common tongues have never ceased to be published.[42] Then, in the full tide of the Counter-Reform, a jurisprudence evolved that was more liberal than the law: on the one hand, bishops and inquisitors (with the at least tacit approval of parish priests and confessors), on the other hand, parish priests and confessors (knowing the favourable disposition of the bishops) gave permission to read Catholic translations, whether to particular individuals or in general. Tacit approbation, letting it go on, even took the place of permission. That was the admitted practice in Germany, and probably in France too.[43] No doubt Quesnel and the Jansenists expressed themselves too absolutely, but a more liberal tendency largely won the day during the second third of the eighteenth century: we have the evidence of Billuart and direct evidence as well, *e.g.*, that of Restif de la Bretonne already quoted, which takes us back to about 1740. It is clear that in many places a contrary custom derogated from the law, if it was not altogether abrogated. There are few more instructive examples than that of vernacular Bible-reading by the laity of what we have written elsewhere about the superseding of laws enacted at a given moment to meet a given situation. The time comes when formal declarations ratify and confirm ways of action that new conditions have made possible. It would be senseless to set these declarations against those of another age, which, indeed, they sometimes explain.

Contemporary popes have several times expressed their strong desire that the faithful should read the Bible every day, and that they should thoroughly absorb the New Testament, or at least the gospels and Acts. So wrote St Pius X in 1907 to Cardinal Francis

[42]See particularly the articles in Hauck, *Realenzyklopadie*, vols iii and xxiii; *Dict. theol. cath.*, vol. xv; and Dunker, *op. cit.*

[43]Dunker (*op. cit.*, pp. 162–163) quotes to that effect Nicholas Serarius, s.j. (d. 1609), whom Baronius calls the light of the Church in Germany. The moralist and canonist Father Layman (d. 1635) said that rule 4 of the Index had never been applied in Germany. St John Eudes (d. 1680) seems to imply that in France the reading of the Bible presupposed authorisation by a spiritual director.

Cassetta and the Society of St Jerome for the Diffusion of the Scriptures. At the fifteenth centenary of St Jerome in 1920, Benedict XV repeated this still more positively. But nothing of the kind has equalled the warmth, explicitness and enthusiasm of Pius XII's encyclical letter '*Divino afflante*' of 1943. It urges study of the original texts expressly and insistently; it advocates translations into modern languages; it encourages the wide circulation of the sacred books, especially the gospels, and daily Bible-reading, when possible as a family affair; like Leo XIII earlier, it calls on lay people to work on elucidation of the text, at least in the various profane disciplines that are the auxiliary sciences for exegesis proper.

Thus rising, above the crisis of the sixteenth century, the Church has gradually recovered her fundamental tradition of a biblical culture and religious reading of the Holy Scriptures for the laity. The measures taken, at any rate in theory, at the time of the Counter-Reform were perhaps excessively strict. But it is clear that even the severest of them were not prompted by opposition to Bible-reading in principle, but were pastoral measures called for by an existing situation and a clear danger. It is obvious from the evidence of history that these restrictive enactments would never have been made had it not been for the Waldenses and their like, and then the Protestant reformers. The Church's tradition would have developed, she would have met new requirements, adopted new techniques of textual study as she was on the way to do when Luther's revolt broke out in circumstances that already forebode a crisis. . . .[44]

*   *   *

The first conditions of all Bible-reading in any Catholic sense[45] are that it shall be read 'in the Church', because the Bible is the Church's book; and that it shall be read within the Church's tradition, because the Bible is part of that tradition, its 'head and source', as St Cyprian says, with a unique value as witness to tradition.[46] But we cannot now discuss the ecclesial constitution of Bible-reading, which

[44]See A. Humbert's excellent book, *Les origines de la théologie moderne* (Paris, 1911).

[45]The disciplinary stipulations are that the version read shall be a translation approved by the Holy See or by the bishop, and provided with notes from the Fathers or approved authors. Non-Catholic texts may be used only for purposes of scientific study (and provided they are not accompanied by systematic attacks on Catholic doctrine). Given the high quality of some Protestant versions)*e.g.*, in English, the Revised Standard Version; in French, the *Version synodale*), it is generally agreed that responsible faithful may use them if no Catholic text be available.

[46]The absence of these consideration from the activities of various Protestant Bible-societies—in other ways so deserving of praise—is the fundamental reason for their condemnation by the Church. Cf. the encyclopaedia *Catholicisme*, vol. ii (Paris, 1950), cc. 26–29.

requires the elaboration of a theology of tradition and of the rule of faith, nor can we give even an elementary account of the principles governing biblical interpretation. What we must do, however, is to find the place of lay Bible-reading in the Church's prophetical function, and for this we again refer to the threefold division of teaching.

Doctoral or professorial teaching depends on competence, in the scientific sense of the word, and in itself there is nothing to prevent lay people taking it up, excelling in it, and seeing their work adopted by the Church for use in her schools. However, it seems that the Holy See prefers to assign the sciences auxiliary to exegesis to the laity, rather than theological interpretation of the Scriptures, which remains the clergy's field.[47] Is this a left-over from the time when learning, even secular learning, was the churchman's business? A relic of the poor opinion of lay people's capacity to search the mysteries, of which we have given some examples? Perhaps. But it is very much more likely that there are deeper reasons at work, reasons bound up with the nature of things. Even doctoral interpretation of the Scriptures is connected with the Church's tradition, with her doctrine, of which priests, and principally bishops, are the proper ministers. The priestly charisms and the celebration of the mysteries mean much to them in this matter, for those things are intrinsically directed towards the communication of the word and the nourishing of faith. (Some theologians see in priestly ordination a *signum deputativum* to pastoral duties, especially to preaching). In that way priests are men of God in a sense that lay people are not, even though sometimes lay persons are spiritually more fervent and intellectually better endowed. The science of the things of God is, in itself, a priestly activity: 'For the lips of the priest shall keep knowledge, and they shall seek the law at his mouth, because he is the angel of the Lord of hosts' (Malachias ii, 7; cf. Leviticus x, 11).

Where *dogmatic* teaching proper is concerned, the Bible-reading of the faithful fits in to what has been said more generally in the course of this chapter. The laity has no public dogmatic authority. But in this field the role of the members of the believing, loving, living, praying Church is far from being insignificant; they can co-operate in maintaining and developing the deposit of tradition, of which the Scriptures are a part.

The biggest field open to the prophetical activity of the laity is that of *the word,* exhortatory, apostolic, apologetical. Grounded in

[47] Cf. Pius XII in *'Divino afflante'* (A.A.S., 1943), and Leo XIII in *'Providentissimus Deus'* (*Enchir. Bibl.*, nn. 113, 117).

life, personal assimilation of the faith, this is co-operation in the witness that the Church bears before the world, in an apostolic setting forth and explanation of truth. A life of faith nourished on the Bible enables the faithful really to co-operate with the magisterium, to co-operate as taught and as teaching. As taught, in the sense that, familiar with the Scriptures, they are the more fitted to profit by the Church's teaching, and thus they do specially good service for the Church, as St Pius X wrote to Cardinal Cassetta. As teaching, in the sense that the voice of a Christian steeped in the Bible will be very much more effective, as experience shows and theology would expect. The mind, the heart, the lips of the faithful become the instrument of a higher teaching authority, of that sovereign part of the Church's tradition which is, too, nothing less than the word *of God*.

But the Bible thus handed on must really be the Bible, the chief part *of the Church's tradition*; and that presupposes that it be read 'in the Church'. It is not an imaginary danger that a *fidelis* (and probably the one least qualified) should become a sort of 'text-chopper' or 'Bible-thumper'. That has always been the way of sects, and the danger justifies a certain caution, reserve or restraint on the part of the Church. The only safe way is to follow the path mapped by tradition and authority. Above all, the laity must avoid setting themselves up as 'doctors of the law'; in the very act of bearing apostolic witness they still belong to the Church taught. It is for them to communicate a *lived* doctrine, but that doctrine has first been *received*.

On the other hand, they need not worry themselves unduly about the way in which the Scriptures are to be understood if they are to live by them. What St Augustine said in addressing some clergy seems to apply here. Charity is the end and object of everything, and Augustine saw a kind of absolute verity of it: from the moment we are dedicated to building up charity, this verity is such that, if we make a mistake in interpreting the Bible, the mistake is not deadly and we do not deceive. It is like the mistake of someone who, getting off the road, walks across fields and reaches his destination safely that way. We must correct our mistake, Augustine goes on, and point out the desirability of not getting off the road, lest it become a habit and we get completely lost. But whoever believes that 'charity is the ful- filment of the law', and reads in a spirit of charity 'out of a pure heart and good conscience and faith unfeigned', can pursue his Bible-reading with a quiet mind.[48]

[48]*De doctrina christiana*, lib. 1, c. 36 (PL., xxxiv, 34, 36, 91, 92, 99).

Chapter IV

THE LAITY AND THE CHURCH'S COMMUNAL LIFE

This heading may appear puzzling. The first part of the chapter will explain it, and at the same time be useful for understanding the Church. The second part will outline some concrete applications and show their interest for a theology of laity, and conclude by posing an important practical problem.

ECCLESIOLOGICAL EXPLANATION

The Holy Scriptures often present the people of God, the Church, as a building, a temple or house in course of construction. The builder is God, Christ, his Holy Spirit. Only God can build a *spiritual* temple —the true spiritual temple is not made by man's hand. *God's* work can be done only by *God* or by men *of God*, men who belong to him, in whom and through whom he acts. The idea of the 'man of God' is one of the finest in the Bible and Christian tradition. Jesus in a perfect sense was 'the holy one of God' (Mark i, 24); those whom he chose, called, and sent out to do God's work after him were only servants, but in their mouth the name of slave was full of glory and religious significance (how fond St Paul was of calling himself Christ's bondman and labourer), and the grandest title that was theirs was God's servant, man of God. In virtue of that alone could they in some manner do the works proper to God, which give life through the Spirit, a life of fellowship with God.

But there are two ways of being a man of God: by a competence [A] of office, or by personal qualification through one's life, *ex officio* or *ex spiritu*. Obviously these ways are not opposed or contradictory, but that does not mean they are not distinct and not able to exist independently one of the other. Their difference must be looked at more closely.

In both cases it is a matter of doing something on Christ's behalf, a visible relay, as it were, of his action. Life can be lived personally on Christ's behalf through the faith and grace that enable us to say with St Paul, 'It is no longer that I live, but Christ that liveth in me. So far as I live now in the flesh, I live by faith in the Son of God. . . .' A man can then relay Christ's influence through his own life and in his own soul. But whatever the degree of fervour of his personal life, a man can also do something on Christ's behalf as a cause or instrument; not because of his life, but because of a functional qualification, not as friend but as doer: in other words, by participating formally in that relationship of Christ towards his Body which consists in actualising it by his power (not in the relationship that consists in filling it with his life). In both cases a man does God's work. But in the first it is the religious subject as such who is active and engaged; he himself, in his life, serves as Christ's relay; in the second, he is still Christ's relay but as minister of a subjective order of means of grace, through a function that is referred (quite apart from what he is himself) to an institution and a source that have their existence outside him.

This distinction is common in the Bible. To build up, to edify, is God's own doing, but it is also done by those who co-operate with him: by all the members of the Church, who build one another up (Romans xv, 2, etc.), by members who have received some particular charism or spiritual gift (1 Corinthians xiv, 3–5, 12), or (under manifestly unusual conditions) by the apostle himself, whose ability to build up the Church is connected with a power ($\dot{\epsilon}\xi o v \sigma \acute{\iota} a$); but he nevertheless prefers to exert the personal spiritual endowments of a religious man.[1] This surely is an echo of Christ's twofold relationship with his body, that of giving life through his Spirit, and that of authority and power. We have pointed out that all receive the gifts of life, and that some receive as well the gifts of the ministry, representing another way of communicating the gifts of God. In the second case, a state of function is added to personal existence, as is seen so well in the example of St Peter, who as Cephas is the

---

[1] This is a very remarkable feature in the apostolical writings. Paul invokes his authority as an apostle to give orders (1 Cor. vii, 10, 17), but he gives advice as a spiritual man, invoking experience and grace (Ibid., 25, 40). He prefers to appeal to the gifts he has received, to what is ex spiritu (often vouchsafed, of course, in view of his apostleship), rather than to the authority that was his: cf. 2 Cor. x, 7–8; xi, 23ff.; xii, 1ff., 11ff.; 1 Thessalonians ii, 7–12; Philemon 8–9. We see something of the same sort in Christ himself: he is the perfect high priest by constitution and authority, but the Epistle to the Hebrews shows him becoming high priest through his sufferings and personal dispositions. Compare the ancient Epistle of Barnabas (i, 8; iv, 6, 9), whose author is a learned teacher but prefers to be but one among his Christian fellows and to address them solely in the name of his love—For St Paul's $\dot{\epsilon}\xi o v \sigma \acute{\iota} a$, see P. Bonnard, Jésus-Christ édifiant son Église (Neuchâtel, 1948), p. 36.

Church's rock, while as Simon he is vacillating and weak. The distinction is not invalidated by the inability of some people of nominalistic tendencies to see the consistency of an order of function and law distinct from actual facts and personal qualities.

Jesus instituted an apostleship, and invested the Twelve with its powers. This was an hierarchical, juridical mission, which made the foundation of the Church as an institution and gave it a sort of framework. Just as Adam was formed before he was given the breath of life, just as the dry bones were brought together and clothed with flesh before new life quickened them (Ezechiel xxxvii), so the Church was given a structure (something like the metal skeleton of our buildings today) before the Spirit was sent upon her. When the Spirit had come, the Church no longer existed simply as an institutional framework but as a body or community quickened by the Spirit of Christ; all the members—and not the Twelve alone—receive the Gift of God (Acts i, 15; ii, 1–4) and at the level of living become subjects, beneficiaries and eventually spreaders of God's activity. The Church has now become the community of the faithful, and henceforth there is a mission of life and love, a mission *ex spiritu*, added to the juridical mission *ex officio*, which had previously constituted, in the Twelve, the Church as institution. The warp had first been set, but it needed a weft. Now the Church sets to work to weave: on the apostolical warp, which ensures her continuity with Christ, the weft ever continues to make a pattern of life aroused in souls by the gifts of the Spirit.

Thus there is a twofold source corresponding to the twofold mission, relatively, to be sure, since in the end everything comes from the same Spirit and the same Lord. But goodness and grace can come from the Lord *in himself* (though *through* men) or from the Lord *in us*. And here we must again appeal to the theology of Alpha and Omega, even at the risk of being repetitious.

Christ is Alpha, the principle of all, and he is Omega; but while he is Alpha by himself he is Omega with us, or rather, we are Omega with him. As to the principle, we do nothing; Christ does all, for our benefit, but the end integrates our free co-operation with the principle, and in a sense our contribution. After all, life is comprised between our baptism, at which we did nothing, and our death, which will be what we have done since baptism, into which the 'doing' of our whole life will be integrated; and that is a reflection in miniature of what happens on the universal, cosmic, scale of the Economy [P], in which Alpha and Omega are, not the baptism and death of an individual, but the pasch of Jesus Christ and the pasch of his fellow-ship-body when he comes again in glory. Everything comes from Alpha in both cases, and it is right to say that Christian life is simply each person's actualisation of his baptism; all then comes from a sheer 'giving'. But all evolves through a free co-operation, through a 'doing', through what the whole of life contributes until the Omega, in which all the Alpha will attain its fullness. To use St Paul's terms, Christ has to reach his full stature in us, to be 'completed' in us and through us, by taking on, so to speak, Adam's substance which he has come spiritually to quicken anew as its new Head. There is a 'Christ that is to be' (the words are Tennyson's), and this through a power that comes from his historical incarnation and passion; but also through contributions and a 'doing' which are—we hardly dare say it—our part in his mystery.

Christ is the first and, in this sense, sole source of everything. There is nothing in that which will at last be the Omega of his return which does not derive from the Alpha of his incarnation, from his cradle and his cross. There is no grace in our sacraments that does not come from Calvary, no dogmatic development that does not come from the one revelation made by him and through his apostles. At the originating source we have indeed to speak of the 'once for all', the ἐφάπαξ, the *Einmaligkeit* of the incarnation and the fact of Jesus Christ. Apostolicity, the hierarchical thing, the sacraments ensure and show forth the continuity of all that takes place between Alpha and Omega with its one source in the Incarnation and the Cross. In the terminology we have used above, that is the role of functional relays, at any rate of ordinary relays, which communicate divine activity through institution, *ex officio*. Such is the significance of the hierarchical juridical mission that gives the Church her framework or warp; and such, too, is the proper part of the priesthood of the clergy.

To this must be added men's 'doing', the contribution of the religious faithful as such. This, of course, is shared by the clergy according to their personal life and gifts and, in that sense, as lay men; not properly as ministers transmitting the energies of the Head through a power received from him, anterior to and outside his Body, but as members living by the vitalising energies within the Body. Here is as it were a second source for the construction of the Church. The source from above, Jesus Christ, is in one sense the only one, for it feeds the second, but it flows in two ways. The stream can come directly from above, transmitted through the apostolic ministry and the sacraments, and through them alone. It can also come through the personal life of men who have received God's gifts, and who according to their various ways and states pass on the fruit of those gifts to their brethren, to the Church. Grace is one in Christ and in its transmission through the apostolic ministry, but it is universal in its virtualities and able to quicken mankind in every fibre for his salvation and union with God. Grace takes on the infinite variety of the mankind on whom it is outpoured, and never is it exhausted, for the fullness of grace and truth that is in Christ Jesus is an absolute fullness, always greater than the sum of its participations. Shared by men according to the multiplicity of their needs and conditions, it develops and actualises the virtualities of its fullness in them and through them. Lived by men and in the 'doing' of men, Christ's grace comes to make the Church by another way beside that of the means dispensed by the apostolic ministry: it comes in the form of all sorts of gifts corresponding to men's 'living' and 'doing', which are themselves bound up with the almost endless multiplication of human situations in the unfolding of the world's history. In this respect, the life of the monk, who goes directly to God by having as little as possible to do with the world and its affairs, does not answer the requirements of a full exertion of Christ's virtualities. The resources of the religious subject—in scholastic language, the Church's material cause—are put to full use in a 'living' and a 'doing' which presuppose, beyond being face to face with God in the wilderness, the whole process of the world and its history. So the lay contribution to the building up of the Church is distinct from that of monks, as well as from that of clergy as hierarchical ministers—we are back again at our first chapter.

We are also back again at the idea of the laity as the *pleroma* of the hierarchical priesthood and at that of 'structure' and 'life', of the Church as an institution making her members and in turn made by them as community. For the making of the linen gown spoken of in the Apocalypse (xix, 8), what Christ did once for all is woven with men's 'living' and 'doing' throughout history, the warp of the hierarchical ministry's part with the weft of what men contribute as religious subjects. In this way the Church is built together not only from above downwards but also sideways, or—not to stick slavishly to our weaving metaphor—in a way from below upwards. From above and from below.

* * *

We have already noticed in Part One Chapter II how it came about that Catholic theologians have confined their considerations of the

Church almost entirely to the first direction and to the theory of her structure. They have looked at the Church only as being built hierarchically from above, with very little reference to the lateral movement, that sort of building from below by what Pope Pius XII called 'a give-and-take of life and vigour between all the members of Christ's mystical Body on earth' (Christmas address to the College of Cardinals, 1945). Perhaps we can get some light on our subject by a closer consideration of the two lines along which the sense of the Church can be developed and of the way in which she is built up, not either line to the exclusion of the other, of course, but together.

The unity of a social body such as the Church results from a two-fold order in its parts, namely, the relationship between the parts, and the relationship of the parts to the principle of order, repre-sented by the head. In other words, the connexion between the members, a network of mutual services and relations, and their subordination to the head, their reference to the centre from which the different parts of the body receive their form of action and their order in the whole.

It cannot be questioned that in the early Church consciousness of inter-part relations was very strong. The feeling of unity, of the homogeneity of the whole Church, was exceedingly active, and many historians have rightly underlined the fact that local communities were recognised as actualisations of a single Church whose existence preceded and included them. All the local churches were looked on as bound to a form of faith and worship which was common to them and came from the Apostles, by 'tradition'. There was also conscious-ness that such a unity must have its sanction, its centre, if you like, and that there was, for the whole Church and at the heart of apos-tolic authority, a responsible place of appeal and guardian of unity, a concrete criterion of the fellowship of all the churches. This con-sciousness is registered in more than a few indubitable facts, and it testifies to what we call the primacy of the Apostolic See of Rome.[2] But, without prejudice to that, the Church of old had a whole net-work of services and relations among the local communities. There were letters of communion, *litterae formatae* or *litterae communicatoriae*, letters exchanged at an episcopal consecration, during persecution, or when something else important happened; there were collections

[2] Among the best of the many Catholic works on this evidence are those of Mgr P. Batiffol; Mgr L. Duchesne, *The Churches Separated from Rome* (London, 1907); and Fr M. Jugie, *Où se trouve le christianisme intégral?* (Paris, 1946). But see also such works by non-Catholics as T. G. Jalland, *The Church and the Papacy* (London, 1944); and F. Heiler, *Altkirchliche Autonomie und Päpstlicher Zentralismus* (Munich, 1940), with Father Congar's account of them in *Revue des sciences phil. et théol.*, vol. xxxi (1947), pp. 276–287.

and other mutual aids, interventions of one church on behalf of another so that it could continue in fellowship and unity; there were the journeys, the visits, the concelebrations and communion together thus occasioned; from the second century in the East, there were the provincial councils. . . . All these were so many expressions of this feeling of mutual care and help, an aspect of *fellowship between*, or amongst, the parts or living members of the Church.

Especially in the West, the growth of ideas, from the time when a theology of the Church began to be expressly elaborated, left this aspect rather in the shade. Beginning with Pope Innocent III, and especially under Boniface VIII, these ideas were dominated by the assertion of the prerogatives and deciding role of the central authority, and by a more and more juridical point of view; and then by the necessity of getting the better of errors that exaggerated the part of subjects in the Church and her aspect as a body made by its members (cf. Part One Chapter II). It is to be expected that the ecclesiology worked out in such circumstances should have put all the emphasis on the Church as made from above, hierarchically, and should have gradually come to see only the relations of the parts to the centre or principle.

That this is what happened becomes clear when things are examined historically. The idea of schism, for instance. In the earlier centuries, schism was looked at principally in the setting of the local church: it was to set up altar against rightful altar and thus to tear fellowship apart. That idea is still perfectly sound in Catholic theology. But towards the end of the Middle Ages the notion of schism was shifted to the setting of the Church at large, and eventually came to be defined exclusively by reference to the Roman Pontiff. The idea of the Church's unity was contracted to its centre, and the life of 'Christendom' envisaged principally in its immediate relation to the visible head of the Church.[3]

Modern Catholicism has certainly developed its consciousness of unity and catholicity in this sense; the life of every body of Catholics is led in direct and constant relationship with the centre. To be Catholic is, above all, to implement and maintain this relationship with the Church's mind and heart at Rome; less thought is given to the other aspect, of relations and contacts between the parts. Until recent years, when there has been some improvement in this respect, there was little contact between the national churches within the one Church. Between the two world wars, for example, we did not

[3] For St Thomas's application of scholastic thought to the matter of schism, see the article 'Schisme' in *Dict. de théol. cath.*

see the bishops of France joining in any public occasion of the life of
the German church, or *vice versa*. Clergy and laity of different local
communities did not mingle much with one another. There was
everywhere a lively consciousness of belonging to a church which is
the world-wide Church, the people of God and earthly Body of
Christ. But this consciousness arose from a feeling of a common faith
and worship, and especially of a common attachment to a single
centre, the more so that it did not express itself in demonstrations of
solidarity among the members and a give-and-take of services between one another. It was predominantly a feeling of communion
with, and little enough of communion *between*.

The two aspects were better brought together by the great
thirteenth-century theologians, who lived at a time of balance between the world of the old tradition and a new world which was in
many respects coming into being at the end of the twelfth century.
At that time, too, the vitality of basic communities was still high, and
their initiative was not cramped by the imposition of a uniform law
from above. The collegiate idea was alive everywhere. We will look
at what St Thomas says about unity or communion, of which schism
is the negation (*Sum. theol.*, II–II, q. xxxix, a. 1), taking as interpreter
his commentator of genius, Cardinal Thomas de Vio, called Cajetan
(d. 1534).

Cajetan finds three zones in depth in ecclesial unity. First, he says,
there is the level of an agreement of all parts of the Church in faith
and worship: we believe the same doctrines, love and worship the
same God, use the same sacraments, and so on. This is all of the
greatest moment to the Church's unity; indeed, it may be said objectively to constitute and form that unity. It does not properly constitute the communion that schism destroys. It makes us alike and
parallel in the acts of our religious life, without formally going so far
as to make only *one Church, a fellowship*. Then, Cajetan goes on, there
is recognition by all of one and the same head: from the point of view
of the Church's external life, our common submission to the Supreme
Pontiff. This, says Cajetan, ensures that the members have the same
head; it is not enough to make them constitute a single community.
The other great sixteenth-century commentator on St Thomas,
Vitoria, gives as an illustration Spain, Austria, Germany and the
Netherlands, different communities all under the authority of the
emperor; again, countries brought under one authority by conquest
do not necessarily form one people: something else is wanted,
namely, a real fellowship among them. In the Church, this something else is the determination and faithfulness of the parts truly to

behave as parts of one whole, members of one body; not to think of themselves each as a whole to itself, with no other law but itself, but as called by the Holy Spirit to be members one of another. 'That', Cajetan writes, 'is what gives to churches so far apart as those of Scotland and Spain more than an agreement in faith, hope, charity, the sacraments and obedience to the same head; there is the bond that unites one part to another in a single community whose regulating principle is none other than the Holy Spirit.'

How this is translated into the concrete is not our concern here. What matters for us is to recognise this aspect of fellowship in the Church whereby her parts have truly to live for one another, to be solicitous for one another, careful to harmonise with the rhythms and needs of the whole of which they are parts.

It is noticeable that the definitions of the Church offered by the best minds of the modern age invoke Cajetan's first two elements but are silent about the third. So Bossuet in the Meaux Catechism;[4] so the many theologians who adopt St Robert Bellarmine's definition of the Church, often word for word: 'The society of men on the way to the Fatherland above, united by the profession of the same Christian faith and participation in the same sacraments, under the authority of lawful pastors and principally of the Roman Pontiff'.

Accordingly we have a conception of the Church which strongly emphasises the similar, converging movement of all the faithful towards God, and the dependence of all on the same one head— inviolably and supremely, Christ; visibly and subordinately, the pope—in a word, the elements of communion *with*; but it neglects the elements of communion *between*—relations among the members and brotherly help towards one another. This is perhaps to be expected in a theology which sets out to define the structure. But this theology has been taken over whole into catechesis, preaching, pastoral work, and so into life, as Dean F. X. Arnold has very well shown (cf. Part One Chapter II, note 21). The same phases and oversights are found in contemporary ways of understanding public worship. The aspect of worship as a duty to God is strongly in evidence; so is its dependence on a priesthood, union with something objective and

---

[4] 'What unites [the faithful] inwardly?—the same faith. What unites them outwardly—The profession of one same faith, one same law, the same sacraments, the same ecclesiastical government under one and the same visible head, the pope.' We would not appear to oppose an archbishop to a bishop, but we find a more complete theology in these words of Cardinal Feltin: 'We believe ourselves Catholics because we say the same Credo, obey the same Father, communicate in the same Bread at the same table. But have we the right to bear that name *when we know each other so badly and have so little to do with one another?*' (Lenten pastoral letter, 1951. Italics ours.)

given; but there is much less weight attached to the aspect of fellowship, of worshipping *together*, of mutual strengthening and of revealing Christ one to another. A most powerful worth as sacrifice and
adoration is recognised in the Mass, but as an effective expression of
brotherly intercourse it is rather neglected: it, too, is fellowship *with*
more than fellowship *between*. Except here and there, in a few rare
parishes and among groups partly constituted 'from below', the
aspect of *synaxis* (assembly) and *agape* [U] is little enough in evidence.

All this has its bearing on the consciousness of the faithful of their
role in the Church and of how she is built up and lives. It was pointed
out in Chapter II that they often have practically no notion of the
Church as something 'to be made' and, at any rate from a certain
aspect, to be made *by them*. It is true that at least the most fervent
among the laity have always been conscious of being able to bring
something to the promotion of God's Kingdom and the building up
of the mystical Body: not to recognise that would be to ignore the
selfless deeds, the burning words, that every priest has seen and
heard at some time or other. But this consciousness seems to be
asserted mainly in the order of inner life, of the communion of saints,
of direct and personal relationship with Christ, the Church's Head;[5]
it is found much less at the level of personal contact through help of
one another or through mutual revelation of God—what we have
called the warp, and what Pius XII calls 'a give-and-take of life and
of vigour between all the members of Christ's mystical Body on
earth'.

APPLICATIONS

The writings of the Apostles and of the Apostolic Fathers show the
Church being built up by the weft as well as by the warp. In St Paul,
this is clearly part of his conception of the Body of Christ. All those
who belong to the community of faithful are living members of that
Body, and members one of another because members of Christ
(Ephesians iv, 25; 1 Corinthians vi, 15, etc.). Because we all depend
on One, because we belong to him in such a way that his will is ours,
in short, because we live in and for Christ, we all share one single life
and work, like the life of an individual in the multiplicity of his
members and activities. In some of his finest passages St Paul shows
each of the faithful members active according to the diversity of his
gifts, for the benefit of all the other members and of the whole Body
(Romans xii, 4–8; 1 Corinthians xii, 4–14; Ephesians iv, 7–12, 16).

[5] This aspect is brought into relief by the fine passage in '*Mystici Corporis*' wher
Pius XII shows the mystical Body co-operating in its own salvation and 'so to say
coming to birth from its own labour'. Other places in the encyclical express the
point of view of mutual help, including external aid and 'lateral' contributions.

Thus the body is built up, the purpose of each one's gifts being simply to ensure the growth of the body by promoting the growth of its members, each in himself for the benefit of all (Ephesians iv, 11–16). What each has, all have, intended indeed for his personal life but also and inseparably for the life and service of others. This great principle—already true at the natural level—shines through many apostolical texts and must needs be enlightening for Christian morality. What, then, are we told?

Let the word of Christ dwell in you richly, so that with all wisdom ye teach and admonish one another . . . (Colossians iii, 16).

Blessed be the God and Father of our Lord Jesus Christ, the Father of compassion and the God of all comfort, who comforteth us in our every affliction, so that we also are able to comfort them that are in any affliction, by reason of the comfort wherewith ourselves are comforted by God (2 Corinthians, i, 3–4).

Encourage each other day by day, so long as it is still 'today' . . . (Hebrews iii, 13).

And let us give heed to each other with a view to the stirring up of charity and of good works; not abandoning our assembly, as is the custom of some, but exhorting each other . . . (Hebrews x, 23–24).

Ye were called to freedom, brethren; only let not your freedom be an occasion for the flesh; rather be ye slaves one of another by charity (Galatians v, 13).

Brethren, even if a man be taken in some offence, do ye who are spiritual set such a one right in a spirit of gentleness. . . . Bear ye one another's burdens, and so shall ye fulfil the law of Christ (Galatians vi, 1–2).

Minister to yourselves according to the gift each one hath received, as good stewards of the manifold grace of God (1 Peter iv, 10).

To these texts there should be added those about generosity and sharing goods (1 Timothy vi, 18, etc.), the collection made for the saints at Jerusalem (Romans xv, 25–27, etc.), fellowship in prayer and sympathy (Acts ii, 42, 46; Romans xii, 9–13, etc.), and all those in which the words 'one another' occur. Then, too, there are those that witness to a whole network of mutual hospitality, help and co-operation:

Love one another with the affection of brothers, in honour fore-
stalling one another . . . sharing with the saints in their needs,
practising hospitality (Romans xii, 10, 13).

Now I commend to you Phoebe our sister, who doth minister
in the church at Cenchreae. Receive her in the Lord as becometh
saints, and help her in whatsoever business she may have need of
you. For she too hath been a help to many, myself among them
(Romans xvi, 1–2; for hospitality, cf. 1 Peter iv, 9; Hebrews xiii,
2; 1 Timothy iii, 2; Titus i, 8).

There are passages that speak in a similar tone in the Apostolic
Fathers, in the Fathers of the classical era and, in more systematised
terms, in the scholastic theologians; there is no point in piling up
examples.[6] They all speak of an order of gifts and activities which
are different from official hierarchical gifts and activities, but which
also build up the Church. In the biblical setting, indeed, every spiritual gift or charism is ordered to this end; there is as it were one single
grace, one single purpose of grace, in function of which various gifts
are given to each individual, all in view of the same work:

For as in our one body we have many members, and all the
members have not the same function, even so we many are one
body in Christ, and members each of the other. But we have gifts
which vary according to the grace that hath been given us . . .
(Romans xii, 4–6).

Now there are varieties of gifts, but the same Spirit. And there
are varieties of ministrations, and the same Lord. And there are
varieties of workings, but the same God, who worketh all things in
all. But to each is given the manifestation of the Spirit for the
general profit. . . . But these are the works of one and the same
Spirit, who apportioneth severally to each as he will (1 Corinthians
xii, 4–7, 11).

And himself gave some as apostles, some as prophets, some as
evangelists, some as shepherds and teachers, for the perfecting of
the saints in the work of the ministry, unto the building up of the
body of Christ, till we all attain . . . to the perfect man, to the full
measure of the stature of Christ (Ephesians iv, 11–13).

---

[6] St Thomas: *mutua subministratio*, see *Sum. theol.*, II–II, q. clxxxiii, a.2, ad 1; cf.
IV Sent., d. xix, q. 2, a.2, sol. 1; *De veritate*, q. xxix, a.4; *Com. in I Cor.*, c.12, lect. iii;
Com. in Eph., c.4, lect. 5; *Com. in Col.*, c.1, lect. 5, and 2, 4.—In his letter to the
Mexican bishops (A.A.S., 1937, p. 191), and elsewhere, Pope Pius XI points out
that Catholic Action is the realisation of a *mutua commutatio*, exchange of services,
which answers exactly to this programme.

This last passage refers especially to 'ministries', perhaps even to instituted ministries, which Paul sets in relation to Christ as *Lord*, that is, in his power; but the previous ones are looking at other spiritual gifts, which are distributed throughout the Body by the Spirit who is the principle of its life. Among these gifts are particular and extraordinary charisms, such as those of miracles and tongues, but there are others much more characteristic of daily life in Christ: the word of wisdom, the word of knowledge, unshaken faith, discernment of spirits, the gift of teaching or exhorting, the grace of generosity or works of mercy, the gift of supervision. . . . St Paul's lists are not systematic and make no claim to completeness. Since such gifts answer to the Church's requirements and growth, it is to be expected that the Spirit will arouse and distribute them according to times and places, bringing forth new ones and modifying the use of others according to need. Before the Apostles were dead, the regime of tongues and prophecy was already modified. Surely it is evident that if Paul had known such a thing as, for example, a Christian king, he would have mentioned the charisms of government; that faced with Catholic Action, he would have perceived charisms of leadership, of witness and many others, as well as new applications of those he mentioned.

To get some faint idea of what working together of the varied gifts of the Spirit is needed for the building of the Body of Christ, one may think of what is required in nature to produce a good apple or in art to produce a masterpiece or, for that matter, of all that contributes to form a really adult and spiritual Christian—a working together, under the life-giving guidance of the Spirit, of the hierarchical Church, of priests and teaching religious, of a family, father, mother, older relatives, elder brothers, of school-fellows and friends, of a scout-leader, perhaps, or a Y.C.W. leader, of all sorts of things, things seen, read, experienced . . . , of a hundred influences almost unnoticed and, over them all, of the whole communion of saints. 'How many contacts there are of one kind and another! This man's example sanctifies the superior who has authority over him; that one brings spiritual encouragement to the minister from whom he receives the sacraments: what varied give-and-take there is between those who preach and those who listen, those who pray, suffer, work, exert authority. God alone knows the numberless ways in which the members of his Church are bound to one another; but we know enough of some of them to guess at the rest and thus to taste one of the greatest delights of life in Jesus Christ' (Abbé G. Long-Hasselmans).

w

This activity of the faithful, lay folk and clergy considered as religious subjects, in building up the Church in what we have called her weft, is indeed very diverse. Fundamentally, all man's 'doing' enters into it in some way, but primarily whatever has a more immediately collective direction or incidence. Natural gifts must not be excluded: such a doctor of the Church as St Albert the Great calls them graces, in the sense of being free gifts, and St Thomas teaches that natural gifts come under the predestination of God's children. Why, for example, should not the charism of supervision (*présidence*) be at bottom a natural gift, but exist in a member of Christ, purified, strengthened, ennobled by a life of faith and charity, directed by the Holy Spirit to the common good, to the ministry of upbuilding the Church? From this point of view also all is grace, or more exactly, as St Paul puts it, a gift made according to grace (Romans xii, 6). Everything can be of service in leading to Christ, and therefore in building up his Body, even though its total and properly social construction cannot be carried on and brought about without the hierarchical apostolic charisms whose function it is.

We can indicate here only two or three among the many possibilities thus opened to all the faithful, and first of all, in the order of perception, the forming of the image of God and of Jesus Christ in human consciousness. We generally confine our consideration to the official communication of knowledge of God by the public teaching of priests and bishops; we are insufficiently conscious of the 'lateral contributions', of how much we can do to show God to one another. How often have I learned more about prayer from seeing so-and-so on his knees (sometimes a very lowly person), or from listening to someone else quite unconsciously testifying to what prayer means in his life! Seeing somebody else's freedom with his time, his goods, his heart, his friendship, I have learned what the spirit of generosity and giving means, learned, too, that I am selfish and mean. And there are the books that have been recommended to me, the questions put to me, the numberless occasions on which, through my brethren, through the noise and glare of the world, through anything, God has been made known to me, has stolen into my heart, to grow there—Jesus Christ was built up in me, and I in him. . . . The Venerable Mary-of-the-Incarnation (Martin) tells how, when she was left a widow at nineteen, she was hesitating whether she should go on living 'in the world', when a friend (knowing little of her difficulty) said, 'One has to be all God's'. This was a flash of light that helped her decision. How many times have we not been similarly shown the way by a word from a fellow Christian!

Here we come upon a general aspect of all the Holy Spirit's working in the Church particularly in her 'weft'—the big part played by
'occasions'. We are God's handiwork, writes St Paul, 'created in
Christ Jesus for good works, which God hath prepared beforehand
that therein we may walk' (Ephesians ii, 10). This text must not be
misunderstood, any more than that good saying of St Francis de
Sales, 'There is no more difference between the written Gospel and
the life of saints than between written music and music sung': there
is no mechanical predetermination, which would destroy freedom.
But there is guidance by the Holy Spirit, which in numberless ways
makes our path cross the path of others, and makes these meetings
occasions for 'the perfecting of the saints in the work of the ministry,
unto the building up of the body of Christ' (Ephesians iv, 12). These
rencounters and occasions are so many missions *ex spiritu* which every
God-fearing man is given in view of a work that is directed by
Another, leading it towards an end that we know in theory but the
details of whose progress are beyond us. Unlike the soldier who sees
only his own little corner of the battle (like Stendhal's Fabrice at
Waterloo), we who are fighting for the Kingdom of God know the
objective and even the general 'strategy' of the campaign, but not
the Lord's 'tactics', and most of the time we have little idea of what
we are actually doing. Nevertheless, each according to his gifts and
opportunities, we are ceaselessly engaged in a mission of helping
someone else in one way or another, of showing him something of
the divine meaning, of using some 'charism', and thereby, in however
tiny a way, helping to build the mystical Body.

Nor must it be supposed that the official, hierarchical mission is
altogether outside this regime of rencounters and occasions. It is true
that it does not depend on them for the constitution and reality of its
mission; but it is actualised and effected by its exercise in them, not
specified thereby but manifested. The hierarchical apostolic mission,
endowed with its appropriate charisms, is constituted from above;
like the stones at the angle of a building, it holds the Church together
by its vertical strength. But when it is in operation it does not stand
alone, like the mast of a wireless transmitter; it brings together all
sorts of connexions, giving and receiving, called upon and answering,
according to occasions and opportunities which, again, the Holy
Spirit provides for 'the perfecting of the saints in the work of the
ministry, unto the building up of the body of Christ'.

The Church is built together by the intercourse of its members one
with another in a whole pattern of services, of mutual enlightenment,
of taking opportunities, by the habitual use for the benefit of the body

of the gifts which each one has received: such a Church cannot be called by any other name than 'community'. And that is why this chapter is called 'The laity and the Church's communal life'. A rediscovery of this aspect of things unquestionably accounts for certain demands and currents in the Church's life today, and a little must be said about these.

(1) One of the features of contemporary Catholic life, especially in some countries, is the multiplication of groups of men and women, or, often, of households and homes, directed to a common leading of Christian life. Everybody has heard of such things: groups or communities of families; 'back to the land' associations; biblical, liturgical, missionary, oecumenical (Christian reunion) circles; university parishes; clubs with particular interests, holiday-camps, and conferences innumerable. Without closing one's eyes to the difficulties that arise or to the amount of work it means for those taking part and their spiritual encouragers, it must surely be recognised that in many places many promising results, amounting to a veritable renewal of Christian society, are due to these groups or to their example and inspiration. In any case, the movement is there, and it is as irrepressible as life itself. Such a movement means something . . .

Essentially, it answers to a need to rediscover the Church and, in a sense, to re-enter and renew her from below. Many of our contemporaries find that for them the Church's machinery, sometimes the very institution, is a barrier obscuring her deep and living mystery, which they can find, or find again, only from below, through little Church cells wherein the mystery is lived directly and with great simplicity. Of these cells Father Montuclard has written: 'They are not one of the least symptoms of the structural insufficiency of Catholic society. In the mind of those who form them, all [these cells] appear as an implicit protest against the rigidity and unadaptability of the forms of ecclesial society. They all find their place outside a properly ecclesiological organisation . . .'[7] Especially does Father Montuclard diagnose a dissatisfaction with the Church's actual structures, and his diagnosis is certainly right. A need is felt to seek, beneath the ready-made administrative machinery, the living reality of basic communities, the aspect in which the Church herself is, at the same time as an objective institution or hierarchical mediation, a community to whose life all its members contribute and which is patterned by give-and-take and a pooling of resources.

Apart from their fruits of fervour and enterprise, to which hundreds of priests can testify, these cells wherein the people can at last.

[7] *Rebâtir le temple: Deuxième lettre aux impatients* (Petit-Clamart, 1948), pp. 47–60.

express themselves and make a personal contribution have a high apostolic value. Pope Pius XII has declared as much, and he sees in them a particularly effective form of lay apostleship.[8]

(2) To this requirement of the faithful there corresponds on the clergy's side a search for pastoral methods adapted to the new needs, particularly that of a Church which is more of a community and wherein the contributions of the people are taken more into consideration, a Church, that is, which is built up from below *as well*. There is no need to repeat here what has been said in Part One Chapter II about reducing the vision of the Church to her aspect as an institution already made and as hierarchical mediation. But all that is being looked for and done in the fields of public worship, apostolic life, parochial organisations, ministering the sacraments, and doctrinal consciousness of the mystery of the Church, all this is in obedience to the same inspiration: namely, without denying anything objective and 'given', to give full weight to the religious subject, his dispositions, what he can contribute, his participation, and the full expression which he can find in a true community. That all means a rediscovery of the Church as community, made in a sense by its members, and to that extent from below. As a German theologian, M. D. Koster, has well put it, it means 'becoming a people again', a *Volkwerdung* of the Church.

Now that is a thing which is done, and can only be done, from the bottom. The more authority is exercised at a higher level, the more it gets out of touch with those below, and the more it tends to become external and to substitute the impersonal bond of law for the ties of community.[9] A community begins with persons, or with elementary communities already living as such. According to G. Le Bras, in old France people were attached to parishes through groups or confraternities; and it is noticeable that today a communal parish is a community of communities, finding its support and strength in more elementary groups, when these are authentic and know how to work together. Canonically speaking, a parish is not defined as a community of faithful, but as a certain territory in charge of a priest appointed by the bishop as his representative. But this canonical notion is modified in a communal direction by the realities of life; moreover, canon law itself provides for the possibility of the faithful freely forming groups of one sort or another, partial communities within the parochial framework, or even marginal thereto.[10] The

See, *e.g.*, his address to the Lenten preachers of Rome, 1951, in *Doc. cath.*, 11 March 1951, cc. 260–261.
[9] Cf. Taparelli d'Azeglio, *Essai théorique du droit naturel*, vol. iii, p. 186.
[10] Cf. K. Rahner in *Zeitsch. f. kath. Theol.*, vol. lxx (1948), pp. 186ff.

faithful, too, who associate themselves with this or that movement, sometimes reaching beyond national frontiers, also can form communities; how much more then within movements for personal improvement or within Catholic Action. It is desirable that as many of the faithful as possible should aggregate themselves to communities and so become active members in the Church.

(3) An ecclesial community formed from below by religious subjects sometimes seeks to bring about certain concrete relations between the mission *ex spiritu* and the mission *ex officio*, between spirit and function. It is especially a question of the priesthood. The spontaneous, partial communities to which we have referred like to choose a priest for themselves; but it goes further. When the members are a community to such a degree that they lead their Christian existence in it, they seek to find among themselves, to as it were carry and bring to birth, a man of priestly soul who may attain to ordination and become in a very special way *their* priest. That is perfectly normal; there were many who became priests in that way in early days and during the patristic age. Hierarchical values are fully respected, since the priest's training, canonical call and ordination remain with the bishop. Priesthood *ex officio*, with its authority and power, comes as a crown to the kind of priesthood *ex spiritu* which grows like a fruit on the communal tree. It is very noticeable how, whenever parishes and other bodies begin to live again as real communities, an instinctive logic impels them to recover ways of doing things which were natural to times of communal vitality.

Here surely is also to be found the answer to a problem which can be an artificial problem, born of a fallacious opposition between hierarchical functions or powers and personal charisms. These two things are often distinguished in such a way that they appear separate, if not opposed, and one does not see how to reconcile them. But in the New Testament there is no hierarchical ministry without charisms, and the highest hierarchical qualification does not dispense one from desiring the greatest possible abundance of them, and charity above all: we may refer to what is said of St Paul in note 1 above. In the New Testament, ministerial responsibilities are entrusted to men who are full of the gifts of the Spirit. It is true that sacramental ordination confers such gifts, but it also consecrates those that are already there. There is any amount of evidence for all this in early and patristic times; and the primitive constitutions of the Order of Preachers laid it down that, after examination, the office of preaching ought to be accorded to those who seem already to have received the grace.

In different terms, and perhaps also in a rather different atmosphere, the same thing is operative today in seminaries, noviceships and scholasticates, through a whole system of studies, examinations, spiritual directors and father masters, and finally of call by the superiors. This somewhat juridical system corresponds to the regime of a Church which has learned from history and experience to organise its life and to regulate its safeguards; actually, it is worth just what the men are worth. But it is to be expected that there should be a revaluation of some things that have always been held and done, in a Church which, after having thought of herself too exclusively as a system of hierarchical mediation, becomes again conscious of the Holy Spirit at one extreme and of the Christian people at the other. As regards the faithful, there will be realisation that the priest is taken from among the people and consecrated for them, that he comes from a community and goes back to it; there will be consciousness, too, of all that is fine and irreplaceable in the control of the subject individual, not by his superiors alone, but by the community, when it really deserves the name. Truly does the Church live from below as well as from above: as St Paulinus of Nola wrote, 'We make up our mind after seeking the advice of all, for the Spirit of God breathes in every one of the faithful' (Letter 23). As regards the Holy Spirit, it will be realised that, the work of God being done by men of God along the two lines set out at the beginning of this chapter, the two ought to coincide. The gifts of hierarchical spiritual power are decisive; in the order of validity, they suffice. But the ancient tradition was to assign charges, not according to purely moral qualities or to character, but according to 'pneumatic' or charismatic qualities, 'according to the degree of the presence of God himself in the candidates' (Abbot Vonier); not reducing the 'pneumatic' to the humanly 'moral' or to the 'juridical'; not accepting an *ex officio* unless it was not merely complemented by, but grounded in, an *ex spiritu*. No priest who is not first a Christian, a religious man, who, before depending on the Lord and the hierarchy who give 'mission', depends personally on God, who gives 'spirit'. . . .

*   *   *

The dangers attendant on emphasising the part that is taken from below in making the Church as community are real and must not be ignored, the more so because the whole purpose of this book is to give the elements of a response at the doctrinal level to the need for giving the laity its full place.

There is the risk of some people claiming a wide independence without any previous training or formation; or of assuming that

bishops and priests have no say about a lot of things that in fact come
into the sphere of ethics, and are therefore within the competence of
the apostolic ministry—marriage questions, for example, or political
and economic doctrines. Sometimes people talk about the 'coming of
age' of the laity (a very ambiguous expression, more false than true,
which we have carefully avoided using), as if they were now twenty-
one and could now shift for themselves . . .

There are drawbacks to the forming of those special groups
wherein, as has been said, the Church undoubtedly experiences a
renewal of her vital effectiveness. In some countries, these groups
like to choose *their* priest. This means a risk for the rest of the urban
parochial priests of becoming a sort of 'non-qualified' clergy, all right
for holy hours, weddings, funerals. . . . To say nothing of the heavy
commitments of so many groups, and of the danger of their becoming
self-sufficient, cliques apart from the parish church . . .

At a deeper level still, there may be a certain danger of 'protestantism', not only in lesser matters of no importance, but in mind and
general attitude to religious life. Directly people begin to rediscover
authentic aspects of the Church's reality that are not to the fore in
the 'received ideas' of ecclesiology and pastoral work, small difficulties become inevitable. But there is a more serious peril lurking in
the truth that the faithful in some way make the Church through the
exercise of the spiritual gifts they receive. If this aspect be elaborated
without previous complementary consideration of the objective institution, the risk is run of seeing in the Church only the aggregate of
personal relations with God and their free sharing through the
exercise of each one's gifts.

To obviate these dangers, one has only to take the various aspects
each according to its own truth, and according to its place in a complete, balanced theology. We venture to hope that the chief elements governing such an equilibrium are given in the present work,
and that it is enough to have pointed out the rocks which may be
avoided by keeping an eye on the theological lighthouses. All the
problems of application and actuality are not solved but, at the
doctrinal level, we have given the elements required for their solution. We think no more can be asked of us here.

*   *   *

We conclude this chapter by referring again to a concrete problem
which also has its difficulties. In a Church structured from above,
unity is ensured by a kind of uniformity, that of the objects received
(Cajetan's *idem credunt*, etc.) and that of the common direction given
(Cajetan's *sub uno*). In a Church structured also from below, from

the moment the contributions of the religious subject are taken into account there is, beyond unity, a problem of communion or fellowship. How does the Church, at the various levels of her life from parish to planet, remain one if men and their groupings are taken into consideration, as well as the objective and hierarchical determinations?—men with their schools of thought, forms of piety, associations for this and for that. The faithful have full freedom, within the bounds of the Church's communion, to associate themselves with this or that theological tradition, with any 'spirituality', to engage in any work of intellectual or cultural creation, to initiate enterprises, to take part in conferences, for peace or social justice or total abstinence or against slums or gambling, to join biblical, liturgical, Marian movements, and so forth. Yes, St Cyprian was indeed right when he said that it is allowable, 'salvo jure communionis, diversum sentire' . . .

Since we are concerned with a theology of laity, we cannot but put the question of the limits of obligatory conformity and divergent choices. To those that may exist in the sphere of ecclesial life, the laity add those of secular life: their state is one of serving God without holding back from engagement in the affairs of the world and of history—sciences and techniques, politics and production, cultural activities, the struggle for existence and service of those engaged in that struggle. . . . This lay engagement must be real and wholehearted; it is not enough to touch the business of the wicked world only with the tips of one's fingers, and to reject the implications of an actual, sincere, loyal commitment lest one soils one's hands. But there is something devouring about such an engagement, one is inexorably fettered. Choice involves strife, with all its complication of motives, means and ends, loyalties and consequences. One is opposed to others, and inevitably sometimes to other Christians; the more so because even Christianity does not exist in a pure state but in an historical state, set in a human matrix, that of an historical 'Christian world' with which one can be at odds on account both of a temporal commitment and an evangelical commitment. The integrity and demands of a Christian's engagement must not be emasculated in the name of charity, peace, agreement among Catholics. Obviously the fellowship between this man and other Christians, between his group and other groups, perhaps even between him or his group and the actual historic Church to which he belongs, will be subjected to a strain which it must be strong enough to withstand without breaking.

The problem arises in a parochial setting, that is, in the setting of the church whose business it is to bestow Christian life pure and simple on people living within a given area. A conflict among parishioners may often enough reproduce a conflict between the parish as centre of Christian life pure and simple and organisms adapted to more particular needs of life. Within a national church, the problem can be not simply a transposition of these disagreements to a larger scale; it may be the result of positions which specialised movements of Catholic Action have had to take up in order to fulfil their mission. Their commitment also should be clear and firm, in religious matters, of course, but frequently also in points determined by temporal considerations which the magisterium itself can approach only from afar and from above. At least in the actual state of Catholic Action, it seems impossible to reduce the obligation of movements simply to the general statements of the hierarchy; even those statements, when they are concerned with matters of fact, do not always receive the unanimous adhesion of Catholics. At the level of the worldwide Church, the problem arises between Christians of different historical traditions and situations, over questions such as those of human rights, tolerance, war, conception of the state, trade unions, practical attitudes to the struggle against Communism, philosophical and theological work to be done, public worship, the balance between authority and free inquiry and other initiatives from below, adaptation and reforms in the Church, and so on. Catholics within one country entertain very various views on such matters, but still more in different countries, according with the diversities of a certain 'geopolitics of Catholicity' of which national temperaments, culture, histories, and political and economic conditions form the main human components.

All this is normal, but it has to be harmonised with the higher law of Catholic communion and fellowship. The more the Church's periphery expands, the more she has to strengthen her centres. The more that Christians undertake personal engagements and obligations, the more they must persist in the essential activities of the Church that are strictly common to them all: public worship and the sacraments, especially the eucharist; faith nourished at its highest source, the Bible and tradition, under the guidance of the magisterium; respect for and obedience to the decisions of the apostolic power of the bishops in communion with the Roman See. These are the essential elements of that *jus communionis* which must always be kept and which is traditionally expressed in community of faith, sacramental communion, and a common submission to apostolic authority. Only in the measure that that is assured can we profit from the freedom of *diversum sentire*.

But within the field of this freedom there are certain things to be taken into account, particularly where political and economic options are in question. It is true that the Church has no competence therein; she can, for pastoral reasons, ask the faithful to make such and such a choice but, without leaving them absolute freedom of choice, she does not thereby impose one. The Church has no power in temporal matters as such; but man's temporal affairs involve questions of ends and means, and these belong to ethics and therefore to the Church's magisterium. The directions as such of the magisterium, if they are formal and imperative, impose an obligation of obedience on the faithful; if they are not formal, they call at least for a submissive ear and respectful consideration. There is a gradation in the pronouncements of authority: at the top, very definite positive principles; then, equally definite and strict determinations, but negative, saying what cannot be allowed but not what must be held; then, more general indications, especially if they are positive. This gradation might be illustrated from the great documents of social teaching: at the top, the condemnations of godless Marxism and of 'racist' Nazism; at the bottom, appeals for a spirit of unselfishness and mutual help about housing, and such indications as that one should vote, and vote for justice.

As one comes down the scale the range of possible choices and opinions gets larger, and in consequence the opportunities for Catholics to disagree increase. When there is no longer question of regulation by an *idem facere* or an *esse sub uno* (to be united in the same objects and obedient to the same authority), it is the duty of members of a community to concentrate on finding an *agere ut pars* (Cajetan again), that is, to have the attitude of a member of one same body. Amidst their legitimate differences of choice and commitment, Catholics still have a duty of unity; and this is the more difficult because that unity is not to be imposed (as some people would still like) by uniformity in everything, from theological systems to an election vote, taking in devotions on the way. This duty of unity and behaviour appropriate to the members of a same body would seem to be reducible to the two following obligations.

(1) In setting forth his own choices and opinions, each must be careful that he *understands* different choices and opinions and their reasons. For example, when the Spaniards define their attitude on the status of non-Catholics in their country, they should take the trouble to understand the historical and spiritual motives for the freer and more tolerant attitude of French or American Catholics. ... Contacts ought to take place in an atmosphere of common loyalty

and mutual trust, in which we can explain ourselves to one another, especially about our points of difference. Over and above that, we ought not to approach these contacts in a spirit of defensiveness and criticism, but in order to establish a 'dialogue', opening the way to agreements and the finding of complements in one another's views. 'Inter-member' relations both raise the problem with which we are concerned and provide possibilities favourable to its solution. The more that individuals and groupings see of one another and discuss together, the less difficult the solution will be.[11]

(2) In setting forth his own choices and opinions, each must be careful to seek to justify them in relation to the whole community, and as part of his service in the actual circumstances of the Church and of the world and of each one of us. But in doing that we must beware that we run the risk of falling into sectarianism, and even fanaticism. Nothing leads to sectarianism like the conviction that *I* am clear-sighted and that I know *the* right way of serving truth. Nothing leads to fanaticism like the feeling in a member of the body that he coincides perfectly with that body and that he carries the whole weight of the cause he wants to serve. That is why it is so necessary to 'see the other fellow's point of view', and to be conscious of the transcendence of our common point of reference in relation to our respective services; in other words, to have that humbleness and real charity without which there is no Christian.

In this as in so many other things, the fundamental need is to try to understand. It is for lack of that effort that, with all our good intentions and fine solutions, we 'get nowhere'. Nothing useful will ever emerge unless, with simplicity, sense of humour and honesty, we criticise our intellectual build-up of self-justification and the unfavourable picture of the other man that we make for ourselves. More and more as every day passes does Christian life, like human life at large, call for understanding.

[11] The archbishop of Paris, Cardinal Feltin, spoke very plainly and persuasively on this subject in his Lenten pastoral letter of 1951 (*Doc. cath.*, 11 March 1951, cc. 268–269). A further pastoral, on unity in the Church (*Sem. rel. de Paris*, 23 February 1952, pp. 175–182, March 1, pp. 203–215), gave authoritative support to the ideas expressed in this chapter.

Chapter V

THE LAITY AND THE CHURCH'S APOSTOLIC FUNCTION

THERE is one Church and one apostleship to carry salvation in Jesus Christ to men throughout the world until the end of time. The Church's mission is an extension of the mission of Jesus Christ, and so, *mutatis mutandis*, it is the same. It is not actualised in the same conditions: Christ is the source, the head; the Church is Christ's body, existing only through its Head but giving it organs and members. Accordingly, Jesus made the sending forth of his Apostles a repetition and continuation of his own: 'As the Father hath sent me, I also send you. . . . As thou [Father] hast sent me into the world, so I also have sent them into the world' (John xx, 21; xvii, 18).

This missionary torrent is a torrent of love, for the Father's sending the Son into the world is a deed of love, of God's *agape* (John iii, 16; 1 John iv, 9): the 'As my Father hath loved me, I also have loved you' (John xv, 9) corresponds exactly to the 'As the Father hath sent me, I also send you'. In complete continuity with these statements Pope Pius XI declared with reference to Catholic Action that, 'By hierarchical apostleship is meant that apostleship that originally came from the heart, the life and the hands of Jesus Christ, which is perpetuated throughout the centuries by the worldwide and age-long expansion of the apostolic college, of the episcopate'.

The mission of Jesus is found in his very name, which means 'God saves', and he expressed it himself when he said 'The Son of Man hath come to seek and to save what was lost' (Luke xix, 10). 'To save' means in the first place to deliver from the degrading tyranny of sin and the Evil One; then, to bring to God and reconcile with him, and in so doing to obtain for things that which they long for—deliverance from 'vanity', that is, from debasement and emptiness, liberation from corruption and disintegration, in a word, that unity and integrity, communion, that they seek (cf. Pt. One Ch. III). We say

'things' so as to exclude nothing of 'what was lost' and so as fully to
honour the title Saviour of the world and the full sense of those texts
where St Paul speaks of creation's groanings and of the reconciliation
of all things (Romans viii, 19–22; Ephesians i, 10; iv, 15; Colossians
i, 20). But, of course, it is men who are principally concerned, in
whose destiny the cosmos is involved, for all creation leads to mankind and, through and with mankind, to God (cf. 1 Corinthians iii,
22–23; viii, 6, etc.). Creation also is an object of Christ's salvation;
not so much for itself—it has not enthralled itself to vanity—but
rather does it await a share in the salvation of men, in 'the freedom
of the glory of the children of God' (Romans viii, 21).

The Catechism of the Council of Trent shows us him who was
given the name Jesus, Saviour, joining thereto the name Christ,
Anointed, as a title corresponding to the three offices for which he
was anointed, and so to the three great powers in virtue of which his
mission as Saviour was to be fufilled—king, priest, prophet. It is in
accordance with those three offices that Christ's mission is continued
in his body, the Church.

The object of the Church's mission is the object of Christ's, with
this difference, that salvation has no longer to be purchased but to
be communicated, not without co-operation. But we have seen that
the conditions in which Jesus, conformably to the Father's will, has
ordered the exercise of his priestly kingship postpone the full physical
and cosmic effects of salvation until the day of the restoration of all
things (Acts iii, 21); during the time until the Saviour comes again
in power and majesty, the 'time of the Church', there is a duality of
Church and world. The ministry of the Spirit that the Church
exercises does not exert the full effectiveness which is by right, and
will be in fact at the day of God's choice, that of the Holy Spirit: of
this we have only the earnest. This is enough to enable the Church
really to be the germinal cell of the Kingdom; it is not enough to
enable her to have as her proper and direct object the fullness of
salvation, even to the renewal of the things that properly constitute
the world. That is why St Paul says we are still awaiting salvation,
to wit, the redemption of our bodies, and that all creation waits and
groans with us (Romans v, 2; viii, 9–11, 21–23, etc.). The salvation
of which the Church exercises an effective ministry is firstly and
directly the salvation of persons, more exactly still, of souls, a spiritual
salvation whose spiritual or cosmic effects are as it were held in
reserve.

However, something very real is effected even in this last sphere.
At present, the Kingdom is only 'coming', but the Gospel makes it

clear that there are perceptible effects of its approach. We only have an earnest of the Spirit, but it really is an earnest. Whence it follows, not only that the Church is the germinal cell of the Kingdom and that total universal salvation will come about through the exercise of the Principle of her existence, but also that she is given anticipations of the final restoration. These are chiefly of two kinds. First, often given in a miraculous way, there are fugitive glimpses and perceptions of the perfect reign of God: literally, sometimes, the blind see, men are freed from the burden that bears them down. Or, more ordinarily, a certain healing, a kind of renewal, of the temporal things of human life, especially of those that touch people most closely, and which can be included under the name of civilisation.

And so when Pope Pius X wanted to make clear the scope of what he already called Catholic Action, or action by Catholics, he said that it 'excludes absolutely nothing of what in any way pertains, directly or indirectly, to the divine mission of the Church'; and he defined this mission thus: 'To restore all things in Christ. . . . To restore in Christ not only whatever is incumbent on the Church in virtue of her divine mission, which is to lead souls to God, but as well that which springs naturally from her mission, Christian civilisation in each and all of the elements that make it up' (Encyclical letter, '*Il fermo proposito*', 1905). Clearly this declaration connects up with several statements in the present work and of theology in general: with what will be said later about the two points of application of Catholic Action; with what has already been said about the role of the laity, and about the relations between nature and grace; with 'Christian philosophy' and the theory of culture; with ecclesiological theses about the object of the Church's magisterium and her action on what is temporal; and so on. All these things are coherent together and correspond exactly. In the absolutely universal scope ('all things') of Christ's redemption and kingship, they imply an area of direct and full efficaciousness, which is spiritual, and an area of indirect, suggested or partial efficaciousness, which touches nature or creation itself.

When we come to examine the energies through which Christ's mission is continued in the Church we find, where Christ himself is concerned, a certain duality, or even more than one. Jesus exerted his activity externally and visibly and also inwardly. As priest, he converted and justified people, and he instituted the sacraments; as prophet, he gave inward light to souls, and he preached in public; as king, he ruled things simply by his will, and he outwardly declared his law and judgement. Moreover, we have seen that he has a two-

fold relation to the Church, of power and of animation or quickening. This second duality is not exactly co-extensive with the first but
rather combines with it, for we shall find it in each of the two ways
of Christ's activity.

When he was about to hallow all by his sacrifice and, having
grounded his work in the power of his blood, to withdraw his physical presence and thus begin the time of progressive accomplishment
of salvation in the Church, Jesus as it were appointed two agents,
two vicars or active representatives who should continue, or rather
apply, his activity according to the two ways we have indicated:
inwardly, the Holy Spirit, outwardly, the apostolic ministry. Sent
through the Father's love, 'knowing that his hour was come that he
should pass out of this world to the Father, having loved his own
that were in the world, he loved them unto the end' (John xiii, 1):
loved them not with a deeply affective love alone, but with a love
creative of the means to its own purpose, begetting a mission that
continues and actualises his saving work until the end of time. That
is why, when he institutes the New Covenant in his blood, Jesus
declares a twofold mission, of his Spirit and of his Apostles (John xiv,
xvi, xvii). Both will do the same work, both will construct the
Church, the one from within, the other from without, but though
their missions are organically complementary they are none the less
different.

Like the institution of the Church herself, the Apostleship of the
Twelve is unfolded at different times during Christ's public ministry;
first, personal choice and calling, then, public choice and calling,
truly creative of the mission (Mark iii, 13–15; Luke vi, 12–13). The
content of the mission, the competence of those sent out, are indicated in several well-known texts: 'Whatsoever ye shall bind upon
earth shall be bound in Heaven . . .' (Matthew xviii, 18); 'This do ye
in remembrance of me' (Luke xxii, 19; 1 Corinthians xi, 24); 'As the
Father hath sent me, I also send you. . . . Receive ye the Holy Spirit:
whose sins ye shall forgive, they are forgiven them . . .' (John xx,
21–23); and especially, 'All power in heaven and on earth hath been
given me. Go ye, therefore, making disciples of all the nations, baptising them in the name of the Father and of the Son and of the Holy
Spirit: teaching them to observe all that I have commanded you:
and behold, I am with you all days, unto the consummation of the
world' (Matthew xxviii, 18–20; cf. Mark xvi, 15–16). The sending
of the Holy Spirit is to actualise inwardly what the Lord had instituted visibly during his days in the flesh. The Apostles were indeed
such 'through the Holy Spirit' (Acts i, 1–2), and when the time

should come for themselves to institute ministers, these in turn would
be such through inward action of the Spirit (cf. Acts xx, 28). But all
this is the effective fulfilment, through the invisible sending and
inward action of the Spirit, of the working of a visibly and publicly
instituted ministry; every operation of grace, whether it be a matter
of the sacraments or of the word, is a 'spiritual' operation, calling for
an inner sending of the Holy Spirit. But this mission comes inwardly
to duplicate—in order to make it effective—another mission, a
visibly constituted institution in the order of ministry or, as Cardinal
Du Perron puts it, of the means of calling to salvation. That is the
important point. The apostolic or ministerial mission, given by the
historic Christ [DD] *to some*, envisages the work of communicating
salvation through the constitution of the *ecclesial* institution as aggregate of *means of grace*. That is why it is an hierarchical mission: not
simply because it is given only to some, but because it entails sacred
powers, spiritual powers tending to salvation, according to the functions of priesthood (sacraments), prophecy (authority of the magisterium) and kingship (authority in spiritual government). The
apostleship thus established is not simply an apostolate of zeal and, if
we may use the words, proselytism or propaganda. It is that, certainly—the ears of the Apostles were not closed to the call to become
fishers of men, to make disciples of all the nations, which means to
convert people. But it also is, and for that reason, an apostolate that
involves authority and powers ordered to the object of the Christian
mission, an apostolate of pastors. Better still, an apostleship that is an
integral part of the institution as such, that is, of the objective,
ordinary and properly ecclesial means of grace, an apostleship constitutive of the institutional ministry: in fact, the apostleship of apostolicity.

The Holy Spirit, on the other hand, has been promised and sent to
all the faithful (Mark xiii, 11, etc.): at Pentecost he comes down on
all those gathered together including, besides the Eleven, several
women, Mary the mother of Jesus, and his brethren, about six score
people, we are told. 'And when the day of Pentecost was come, they
were all gathered together in one place. And suddenly there came a
noise from heaven, as of the rushing of a blast of wind, which filled
the whole house where they were seated. And there appeared to
them tongues, as though of fire, which parted and sat upon every
one of them. And they were all filled with the Holy Spirit . . .' (Acts
ii, 1–3). Similar kinds of pentecost, partial but still collective, follow:
after Peter and John were set free (*ibid.*, iv, 31), in the house of
Cornelius (x, 44–46), among the disciples at Ephesus (xix, 6). Each

x

of these comings of the Spirit is followed by activity of the word. The
faithful who are thus visited speak with tongues, prophesy, praise
God, and speak his word with confidence (iv, 31). There are other,
less remarkable, comings of the Spirit, which go on being given to the
Church as daily bread, an apostolic manna; not only Peter (x, 19;
xi, 12) and Paul (xiii, 9; xix, 21, etc.), but Stephen (vi, 5), the
evangelist Philip (viii, 29), Ananias (ix, 10) are visited by the Spirit
and *in this way* receive a mission of testimony or apostleship according
to the needs of the Church's life. No doubt these men and occasions
are a little out of the ordinary; but it is clear that all the faithful in
their own way are given a mission to build up the Body of Christ and
bring it new members, being refreshed and guided by the same spirit
and endowed by him with the spiritual gifts spoken of in the previous
chapter. This mission may be characterised as personal, spiritual and
universal. Personal and spiritual as distinct from social and juridical:
not a mission given as a public charge, *ex officio*, and involving powers
or competences pertaining to an instituted office, but a mission
deriving from the personal spiritual possession of inner spiritual
energies and life, *ex spiritu*;[1] a mission to action that requires no
hierarchical powers, to action, therefore, through influence. Universal, in the sense that this mission is not confined to some but is given
to all on whom the Holy Spirit has come and to whom he has given
something of his gifts.

We see two different missions, and yet in the end they are only
one. How do their two exercises harmonise into this unity? That they
are one is obvious, for their object, end, content are the same—
salvation in Christ Jesus. But there are as it were two degrees or
'titles', which the New Testament shows to be combined as follows:

(1) The mission of the Twelve has an absolute priority; it is total,
not only in the sense that it embraces the totality of the object
assigned to the apostleship, but also as comporting the totality of the
means, powers and charisms pertaining to this mission. With it,
there is the Church, which also Jesus instituted essentially in the
Twelve. Their apostolic mission with its ministerial powers suffices to
constitute in its essence the Church's apostolic mission.

[1] F. M. Braun in *Revue thomiste*, 1951, pp. 41–42, on the difference between the
gift of the Spirit to the Apostles on the evening of Easter day and that to the whole
community at Pentecost—The need for clarity makes it necessary for us to distinguish what scholastics call formal reasons. Nothing is further from our mind than
to push distinction to the length of separation and opposition. We repeat: Not only
is the priest one of the faithful in the first place, seeking salvation by a life of personal holiness; but he also has to discharge hierarchical functions in the spirit they
require and accompany all that he does *ex officio* with righteousness *ex spiritu*. Moreover, the Holy Spirit is at work in all the sacred things done by the priest through
his hierarchical powers.

(2) Several very similar expressions recur characteristically in the New Testament: the Church exists since the Apostles, and to become a member thereof is to be with the Twelve, 'to be added to', to join the first community (Acts ii, 41, 47; cf. ix, 26, etc.). Thus the apostleship of the faithful is also an adjunct to that of the Apostles, it is added to it and completes it. The Church's mission is perfected in the Apostles as to its essence, but those twelve men had the limitations of men and were not able to carry it on everywhere and for ever; even during their lifetime other apostles were needed, not so that the mission should be constituted in its integrity but so that it should be carried out in its integrity.

(3) So the mission of the faithful makes them co-operators with and complementary to the Apostles; like their charisms, like all their Christian life, it has to be exercised in such a way as to assimilate it to the work and activity of the Twelve, which is the norm. It does not come from them, it is not constituted (as the mission of ministers will be) by a participation in their original mission; but it is none the less given for the same object, the object of which the Apostles were given first and total charge, in respect of which their authority and action are normative. On the side of its object and rules for action, an apostolic mission is given to the faithful only as a sharing in, an association with, complementary to, that of the Apostles.

Once again we verify this law of the Church's existence: the inseparable duality of the hierarchical principle and the communal principle, an hierarchical structure and a life of the whole body; more: the inseparable duality of the institution, aggregate of the means of grace, and of life; of what is given to constitute the Church and of what is given so that, the faithful community being formed, all its members may bring forth living activities. It is clear that the Church's apostleship of constitution brings the three messianic offices into play in their form as powers: the apostolate of the simple increase of God's people, the messianic functions as the spiritual form of *life*, most particularly the prophetical function and the priestly function as directed towards others. They are made one in the Apostles and in their heirs, the bishops, who are at the same time both endowed with the fullness of ministerial powers and dedicted to all the activities of devotedness and zeal.

The Apostleship of the Faithful in History

Pope Pius XI often pointed out that, fundamentally, Catholic Action was nothing new and that apostolic texts show the faithful

actively co-operating in apostleship; he was specially fond of appealing to the passage in the letter to the Philippians (iv, 3) where St Paul
refers to the women Evodia and Syntyche, who 'have toiled along
with me in the gospel, as hath also Clement and the rest of my
fellow-workers . . .'. Evidence for the apostleship of the faithful in the
New Testament and first centuries is fairly plentiful, though not
always clear in detail; but the general impression is plain. Around
Paul and the other ministers of the Gospel, many of the faithful were
striving in one way or another. Before the coming of Paul, some had
spread the faith and begun to get a community together, such as
Epaphras at Colossae (cf. Colossians 1, 7; iv, 12); others are com-
mended for their pains (Romans, xvi, 4–6; 1 Corinthians xvi, 15;
Colossians v, 13); others because they are 'approved in Christ' and
have 'laboured much in the Lord' (Romans xvi, 10, 12); Paul calls
Prisca and Aquila his 'fellow-workers in Christ Jesus', and two of his
relatives, Andronicus and Junias, he calls 'distinguished among the
apostles' (*ibid.*, vv, 3, 7). In the letter to another fellow-worker,
Philemon, we see Paul gaining a soul both to the Gospel believed
and to the Gospel preached: the fugitive slave, Onesimus, is not only
his son but also his associate in Christ's service.

St Paul was putting into practice one of the most fundamental
things of the Gospel, whereby to be a disciple is equivalent to being a
servant, to being engaged in the service of the Gospel in one way or
another. We are not referring to that universal basic principle which
associates a truly religious relationship to God with love of one's
neighbour, giving that love a kind of primacy in the order of practice, nor to those texts which identify discipleship with loving service
of our brethren and determine degrees of discipleship by degrees of
that humble service. Rather are we thinking of how a man who is
conscious of being called to be a disciple of the Lord is at the same
time conscious of being a link in Christ's work and of being sent to
someone else. Thus we find Andrew recruiting Peter, and Philip,
Nathanael; the woman of Samaria bears witness to Jesus among her
countrymen (John i, 41, 45; iv, 39); the women who follow the
Master serve him at the same time; when he appoints disciples, Jesus
gives them an apostolic mission so like that of the Twelve that, if
there were no other references, we could hardly tell one from the
other (Luke x, 1–22). He does not call people that they may stop at
home (Luke ix, 57–62; Matthew viii, 19–22), and the case of Nicodemus, a 'private' disciple, appears almost abnormal. Jesus likens the
disciples to a lamp in a dark room, to a city set on a hill, a landmark,
to the salt added to a tasteless dish, and, speaking of the Kingdom

whose workers they are with him, to the leaven in dough. Because of
Jesus, one is a disciple, but also for the sake of others; as in the multiplying of the loaves (Mark vi, 41), one has always to break and give
out the bread received from his hands. The daily bread that the Lord
taught us to ask for is surely the bread which is common to us all *and
to him*, the bread of his mystical Body.

Among the Fathers, St John Chrysostom is the one who most
insistently and faithfully applies these fundamentals of the Gospel in
his pastoral work. The following are a few relevant passages:

> The most perfect rule of Christianity, its exact definition, its peak,
> is this: seek that which is for the benefit of the community. . . .
> Nothing can make one more Christlike than to look after the
> welfare of others (*In 1 Cor.*, hom. 25, n. 3; PG., lxi, 208).
> Nothing is more useless than a Christian who does not try to
> save others. Don't tell me that you are poor: the widow's two
> mites confront you; Peter, too, who said 'Silver and gold have I
> none', and Paul, so poor that he was often hungry. Don't plead
> your modest circumstances: they too were lowly and of humble
> station. Don't plead your ignorance: they too were uneducated.
> You may be a slave on the run; so was Onesimus. You may be ill;
> so was Timothy. Anybody can help his neighbour if he is only
> willing really to do what he can. Look at those beautiful, strong,
> tall trees, with their smooth bark—but they bear no fruit. If we
> have a garden, we want pomegranates and olives in it rather than
> trees which, however pleasant, have no practical use, or not much.
> People who are entirely taken up with their personal affairs are
> like that. . . . So are the well-dressed maiden ladies, chaste and well-
> behaved, but. . . . Such are the people who do not nurture Christ.
> Notice carefully that they are not accused of any self-regarding
> sin, impurity or forswearing and so on, but simply of not doing
> anything for anybody else—like the man of otherwise irreproach-
> able life who did not use the talent given him. How can such a
> man be a Christian? If the leaven does not 'work', is it really
> leaven? . . . Don't say that you can't make any impression on
> others: if you are a Christian it is impossible not to have some
> effect . . . , it is part of the very essence of a Christian . . . and it is as
> contradictory to say that a Christian can do nothing for others as
> to say that the sun cannot give light (*In Acta Apost.*, hom. 20, no. 4;
> PG., lx, 162).
> I cannot believe in the salvation of anyone who does not work

for his neighbour's salvation (*De sacerdotio*, lib. 3, n. 10: PG., xlviii, 686).

'Go ye, therefore, make disciples of all the nations' was not said only to the Apostles, but to us as well. That the promise is not for them alone but for all those who come after them is seen from the words that follow it, 'unto the consummation of the world' (*In ii Thess.*, c. 3, hom. 5, n. 4; PG., lxii, 498).

So be very careful, all you simple faithful, and do not forget that together we form one single body and that we differ from one another only as member differs from member. Therefore you must not leave concern for the Church to the clergy alone . . . (*In ii Cor.*, hom. 18; PG., lxi, 527.

If you only would, you can do much more for people than we can. You have more opportunities for meeting one another, you know each other's condition better, you know each other's faults, you have more freedom, charity and ease among yourselves. . . . You can reprove and encourage one another better than we can. . . . In this way you lighten our task, you help us, you rally round us, sharing our labours as comrades, together working out one another's salvation and each one striving for his own (*In Hebr.*, hom. 30, n. 2–3; PG., lxiii, 211–212).

*   *   *

After the conversion of Constantine, the fall of the Roman empire, and the conversion of barbarian leaders and peoples, under the Merovingian and, more especially, the Carolingian kings, the West established a Christian regime that from our point of view can be described thus: the temporal world and the Church together formed one single society, often called *Respublica christiana*, or simply *Ecclesia*; in this one body, the temporal element expressly called itself Christian and acknowledged spiritual rules. It followed, at any rate in principle, that everybody was a Christian, being such through birth, institutions and laws. It also followed that lay apostleship for the increase of the faithful had hardly any place within Christendom: the laity built up the Church by observing her laws and living her life within the protecting bounds of the Christian commonwealth; if they had to defend her, it was rather by military crusades. The active part of the laity's proper role was taken over by their kings and leaders, leaving to the laity the duty of being obedient to the Church, that is, to the clergy. This regime lasted till towards the end of the sixteenth century. In Part One Chapter II we noticed in passing how

St Robert Bellarmine (d. 1621) was, where the laity were concerned, confined by the outlook on the relations between temporal society and the Church that still governed his thought.

With the establishment of Protestantism in several countries, followed by a spread of unbelief and indifference accepted as a social fact, religious divisions became a characteristic of the Western world, and an *élite* of laity began to concern itself with apostleship and defence of the Catholic faith by means other than those of the political powers. The history of this lay apostolate of the seventeenth and eighteenth centuries has been written only fragmentarily, in monographs on the great discoveries, conquests and colonisations, the devotional movement, the Company of the Blessed Sacrament, the missions of such men as Gaston de Renty, the sodalities of Mary, apologetical writing, and so forth.

It is quite another thing when we come to the nineteenth century and are face to face with a society born of the Enlightenment, rising industrialism, the French Revolution and its Napoleonic prolongation, aggressive and widespread unbelief, and the disappearance of the props to the faith provided by political powers. Christians were shaken. The world's structure had changed: it was now deeply divided, separated from Christ by hostility or indifference, full of new forces at work, enthusiastic for values unknown to classical theology, heedless, often ignorant, of the traditional Catholic set-up. Many priests and lay people appreciated the urgent necessity for making contact with this world, for finding ways of acting on it, for defending and explaining the faith in a language it could understand, for applying themselves to the Christian regeneration of society by forming islands whence Christian life should shine. They knew, too, that reliance could no longer be put on the upholding of priestly authority by power, and that henceforward it must rely on a laity full of zeal for God and his Church.

In the forefront of their activities was work directed at that new master factor, opinion: *apologia* for and defence of Catholicism, in which Chateaubriand and Joseph de Maistre were among the first to make their name, followed by men like Goerres, Donoso Cortes, Auguste Nicolas;[2] journalism, with *L'Avenir*, Louis Veuillot, the undertakings of St Antony Claret and Father J. S. Bailly; parliamentary and political action, so novel that at first some people denied that a lay man like Montalambert could engage in it as a defender

---

[2] In his introduction to his work *Du Pape*, de Maistre justifies himself as a man of the world assuming the right 'to write about things which up to now have seemed exclusively reserved to the zeal and learning of the priestly order'.

of the Church, but others were soon doing it with success—O'Connell, Goerres, Windthorst, Lueger, Albert de Mun; teaching, from the humblest schools to universities, where from the first Newman saw a chance for the laity to make a link between the contemporary world and the world of priesthood and faith.[3] All this is well summed up by one who always tried to give their due place to the laity, Father Lacordaire: 'The lay man has a mission to fulfil; he has to supply whatever may be lacking to the diocesan clergy and the religious orders, for their resources and for many means of action. Men of faith must join their efforts to defend truth against the ceaseless influence of evil teaching; their charity must work in common to repair the breaches in the Church and the social order.'

Charity in the form of multiple social works was joined to the work of ideas for the renewal of society: in France by such as Ozanam and Armand de Melun, in Italy by, among others, Bd Vincent Pallotti, whom Pius XI hailed as the 'pioneer and herald of Catholic Action'. In fact, the matter of Catholic Action was prepared in these multitudinous enterprises and activities of the nineteenth century, and a good deal of its idea as well: the collaboration of the laity with the clergy under the direction of the hierarchy for the reign of Christ and for social salvation.[4] Catholic Action, coming at the end of a century of effort, was to be deeply marked, as lay action, by a thirst for the renewal *of society* by faith in Christ and for his reign.

The aspect of this activity that particularly interested the Holy See at first was political and apologetical-literary defence, as may be seen from Pope Pius IX's few references to it. The same is true of Leo XIII, but he added a new element, namely, insistence on an organisation of 'action by Catholics' in definite undertakings, societies and conferences. Amidst a secularised and often hostile world, Catholics should seek thus to remake the framework of a Christian society capable of maintaining the faith, of defending it, and even of regaining, as well as the adhesion of the faithful, some degree of sympathy and even of a favourable situation from the world.

St Pius X's aim, 'to restore all things in Christ', was more positive still, one might almost say more militant; starting from its own principles, it meant the reassertion of 'being Christian', the total

---

[3] See a letter in W. Ward, *Life of J. H. Newman* (London, 1912), vol. ii, pp. 397–398, wherein Newman deplores the absolute refusal by the archbishops of lay cooperation in the matter of the Catholic university in Dublin.—Cf., too, a letter to J. M. Capes, editor of *The Rambler*, in Ward, *op. cit.*, i, 262–263.

[4] These terms were used by Francis Veuillot in 1871. Cf., *Sous le signe de l'Union* ... (Paris, 1948, ed. G. Courtois), a work which shows that the themes of Catholic Action were all expressed or foreseen during the previous seventy-five years.

dynamism of Christian life. From his first encyclical letter, '*E supremi apostolatus*' of 4 October 1903, Pius X was setting out the main lines of our Catholic Action; he often used that very expression, though generally only in the sense of activity of Catholics, or else specified as 'Catholic social action', thereby stressing that 'Catholic action [is] the practical solution of the social question according to Christian principles' ('*Il fermo proposito*', 1905). Everybody knows that Pius X called on the faithful to take their full part in the ecclesial activities of worship and sacramental life; and at the same time, whilst there was a Catholic revival among the cultured, the clergy found a new awareness of pastoral needs, especially in the cities, where very many people not only did not go near a church but had lost all contact, and the possibility of contact, with religion. H. Swoboda's book, *Grosstadt-Seelsorge* (1909), is hardly known in this country, so cut off from one another were Christian peoples then; but it was certainly the first of those documented analyses of the real state of the pastoral situation which have led to a re-examination of the actual structures and conditions of pastoral work. Swoboda was much concerned to point out the laity's place in the pastoral organisation of big towns, but he looked at it mainly in terms of reaching the scattered and lost sheep; to read him today is to realise what a change is represented by Catholic Action as defined and instituted by Pope Pius XI.

For that is what this great pope did. Up to his time there had been very many active Catholics—those of the nineteenth century will not be easily bettered as Christian personalities and men of enterprise; there had been activity of Catholics, in this sense, Catholic action (with a small 'a', as Jacques Maritain says): but Catholic Action was created by Pius XI. Certainly it had a continuity with what was in existence before; but it was also strongly influenced by contemporary circumstances. Not the least of these was shortage of clergy, and to hear some people talk one would think that if there had been enough priests the laity would have had nothing to do in the Church's apostleship. Actually, Pius XI's Catholic Action revived something fundamental in the Church, and led to the throwing open of the whole question of the laity. In contrast with what had existed before, three features in particular seem new: the insistence on the properly *apostolic* nature of Catholic Action; the generalised character of the appeal and the wide scope of a movement that was to include all categories; and the pronounced aspect of a *lay task*, corresponding to the Christian's engagement in the more clearly recognised secular field. Pius XI's Catholic Action thus went beyond all partial, accidental and peripheral considerations and touched the very heart of the laity's ecclesial status.

What Catholic Action Is

Pius XI's repeated definition of Catholic Action, which, he said, was not adopted without divine inspiration, was 'the participation of the laity in the hierarchical apostolate'. In seeking to determine the true meaning of this famous definition it goes without saying that the opinions here expressed commit no one but ourself and are subject to correction by competent authority.[5]

It seems to us that the philosophical look of the definition, with the word 'participation' taken from the vocabulary of metaphysics, for a time upset the understanding of a highly condensed formula. Some have been led to see in it an essential definition in which the important word is 'participation', indicating, with the rigour and fullness of a scholastic concept, that which formally constitutes Catholic Action. From this point of view, Catholic Action represents as it were an ecclesiastical order or office constituted by a new, creative 'participation'; as we shall see, the 'mandate', which certainly has its importance, was accordingly endowed with a quasi-sacramental value. In our opinion, the pope's formula was rather a descriptive definition, in which the word 'participation' indicated the fact of the laity taking its part in the needs and works of the Church; Catholic Action was constituted by the existence of this organised taking-part by the laity, sanctioned by the mandate, in the conditions that we shall see; it was less a sort of order or organisation than an activity, a co-operation, an organised whole of multiple activities and co-operations.

This is how Pius XI spoke of it, side by side with his striking formula, when he expounded his mind on the subject. He pointed out that Catholic Action in the first place is activity, the exercise and manifestation of a full, consistent Christian life, the activity of all Catholics in all ways in so far as it is properly religious (DC., pp. 21, 139, 150, 161, 163, 167, 168, etc.). As activity, Catholic Action excludes from its bounds purely devotional groupings, confraternities for prayer and the like (they are as it were preparatory); as properly religious activity, it excludes such authentic Catholic enterprises as professional associations or trade unions, since their aims are

[5] In the rest of this chapter the initials DC stand for *L'Action catholique: Traduction française des documents pontificaux*, 1922–1932 (Paris, 1933); TP stands for *L'Action catholique: Textes pontificaux classés et commentés* by E. Guerry (Paris, 1936). *Doc. cath.* is the periodical *Documentation catholique* (Bonne Presse, Paris).

temporal and secular. But it is in the first place the activity of Catholics, and only secondarily the organisation created for the co-ordination, support and discipline of this activity; more exactly still, the organisation of the whole, directly and expressly united with the episcopate in each country, and through the episcopate with the Holy See, each national church including a number of relevant societies and branch organisations.

Again, some have got a wrong idea from Pius XI's very strong insistence on the organisation of Catholic Action in every country and throughout the Catholic world; his mighty effort in this direction between 1925 and 1935 has left enthusiasts with an impression of a veritable creation. It is supposed that the pope created something entirely new. But in fact he never tired of repeating that 'Catholic Action is nothing but the help the laity brings to the apostolic work of the hierarchy. It has existed from the beginning of the Church, and today it takes new forms, better adapted to the present era' (DC., p. 387). Indications of the historical evidence for this have been given above in the preceding section. Had we elaborated our brief references to the nineteenth century and to the pontificate of St Pius X, it could have been easily shown that Catholic Action today was outlined and prepared then, even to its name. Pius XI hastened and completed a development that was already well advanced; he took over and gave life to the whole thing; he unified it and gave it a clear framework: he brought it to adulthood. His great work was indeed creative, as an empire-builder's is creative. But it was less the creation of something entirely new, constituted by 'participation' in the apostleship of the hierarchy, than the more efficient, active, official organisation of something already known and in operation—lay activity under episcopal direction in the fields of apostleship, of defence of the faith and of bringing the faith to bear on the whole of social life.

But Pius XI spoke of the faithful participating, taking their part, in the hierarchical apostolate. We must come to grips with that. What exactly are they participating in? Is it the apostolic mandate of the bishops, or is it rather the content and certain activities of the hierarchical apostolate? There is no doubt that Catholic Action is outside any participation in the constitutive functions and powers of the bishops (reserving what has been, and will be, said about the laity's part in the Church's prophetical function). 'Catholic Action is participation in the hierarchical apostolate, but not in the hierarchy itself', declared the German bishops (*Doc. cath.*, 1933, c. 913); and the French cardinals and archbishops, 'Catholic Action is not a participation by the laity in the power of the hierarchy in its function as magisterium' (*ibid.*, 1946, c. 741). There has never been any question that service of the Church and participation in the hierarchical apostolate through Catholic Action give lay people a place in the hierarchical ranks of the ministry and withdraw them from their lay condition or 'order'. They share in the activity of the ministry, not in its powers.[6]

Why then, and in what sense, is Catholic Action said to be participation in the *hierarchical* apostolate? According to the statements of Pius XI, what the adjective does is to qualify the noun in accordance with the following line of thought: (1) It is a matter of taking part in the authentic apostleship, that and no other, that continues our Lord's work and for which he sent out his Apostles (DC., p. 310; and cf. pp. 47, 150, 234). It is a participation in the Church's *own* mission, none other, which is defined by its object, namely, to communicate the stream of living water flowing from the Redemption, to bring about the reign of Christ Jesus (DC., pp. 248, 284, 306); (2) This mission was given to the Apostles, and it is the Church's mission everywhere and always, because the Church is apostolic and the mission as (at least in part) authority and the charisms of the Apostles are handed on in her through the succession of rightful pastors (DC., p. 310, and cf. pp. 119, 139 etc.); (3) Therefore Catholic Action has to be carried on in subordination to the bishops: in this third sense, too, linked with the first through the second, it is a participation in the hierarchical apostolate.[7]

If our explanation of Pius XI's formula is correct, it can be seen how Pius XII was able to replace the word 'participation' by 'cooperation', not only without altering but in fact clarifying the meaning put on participation by his predecessor. The fact is well known. As Cardinal Pacelli he spoke of 'co-apostolate of the laity'; as Pope Pius XII he freely used expressions designating Catholic Action as collaboration or help given to the apostleship of bishops and priests.[8] It is quite unjustified to see any lessened esteem for Catholic Action in this slight change of words, or to find it a reason for opposing Pius XII to Pius XI; for in fact Pius XI himself often used the word

[6] Cf. Cardinal A. G. Piazzi's commentary on the new statutes of Italian Catholic Action, quoted in R. M. Spiazzi, *La missione dei laici* (Rome, 1951), p. 200.

[7] Cf. the references given in (2), and DC, pp. 43, 66. For Pius XII, see *Doc. cath.*, 1951, c. 579.

[8] See the *Acta Apostolicae Sedis*, 1939, pp. 86, 142, etc.; 1940, pp. 367, 432; 1941, pp. 155–156; 1942, p. 237; 1943, p. 201; 1948, p. 398; and elsewhere. Cf., too, *Doc. cath.*, 1950, c.258; 1951, c.579.

'collaboration', sometimes simultaneously with 'participation', without showing any substantial difference between them.[9] We will therefore not enlarge on the sometimes contradictory interpretations of these words to be found in over-subtle commentaries; we are content to accept the different expressions of Catholic Action as help or collaboration as more clearly expressing the meaning we find in Pius XI's classic formula.

There is a head under which the *nuance* is not without importance, as touching not only a right notion of Catholic Action but also our estimate of the laity's position in relation to apostleship, and so of a crucial element in any theology of laity. Pius XII's definition brings into better relief something which Pius XI's declarations clearly set forth but which his definition by participation did not clearly confirm: namely, that Catholic Action reproduces, consecrates and gives new qualification to an apostleship already exercised by the faithful in virtue of their faith and the fervour of their Christian life; but that it does not confer on these faithful an absolutely new title of apostleship through participation in a mission which belongs to the hierarchy but not to the whole body. If 'participation' *constituted* an essentially new apostolic title which would be as it were episcopal property, 'the hierarchical apostolate' understood in this sense, we should have either to deny the faithful any apostolic title anterior to receiving the Catholic Action mandate, or else we should have to find a difference, not simply of quality but of kind, between the people's spontaneous apostolate and the hierarchical apostolate in which this mandate enables them to participate: and if so, what difference? On the other hand, to speak of co-operation with the apostolate, the pastoral mission, of bishops and priests gives a better picture of lay people, already destined apostles in virtue of the personal gifts of their baptism, their faith and charity, being called by the Church to integrate their activity into an organic effort, which is no longer so-and so's but the effort *of the Church herself*, in union with and subordination to the ministers divinely instituted as pastors. A lay apostleship exists, and has always existed, anterior to Catholic Action, and in some respects wider than Catholic Action, based on the sacramental and extra-sacramental gifts which make the Christian; in Catholic Action, and on the new basis of its mandate, this apostleship is raised to the level of a fully ecclesial activity.

The first of these statements is borne out by the facts, by the biblical and traditional texts we have quoted, and by pontifical

[9] See A.A.S., 1930, p. 581; 1932, pp. 177–178; 1934, p. 586; DC., 1931, pp. 283–284, 308, 312; TP., pp. 14, 15, 152–153; etc.

documents. These last and their commentators (*e.g.*, TP., pp. 256ff.) show that Christians are pledged to bear witness and to help their neighbours to be disciples of Jesus Christ: pledged first by baptism, which makes them members of the mystical Body, solicitous for the growth of the body (TP., pp. 58–59); then by charity, which enables us to recognise our living neighbour and to look after him for God's sake (DC., p. 392; A.A.S., 1942, p. 248); then by confirmation, which makes us soldiers of Christ, charged with the common good of the holy City, fellow-fighters in the battle for his reign (TP., pp. 58–59); pledged, too, by our gratitude and thankfulness to the Redeemer (TP., pp. 58, 263), by the spiritual endowments given us for the benefit of all, by the circumstances which lead us, in faithfulness to ourselves, to testify before others. These are the heads of Christian life pure and simple, and on each of them every true *fidelis* is called to apostleship, an apostleship which is, in the words of Cardinal G. Pizzardo, 'generic and varied', that is, both without precise qualification and as wide and diversified as it could be. In this context, every faithful Christian can and ought to adopt the magnificent saying of John Wesley, 'I look upon all the world as my parish'.

People thus apostolically engaged have naturally tended to organise themselves into groups, and very many societies have come into existence, within a parish or in a bigger field or sometimes purely privately. Such groups were engaged in Christian, therefore Catholic, activity; but they were not yet Catholic Action. There are still many groups, of young married people or professional men, for instance, that are not properly Catholic Action formations.

All this stays, and in a way furnishes the matter of Catholic Action. Pius XI wrote to Cardinal Van Roey that Catholic Action 'is nothing but the apostolate of the faithful who, under episcopal guidance, put themselves at the Church's service and help her integrally to fulfill her pastoral ministry' (DC., p. 43). So Catholic Action exists when the apostleship of the faithful puts itself under the direct guidance of the bishops, to work for the objects which they appoint in the way they determine, so as to assist and complete their episcopal activity, instead of the work being done in fits and starts, without direction, here and there, as a matter of private enterprise alone. In its nature and foundations, Catholic Action is basically a continuation of that apostolate *ex spiritu* which is the spontaneous act of all truly Christian life, but new qualification is added: as a title to apostleship, the mandate; as to the quality of the Church's activity, it becomes a matter of public law.

The foundation is always baptism, charity, confirmation, thankfulness, spiritual gifts received. Several of the texts referring to these matters cited earlier refer also to Catholic Action, and some of them particularly insist on confirmation:[10] some theologians even see it as 'the Catholic Action sacrament'. Real support for this idea can be found in the classical theology of confirmation, especially in scholastic systematisations. St Thomas sees in confirmation both a sacrament which completes the *fidelis* as a Christian and as one of the consecrations which settle and arrange the various 'offices' in the Church. Catechisms say this sacrament makes us 'perfected Christians', that is, finished members, *active* members, of the Church. From the first point of view, confirmation marks the young Christian's passage from living in and for himself to living in society (*Sum. theol.*, III, q. lxxii, a. 2); from the second (connected with the first), the confirmed Christian is invested with a certain social mission of witness to and defence of the faith. These are profoundly evangelical conceptions, emphasising that we cannot progress in Christian life without living for others and accepting responsibility in the Church militant. St Thomas, who does not use strong expressions without reason, goes so far as to show the confirmed person as being constituted a defender and witness of the faith 'quasi ex officio';[11] so that, conformably with what has been said in Chapter I of Part Two, the Christian is qualified for general Christian life pure and simple by baptism, and for certain activities of the Church by other sacraments, which constitute him in offices or ministries: by confirmation for the Church's militant life, by holy order for the hierarchical ministry of sacred things.

From the background of St Thomas, the three consecratory sacraments of baptism, confirmation and order being diverse progressive participations in Christ's priesthood, we can see why Pius XI and the theologians present Catholic Action as an exercise of the royal priesthood of the faithful (DC., p. 9; A.A.S., 1937, p. 191). In fact, it is easy here to apply what we have said about the priesthood of the faithful, especially in its aspect of including that service of the Gospel whereby one can lead another to offer himself to God as a sacrifice

[10] This is supposed to be a classical point, but the pontifical texts do not emphasise it. Cf., TP., p. 58, and Cardinal Faulhaber, quoted by M. Laros in *Pfingstgeist über uns* (Regensburg, 1935), pp. 67–68.

[11] Principal references: *IV Sent.*, d.25; q.1, a.1, sol. et ad 4; *Sum. theol.*, III, q.lxxii, a.2, 4, 5, 9 ('confirmatus accipit potestatem publice fidem Christi verbis profitendi, quasi ex officio'). We have already noticed that some medieval theologians associated prophecy (witness) with confirmation.

'sanctified in the Holy Spirit' (Romans xv, 16): a 'spiritual' priest-hood, without 'powers', just as there is a 'prophetism' of life in the Holy Spirit, without authority. These ideas are now familiar.

In Catholic Action proper, there is a new title, additional to these fundamental ones—the mandate. This word and its meaning aroused considerable discussion in France, which in 1946 brought a state-ment from the French cardinals and archbishops: 'The word "man-date", appearing in some documents of the Holy See and the French episcopate, was seen suitably to describe the relations of the hierarchy with the organised laity'. The word in fact figures in only a few Roman documents: not to *define* Catholic Action by an idea of dele-gation, but to designate one of the elements whereby the laity in Catholic Action is co-ordinated with and subordinated to the hierarchy.[12]

It would be an exaggeration, in our opinion a formal deviation, to turn this mandate into a means of complete subordination, whereby the laity in Catholic Action would be no more than a tool, conjoined but inanimate: 'the *longa manus* of the ecclesiastical hierarchy'.[13] This would be practically to confuse Catholic Action with its organisa-tion, and to forget that it is the organisation of an already living apostleship, one grounded in the deepest realities of Christian life. It would also be to ignore that, while Catholic Action is a lay movement subject to the hierarchy like any other activity in the Church, and subordinated to the bishops in its specific existence as an apostolic movement, its subordination is of a kind befitting faithful people endowed with intelligence, who have abilities and a sense of Chris-tian responsibility, and who are fit to conduct their own enterprises. The cardinals and archbishops of France spoke quite clearly: 'Mem-bers of Catholic Action movements are not lay curates. . . . So far from impairing the dignity of their proper mission as lay people or altering its nature, the mandate gives official value and public character in the Church to this organised lay apostolate, without its ceasing to be lay' (*Doc. cath.*, 1946, cc. 741, 744).

It would be equally an exaggeration to represent the hierarchical mandate as a sort of sacramental thing creative of a kind of lay order,

[12] Cf. Pius XI's letters to Cardinal Bertram (A.A.S., 1928, p. 385), where the context shows that 'mandate' is there used in the sense of 'mission', and to Cardinal Schuster (A.A.S., 1934, p. 586). Cf. also DC., pp. 218, 227; TP., p. 64; and Cardinal Pizzardo, reported in *La Croix*, 19 October 1947.

[13] Mgr L. Civardi, *Manuel d'Action catholique* (Brussels, 1936), p. 99. What we object to is the idea of a 'lay hand' which is held and moved by the clergy as a human arm uses a stick. Pope Pius XII spoke otherwise to the congress of laity in 1951: 'We understand the comparison in this sense, that ecclesiastical superiors use the 'hand'] in the way that the Creator and Lord uses rational creatures.'

having its *ex opere operato* and inspiring a veritable '*mystique*' fed on mistaken applications of notions that are often disputable. Good intentions apart, there are here real and serious dangers of departing from the very conception of Catholic Action, and these spoil whatever may be good and right in the ideas themselves. This view encourages the belief that the apostolic mission is strictly proper and personal to the hierarchy, whose mandate conveys a part of it to this or that group of organised and directed lay people, who up to that moment are without apostolic mission. We have explained why we believe such an interpretation to be wrong. It gives a meaning to the word 'participation' which is not that of the pontifical documents; it leads to a practical denial of all the apostolic titles attached to being a Christian; it takes no account of the popes' insistence that Catholic Action is as old as the Church, or of the past hundred years of history; and, instead of recognising that the laity have a mission of their own, co-operative with and complementary to that of priests, it improperly attributes to them a share in the mission of bishops.

This is not at all another way of saying that the mandate is nothing and does nothing. It adds to the titles of mission *ex spiritu* a new title, of which we may say, as St Thomas did of the witness of those confirmed, that it is *quasi ex officio*. If people join together of their own accord to exert Christian activity *ex spiritu* on the basis of the baptismal and confirmatory consecration, of faith and charity and spiritual gifts, their activity is that of Christians *in* the Church; it is not properly speaking activity *of* the Church; we might say that it remains a matter of private law. But it can become a matter of public law, an activity of the Church herself, if it be 'instituted' by an hierarchical intervention and call. This may come about in two ways: either by a call to the priestly ministry, followed by a consecration conferring ministerial powers and participation in the mandate, functions and powers of the hierarchy; or by a call to Catholic Action, which leaves the lay man a lay man, even requiring him to be such. In either case, the gifts of God, an attraction, perhaps an inward voice or providential circumstances, have brought about a call within; in either case, the call has to be sanctioned and completed in its own line by an hierarchical act which makes it a vocation having public status in the Church. Enrolment and receiving the insignia are analogous to being clothed with the habit, or to religious profession or the tonsure: they turn a spontaneous personal resolution into a state acknowledged by the Church.

Religious life under vows comes in usefully here as an illustration.

The relation of mandated Catholic Action to free personal apostleship has an analogy in the relation of the religious life, under vows according to an approved rule, to a personal religious life led in the spirit of the counsels. Public vows are neither virtuousness nor the call to perfection; but they ratify and provide for them in a publicly recognised state of life. In Ch. I of Pt. Two we came across something similar in worship. We remarked that there is the spontaneous prayer of the faithful, which remains private prayer, originating from below, even if a number meet together for it; and there is sacramental worship as such, celebrated by the hierarchical priesthood in a form given from above. But we noticed how the hierarchical priesthood, by adopting, directing and dedicating the prayer of the faithful, introduces an intermediate form between private and sacramental worship, public prayer, to which corresponds the priest's function as leader of prayer. Catholic Action is something like that. It too is constituted both from below and above: from below, in that it is the work of the spontaneous apostleship of the faithful banding together for different works; from above, in that it is this apostolate adopted, directed and properly instituted by the hierarchy as an extension, complement and aid to its own task.

This is where the mandate comes in: not as a kind of sacrament or ordination of lay people, but as one of the means—juridically the decisive means—by which their external Christian activity is organically articulated with the apostolic hierarchy and becomes properly an activity of the Church.[14] That is why we agree with those authors who think it right to interpret Catholic Action as the form of lay apostolic activity that has been made a matter of the Church's public law, and therefore, as a whole, an activity and a good of the Church. That is why, particularly during his struggle with fascist totalitarianism, Pius XI declared on several occasions that to touch Catholic Action was to touch the Church herself, and why the freedom of Catholic Action was stipulated by him in several concordats.

As well as answering to the meaning of Catholic Action and its definitive texts, this way of looking at it seems to correspond to the law governing the Church's apostolic life as found in the New Testament. There is an instituted apostleship in which the Church's apostolic mission exists in its fullness; those who have received its charge are, by excellence, the Apostles and their heirs and successors:

[14] Catholic Action is *one* mode of articulation of the *ordo laicorum* with the *ordo hierarchicus*; there are others, spoken of herein with reference to the priesthood and prophecy of the laity.

it is the apostleship of the hierarchy. By the fact of being living members of the Church, the faithful are called to do her work and so to share in the apostolic function, one in its content and end, existing firstly and fully in the hierarchy. The faithful can do this, simply, *ex spiritu*, on their own account, subject to the apostolic ministry as in any other Christian activity. But their co-operation can also be expressly ratified and directed, provided for and organised, by the apostolic hierarchy; the faithful are then more closely associated with the Church's apostolic mission, being expressly associated in some sense with the mission of the bishops themselves. To their general mission *ex spiritu*—specified for each individual by his abilities and circumstances—there is added a certain juridical title, a mission *quasi ex officio*; and this apostolate being as it were 'instituted', is recognised by the hierarchy, which makes use of it, directing and supervising it closely. The mission *ex spiritu*, whereby the *fidelis* already has some part in the Church's apostolic charge, is then carried out in a certain association, recognised and approved by the Church, with the mission of the Apostles, with that charge considered as instituted by the Lord—but without receiving the powers of the ministry.

*   *   *

The notion of Catholic Action and its mandate will become clearer if we try more exactly to see its mission in face of the hierarchical mission.

The kind of internal general mission which every Christian has as a Christian, *ex spiritu*, is very indeterminate indeed, except, in ways partly unforeseeable, by each one's state of life and the circumstances in which Providence has placed him. Circumstances have been referred to in the previous chapter; we must consider state of life and its duties here and in the next chapter.

The external mission, conferred by the hierarchy on priests and lay people according to their order, is at the same time both vague and specific. The priestly mission is to exert the ministry of the objective means of salvation, for which sacred powers have been given them, and to strengthen and guide the members of the community of faith, hope and charity, in accordance with the Church's two aspects, as institution of the means of grace and as community of *agape*. For bishops and their ministerial collaborators, the parochial clergy, their apostolic mission is precise and clear, in that they are given charge of a definite area and its inhabitants; but their mission is vague and uncertain in that it relates to an undifferentiated collection of people. The mission of Catholic Action is just the opposite. It

is not associated with a charge and a collation of powers, but presupposes personal spiritual gifts, and simply resumes the mission *ex
spiritu*, without altering its objects or the qualifications with which it
acts; it is exercised in the order of Christian life, in its collective
conditions and ordinary working. It too is both vague and specific:
vague, in that it is not directed towards the inhabitants of a definite
area; specific, in that it relates to a determined *milieu*, of a particular condition and with differentiated human needs.[15]

It may perhaps be added that these two missions correspond to the
modes of participation in the messianic energies of Christ, by the
hierarchy on the one hand, by the body of the faithful on the other.
The priestly mandate is fixed and clear because it has reference to a
given people over whom the Church has jurisdiction and pastoral
authority; the mandate of Catholic Action has reference to a sphere
upon which the Church acts more by influence than by using her
powers: it is associated, 'not with the functions and authority of the
hierarchy but with its pastoral care and apostolic activity'.[16] The
Church has jurisdiction only over men as such; but she has also an
apostolic charge of influence in regard to *milieux* and institutions.
Much of this charge is incumbent on the laity of Catholic Action,
organised in their different movements. We say *laity* and *movements*;
for while the internal spontaneous mission is personal, while the
priest's mission is individual, that of Catholic Action is collective:
'the mandate', declared the French archbishops, 'is given to the
movement', for the exercise of Christian influence in a particular
sector of life. This particularised direction does not alter every
Christian's personal mission with respect to every other man; but it
does consecrate the relative providential determining of the mission
ex spiritu by position, occupation, circumstances, abilities and actual
possibilities of service. Each man and woman has his own irreplaceable job in this great network of brotherly intercourse, wherein
all may be co-operators with God. The whole world is upheld and

[15] The old world, before the days of democracy and, especially, industrialisation,
had a very strong communal sense: human beings were really one people. The
modern world has added, or substituted, a sociological differentiation and conditioning that are much more determinate. That accounts for the new consciousness,
over the past century or so, of man's social dimension and new conditions of life on
a socio-economic basis; these characterise the 'christianisable' mankind for whom
the apostolic ministry works. The emergence of an apostolic mission not determined
by a given territory but by conditions of life is a matter of the greatest moment to
clergy as well as laity, particularly in Catholic Action. Cf. the last section of this
chapter.

[16] Mgr E. Guerry in *Catholicisme*, vol. i (Paris, 1948), c.99. The mandate of the
hierarchical priesthood involves the exercise of powers, therefore of rights; the
Catholic Action mandate involves the exercise of influence and of duties rather
than rights.

served by men in their totality. Christianly speaking, the world is given the fullness of all it can receive from Christ only through the efforts of all those people whom the Lord has put in it and endowed with diverse gifts and callings for the doing of his work therein.

Thus we find a new application of an idea already familiar, the idea expressed by St John Chrysostom, that the laity form the priestly *pleroma* of the bishop. In many passages Chrysostom takes it for granted that bishop and priest share the exercise of their pastoral charge with the laity, that their work is extended and fulfilled in this way. We have given some examples earlier in this chapter, and we saw in Part Two Chapter I that churchmen of the weight of Pope St Leo the Great, St Gregory of Tours, St Peter Damian and Cardinal Pole attributed a priestly quality to kings and princes who shared the priestly solicitude of the pastors. In reference to Catholic Action, popes have spoken as follows.

By an altogether special grace of God, [those who work in Catholic Action] are called to a ministry little different from the priestly ministry; for fundamentally Catholic Action is simply the apostleship of the faithful, who, guided by their bishops, bring their assistance to God's Church and in a certain way perfect her pastoral ministry (Pius XI; DC., pp. 43, 56).

The resources of numerous clergy will indeed be greatly augmented if, side by side with them, there are serried groups of tried and trusted lay people on whom priests can rely to prepare for and complement their work, and even to take their place, when that is necessary in certain fields, for instance, religious instruction (Pius XI; A.A.S., 1936, p. 160).

Apostolic work, carried on in the spirit of the Church, so to speak consecrates the lay man and makes him a minister of Christ, in the sense St Augustine explains (Pius XII; A.A.S., 1939, p. 444. The Augustinian reference is to *In evang. Joan.*, tr. 51, n. 13).

And you members of Catholic Action, you form as it were one single thing with the bishop and the pope (Pius XII; *Osserv. Rom.*, 6 May 1951).

Pastoral reality illustrates these official statements. Everywhere the pastoral position demands, and doubtless will demand more and more, that the work of the Gospel be considered as belonging not to the clergy alone but to the clergy and laity together; that the actual situation in a given country at a given moment may require that whole slices of apostolic and even pastoral activity be entrusted to lay people;[17] and that the nature of the apostolic undertaking itself requires it. It is not simply because of the shortage of clergy, or of any clerical inadequacy; it is because there is a qualitative insufficiency in the pastoral field, an intrinsic ineffectiveness in the apostolic set-up, if the laity is not organically associated in the work of the Gospel—not just a few of the laity, 'safe people', but the Christian laity taken as a whole. On the one hand, the sociological conditions of life, its removal from and independence of a local, 'ecological' framework, means that men cannot be properly reached unless the integral human whole be touched—and that can be done only by the action of lay people; on the other hand, catechetical formation seems bound to remain academic, abstract, to give an impression of unreality and artificiality, if it be confined solely to the priest ('the schoolmaster for religion') and has no support in the home and no background of a whole parish concerned in the work of the Gospel.[18] 'So the priest's apostolic task is clear', wrote Cardinal Suhard, 'Confronted by men and women to be saved, he does not say "I", but "We"! The full artificer of evangelisation is neither simply the baptised person nor the priest alone, but the Christian community. The basic cell of apostleship, its unit of measurement, is everywhere, like a sort of "organic compound", the inseparable two-fold of priesthood-laity.'

In the language of the Schools the word 'subject' designates the person from whom an activity emanates and on whom there falls a charge or responsibility. Can one go so far as to say that the pair priesthood-laity forms alone the adequate subject of Christian apostleship in this exact sense? After the renewal of the idea of the Church in German Catholic romanticism during the first half of last century, several writers of pastoral theology did not hesitate to answer Yes: theologians such as A. Graf and J. Amberger defined pastoral work as an activity of the whole Church, expressly including all the faithful. We think so too, and the idea seems to be found on more than one page of the *Directoire pour la Pastorale des Sacrements* issued by the French episcopate in 1951, with an explanation added that was not outside the thought of Graf and Amberger. We should

[17] This is one of the conclusions drawn from pastoral experience under the Nazi regime. Cf. *Aufbau im Widerstand: Ein Seelsorgebericht aus Oesterreich 1938–1945* (Salzburg, 1947).

[18] See L. Rétif, *Catéchisme et mission ouvrière* . . . (Paris, 1950), particularly pp. 264ff., 420, 425ff. 'The true scope of parochial catechetics provides an indispensable role for the laity: they create a Christian community without which all catechetical formation is half useless' (p. 265). [What Father Congar says about religious instruction confined solely to the priest would seem to apply also to that given by teaching religious of both sexes and by lay schoolteachers as such.—*Translator's note*.]

not speak of the priesthood *and* of the laity as forming a single subject of the exercise of government, for that requires authority and power; or as forming a single priestly subject, in as much as the priesthood involves power to consecrate the eucharist; or as forming a single subject of prophecy, in that this involves an authority of magisterium and a charism of infallibility for the explanation of the meaning of Revelation. The hierarchy alone, which is bound up with priesthood, is the subject of the messianic energies communicated to the Church under the form of *powers*. On the other hand, we do speak of the priesthood *and* of the laity as a single subject of the exercise of Christian life and of the activities it includes: spiritual kingship; inward priesthood and, in the sense we have explained, sacramental priesthood; prophecy as life in the knowledge of God; apostleship and, in this sense, pastoral care. The whole Church, and as concerns daily life the whole parish, is the subject of the activities of worship and charity, of apostolic and missionary activities, of those of catechetics and religious instruction.[19] Remembering all the time that priesthood and laity are not on the same plane, even for those things that they do together: and this not simply that the one has powers that the other has not, but because their duties are different—and complementary.

The Duty of Catholic Action

It cannot be denied that apostleship is an obligation laid on every Christian by his baptism and by charity. Therefore any tendency to identify Catholic Action with apostleship itself means a tendency to impose a universal obligation of being an apostle in the ranks of Catholic Action.

If we again examine the pontifical texts we find certain statements that, materially, do not exactly coincide: some speak of an *élite* of the faithful, people who are objects of a particular grace, chosen and called; others seem to include every work, every Christian activity, 'every Catholic'. It is not to be supposed that the Holy See contradicts itself, so it is necessary to try to reconcile these texts.

As in many documents emanating from the hierarchy, doctrinal instruction is mixed with pastoral direction. When they speak from the second point of view, it is not surprising that there should be some diversity, for the external forms of Catholic Action, its organisations and the needs they serve, vary from country to country

[19] See, respectively, Fr H. C. Chéry on the work of the Abbé Remilleux, the writings of the Abbé Michonneau, and the Abbé Rétif, *op. cit.*

and at different times in the same country. That, no doubt, is one of the reasons why Pius XI and Pius XII generally chose to formulate their instructions in letters addressed to a national episcopate, to the president of a Catholic Action organisation, to a congress, to a group of pilgrims, involving the burdensome necessity of speaking to each according to its particular needs.

In the more theoretical texts, it is clear that materially divergent passages—where there are any—are not referring to precisely the same thing. Sometimes they speak of Catholic action, that is, of Christian apostleship in general, and it is to be expected that that should be referred to as an obligation of all Christian life. Sometimes they speak of Catholic Action proper, juridically adopted movements and organisations; and if a strict obligation is there stated, it would be an obligation created by the Church in the name of her power of spiritual government, whereas in the first case she simply declares an obligation of divine law in the name of her magisterium.

In the light of these elementary distinctions, the chief pontifical texts seem to make three principal affirmations. (1) All are called. Called to Christian activity and to the apostolate in general, yes; but also, in principle, to engage in the works and movements of Catholic Action: that, said Pius XI, is one of the primary duties of Christian life (DC., pp. 7, 28; TP., p. 266). We say 'in principle', because all are not called in the same way or with the same urgency: each must respond 'according to his opportunities . . . where there are no opportunities, the obligation ceases', as Pius XI declared (DC., p. 63; TP., pp. 24, 264–265). (2) When one is fighting in its ranks, Catholic Action is found to be 'activity in the perfection and fullness of Christianity, in accordance with Christ's will expressed in the Church's legislation' (Pius XI; DC., p. 90; TP., p. 13). (3) If Catholic Action includes the totality of the faithful in law and as a possibility (DC., pp. 47–48; TP., p. 10), in fact it is made up of a large number of faithful whose moral qualities and will to serve Christ make them belong to that *élite* of which pontifical texts speak. In fact, Catholic Action does not cover the whole area of apostleship and Christian activity.

If 'call' be understood, not as general aim and ideal principle, but as actual duty, taking account of circumstances and personal factors, it cannot be said that all are called to take part in Catholic Action and that they are necessarily at fault if they do not do so. And in Catholic Action itself there are 'many mansions'. . . . Pope Pius XII made the position quite clear at the Congress of Laity in 1951, after the above had been written: there is a universal obligation to apostleship in the wide sense, but not to the specific apostolate of Catholic Action.

FORMS OF CATHOLIC ACTION

Catholic Action is not a uniform, monolithic, unchangeable construction; it is a whole made up of varied, adaptable and alterable organisations in which the ineluctable apostleship of the laity and of Christian activity are in part exerted. This must be borne in mind if one is to avoid an undue maximising of the institution, practical disappointments, and a certain confusion in face of official declarations which, as has just been explained, are purposely many and varied. Even looked at in its most general aspect, its common denominator, Catholic Action is very diverse, with various possibilities and opportunities for its members.

Aspects of Catholic Action

Pius XI often stressed that Catholic Action is first a school of personal formation, and then of activity (DC., pp. 309–310; TP., pp. 33–34). The need for serious formation and training is so obvious and has been so often discussed that there is no need to insist on it here. It is in the pastoral field of the clergy that there are new and urgent matters to be discussed. The development, the blessed development, of Christian activity among lay people has added heavy burdens to the priestly ministry, and it has also raised difficult problems, of which the extent is far from being fully appreciated. Things would be easy if lay Catholic Action had simply left the priest to his sacred duties, the sacraments, preaching, charity in its many forms; but it has opened out new aspects of his role as educator and spiritual trainer, and has enlarged and complicated his duties in this matter to a remarkable degree.

It begins with the young people, and even the children, for the age of catechism, school and scouting is also the age of awakening to a sense of Christian responsibility. The great problem over which many priests stumble is the passing from the levels of childhood and adolescence, with their own difficulties and needs, to the level of adults, with theirs. It has been well put that, 'One of the greatest obstacles to Catholic Action is the survival among adults of a child's mentality, of ways of doing things and of a spirituality such as are imparted to the young. . . . Perhaps we have put too much trust in the belief that it is enough to train young people as such, that is, as if they will never grow up, and to ensure a stagnating perseverance afterwards.'[20]

[20] P. Durosoy, in *Écho de l'USIC. Responsables*, May–July 1948, p. 134.

Catholic Action of the young is governed by awareness of the demand for Christian activity and of the need for initiation into the huge problems it is up against. This youthful Catholic Action is not artificial: it is a true apostolate, and it is concerned with real problems, those proper to youth, of course, but there is also realistic initiation into those raised by the society in which they live and have to work. But Catholic Action for youth is necessarily more synthetic than that of adults; young people's life is less particularised, and their consciousness of the problems of Christian activity needs to encounter the ideal of that activity in an inspiring and adequate form.

The commitments of youth can be subjectively as serious as those of grown-ups, but the latter collide more roughly with solid realities. Adults are better at differentiating between things; they are more engrossed, hurt, beaten down by life; they have perhaps lost their ambitions, but they have a better idea of the worth of a limited activity, commonplace and small, no doubt, but real. It is not everybody who can get to work on the social structures; for many, Catholic Action must consist in bearing witness by one's life, by the word as opportunities occur, by an irreproachable professional record, and in the different established Christian services, whether parochial or in a wider field.

Different Possibilities

From the beginning, by its very nature, it has been possible for Catholic Action to develop along two lines, or more exactly on two planes, which are far from being opposed but are quite different: missionary activity and action on structures.

Evangelisation, apostleship proper, that is, whatever a believer can do to bring another person into the obedience of the faith, is an essential object of Catholic Action. Time and again pontifical utterances have solemnly declared this aim, the salvation of souls, the reign of God, the evangelisation of the world, the communication to others of the riches of the Redemption. There is then in the very forefront of Catholic Action a realisation by the *fidelis* of his responsibility in respect of every one of his neighbours; of what he can be and do for the personal destiny of others, where the relationship of a soul with God, *sola cum Solo*, is grounded in faith. That has an absolute primacy. And that is what the Gospel is interested in: 'What shall it profit a man if he gain the whole world, and lose his soul?'

Pontifical documents accordingly put the word, witness, among the first means of Catholic Action, a day-by-day observance of Christ's command to preach the Gospel to every creature (DC., pp. 103, 141, 310; TP., p. 41, etc.). Pius XI liked to present Catholic Action as working for a much-needed 're-evangelisation' in the same way that Christianity was spread at its beginning: he saw Catholic Action as 'the renewal and continuation of what took place in the first days of Christianity, of the earliest proclamation of our Lord's kingdom', when 'officials, soldiers, women, children' took part in 'this work of penetrating everywhere, among the people at large as well as in Caesar's palace' (D.C., pp. 146, 150). In those days Christianity was spread to a large extent by personal contacts, the faith that radiated from one soul taking root in another, something like the process that gardeners call 'layering'. We have noticed above how Andrew brought in Peter, Philip brought in Nathanael, the Samaritan woman told her neighbours, the other Philip converted the eunuch of Queen Candace; a whole study could be made of early Christianity from this point of view, and it could be carried on down to our own day.

This purely apostolic aspect of Catholic Action must not be mini-mised, nor its primacy in principle overlooked. As for how it is actually exercised, vocations and charisms are diverse: every man is responsible in respect of God's will for and call to himself. There must always be a missionary *mystique* in Catholic Action formations. The contemporary Church has made some very fine experiments in this matter and has been given missionary graces that put responsi-bilities upon all Christians. In one country alone, the names of such as Godin, Loew, Michonneau, Depierre, Voillaume, the Mission de France, the Mission de Paris, and the message of the *turba magna* of the nameless and obscure, ought to mean something to us.

Conversion is always a personal process; souls are converted by ones, just as they come into the world and go out of it to judgement by ones, as Cardinal Vaughan once put it. He was writing with reference to the idea of a corporate reunion of the Anglican Church; and as a matter of fact, the problem of oecumenism in face of a mis-sionary effort bent on individual conversions has a certain parallel in the problem of Catholic Action working on the structural plane in face of an individual apostolate 'angling'. We believe that in either case *both* lines of action are valid, necessary and willed by God. We personally feel called to oecumenical work, but we do not depreciate the missionary work of conversion. May it always have its place in Catholic Action, and that place the first!

But the mission of Catholic Action has always required a wider outlook than that of individual conversions alone. It was inevitable that an organised collective apostolate, strongly attracted in the missionary direction, should be ambitious to 'conquer' the whole of a given *milieu* for Christ. When one has sung a few times with a body of Young Christian Workers that 'We will make our brothers Christian again; by Jesus Christ we swear it', one is in no mood to be sceptical about the quality of these ambitions of the creative years. Thanks especially to Catholic Action's inquiry method, it was soon found that a *'milieu'* was quite another thing from the aggregate of men in a given category. Every inquiry showed more clearly how much the social aspect was a dimension of man himself. Certainly the individual man answers to the bare definition of 'reasoning animal', but when he is severed from his normal social relations he is incapable of fully actualising it: that is plain enough when one meets children who have never known a home or convicts cut off from society for years on end. Man's development, even spiritual—no, especially spiritual—is deeply conditioned by the *milieu* in which he lives, here meaning by *milieu* the structures and institutions beyond his social group, the totality of relations and involvements determined by the general set-up, laws, material conditions, social pressure.

'To ease social pressure, to influence it and make it propitious to the flourishing of Christian life, to use it to create an atmosphere and background in which men can develop their human qualities . . . in which Christians can breathe comfortably': those are the terms in which Cardinal Saliège proposed to define Catholic Action, and many others have put it in a similar way. In the days of 'Christendom', when the whole of life was conducted in accordance with the Church's teaching on man's spiritual good, social structures, institutions and influence were expressly favourable to faith. What Christian kings and princes did in feudal times must, in our modern feudalism, be done by social groups and influences,[21] by the personal service and effect of convinced and able men of faith on this social environment of neighbourhood, classes, leisure, culture, cinema, radio and the rest. An integral apostolate, one that faces the real dimensions of the contemporary problem of faith, realises that it has not simply to deliver the Christian message but to stir up an inclination to listen to and accept it, and then to stick to it and live it. In the modern world, apologetics has had to give attention to subjective preparation and to expounding the palatability of the faith; as a buttress to her dogmatic teaching, the Church's magisterium has had to undertake a defence of reason and the establishing of *praeambula*

---

[21] Modern feudalism: see J. Leclerq, *Essai sur l'Action catholique* (Brussels, 1928), especially p. 18.

fidei [HH]. In the same way, Christian apostleship has to make use of kinds of *praeambula apostolatus*, the preparation, defence, 'disinfecting' of men in their secular social structures, in their actual life as persons, so that the faith may strike root, grow and bear fruit.

And when the Church has achieved her task, mankind will take responsibility for itself and its affairs. The injured man who was picked up on the road from Jerusalem to Jericho left the inn to which he had been carried, and everything paid in advance, grateful, no doubt, but glad to be walking on his own feet. . . . Schools, hospitals, institutions of all sorts—Western civilisation is made up of things taken over or created by the Church and then handed over, full of health, to the world of men. Some people see this as an historical process of secular things returning to their secular state, and want the Church to give up concerning herself with them. Is not this perhaps to ask to have the finale in the first act, and to dispense with the effect that one can have on the other?

Anyway, the need for christianising the *milieu* leads to specialised Catholic Action, influenced by the two features of that *milieu*: collectivity of persons, a whole made up of structures, conditions and connexions bringing about a social pressure. This orientation of Catholic Action is required by the realism of its apostolic outlook, and it is fully justified doctrinally both by explicit papal declarations and by the nature of things and the Church's mission.

Emphasising the essentially religious concern of Catholic Action, Pius XI showed how, displaying a fully Christian life among the faithful, it brings Christianity to wherever they live and work (DC., pp. 47–49, 303, 313). In particular, said the pope, Catholic Action, without meddling in party politics, trains people to a Christian pattern and enables them to become good servants of the political common good, good magistrates and officials, and the like (DC., pp. 92, 101, 116–117). Shining with the redemptive grace active in Catholicism, it is thus a principle of renewal and well-being for family, school and state. It is, Pius XI often declared, the remedy for 'the plague of laicism' which seeks to confine religion to personal feelings and conscience. This pope, however, argued less from a theology of the relations between nature and grace than from the needs of religious defence and the charity that demands a concern for human society. Pius XII gives more attention to the idea that God's reign matters in all the affairs of men, that it would be a misunderstanding and disembodiment of the supernatural to make it wholly transcendent and outside earthly life; that, on the contrary, Christianity ought to be a principle of health, stability and unity in that life. This is what he said to the newly-made cardinals on 20 February 1946.

In carrying out the mandate of her divine Founder to spread throughout the world and conquer every creature for the Gospel, the Church is not an empire, especially in the imperialist sense that word ordinarily has nowadays. Her progress and expansion is in the opposite direction to that of modern imperialism. Before all else she progresses in depth, only thereafter in extent. In the first place she seeks man himself, using all her endeavours to form and fashion him, to perfect the divine likeness in him. She does her work in each one's heart, but it affects the whole of life and every individual activity. In men thus formed, the Church prepares a secure foundation for human society. Modern imperialism is just the opposite: it seeks extension and size. It is not interested in man as such, but in what he can be used for; and this means that imperialism carries germs that endanger the basis of the human community. . . . The Church works in the innermost part of man, of man in his personal dignity as a free being and, infinitely higher, a child of God. The Church forms this man and brings him up, for he only—complete in the harmony of his natural and supernatural life, in the ordered development of his instincts and inclinations, of his high qualities and varied aptitudes—he only is at the same time the origin and end of social life, and therefore the principle of its equilibrium.

. . . Again it is the Church who can treat and heal such a wound. And again she does it by going to the depths of the human being and putting him at the centre of all social order. Now this human being is not man in the abstract or man considered solely in the order of pure nature, but man complete, as he is in the eyes of God, his Creator and Redeemer, as he is in his actual historical reality, which cannot be lost sight of without compromising the normal economy of the human community. . . .

And now, what are the consequences of all that for the Church? Today more than ever she must live her mission; more energetically than ever she must repulse this narrow and false conception of her spirituality and inward life which would keep her, blind and dumb, in the recesses of the sanctuary. The Church cannot shut herself up, inactive, in the privacy of her churches and thus neglect the mission entrusted to her by divine Providence, the mission to form man in his fullness and so ceaselessly to collaborate in building the solid basis of society. This mission is of her essence.

Looking at her from this point of view, it can be said that the Church is the society of those who, under the supernatural influence of grace, in the perfection of their personal dignity as sons of God and in the harmonious development of every human inclination and energy, build up the mighty framework of the community of men.

From this aspect, Venerable Brethren, the faithful, and more precisely the laity, are in the front line of the Church's life; through them, the Church is the vital principle of human society. Consequently, they particularly must have an ever more clear consciousness, not only of belonging to the Church, but of being the Church, that is, the community of the faithful on earth under the guidance of the common head, the Pope, and of the bishops in communion with him. They are the Church, and thence it comes that from the earliest days of her history the faithful, with the agreement of their bishops, have joined together in associations concerned with the most diverse affairs of life. And the Holy See has never ceased to approve and commend them.[22]

This remarkably weighty passage elucidates the conclusions of this chapter. It shows the fundamental reason why, quite apart from any tactical necessity, action on temporal structures is part of the mission of the Church and of the lay apostolate in Catholic Action. We must recall what has been said about the Church's mission in Chapter III of Part I and at the beginning of this Chapter V.

Christ redeemed and saved all: he is the perfectly sufficient principle of a fellowship of all things with God and with one another. He did not stop short at declaring God's forgiveness to the world; he took on our nature, that he might heal it, raise it up, divinise it by a perfect oneing with God. The Church in her turn does not stop at declaring salvation by word of mouth; she communicates its living reality in the sacraments and in every other way by which she is the channel of grace. Her mission of love is like Christ's, it embraces all mankind, it is 'love for men' (Titus iii, 4).

We know that total restoration will take place only in the Kingdom, since not till then will Jesus exert the fullness of his power. But we also know that the Church is the germinal cell of the Kingdom, having the principle of the restoration of all things already present and active in herself, though only in an initial, partial way, precarious first-fruits. In this life, salvation is hardly more than inward

[22] *Doc. cath.*, 1946, cc.172–176. Cf., also the same, 1947, c.260, and 1951' cc.579–580.

and spiritual, grounded in personal obedience to the faith and in the gifts of the Spirit. That is why it is legitimate to speak of the salvation *of souls* as the aim of apostleship. There can be indwelling and sanctifying of the soul by the Holy Spirit without his presence producing all its effects, particularly bodily immortality and glory; but there cannot be real sanctification without the whole man and human achievement, in the measure that it is really such, undergoing something of a healing, being resettled on its foundations and directed towards its true ends, ennobled, strengthened: in short, as it were saved. So the Church's mission includes action on this human achievement, this environment that we can, with St Pius X, call civilisation, whose structures or sociological conditionings are an apostolically crucial factor. We must examine the conditions and bounds of this action.

When it is a question of operations supernatural in their very matter, as, for example, incorporation into Christ by baptism, the Lord's presence in the Eucharist, forgiveness of sins, the Church acts directly and through powers, an operative presence of the Holy Spirit, given to her precisely for that purpose; this holds for the whole order of personal sanctification of the soul. But when it is a question of the hallowing and saving of what is outside and appurtenant to the soul, the Church's action is no more than indirect, the more so the further one gets away from the personally spiritual. Because of the postponement of the full exertion of Christ's kingly power and the consequent distinction between Church and world, the Spirit, though given to the Church, is not given as *effective* cause of such a transformation. It does not make our bodies 'pneumatic', though it will one day (1 Corinthians xv, 44, etc.). If there be action, it is indirect and as it were reflex, not the object to which a competence is directed; less an action directly brought about by a power than an influence at work. That, too, is why things thus influenced retain their secular or temporal nature: the institutions, structures, techniques and achievements of civilisation, philosophy, the sciences, works for aid and welfare, all remain natural as to their matter. The fact that they are the work of baptised people, saints perhaps, does not alter their nature: an argument of St Thomas is still an argument, for St Camillus of Lellis his hospital is still a hospital. Yet all the time it is part of the Church's mission and of the Christian calling to nurse the sick and to philosophise, or to be a worker, a trade-union official, a magistrate, a politician. . . . But in none of these fields, departments of human work in the world of men, does the Church act with properly supernatural power, nor do her members

exercise a ministry in the strong sense of the word. The Church and
the faithful simply seek to direct these human matters in accordance
with the mind of Christ, which is, they know, a mind for their
salvation; they tackle these undertakings candidly, determined to
be loyal to their own proper nature—to produce a valid argument,
good medicine, sound workmanship, just laws; but always according
to what they themselves are and must remain, sons of God in Christ
Jesus, baptised, members of the Church, called to give glory to God
by their whole life.

So all this substantially natural work is directed in the end towards
God in Christ. Fellows with all other men, sharing their earthly
labours, no different from them in intelligence or technical skill,
Christians nevertheless approach those tasks with resources and
demands taken from elsewhere. Pius XII associates all these things
with Jesus Christ, and goes on: 'The Church accepts and hallows
everything that is truly human; she directs and orders multitudinous
aspirations and particular aims towards man's common and all-
embracing aim, the closest possible likeness to God' (*Doc. cath.*, 1946,
c. 171). The Church does not give technical explanations of the laws
of natural things, which are what they are; but she gives the *meaning*
of everything, and this meaning is God, in Christ Jesus: she teaches
the faithful to 'christofinalise' everything they do. At the same time,
through her magisterium and pastoral supervision, she declares what
an order conformed to God calls for, and through her priesthood up-
holds the faithful with the ecclesial means of grace. Catholic Action
'has the duty of inspiring society with the Christian spirit and im-
planting the Christian idea of man, with all it calls for from individuals and families and on the national and international planes,
according to the principles of the Church's social teaching'; and this
without losing its character as 'an organ of the Church in the surroundings of the world', and without becoming a secular movement
by assuming the task of direct 'technical transformation of the political or economic structures of earthly society' (*Doc. cath.*, 1950,
c. 650).

So Catholic Action remains a Church thing even when it is exerting influence on temporal affairs. Purely temporal activities of
Christians are not Catholic Action. Events bear out the hierarchy's
definite statements on this point. More than once in recent times
movements of Catholics in secular matters, begun as Catholic activity, have eventually been forced by their own nature to recognise
themselves as unreservedly temporal enterprises; examples of this in
France are the Sillon in 1907, and the Mouvement populaire des

z

Familles, which in 1950 became the Mouvement de Libération du Peuple. Even those official statements which emphasise that Catholic Action forms the best citizens and can regenerate society also declare that it does not and must not engage in politics (DC., pp. 32, 57, 91ff., 116, 342ff., 389). They tell us, on the one hand, that Catholic Action teaches as a duty that Catholics must take part boldly in secular affairs; on the other, that such activity 'is in a field distinct from the apostolic sphere of Catholic Action'. As Bossuet would have said, 'Christians, what is this mystery?'

It is the mystery of the point where the competence of the Church and the autonomy of the temporal articulate with one another. A classical scholastic distinction comes in useful here, the distinction between the end of the work itself and the end of him who does the work. At any rate in the last resort, the end that the Christian puts before himself must always be the glory of God. This end is transcendent, which in itself implies a certain indifference about what is done (except that if what is done be intrinsically evil, the intention is vitiated): St Paul tells us to glorify God whether by eating or by not eating. That is why Christians are so often accused of not being really interested in *what* they do, and of treating *things* simply as occasions of merit. But there is the end of the work itself, the object which gives content and specific quality to what we do, which directly governs means and execution. From this point of view the Christian can not only make acts of praise and love of God, he can, even in some earthly matter, take action whose intrinsic and specifying aim is ordered to God, to lead to Christ, action, then, that is *intrinsically* apostolic. He can also, while having the inward final intention of God's glory—indicated, for instance, by writing the letters A.M.D.G. at the beginning of a book—take action whose *intrinsic and specifying* aim is, not to lead to Christ, but to obtain some temporal result as such: a scientific treatise, for example, or a rise in wages, a housing law, or better care for the sick.

Since the subjective final intention can be the same in either case, we will leave that aside, supposing it to be Christian, and consider *what* Peter or Jim does when he hears the Church's call and goes on from his inward faith to the social consequences of that faith. Aware that temporal structures ought to be such as to constitute a *milieu* in which it is possible really to believe and live as a Christian, even to be one that foreshadows the reign of Christ, Peter, Jim and their fellows join together *in order to* form themselves integrally to Christian life, to learn more about its demands, and to be strengthened in work that aims at leading to Christ those whom God throws in their way, and at exerting Christian influence over secular institutions. *At this stage*, the *content* of what they are doing is expressly and intrinsically apostolic; it is of the order of Catholic Action, a Church activity. But when one of them works in this spirit as an active trade-unionist, another as a lawyer, another as a nurse, then *what* they are doing is intrinsically temporal. It may be, it ought to be, in living continuity with the Church work, and thus the Church can act on temporal things through her lay members. But the intrinsic, specifying aim of the activity must be taken into consideration.

When properly and intrinsically religious things, things, that is, within the Church's spiritual competence, are done in order to influence the temporal in a Christian direction, then *what is done* is Catholic Action. The temporal matter influenced and its conduct do not pertain to the Church's sphere, or, then, to Catholic Action, but to the sphere of this world; they are properly a matter of the *temporal activity* of Christians. So Christian social action and movements are associated with Catholic Action proper, outside its own bounds; they have a continuity of spirit with it in the heart and life of Christians, but they are distinct from it, just as one country is distinct from another even though the one is culturally influenced by the other. Is it a valid and suitable comparison to see the Christian's temporal activity joined to the womb of Mother Church by Catholic Action, as by an umbilical cord through which the mother's blood nourishes a complete living creature constituted in its own autonomy?

Pope Pius XII has been quoted above to the effect that the Church is not an imperialism that forms temporal society; external secular work is not hers; she acts internally and forms man himself, the *whole* man. There is not something separate, the so-called religious man, a sort of 'walking conscience', who has nothing to do with this world. Whereabouts would such a man live? Between the porch, the confessional and the sacristy? But who would find that a living-space for his conscience? To the pagan who said to him, 'Show me your God', Theophilus of Antioch replied, 'Show me your man, and I will show you my God'. The God of Christianity is the Lord of Heaven and earth, whose image is not reflected only in him who prays alone but in the whole behaviour of a living man. The Church has no authority over secular things; in her pilgrimage to the Kingdom she is confronted by a world of temporal reality which remains such, a world which keeps its own order of explanations, techniques and the nature of things: so much so that the Christian cannot serve God *in this world* (unless his vocation be to leave it to serve God alone in himself) without respecting the nature of things in which God must

be served, and observing their corresponding explanations and techniques in his thought and deeds. As Étienne Gilson has written:

> If one wants to practise science for God's sake, the first condition
> is to practise it for its own sake, or as if for its own sake, because
> that is the only way to learn it. . . . It is the same with an art: one
> must have it before one can put it to God's service. We are told
> that faith built the medieval cathedrals : no doubt, but faith
> would not have built anything had there been no architects and
> craftsmen. If it be true that the west front of Notre-Dame is a
> raising of the soul to God, that does not prevent its being a
> geometrical composition as well: to build a front that will be an
> act of charity, one must first understand geometry.
> We Catholics, who acclaim the high worth of nature because it
> is God's work, should show our respect for it by taking as our first
> rule of action that *piety is never a substitute for technique*; for technique
> is that without which the most fervent piety is powerless to make
> use of nature for God's sake. Nothing and nobody obliges a Chris-
> tian to occupy himself with science, art or philosophy, for there is
> no lack of other ways of serving God; but *if he has chosen this way of
> serving him*, the end he puts before himself obliges him to excel; the
> very intention that guides him compels him to be a good scholar,
> a good philosopher, a good artist: it is the only way he can become
> a good servant.[23]

It does not follow that one is doing Catholic Action simply by
doing one's job well and observing the intrinsic truth of temporal
work, though this idea starts from a right supposition. Since the
Christian has got to leave secular things in their own nature and
order, and not turn them into Church things, his activity is in itself
authentically temporal. In that sense there is no question of sacralising the temporal, or even of christianising it in itself, but simply of
'christofinalising' it: the texture of the work done is temporal. In this
way Christians can do the authentic work of earthly society with
other men. But Catholic Action is not like that. Its content is not the
temporal engagement itself: apart from express direct apostleship, it
is Church work in view of the Christian animation, direction and
nourishing of that engagement. Looked at from outside and below,
abstracting from its spiritual animation, the temporal engagement of
the lay Christian is of exactly the same nature as that of the civic

[23] 'L'intelligence au service du Christ-Roi', in *Christianisme et philosophie* (Paris,
1936), pp. 155–156.

official or artisan with whom he works. Many Christians bring to it no other spiritual motives and resources than are implied by a general intention of submission to God in all that they do—to say nothing of those who scarcely relate a daily life lived 'all anyhow' to a very feeble life of faith. Some make an explicit and even lively connexion between their religion and their job in the world, but in a purely personal fashion; these are not 'militants' of Catholic Action, for whom the Christian animation of their secular commitment in the hope of 'christofinalising' social structures is completely a work of the Church, guided by her as such, and so regulated by her. In the movements and organisations of Catholic Action the Church gives herself the organs that are required to fulfil, not only 'her divine mission which is to lead souls to God', but also the task 'which springs spontaneously from this divine mission, the task of Christian civilisation' (St Pius X). Such is the sphere proper to Catholic Action with respect to influence to be exercised over social structures.

*   *   *

All this will have been rather lengthy and complicated for the taste of many readers, but it enables us to give a better account of the laity's *own* vocation in the work of the Church: more exactly, in the work of the Church militant, for it is only in the Church's earthly phase, characterised by the existence of an apostleship and by the distinction between Church and world, that the laity has a particular vocation. The heavenly calling to the glory of the Kingdom is to lay and cleric alike. There is a calling to apostleship that is made to all Christians without distinction, that, namely, which is associated with baptism, faith and charity. But there follows a twofold distinction in apostleship, which somewhat corresponds to the two ways in which the lay state may be defined (cf. Part One Chapter I).

Lay people are those faithful who do not have hierarchical powers. The apostleship of bishops and priests brings into play the means of grace whose ministry was conferred on the Twelve, while that of the laity calls simply for those spiritual gifts which each receives and makes his own. It is in this sense that we said that even where there is a mandate of the Church and to that extent a mission *ex officio*, lay people have only their personal spiritual resources to use: the mandate is a participation in the hierarchy's mission, not in its powers. From this point of view, then, the lay state is characterised in a rather negative way.

Not so with the second definition. The laity are then seen as Christians who, without prejudice to service of God *in himself*, have their *own proper* calling to serve him and to fulfil the Church's mission, in and through engagement in temporal tasks. The monk goes to God, so far as may be, directly. Many religious orders and congregations translate their service of God and search for perfect charity into service of their neighbour—doctrinal service, as the Friars Preachers; charitable service, as the teaching religious and hospitallers; but the properly monastic way remains a way of solitude, with a minimum of temporal commitment and use of the world. *Tamquam non utentes*. The priest apostle, co-operator in the episcopal charge, mixes with the world and lives amidst its history, but he does not engage in the world's work, for he is dedicated to service of the Kingdom. Minister of the eternal and of the City that shall have no end, he is the servant of men and has to mingle with them, not in order to help them build this world which cannot endure, but to make them living stones for God's temple. The resources he puts at their disposal are not strong arms, skilful hands, or any trade, however noble its purpose: but spiritual resources, whether personal—understanding, love, prayer—or ministerial, those of his priesthood and hierarchical order. Unlike the monk, the priest apostle is 'in the world', without being of it; he is there, he has to be very much there, that he may arouse and prepare the third dimension therein, that whereby men, for whose good society exists, are made for God. He is 'ordained for men in the things that appertain to God' (Hebrews v, 1). The priest's vocation is to make his way to God, guiding others with him by the use of spiritual means.

The vocation proper to lay people, corresponding to their state as such, is to make their way to God while doing this world's work; to live according to the third, vertical, dimension while making the stuff of the world and its history, and for that purpose living according to life's horizontal dimensions. *Et divisus est*. St Paul's word *à propos* marriage is true of the whole life of the Christian engaged in the world. Ideally speaking, the monk unifies himself easily: he lives in the oneness of the world to come. The priest apostle lives among men and their affairs, but in order to refer all things spiritually to God. But the lay person has to live for God without being dispensed from doing the work of the world; his particular Christian calling is to bring glory to God and the reign of Christ *in and through that work*: to be the Church—not the Church inert, present but not present in a world wherein she would have nothing to do, but—the Church active, there where the clergy are not, in ways the clergy cannot be, namely, in temporal affairs and daily events, doing the work of the world and of history. That is why Pope Pius XII said that the laity do more than belong to the Church, that they *are* the Church, *in as much as* she is 'the society of those who, under the supernatural influence of grace, in the perfection of their personal dignity as sons of God and in the harmonious development of every human inclination and energy, build up the mighty framework of the community of men'.[24]

Since the Church's apostolic mission carries with it, beyond its purely spiritual duties, influence upon temporal civilisation, it follows that this mission is *fully* exercised only through the lay people doing their own proper part in it: they are irreplaceably the Church for a whole order of ecclesial activities. It may be said, with Jacques Maritain and the Abbé Journet, that the clergy have specially to show forth the exalting influence of grace and the spiritual transcendence of Christianity, while the laity show forth its healing and salutary influence on civilisation, the fineness and nobility of a Christian temporality. The clergy's part and the laity's part are integrated in the Church's total mission, without detriment to what is common to both; the laity's mission complements that of the priesthood, which would not be fully effective without it. Once more, the laity form 'the priestly *pleroma* of the bishop'.

We have remarked several times that neither the laity's Christian task nor Catholic Action need be confined to influencing temporal things. There are some writings, otherwise excellent, which seem to us too much to equate Catholic Action with Christian influence on what is temporal: Catholic Action, they say, is 'secular (*profane*) in its object . . . a secular apostolate that is authentically supernatural'. This is right enough in its positive sense; but surely it is regrettable that it should appear to overlook the place of a direct, purely spiritual apostolate *in the very idea of Catholic Action*, and also of a more diffuse but real apostolic influence that has little reference to secular affairs and social duty. There are said to be two definitions of Catholic Action current among its 'militants', namely, '*Apostleship* of the laity' and 'Christian *animation* of the laity's temporal engagements'. We believe we have shown in this chapter that neither of these definitions is adequate—which, indeed, is suggested by the fact that there are two of them. Official definitions, which are more descriptive than scientific, combine the two aspects, and we will not separate them. In any case, they are not separated in the great Catholic Action movements, especially in such a one as the Young Christian Workers, where concern for the humanisation of institutions at all

[24] Note 22, above. Cf. Cardinal Suhard, *Le prêtre dans la Cité* (pastoral letter 1949), pp. 53–55.

levels is always accompanied by personal witness in one's *milieu*—personal gifts and particular vocation being at work to put emphasis on the one or on the other.

This duality of orientation is real, and is not unconnected with the distinction between general Catholic Action and specialised Catholic Action. Each of these forms raises plenty of concrete questions: the first being more directly connected with the parish and Church undertakings, the second with 'movements' which from their nature depend on the Church *comme cité*[25] rather than on the parish, and therefore on the diocese or on a national or international organisation. The relations between the two forms of Catholic Action also raise problems, often due to reciprocal misunderstandings. Interesting as they are, these matters are outside the scope of this book.

PRIEST AND PEOPLE IN CATHOLIC ACTION

Officially and actually, lay people are 'directors' or 'leaders' ('*dirigeants*'. Cf. DC., pp. 218–219; TP., pp. 62, 66; A.A.S., 1946, p. 423). They have a responsibility of their own, a certain autonomy, even a certain authority. Nevertheless, in participating in the Church's apostolic mission they do not participate in hierarchical powers, and Catholic Action remains subordinate to the hierarchy. Though 'directors' in a certain sense, they clearly continue to be directed. They are 'directors' in an organism whose role in the Church is not directive but executive; Catholic Action is co-operation in apostleship under the direction and control of the hierarchy. Its lay 'directors' are something like military leaders, who have full tactical direction of their forces under a supreme political authority that determines the general conduct of the campaign and the broad lines of its strategy. Official documents declare accordingly, that Catholic Action 'is not directive action in the theoretical order but executive action in the practical order' (DC., pp. 218–219, 234; A.A.S., 1946, p. 423). Catholic Action has not altered the Church's hierarchical structure. Cardinal Verdier said to his clergy: 'You will have a rather new ministry. Hitherto you have been unquestioned masters, almost kings by divine right. . . . When tomorrow the laity stands beside the hierarchy to direct external Catholic Action, you will then be constitutional kings' (*Doc. cath.*, 1931, c. 588). These words must be understood with the same nicety with which they

---

[25] For what we mean by that, see our brochure *Sacerdoce et laïcat*, p. 33, or in *Mission de la paroisse* (Lille, 1948), pp. 48-65.

were uttered, as a psychological truth, not a juridical pronouncement. Authority in the Church remains with the hierarchical priesthood.

More exactly, it remains with the hierarchy, which is priestly, for we are thinking here of the pastoral authority of spiritual government. No priest whatever has authority simply because he is a priest. The hierarchy is the bishops, and it is to them that Catholic Action is subordinated. But they exercise direction and control through their co-operators: nationally, through some organisation instituted by the local episcopate; in a diocese through chaplains and diocesan directors; locally, through the section chaplain or parish-priest.[26] These representatives of the bishop exercise different degrees of intervention, strongest in training the young; and general Catholic Action, with its parochial interests, is more closely supervised by the parish-priest than specialised Catholic Action by its chaplains, since the latter is more expressly concerned with influencing social structures. These last chaplains are called 'ecclesiastical assistants' in Italy and France.

The priest in Catholic Action—chaplain, ecclesiastical assistant, pastor—has to advise, spiritually quicken, transmit episcopal directions, keep an eye on doctrine (DC., pp. 390ff.; TP., n. 91, pp. 65ff., 275ff.). In France at any rate, there is more and more general agreement on the primary importance in practice of the priest's work of forming, counselling and encouraging Catholic Actionists in their day-to-day problems. He has to be for this little *pleroma* of faithful something of what Jesus Christ was and is for his: not only the Christ who objectively revealed the Father, who was actually there in flesh and blood, but the Christ who formed his Apostles day by day and, when his bodily presence was withdrawn, was still with them, comforting them, counselling them, leading them to prayer, helping them in every way through his Spirit. With the modest resources of man of God and 'universal brother', the priest has to try, as a good servant, to do from outside what Jesus and his Spirit do inwardly, according to the law of the ministry.

It must not be glossed over that the programme of Catholic Action exacting for the laity, is overwhelming for the clergy. The call of the faithful to action comes at a time when we have really emerged from the Middle Ages and a regime of Christendom. We can no longer look for help to the institutions of a world over which the Church wields authority, or leave the business of making Christians to structures all ready-made. Without despising whatever solid fragments

[26] This point was expressly mentioned by Pius XII at the Congress of Laity in 1951.

may remain from that state of affairs, we have to adjust ourselves to a world that has returned to secularity and to try to do God's work from a base of personal consciences formed according to Christ. To do that, it is needful that a creative spirituality grounded in the faith should outweigh formations and programmes. The clergy have increasingly to be educators of adult consciences, enabling them to bring forth Christian activity from their own convictions. They have to give the faithful a grown-up religion, 'not frills, but solid piety drawn from the Bible', as Pius XI said (A.A.S., 1937, p. 191). There has been a call for 'catechist-prophets'; Catholic Action needs priests beyond compare.

But however sincere and good they may be, it is impossible for them alone to be a source of response to all demands. In the first place, we know only too well that we are always being asked to give what we have not got; we have seen the 'miracle of the empty hands' repeated more than once. We are mediators of a daily manna of which we cannot lay in a store. But we do not receive this manna of the apostolate only from on high: the very ones who ask it of us create the gift in us. We listen to their questions, and the reply begins to dawn on us; they bring more than half of what they come to ask for. The ministry of spiritual animation implies a sort of dialogue in which answer is begotten by question. Since the real elements of the lay engagement in a large measure escape the priest, only the laity can tell us many things without knowledge of which our counsel will often be rather unreal and ineffective. Hundreds of priests can testify to the depth of apostolic and spiritual, yes, and theological thought that they have found in free and frank conversation with lay people fully engaged in the world. One of those priests has said that 'Being without laity for three years, I had the feeling of an empty priesthood'.[27] Priests who have had this experience and cannot doubt the fullness and depth it has brought to them, spontaneously speak, not only of a 'team' but of the 'priesthood-laity couple'. This well expresses the fellowship in the same work, the mutual contributions, the complementing of one another, the rising above self, that are due to the fact that they are not separate and alone but together.

How many times we have quoted Chrysostom's words that the laity are the bishop's *pleroma*. The Church is indeed built hierarchically; but she exerts the fullness of her life and mission only when she nourishes them at that source below, from mankind increasing and multiplying and filling the earth and subduing it.

---

[27] Compare the testimony of Canon Sempay at the Congress of Laity in Rome in 1951.

Chapter VI

IN THE WORLD AND NOT OF THE WORLD

THIS chapter is concerned with 'spirituality'—but we are not going to join in any discussion about that word. We agree with those who, giving the word its full theological exactness and implications, reject the idea of a 'spirituality' of the diocesan clergy, a 'lay spirituality', and so on. At the same time we have every sympathy for those who, taking the word in a concrete descriptive sense, seek to identify the elements of 'spirituality' among parish-priests, in the apostolate, among the laity. For ourselves, we use the word or refrain from using it almost indifferently. We have used it, not without inverted commas, in the first line above principally so that those to whom the word is familiar and clear may know that our purpose is to talk about the things they understand by that word: in what particular conditions do lay people have to sanctify themselves?—What values and what characteristics do these conditions produce in Christian life as led by the laity?

A primary truth governs the whole question, and it is this: there is only one Christianity, one obligation to seek union with God in Christ, and so to tend to holiness; it is not the onerous privilege of priests and religious alone, it is the obligation of all Christians whatever in virtue of the one Christianity that is common to them all. But their vocations are diverse, their states and conditions of life are diverse, their actual duties are diverse: and accordingly, while it is true that there is no spirituality proper to the laity because theirs is the common Christian spirituality,[1] it is also true that there is a spirituality of lay life, as there is of priestly life or of monastic life. Each form of life has its own conditions, duties and resources, and the *vita in Christo* is influenced accordingly. The monk or nun is simply a Christian who concentrates to the uttermost on the one thing necessary, without the primacy of which there is no Christian

[1] Lay people are in agreement about this: see *Vie spirituelle*, February 1946, pp. 312ff.

life worth the name; and in the same way the spiritual life of the priest is simply the intensification of Christian life.[2] But lay people do not take monastic vows and have neither the helps nor the obligations of monastic life; they do not celebrate the sacraments or exercise the spiritual fatherhood of the priestly order, with its difficult and rewarding demands. Instead, they are employed in the occupations and activities of the earthly city, and are deeply engrossed and marked thereby; man and woman, they form the natural pair in which the race exists completely and perpetuates itself; they have children whom they look after till the time comes for them to have children in turn, and that too engrosses and marks their existence to its very heart. Obviously their 'being in Christ', while of the same essence as the being in Christ of priests and monks, is not in its conditions and actual living exactly that of priests and monks.

That is enough. We are bound to devote a last chapter to the consideration of this Christian life which, being conditioned in its broad lines by the circumstances of lay life, is properly, but not specifically, lay. The division of the subject is naturally provided by the two terms of comparison that we have again adverted to after first meeting them in Chapter I.

THE PROBLEM OF LAY HOLINESS

The Gospel teaches that the Christian position is one of opposition to the world, which presupposes—and the Gospel says so—that the faithful are called to live 'in the world'; it is concerned with this present life in relation to life everlasting. It is striking to what a degree our Lord concentrated on the right ordering of things in this world, always, of course, in view of the next. In St Matthew's gospel there is nothing but this between the opening pages, which introduce Christ's mission, and the chapters that narrate the events leading to Calvary: the Sermon on the Mount (v–vii) sets forth precepts of conduct in this life; the following chapters (viii–ix), and many other passages in the gospels, show us Jesus fulfilling one of his essential messianic functions, that of healing *nature*; finally (x), he instructs his apostles for the spreading of the Good News. The Gospel insists that effective primacy be given to service of the Kingdom and of God's reign (Matthew vi, 24–34), but it leaves Christians to pursue their life of obedience to Christ *in the world*. Nowhere is this stated more clearly than in the prayer for the apostles, John xvii, 6–19. We

[2] Cf. G. Morin, *L'idéal monastique* . . . (1913); J. A. Robilliard in *Vie spirituelle loc. cit.*, pp. 186–193.

see there how the disciples are not of the world and yet are altogether
in the world. They are not of the world because, chosen and called
by the Father, having heard and kept the word, they belong to Jesus
Christ; they are of his people and of his Body. But Jesus does not tell
them to withdraw from the world; he wants them to stop there and
he gives them a mission to it.

It is just the same in the apostolical writings. The faithful are in
the world and they are not to leave it, not even to avoid mixing with
pagans, though they must avoid any spiritual fellowship with them
(1 Corinthians v, 9ff.; 2 Corinthians vi, 14ff.). Especially must
Christians be distinguished from idolaters by their way of living.
Here the Scriptures do not stop at injunctions and exhortations;[3]
they also tell us how things were in fact, as each could see for himself:
unlike the heathen, Christian conduct is gentle and light-bearing,
and its different characteristics, spiritual as they are, do not fail
together to form an ideal of humanism.[4] But this humanism, if
humanism it be, is hardly more than an unsought consequence, as it
were the over-measure promised to those who seek first the Kingdom
of God and his righteousness. It does not appear from the apostolical
writings that Christians interested themselves in the progress of the
world they lived in. They respected its order, both the creational
order, which is good like all other things made by God, and the
human or political order, which also is good as such (1 Timothy iv,
1–5; Romans xiii, 1–7, etc.). With regard to society, the recommended attitude was one of respect and conformity modified by a
certain indifference to things, with a bias towards sympathy, a great
will to peace, and a desire to be well thought of among men.[5]

The apostles, especially St Paul, have very positive ideas about the
position and destiny of the world as cosmos: it must be wholly subjected to God (1 Corinthians xv, 27–28; Ephesians i, 10; Colossians
i, 20), but, in spite of 'all things are yours, and ye are Christ's, and
Christ is God's' (1 Corinthians iii, 23), it is not expressly stated that
the duty of bringing about this subjection falls on the faithful, and it

[3] 2 Corinthians x, 3ff; Galatians iii, 3; v, 16ff.; vi, 8; Colossians, iii, 2, 5ff.;
1 Thessalonians iv, 1–12; and the characteristic words of Paul in Romans xii, 2:
'Be not conformed to this world, but be ye transformed by the renewing of your
mind, so that ye find out what is the will of God, the good and the well-pleasing
and the perfect'.

[4] See, for instance, Ephesians iv, 17; vi, 9; Philippians iv, 8; 1 Thessalonians v,
12–22; 1 Timothy iii, 1–13; and most of 1 Peter.

[5] Cf. Romans xiv, 6ff., 17; James i, 9–12; ii, 1–7; v, 1ff.; 1 Corinthians i, 26;
vii, 17–24; 1 Peter ii, 18ff., etc. The apostles urged the doing of good in men's sight
in order to earn their respect and to be at peace with them: Romans xii, 17–18;
xv, 2; Philippians iv, 5; Colossians iv, 5–6; Titus iii, 2; 1 Peter ii, 12, 15; iii, 15–16,
etc. And cf. Matthew v, 16.

does not appear as an historic process: rather is it presented as belonging to Christ's power exercised at the end of history. It is for the faithful to refer all things to God, making use of them for good and with thankfulness (1 Corinthians x, 31, etc.); it is legitimate to use the world's goods, and praiseworthy to manage one's business and household efficiently (1 Timothy iii, 4, 12; 1 Thessalonians iv, 11). Nothing is said about systematic self-deprivation or flight from the world's activities; but neither are the faithful told to seek those activities and to excel in them for the promotion of God's reign. Living frankly and sincerely in the world, Christians are citizens of another country, which is above (Philippians iii, 20); the life now lived in the flesh is lived in hope of a better, earnest of which is already theirs. 'The world as we see it is passing away' (1 Corinthians vii, 31). Hence a state of discomfort, expressed in paradoxical rules of behaviour: to use the world as using it not, to be married as if not married, to be ill-treated and yet cheerful . . . (1 Corinthians vii, 29ff., etc.). Moreover, to the first generation of Christians the end of history seemed not far off (Romans xiii, 11ff.; 1 Peter iv, 7, etc.).

Christianity was, is and always will be dominated by faith in an everlasting life whose beginning and preparation is here below. No longer feeling that an end in time is at hand, it has a conviction of the reference of everything to the one necessary thing: that is of its essence, and is found at every stage of its history. But history also shows that from time to time there have been shades of difference in the application of that conviction to the estimate of earthly life.

The Church of the martyrs lived in conditions too like those of the first communities to show any variation in this matter. There was a strongly-felt difference between the ways of living of those who were Christ's and of those who knew him not, and the Jewish theme of the two paths was adapted to this sentiment.[6] There was a strong consciousness of Christian life as a new life through the Holy Spirit and, moreover, as an earthly anticipation of the life in Heaven whose full triumphal manifestation was awaited. Christians lived for the Lord's coming and the resurrection; from this point of view, the ideal was a sort of monastic life in the world, 'a righteous, clean and temperate life, looking for the coming of the Lord'.[7] In these conditions, all the faithful wanted to be holy with an absolute holiness, that is, to order the whole of life to the one thing necessary to the uttermost degree. It is true that they held the place in the world that was theirs when they were called; Tertullian, with some oratorical extrava-

[6] Cf. the *Didache*, i–vi; J. P. Audet in *Revue biblique*, 1952, pp. 219–238; etc.

[7] Cf., for example, Clement, *Cor.*, 1–32, and the Letter of Polycarp.

gance, speaks of them as filling the whole city. But these same faithful were not interested in the world—the pagan Celsus reproached them for it; the only question they put about secular activities, the only one that Tertullian himself put, was 'May a Christian engage in them?'

It is not surprising that, before the end of the era of persecution, Christians were looking for an equivalent of the absolute self-giving of the martyrs in a flight from the world and conditions of life as near as might be to those of angels. Thus, at its beginnings, the hard ideal of monachism was a sort of substitute for martyrdom, and also the answer to a certain sickliness that had overtaken the idea of opposition to the world and the eschatological reference of Christian life, in consequence of contact with the Graeco-Roman world and the Church's new situation in the empire of Constantine.

Even though it was wholly taken up with spiritual things, Christianity could not but inspire a new order in the world, since it involved a new way of looking at life and the regarding of others as one's neighbours. It is obvious that, from this point of view of influencing earthly affairs, the Christian empire, and later the conversion of its new barbarian masters, gave Christianity the opportunity for a new experience that the apostles and martyrs did not have. They did not and could not have any idea of an organic symbiosis of the Church with the City such as was realised in what we call Christendom or the Christian State, generally referred to in the Middle Ages as the Christian Commonwealth (or even simply as Church). There was no confusion of powers: there was always an emperor and princes on one side, a pope and bishops on the other; but they were two sides of one body, the Body Christian.

This state of things unquestionably presented lay people with big possibilities of engaging in temporal business, and Pope Pius XII has recalled some notable characteristics of this engagement (A.A.S., 1951, pp. 511ff.). Christian influence on law-making, the establishment of hospitals, military expeditions for the defence of Christendom, the organisation of society from top to bottom, the encouragement of education and the sciences—these are certainly not mythical. What more worth could be adduced for the laity's role as Christians engaged in the world?

But in fact that world was not *the* world; it was, if we may put it so, a Church world, one in which society and its sciences were directly and strictly governed by the finalities of the Church, salvation and reference to eternal life; a society, then, sciences and a world, which did not seek or really develop their own proper finalities, of which

Leo XIII was to say later that they are sovereign and autonomous in their own order. But they were not treated thus; their order was regulated by the spiritual finality of the Church, and this led to a certain stifling of immediate and proper causes by the first Cause, a certain transference of the activities that have these causes in view to that higher activity that has the first Cause in view, in short, to something of an eclipse of the priesthoods of second causes by the priesthood of the first Cause, a matter to which we have already referred. At bottom, the Church of medieval Christendom, which entered into symbiosis with the world and has so often been accused of being secularised, kept to the primitive line of an earthly life altogether relative to the life on high. Monasticism was consciously related to the ending of persecution and a weakening of the feeling of opposition to the world among Christians as a whole, but in order to maintain its ideal it did not have to pursue it outside the Church, like the sects. In fact, it was monachism that really dominated early Christendom: not perhaps in the Empire before the barbarian invasions, though a good number of influential bishops at that time were monks; but certainly, in the West, after the conversion of the barbarian leaders, and particularly under the Carolingians. It was the monks who preserved the elements of culture, who educated princes and who, literally, formed Christendom, and therefore Europe, spiritually. Charles Martel's successor, Carloman, was so attracted by monastic life that he ended up by renouncing his throne to become a monk. St Benedict of Aniane's reform was crucial in this regard; it was developed under Lewis the Debonair, who had been trained by monks, and he was a sort of monk-emperor on the throne of Charlemagne, a 'supreme abbot' of the Christian world.

Thus medieval Christendom was brought under strong monastic influence by the historical conditions of its development and by its own inner logic, which was to bring this world's affairs under direct and strict control by the ends of eternal salvation. It was shot through with a spirituality that was deeply monastic in its inspiration, well expressed by the Cistercian principle, 'He to whom God is enough lacks nothing'; it reflected the characteristics of the monastic state, the referring of this life to the other, lack of regard for earthly things for their own sake and in themselves.

An example of this is provided by marriage, a subject on which ideas have undergone considerable development between the patristic period or the Middle Ages and our own time. It was not only the earlier or medieval heterodox sects that depreciated marriage. Plenty of orthodox writers, including some of the Fathers, exalted virginity or continence, which is certainly in accord with Christian tradition, but they did it at the expense of marriage. Some of the earliest writers were, no doubt, not free from encratic error. A few Fathers thought marriage was a consequence of original sin. St John Chrysostom who, in the light of his pastoral experience, came more and more to appreciate the vocation of the Christian in the world, looks on marriage as a refuge—a legitimate refuge—for those unable to be continent, and he does not speak of it with high favour. St Jerome, who went in for extreme statements, generally refers to marriage in terms that recall Tertullian, as if it were a lesser evil that God tolerates and allows. Most of the writers of the fourth and fifth centuries—Fathers, historians, chroniclers of monastic life and holiness—treat the bodily part of married life as if it were 'low', nothing but a danger and enthralment, almost sinful. It is true that the Fathers, including those just referred to, at times strongly affirm the complete lawfulness of marriage and its compatibility with holiness, but the weight is given to virginity and continence, to monastic values and *askesis*. One could draw up a catena of texts based on a scale of states of life in an ascending order: lay people, clerics, monks; or *conjugati*, *continentes* (or *paenitentes*), *virgines* (*rectores*, *praelati*); or of others which, in line with St Jerome, present marriage as something indulgently tolerated.[8]

In a more general way, the Middle Ages inherited from the Fathers, and from a spiritual and pastoral tradition in which the part of St Gregory the Great can hardly be exaggerated,[9] the sense of another life to which this life was wholly ordered, a life that was spiritual and contemplative, not earthly. It had to be prepared for by observing its law so far as possible. What we call monastic spirituality strongly imbued life with an ascetic ideal which became a determining feature in how it should be lived and a dominant factor in judgements of value and behaviour. Medieval man was himself aware of being under the banner of monachism, and he measured the progress or the renewal of Christianity by the extent of conquests made by the religious life. The antithesis between good and evil, translated concretely into a war between virtues and vices and into

[8] In justice we must add that two remarks: (1) Throughout the Middle Ages, and especially in the fourteenth and fifteenth centuries, many texts esteem marriage as a Christian state of life, in which and through whose activities eternal life is attained; (2) All theologians recognised that, if virginity and the religious life are, in themselves, higher than life in the world and the state of marriage, these last can be better for an individual, and a lay person can far surpass a nun or a bishop in holiness.

[9] Rather like Chrysostom, Gregory as time went by, and as his pastoral experience increased, somewhat modified his attitude of contempt towards the world.

an ascetic hierarchy of states of life, dominated the spirituality and the iconography of the eleventh and twelfth centuries. The naturalism that began to appear from the twelfth century did not prevent the continuance of an ascetic ideal of generally monastic pattern, and an enthusiasm for virginity so strong that it threw something of a shadow over the Christian ideal of marriage: this can be seen in teachers so well-balanced and sympathetic towards nature as Albert the Great and Thomas Aquinas. It must be recognised that these teachers were repeating traditional affirmations, but those of a tradition that had not yet developed a positive theology of what married people as such can bring to the mystical Body, as is being so notably done today and by pontifical teaching itself ('*Mystici Corporis*'). There was no question of manichean dualism, and marriage was recognised as something good, willed and blessed by God. But the asceticism of actual ideals favoured a prejudice against the body, or just against the physical world altogether: this prejudice could be accentuated until it became a phobia, one little in accord with Christianity in the measure that a 'spirituality' or an 'ascetic' severed itself from theology and developed practical considerations and rules for moral conduct without embodying them in a doctrinal whole concerning nature and created things.

Hence in later times, right down to our own day, there is a certain shamefacedness in speaking—or in not speaking—about marriage and the things of love, a certain insufficiency in the attitude of Christians towards man's earthly engagements. Listen to Port-Royal on the subject, or a theologian of the Sorbonne, Dr Duval, on the place of marriage in the life of the mystic Bd Mary-of-the-Incarnation.[10] It must not be overlooked that there were at the same time teachers and pastors who put forward a very positive ideal of marriage, as Henri Bremond showed in volume ix of his *Histoire littéraire du sentiment religieux*; but the diffused influence of Jansenism was strong, and in some places it has continued down to the present time. It was not the thing to talk about such matters, and the chapter of the catechism about marriage was often left out when teaching girls. When writing his Life of St Elizabeth of Hungary, Montalembert determined to break with these unhappy customs, but the very mention of Elizabeth's love idyll aroused bitter criticism. Today there are still unnecessary *tabus* here and there, and there is sometimes a flavour of manicheism in the way purity is talked about and in

<hr />

[10] [Duval has been faithfully dealt with by L. C. Sheppard in *Barbe Acarie* (London, 1953).—*Translator's note.*]

slighting references to marriage.[11] Such ideas were bound to have a harmful effect on appreciation of the laity's place and part in the Church, for marriage and the charge of earthly things is their normal state.

There is no need to exaggerate. The texts and the facts are there, and they bear witness that from the beginning Christianity has been looked on as a religion for this life, and not regarded solely in its eschatological and monastic aspects. We have seen that the earliest monks declared that married lay people could equal them in holiness; and that St John Chrysostom, in spite of his reserves about marriage (especially in his earlier days), was a thoroughgoing upholder of perfection in lay life. Many of the Fathers wrote letters of spiritual direction to lay people. In the Middle Ages there was less intermingling in society and, especially in the West, little of that secular culture that flourished in the age of the Fathers; but we do come across treatises on Christian life addressed to the laity.[12] These have been multiplied in later times, from the *Introduction to the Devout Life* down to our own day.

But this call to holiness of living, even 'in the world', was not accompanied by full and candid examination of all the Christian possibilities for those engaged in this world's affairs; St Francis de Sales remarks in the preface to his famous *Introduction*: 'Almost all those who have written about devotion have had in view the instruction of people who are quite withdrawn from the world's traffic, or they have at any rate taught the kind of devotion that leads to such a withdrawal'. When the wealthy senator Paulinus of Nola wanted to dedicate himself with his wife to God's service, he asked the advice of St Jerome. Jerome's fine reply was full of the gospel spirit, but he saw only two possible alternatives: to serve God in the priesthood or as a monk. One may well think that the contemporary Chrysostom would have offered a third possibility, service of God 'in the world', which has its difficulties and also its own opportunities. We find great and holy pastors doing that more than once in the Church's history, but the circumstances must be examined. The most significant example is probably that provided by Pope St Gregory VII. At the same time as his enterprises on behalf of ecclesiastical reform and the

[11] A. Adam in *Spannungen und Harmonie* . . . (Nuremberg, 1948) quotes a very well-known preacher, Mgr Tihamer Toth, as saying that 99 per cent of men are damned for sins of impurity. It is not surprising that Dorothy Sayers spoke up, so to speak, for the other sins in her essay *The Other Six Deadly Sins* (London, 1943).

[12] Histories hardly mention them. See, for an example, the *De institutione laicali* of Jonas of Orleans in PL., cvi, 121–180. There were, too, the sermons addressed *ad status*, increasingly common from Rathier of Verona onwards, and the *Miroirs* or *Spiegel* of conduct, adapted to various states.

primacy of sacerdotal power, he undertook far-reaching action for the renewal of Christian society, the defence and unity of Christendom under the authority of the See of Peter. At a time when monastic life was looked on as the highest service to which a lay man could be called, Gregory, himself a monk, called lay men to militant service of the Church, and looked on Hugh, duke of Burgundy, as a deserter because he had gone into a monastery: to do that, said the pope, was selfishness and a putting of one's own peace and quiet before the safety of the brethren, whereas charity ought to come first. Gregory made other declarations of a similar sort; the needs of the poor and of an imperilled Church, he said, are more important than any personal consideration; he gave a practical primacy to forceful action and the service of others.

These pastoral instructions were backed up and illustrated by the canonisation (the first of its kind) of a fighting-man, Erlembaldo, military leader of the Patarines against simoniacal clergy, who was murdered at Milan in 1075. One could speak here of a politics of canonisation, were it not that canonisation is firstly a result of God's will, who chooses to give external recognition to his servants by means of miracles and popular veneration; but the point is worth noting, for we shall come to a yet more significant example in contemporary times. After all, canonisation is what the theologians call a grace *gratis data*, given for the good of the Church and not for the benefit of the person concerned; it is possible, nay, it is likely, that at a given moment there are plenty of other people as much loved by God, as closely united with him, as holy as the one whom God chooses to be recognised publicly. In canonisations there is an aspect of the providential overseeing of the Church, to which God gives the particular patterns and intercessors whom he sees that the times require. As always, God does not impose these gifts by force; they are made from above, freely, but very often in such a way that they appear to come from below, as flower and fruit of history.

During the eleventh century the devotion of the faithful was kindled towards soldier saints, the patrons of chivalry: as well as the archangel Michael (already much honoured in the age of Charlemagne), such as St Maurice, St Theodore the Recruit, St George. From Charlemagne to St Lewis of France, and especially during the Crusades, there was an increased appreciation of lay life as Christian, but almost solely from the military or chivalric point of view: it is the knight whom art and literature show to have been the ideal of Christian humanism at this time. Other aspects could have been seen and appreciated, but they hardly were—we have learned above about the married state. Learning and culture? No, the laity in the West in the Middle Ages were too ignorant, unlike their fellows in the patristic age, in Italy till the beginning of the sixth century, in Byzantium contemporaneously. It was this ignorance that made so many medieval writers distrustful of lay people studying the Bible, and that objection was voiced so late as the Council of Trent, as we have seen. We have also seen that the acquiring of a personal culture by lay people, especially after the invention of printing, contributed to a crisis in the Church. Whole sectors of normal lay activity, represented today by their wide sphere of Christian engagement and sanctification, were practically not developed at all, including apostleship itself properly so called: we must recall that, under the regime of Christendom, this was practically left to kings and princes, and their activity was rather legislative and military than properly apostolic.

The Middle Ages were too taken up with thoughts of Heaven to be able to attach much value to engagement in this present life. The Church militant, and the Empire itself, were seen principally as representing the Church triumphant and the heavenly order, where there is no thought for anything but direct praise of God. Hagiography particularly, whence we get the *legendae* of our Breviary, put forward the example of a holiness that consisted of unusual actions, strange to ordinary life and sometimes in contradiction with it, and strongly marked by asceticism. The models proffered were chiefly patterns of renunciation of the world, not simply in its evangelical sense of the kingdom of disorder opposed to the reign of God, but in its natural and cosmological sense as the totality of earthly conditions. Up till recently husbands or wives were hardly ever canonised unless they had left their families (Jane de Chantal, Nicholas von Flüe), great men of action unless they had atoned for their activity, normal healthy men unless they had ill-treated their bodies to the limit that life allows.

* * *

These historical considerations were necessary in order to avoid any appearance of arbitrariness, and they show us that, until the modern age, the Church was not properly and fully in a position to inspire and foster a lay holiness of men engaged in the secular work of the world, having to sanctify themselves in and through this engagement itself. It is true that this aspect of holiness was never wholly absent, but Christians as a whole looked to a monastic spirituality and shared after a fashion in the monastic state. There was continuity from the clergy who sang God's praises in choir, through the *conversi* (lay-brothers) who laboured in workshop and field, leading a life of dedicated self-denial and joining prayer with their work, to the married people, who observed the fasts and other precepts of the Church and at the sound of the bell interrupted their work to pray. In those days there was general what can now be seen only in a few countries (Spain, Ireland) or among special groups (such as the Distributists whom we once visited in England) or in a few surviving spots (villages in Flanders or Vendée, such a place as Mesnil-Saint-Loup). Lay life was a sort of degenerate monastic life, which simply permitted the married state and of which the part not given up to prayer, instead of being lived in the cloister under direct discipline of superiors, was lived at work and at home, but not out of sight of spiritual authority.

The classical systematisation of the sanctification of the priests who are, so disputably, called 'secular' also derives from monastic spirituality and practices. Fundamentally, clerical life as it has been progressively fixed in the West, which has been adorned by so many holy men since the Council of Trent, is a reduced monastic life too. There are no 'secular clergy' such as those of the East: married priests, with no daily Mass or Breviary obligation, sharing closely in the life and work of the village and its people, essentially responsible for spiritual guidance, maintaining Christian discipline and ministering the sacraments. Here in the West since the Middle Ages, and especially since Trent, the ideals and means of priestly holiness have been borrowed from monachism, adapted from a spirituality that is monastic, or at any rate 'religious' in the technical sense. That is one of the reasons why the 'religious life-diocesan clergy' debate, whose ideological terms have been taken from a past age, before Trent, so often appears to be beside the point and hardly to admit of a satisfactory conclusion.

There are preparations, anticipations, checks to progress and delaying of consequences in historical processes: at a given moment the birth of a new world may be perceived, but it is never the result of spontaneous generation. We can see that the problems of lay sanctification arise with unexampled acuteness today as a consequence of engagement in the work of a world that is thoroughly secular. But the world has not become secular overnight. The more that scholars make known the real twelfth century, the clearer we see that it was marked by a rediscovery of nature and a more positive appreciation of the things of this world. With the thirteenth century this process was strengthened, and our attempt to examine the problem of a properly lay spirituality can invoke the aid of him whom the Church has made her 'Common Doctor', St Thomas Aquinas.

His importance in this connexion has been shown by Father R. A. Gauthier in his full study of magnanimity.[13] It is from that unexpected—and perhaps rather narrow—angle that the question of the Christian and moral value of earthly work is tackled. The word seems a bit too much in the style of Corneille; conformably with its real meaning, it can be expressed in terms of human hope, spirit of enterprise, man realising himself through his engagements; one might almost say, in terms of man's demiurgic [II] function but that it is a question of a humanist value for life rather than of external actualisation. Pagan magnanimity envisaged man's greatness, a greatness he found in himself through his own efforts; it expressed the ideal of a humanism of man only. Brought up on the Bible, wherein man is good, strong, holy only through God who alone is good, strong and holy, the Fathers transposed this ideal of magnanimity into terms of relationship with God, in what he does for man and in man. While the pagan philosophers were concerned only with man's greatness and a pure humanism of human endeavour, we find in the Fathers and the monastic ideal what may be called a pure 'divinism', in which everything is looked at from the angle of an immediate ordering to God, of an *immediate* adherence to him: no attention is paid to any greatness *of man himself*. Father Gauthier takes the ideas about the historical signification of Thomism that have been brought out by Father Mandonnet, Professor Gilson and Father Chenu, and extends them to his own field; he shows how in St Thomas there are affirmed an autonomy and a value of created things *in themselves*, and most particularly of man. The Fathers and the monks had simply laid the foundations of a spirituality of immediate adherence to God, implying renouncement of the world. In medieval Christendom this spirituality was lived as fully as possible, and earthly society itself was conceived in function of it; this was expressed 'through the absorption of society into the Church and the effacing of secular tasks and aims by supernatural tasks and aims'. Father Gauthier goes on:

> St Thomas does not belong to those middle ages; indeed, the proper import of his teaching is to sound their knell and usher in the modern world. Following Aristotle, he restored credit and its own value to nature, in particular to man's nature, and by so

[13] *Magnanimité: L'idéal de la grandeur dans la philosophie païenne et dans la théologie chrétienne* (Paris, 1951). There must be no illusion about St Thomas's earthly humanism: not only is he theocentric, he is basically monastic in his concrete ideals, which were embodied in St John the Baptist, St Antony, St Benedict. Cf. I. Eschmann in *Medieval Studies*, vol. vi (1944), p. 106; *Sum. theol.*, II–II, q. clxxxviii, a.8; *Polit.*, i, 1.

doing he in effect laid down the constitutive principle of modern
society: the whole historical process of this society is simply a
translation of its principle into fact, ever since the end of the
thirteenth century secular structures have been receiving their
autonomy. The thomist teaching on magnanimity supplied this
nascent world with the spirituality that it called for. Of course, as
we have already emphasised, St Thomas in nowise disowned the
spiritual doctrine of the Fathers. His teaching on the theologic
virtues (Christian hope, in this case) not only kept all its religious
wealth, but he set it forth with greater clarity and force than did
the Fathers themselves. But—and this is his particular work—he
adopted a 'humanist' spirituality, showing how it could be reconciled with the 'divinist' spirituality of the Fathers. Therein lies the
whole significance of St Thomas's doctrine of magnanimity. By it
he made possible, side by side with the monastic spirituality made
for those who have renounced the world, which is characterised by
an almost exclusive dominance of the theologic virtues which order
us *immediately* to God, he made possible the emergence of a typi-
cally lay spirituality: a spirituality characterised by the place
given to the virtues which, animated like all Christian virtues by
the theologic virtues, seek God, but seek him, not *immediately*, but
through something other than him, through man and through the
world which are their proper object. Now, on the plane of individual life, the first of these virtues, governing all the others, is
magnanimity, just as on the plane of communal life it is social
justice.

Like so many other aspects of St Thomas's wisdom, these views
were not fully elaborated and applied at once. New things are first
lived in individual minds and consciousness before they are expressed
in social history. Time had to go by, and several stages be lived
through,[14] before a really lay world would emerge, and not without
men's violently throwing off monastic and theologic tutelage and
experimenting with a pure humanism without God. Here would be

[14] The writings occasioned by the troubles of Philip the Fair and Lewis of
Bavaria with the papacy are generally considered only from the viewpoint of
political theory; but fundamentally they involved a vindication of the autonomy of
the lay order and a refusal to see it as receiving its validity from the priesthood. As
well as the *De potestate regia* of John of Paris, see book iii of Occam's *De potestatae
papae*. Here the way St Robert Bellarmine speaks of the laity is again interesting.
He was writing only from the point of view of their temporal and political role, but
in a measure it was an acceptance of progress made since St Thomas; in a measure
only, for Bellarmine was dominated by the mentality of hierocratic Christendom
even when his principles were beginning to anticipate Leo XIII's teaching on the
autonomy of the temporal in its own order.

the place to go over the stages of this 'recovery of the human' which had been swallowed up in the divine and, in this sense, as it were made alien to it. But it is sufficient to recall the elements of its 'pre-history' and the inevitable character of the process.

The first movement of faith is to give all to God. What Pascal lived through alone during the night of 23 November 1654, the Church had lived collectively and numberless souls have lived at the beginning of their Christian life: 'To forget the world, to forget everything, except God . . .' From a purely eschatological and monastic point of view, the less of the world, the less of the body and earthly activities, the better: primitive monachism was a total with-drawal from the world, and this has always been held in honour in the Church as a vocation and an example. But in the religious life itself there has been a progressive movement away from this absolute attitude towards a certain being in the world. First, agricultural work in common was introduced, then intellectual and cultural activities, then, with the Preaching Friars, scientific work of the reason (this raised protest and opposition). We are seeing experiments with religious life 'in the world', truly lay. At the same time there is a rediscovery of the excellence of marriage, and of the excellence of the body, round which a kind of theology and spirituality are being made. Christians, who had said No to so many things, are gradually coming to say Yes to them; a recovery of the human and of nature is at work in history. And so, little by little, the Church enters into the experience of a secular world and of a fully lay condition of the faithful in this secular world. For the purely human humanism of paganism she substituted the pure 'divinism' we have referred to; then came the Renaissance and the emergence of a new, godless humanism; and now, recognising the fact of a secular world and an order of properly human and earthly values, she faces the task of developing a suitable programme for its hallowing, for a God-centred humanism and a 'christofinalised' human work on earth which yet remain truly human and of this world.

This task is largely unprecedented, for, in our opinion, there has been a secular world and a fully lay life only since the time that social and political life was laicised, and especially since the inauguration of a mechanised civilisation which, born outside the Church, has never been consecrated and regulated by her. One is extremely con-scious of this when, mixing with the crowd on a workmen's train or when a factory knocks off or at a football match—still more, no doubt, if one is engaged in business or industrial production—one asks oneself what is the relation of all that with the Church and with her sacral life and priesthood. We know well enough that men are turning away from God and that the contemporary world is a world of unbelief, of rationality turned in on itself, bent on the use of its demiurgic powers and the pursuit of happiness, all without God. But there is more to it than that. There is the fact that, for the first time, the Church is really confronted by a secular world, and by the task of developing a fitting spirituality and means towards the reign of Christ in the lives of those engaged in the work there. It is not difficult to see that new forms of holiness are called for and that, if they are really to touch men where they actually live and move, the clergy have to find not only new pastoral forms but even new forms of priestly life.   *   *   *

There is only one Christian life, which is developed according to the conditions and requirements of particular times and callings. The signs of the quest for new actualisations of holiness that is going on today can be grouped under three main heads.

(1) For a time and as a whole, Christians did not react in face of a laicised daily life. They asked no questions, and in practice accepted a division between their religious life, consisting chiefly of obligatory cultural observances, and their daily earthly life of work, family, recreation. Between the years 1925 and 1935, Catholic Action struck a heavy blow at this calamitous attitude. Catholic Action marked the simultaneous realisation of the secular condition of the contemporary world, consciousness that it must be hallowed and that we must sanctify ourselves in it, and the rise of a laity which, with its clergy, was seriously considering the problem of its Christianity. During those ten decisive years, the theme of exhortations, of writings, of retreats and days of recollection was unwearyingly the same: Put Christ back into the whole of life; don't be Christians only on Sundays; the faith is not an overcoat, to be hung up in the cloakroom of office or factory, it is a total quality which must inform the whole personality and its integral life.

Thus was spread the idea that daily life, working, civic, domestic, is simply an aspect and a part of one single Christian life in which the faithful have to sanctify themselves and give glory to God—after all, a rather strange idea to the old monastic world, and still more to the laicised world between a dying sacral Christendom and the first hints of a new Christendom.[15]

[15] We have pointed out that the patristic era and the Middle Ages did not ignore the sanctification of professional and family life, but even to that they brought the points of view of their monastically-dominated spirituality. The differences between then and now are obvious. Compare how medieval lay groups were drawn to the religious orders, the rise of the third-orders (tertiaries), for instance.

This awakening of Christian consciousness was not without its dangers. There was—there always is, of course—profound truth in the things so often heard during those years: 'When you are at the factory, it is Christ who is there'; the criticism of a 'disembodied Christianity'; the idea of a 'continued Incarnation'. But there was also—and there is always—a danger, when the secular order and the Christian's full engagement therein were (re)discovered, of reducing Christianity itself to that: a danger of identifying the mystical Body with industrial work 'christofinalised' in the soul of the Christian worker; of seeing in holiness an exaltation of man, a service of men, and of this service itself being humanised and laicised, in the bad sense of those words ('I've done with a faith; I'm at the service of a social world'); a danger, finally, of believing that the maximum of Christianity is necessarily found in a maximum of effective engagement in the world's work. These dangers were and are real; many concrete examples of them could be given, and they have been severely denounced.[16] But it must also be stressed that they have been effectively set off in individuals and groupings by a very active life of prayer, frequentation of the sacraments and union with Jesus Christ and his cross. Among the Young Christian Workers in particular, the eucharist, prayer and Calvary in their purest form have never been separated from the truth that they extend to the daily life of work and human relations.

(2) During the war of 1939–1945 and the years that followed there was a deepening of the consciousness of the secularity (*profanité*) of the world and of the full 'laicity' of the faithful; but there has been added thereto consciousness of the missionary commitment of the Christian and the Church, and, too, a probing of the mystery of the Church and of the fact that the laity as laity are 'of the Church'. Hence the desire of so many lay people for a spirituality that would enable them to answer their call to holiness in their own way, by being adapted to their lay condition and to their responsibilities as real members of the Church, the people of God and the Body of Christ. They have a new awareness of being called to holiness, to a holiness not less than that of priests and religious, but doubtless a little different. Many people have now got over the idea that evangelical perfection, particularly the spirit of the Beatitudes and what are called the counsels, is not for them. Accordingly, they feel an inadequacy in the classical classifications, the distinction between the evangelical life, identified with monasticism, and the life of

---

[16] See, *e.g.*, especially A. Z. Serrand in *Vie intellectuelle*, October 1945, pp. 40–61, and L. Bouyer in *Revue des sciences relig.*, 1948, pp. 313–333.

Christians in the world, or the distinction—often leading to separation—between action and contemplation. To deserve the name of contemplation, need prayer, the adherence of mind and will to God, grow somewhere between Heaven and earth, feeding solely on speculative considerations? Cannot it be nourished by all the doings of a dedicated life, dedicated to God in himself and in our brethren, God sought 'on earth as in Heaven'? There is only one God and there is only one holiness, and it consists in total cleaving to God, who alone is holy, holy by himself and in his existence, simply, in his own 'order'.

Today search is being made for an understanding and a living of this holiness that properly befit the lay person and lay service in the Church.[17] In the middle ages a man who felt the hand of God answered by 'leaving the world', he was converted and did penance by renouncing earthly things to the uttermost; and we have seen how Pope St Gregory VII reacted from this in favour of militant and missionary engagement. Today, when the hand of God touches a man, he certainly thinks of the priesthood or the religious life: sometimes right away, like Lacordaire; sometimes after first thinking of remaining a lay man, and then realising that a total commitment of service and godliness is required of him elsewhere. But many people, often by express choice, remain in the lay state, there to try to live Christ's holiness. They want to serve God and to be wholly his in the state of life wherein his call has come to them. Lay saints, 'among working people, scouts, students, fathers and mothers . . . , in every social class, and in the trades and professions which seem never to produce saints . . . , holy men and women who have lived their lives in the ordinary conditions of the world . . .'. We think of our Lady St Mary, queen of all saints, who was the first lay person in the Church and who led a perfect life in those ordinary conditions. At the present time, a desire for service and Apostleship is very often added to the seeking of holiness 'in the world'. In a medieval world imbued with Christianity, the God-touched man devoted himself to God alone. Now, in a world not simply 'pagan' and indifferent but godless, it is still like that; but the man also—perhaps especially— wants to be an apostle, to bear witness, to serve others, to live and bring to them the saving love of Jesus Christ. Canon F. Boulard has rightly written that, 'Other ages were inspired by the superhuman virtue of the solitary and the ascetic; ours is won over by all-embracing charity and goodness'. As we shall see, service of others as

---

[17] Cf. the inquiry referred to in note 1 above.

well as being in the highest degree evangelical is a crucial part of lay 'spirituality'.

(3) Contemporary aspirations would seem to receive divine guidance particularly through the example of the saints who have been given to our age and through the directions of pastoral authority.

It is clear that, looking at holiness in practice, there is something new about it, in the way that new things come about in the Church: that is, they do not abolish the old, they simply develop to meet a new situation those given resources that are beyond the reach of time.[18] It is said that St Aloysius Gonzaga would not look his own mother in the face, that the Curé of Ars would not kiss his; but Piergiorgio Frassati, who is recommended to us as a model today, did not avoid young women and went camping with them. St Katharine of Siena lived like a nun 'in the world' and engaged in all sorts of difficult affairs; but when she undertook the spiritual direction of a Florentine lawyer, the first thing she told him to do was to give up his wife and his profession. Such a thing could happen today, but we lay special emphasis on the home and professional duties, on sanctification through the family and one's work. A hundred years ago a religious man, retired from work, would spend his time in devotional observances and in the company of other like-minded persons; today we are urged to be up and doing among men in a world of men, to use our energies to the full in the field of apostolic work.

Would it be wrong or exaggerated to say that fresh values are being recommended to the faithful in view of new calls of grace in these times? We are thinking of the many writings which, without for a moment forgetting the law of the Cross, offer Christians a humanist ideal, a candid engagement in earthly activities and a positive view of their worth.[19] We are thinking of the renewed vision of the world of nature, the keen concern about work and the world of work, the interest taken by the clergy in men's real life. We are thinking of the many pronouncements in which the leaders of God's people, and notably Pope Pius XII, declare the goodness of earthly activities, of the body and of sport, of marriage as being in its own way an occasion and means of perfection.[20] We are thinking of that impressive

---

[18] See the passage in Newman's essay on the mission of St Benedict where he contrasts the characteristics of Benedict, Dominic and Ignatius Loyola.

[19] See, for example, the references given by S. Ligier in *L'adulte des milieux ouvriers* (Paris, 1951), p. 162, n.2; the work of Fr P. Doncœur in France, of Fr A. Rademacher in Germany, and others.

[20] Pius XII in *Doc. cath.*, 1945, cc.513–518; and his address on 3 March 1940, when he spoke of that charity 'which affection does not corrupt but enlivens, which the marriage bed does not contaminate but heightens'.

collection of texts in which the Church's pastoral magisterium encourages the faithful to recognise the value of initiative, of strength, of confidence, of cheerful and energetic collaboration in human work and earthly progress (cf. Appendix III). All this is supported by the actual lived experience, not of lukewarm lay people of 'worldly' tendencies, but of those who are very fervent and deeply committed Christians. It is plain that all these things mean something and indicate a current that is being providentially guided in the Church of our time.

We have already remarked how canonisations and examples of holiness have a significance equivalent to providential guidance. The Church's life has always included many examples of holy life 'in the world', the greater part of them, however, belonging to that *turba magna* spoken of in the Apocalypse and the liturgy of All Saints, known in their glory only to God;[21] but during the past few generations it seems that a new series is being opened in the shining roll of holiness. As we have said above, the hagiography that is represented by the Breviary *legendae* presents a type of holiness that is expressed in special ways, those of asceticism and monasticism; and the laity accordingly often get from it an impression of unreality and unapproachability. God now seems to be giving us, beside the saints of the sacral ages, examples from among people whose holiness was achieved through ordinary activities, just the same as those to which we are called, but carried out for the sake of God and his reign, with perfected love and obedience to his holy and hallowing will. Such persons as St Antony Claret, St John Bosco, the boy St Dominic Savio, and our contemporaries St Pius X, Bd Contardo Ferrini and St Teresa of Lisieux, she whose way of childhood would appear to be an interpretation of the evangelical ideal given by God to our world and lit up by a wonderful shining holiness. And perhaps among the saints of tomorrow there will be such as Ozanam, García Moreno, General de Sonis, Philibert Vrau, Leo Harmel, Frassati, Elizabeth Leseur, Marius Gonin, Jaegr, Brother Mutien, Antony Martel, Father Maximilian Kolb, and some of the stalwarts of Catholic Action (only yesterday, John Colson).

If one examines, from the point of view with which we are concerned, the canonisations carried out by the twentieth-century popes, one will notice, as a Protestant observer has done,[22] a sort of 'politics

[21] [Perhaps attention may here be drawn to the people of godly life who are publicly venerated because they accepted martyrdom. An outstanding example is St Thomas More.—*Translator's note.*]

[22] H. Hermelink, *Die katholische Kirche unter den Pius-Päpsten des 20 Jahrhunderts* (Zurich, 1949).

of canonisation': it consists in giving contemporary people models of holiness and patrons for the different conditions of their vocation, occupation and duties. These patterns are not so much in line with asceticism and unusual deeds as with St Teresa of Lisieux's childlike spirit, in complete giving of oneself to God's will, the exact doing of the duties of one's state, the following of Jesus in his love and humbleness.

Dostoevsky sometimes had strange ideas but he was often prophetic about the state of the world, and in *The Brothers Karamazov* he sketched the idea of a new Christian vocation. The old monk Zossima, on his death-bed, tells his disciple Alyosha to leave the monastery and return to the world; there, in contact with evil, he will have to fulfil his vocation of raising up a reconciled and brotherly mankind: he will have to serve God in the persons of men. Zossima dies; and Alyosha, after reading the story of the wedding at Cana beside the body, throws himself to the ground and kisses the earth in a passion of love. Dostoevsky did not write the continuation of a story in which life would no doubt reveal more about things than do books. But the broad outline of the idea is clear enough to enable us to see the pattern of the whole.

SANCTIFICATION IN THE WORLD

It is easy to define the two sides of our inquiry. We learn from the Bible and from the experience of the Church of the saints and martyrs that the Christian, while living in the world, is not of the world—he is in it as a stranger and sojourner. Recent experience, especially of new demands made on Christians, speaks to us of sanctification through our very employment in the world and involvement in its affairs. The first of these voices has an absolute value, as a permanent imperative; the second is a relatively new imperative, made manifest in an historical situation which Christians had not yet fully experienced; the first is the expression of a universal law, covering all cases, the second is a full valuation of the particular aspect, included in the universal law but hitherto less realised, expressed in God's own word: 'I pray not that thou take them out of the world . . .' (John xvii, 15); 'Increase and multiply, and fill the earth and subdue it . . .' (Genesis i, 28). How can the truth of these two voices be reconciled, how can both be obeyed at once? How can the lay man fulfil his calling to be fully a citizen of the City that is to come, not in spite of his commitment to the earthly City but actually in it? There are some answers offered to this question that do not entirely satisfy us.

Some are too optimistic; they put forward service of God in and

through the world's work in such a way that this work seems to be
identified with that of the Redemption and of the Kingdom of God:
they would as it were see most Christianity there where there is most
effective engagement in the business of the world. Convictions of this
kind make ready appeals to the ideal of Catholicity and of 'continued
Incarnation'. But this is to forget that the Church is a different
thing from the world, and that the world is not holy by itself but has
to be hallowed and saved from without, by Jesus Christ. The Son of
man, the New Adam, does not come from the earth but from on
high; his work is not the world's work, which also is not holy by itself:
it has to be hallowed by being put into relation, in a way that
remains in a sense external to it, with the unique holiness of God and
Jesus Christ. Moreover, many great lay saints, beginning with the
Virgin Mary herself, while they were sanctified in the duties of their
state, yet did not undertake big things from the point of view of the
world's demands.

Other answers seem too negative, or at least too dualistic. First
among these is the ascetico-monastic answer. When for instance
St Gregory the Great resolves the Christian antinomy (to be in the
world—not to love the world—to use it as not using it) by saying that
earthly things are there for the Christian to use according to his needs
but not for him to desire and cherish, we are in general agreement
but not completely satisfied. For we are seeking a spirituality that
shall recognise more worth in earthly things than St Gregory
accords them: we want the Christian to be able to put his heart into
the world's undertakings and achievements but without being enthralled by them as if they were a last end. St Gregory's solution is
wholly monastic; at bottom, it assumes that there is only one order
of values, that of supernatural life, faced by which the use of temporal things is no more than an indulgent concession; eventually, it
leads to what has been called 'political Augustinism', whereby temporal power itself has only the consistence it receives from the supernatural order. But this was given its death-blow by the great
thirteenth-century doctors, Albert, Thomas, and after them John of
Paris and many others. We have learned that though the work of the
world is not the last end, neither is it *solely a means*; subordinate to
the absolute end, it partakes of the character of means, but also of
intermediate end, having its *own* value in its order. Accordingly it is
appropriate that our commitment to it—in complete subordination
to our supreme commitment to the faith—should be real and valid in
its order too. We are engaged neither as to sheer means nor as to
absolute end, but as to an intermediate end.

The 'cosmic incarnation' position does not sufficiently distinguish between Church and world. The monastic solution does not see the whole of the Church's mission to the world: to the world as sinful, to preach repentance to it, yes; but also to the world as cosmos, to achieve its purpose in Christ Jesus. The one explanation has an idea of Catholicity that is too wide; the other has an idea of holiness and of Christ's work that is too narrow, in as much as it makes the monastic ideal that of all Christian life, even lay. Jesus is the saviour *of the world*, his incarnation and his cross are to restore creation in accordance with God's design. This restoration is indeed eschatological; but not in such a way that the work of Christians engaged in the world is unconnected with it: it is particular material of holiness and Christian value to those who are called to it.

So we have to find a way between positions that are too favourable to the world or too negative, which, however, at least remind us that the antinomy of the Christian condition here below is irreducible. St Paul was not just playing at paradox or literary conceits when he wrote of this condition in dialectical terms: having as having not, weeping as weeping not, using the world as not using it, treated as deceivers and yet truthful. It is all quite true, and we can add to St Paul contradictions inherent in the conditions of our life today: finding life hard yet being assured, worried for our children yet full of trust, badly off but finding the wherewithal to give. . . . This is perhaps to go beyond St Paul's strictly personal terms of reference, as it is to extend his thought to speak, with Walter Dirks, of the Christian being lost to the world and at the same time the friend of every created thing.[23] There is no world-loving spirituality for lay people, he writes, for they too have to renounce the world and set it at naught; but, unlike monks, they have to work in it, to use it, and to serve God without cutting down their earthly commitments. Once again, to be of it and not of it, to be truly of it and truly not of it. How?

We have to start from the will of God, for it is that that sets the Christian apart from the world to make him a citizen of another City and, at the same time, does not withdraw him from the world but leaves him to work therein. To all, God directs a call that raises them above the world; it is this call that properly constitutes the people of God, following that first call by which this people came into existence in the person of our father Abraham, father of believers: 'Go forth out of thy country and from thy kindred and out of

<hr>

[23] 'Der Welt verloren und aller Welt fruend', in *Geist und Leben*, vol. xxiii (1950), pp. 288–298.

thy father's house'.[24] Nobody who fails to answer the call is fit for
the Kingdom of God; but neither is everyone called to work for that
kingdom *directly and exclusively*. Those to whom the call comes in this
sense must answer it: no yoke of oxen to be tried, nay, not even a
wife to be cherished, may be allowed to come between the Lord and
them (Luke xiv, 16ff.; etc.). Others have to work for the Kingdom
without leaving family and relatives, business and property—their
'nets'. John the Baptist sent the tax-gatherers and soldiers back to
their occupations, only telling them to be more honest in their dealings (Luke iii, 10–14). Jesus did not call the centurion away from his
command or Nicodemus and Joseph of Arimathea from their respectable positions or the ordinary people who listened to him from their
hardworking lives; he sent the paralytic back home, the woman
taken in adultery and the Samaritaness too. St Paul wrote that it
does not matter whether we eat and drink or whether we abstain, he
told the faithful to stop where they were; and it is clear the Apostles
did not alter the state of life of those whom their preaching numbered
among the faithful.

After having set the faithful apart from the world by his call, God
puts them back there and assigns to each a task and duty which also
is, in its order, a vocation according with the divine will. God leaves
the monk in the world, but here the world is only a setting; he leaves,
he sends, the apostle—priest or lay person—in the world, but here
the world is only an object on which one works in view of something
else; he leaves, or rather he puts, a vast number of men and women
in the world, assigning to them the task of co-operating in the work
of the creation in such a way that it is not alien to their sanctification
and salvation, to their co-operation in the Kingdom of God.

The Christian is in the world and does its work in conditions very
different from those of the man who knows not the living God. The
Christian's engagement therein is real, but it is not to a closed world,
regarded solely in itself and as final and definitive, but as being under
the will of God, a temporary world, which man can look after
lovingly but wherein he is awaiting a call whose delay does not hide
its real imminence. 'All things are yours', writes St Paul, 'and ye are
Christ's, and Christ is God's.' That does not mean that every earthly
joy is to be banished, that every thing is to be decked in ashes and to
take on the mourning of Good Friday. People are afraid of that,
partly through worldly attachment to loveless pleasure, partly

---

[24] Genesis xii, 1; cf. Hebrews xi, 8–10. This is in line with the well-known texts
Luke xiv, 26; ix, 62; xviii, 29; Mark x, 29. The association of the word ἐκκλησία
itself with the idea of calling together should be noticed.

through wrong understanding of what for us is 'being Christ's', and
for Christ is 'being God's'. We are much too inclined to separate
Good Friday from Easter; we do not perceive the deep bond between
the redeeming Incarnation and the Creation, that the second requires
the first, not that it may be rejected and destroyed but that it may be
saved and fulfilled in truth.

It therefore seems to us that the paradox of the Christian condition
can be resolved by starting from God's will, which gives or restores
the world to us as duty and as task. From this first great unbreakable
link the main elements of a 'spirituality' of Christians 'living in the
world' follow like a chain thus: the holy and hallowing will of God→
vocation→service and its demands→engagement and responsibility:
the whole beneath the sign of the Cross.

The Will of God. – When we set ourselves to learn how the Bible
understands things, in particular such fundamental notions as faith,
truth, holiness, the word, strength, we arrive at the following general
idea, which in its simplicity lights up many texts:[25] God is the primary
and supreme source of all activity, nothing has life and dynamism
except through him; he alone is wise, mighty, good, and man is wise,
mighty, good *only through him*. God alone is holy, and especially is
nothing holy except through him, that is, by belonging to and par-
taking of him. Now, in God, holiness is not an attribute that can be
explained by another attribute, indeed, it hardly is an attribute: it is
in Pascal's sense of the word, the order proper to God, his order of
existence, wherein he is grounded as an inexistence itself, necessarily,
by reason of what he is. It is a mystery, his mystery, a mystery being
something whose explanation is carried in itself. Surely there are few
verses more expressive of biblical spirituality than Psalm xviii,
verse 10 (Vulgate): 'The judgements of the Lord are true, justified in
themselves'. God's will is holy; not because it is good by reference to
a right and good object, but because it is the Lord's will, he who is
in himself absolute holiness.

Nothing is holy unless in dependence on and in conformity with
God, who alone is holy: and accordingly spiritual men all declare
obedience to his holy and hallowing will to be the content and final
test of holiness. Is not this what all the prophets preached, beginning
with the first, Samuel? 'Obedience is better than sacrifice . . .'[26]

God's will is a will of love. As Father F. Varillon has said, love is
not an attribute of God, it is his very name, that is to say, his essence,

[25] Cf. J. Pedersen, *Israel, its Life and Culture* (2 vols., London, 1940).

[26] 1 Samuel (Kings) xv, 22–23. Cf. Osee vi, 6; Amos v, 21ff.; Isaias i, 10ff.;
Micheas vi, 6ff.; Psalms xlix, 9; l. 18; Matthew ix, 13.

and the classical attributes (justice, all-powerfulness, and the rest) are rather the attributes of love. 'God is *agape*', wrote St John, precisely that source of goodness whose loving movement is directed and justified by itself, like water rising from a spring: God's love is not aroused by the existing goodness of what it sees: flowing from the source of all goodness, it makes good that which it freely loves. God loves and sheds goodness everywhere because he is God. There is no need to stop at the philosophical aspect of certain passages of St Thomas which invoke the Dionysian axiom that the good communicates itself;[27] he uses these perfectly valid philosophical notions only in order to elaborate an exposition of the most fundamental data of the Judaeo-Christian revelation. This revelation shows God, perfectly blissful and self-sufficient in the absoluteness of his glory, freely making creatures, and in particular a creature in his own image, in order that he may communicate his goodness to them.

In a succession of ever higher and more beautiful degrees, God gives his creatures being: not simply the minimum of being necessary for existence, but with the ability further to perfect their being through their own activity, to accomplish themselves and the world through a demiurgic [II] power that is in them. Yet more, God made man in the divine image, destining him from the first to be raised to sonship, in such a way that he could accomplish himself and the world by his efforts *freely*. For freedom is the mode of action that befits a spiritual being and a person who exists in his own being, with choice and judgement of his own activity. By a further communication of God's goodness, man is called to do his work of accomplishment not simply through the exertion of the demiurgic energies implanted in him and the world, but according to another scale of knowledge and powers, that of the divine intercourse that we call grace: on the basis of a choice, a call, a personal communication through his word, then of the gift of his own Spirit, grace is a new and more intimate communication by God of his goodness.[28] That goodness goes further still, even to a real and substantial communication of himself to mankind through the union of the person of the Word with the son of David, in Mary's womb. Nothing more could be given, for this union is the only communication of his divine being itself that God could make short of pantheism.

These communications are so linked up that the first tends towards

[27] See particularly *Sum. theol.*, III, q.i, a.1, with Cajetan's comments; and C. V. Héris, *Le mystère de Dieu* (Paris, 1946).

[28] Chrysostom distinguishes God's kingship exerted over his creation according to demiurgy and according to 'familiarity': *In i Cor.*, hom. xxxix, n.6 (PG., lxi, 341). Cf. the *Journal of Theological Studies*, 1948, p. 59.

the second and finds its meaning there; together they show forth the bounty of God's successive approaches. They make part of a single design, which can be expressed, as by St Thomas, in terms of that which comes from God returning to him, or in terms of temple, as summed up by St Paul, 'All things are yours, and ye are Christ's, and Christ is God's': Christ gives back to the Father all over which he has established his reign, that God may finally fulfil the communication of his goodness in blessedness and glory, and that his reign may be ours too.

Such, so far as we can know it, is the general effect of God's holy and hallowing will. It is expressed for each individual in a variety of ways in his daily life, particularly in that which may well be called a vocation. We shall come back to that. But all vocations have their place within the total purpose that embraces the whole destiny of the created universe, so that God's will for each one always involves imperatives having in view the actualising of his mercy for the whole world and for all men. To each he accords gifts, possibilities, opportunities, which are the setting for the fulfilment of oneself, of one's task and one's happiness,[29] but also of one's part in the accomplishment of God's will for the whole world: the will that all things that breathe shall be filled, that all men shall be saved and come to the knowledge of truth.

Every believer must needs be a servant of this holy, santifying will, and find a cheerful strength from the certainty that, whatever form it takes, it is a loving will. We know, and they know, that lay people do not have a special 'spirituality'. They nourish their spiritual life and seek their sanctification by turning ever more directly towards God's will, lovingly endeavouring here and now to co-operate with it on earth as in Heaven. That is the essential consideration in a 'spirituality' of Christians busied in the world: it is hardly its 'own' or its 'proper' value, for it is not peculiar to that 'spirituality', but it may be said to be the most sufficient and the most fitting to it. In the inquiry conducted by *La Vie spirituelle* already referred to (note 1, above), it is noticeable that obedience to God in one's state of life is very often put forward as the proper characteristic of holiness. And it is noticeable, too, that several answers personify this ideal in our Lady St Mary: she 'led a normal life in obedience and detachment . . . in the world, amidst the day-to-day comings and goings of an artisan's household'; but above all, perfectly in right relation towards

---

[29] Some wise man has said that 'The secret of happiness is to love one's duty and to try to find satisfaction therein'. In the collect of the 13th Sunday after Pentecost we ask 'ut mereamur assequi quod promittis, fac nos amare quod praecipis'.

God from her conception, she was at every moment exactly what he wanted her to be. One answer invented a word that is expressive, even if not beyond criticism: it spoke of 'the Blessed Virgin's increasing participation in the grace of *immaculisation* of the will', meaning thereby growth in perfect conformity to what God wills for us at every moment and in all circumstances of life.

It is also to be remarked that the aspect of God's will has been stressed whenever there has been a call in the Church for service that is militant, and therefore temporal and generally lay. Pope St Gregory VII, for example, wrote that 'It is not for a man to decide what path he shall take; he has to accept the decisions of Him who directs his steps'. Nowadays people like to refer themselves to Christ the King, to the rule of his sacred heart; and French scouts have made their own a prayer of St Ignatius Loyola: 'Lord Jesus, teach me to be generous, to give without counting the cost, to serve you as you ought to be served, to fight without caring about wounds, to work without respite, to spend myself without looking for any reward except the knowledge that I am doing your holy will'.

Vocation. – We might say that everything is vocation, as George Bernanos said that everything is grace. Bernanos was no Father of the Church, but the Fathers and many of the great scholastics would not have disowned him. However, there are narrower and more precise meanings of the words grace and vocation. The term 'vocational council' points to the sense of vocation as profession, trade, occupation, 'calling' in fact, and that usage is fully justified. But when we speak in French (and English) of 'the work of vocations', or say that so-and-so has, or has not, got a vocation, we are thinking solely of the priestly or religious vocation, the 'call to higher service. Accordingly there are some who want to reserve the name of vocation to the priestly and religious state of direct service of God and rejection of temporal things, and refuse it to lay life and to marriage. Others, on the contrary, speak of vocation to marriage and to the various states of life characterised as callings, and point out that the very existence of celibacy implies a vocational character in marriage. Surely these are two elements or aspects of a truth to each of which, here as elsewhere, justice must be done, while keeping them together in an integral synthesis.

This is not so difficult if we start with God's will as pursuing the realisation of a design which is carried on at two different levels but is none the less one in the end. Every man has a vocation, because there is a will of God in respect of each one, ordered to the carrying out of that design. This will may be manifested in a particular way;

but ordinarily it is expressed in the inclinations which an individual gets from his temperament, education and circumstances, in the invitations he receives, expressly or tacitly, from others, and so on. That is St Thomas's idea, and at bottom it is the idea of Catholic tradition. It may be remarked that it is especially preaching religious, spiritual writers and mystics who have held to this idea of a vocation of every man according to his state, and of sanctification in carrying out the duties of that state 'in God's name', that is, in loving obedience to His will. We find it, for instance, in Eckhart and Tauler: when a man turns to God, God gives him the world anew as a duty and service. Tauler speaks of this explicitly as a call or vocation from God.

The Bible enables us to distinguish the two different planes on which the single design is worked out. Genesis, the Book of Beginnings, sets forth, in their relation to God and his to them, the origins of two orders of things; it deals with them in successive parts, the first comprising chapters i–xi of the book, the second being from chapter xii to its end—or even to the end of the whole Bible, where the 'unveiling', the Apocalypse, of the purpose announced at the beginning is completed. The first eleven chapters of Genesis explain—essentially from the point of view of God's free and gracious willing—how there came into being what may be called the creational order, all those things that man experiences about him in the world: an order, moreover, that is disturbed by sin, deprived of its 'integrity' and in bondage to 'vanity', in the sense of those words given in our third chapter. Genesis explains the cosmos itself, the earth, light and darkness, the firmament, land and water, life vegetable and life animal, and then man, with his spiritual nature, his male and female forms, the mutual attraction of man and woman, marriage, work as creativeness: and then sin, evil, pain and affliction, work as a burden, sexual shame; finally, the seeds of war and death in the world, something of a mechanised civilisation, differences of race, the variety of language that makes a barrier between peoples, with whose multiplicity and dispersion the section ends.

But with chapter xii something absolutely new begins, a new creation, as one may say: 'The Lord said to Abram: "Go forth out of thy country and from thy kindred and out of thy father's house and come into the land which I shall show thee. And I will make of thee a great nation." . . .' It is no longer a matter of the creational order, with its surroundings and laws whose regularity was guaranteed by the Noachic covenant [W]: so far as a collective economy is concerned, the order of free purpose of grace has begun. God no longer acts simply as Cause of all things, but as Lord, as the living

God. Freely he chooses and calls, with a word he makes this choice and calling known. It is the beginning of the history of the people whom God summons, whom he calls from the world to his service (*ecclesia*): to correspond with the creational order, it may be called the vocational order, the order of the purpose of grace whose story fills the Bible and which is actual today in the Church.

It would seem that this distinction of two orders can be helpfully applied to the matter of vocation. It shows us vocation in a wide sense, depending on the creational order and God's general providence; and vocation in a strict sense, properly and directly ordered to the realisation of the purpose of grace, depending on a special intervention by God. God's call to those whom he has chosen to work for his purpose and reign is clearly presented as vocation in the Scriptures: all the faithful (who as such are called) and the instruments or ministers whom God joins with himself as collaborators.[30] If the word vocation has been more particularly applied to the monk, to the extent of being almost reserved to him, it is not (as K. Holl supposes) through an ignoring of the faithful people and an improper confining to some of what belongs to all: it is principally because the monk's life realises the Christian vocation integrally and to the letter. God's word to Abraham, quoted above, has been traditionally applied to monks. Holl was making the most of the views of Luther who, as against what he believed to be the traditional meaning, denied that monk or priest has any special Christian vocation different from that of a cobbler or a housewife. But it is the opinion of contemporary exegesis that Luther exaggerated the importance he attached to states of life 'in the world' as Christian vocations, these things not being so strongly brought out in the Bible.[31]

Vocations to the direct service of God's purpose of grace have something special about them. They are much more imperious. They are organised socially in and by the Church, which thus again collaborates with God and again carries out visibly what the Holy Spirit does inwardly; they therefore entail entry into an 'institution' and

[30] Use of κλησις for the faithful: Romans xi, 29; 1 Corinthians i, 26; Ephesians i, 18; iv, 1, 4; Philippians iii, 14; 2 Thessalonians i, 11; 2 Timothy i, 9; Hebrews iii, 1; 2 Peter i, 10. Use of κλητός Romans i, 6, 7; viii, 28; 1 Corinthians i, 2, 24; Jude 1; Apocalypse xvii, 14; and the numerous use of καλέω. For the collaborators, cf. for example Abraham, Genesis xii; Isaias li, 2; Moses, Exodus iii; Samuel, 1 Kings iii; Isaias, Isaiah vi; Jeremy, Jeremiah i; the Apostles, Matthew iv, 21; Mark i, 20; iii, 13; Paul, Romans i, 1; 1 Corinthians i, 1; Galatians i, 15.

[31] K. Holl, 'Die Gesch. d. Wortes Beruff', in *Ges. Aufs.*, vol. 3, pp. 193, 196. Cf. Kittel's *Wörterbuch*, vol. iii, p. 493, note.

there constitute a particular sacred state.[32] Nevertheless, the tasks willed by Providence in the creational order for the fulfilling of the whole divine plan are also the object of true vocations, though in a less strict sense and in a less urgent way. There are as many of them as there are men and women, for God calls each one by his name, but they have a common object and they can be arranged into several large categories.

Their common object is to seek the perfection and harmonisation of the creational orders by striving to withdraw them from 'vanity' and so far as possible to procure its 'integrity' for everything: this can be done only by putting a thing in its right place with regard to other things (peace, unity), especially with regard to that which is above it (order). This, as we have seen, constitutes a preparation of the Kingdom of God in respect of the cosmos. Concretely, it is man's effort to liberate and develop the energies latent in the world (demiurgic power), to free himself from the world, to accomplish creation and accomplish himself by giving, at the call of his Creator, the free response of his co-operation and self-dedication, as leader in a world that he draws after him in the wake of his own destiny. Here we would draw attention to all the texts of the Old and the New Testaments that sound a note of 'cosmism': they encourage a very positive idea of the Christian's creational vocations.

These vocations may be distributed accordingly as they belong to the elementary human, the political or the economic organisms. The elementary human organism includes the states of husband and wife, of father, mother and child. All the states we are going to mention here can be called 'orders', in the sense explained. But the state of husband and wife, being consecrated by a sacrament of the Church, constitutes an order not only in the world but in the Church; it is traditionally so called in a sense that has an ecclesiological as well as a sociological significance. On the other hand, the governmental and civic states of the political organism have no ecclesiological significance, except possibly that the sacring of sovereigns may institute them in a sacred office and dignity. The economic organism includes the states of employer and employed, or rather, within an enterprise, of an initiator and director and of the co-operators; and this organism also includes the different trades and professions that are integral parts of it (the first division is rather that of its potential parts).

[32] Writing of the priestly and the religious states, Fr de Montcheuil observes that 'One does not enter them simply at will, and one cannot leave them at one's own pleasure'.

These great categories, and others, were seen of old as so many 'orders' or 'estates'. The word *ordo* had more than one meaning: in a general sense, recognised in the secular as well as the ecclesiastical sphere, it signified a state of life corresponding to a function (*officium*), having defined conditions of life and its own regulations. Accordingly, *ordo* was at one and the same time (e)state (*status*), charge (*officium*), business or profession (*ministerium*), dignity and honour (*dignitas, honor*), and with all that, vocation. *Ordo* was grounded in a certain state or condition which involved a given way of life, emoluments, expenditure and honours, but also duties (to live according to one's condition or state), and it represented a certain degree (*gradus*) in a social hierarchy that was highly organic. Every man had his place and his function: the carpenter, the mason was carpenter or mason of a community that also had its fighting men, its judges, its king, its men of prayer and its priests. Each one represented this or that function or service for the others. This notion of an organism is always cropping up in the mind of the middle ages; it is the secret of a society whose fixity rather repels us but whose essential idea was perfectly sound.

The Middle Ages thought of sacred functions and secular functions as completing each other to build up one single society, as the north and south sides make up a church building or the right and left sides a human body. We cannot follow that era in giving the name Christian Commonwealth or even Church, to the whole of which the orders of labourers, soldiers and the rest would be members side by side with the orders of monks or of nuns. But we can do justice to the deep element of truth expressed in this view; after sharply distinguishing the vocations of the creational order from those directly referred to the purpose of grace and the Kingdom of God, we can agree that the first of these orders is not unrelated to the second.

We have only to recall what has been said in Part One Chapter III. We saw that the Incarnation has a relationship to the Creation, that Christ 'brings all things to a head', so that in him Creation is accomplished and finds its full meaning. Thereby the creational order, the order of explanations and techniques, receives a divine *significance*, which belongs to the wisdom of faith and answers to that 'supplement of soul' of which Bergson speaks; it was Bergson, too, who did not hesitate to call the universe 'a machine for making gods', thus recalling many passages in the Fathers. 'Just as God's will is an act and is called the world, so his intention is man's salvation and is called the Church', wrote Clement of Alexandria. It is very remarkable to see how the ancient liturgies, no doubt taking a theme from Jewish prayer, put thoroughgoing Christic praise into a setting of cosmic praise. So far as we know, this point has not been studied; but it is important and deserves careful examination. One can speak of an 'Adamic function' of creation and a 'Christic function' of redemption, provided that the connexion of the first with the second is made clear, and that they are not referred respectively to the laity and the clergy: creational tasks ('Adamic function') are more especially the business of the laity, but their final meaning is in Christ and they do not prevent lay people from having their part in the redemptive function and the duties of the Church, as we hope we have shown. In any case, the creational function or vocation of the laity is itself in one sense a function or vocation of the Church, or at the very least in the Church. Not only does spiritual vocation generally find its place in the natural vocation that arises providentially from our gifts, opportunities, etc., but it is each one's providential 'Adamic tasks' that provide the setting of the laity's mission of 'being the Church', in the sense of Pope Pius XII's words. Care, then, must be taken in distinguishing the two planes of vocation, lest we put too far from one another what God himself brings together in that unitary design wherein the same creation that was lost is to be saved in Christ.

In this matter of vocation, one of the most necessary of priestly duties is to give the faithful an over-all view of God's design for the world, to help them to find their place in that design and to learn what is the Christian's service and responsibility in the world.

Service and its demands. – We are emancipated from the tyranny of the world by the call from on high; but God gives the world back to us as our task, and we accept it as his holy and hallowing will, with the vocation to co-operate with Love's design for his creation. That is the field of the engagement for which we have been set free, in which we exercise that Christian freedom spoken of before with reference to our spiritual kingship.

Christian freedom is not the freedom of a man without responsibility or of a tourist—we are pilgrims, travellers, in the world, but not in that sense. Ours is the position of one who, delivered from bond-service, is given a new task, or simply the same one, as a vocation and labour of love. For the Father does not restore the world to us as selfish, worldly beings but as his children, his family, the body of his only-begotten Son, to us-all-as-a-single-one, to us as living in charity: 'ut te tota virtute diligant, et quae tibi placita sunt, tota dilectione perficiant', says the Missal. And what is restored to us is the same world and not the same world: it is the world as realm of the Father. Every part of it belongs to him: we live there very happily, as children with their Father, but in as much as, babes as to malice, we are grown-up in mind (cf. 1 Corinthians xiv, 20), we indeed also live there as stewards of the things that are not ours but the Father's, intended by him for all his family.

Such is the very profound meaning of the parable of the Unjust Steward. We have seriously to strive for life everlasting by making use of goods that, radically, do not belong to us but to the Father of all. It is service, therefore, *of God* and of our brethren, his children, not solely in themselves but in that part of the common estate which it has fallen to us to take care of; this, of course, without detriment to direct service of God and neighbour, in which the part of the clergy and religious is more especially found. The fact that all this is service of God does not mean that nothing else is added to it, especially at the inspiration of God himself, who is the author of all healthy natural inclinations (interest in things, fellow-feeling, love for the world of men); nor does it mean any lack of enjoyment of the work given us to do. It is right and proper that we should come from prayer or the eucharist with a longing, like Dostoevsky's Alyosha, to kiss the earth: for we have just communed with the source of all fellowship and with the will of Him who day by day, together with the day's bread, gives us all things for our task: 'Give us this day our daily bread'; 'My food is to do the will of him that sent me and to accomplish his work'.[33]

The Christian's position as God's faithful servant in the world makes two principal demands, corresponding respectively to an aspect of detachment or transcendence and one of engagement or immanence. In relation to engagement, that is, fidelity of service and its discharge taken in themselves, the great requirement is to have respect for things and to be competent and efficient. To serve God in the care of his household and children certainly means referring and offering the work to God in prayer; but it also means, essentially, to do the work well: one must be prepared for it, work hard at it, and so far as possible be well qualified for it. It is the same for any other employment—teaching, research, journalism, commercial or industrial activities . . . We need only refer the reader back to the quotation from Professor Gilson in the previous chapter: we Catholics would do well to search our hearts in the light of it. How often do forms for examination of conscience in our prayer-books take notice

---

[33] John iv, 34. On the daily bread, see V. Solovyev, *God, Man and the Church* (London, 1938), pp. 45–46; this is a book well worth reading. See, too, M. Glanndour, 'Notre messe continue', in *Vie spirituelle*, 1951, pp. 466–471.

of this aspect of our duties? Who ever questions and accuses himself on this head?[34] Why is it that so often good intentions are a substitute for a serious effort to be technically efficient, and that the motive of God's service is a cover for mediocrity, uninterestedness and sometimes real objective dishonesty? Péguy went to the heart of the matter when he wrote:

> If one would raise oneself to the eternal, it is not enough to depreciate the temporal. To raise oneself to grace, it is not enough to depreciate nature. To raise oneself to God, it is not enough to depreciate the world . . . [People] believe that, because they have not the strength (and the grace) to belong to nature, they belong to grace. They believe that, because they lack temporal courage, they have passed the threshold of the eternal. They believe that, because they have not the boldness to be worldly, they are godly; not brave enough to be on man's side, they believe they are on God's side; not belonging to man, they think they belong to God. Because they love nobody, they believe that they love God.
>
> And yet Jesus Christ was a man.[35]

The requirement of transcendence concerns, not the actual discharge of one's service, but the spirit that animates it. It is a matter of respecting in all that we have the quality of its being something belonging to one of God's children, a member of his family and of Christ's mystical body: being ours, it is yet not altogether ours, it belongs to God and to all our brethren. The Christian's kingly condition is such that he not only owns things, he dominates them and looks on them as a service or an opportunity for service. That is the concrete programme of that spiritual kingship—so close to inward priesthood—whereby we rule by offering and giving: and that is a thing we have to learn to do properly, just as we have to learn technical competence. There are the words of Jesus, 'What shall it profit a man if he gain the whole world, and lose his soul? Or what shall a man give as a price for his soul?', and the other places where he emphasises the importance of 'being' over 'having', of the person made to love and serve by love over the individual who is slave of a selfish affection (Matthew vi, 19–21, 25; xviii, 8–9, etc.). And after the Master, his apostles: 'All things are lawful to me, but to nothing

[34] [It was not always thus. In the examination of conscience in the first edition (1740) of Bishop Challoner's *Garden of the Soul* there occurs the question: 'Have you profess'd any art, or undertaken any business without sufficient skill or knowledge? And what prejudice has your neighbour suffer'd from it?'—*Translator's note*.]

[35] *Œuvres complètes*, vol. ix, pp. 180, 181.

will I become enslaved' (1 Corinthians vi, 12); 'By whatsoever thing a man is overcome, to that same is he made a slave' (2 Peter ii, 19). Surely these considerations on Christian freedom and spiritual kingship give a concrete meaning to some rather enigmatical sentences earlier in this chapter: Having as having not, weeping as weeping not, and, in contemporary terms, finding life hard yet being assured, worried for our children yes full of trust . . . . We can now see how those whose vocation keeps them 'in the world' can still answer the call addressed to all believers in the person of their father Abraham, 'Go forth out of thy country and from thy kindred and out of thy father's house'. Go forth as not going forth, use as not using—in other words, not to let oneself be tyrannised over by the very things through which we are called to work and serve God with our whole heart.

Engagement and responsibility. – God's will, vocation to service, engagement, feeling of responsibility—these are firmly linked with one another. There is a logic as living as it is sound in the fact that, while our era has taken up the idea of the lay condition as a question of Christian situation and sanctification, it is at the same time particularly drawn to an apostolic (missionary) engagement and shows itself alive to a duty to 'take charge' of this or that corner of the field wherein one is called to work. We have seen that these aspirations would appear to have been given providential encouragement by certain canonisations and other examples of holiness, as well as by pastoral pronouncements (Appendix III). Every generation has its master words. The mind of the Middle Ages answered to 'unity' and 'order'; during the first third of the sixteenth century, everybody was stirred by 'the Gospel' and 'Christian freedom'; the eighteenth century was all for Reason, Nature, the Sublime; today we hear on all sides 'engagement' or 'committed', 'mission', 'community', 'taking responsibility'.

These are not simply fine Christian words: they express searching realities, of which the essence is that every person has been given a task and talents for which he will have to account, and that they are given for the benefit of the whole family of God's children. Each person is responsible for something to somebody, namely, to the authority who gave the charge in respect of which he is accountable. So in a last analysis we are responsible to God in person, for all authority comes from him. But it must not be overlooked that between God and us there is mediation through the order of things in which he has put us, and this mediation, if it be authentic, partakes of the absolute character of his authority. That is why it is not ridiculous to hold oneself responsible before Society, the World, Mankind, History, or to write those words with capital initials—they designate so many faces of God, since they represent so many orders of his will. Unless withdrawn from them by a higher order, every person is pledged to these general orders as to God himself.

One's obligation to these universal orders is sacred. It is not only found in such general duties as speaking the truth or doing a fair day's work for a fair day's pay, but in occasional happenings in which a man finds himself involved, whether he is bound by any express law or not. If we see a child in danger we know we are bound to help; if we know something about an accident or a crime, we feel bound to say so: to do nothing would be to betray something towards which we are responsible. If I do not do it, it will not be done, if I slip away, something will be lost, and I feel a responsibility is on me; if I avoid it, I betray the best in myself. The human person, and still more the Christian person, is not free in Sartre's sense of freedom: he is free and bound, both at once. St Paul wrote: 'Ye were called to freedom, brethren; only let not your freedom be an occasion for the flesh; rather be ye slaves one of another by charity' (Galatians v, 13). It is written into the structure of his personality that man has a relationship to universal and absolute goods, whose nature is determined for each one by the circumstances in which he is.

Dostoevsky wrote in a book that we are responsible (and we may be to blame) for everything and everybody. It is not a matter of books. Many Christians—and non-Christians too—live it. When they see that something they value will not be done if they do not do it, they feel personally called by a higher power; and at God's word they voluntarily add other responsibilities to those already incumbent on them. A household, for example, or group of households, takes charge of the religious upbringing of neglected children, or an individual undertakes to represent Christians in some political or social organisation or a trade union. Free vocations? Yes, but they feel *bound* to undertake them, because each is responsible for all and all for each, the circumstances, external and internal, of every man determining his obligations, as we have said of apostleship.

Engagement, mission and the rest are indeed great Christian words, and moreover they deliver us from that vapid vocabulary which is so embarrassing to an adult. One has to be gradually initiated into all these things by a process of education, and the words accordingly stand for values which are those of adult life. Engagement, to be committed, is at the same time a means to and an indication and fruit of 'growing up'; maturity of personality is both a result and an expression of it. An adult is he who takes full responsibility for what he does and who realises—in both senses of the word, 'understands' and 'effects'—the part he is called on to take in the little world of his daily life, and perhaps on the bigger stage of society and history. He is a man fully born into the world: not the birth to separate physical life after a few months of gestation, but a gradual birth through a slow personal acquiring of the capital of cultivated life garnered by mankind, through difficulties successively overcome and stages reached and passed one after the other; a birth which brings him into the world of action and history, that he may take his place in it and in his turn do the work of creation according to his measure.

To shoulder responsibility means first of all to take a stand: in the home, at work, in economic and political matters, in social life; in the matter of personal witness, too, in parish affairs, perhaps in Catholic Action. To take a stand means to come into collision with differing choices and elements, and so to have opponents: it means a state of strife. That is a test of character, for 'to have character' means to uphold one's convictions in one's own life and to maintain them in face of things, however murky or difficult they may be. To take on responsibility for something often leads to setting bounds to the accepted commitment and to laying down its conditions. A true sense of responsibility is not consistent with an attitude of all-round acceptance; passive obedience kills the psychological and moral roots of responsibility. Authorities who are tempted to abuse their power would do well to reflect on the way God acts: so great is his respect for our freedom that his own mastery gives way before it, as H. Gohde has so well said (*Der Achte Tag*, Innsbruck, 1950, p. 242).

But above all, responsibility or engagement means personal judgement and making choices. Those who always have a habit of asking for answers and directions ready-made, who are always afraid of taking an initiative on their own, run the risk of becoming infantile, poor-spirited, ineffectual and at last of drawing back altogether from any new undertaking that requires decision and wholeheartedness. Many have written about the harm done by legalism with its cut and dried answers, and by the habit of living and thinking as it were by proxy, which makes it impossible to produce a laity up to the requirements of the present day.[36] There is much that needs doing to cure lay people of their mania for looking for directions that dispense them from thinking out their own problems, and to dissuade the clergy from their habit of deciding and prescribing for everything. It would be a good thing were the excellent thomist theology of prudence again to find its place among theologians and in manuals for clerical students, and then to be propounded to the faithful and livingly applied to the needs of contemporary consciences. Something has been done in this line;[37] but St Thomas's lofty and delicate treatment of the subject is far from being really understood by all the doctors in Israel, and therefore far from being properly put to the confused consciences of today.

This is one of the reasons why some people can see no way out of 'moralism', or no alternative to plain obedience to the dictation of cut and dried determinations tempered by casuistry, except in a *mystique* of evangelical freedom or in a pure 'ethic of the situation'. For the first of these, conscience at every moment is given its rule of action according to love; for the second, each situation, often full of insoluble contradictions, is to be judged simply in a spirit of loyalty to oneself and of obedience to God's immediate will. There are several factors drawing people in this direction, real factors, but some of them regrettable. They are, in Father K. Rahner's opinion, the following: the superseding of a hierarchised and stable world by a moving, changing world, full of revolutions and disasters, in which man is confronted by unprecedented, complex and often tragic situations in which it is very difficult for him to know what he ought to do; the influence of Existentialism, of Kierkegaard, and of some Protestant pronouncements, with their suspicion of all metaphysic of essences and of all 'morality' of general rules, and their insistence on the individual's obedience to a positive willing and an immediate call by God, recognised as such in his conscience;[38] and the feeling of

[36] In addition to the writings of Mgr Guardini, Father Doncœur and Charles Péguy, there may be mentioned among many others M. de la Bedoyère, *Christianity in the Market Place* and *The Layman in the Church*; E. Mounier, *L'affrontement chrétien* (Neuchâtel, 1945), pp. 70ff.; and R. Egenter, *Von der Freiheit der Kinde Gottes* (Freiburg i. B., 1948), pp. 132ff., 216ff. Among many references in *La Vie spirituelle*, see especially the issue of October 1951 and May of the same year, supplement, 'Loi et Amour'.

[37] See G. Leclercq, *La conscience du chrétien* . . . (Paris, 1947); A. Gardeil, *La vraie vie chrétienne* (Paris, 1934); the Cahier de la Vie spirituelle, *Prudence chrétienne* (Paris, 1948); T. Deman's French translation of the treatise in the *Summa*; and the writings of Canon J. Leclercq, Fr H. D. Noble and Dr J. Pieper (in German).

[38] Protestant writers often prefer to speak of 'ethic' rather than of 'morality', ethic envisaging Christian behaviour in conformity with God's will, morality considering the objective content of man's works and deeds. Protestant theology rejects (in principle) distinction between sins and appreciation of their gravity according to their matter or object.

insoluble antinomies, aggravated by the difficulties of existence and
by the loss of clear and ordered objective certainties. To these factors
two others must be added, at any rate in France: the renewed appreciation of religious and mystical values over 'morality', and the
return to the Bible. In this last, the rediscovery of the Old Testament
has been very important: from beginning to end it shows that man's
good is what God wants him to do; its conception of the religious
situation is hardly at all essentialist or sapiential, but is determined
by the willing and action of God.[39] There can be no doubt that that
has moved people's minds in the direction of a 'situation ethic': not
that it has led them to substitute the magisterium of conscience for
the magisterium of objective laws; but in the sense that, beyond
objective laws and general principles, people are ready to refer
themselves to what God asks of them *hic et nunc*, to what he wants as
perceived in a conscience that is possessed by the desire to make
loving obedient response to his will.

Our own opinion, formed in the school of Holy Scripture, is that
there is some truth in this point of view of a 'situation ethic'. It can
be seen against the background of Christian life in the work of the
world, with its series of God's holy and hallowing will→vocation→
service→engagement and responsibility. God's will is a daily bread,
given from on high—Christian conduct in its truth is to be ceaselessly formed through a progressive deepening of the subject himself
confronted by God. 'Be ye transformed by the renewing of your
mind, so that ye find out what is the will of God, the good and the
well-pleasing and the perfect' (Romans xii, 2); 'We have never
ceased praying for you, asking that ye may be filled with the full
knowledge of God's will in all wisdom and spiritual insight. Thus
may ye walk worthily of the Lord and in all ways please him . . .,
increasing in the full knowledge of God' (Colossians i, 9–10).

But it is quite clear that St Paul thought the will of God to be
known to us firstly in the commandments he has given, and that
there is an imprescriptible objective law of actions by which he is
pleased or displeased: Father Rahner rightly invokes the list in
1 Corinthians vi, 9ff. (and compare Galatians v, 18–21), as well as
the texts where St Paul presents law-abidingness as the condition of

---

[39] It is no matter for surprise that the best exegete among the Fathers, St John
Chrysostom, wrote that a reputedly wicked deed is good if God wills it, and inversely: 'it is not the nature of things but God's decision that makes an action good
or bad' (*Adv. Juadaeos*, 5; PG., xlviii, 873). He refers to the examples of Ahab
(3 Kings xx, 32ff.) and Phineas (Numbers xxv, 6ff.); he could have added Abraham's sacrifice (Genesis xxii), Osee's marriage (Osee i), and others. For the explanation of such cases in classical theology, see, *e.g.*, T. Deman, *Le mal et Dieu* (Paris,
1943), pp. 49–50; A. D. Sertillanges, *Le problème du mal*, vol. ii (Paris, 1951), p. 39.

life, plainly echoing the formal teaching of our Lord himself.[40] It can scarcely be denied that any 'situation ethic'—or rather, as we should prefer to call it, 'ethic of the immediate will of God'—must *in the first place and always* be an ethic of obedience to God's will objectively expressed in the commandments, on which Christian tradition, itself elucidated by the apostolic magisterium, is like a living commentary. There is not simply an 'ethic', there is a true 'morality' (cf. note 38, above); and at the edge of a science of objective moral laws there is a legitimate discussion of cases wherein the truth of these laws is applied to more complex objective situations: why, St Paul himself uses a certain 'casuistry' . . .[41]

We are convinced that the authentic demands of an ethic of God's immediate will (or 'situation ethic') are met by the thomist theology of action, with its enlightening ideas in the practical order, of prudence and of the gifts of the Holy Spirit. Prudence according to St Thomas is something quite other than an inclination towards 'how much or how little' and mediocrity generally: it is a virtue—that is, an energy—of commitment and effectiveness arising from a conviction about ends in view; it is not at all a collection of recipes or ready-made opinions, nor is it a passive submission to utterances of some acceptable official origin, after the manner of the childish mob in Dostoevsky's Legend of the Grand Inquisitor. Prudence is a virtue, a living adaptation of the subject to his existence in the sense of Good; a moral virtue of the practical understanding, in which the vital right-ordering in respect of Good is of moment to the perception of truth and concerns a sphere wherein truth is *to be made* and built up by the subject himself: a very different thing from copying it line for line from the pattern in some elementary textbook of design. Accordingly, the job of priests with respect to lay people is not to make them the *longa manus* of the clergy, telling them what they've got to do; but to make them believing men and women, adult Christians, leaving them to meet and fulfil the concrete demands of their Christianity on their own responsibility and in accordance with their own consciences.

[40] Matthew xix, 17; John xiv, 15, 21; Romans ii, 13; Galatians iii, 12; etc.
[41] A. Adam, *Spannungen und Harmonie* . . . (Nuremberg, 1948), pp. 111–115, refers to 1 Corinthians vii and x, 27ff., and shows how Paul's 'casuistry' does not stop at a sort of 'prudent dosing'; it takes the cases of conscience seriously, and in each one shows the principle, drawn from the heart of Christian existence itself, from which the faithful soul can and must himself form a conscientious judgement: in the end, this principle is always charity, which 'builds up'. Cf. R. Egenter, *op. cit.*, note 36. It was after these pages were written that Pope Pius XII pointed out the exaggerations in the *Situationsethik* and the errors to which it can give rise (A.A.S., 1952, pp. 270–278, 413–419; *Doc. cath.*, cc. 449–456, 589–596.

Prudence is, moreover, an intellectual virtue, which means that the person will inform and cultivate himself for his own enlightening, that he will use all his knowledge, and that he will turn to advisers when necessary. But advisers should never, even where children are concerned, become dictators, making unnecessary the living movement of a conscience animated by enthusiasm for its ends and by the will to serve them. It is right and proper that the priest should come into the picture, and he will be the faithful mouthpiece of the Church's teaching; but he will do all he can to enter into people's problems and to help them to think *practically*, with God's eye upon them. That can all be done only in an atmosphere of prayer, and of habitual submissiveness to God and to the best in oneself. In these conditions, the virtue of prudence, with all its human limitations, is helped by the gifts of the Holy Spirit, especially wisdom and counsel. These gifts represent openness of the soul to God's comings and to what they call for: openness, then, to the 'event', and submissiveness to the Lord's immediate and positive will. St Thomas sees the field of the gifts as coextensive with the whole spiritual life, as one of the conditions of Christian existence.

It is desirable that this context of morals should be affirmed anew. The problems set by lay engagement and a spirituality dominated by the will of God can thus be solved without falling into the *in pace* of subjection to the cut-and-dried or embarking on the venture of a purely 'situation ethic'.

*   *   *

Emphasis on missionary commitment, on service and on vocation is accompanied by the rediscovery of the meaning of community and by an imperious need to 'form a team'. These solidarities are facts that must be accepted; they have persisted together throughout history, and they have only to be looked at to be understood.[42] It is a very important point, and among all the things that must be forgiven us not the least is that we have paid so little attention to it in this book. We have talked about the priesthood of the faithful, about their spiritual kingship, about their *prophétisme*, about their apostolic role and their contributions to the life of the Church as community, but principally from the point of view of persons. That is the most

---

[42] See *Vraie et fausse réforme*, pp. 292ff.; E. Masure, *Prêtres diocésains* (Lille, 1947), pp. 244ff.; Michonneau-Chéry, *L'esprit missionnaire* (Paris, 1950), pp. 157ff.; *Vie spirituelle*, 1946, pp. 202, 254, 280ff.—It is worth noticing that, while some of the numerous medieval lay spiritual movements after the Gregorian reform ended up as sects outside the Church, the others were eventually 'nobbled' as societies by the religious orders (cf. note 15, above). When such movements reappeared in Italy early in the sixteenth century, they were marked by communal relations and charitable work.

important, indeed, the essential point of view. But a more concrete experience than ours would have had more expressly to show their place in the communal aspect, in actual associations, in the witness and contributions of communities as such. Here are a few testimonies drawn from books or from personal correspondence.

Amidst our pagan conditions of life, the holiness of isolated individuals would appear to be more than endangered. It does not seem to me possible except in an organisation. And that is just the life-buoy that is offered by Catholic Action, whose object is none other than to form 'a band of organised saints'.

For me the most important means of sanctification is membership of a Christian community, provided it is properly united and that it includes certain elements that I feel to be superior to myself. It is very hard to climb alone . . .

It seems to me that the essential element of man's sanctification follows from God's word at the creation: 'It is not good for man to be alone'. This is applied almost exclusively to marriage, but that seems to me to restrict its meaning unduly. Life together with others is for me a primordial element of holiness; it is at the same time a challenge, an enlightenment and a principle of unity . . .

I would like to talk about the particular problems raised by the life of the more and more numerous Christian lay people who are permanently attached to organisations (themselves more and more numerous and diverse), from the direct religious apostolate to international concerns like UNO and UNESCO, including in passing work on newspapers and reviews, trade unions, cultural associations, whether confessional or not. Many of these people are also engaged in—forgive these fine words—the social 'revolution' and religious 'reform' . . . Many of them are so overworked that their physical health and sometimes even their general development and spiritual life are endangered.

My personal experience of thirty years, and what many of my fellows tell me, lead me to the conclusion that only in a team (*équipe*) is it really possible to react effectively, *for oneself in the first place*, and to be capable of directing and animating one's work along the line of reform and revolution. Without being too cut off, this team-life should have a certain autonomy in relation to the organisations, even if these be Catholic. Secular religious institutes might come in here, especially for women. But far too many people remain totally isolated and forsaken from the spiritual and apostolic point of view. I have just seen X, who is certainly one of the most capable and influential trade unionists. He has just been led to resign, at forty-five years old, in deplorable circumstances. He told me that 'Except at Z., with A.B., I've always had to fight alone since I was twenty. When I made mistakes—which I did— nobody helped me to see more clearly; when I was right, nobody backed me up in the row that followed.'

It is necessary for priests to have a hand in these teams; in many ways this clergy-laity collaboration is very good for both, but the priest also must be prepared to 'receive'. It is only on that condition that he is able fully to give.

There are plenty of problems in all this. The evidence also gives their solution so far as it can be formulated, for at the theoretical level it is possible only to point out the direction: the difficulty is all in the carrying of it out, which depends on people. It is less a question of 'how' than of 'who'. All the same, it is important to have become aware of the problem and its theoretical solution, for every one, priest or lay man, whether he wants to form a team and a community or not, can do much to make everything easier or everything more difficult.

A team and a community are not a society or an association but a friendship. These different types of union are born of coming together in the pursuit of the same end, of fellowship in the same objects. The union is not the first thing aimed at, but is the result of an activity or life specified by similar aims. The first thing to do then is to share the same aims, which supposes an effort of the understanding, but it can also come about through empirical action: how many friendships and groups are formed among men who have not clearly formulated their common ideals, but who find themselves together in the same tasks of help and human improvement to which each has given his heart?

But there are several ways of sharing aims and corresponding ways of attaining unity. People can share objects which for the individuals concerned are simply external means to a better and more satisfying life; there is then a general sympathy but not a personal fellowship; the persons are interchangeable without their social relations being affected. They give their services, they do not give themselves. Or they may share directly in objects which are for each one the very heart and matter of his engagement, perhaps the most valuable things in life. Then the persons themselves are involved, they give themselves, and they have fellow-feeling for one another through their common heartfelt convictions and aims. There is something absolute about this giving and sharing, which are of the order of being itself, and they suffer at the touch of any individual, self-interested, holding back. It is the order of friendship; an order of intimacy because the persons themselves share together and so do not remain wholly external one to the other. Here, so far from being interchangeable, the persons are part of the relations, of the mutual exchange, of that which is put in common; and the putting in common means not to lose but to find oneself and to achieve one's best.

In a union of the society type, individual liberties are limited by the obligation to respect the others and to give certain services; in a union of friendship or of true community the aims or ends shared are those personally chosen and adopted. In friendship, the community is above all one of tastes and inclination, and the elements of affection and of intimacy are alike stronger; that is why friendship is a sort of communion or give-and-take in its pure state, it has less need of common action and is sensitive to absence. A community is a larger friendship, more dependent on action together, more external and less intimate, though it has the same fundamental law. A 'team' is formed still more strictly round a definite commitment and end to be worked for: it is to that that the common effort is directed; but, without making the same demands on mutual affection as friendship, it requires a wholly sincere and disinterested contributing of all that a common undertaking calls for. It is the normal form of support for adults of developed personality who are conscientiously engaged in a work beyond their powers as individuals, whether those powers be moral or intellectual or physical.

Where religion is concerned, a 'team' should be made up not simply of individuals or, better, of groups or households, but of lay people and priests. That is what was done in many lay associations of the past, notably in the Oratory of Divine Love. History shows it has only been possible when a fervent laity has been matched by a no less fervent clergy: in medieval times by religious particularly, in the sixteenth and seventeenth centuries by the zealous priests produced by the Catholic reform. Without priestly participation the lay group or team will lack confidence, and it will not be fully achieved *in the Church*. With it, tremendous good will result both for laity and clergy, provided the priest comes in as a religious man and not simply as servant of a system, and that, without derogating from his priesthood, he enters into the spirit of loyal community. Happy

is the man of the Church who is also the man of a true community
of men in the Church.

The parish should be a community of this kind, the more so because in theological sociology it corresponds to the family. Unhappily, many lay people complain that they find little support in
their parish;[43] some of them add that their spiritual life owes a great
deal rather to Catholic Action groups. Is not that because in Catholic
Action the Church takes a more communal form and the clergy-laity
combination is more real? What has been said about the Church's
communal structure, Catholic Action and the clergy-laity combination (Chapters IV and V) finds concrete expression here at the
level of lay people's 'spirituality'. In such a spirituality, communal
values are called for by the vital logic of the Gospel and the deepest
needs of Christian living, and by the most characteristic elements of
the Christian's life in the world—God's will, vocation, service,
engagement and responsibility.

And then there are all the difficulties. How to find time, how to
overcome self-interest, how to get a happy balance between the
requirements of close intimacy and of welcoming openness, and so on
and so on. The answers are as numerous as the difficulties, and like
the difficulties they can only be lived. . . . But they all reflect God's
one answer: love and sacrifice.

Under the Sign of the Cross. – Whether the lay condition be considered under the aspect in which No is said to the world, or under
that in which one says Yes to it, we find the Cross.

The No to the world is the triumph of the spiritual man over the
carnal man: 'They that are of Christ Jesus have crucified their flesh
with its passions and desires'; 'If thine eye scandalise thee . . .' All
that we find in the Gospels or in St Paul apply as much to the Christian 'in the world' as to the monk, and the Church proposes it to the
one as to the other. There is not one life, religious, which recognises
the bindingness of these imperatives of God's Kingdom, and another
life, lay, wherein for practical purposes one holds oneself dispensed
from them. The words 'regular' and 'secular' belong to the vocabulary of canon law; their transference to that of spiritual life and moral
problems has certainly done more harm than good, and its dangers
must be pointed out. From the moral and spiritual point of view,
every Christian is a 'regular', for all of them, laity and clergy, are
bound by the Rule (*regula*) of the Gospel, of which all other rules are

---

[43] There is an impressive display of evidence for this in the *Vie spirituelle* inquiry (1946), pp. 286ff. But of course it generally happens that those who have
complaints express themselves more freely than do others.

only particular applications. The monk promises 'conversion of manners', and thus to tend to perfection in love of God and of his neighbour. But this perfection and the day-to-day improvement in one's ways that it implies are not reserved to monks: they are the rule of all Christian life. In marriage, for example, after the striving for understanding and consideration that comes easily to young love, there is not a moment when one can return to self-centredness and give way to impatience, roughness and whims, careless of the other and careless of one's own perfecting. In business or professional life, there is not a moment when the rule of hard work, good service and selfless love can be dropped, as a youthful enthusiasm outgrown. The movement called Moral Rearmament provides an expression of the spirit of the Beatitudes that no doubt is an over-human version of things—'absolute love, absolute disinterestedness, absolute purity, absolute loyalty'; but it at least shows appreciation of the character, the absolute character, of the gospel rule: its form is striking and positive, and in a general way it declares the law of the Cross. For all Christian life that is the imprescriptible part of the spirituality of the *Imitation of Christ* (after which, but only after which, it can be admitted that that book does not in all respects meet the needs of the faithful engaged in the world).

We said at the beginning of this book that in a way the faithful have a right corresponding to what canon law lays down as the obligations of the clergy. We add here that to the obligations of all Christian life there is a corresponding duty of pastors to be ready to guide souls in this way and to attract them to it: to be prepared to show them the life of prayer, the meaning of God's advances, what a real evangelical 'conversion of manners' calls for. If the spiritual obligations of all spiritual life are similar to those of monastic life, every priest should be, or be able to be, something of a father abbot to his people.

The No to the world may be called the willed part of the Cross. The Yes which is also said to the world by the christian called to serve God in it is rather the accepted part of the Cross; willed, too, in the sense that it is not just taken as an animal takes a blow: one consents to it, one loves it with heart and understanding, but one receives it from God and from events, those masters from the hand of God. It can be said that the lay person's positive engagement in the work of the world is marked with Christ's cross from beginning to end, as the world itself is marked. For the Christian, there is no 'Adamic' function which is not 'Christic'. . . . There is no true charity without learning in the school of the Cross; and among several aspects of our encounter therewith we select three.

First of all, without suggesting for one moment that the things of man (undertakings, health, prosperity, etc.) have to be *expiated*, it must be clearly recognised that they stand in need of purification. Directly one seeks the Absolute through the relative there must be purifying of attachments, which can so easily become a deadweight of hindrances. There is never any serious spiritual life without a purification of faith, hope and love, the virtues by which we cleave to God, in order that it may be *to God* that we cleave, in himself and for himself. Purgatory answers to a like necessity, and one may well see it as a 'time' and 'place' of cleansing even more than of atoning.[44] It is against this background that we must look at the endless difficulties, troubles, trials and temptations which are part of the Christian's daily bread. But in the very midst of dark and weakness God gives light and strength to those whose heart is disposed to welcome the one with the other from his hand as a demand of his love. 'Amidst all this we more than conquer through him who hath loved us. For I am confident that neither death, nor life, nor angels, nor principalities, nor things present . . . nor any other creature shall be able to separate us from the love of God in Christ Jesus our Lord' (Romans viii, 37–39].

Voluntary sacrifice considered in its aspect of painful deprivation has the same cleansing function in life. Apart from tiresome things which we do only out of duty, the engagement in the world by which we serve God runs the risk of itself becoming the end and aim of our activity. We study, write, look after the children, run our business, with an at least general intention of obeying God's will and serving him; but we are none the less occupied, in the concrete, with certain things that are very absorbing of attention, and often interesting, in which, moreover, there is food for one's love of oneself, and sometimes for self-esteem. That is not a bad thing. It is to be hoped that we shall never do anything 'for God' in the sense of St Vincent de Paul who, watching a nun doing a job very casually, remarked, 'Well, sister, it is easy to see that you are working for God!' No, we must put our heart into it. And the more we do that, the more necessary it is once in a while to sacrifice something, to do a bit for God without any element of human satisfaction coming into it. Pursue culture, yes—and don't aim too low! But now and then we should deprive ourselves of something interesting for God's sake, or put off some piece of reading we are looking forward to, or let ourselves appear

---

[44] See the writer's *Le mystère de la mort et sa célébration* (Paris, 1951), pp. 279–336, especially p. 289.

not quite up-to-date in our information. . . . Thus all will truly go to God and intermediate ends will not usurp his supreme place; and we shall continue to be spiritual kings and priests over our creation. The field of voluntary sacrifice is boundless, access to it is easy, and a sure tradition guarantees its fertility. In it we find an essential condition of freedom in respect of the world and of a real submission to God's will of all that we do and are.

The world of men is a world of bitter conflicts and injustices; by engaging in and disengaging from it, immersing himself in and rising above it, in accordance with the law of his kingly priesthood, the Christian has the opportunity to play the part of the peacemaker which the Gospel attributes to God's true children. The world is atrociously divided; progress, bound up with technicised industry, brings an element of division into what should be a uniting factor, and the world itself is characterised by plurality and by rejection of hierarchies. It is a world, too, of grinding competition, where children soon learn to 'look after Number One'. Hence a frantic utilitarianism which judges only by the biggest and quickest output, which makes it difficult for human character to mature and the most elementary ideas to develop. In such a world, with its immense and wonderful resources, Christians have a part to play which, even from a human point of view, can be a magnificent contribution. Provided they are as effectively engaged in it as they are authentically disengaged and disinterested, provided they live in God as truly as they live in the world, it is possible for them to be a factor for peace and unity; their character, their loyalty, their ability, together with their worth as spiritual men, should enable them to be accepted as reliable judges of things, to be a sort of arbitrator. In a frenzied world, it is for them to pursue a long-term policy of true humanism, sanity and serious work, if they believe in God whole-heartedly enough to believe in man as God believes in him, that is, more strongly than any man can do who uses only human standards.

The sign of the Cross also marks the Christian's efforts to 'christofinalise' the work of creation and bring about God's reign therein, and this, of course, less in the more technical and 'physical' aspects of temporal activity than in the more human and 'moral' aspects, those most concerned in the achievement of 'civilisation' (in the sense we have given the word in Chapter V, which is not the same as that of the Germans when they oppose 'civilisation' to 'culture').

The properly spiritual order is dominated by what St Paul calls the wisdom of the Cross, which is expressed in our lives very concretely by the paradoxical truth that, God's strength being perfected in weakness, 'when I am weak, then I am strong' (cf. 2 Corinthians xii, 9–10). The purely temporal, the object of the energies that God has put into nature, seeks achievements of power, tangible and satisfying success. When the spiritual tries to influence the temporal and to produce its normal fruits therein it sometimes has considerable successes, but often they are partial and uncertain. Nowadays, for example, we see little centres of integral Christian life here and there; should the day come for organising them as a whole, making their idea a general programme, creating a City on an entirely Christian system, it is probable that there would be grave disappointment and disillusionment. One wonders if these successes can be anything more than, as it were, parables of the Kingdom and its righteousness, and whether the Gospel is susceptible of being expressed in a scheme of earthly actualisation that would be adequate. In a general way, man's objectifyings of the spiritual intentions of thought, culture and so on within him are always exceeded by the intention, which arouses and animates other expressions beyond them. A perfect work of art is perfect within limits, it has a sort of congenital poverty: it is not the work which piles on qualities and thinks thus to have realised the ideal (the west front of Rheims, the name of Amiens[45]), but the work that most purely and shiningly embodies an ideal *in relative and limited concrete conditions*. In the same way there is the absolute of the Gospel and there are the relative realisations of it that history records. Their interest for us is in proportion to the shining purity with which, knowing that the one Absolute cannot be matched, Christians have tried to realise its abiding demands within the limited conditions of history and their own *hic et nunc*.

Those who think of a good result in terms analogous to those of success in power and technique may perhaps experience some disappointment here. They often feel they have had a set-back; they have a sense of frustration, sometimes justified, in their professional or family life as well. So, without canonising ill-success and making a false ideal of the contented failure, the law of the Cross must be included in the very conception of Christian action.[46]

[45] [In England, Henry VII's chapel at Westminster or the Albert Memorial.—*Translator's note*.]

[46] These few pages make no claim whatever to be a treatise on spiritual life, even for lay people living in the world; that would have meant talking about charity, the eucharist, God's dwelling in us, prayer, and many other things. About them there are numberless good books in many languages.

[The author then furnishes a list of such books specially adapted to lay people. As they are nearly all in French only, the list is omitted here.]

Chapter VII

CONCLUSION

LET us summarise the principal conclusions of our laborious inquiry into the position and proper role of the laity in the Church. That the end may correspond with the beginning, we will recall how priests, monks and laity are and make the Church, or, in technically more exact terms, how they are the subject of the operations by which the Church is constructed, and by what title they are necessary to her.

The laity (and monks as such) are not the subject of the acts by which the Church receives her structure as institution of salvation, which involve the exercise of apostolical powers; they are not the subject of the juridical mission constitutive of apostleship, which is carried out in various organs of apostolicity. In the gospels and Acts we see that the Apostles, and those joined with them or appointed afterwards to exercise part of their ministry, partake of competences [A] that the other faithful do not share, competences that enable them to play the part in the building up of the Church that St Paul calls that of master-builders (1 Corinthians iii, 9–17) and of foundations (Ephesians ii, 20). The faithful are indeed living stones and are all part of the temple (1 Corinthians iii, 16–17; Ephesians ii, 21–22; 1 Peter ii, 5; etc.); they are neither master-builders nor foundation, but rather are themselves built and based. There are gifts of authority and mediation in the Church, and they are accorded to some members only. This is the hierarchical principle.

But apostolicity is an organic function, a service, a ministry. It is not an end in itself. It exists for the body and in the body; for the body, in somewhat the same way as the master-builder exists for the house; in the body in somewhat the same way as the foundations exist for the house once it is built. Foundations that are not organically part of the building do not make a house—they belong to an unfinished plan, or a ruin. All the stones are the house, and each one for itself makes the 'act of the house', so to speak; some of them do

this as foundation, but in order that all the others may be a house
and not simply a formless mass of materials. The Church's hierarchical principle is of necessity accompanied by a communal principle.

These two principles are in no wise opposed, since the first is
expressed in an organic function of a body wholly living throughout.
Nothing is more noticeable than the persistence with which the
Bible joins in the same passages mention of the functions or competences proper to the apostolic ministry with affirmation of a life and
spiritual quality in which all share.[1] The Scriptures and tradition
speak of the Church essentially as a living organism. She is the Body
of Christ; she is a city or a family all of whose members are active,
though not all equal; if she is called a temple, it is a temple whose
stones have life.[2] All do not take part in the laying of the foundations and in directing the building, but all share in the dignity of
the whole, in the functions that compose it and in the activities of
its life.

In the Church's *dignity*. We are inclined to overlook this aspect,
but the Fathers were very conscious of it.[3] As members of the Body
of Christ, the faithful share in his kingly and priestly dignity. There
is in the world an order of inert existence, then an order of sensitive
and perishable life, then an order of spiritual life; but beyond that
there is an order of properly divine life, in and through the Son of
God made man, Jesus Christ. The name of Christian that every
baptised person bears raises us to *that* height of dignity.

In the Body each one fills a part determined by his vocation, by
the gifts accorded him, and by his state and *function*. We have seen
with what vigour this teaching of St Paul and the Fathers was taken
up in the encyclical letter '*Mystici Corporis*'. Hierarchical functions
alone assure the Church's structure as institution of salvation and, in
that sense, they alone are essential to her existence pure and simple;

[1] I Corinthians iii, 9–17; xii; Ephesians ii, 19–22; iv; Romans xii, 1, 3–8;
Hebrews xiii, 7; 15–17; I Peter ii, 4–10; v, 1–5; etc.

[2] It may be remarked that all the comparisons wherein the Scriptures unveil
something of the Church's mystery have four decisive traits in common: (1) the
image is relative to somebody and to *one* Person; (2) it is collective, made up of
many; (3) in regard to which *some* have a function, authority or ministry; (4) which
is *dynamic* and implies growth and accomplishment. For example, in the image of
the body, (1) is Christ, the head, (2) the various members, (3) the muscles for
particular purposes, (4) growth (Ephesians iv; cf. Romans xii; I Corinthians xii).
A further common trait, following from these, is beauty. Many of these comparisons
(bride, temple, city, kingdom) involve the idea both of an existing thing and of a
reality to come.

[3] See, for example, St Leo, *Sermo iv*, 1 (PL., liv, 148–149). It was Leo who said,
'Agnosce, Christiane, dignitatem tuam . . . memento cujus capitis et cujus corporis
sis membrum' (*Sermo xxi*, 3). There are numerous texts in Dabin, *Le sacerdoce
royal* . . .

but other functions enter into the concrete morphology of the Church and form part of her internal organisation. The encyclical mentions charismatics (apparently in the modern sense of the word, which implies exceptional gifts); religious who make public profession of the evangelical counsels, whether in contemplative life or in the doing of works of spiritual or corporal mercy; married people, fathers and mothers, godparents; all the members of the 'order' of laity, and especially those who strive in Catholic Action. Here we see, with the addition of a new category, the classic list of 'ministries, grades, professions, states, orders and functions' (these words occur in the encyclical), of which tradition has always seen the Body of Christ, the Church, to be made up (sometimes with the addition of preachers, widows and deaconesses). The Church is, then, presented to us as an organism in which certain functions ensure the existence of the institution and others ensure its perfection, in accordance with the will of God who bestows his gifts and his vocations as he pleases. So far as concerns its essential structure, the Church existed in the Apostles, whose heirs and successors are the bishops: their priesthood is necessary to the institutional structure. But from the beginning Jesus willed that, side by side with the Apostles, there should be the seventy (or seventy-two) disciples, the holy women, and others. The list of the different 'orders' of which mention has been made could be increased, or all could be reduced to two, religious life and life in the world; but in any case they too are necessary, not that the Church as institution may exist, but that she may fulfill her mission to the uttermost and fully carry out her work as Body of Christ.

The lay function is necessary for the carrying out of this mission and work. Were it only a question of a receiving subject, a beneficiary, of the work of grace carried out by the priesthood, the monastic function would be enough. Monks are, one might say, mankind passing into a pure state in the Church, so offering themselves that Christ's life may inform them directly and wholly. But God's design is not that there should be only a Church here below, but rather a Church *and* a world, a Church with a mission to the world and making use of its resources; and at the last a Kingdom, which each after its fashion will have prepared. The work of the mystical Body involves the bringing together under Christ of all that the wealth of creation and the virtualities of mankind can achieve: the first Adam needs the Second Adam that he may be saved, but the Second Adam supposes the first, that he may save him and have something to reign over. As for the Church's mission, it is fufilled only if the Gospel be declared to every creature, if creation with all its growth and increase be offered in Christ; it is not fulfilled in all its requirements and consequences unless there be a Christian influence opening the way to faith at the level of human structures, at work throughout civilisation to turn it Christward.

These things can be done only by lay people, for they belong both to the world and to the Church in a way that is true neither of the clergy nor of monks. And so the lay function as such is necessary to the Church's mission and to the economy [P] of grace. Lay people are the proper and irreplaceable subject of some of the activities through which this mission and this work are accomplished in their fullness. We have seen how this, their own, mandate is determined by the providential circumstances of their mundane engagement; how it corresponds to the part of the Church's mission in which she acts through her spiritual 'powers'; and how this mandate *ex spiritu*, *ex circumstantiis*, is confirmed by the hierarchical apostleship, which joins that of the laity to itself and therein finds its complement. We asked by what title lay people are the subject of functions by which the Church is constructed and how far they are necessary to her, and we find the answer is to a considerable degree positive. But that is not all. The laity also share, and fully, *in the acts of the Church's life*.

So far as its final determinations are concerned, that life reaches the body through the channel of apostolicity; but this is an organic function ordered by the Holy Spirit to the quickening of the whole body with the life of its Head. Thus animated, the entire body is, in the strongest sense of the word, concerned in the prophetical, priestly, apostolic, saving activity in which Christ takes those who are his as partners; the Body is the true subject of all life in Christ, and is alone its adequate subject. This life is actualised in its fullness only in the totality of the body. And therefore, on the one hand, the Lord can be wholly found and truth fully known only in the fellowship of the whole; on the other, the hierarchical instances of apostolicity themselves, being what they are only in view of the body, can be exerted only in and with it.

That is a truth that we came upon at the end of all our inquiries, and principally under two forms, namely, the idea that the faithful are the *pleroma* of the hierarchy, and the idea of an association of communal principle with hierarchical principle. This is more particularly noticeable in the spheres of liturgical worship, of the life of faith, and of apostleship. There we find both duality and unity of subject. Duality, since the hierarchical priesthood and the magisterium are not at all a delegation by the people; the apostolic mission of the Twelve, continued in the episcopal hierarchy, is complete and whole in itself; and yet there is a priesthood of the faithful, an infallibility of the believing Church, and an apostolic mission of all. Unity, since we have recognised that there is a sense in which the faithful with their clergy form one single subject of worship, of infallible faith and witness, and of apostleship. There is but one Lord, one Spirit, one Body (Ephesians iv, 4–6); the Holy Spirit that quickens the hierarchical organs in order that the body may have life, and the Holy Spirit that quickens the whole body in order that it may do the works of that life, can only go together, if we may venture to put it so, for they are the same. As in the whole of creation, so in the Church, God goes from unit to unity through the many; he distributes his grace by communicating it to many individuals and he brings that many to unity in communion, in a kind of concelebration of the mystery of the same life. In so doing, God is only reflecting his own mystery in the Church, for everything in him is a proceeding from one Principle, a communication to several, and a perfect communion in unity. *O beata Trinitas!*

The association of the laity with the hierarchy extends to a certain co-operation with it, at any rate at the level of execution, in the order of the juridical mission of which the hierarchy is the proper subject. We remember what we have found in the liturgy of worship, in teaching, in the apostolate and even in the regulation of God's household. There were the hierarchical power and acts coming from above, and the acts of life of the whole body from below: but also a sort of taking over of the second by the first which leads to, for instance, a liturgical worship of the Church as such, coming between properly sacramental acts and private personal prayer; or again, between apostleship of purely personal inspiration and the hierarchical apostleship, a certain 'sharing' of the latter, and the instituted apostolate of Catholic Action. There were, too, the participations—however tenuous—in teaching authority and the functions of regulation. Thus the principle of association is found even in institutions and is expressed canonically. But it is most fruitfully at work in the wider sphere of life, in an association of clergy with laity, wherein the priest energises most effectively as spiritual man, as thoughtful and cultivated man, as apostolic man, his people's guide, joined with the faithful in seeking ways and means for the Church's well-being in the actual circumstances and events of history.

DD

It is true that the development of ideas has worked rather against the combination of the communal principle with the hierarchical principle, and for an elaboration of the latter alone, especially in the West. For a long time the idea prevailed that hierarchical acts, sacramental celebrations in particular, were acts of the mystical Body and that they could be accomplished only in the fellowship of the body. It became necessary to make it clear that their validity does not come from the body as such, but from on high. This necessary precision was secured at the beginning of a whole movement which developed the theology of hierarchical powers and means of grace—and therefore of the Church as institution—and it certainly contributed to the isolation of the hierarchical principle. During the same era (eleventh and twelfth centuries), the old discipline that connected it clearly and effectively with the communal principle gave place to other usages. There was a change from priestly ordinations made for the service of a given church to ordinations 'without title'; from episcopal elections with a lower clergy and people's element to elections reserved to the cathedral chapter; from canonisations made in various ways from below to canonisations reserved to the pope; from the idea of authority as guardian of tradition to that of authority as source of law; from communion bound up with the eucharistic celebration to communion out of Mass, from reserved hosts. These points could be illustrated by many references and the list could be easily lengthened: they all represent an impulse in the same direction, namely, towards isolated affirmation and exercise of the hierarchical principle.

In this matter there is considerable difference between the West and the East, which became so unhappily separated from one another at the time to which we have just referred. The West has tended to emphasise the hierarchical principle, the East the communal principle. The West looks at and stresses above all that there is only one principle and that the body receives from it: this can be seen in the idea of priesthood, in the theology of papal power, even in Mariology, wherein one can easily tend to make God's gifts a personally held privilege; it can readily be seen in the liturgy, in the eucharistic celebration, for example, where it looks as if nothing can be said or done unless the priest says or does it, to the length of his saying 'Domine, non sum dignus . . .' and 'Amen' at communion instead of the people doing so. The East, however, looks at and puts more stress on how all share that in which the hierarchical principle resides.[4] But she does not deny the hierarchical principle, any more than the West entirely disregards the communal principle. The two are complementary, just as, fundamentally, the East and West are themselves complementary, having been providentially willed by God to be thus *without separation*, in a duality and fellowship which themselves form part of the concrete pattern of the Church.

Every idea ought to be both expressed and safeguarded in outward signs. For its proper expression in the Church, the union of our two principles has to have its significant signs, and there are no finer and better ones than those of the liturgy. As Pope Pius XI said to Dom Bernard Capelle, the liturgy is not simply 'the Church's *didascalia*'; beyond its defined ideas, it is the sacred ark wherein the spirit of the Church is kept and expressed. We have seen how at Mass all the forms of priesthood are operative in their mutual organic relationships and connexions. When priest and people assure one another that the Lord is with them and, thus assured, the priest says 'Let us pray', the hierarchical principle is effectually completed in the communal principle and the true nature of the mystical Body is made manifest. The whole Mass is a wonderful expression and making real of the Church's symphonic unity, different members filling diverse roles in the oneness of the whole: one precents, another picks up the chant from his lips and continues it; one reads, another blesses; one consecrates, the others communicate; the priest, the deacon, the acolyte have their various offices and the service is made a whole only through their respective actions. In this connexion, what a matter for rejoicing it is that in the paschal vigil service, as restored in 1951, the celebrant listens to the prophecies read by another minister, without reading them privately himself.[5] It is very regrettable that circumstances that no longer exist should have led to the prescription that the priest at high Mass should himself read inaudibly those things that the various ministers or the people sing. It is a liturgical anomaly; it is also a sort of symbol of the fact that the hierarchical priesthood has as it were taken over everything. It

[4] It would require a special study to show how different theologies of the Holy Spirit are respectively at the root of these two conceptions. In the one, the emphasis is put on the fact that all comes from one alone and on the dependence of the body on its head for the life that animates it; in the other, the emphasis is on life distributed throughout the body by the Holy Spirit, who is seen as an autonomous reality in relation to the Word. It is clear that a theology of laity calls for a theology of the Holy Spirit, both of which would simply be a revelation of profound and authentic traditional elements.

[5] See Dom Lambert Beauduin's commentary in *La Maison-Dieu*, no. 26 (1951–1952), pp. 106–107. For the rather humiliating circumstances which led to the priest's reading of pieces executed by other ministers, see Fr L. Bouyer in *Dieu Vivant*, no. 19 (1951), p. 87.

makes it look as if nothing can be done in the Church unless the priest does it and, from the point of view of apostleship, expression of thought and so on, as if the Church is not present there in any place if there is no cassock about. Personally, we attach great importance to significant signs. They are guardians of the spirit. Not to raise one's hat shows that respect is waning. The laity will not be re-established in the fullness of its quality as the Church's laity until the spirit of that small Easter reform of 1951 shall have been extended to all the spheres where it is relevant.

I am happy to finish this big volume with the evocation of the Easter vigil, between the tomb and life renewed: it is the dawn of spring, too!

Appendix I

GLOSSARY

[A] COMPETENCE. Faculty or authority pertaining to a function or office. The word has nearly the same meaning as 'power', but it is less definite and has not the same *nuance* of compelling force. Thus the magisterium is an initial competence in the Church, but takes on the *nuance* of power only when jurisdiction is added to it.

[B] CHARACTER, SACRAMENTAL. A spiritual sign conferred by the sacraments of baptism, confirmation and orders; it shapes the soul in the image of Christ, very especially of Christ as priest offering up perfect worship to his Father.

[C] ARTS-MEN. Professors of the faculty of arts in a medieval university: hence, any man pursuing rational sciences.

[D] HEILSGEMEINSCHAFT. Community of salvation; the word expresses the Church under her communal aspect.

[E] HEILSANSTALT. Institution of salvation; the word expresses the Church under her aspect of hierarchical society and as means, ministry or mediation of grace.

[F] PLEROMA. A Greek word signifying, in the active, that which fills or makes complete; in the passive, that which is full of something, plenitude, full measure or totality of a thing.

[G] SYNOPTISTS, THE. From a Greek word meaning 'general view' (cf. 'synopsis'). It designates the gospels according to Matthew, Mark and Luke, which can be set out in parallel columns because of their resemblances to one another.

[H] SACRAMENTUM. When this word is associated with *res* [I], it designates the external aspect or moment of a sacrament, the sign or visible rite, as distinct from the reality of grace that it is called on to produce.

[I] RES. The inner spiritual effect normally produced by a sacramental rite or sign, of which it is the principal *raison d'être*. Cf. [H].

[J] ALPHA. A, the first letter of the Greek alphabet, as Omega, Ω, is the last. The Bible and the liturgy use these letters symbolically to denote that the mystery of Christ is the beginning and end of everything.

[K] ESCHATOLOGY, ESCHATOLOGICAL. Relative to the end, terminal. Cf. [AA]. Eschatology is our knowledge of the last things. According to the Christian revelation, God's design and the world in which it is worked out are moving to a term and end. This term and end will indeed be the final point or last chapter of the history which concerns us, but also and especially they are that to which this history is moving, so that the end or term in aspiring towards itself elucidates and qualifies the whole unfolding of things. Spiritual history is illumined by its term, present time by eschatology.

[L] PNEUMA. Greek word meaning 'spirit': in the Christian language of the New Testament and of the Fathers, either man's spirit as rising above the body and matter or, more especially, the Spirit of God, the Person of the Holy Spirit; and also God's gift of grace to us, which is attributed to his Holy Spirit. The *Pneuma*, then, is as it were the stuff of supernatural creation. *Pneumatic:* pertaining to the order of grace and of supernatural creation.

[M] RÉCAPITATION. The author sometimes uses this or equivalent terms to render St Paul's ἀνακεφαλαιώσασθαι (in Ephesians i, 10), which etymologically means to 'sum up' or to 'resume all under one head'. Cf. Chapter III, note 9.

[N] NOVISSIMIS, DE. The theological treatise on the last things, which deals with matters relative to death, judgement, Purgatory, Hell and Heaven.

[O] TIME OF THE CHURCH, THE. The duration of time for which Christ has instituted the Church in her earthly form, the period from his Ascension to his Second Coming. The expression also means the regime existing during this chronological era, 'the state of things' (cf. [X]).

[P] ECONOMY (Latin, *dispensatio*). The order and unfolding of God's design of salvation.

[Q] PALINGENESY. A Greek word meaning 'new birth'; by extension, a 'general renewal'.

[R] PAROUSIA. A Greek word meaning 'presence' or 'arrival'. In Christian speech it designates Christ's second coming at the end of time, 'in glory to judge the living and the dead, whose kingdom shall have no end'. *Anteparousial:* before the second coming. *Parousial:* pertaining to the second coming or to the order of things begun thereat.

[S] DISPENSATION, OLD. The biblical Greek διαθήκη is generally rendered 'Covenant' in English; sometimes, less happily, 'Testament'. The French here has *Disposition*, as better than either *Alliance or Testament*.

[T] PASCH. Greek version of the Hebrew word designating the Mosaic feast called in English the Passover, a name which expresses the biblical meaning: the passing of the Lord over Egypt, the passing of the Hebrews from Egypt through the wilderness to the promised land. This significance of 'passing' is retained by the evangelist for Christ's pasch (John xiii, 1) and then by tradition and liturgy, in the abundant symbolism of The Pasch (death-entombment-resurrection) as epitome of the whole Christian mystery. Cf. L. Bouyer, *The Paschal Mystery* (London, 1952); J. Daniélou, *Bible et liturgie*.

[U] AGAPE. A Greek word which in Christian speech signifies charity, with a *nuance* of 'given freely through love'. Cf., for example, Romans v, 8; 1 John iv, 8–10. *Agape* also designates the meal that was taken together before the Eucharist (love-feast), and so a friendly meal in common.

[V] EINMALIGKEIT (ἐφάπαξ : ἅπαξ). Once only, once for all.

[W] NOACHIC. Adjective from Noah, Noë. The Noachic covenant is the covenant made with Noah after the flood, whose essence was God's promise not again to disturb the cosmic order; Genesis viii–ix.

[X] AEON. Greek word signifying a long duration of time, then a particular period. In the New Testament the word signifies, beyond a chronological space, the characteristics and regime of the period in question (cf. [O]).

[Y] PARAKLESIS. A Greek word that is often difficult to translate in the New Testament: it combines the sense of 'warning and advice', 'urgent appeal', 'consolation'.

[Z] ACTA ET PASSA CHRISTI IN CARNE. 'Those things which Christ did and suffered [for us] in the flesh' (St Thomas Aquinas, *Sum. theol.*, III, prol.).

[AA] ESCHATON. The last thing after which there is no more; that which is at the term. Cf. [K].

[BB] CHARISM. A gift of God's grace. The term is often limited to such special personal gifts as those referred to by St Paul in Romans xii, 6ff. and 1 Corinthians xii. *Charismatic* (adjective): relative to charisms; (substantive): one endowed with such particular gifts of the Holy Spirit.

[CC] Soteriology. The theology of salvation and the things relating thereto (Greek, *soter* = saviour).

[DD] Historic Christ, The. Christ before his resurrection, who was born and grew up, who was seen and heard, and who suffered on the cross. After his resurrection we speak of the risen Christ, and after his ascension of the heavenly Christ. It is our faith that these are one and the same Christ.

[EE] Lapsi. Latin, 'fallen', 'backsliders'. The term was used to designate those who during the early persecutions, especially that of Decius, gave up the Holy Scriptures or acquired certificates of conformity.

[FF] Epieikeia. Greek word meaning suitability, moderation, equitableness. Moralists apply the term to the appreciation of what is equitable, waiving if necessary a rigid application of what is strictly legal, for in some cases *summum jus, summa injuria*, 'the more law, the less justice'.

[GG] Apatheia. This word, from the terminology of the Greek philosophers, especially the Stoics, means unfeelingness, passionlessness, indifference.

[HH] Praeambula fidei. Preambles to faith. In theology, certain truths that are in themselves attainable through rational demonstration, and so constitute a basis from which the adherence of faith proper is possible. These truths are essentially the existence of God, his providence, his chief attributes and the immortality of the soul.

[II] Demiurgic. Adjective from 'demiurge', which originally meant in Greek one who works for the public; thence, one who exercises a trade, and so one who produces or creates. In its philosophical sense, 'creative power'. Strictly speaking, man creates nothing: but he transforms wonderfully all that he touches, and from nature's virtualities draws endless energies which he uses to produce new effects. This power and activity (illustrated in the person of Faust) are what are called 'demiurgic'.

[JJ] Theological Criteria, Treatise on. The chapter of theological methodology that deals with the value of the various authorities and of the different documents used in theology, and of the theses therein sustained (sometimes called *loci theologici*).

Appendix II

THE 'SENSUS FIDELIUM' IN THE FATHERS

THE following are the principal texts of the Fathers, come across in our reading or quoted by writers on the subject.[1] They fall under two main lines of argument.

(1) To refuse to believe as Catholics believe is to nullify the faith of a whole people, and that is impossible.

TERTULLIAN, *Praescr.*, 28: 'Age nunc omnes Ecclesiae erraverint; deceptus sit apostolus de testimonio reddendo quibusdam; nullam respexerit Spiritus Sanctus uti eam in veritatem deduceret, ad hoc missus a Christo, ad hoc postulatus de Patre ut esset doctor veritatis; neglexerit officium Dei villicus, Christi vicarius, sinens Ecclesias aliter interim intelligere, aliter credere, quam ipse per apostolos praedicabat. Ecquid verissimile est ut tot ac tantae in unam fidem erraverint?'

ST GREGORY NAZIANZEN, *Ep. cii* (PG., xxxvii, 200): 'If that is not true [the Catholic faith on the Incarnation and Christ's godhead], our faith is vain, the martyrs died in vain, bishops have ruled their people in vain . . .'.

ST BASIL, *Adv. Eunomium*, lib. 3, c. 1 (PG., xxix, 654): 'Scorning the conviction of the multitude that glorifies the Holy Spirit [as God], he professes to follow the teaching of the saints . . .'

ST JEROME, *Contra Vigilantium*, n. 5 (PL., xxiii, 343): 'Were then the people of all the churches crazy when they flocked to holy relics . . . ?'

(2) Argument for a doctrine from communal practice and belief.

ST EPIPHANIUS, *Adv. haer. Panar.*, haer. 78, c. 6 (PG., xlii, 705): 'Has anyone at any time ever dared to call on the name of blessed Mary without adding "the virgin" . . . ?'

ST NICEPHORUS argued against the image-breaking emperors from

[1] The best recent work is J. V. Bainvel, *De Magisterio vivo et Traditione* (Paris 1905), nn. 92–94.

'the faith of the people, their spontaneous inward inclination, the eagerness, the religious care with which [the images] are treated, the old and continuous custom handed on in the Church . . .' (quoted by R. Wehrlé in *De la coutume en droit canonique*, Paris, 1928, p. 75, n. 1).

St Augustine has many relevant texts. He invokes the Church's practice, what he sometimes calls *dogma populare*, on four points particularly. (1) Not rebaptising heretics: *Contra Crescon.*, lib. 2, c. 32 (PL., xliii, 490); *De bapt. contra Donat.*, lib. 2, c. 9, n. 14 (xliii, 135). (2) The necessity of grace, evidenced by the meaning given by the faithful to prayer: *De dono persev.*, c. 23, n. 63 (xlv, 1031); *De natura et gratia*, n. 52 (xliv, 272: 'Iste vero [Pelagius], objecta sibi quaestione in qua intolerabilis videtur cordibus christianis . . .'). (3) The canonicity of biblical books, such as Wisdom, which are listened to 'ab omnibus christianis, ab episcopis usque ad extremos laicos fideles, penitentes, catechumenos, cum veneratione divinae auctoritatis' (*De praedest. sanct.*, n. 27: xliv, 980). Incidentally, this point about the part taken by basic communities and the faithful in the determination of the biblical canon deserves study. (4) The necessity and efficacy of baptism for salvation, particularly of babies: *Sermo ccxciv*, c. 17 (xxxviii, 1346: 'premitur mole matris Ecclesiae . . . auctoritate reprimuntur Ecclesiae'); *De peccat. meritis et remiss.*, lib. 1, c. 24, n. 34 (xliv, 128: the Punici know that baptism is salvation and that the eucharist is life); *Epist. cxciv*, n. 31 (xxxiii, 885: 'auctoritate evangelica territi, vel potius christianorum populorum concordissima fidei conspiratione pertracti'); *De nuptiis et concupisc.*, lib. 2, n. 4 (xliv, 438: 'aures catholicas . . . cuncta Ecclesiae catholicae pectora . . . omnes currunt'); *Opus imperf. c. Julian.*, lib. 1, § 19 (xlv, 1058: 'Nullo modo autem diceres vulgi a nobis in vos pectora commoveri, nisi scires multitudinem christianam in utroque sexu fidem catholicam non latere'); *ibid.*, § 33 ('Plebicularum quas irrides catervae noverunt catholicam fidem, quae a Salvatore salvari confitentur infantes; et ideo pelagianorum, qui hoc negant, detestantur errores'); *Contra Julian.*, lib. 1, c. 7, n. 31 (xliv, 662: 'Quamquam et ipse populus adversus vos propterea murmuret, quia non est talis quaestio quae possit etiam cognitionem fugere popularem. Divites et pauperes, excelsi atque infimi, docti et indocti, mares et feminae noverunt quid cuique aetati in baptismo remittamus . . .' Cf. n. 32 and lib. 2, n. 36; lib. 6, n. 22); *De cura pro mortis gerenda*, lib. 1, n. 3 (xl, 593). See also *De utilitate credendi*, c. 17, n. 35 (xlii, 90–91).

All those influenced by St Augustine had this sense of the faith of the whole Church. Cf. his contemporaries, St Paulinus of Nola, *Epist. xxiii*, n. 25 (PL., lxi, 281: 'De omnium ore pendeamus, quia in omnem fidelem Spiritus Dei spirat'); and Pope St Celestine I, *Epist. ad episc. Galliae*, nn. 12–14 (PL., xlv, 1759). The idea of the infallibility of the faith of the Christian people in its wholeness was elaborated systematically particularly by the Lérins school, and it is at the bottom of the famous canon of Lérins, 'Quod semper . . .'. The following two classical passages should be especially noticed.

St Vincent of Lérins, *Commonitorium*, c. 24 (PL., l, 670): Heterodox doctrines are those 'quae nihil habent sacri, nihil religiosi, ab Ecclesiae penetralibus, quae est templum Dei, penitus extraneas . . . quae si recipiantur necesse est ut fides beatorum patrum, aut tota aut magna ex parte violetur; necesse est ut omnes omnium aetatum fideles, omnes sancti, omnes casti, continentes, virgines, omnes clerici, levitae et sacerdotes, tanta confessorum millia, tanti martyrum exercitus . . . totus postremo jam pene terrarum orbis, per catholicam fidem Christo capiti incorporatus, tanto saeculorum tractu ignorasse, errasse, blasphemasse, nescisse quid credunt, pronuntietur . . .'.

Cassian, *De incarnatione*, lib. 1, c. 6 (PL., l, 29): 'Hanc ergo confessionem, id est catholicorum omnium fidem, et omnes Africani episcopi, unde scribebat, et omnes Gallicani, ad quos scribebat, comprobaverunt. Neque ullus adhuc omnino exstitit cui fides haec sine infidelitatis crimine displiceret quia professio impietatis est, probatam negare pietatem. Sufficere ergo solus nunc ad confutandam haeresim deberet consensus omnium, quia indubitatae veritatis manifestatio est auctoritas universorum, et perfecta ratio facta est ubi nemo dissensit'.

The theme of the faith of the universal ecclesial community is always present in Catholic theology, more especially in authors of the Augustinian tradition, such as, at the time of the Reformation, John Driedo. Confronted by Protestantism, the Council of Trent had to formulate the Church's common tradition at the stage of development it had then reached, and it did not fail several times to invoke the *sensus Ecclesiae*. For instance, in Session xiii, c. 1 (Denzinger, 874): 'Ita enim majores nostri omnes, quotquot in vera Christi Ecclesia fuerent . . . contra universum Ecclesiae sensum detorqueri . . .'. (It is a question of the interpretation given to the eucharistic texts *by the whole Church*.)

Appendix III

SOME UTTERANCES OF THE CHURCH'S PASTORAL MAGISTERIUM CALLING ON CHRISTIANS TO BE ACTIVE IN THE WORK OF MANKIND

'WHILE observing all necessary discretion in respect of dissidents, we must be solicitous for them and ceaselessly concerned ever to understand them better; we must approach them respectfully and in a spirit of friendship; we must beware of too hastily attributing perverseness to them; without deceiving ourselves in their regard, we must treat them with the kindness and consideration that Christ always showed to the strayed sheep whom he came across on his path . . . This era is one of the most disturbed that mankind has known; it is also one of the finest: for it is an age wherein mediocrity is allowed to nobody, wherein Christian lives flower in all their beauty and triumphs are made ready for the Church. But we need holiness for that . . .' (Pope Pius XI to the bishops of France, December 1937).

'There is no conflict between the laws that rule the life of the Christian faithful and the essential postulates of mankind; on the contrary, they are in common and support one another' (Pope Pius XII, encyclical letter '*Summi pontificatus*'; A.A.S., 1939, p. 503).

'As if feeling for the collective responsibility of all for all had not been living and persisting in the Church's soul for two thousand years . . . At least you, conscious and convinced of this sacred responsibility (of co-operating in the future organisation of that new order that the world awaits amidst the terrible upheaval of current conflicts), you in the depths of your souls can never be satisfied with a general inadequacy of public conditions, in which the mass of men can only through heroic virtue keep the divine commandments, which are inviolable always and in every case' (Pius XII, discourse at Whitsun 1941; A.A.S., 1941, p. 215).

In his address to newly married couples on 30 July 1941, Pope Pius XII said it is a characteristic of pagan and insufficiently Christian societies that they are unable to remain strong and enterprising and at the same time to 'keep a truly human heart, a heart capable of wholesome affection and genuine religious dutifulness'.

'A living faith in the one personal transcendent God leads to a firm and frank moral energy that gives the pitch to the whole course of life. For faith is not simply a virtue: it is the divine door to the temple of the soul, giving entrance to all the virtues that build up a strong and tenacious character, one that does not waver in the ordeals that right reason and goodness undergo' (Pius XII, Christmas message 1941; A.A.S., 1942, p. 18).

'For the Christian soul who weighs history against the mind and spirit of Christ, there can be no question of a return to the past, but only of a desire to go on into the future and to excel oneself' (Pius XII, broadcast of 13 May 1942; A.A.S., 1942, p. 158).

The 'tranquillity' of the order we have to seek has nothing in common with a 'hard and obstinate fixedness, holding on tightly to itself; it has nothing in common with a repugnance—child of ignorance and selfishness—to applying the mind to the problems set by the rise and development of new generations, with their fresh accomplishments and needs. A Christian who is conscious of his responsibility towards the least of his brethren cannot tolerate an indolent tranquillity. So far from standing aside, he will be up and doing, pitting himself against inertia in this great spiritual struggle whose aim is to build up society, or rather, to give it a soul' (Pius XII, Christmas message, 1942; A.A.S., 1943, p. 15).

'Get to work then, dear children! Close your ranks! Don't lose heart or sit idle among the ruins. Go out and build a new world of society for Christ' (Pius XII, Christmas message, 1943; A.A.S., 1944, p. 20).

'It is the clearsightedness, courage, devotedness, inventive genius and brotherly charity of upright and loyal hearts that will decide in what measure and to what point the Christian spirit will succeed in establishing and consolidating the huge work of renewing social, economic and international life on a basis consistent with the religious and moral content of Christian civilisation' (Pius XII, message of 1 September 1944; A.A.S., 1944, p. 251).

'In God, in the God-man, Christ, the Church has the unseen but unshakeable principle of her unity and integrity, of the unity of head and members in the full plenitude of her life. She welcomes and hallows all that is truly human; she brings together many and varied aspirations and particular aims, and directs them towards man's common and all-embracing aim, which is to become as like as possible to God . . . The Church cannot shut herself up, inactive, in the privacy of her churches and thus neglect the mission entrusted to her by divine Providence, the mission to form man in his fullness and so ceaselessly to collaborate in building the solid basis of society. This mission is of her essence' (Pius XII, address to the new cardinals, 26 February 1946; *Doc. cath.*, 1946, cc. 171, 176).

'Among the many ways of acting by which we are confronted, it is today less difficult to decide what should be our line of conduct. The first way is ruled out: it is the way of the deserter, of him who is rightly called "the refugee from inside"; the behaviour of the dissatisfied or disheartened person who, out of sulkiness or spite, won't use his abilities and powers and takes no part in the life of his time and country . . . Abstentionism is even more unworthy when it is the result of lazy and careless indifference' (Pius XII, discourse to the Roman nobility, 8 February 1947).

'Rarely in the course of history has the position of Catholic students and intellectuals been so heavy with responsibility as it is today . . . Yes, be there at every point in the intellectual conflict, at this time when the problems of man and nature are being envisaged in the new settings and scope that will be theirs henceforward' (Pius XII, letter to Pax Romana congress, 6 August 1950; A.A.S 1950, p. 635).

To these papal texts there could be added many others from bishops expressing the Church's pastoral magisterium. See, for example, Cardinal Bertram, Archbishop of Breslau, pastoral letter *Laienapostolat* . . . (Breslau, 1921), who enumerates the virtues appropriate to the lay apostle as shining faith, true brotherly love and real social sensibility, perseverance and courage, and a sympathetic and cheerful disposition; Cardinal Liénart, Bishop of Lille, pastoral letters: 1947, *Essor ou déclin de l'Église*, especially pp. 40–46, 56–59; 1948, *Le sens de Dieu*, pp. 37–40, 53–60; 1949, *Le prêtre dans la Cité*, pp. 1–3, 57–64, 70–72.

There are many texts of Popes Pius XI and Pius XII appealing to all men of good will and asking Christians to collaborate with them for a sound social order. The chief of these texts may be found in the author's study on *Les conditions théologiques du pluralisme* (Paris, 1952), pp. 191–223.